9/2

UNITE

30°N

O'ahu

Hawai'i

HAWAI'I

...ston

MEXICO

15°N

Mexico City ⊚

North Pacific Ocean

Clipperton

Kiritimati

Line Islands

I

...ands

0°   equator

C O O K   I S L A N D S

Marquesas Islands

Galapagos Islands

F R E N C H   P O L Y N E S I A

MERICAN SAMOA

Tuamotu Archipelago

UE

Society Islands

Tahiti

15°S

Rarotonga

Austral Islands

Gambier Islands

Pitcairn Islands

...uth Pacific Ocean

30°S

Rapa Nui (Easter)

THE PACIFIC ISLANDS

W   E

155°W

140°W

125°W

45°S

110°W

95°W

Colonialism, Maasina Rule, and the Origins of Malaitan *Kastom*

Pacific Islands Monograph Series 26

Colonialism, Maasina Rule, and the Origins of Malaitan *Kastom*

David W. Akin

CENTER FOR PACIFIC ISLANDS STUDIES

School of Pacific and Asian Studies

University of Hawai'i, Mānoa

UNIVERSITY OF HAWAI'I PRESS • Honolulu

18 17 16 15 14 13   6 5 4 3 2 1

Library of Congress Cataloging-in-Publication Data

Akin, David, [date–] author.
  Colonialism, Maasina rule, and the origins of Malaitan kastom / David Akin.
    pages cm. — (Pacific islands monograph series ; 26)
  Includes bibliographical references and index.
  ISBN 978-0-8248-3814-0 (cloth : alk. paper)
  1. Malaita Province (Solomon Islands)—Politics and government.   2. Malaita
Province (Solomon Islands)—Social life and customs.   3. Self-determination,
National—Solomon Islands.   I. Title.   II. Series: Pacific islands monograph
series ; no. 26.
  DU850.A684 2013
  995.93'7—dc23
                    2013008708

Maps by Manoa Mapworks, Inc.

University of Hawai'i Press books are printed on acid-free paper and meet the
guidelines for permanence and durability of the Council on Library Resources.

Design by University of Hawai'i Press Design & Production Department
Printed by Sheridan Books, Inc.

To Ma'aanamae, Sulafanamae, and Saetana
'Ola moru siria lo'oo, fu'u wane.
and
Kisini

Editor's Note

David Akin's *Colonialism, Maasina Rule, and the Origins of Malaitan* Kastom provides a sophisticated reading of Pacific Islander interactions with and responses to foreign influences and colonialism. It adds to the rich histories and ethnographies of the interactions between Islanders and Europeans and exemplifies how Islanders often capture and use foreign ideas and institutions, blend them with local cultures and structures of power, and use them as vehicles for protest. This book, while focusing on Malaita in Solomon Islands, links the Pacific Islands with colonial experiences elsewhere, especially British colonies in Africa and Asia. It illustrates the complex relationships between colonial powers and their subjects and the ways Pacific Islanders engage with foreigners, their ideas, and institutions while at the same time drawing from their own cultures and institutions to make sense of these interactions and formulate responses. While couched within the broader context of colonial studies, the book emphasizes Islander agency and voices.

In this book, Akin weaves a captivating story that blurs the boundaries between anthropology and history, displaying an extensive knowledge of the interactions between Solomon Islanders and Europeans and an acute understanding of Malaitan societies and histories from the late 1800s into the mid-1900s. He draws on meticulous archival research and years of ethnographic work in Solomon Islands, allowing him to tell these stories in an insightful and refreshing manner.

Akin begins by examining the period from the late 1800s to the 1930s, especially Malaitans' involvement as plantation laborers in Queensland, Fiji, and Samoa and, later, in other parts of Solomon Islands. This provides a fascinating ethnography of how interactions with Europeans shaped Malaitans' political consciousness and identity. It illustrates the complexity of the relationships among Solomon Islanders, plantation owners, labor recruiters, Christian missionaries, and the colonial administration. By the early 1900s, the British Protectorate government had established its administrative structures and imposed colonial rule. In the 1920s, in order to help finance the administration, the government introduced the head tax. The only way many people could pay tax was by seeking formal employment in the plantations. This provoked protests, especially in Malaita, resulting in the 1927 killing of a government officer and 14 members of his tax-collecting party in Kwaio. The British government responded with punitive expeditions, which further influenced Malaitan perceptions of and relationship with the government for decades afterward. These events generated a broader political consciousness among Solomon Islanders about their relationship with the colonial government. The Fallowes Movement of the 1930s was a more widespread expression of discontent that included people from other islands as well as Malaitans. Akin tells of how Solomon Islanders were becoming more aware of the power relationships between them and the colonial administration.

By the early 1940s, the Second World War reached the Pacific Islands. As elsewhere in the Pacific, the war had an enormous impact on the islands and Islanders. In Solomon Islands, the war marked a break in British colonial rule. Most of the British colonial administrators left, leaving a power vacuum; the Islanders were caught between the invading Japanese and US military forces with their military might, massive supplies of "cargo," and ideas about freedom and equality. Many Malaitans worked for the Solomon Islands Labour Corps. Akin documents how interactions with American soldiers influenced Malaitan political consciousness and led to greater resistance to British attempts to reestablish their rule after the war.

From this background arose Maasina Rule, a protest movement that started on Malaita and spread to some of the nearby islands. This was the first major protest against the colonial administration in Solomon Islands. Although the Maasina Rule story has been told in previous publications, Akin's narrative provides a fresh perspective on the movement, giving voice and agency to the Malaitan characters in a way that I have not seen before. Information gathered from his extensive archival research is reinforced by his distinct knowledge and understanding of Malaita societies and histories. He tells of Maasina Rule's interaction with the government and their launch of Operation Delouse as well as Malaitans' refusal to be involved in labor on plantations. The colonial government responded with a campaign to suppress Maasina Rule, particularly in 1948 and 1949, by jailing leaders and trying to force Malaitans back under colonial control. In spite of this, Malaitans continued to defy the government, proving that Maasina Rule had popular support. This led to the release of the movement's leaders, changes in the colonial administration's tactics, and the establishment of a Malaita Council, giving more autonomy to the island. Akin finishes by outlining the successes and failures of Maasina Rule.

The Pacific Islands Monograph Series is privileged to add this volume to its list. This book will appeal not only to those interested in Solomon Islands and the Pacific region but also to those interested in colonial studies more generally. As one of the reviewers for this manuscript stated, "There is no other equivalent study of this detailed and important Pacific protest movement."

TARCISIUS KABUTAULAKA

Contents

Illustrations

Acknowledgments

I thank first the two editors who applied their skills to this book. Countless times my wife Terre Fisher set aside her own work to slog through painfully rough chapter drafts, imposing order and readability and purging silliness. Despite the trials of living with a distracted writer, she maintained good humor for the duration. My editor for the Pacific Islands Monograph Series, Jan Rensel, first encouraged me to write this work (just how many years ago I decline to say). She made the prose decidedly better and made what might have been a tedious production process enjoyable. She is an editor's editor, and much more. Without Terre's and Jan's help, you would not be reading this book.

Ben Burt and I, by coincidence, landed on Malaita on the same day in 1979, and over the years since he has been as generous a colleague as one could wish for. To this book Ben gifted his deep knowledge of Malaita and its history as well as a good deal of time, reading several chapters more than once and offering point-on criticism when most needed. I also thank him for sharing many archival documents and, along with his home institution the British Museum, for making available several of the photographs that illustrate the text. I am beholden as well to historian Clive Moore for his patience with this anthropologist's attempt at history writing; he read and commented on all the chapters and provided many documents. Another fine historian of the Solomons, David Hilliard, read several early chapters, sent me feedback and encouragement, and shared his letters from Richard Fallowes.

During my last several residences in Kwaio I have lived with the people of 'Ai'eda, which must surely be the nicest community on the globe. Among the many there whose help was crucial to my research for this book, I am most indebted to John Aniwa'i Laete'esafi, Bebea Animae, Kotomae, Taawa'i, Jackson Waneagea, 'Otomoori, and especially the late Ma'aanamae. A list of all of the people in Kwaio who have helped me would fill pages, and so I thank here only those who contributed most directly to my research into this book's subjects: Agiaboo, Alasiaboo, 'Abaeata Anifelo, Arimae, Arubata, Arugeni, Basiberi, Basiitau, Bati, Busumae, Dangeabe'u, Demuele, Dooka, Biri Fa'afusia, Feefela, Jonathan Fifi'i, Gemu Fiinaabata, Folofo'u,

'Ita Foolamo, Beni Fo'aanamae, Funaafela, Sale Genifataa, Geniilefana, Genima'asua, Geni'iria, Gwanu'i, Ilobata, Inaarobo, Sale Kaakalade, Kwai-ofo, Kwaru'ume, Kwa'aruga, Laefiwane, Laeniamae, Laetemu, Larikeni, La'afilamo, Le'aa, Logomae, Saelasi Lounga, Maato'o, Simone Maa'eobi, Sale Maeana, Maefanaomea, Japhlet Maefe'ua, Maefooru, Maenaalamo, Batamani Maenaa'adi, Molaina'o, Mongaboo, Moruka, Na'oni'au, Ngiri'a, Noomae, Notofaka, Oleka, Oloi'a, Orinaasikwa, Orite'elamo, Rifuala, Riginai'a, Riufaa, Ri'ika, Rubea, Bita Saetana, Safaasafi, Sangosoea, Siufio-mea, Peter Soea'adi, Nene'au So'ogeni, Sulafanamae, Surube'u, Su'umete, Taanga, Tagii'au, Ta'ika, Telegeni, Tome Toloasi Teeboo, To'oni, Wadoka, Wa'ifurina, 'Aditalau, Biri 'Asuani, 'Edaori, 'Oifofo, Sale 'Oirukua, 'Oisafi, 'Oitalana, 'Otaalea, 'Otamae, 'Otolo'u, and 'Ubuni. Many of these people are also cited in endnotes for specific information they provided.

I give special thanks to three former district officers, three true gentle-men, for their help. The late Martin Clemens read early versions of early chapters and, both in person and in letters, provided me with information about prewar Malaita available nowhere else. Tom Russell and James Ted-der each read the entire manuscript, and though they no doubt would have written parts of it differently, both were generous with their time, knowl-edge, and good advice. Like any serious student of Maasina Rule, I also owe much to Tom for the remarkable administrative reports he wrote from Malaita and also his later writings. James's book about his Solomon Islands years, too, is a valuable source, and I thank him for letting me publish his photograph of the first Malaita Council (figure 8.1).

David Hanlon and Tarcisius Kabutaulaka, successive editors of the Pacific Islands Monograph Series, supported this project over an extended period. University of Hawai'i Press editors Ann Ludeman and Masako Ikeda guided the manuscript through the publication process. I was helped with archi-val research by George Gwailau at the Solomon Islands National Archive; Renée Heyum and Karen Peacock at the University of Hawai'i Hamilton Library's Pacific Collection; Karen Evans and Caese Levo at the Anglican Church of Canada Library in Toronto; Kylie Moloney at the Pacific Man-uscript Bureau; Stuart and Patricia Braga, Gordon Griffiths, and Stuart Piggin regarding the South Sea Evangelical Mission archive at the Baptist Community Services Archives in Sydney; and especially Kathy Creely at the Tuzin Archive for Melanesian Anthropology (formerly the Melanesian Archive), Mandeville Special Collections Library, University of California, San Diego (UCSD). Jeff Wilmot and the descendants of Edge-Partington kindly allowed me to publish photos from their families.

I owe a great deal to people who have read and commented on differ-ent parts of this work in its different versions, or on segments that were first parts of other projects: Wallace and Peggy Akin, Andrew Arno, Gra-ham Baines, Jack Bilmes, Laura Brown, Mike Butcher, Bill Davenport, Kate Dernbach, Lawrence Foana'ota, John Mofat Fugui, Tony Hopkins, Dan

Jorgensen, Lamont Lindstrom, Nancy Lutkehaus, Pierre Maranda, Debbie McDougall, Eric Montgomery, Joel Robbins, Michael Scott, Rupert Stasch, Matt Tomlinson, and particularly the late Don Tuzin. Christine Jourdan gave me comments on several chapters and moral support throughout, and also provided figure 1.3.

My thinking on the various topics that make up this book has benefited over the years from discussions and exchanges with numerous friends and colleagues. I would especially like to thank Sandra Bamford, Jolene Braun, J Peter Brosius, Mike and Anna Clark, Jeff Conway, Gillian Feeley-Harnik, Rick Feinberg, Jonathan Fifi'i, Robert Foster, Clacy Fotanowa, Ian Frazer, David Gegeo, Kathleen Gillogly, Chris Gregory, Raymond Grew, Pei-yi Guo, Jim Hagen, Shah Hanifi, Keith Hart, Jo Herlihy, Randall Hicks, Alan Howard, Dan Jorgensen, Roger Keesing, Mariano Kelesi, Raymond Kelly, Jari Kupiainen, Jocelyn Linnekin, David MacLaren, George Maelalo, Debbie McDougall, Farina Mir, John Naitoro, Douglas Oliver, Derek Rawcliffe, David Roe, Bill Savage, Ryan Schram, Shelly Schreiner, Tom Titiuru, Susanne Unger, Tome Waleanisia, Ansene Wa'ii'a, and Aram Yengoyan. Bishop Terry Brown allowed me to tap his knowledge of Malaitan Christianity and also supplied several documents and figure 7.1. Michael Scott and I swapped many documents and ideas, and I was also helped by talks with Krista Ovist. Geoffrey White shared insights, his documents on Isabel and World War II, and his letters from Richard Fallowes, and he also facilitated some of my research. I am grateful to Joel Robbins for ongoing discussion, advice, encouragement, and friendship, and to Andrew Shryock and Thomas Trautmann who have each supported my work in incalculable ways.

This book draws on research funded by the National Endowment for the Humanities (grant FB-32097–95), the National Science Foundation (INT-9504555), the Wenner-Gren Foundation for Anthropological Research (5800), the East-West Center, the University of Hawai'i Program on Conflict Resolution, and support from the Friends of the UCSD Libraries and travel funding from the Tuzin Archive for Melanesian Anthropology, University of California, San Diego.

To Kimo, formerly the priest at the Kwalakwala Catholic Mission at Uru, who was so welcoming to my mates and me whenever we descended on him wet and hungry, I hope to some day properly reciprocate.

Thanks for reading.

Notes on Spellings and Translation

The following is a short pronunciation guide to Malaitan and Solomon Islands Pijin words:

a   pronounced as in mama
b   pronounced mb, as in timber
d   pronounced nd, as in candy
e   pronounced as in egg
g   pronounced ng as in mango
i   pronounced like e in me
o   pronounced as in go
u   pronounced as in true
'   glottal stop (a consonant, treated as the last letter of the alphabet)

Doubled vowels are pronounced as lengthened and accented (eg, Maasina Rule)

Many Malaitan names have English origins—Dio (Joe), Falage (Frank), Biri (Billy), Tome or Tomu (Tom), Sale (Charlie). I spell these phonetically by Malaitan pronunciations (they vary by area) unless the person adopted an English spelling. For some personal and place-names I have only spellings used by government officers in documents, which are often wrong or inconsistent. I have been able to correct many but not all of these, and no doubt some remain misspelled. Quotations maintain original spellings. Where possible I spell place-names as those who live there pronounce them, but for some I know only Kwaio or Kwara'ae pronunciations.

Regarding quotations of statements given to me, those of Kwaio people I have translated from Kwaio language and those of other Solomon Islanders from Solomon Islands Pijin, unless otherwise indicated. Solomon Islands Pijin pronunciations vary on Malaita and in the Solomons, typically by local language conventions. Thus there are not universally "correct" phonetic spellings, and I follow pronunciations I am most familiar with, from central Malaita.

Regarding the Endnotes

There are many endnotes in this book, for several reasons. First, all source citations are in the notes; their number would have made in-text placement too interruptive of the flow of text. Second, one target audience for this book is the fast-growing number of young Solomon Islander scholars who are interested in this history. Details regarding local people and events are important to many of them but will not be to all readers; I have put some of these in notes so those uninterested can pass them over. Finally, an astonishing amount of misinformation has been written about Maasina Rule and related topics. Many of my endnotes correct these inaccuracies. I think it important to address them, but so great is their number that to do so in the text would have made for tedious reading for those unconcerned with this history of errors.

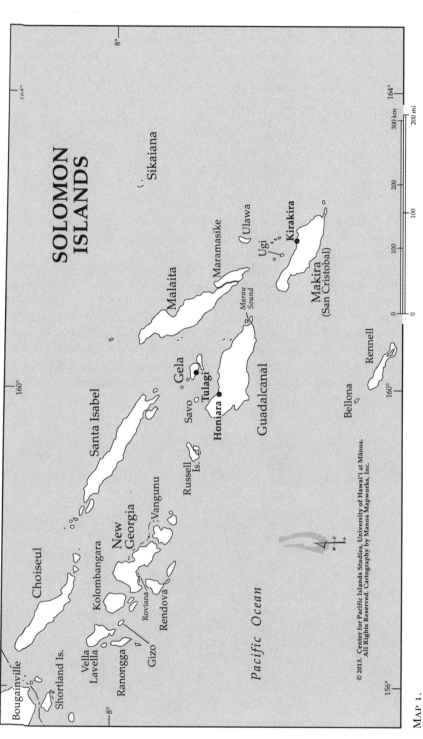

SOLOMON ISLANDS

Bougainville

Shortland Is.

Choiseul

Vella
Lavella

Ranongga

Gizo

Kolombangara

New
Georgia

Roviana

Rendova

Vangunu

Santa Isabel

Russell
Is.

Savo

Gela

Tulagi

Honiara

Guadalcanal

Marau
Sound

Malaita

Maramasike

Ulawa

Ugi

Kirakira

Makira
(San Cristobal)

Sikaiana

Bellona

Rennell

Pacific Ocean

8°

164°

160°

156°

8°

160°

164°

0   100   200   300 km

0   100   200 mi

© 2013. Center for Pacific Islands Studies, University of Hawai'i at Mānoa.
All Rights Reserved. Cartography by Manoa Mapworks, Inc.

MAP 1.

Introduction

This book is a political history of the island of Malaita in the British Solomon Islands Protectorate (BSIP) from 1927, when the last violent resistance to colonial rule was crushed, to 1953 and the inauguration of the first island-wide, representative political body, the Malaita Council. It is a case study of the inner workings of the colonial administration and how its officers and policies interacted with Malaitans and their desires for change. At the book's center are a political movement known as Maasina Rule that sought to bring about that change, and the movement's core ideology, known by the Solomon Islands Pijin term *kastom*. Maasina Rule dominated Malaitan affairs from the mid-1940s into the early 1950s, and *kastom* remains important in Solomon Islands politics today. Historians, anthropologists, and former colonial officials have all written extensively about Maasina Rule over several decades, and yet, though some of this work has been excellent, the literature has been plagued with errors, and basic aspects of both the movement and Malaitan *kastom* have remained poorly or partly understood.

I am a cultural anthropologist by training, and over the past three decades I have spent several years living and studying in the mountains of Malaita. But much of my data for this book comes from period government documents, complemented by oral historical accounts and additional materials provided by Malaitans, Christian missionaries, former colonial officers, and others. These latter sources bring to light much that is absent from the colonial archive and often contradict the picture it presents.[1]

My concentration on Malaita has advantages and disadvantages. The demarcation of the island as my subject is artificial in that throughout the period under study Malaitans maintained important political and other links with neighboring islands: Langalanga with Gela, north Malaita with Isabel, southern Malaita with eastern Guadalcanal, Makira, and Ulawa (see map 1). Furthermore, these other islands all had their own versions of Maasina Rule and *kastom* ideologies, and other Solomon Islanders shared many of the Malaitan experiences I will examine. While I do not ignore interisland connections and broader economic, political, and religious contexts, my focus remains on Malaita throughout.[2] The advantage of the tighter focus is that it lets me undertake a deeper, more nuanced analysis of events, processes, and people than would be possible in a geographically broader study. Key aspects of this history emerge from the details: many documents

1

that I draw on may seem trivial on their face—telegrams, handwritten notes, fleeting updates—but it is often in such items, more than in formal reports, that something closer to truths may be found, not yet sanitized or varnished for consumption by more senior officials or the public.

I highlight not only the workings of the colonial administrative system but also the actions of individual colonial officers, and in many places I delve into their shortcomings and failures. My intent in doing so is not to employ hindsight to harp on deficiencies, prejudices, or injustices of colonial rule for their own sake. Rather, understanding what drove Malaitans' political actions and generated the *kastom* ideologies that anchored them requires frank examination of what they rebelled against. Only in this way can one appreciate why most of them during Maasina Rule took up the call for resistance and change so earnestly and tenaciously, despite extreme government efforts to rein them back. At the same time, we want to know why officers acted in the ways they did, including why many at times believed acute repression necessary. For this, one must also consider European attitudes of the day toward Melanesians in general and Malaitans in particular, in tandem with the Malaitan actions that officers were reacting to.

To argue, as I do, that the colonial project badly failed on Malaita is not at all to say that all officers who worked on the island were failures—many were diligent and dedicated young men (most in their twenties) who tried to and often did do good on the island. Also, readers will become familiar with a pattern of district officers finding their decisions overruled by superiors with no grasp of Malaitan realities, who were disinclined to allow more progressive initiatives, let alone fund them. Officers served an administrative system that developed its own dynamics, concepts, values, and blind spots. Nonetheless, throughout this book I highlight individual officers because with only a handful in charge of Malaita over many years, and with their workplace so opaque to their superiors, their individual personalities, attitudes, and skills had great consequences for what took place there. We will see that changes in personnel sometimes triggered radical shifts in policies and events.

As the field of colonial studies has flourished over the last few decades, a most productive research topic has been how colonial states created and applied ethnographic, historical, linguistic, and other forms of knowledge to construct, categorize, represent, restructure, and manage the societies they ruled. Building on Gramscian and Foucauldian theories of knowledge and power, Edward Said's insights on Orientalist discourses, and Bernard Cohn's pioneering writings on India, scholars have studied the "cultural technologies of rule" with which colonial officials gathered, selected, ordered, modified, and invented knowledge of subject societies for their own purposes. This literature has highlighted colonial censusing; ethnography; attempted standardizations of languages, texts, and religious codes; and the creation of ethnic groups and boundaries, "traditional" leadership structures, codes of "customary law," and models of race and gender. All of these are part of the history I present here.[3]

The seminal studies of the field addressed British India, where the collection, systematization, and application of colonial knowledge were particularly wide-ranging and intense, to the degree that Cohn asserted, "The conquest of India was a conquest of knowledge," and Nicholas Dirks described India's late-nineteenth-century government as "an ethnographic state."[4] Early work in this area emphasized the effectiveness of knowledge-based regimes in imposing hegemonic orders on relatively passive subjects. Later studies from India and elsewhere have painted a more complex picture and have critiqued previous analyses as having been overly focused on European domination and agency. They have stressed ways in which colonial systems developed out of dialogic processes involving both colonizers and colonized. Some studies document subaltern participation in the compilation and construction of colonial knowledge, while others highlight indigenous precursors to and continuities with colonial models and institutions. Still others question the degree to which colonial regimes really attained the sorts of hegemony or control they sought or claimed. In the same vein, there is much interest in what Cohn called the "unintended effects" that a colonial "discursive formation" could have, since "those who were to be the objects produced by the formation often turned it to their own ends." Maasina Rule presents a remarkable case of this.[5]

Common themes run through different expressions of colonialism, and any student of the topic will recognize many of them in the Malaitan case. Diverse colonies were connected through core ideologies, centralized if often inharmonious policymaking by ruling powers, and—especially significant to the Solomons scene—direct transfers of ideas and personnel from one colony to another. Nonetheless, once one understands colonial systems as the products of interactions between disparate colonists and diverse colonized peoples, it becomes problematic to think of colonialism as a unified phenomenon or logic, even when looking at territories ruled by the same power. We find that, in Nicholas Thomas's words, "colonialism can only be traced through its plural and particularized expressions," as assorted colonialisms.[6] A case in point is the Solomons, where distinctive strategies and forms of rule developed on islands in clear sight of each other and even, as on Malaita, regarding different groups inhabiting a single island. One task for postcolonial studies has been to work out the relationships of colonialism's general themes and policies with their specific expressions and practice in different settings.

Concepts and techniques of rule developed in India were later transferred uneasily to African colonies, where they contributed to the construction of formal schemes of indirect rule that purported to adapt African political and legal structures to colonial administration. These African models were subsequently, if haphazardly, transposed to the Solomons. They did not arrive only as concepts and directives emanating from London; from 1929 throughout the period dealt with here, all of the Protectorate's senior officials were transferred there from African colonies, and they brought with them firm views of and guidelines for how "natives" were best ruled.[7]

By the 1930s, and especially after World War II, the Solomon Islands were a British embarrassment (when London noticed them) in that direct rule of a colony with no provision for social services or means of advancement had become anachronistic. There was a felt need and mild pressure from above to catch up with the times and begin instituting less direct rule, but to do so was difficult in that no foundation for such a shift had ever been laid. The BSIP government had provided neither education nor medical care; serious development for the benefit of inhabitants had never been on the agenda; and the state had always disqualified "primitive" Solomon Islanders from having any formal role in their own governance. A system of indirect rule was nevertheless slowly put into operation—at first casually and then, not long before and just after World War II, officially—that loosely but explicitly followed African models. As in parts of Africa, the Solomons system entailed a "native administration" grounded in selected and modified "native custom." Particularly important to the official system was the government's recognition and appointment of "traditional leaders" ("chiefs" or "elders"), the codification of selected "customs," and the institutionalization of bodies and methods of dispute resolution through which the leaders would apply them, all under close official supervision. The leaders and "customs" were to be deployed most importantly in "native councils" and "native courts" appointed in each subdistrict. It was expected these bodies would ease the workload of overburdened officers at minimal cost and also mollify Islanders who were calling for more voice in running their own affairs. Thus did the government import and institute a structure through which to apply colonially ordered ethnographic knowledge to govern Solomon Islands societies. But on Malaita, as well as other islands, a fundamental obstacle to putting this plan into operation was the government's glaring lack of such knowledge.

I first worked in the Solomon Islands National Archives in the 1980s, at a time when history and anthropology were still divided by a sharper disciplinary boundary. One day, a well-known historian of the Solomons visited the archives and asked me if I had discovered anything useful. When I indicated a quantity of materials, he replied with a puzzled look, "I didn't think there was that much anthropology *in* here." He was right in the sense that colonial documents related to Malaita contain surprisingly little ethnographic information of the sort most people then considered to be within the anthropologist's purview. The problem was that most colonial officers knew little about the inner workings of Malaita societies, and what past officers had managed to learn was never systematically recorded. In most colonies, administrators typically knew much less about their subjects than they believed they did or claimed to, particularly regarding areas they considered most backward. Yet it is striking nonetheless to realize the degree of colonial ignorance regarding Malaitans and the lack of effort that was made to obtain, record, or create any body of ethnographic knowledge about them. Many officers were conscious of this, though they varied as to whether or not they saw it as a serious handicap; one finds fewer claims to or attributions of "ethnographic acuity" in these documents than in those for other colonies.[8]

This was not really the fault of district officers. They were never assigned the task of, or given adequate means for the concerted gathering of such information, and most seem to have given it little serious thought. Even those who would have liked to closely study and document Malaitan societies did not have time for it, given their many and at times overwhelming duties: on Malaita, two (or at times three) officers had to administer and tax some 50,000 culturally diverse people, speaking ten languages and living in thousands of shifting hamlets and villages scattered across 4,225 square kilometers of rugged terrain. Moreover, officers were transferred often, and with no organized system in place to record for successors what cultural information one had collected, research was an unwise use of time and resources. At a more basic level, the sorts of unofficial, personal relationships and interactions through which colonial officers might have learned more about Malaitans and their lives were precluded by a high wall of separation maintained from both sides. Most colonists frowned on "familiarity" with the natives, and many Malaitans avoided interacting with officers more than was absolutely necessary.

To make matters more difficult still, Malaita, unlike many British possessions, attracted few anthropologists, linguists, historians, or religious scholars who could assist the state. There were a few Anglican clergymen, particularly Walter Ivens, who learned languages and wrote useful studies, and anthropologist H Ian Hogbin came in 1933 and spent several months studying in the far north of the island, yet the government scarcely made use of their published work.[9] Finally, although an important qualification for Malaitan leadership was possession and control of knowledge, very few Malaitans were literate and there was no tradition of written scholarship, and so the government could not realistically look to Malaitans for a substantive corpus of texts about their own societies.

Much of what officers did learn they acquired piecemeal in the course of their duties, especially when holding courts. Not one of them learned a Malaitan language, and some spoke even Solomon Islands Pijin poorly. This is not to say district officers were unintelligent or invariably uninterested; the obstacle was the system in which they served, which assigned minimal value, training, or resources to building serious knowledge about Malaitans and their everyday lives beyond what was required to maintain order and a steady supply of plantation laborers and to collect taxes.

Given the lack of ethnographic expertise, broader understandings that officers did have of the people as human beings could be deeply flawed. We will see that the gaping holes in their knowledge were often filled with crude stereotypes, some of which were fully contradictory: Malaitans were wholly mystical in their worldview; they were crassly and wholly materialistic. Malaitans cared little about money or wages because they could meet their own wants; they coveted white wealth and progress but were too lazy to work for it; they were by natural fact the best workers in the Protectorate. Malaitans were inherently uncreative, trapped in a world of unchanging "custom," fearing change and yearning for a return to the past; their demands for change were unreasonable since they were already changing too fast. Malaitans had no sense of community and their societies were fettered by atomism and disorder; they were radically communalistic in that they could not think as individuals but only in conformity with their group. Malaitans lacked strong leaders; they followed their leaders slavishly. These stereotypes, which of course ascribed traits that Europeans attributed to many other nonwhite peoples they ruled over, provided an always-handy grab bag of tenets through which to "know" Malaitans, and for making and justifying decisions as to how best to deal with and control them.

In sum, there had been no "conquest of knowledge" on Malaita. So when the colonial government imported a framework designed to impose aspects of an "ethnographic state," there was little ethnographic information with which to give it substance, and understandings of local societies were mired in misinterpretation and confusion. To obtain the knowledge necessary to constructing the new system, the government was forced to turn to Malaitans themselves. Just before World War II, Malaitans, despite their minimal literacy, were instructed to codify their "customs" and were told that after government had approved these they would be allowed to apply them to managing aspects of their own lives. Unlike in some other colonies, officers did little to engage with the codification process itself, and this gave Malaitans, fully aware of British ignorance, a political opening: indirect rule was set down on Malaita as an empty vessel, and Malaitans seized the opportunity to fill it with "customary" contents to their own liking.

After the war, officers revived the indirect rule scheme with renewed vigor but soon lost control of it to the Maasina Rule movement. Examples are legion of colonized people appropriating and "turning to their own ends" colonial concepts and institutions, including for manipulating or resisting their colonizers,[10] but what occurred on Malaita was extraordinary. Malaitans did not just shape, harness, or exploit the native administration scheme. Rather, as Maasina Rule took hold, they commandeered, expanded, and extended nearly all facets of it—chiefly offices, legal codes, courts, censuses, social engineering projects—and added many elements of their own making to create a system for self-government and sweeping social reform, one that would no longer require British overseers.

In addition to the mechanisms and institutions of indirect rule, Malaitans appropriated the concept of "custom." "Custom" expressed a British vision of Malaitan societies as ahistorical, static, and to some degree unchangeable, and "true customs" were conceived as surviving, authentic, pre-European ways of life. Malaitans recognized this as a contrivance, and their concept of *kastom* expressed their more realistic understandings of their own societies as dynamic, flexible, and rapidly changing. Malaitans demanded no ancestral pedigree for something to qualify as *kastom,* which encompassed fully new political structures and leadership, social and legal rules, innovative programs for great change, even labor strikes. *Kastom* labeled a political ideology and actions founded on Malaitans' determination to pursue change on their own terms, according to their own sensibilities.

Kastom was like "custom" had been, in the sense that Malaitans would oversee it, with the critical difference that whereas "custom" had been kept on at the government's pleasure, *kastom* would now move forward fully in Malaitan hands. While district officers wanted "custom" codified to make it more accessible to and manageable by the state, Malaitans codified *kastom* to demarcate a realm that the government was to leave fully to Malaitans, and that furthermore would include almost everything. *Kastom* became a voracious category, encompassing all things over which Malaitans now claimed authority. In other words, Malaitan *kastom* was fundamentally different from British "custom," and it rapidly became a label for the entire Maasina Rule project and its ideology, eventually including people's refusal of European rule, at least on its old terms.

Colonial officers persistently confused *kastom* with their own concept of "custom" and saw in the Malaitan usage an ignorance of the term's meaning, or, increasingly, crude political deceit. To them, *kastom* was a disingenuous invention of tradition for purposes of political manipulation. The colonial confusion of *kastom* and "custom" was a precursor to anthropological conflations decades later of *kastom* with "culture," which led to similar misunderstandings. Many of the later anthropological errors stemmed from an insufficient understanding of the deep historical-political roots of the *kastom* concept in places like Malaita, and one purpose of this book is to help to remedy that problem.[11]

The rest of this introduction previews the chapters to follow and places the abovementioned themes in the context and trajectory of the book as a whole. Chapter 1 provides an overview of the early history of Malaitan-European interactions, highlighting the labor trade and the imposition of Pax Britannica. From 1870 into the first decade of the twentieth century, ships carried thousands of Malaitans and other Solomon Islanders to work on Fiji or Queensland plantations. For decades before Europeans gained any foothold on Malaita, the labor trade brought new tools, weapons, crops, wealth, and diseases, as well as ideas about everything from proper social relations to religious practice. All realms of life were transformed. We will see that

Malaitans during this period displayed remarkable flexibility and creativity both at home and abroad, and there is no better historical argument against the notion (which appears often in this book and is still held by many Europeans today) of Malaitans as inherently conservative and unable to adapt, and the companion idea that "custom," in the sense of precontact ways of life, remained intact well into the twentieth century and had to be protected by Europeans from unmanaged change.

The period is also important to us because it saw the first emergence of a broader Malaitan political consciousness out of the shared Melanesian experience of low status in European-dominated settings, and recognition of not just the opportunities but also the dangers that white people presented to their homeland. Here we find roots of Malaitans' insistence that they themselves decide what to adopt or reject from elsewhere, an idea that still infuses Malaitan *kastom* ideologies. But Malaitans have often disagreed as to what is suitable to them, the most obvious early example being conflicts between those who adopted Christianity and those who rejected it, first abroad and then at home. Important here, too, is how early Christian churches on Malaita built organizational structures and networks that were later harnessed in the service of social protest and resistance movements.

In chapter 1, I also summarize shifting patterns of violence during these early decades, both among Malaitans and between Europeans and Malaitans. Just as the overseas labor period was ending, the BSIP government initiated its first attempts to bring Malaita under its control. At first unsuccessful, these efforts were intensified in the late 1910s and 1920s, culminating in the final imposition of colonial rule by means of a brutal punitive expedition launched in 1927 after a district officer and most of his party were killed as they tried to collect taxes. From that point onward, organized Malaitan resistance to the colonial system would remain nonviolent.

The second and third chapters examine the government's attempts in the years before World War II to erect a system of native administration. The main goals were to maintain order, to carry out taxation, and, above all, to ensure a continuing flow of laborers to the Protectorate's plantations. At first a system of "indirect rule" of the African type was planned, but due partly to funding problems during the Depression and partly to officers' low opinions of Malaitans and their abilities, that plan was delayed for several years. The only Malaitans given power were government-appointed "headmen," many of whom had little community standing. Neither Malaitan leaders nor institutions were officially recognized, but necessity demanded much unofficial reliance on both as officers and headmen tried to apply "native custom" to settle disputes and other matters and had to depend on local leaders for assistance. Only in the late 1930s did the administration finally begin trying to set up a formal system of indirect rule.

Chapter 2 looks at how the administrative system worked on the ground and also its flaws. Especially problematic was that officers privileged and granted political agency to "custom" but, as already noted, possessed insuf-ficient knowledge of Malaitan life to make the system work well. Further, partly as a result of this ignorance, the "custom" concept was riddled with fictions and contradictions that were on constant display for Malaitans to see. I describe Malaitan interactions with and changing assessments of gov-ernment during the prewar period, giving special attention to legal matters because "custom" was particularly important in that realm and because law, or *loa*, soon became a focus of conflict between Malaitans and the state. The chapter also introduces several individuals who remain important through much of the book. This story has characters, and as readers get to know them they will better understand why they acted as they did, and why Malai-tans reacted to them as they did.

Chapter 3 begins with the Great Depression, which ruined the BSIP econ-omy and directly affected Malaitans, who were dependent on indentured plantation work. Wages were halved and throughout the 1930s resentment grew toward the white establishment, especially for its exploitive labor sys-tem. Malaitans and other Solomon Islanders now began to openly express dissatisfaction with their lot under colonial rule. I consider two examples of that expression from 1939: one movement started by an Anglican priest named Richard Fallowes on the island of Isabel, and another on Malaita that was directed by messages from the spirit of a powerful ancestress. The first demanded education, medical services, and Islander participation in government; the second predicted that American invaders would soon vio-lently oust the British. Each in different ways foreshadowed Maasina Rule.

As the 1930s progressed, the administration faced two other press-ing problems: a chronic shortage of staff and funding, and what officers believed to be an ongoing and rapid depopulation of Malaitan peoples. This chapter analyzes two solutions officers devised to meet these problems, and how together they led to the reified "custom" concept becoming a key-stone of administrative policy, particularly as it directly affected Malaitans. Settling disputes was a great drain on officers' time and resources, and it was decided to institute a system of "native courts and councils" presided over by government headmen, with recognized "chiefs" and "elders" act-ing as assessors. Communities were instructed to compile written codes of "local custom" for the courts and councils to apply once the government had modified and approved them.

The second problem, depopulation, officers blamed partly on a psycho-logical factor: Malaitans were dying off because they had lost interest in life or were emotionally exhausted due to a "cultural fatigue" caused by the European "fatal impact." Melanesia's cultures were thought to be stagnant and rigid, and its people lost and bewildered without the "rule of custom" that had once "regulated every detail of existence." The key to combat-ing depopulation, therefore, was cultural stabilization, preservation, and revitalization, and paradoxically, radical social reorganization. Government policy became that "old native custom" would be authorized, encouraged, and modestly empowered. Malaitans were told that officers would avoid interfering with their "custom," "so long as it did not run counter to the dictates of humanity," and that they would be accorded some powers to administer it themselves through the courts and councils.[12] In this way, the pursuit of greater order and control with meager resources and the apparent need to save local societies from themselves dovetailed to push "custom" front and center in government administration and social engineering schemes. One section of chapter 3 considers the courts and councils and how Malaitans received them. Another examines a major project carried out at the decade's end to reorganize and revive native populations, which involved relocation of the populace into large villages tending communal gardens and "the stabilization of custom" through the development of codes to be applied by the native courts.

Chapter 4 takes readers into the period of World War II, which scattered the colonial apparatus and exposed Solomon Islanders to a novel racial and social order. Several thousand Malaitans, and other Islanders as well, worked for the US military in the Solomon Islands Labour Corps on Guadalcanal and Gela. There they were astonished by the great material wealth in evidence and, more important, by the generosity and camaraderie they found among some of the American soldiers both white and black. Few soldiers knew or worried about maintaining the colonial racial codes that Solomon Islanders lived under. At the same time, with district officers away or focused on the war, Malaitans reasserted control over much of their island, which the fighting left mostly untouched. Overall, the war experience suggested to Islanders alternatives to life under British rule and left Malaitans determined to resist a return to the prewar status quo.

This was a period of strikes and political discussions—some of the latter with Americans—and people went so far as to try to secure a continued US presence and future help by making mass donations to the Red Cross. Though Maasina Rule had yet to formally organize, it began here among the wartime laborers. As the war moved off to the north, the colonial administration, recognizing and fearing but still underestimating rising discontent, renewed its pledge to provide education and medical services. These had been promised since the 1920s but never delivered, and I explain Malaitan anger at this perceived betrayal. Officers also worked with new vigor to restart native courts and councils, based again on "custom," which would give Malaitans more say in their own affairs. But what they now offered was, for Malaitans, not enough and far too late, and in any case officers soon found that "custom" matters had been taken out of their hands, to be reasserted now as *kastom* controlled by Malaitans.

Chapter 5 describes Maasina Rule's rapid rise, its programs, and how it transformed life on the island during its heyday of 1946 and 1947. It was launched in 1944 in the south where the government's prewar repopulation efforts had been most intense. At this time, political movements were forming in almost every part of Malaita, and Maasina Rule soon melded them into a single initiative to reject the colonial order and work for a more liberated and prosperous future. It was estimated that, at its peak, 95 percent of Malaita's people were adherents, and the movement in various forms dominated the island's affairs into the early 1950s, in addition to spreading in various permutations to neighboring islands. It commandeered and expanded nearly all aspects of the government's prewar administrative and social engineering schemes: "chiefs" were appointed, *kastom* councils and courts were created, and endless meetings were held to compile *kastom* codes that registered new rules for community life and forbade many old ways deemed unsuitable for the new society. People gathered in large coastal villages, or "towns," and tended communal "farms." Maasina Rule during this phase was heavily engaged in building forward-looking social programs and cannot be understood simply as a resistance movement. Malaitans also told Europeans that no men could work for them now because their labor was needed for Maasina Rule's projects at home.

Malaitans put forward "custom"—now *kastom*—as a symbol of unity. Before Maasina Rule, the island had been divided by religious and political factionalism, with sometimes-bitter relations not only between Christians and those following ancestors, but also between the different Christian churches. There were also long-standing enmities between and within different groups, and intergenerational tensions were rife. The most daunting challenge Maasina Rule faced was how to unify all of these groups into a cohesive and effective movement to pursue radical change, led by "chiefs" with little coercive power. I explore at length how they accomplished this. Europeans, who had long taken comfort from the assurance that xenophobic Malaitans would never be able to unite as a political force, were shocked and dismayed.

Having looked at Maasina Rule from within, I turn in chapter 6 to the movement's interactions with the government, which have been greatly oversimplified and otherwise misconstrued in past writings. An important task of this and the next two chapters is to present a nuanced account of government-movement relations and how they shifted dramatically over time. Early government understandings of Maasina Rule and the forces driving it can be divided into four general phases. The first, detailed across chapters 3 and 4, was the dawning recognition, just before, during, and immediately after the war, that Solomon Islanders were profoundly dissatisfied and were starting to organize to demand change. This was brought home first by the Fallowes movement and then more powerfully by the defiant actions of men in the Labour Corps. Officials were confident that they could manage the situation, which they blamed more on the war's unsettling impact than on deficiencies in the colonial system—they thought their difficulties would subside if they instituted countermeasures, particularly native courts and councils and—at some unspecified, later time—schools and medical services.

Chapter 6 begins at the second phase, with a belated government realization that Maasina Rule had organized and extended throughout the island. At first alarmed, officers came to believe they could guide the movement toward government objectives, many of which harmonized with Maasina Rule, and that eventually it would fade as a viable threat to the colonial order. Discussions became more urgent regarding the need to grant still more powers to courts and councils and to act on long-standing promises of social services.

A third phase began in mid-1946 when officers recognized with alarm that Maasina Rule was overflowing the channels of government control. Nonetheless, for many months district officers kept working with the leaders to try to redirect and harness the movement's force, and many Malaitans envisioned a continuing if much reduced role for the government. However, in mid-1947 the scene rapidly shifted when crucial officers left Malaita and open opposition to government policies intensified in northern parts of the island. A fourth phase began when a new district commissioner in August resolved, with the resident commissioner's assent, to arrest Maasina Rule leaders and crush the entire movement by means of a series of raids labeled "Operation Delouse." This extreme response was based on gross misunderstandings of the movement as well as the resident commissioner's frustration at the remarkable Malaita-wide refusal to resume working on plantations. I explain the Malaitan resolve to resist a return to the old indentured labor system.

Chapter 7 examines a prolonged period of intense government repression and Malaitan resistance that followed Operation Delouse, particularly during 1948 and 1949. It quickly became clear that officers had badly misread Maasina Rule; it was not, as they had believed, propelled by a clique of bullying leaders but was instead a truly popular movement that Malaitans were determined to carry forward even in the face of government attacks, with or without their jailed leaders. When the main leaders were sentenced to prison for sedition, a massive civil resistance campaign was organized, and thousands lined up for arrest and jail. Officers announced that the government would force every last Malaitan to concede its authority and legitimacy by ceasing disobedience, paying the head tax, and submitting to a census. Disrupted by the government campaign, Maasina Rule could no longer effectively pursue its constructive projects, and Malaitans turned their energies to defiance. Once the suppression campaign began, moderate factions that the government might have negotiated with disappeared.

At this time Malaita was also rife with rumors about everything from impending arrival of American military ships and troops to drive away the British, to government plans to launch murderous attacks on movement followers. Some officers claimed such ideas demonstrated how irrational the movement was and why it had to be suppressed. Many anthropologists followed their lead and for years analyzed Maasina Rule within the "cargo cult" literature. Later writers rejected such portrayals, arguing instead that such ideas were never important to the movement and that they distracted scholars from grasping its political and liberationist nature. I examine these divergent readings, and truths that lie between them, at the end of chapter 7.

By early 1950, it was clear that the government's strategy—the years of mass arrests and refusals to negotiate until all Malaitans capitulated—had failed. Officers, but not Malaitans, had always said that if people began again to pay tax and to labor on the plantations it would mean the death of the resistance. Something under half of Malaitan men by this point had paid the tax to avoid further imprisonment; more men were signing on as shorter-term, non-indentured laborers; and people no longer lined up for prison. But, in a coordinated movement strategy, they instead fled from any contact with officers and would have nothing to do with any government endeavor. Further, resistance was now being guided by what was called the "Federal Council," and its leaders were as unwilling as the government officers to compromise. The government had failed to attain its goal of forcing Malaitans to capitulate and acknowledge its legitimacy.

London wanted resolution and commencement of the political and economic development that postwar colonial policy dictated, and the Colonial Office sent a new resident commissioner to seek a way out. He decided to release the head chiefs from prison on license and to initiate educational, medical, and agricultural projects on Malaita, though most of its people still refused to cooperate. This began a long, slow shift in government policy away from coercion toward conciliation, with many fits, starts, and regressions along the way. Chapter 8 traces the three-year process of attrition and compromise that culminated in 1953 in the formal inauguration of an island-wide Malaita Council, most of whose members had been resistance leaders.

The book's final chapter assesses what Malaitans, the government, and the Solomons gained and lost through Maasina Rule. The movement has usually been pronounced a failure, but most assessments of its outcomes have been poorly informed and cursory, with little analysis of adherents' multiple, shifting, and at times contradictory goals. Likewise there has been no comparative examination of the colonial government's varying goals and its successes and failures in attaining them. A more careful look at the changes that Maasina Rule brought about reveals both important gains and tragic losses for Malaita and for the Solomons as a whole. As part of this appraisal I discuss how *kastom* has remained a foundation of Malaitan political thought and practice in the decades since Maasina Rule.

Chapter 1
The Half Century Before

This book's main focus is a period that begins just after the colonial government crushed the last martial resistance to its rule in 1927. By then, Malaitans had been interacting with Europeans for well over 50 years, and their societies had been radically changed by their men laboring abroad and by new technologies, weapons, crops, and political ideas. Many themes that appear in the chapters to follow first emerged during these early decades, and I want to summarize key aspects of the period for readers unfamiliar with Solomon Islands history. Particularly important are the impacts of the labor trade and, in the 1910s and 1920s, the imposition of government rule.

The Labor Trade

Pacific historians have exhaustively studied the labor trades of Fiji and, particularly, Queensland, Australia.[1] Sustained Malaitan contact with Europeans began about 1871 when the Solomons became a new frontier for labor recruiters. From the mid-1880s into the early twentieth century, Solomon Islanders, especially Malaitans, made up the majority of Queensland recruits; by 1904 over 9,000 had gone there. About half that number of Solomon Islanders went to Fiji, some 60 percent of them Malaitans, and a few ended up in German Samoa or New Caledonia. Malaita has been the premier reservoir of Solomon Islands plantation labor ever since.[2]

European writers have often portrayed the labor trade simplistically, either as based on kidnapping or as a matter of young men, and a much smaller number of women, taking to the ship for adventure or respite from pressures and responsibilities of home. There is some truth in both portrayals, but the bigger picture was much more complex. In some areas men were indeed kidnapped, or "blackbirded" early on, but as the Queensland trade swelled in the 1880s, although deceptive recruiting methods continued, most Malaitans went as volunteers or were offered up by their communities (sometimes with little say in the matter themselves). Nonetheless, the early abductions and the continuing exploitive nature of the trade and mistreatment, humiliations, and violence on the plantations deeply stained Malaitan historical memories of the labor trade and their long-term perceptions of Europeans. The labor trade's abuses remain politically evocative even today.[3]

The labor period clearly brought revolutionary changes to Malaita, but details of how or when many of them occurred, and even at times their precise nature, have eluded anthropologists and historians, as have core aspects of precontact Malaitan society. Daily life during this period, especially in the mountains where most people then lived, is mostly invisible in written records, and decades of great change took place before Europeans ventured beyond the coastal margins. In most parts of Malaita, colonial government became a significant force only in the later 1910s and 1920s, a half century after the labor trade began. Up to that time, Malaitans generally were able to deter European intrusions and manage foreign visitors via coastal middlemen; historian Clive Moore aptly labeled the island in the early decades after European arrival in the Solomons "fortress Malaita." Here we find roots of Malaitans' insistence that they decide for themselves what to adopt or reject from the outside, setting a pattern of what Roger Keesing called "compartmentalization"—selective demarcation of outside places, ways, and people as conceptually distinct and separated from the homeland and home ways.[4] But we will see that Malaitans came to sharply disagree over where such boundaries should be drawn and what was suitable or unsuitable for them.

What is apparent is that Malaitans adapted with amazing speed to the changes brought about by European incursions. Beyond initial contacts, there is little evidence that they held Europeans in any awe, though for many decades, some whites would imagine people gazing at them in childlike wonderment. Malaitan concerns quickly turned to acquiring new wealth, weapons, and other technologies through both peaceful and violent means. They soon became adept at dealing with whites and the demands of laboring, though this at times required considerable reassessment and revision of ancestral and other cultural rules. Many fundamental principles for changing and adapting ancestral religions (and later, Christianities) in contexts of rapid change evolved during this period.

A prime motivation for labor recruits and leaders who offered them up was a desire for trade goods, some of which dramatically changed Malaitan life. An early incentive was to obtain steel tools, at first tomahawks and then axe blades. Steel allowed men to clear jungle for gardening much more quickly, which meant increases in crops harvested and pig herds fed with them. Steel also revolutionized the making of many shell currencies used on the island (though Langalanga people used stone tools to make shell beads into the later twentieth century). These and related changes led to enormous expansions of and inflation in feasting, brideprices, compensations for dispute resolution, bounties paid for killings, and other socioeconomic institutions.

Before long, many men were signing on largely to get guns. For years it was legal to import and sell them, and Malaitans acquired imposing arsenals. Most were smoothbore muskets and the more powerful steel-barreled

Snider-Enfield breach-loaders (accurate to 100 meters) cast off by the British army for the 0.45 Martini-Henry in 1871 and sold by thousands to recruiters. They also obtained Spencers, Winchesters, Martini-Henrys, pistols, and other arms. In 1883 Anglican Bishop John Selwyn claimed that every returnee carried one or more guns and several hundred rounds of ammunition, and many more weapons were given as beach payments for new recruits. An 1884 act prohibited British firearm (and liquor) sales, despite raucous opposition from whites in Queensland and the "sullen indignation" of Melanesians, but guns kept coming via French recruiters, and illegally from Australian recruiters and rampant smuggling by returnees. In 1902 the Protectorate's first resident commissioner, Charles Woodford, guessed that Malaitans held 4,000–5,000 Winchester repeating rifles, and his deputy, Arthur Mahaffy, claimed that 80 percent of men owned guns. As late as 1927, men of one north Malaita district surrendered 1,077 guns in fear of government reprisal for the killing of a district officer farther south, though by then there was little ammunition on the island.[5]

It is usually assumed that guns triggered increased violence on Malaita and elsewhere in Melanesia, but this is hard to gauge and difficult to detach from changing modes of conflict and destabilizing impacts of other rapid

Figure 1.1. "Men of Central Malaita, Armed Bushmen at home," ca 1911, near the west Kwaio-Kwara'ae border. (Photo by Northcote Deck, courtesy of the SSEM Archive, 5MENFR~1.)

changes taking place. It is notable that later, as ammunition grew very scarce, violence continued at high levels. Patterns of fighting varied through time with shifting supplies, distribution, and models of guns and ammunition, as well as with changing social conditions. Guns extinguished certain modes of violence. For example, one style of Malaitan warfare resembled that in the New Guinea Highlands: groups formally faced off at established fighting grounds to duel with bows and spears, layered tapa cloth body armor, and painted shields of wood and bark coated with flint shards or canarium almond shells, while women repaired arrows behind the lines. But guns put an end to all that.[6]

Soon, new sorts of leaders emerged. Most Malaitan harbors had one or more "passage masters" (referring to passages through reefs or into harbors), who acted as middlemen between communities and recruiters. Called "interpreter men" (Pijin: *tobetamani*), most were former laborers familiar with Europeans and Pijin. Men like Kwaisulia of 'Adagege in northern Lau and Fo'alanga of Walade in the south expanded their spheres and degrees of influence far beyond what had been possible before on Malaita by redistributing guns and other goods they received for recruits.[7] Such men were sophisticated negotiators and though recruiters and missionaries denigrated many as manipulators or cheats they could not avoid them.[8] At some passages, several men might assert rights to negotiate with Europeans and claim the title of *sifi* (chief). When the *Helena* called at Uru in east Malaita in 1892, "At least five men claimed to be 'masters' of local villages," and a few years later, after Anglican Bishop Cecil Wilson visited 'Ataa farther north, he reported, "Every man I met said he was a chief, and wanted presents of hooks, etc." A government officer in 1909 wrote of Malaita, "The district appears to be inhabited solely by chiefs." Some leaders marshaled goods brought home by returned laborers and deployed them in feasting and other competitive exchanges. In places young men converted their trade goods into local wealth and entered economic realms formerly dominated by older men. Others found new power through their guns, which some used to kill to collect blood bounties. In these and other ways, the political-economic scene was remade.[9]

The labor trade brought many other new things. Initial disquiet that whites smoked from fires within was soon laughed off, and many Solomon Islanders became addicted to tobacco. Getting it soon became an important motivation for leaving to labor on plantations. For decades Virginia tobacco sticks served as a currency, and naturalist Henry Guppy wrote, "A white man without tobacco in these islands is worse off than a man without money in his purse in London." Food crops that were introduced included pineapple and papaya, and new varieties of taro, yams, bananas, and sugarcane. Sweet potato, later a Malaitan staple, first came to most places during the labor trade, though for most inland people it did not become an important food crop right away, and in some places not until blights devastated taro in the mid-1920s. Imported ornamental plants and trees were also popular.[10]

Taro and yam gardens were a source of prestige and men worked hard in them, but the potato was considered a mundane "women's crop," so the more it was planted, the more garden work fell to women. As potatoes grew in importance, once-vital taro rituals conducted by priests in special shrines were abridged or faded away. Yam ritual complexes built on shrine hierarchies integrated different regions of Malaita, but these disappeared by the early twentieth century. Bigger and more aggressive pig breeds arrived also, and soon Malaitans demanded them as payment for recruits. Because of them, gardens needed stronger fences, which were hard work to build, and roving swine destroying gardens became a major cause of disputes. Unwelcome arrivals included the aggressive weeds that returning laborers used to pack their boxes of trade goods, which greatly increased garden work, and also rats. Imported cats helped control the latter but wiped out ground-nesting birds. The terrible new diseases that came are discussed in chapter 3.

Real and perceived excesses of the labor trade raised an outcry in some European circles, especially among missionaries, and this was one factor that pressured Britain to expand its realm into the Solomons. Important here too was the violence the trade spawned, especially that directed against Europeans. Over the first 30 years, Malaita acquired a sanguinary reputation among whites, who wryly referred to killings there as "death by natural cause." Early on, Malaitans assaulted recruiting vessels for plunder, prestige, and revenge for past abuses and attacks, particularly along the east coast. Open bounties placed on unspecified Europeans or ships became common and motivated many attacks, and some of these stood into the later 1920s. This reflected the Malaitan view that a person's relatives or allies could be held liable for their misdeeds. Europeans pointed to such bounties as indicative of the brutal nature of Malaitan societies, but they were a crucial leveling mechanism since via them militarily weak groups could use wealth gained through production and exchange to defend themselves against communities with more fighters and, later, those with more guns. Bounties assured a rough balance between martial and economic power, and integrated them. They also led (especially when bounty hunting intensified during the labor period) to murders of hundreds of innocent people, including many women and children. As with bounties placed on Malaitans, groups pooled resources to sponsor bounties on Europeans.[11]

Europeans had few options for avenging attacks. In the phrase of Anglican missionary Arthur Hopkins, based in northeast Malaita starting in 1902, coastal people and those on tiny offshore islands in the Lau and Langalanga lagoons were "get-at-able," though it was often impossible to know exactly who to punish. Inland people were mostly unget-at-able, and at that time many parts of Malaita had no coastal settlements. Warships occasionally lobbed shells into the hills but rarely did serious damage. The

FIGURE 1.2. "Malaitans on the beach just after returned laborers have been landed with their boxes of trade goods, northwest Malaita," 1907. (Photo by George Rose, Rose Stereographs 12257, Thomas Edge-Partington collection, courtesy of the Edge-Partington family.)

European quandary resembled that faced by Malaitans wronged by Europeans unknown or out of reach, and they responded in much the same way: whites were quick to ascribe sweeping group responsibility for attacks by individuals or small groups. As local informants became available—often returned laborers or passage masters—it was easier to learn who was culpable, and Europeans sometimes posted bounties of their own. But often such knowledge was brushed aside and innocents were punished "to teach the natives a lesson."[12]

Military attacks would later prove effective in bringing under European control some parts of the Protectorate, such as coastal areas and the Western Solomons. But submission in those places was partly due to Islanders' recognition that warfare was hindering their participation in an economic scene increasingly dominated by European trade and cash cropping. Likewise on Malaita, by the mid-1890s European-Malaitan clashes were on the decline. Recruiters got better at avoiding attacks, but more important, as relations became more routinized, Malaitans in power, particularly along the coast, came to see that violence against whites hampered doing business with them. However, Malaitans continued to kill Malaitans into the 1920s, and due to Malaita's place in the colonial economic system—as a labor pool rather than a site of plantations—Europeans saw little need to pursue internal pacification there. For them, and for those Malaitans who most benefited from labor recruitment, the pressing need was for peace between Malaitans and Europeans. Internal fighting could even be profitable since two important motivations for signing on as labor were flight from violence and a need for guns.[13]

Life Abroad

I cannot detail here the lives of Melanesians in Queensland and Fiji. Historians have distilled and published voluminous archival materials on the topic, and what follows draws much from their work. My primary interest is in the impacts of labor experiences abroad on Malaitan societies. Islanders' plantation experiences varied greatly. As Peter Corris described, the degree to which laborers were exposed to foreign ways, and thus often the extent to which they returned home changed persons, depended on many factors, most basic being their location and period of employment and the length of time they spent abroad. Rural Fiji was more like the Solomons than was Queensland, and within Australia men who worked on isolated farms led different lives from those on large plantations near Bundaberg or Mackay. The work and social conditions in both Queensland and Fiji also changed over time; recruits in 1900 had experiences quite unlike those in 1871. For instance, as the Queensland sugar industry blossomed in the early 1880s, men increasingly found themselves working larger estates, but when plantations were subdivided in the 1890s, more Islanders again worked on smaller farms.[14]

At first Melanesians taken abroad filled many roles such as servants, fishermen, cotton pickers, and shepherds. An 1884 Queensland bill barred the men from all but unskilled agricultural work, though noncontract workers continued to do other jobs. By the time more Malaitans were arriving, sugarcane was moving to the fore. As a Kwaio friend explained to me, most "worked on the sugar for the white people to put in their tea."[15] Treatment of laborers varied; severe physical brutality was not the norm but did occur, and working conditions were often deficient or demeaning. Over time improvements were made and mortality rates fell, though Ralph Shlomowitz has argued that the drop owed more to increased resistance to diseases than to better treatment.[16]

The experience was hardest for first-time recruits adjusting to new social scenes, climates, housing, diets, and infections.[17] But as time passed, ever more Melanesians in both Queensland and Fiji were so-called "old chums"— those who lived there for longer periods or reenlisted one or more times. Newcomers learned from them, and in later years many arrived abroad already knowing the English, Pijin, or Fijian being spoken and taught in the Solomons and on ships. Some decided where to sign on for based on detailed information from previous recruits.[18]

Melanesians differed widely in how and to what extent they adopted foreign practices abroad (including those of other Melanesians), put aside their own, or combined them with innovations distinct to plantation identities and cultures. Some, particularly those who stayed longer, took up housing and lifestyles that looked more European. A few acquired land and hired workers, or owned businesses in the "Kanakatown" districts Melanesians frequented, where stores catered to Islanders and became sites for socializing. During the 1890s, one-third had bank accounts holding an average of £8 (new indentured workers earned £6 a year; white plowmen up to £66).[19]

Christian missionaries pressed Melanesian laborers to repudiate indigenous practices and take up European ones, but as in most colonial situations they did not want them to fully adopt white ways. They could, in Mahmood Mamdani's words, be "almost the same but not quite," though here the distance of separation was to remain great, and whites often belittled those who transgressed boundaries as absurd mimics. Many whites were preoccupied with the clothing Islanders wore—oblivious to their rich senses of style and fashion, Europeans saw their attire as a façade that concealed and falsely denied the savage beneath. To missionaries, dapper Melanesians lacked the humility proper to Christians, as one explained: "Many Melanesians waste an enormous amount of money in dress. It is pleasant to see them clean and tidy; but when a 'boy' comes to Church in a faultless suit, with a white starched shirt and collar, an expensive orange and red tie, and, to crown all, with his mustache waxed to an extreme point, it is sad to see his vanity and what a fool he has made of himself. He is not going to spoil his trousers by kneeling down."[20] These views betrayed not just contempt but fear, for such men threatened the black-white distinctions and segregation so vital to those Europeans who wanted Melanesians to aspire to status no higher than servants. These white fears later became more palpable back in the Solomons with rules that forbid Melanesians to wear shirts, usually citing health concerns.[21]

FIGURE 1.3. Three Melanesian men in Queensland, nd. (Courtesy of the State Library of Queensland, negative 18044, photographer unknown.)

We have limited data on how Melanesians maintained or discarded cultural and religious practices abroad. Here again, individuals varied, much as Malaitans still do when traveling. It is important to know that these men were not so cut off from their home communities and social networks as we might suppose. Many recruited together with relatives, and men who went on the same ship often stayed together and even refused to be separated. From Langalanga, Deryck Scarr found, "Scores of people would engage together, so that there was a constant flow of young men, especially, between their villages and the plantations." Also, many Melanesians became literate and were, Hopkins later recalled, "great letter writers," and thereby exchanged news of deaths, births, and other events both at home and abroad. It is said that bounties were posted on Malaita for killings in Queensland.[22] Then again, one can exaggerate links to home. At least into the 1890s, deaths abroad often went unreported or misreported on Malaita. For example, in 1886 the ship *Young Dick* was attacked at Sinalagu Harbour to avenge a death falsely reported from Queensland. The ship kidnapped Sinalagu passage master Geni'eloa, who spent years in Fiji and Queensland before returning home in the 1890s to find his family thinking him dead and his mortuary rites long concluded. People at times turned to divination for news of faraway kin.[23]

Malaitans quickly developed new strategies for managing religious rules in places where they had little control. The chief difficulty was interactions with foreigners, both European and Melanesian, who did not know, let alone observe, the behavioral rules or taboos that ancestral spirits enforced among descendants. At home, even Malaitans from the same language group followed different taboos enforced by their specific ancestors, and rules that a person observed at home and abroad were key identity markers. In recruiting, taboos could become problematic as soon as a man entered a ship's hold if women were known to have trodden the deck above, since men could not be underneath women or places they had walked. All ancestors also forbade male descendants being exposed to menstruation, and so women aboard the same ship could present difficulties.[24] Fewer women were recruited from Malaita, but they might in any case be aboard ships that called there, and innovative solutions had to be devised if men were to travel with them. This did not mean that taboos were fully waived. For example, the most profound taboo violation for Malaitan men was to have contact with childbirth, and Corris found that resulting problems led to government agents being told in the early 1880s to bar pregnant women from the ships.[25]

People negotiated with their ancestors new ground rules for proper behavior abroad, to follow taboos when possible but waive them when necessary. Like so many other things, taboo observation, and taboos themselves, changed over time and varied from person to person, and those who stayed in Queensland or Fiji longer were less likely to observe taboos, among other reasons because more of them became Christians. Models developed for religious practice abroad extended older principles for adjusting, mitigating, or waiving ancestral taboos at home, in ways that allowed men to live a normal life while away. Many of these models are still applied by non-Christian Malaitans on plantations or in towns. Later, when "foreign" things, ways, and institutions proliferated in the Solomons and then on Malaita itself, the rules and procedures for adapting them abroad were extended once again, but now in reverse, applied back to spaces defined as "foreign" in the homeland. These eventually included plantations and district stations, and, most important, the Christian villages that began to appear around Malaita. As the twentieth century progressed, an increasing proportion of the world Malaitans moved in came to be defined as, to varying degrees, outside of the ancestral domain, and thus as places and spaces where ancestral taboos might be selectively relaxed or put aside. In areas where they were still followed, taboos at times became stricter, as they became both for ancestors and their descendants symbols of rivalries with Christian communities and markers to hold the line against further decadence. What emerged over time was a highly contested politics of space and taboos.[26] This all interests us in part because we will see that Europeans often portrayed Malaitans as innately conservative, as servile to "rigid custom," and as most conspicuously so in their religious behavior. But the labor period as a whole, and particularly how quickly people adapted religious beliefs and practices to change, gives lie to that perspective. Christians applied similar principles of taboo interpretation to their new religious rules, often to the consternation of missionaries.[27]

Some Christian Malaitans abroad believed it sinful to accommodate ancestral taboos, a precept that later caused endless conflicts back on Malaita. Once back home, most returned to their ancestors, but over time a growing number maintained their new religion there, often in the face of great danger and social hardship. People could not fully rejoin their home communities as practicing Christians, and instead they formed small, mostly coastal communities. Some Malaitans opposed their fellows adopting Christianity even while abroad, perceiving in it threats to their ancestral religions, morality, and power; after returning home they disparaged the churches and warned others against tolerating them. This set the scene for future hostilities.

The Fiji labor scene has been studied much less than Queensland's, but a different situation unfolded there—laborers in Fiji more often lived on smaller, isolated plantations, especially after the mid-1880s, sometimes on islands far away from any town. Another crucial difference with Queensland arose from similarities among Fijian and Solomons cultures. Relatively few Fijians worked on plantations, but Malaitans interacted with them and some married or otherwise integrated into Fijian society. Corris wrote that laborers found it easier to maintain their cultural practices in Fiji than in Queensland. Anglican missionary Walter Ivens, based in south Malaita, wrote that many laborers in Fiji "merely changed one set of native con-

FIGURE 1.4. Malaitans performing a *sango* dance in Fiji for a mostly Melanesian audience, ca 1904. One dancer wears a beaded Christian cross. *Sango* was performed throughout north Malaita into southern Kwaio for mortuary feasts and after killings. (Postcard in author's collection, photographer unknown.)

ditions for another—living on a plantation and learning Fijian or mixing almost entirely with natives and learning but little English. Practically they still were natives instead of being bad copies of a certain class of whites." Later, so many Solomon Islanders knew Fijian (some learning it in the Solomons) that there was talk of making it the Protectorate's official language.[28] Malaitan returnees brought home aspects of Fijian religion and other culture borrowings, but few details are known about the extent to which Solomon Islanders and Fijians felt a common identity, and there were rivalries and fights among them.

What is certain is that in both Queensland and Fiji, Islanders forged new, broader ethnic identities as Malaitans, Solomon Islanders, and Melanesians. In 1971 Aduru Kuva interviewed surviving Kwara'ae and Kwaio recruits still in Fiji, who recounted how ethnic barriers weakened as soon as they boarded recruiting ships:

> Mutual animosity of people from different tribes would normally have been too great even for them to consider a long voyage together, yet on the ship these people become almost a closed community, very much isolated from shore communities and their influences. Any desire to harm former enemies was superseded by the overriding need to live peacefully and safely on the ship. Recruits were also under the explicit instructions of the recruiters, the captains, and the "old hands" aboard not to quarrel or fight.... The recruits found that on the two to three month voyage tribal feelings tended to dissolve because they had to integrate in their daily activities. All became Solomon Islanders with a common purpose and a common identity which they would not have recognized on shore.[29]

Such bonds were sometimes maintained back home, and Kwaio and 'Are'are people today trace their long alliance on plantations to the early labor period. Some enmities remained and new ones emerged, most famously in Queensland between Malaitans and men from Tanna in the New Hebrides.[30] What endured, and resurfaced in later political movements, were new, shared identities grounded in the common political lessons gained from like dealings with Europeans.[31]

In Queensland and Fiji there emerged a third culture, neither strictly European nor Melanesian, but rather what Ted Schwartz referred to as "contact culture" and Keesing later called "plantation culture." This was the culture of Melanesians, predominantly men, living together aboard ships, on plantations, and in towns. To some extent it encompassed Europeans within these settings. At the same time, it was not fully separated from life back home—labor migration and plantation culture became integral aspects of Melanesian societies, not merely a break with or escape from them, and this remains true today. Within plantation culture, codes of social relations evolved between Islanders and Europeans and between different Islander groups, along with new structures of commerce, politics, marriage, conflict, and religious practice. Malaitans devised individual and group guidelines as to how social and religious rules were to be adapted to foreign settings, and how to reestablish social relations with living kin and ancestral spirits on one's return home. At the same time, various political, philosophical, and religious ideas and practices diffused throughout Melanesia, facilitated by new crosscutting identities and relationships, and shared languages like Fijian, English, Hiri Motu, and other pidgins.[32]

Christian Missions and the Labor Scene

A key connector of many Melanesians abroad was their shared adoption of Christianities, and Christians were among the Malaitans who came home most outwardly changed. They varied considerably, as they still do, in the degree to which they embraced the new faiths, and in their understandings and interpretations of different denominational teachings. Malaitan Christianities from the start embodied Melanesian ideas that distinguished them from European versions. Although in this book I sometimes refer to "Christians" as a group and "Christianity" in the singular (as Malaitans, both Christian and not, often do), this diversity must be kept always in mind.

The established Christian missions maintained odd relationships with the labor trade as both its staunchest critics and some of its most obvious beneficiaries. Many missionaries were relentless and important public advocates for Islander rights and were influential in bringing about better recruiting and labor practices. At times they exaggerated in sweeping terms the trade's brutality, for example by emphasizing blatant kidnapping even after it had largely stopped, and they also inflated its negative impacts on Melanesian societies. Some saw the trade as undermining Church control over Islanders. In many places, missionaries had been the first and the only Europeans to deal with local communities on a regular basis and their influence could be enormous. But the labor trade gave Melanesians alternative means of obtaining European knowledge and goods. It exposed them to being "stained by contact with Chinese and low white folk" in whom missionaries saw a corrupting influence and spiritual danger, exemplified by "the man who went home from Queensland and told his friends that Christianity could not be so very important after all, for white people didn't think much of it."[33] In essence, many missionaries wished to be European "passage masters" and thereby mediate all Islanders' contacts with outsiders, and they felt this was imperative if they were to be protected and properly civilized. It was hoped that under missionary guidance, rather than signing on as labor, they would "sign on for Jesus."[34] These ambitions and anxieties fed ongoing missionary tensions with each other, as well as with colonial officials, traders, and the laborers who came home more sophisticated in and critical of European ways.

Yet the labor trade also gave missions opportunities to infiltrate societies previously inaccessible, indifferent, or hostile. The Anglican Church had enjoyed some success in removing individual Melanesians from their homes for religious training on distant Norfolk Island, after which they were sent out to proselytize. But that process was slow, expensive, and piecemeal, and once back home, "native teachers" often gave in to family and other pressures to return to ancestral ways.[35] Queensland and Fiji offered attractive settings for pursuing a similar strategy more cheaply and on a much larger scale. Away from their homes, Melanesians were easier to access and control, and many were eager to experiment with new ideas.

Missionaries, like many Europeans, nonetheless found Melanesian social freedoms abroad problematic. One author in the Anglican journal *Southern Cross Log* wrote, "There is in Queensland an almost entire absence of control. A Melanesian...soon finds out that when his work is done he is a free man in a free land; so long as he does not offend against the civil law he may go where he pleases and do as he pleases. He has left public opinion behind in his island. He is like an undergraduate at the university." Without proper guidance and control, a man abroad might be open to new religious ideas but also to new vices. The same writer observed men dodging missionaries who pursued them: "When the plantation where he works is visited, he knows of the visit and can keep well out of the way. There is no opportunity of seeing him unless it be a chance meeting, and then he might run for it." Some time-expired workers, he claimed, relocated to other plantations to escape the missionary's persistent "warning or advice."[36]

Established mission societies were slow to grasp the opportunities Queensland offered them. Due to logistics, Anglicans made no concerted official effort to provide teachers for Melanesians on Queensland plantations until 1896 (though individual Anglicans taught before then); the London Missionary Society did not want to compromise its vehement opposition to the labor trade; and the Catholics in Fiji would not baptize Solomon Islanders for fear that, as Bishop Francis Redwood put it, "on returning to their pagan lands, and deprived of [Catholic] missionaries, they would revert to paganism."[37] But they soon noticed the success of independent missionaries working on plantations, some of whom they correctly foresaw as future competitors. Anglican Bishop Henry Montgomery of Tasmania encountered women teaching laborers in Fiji in 1892: "I was more and more interested as the hours passed at Suva, to learn about the hundred and fifty Melanesians attending their school night after night, of the earnest-minded ladies who assisted, and of the communicants among these Mala men. It was then borne in upon me with force that the labour traffic could be made a mighty engine for the conversion of the South Seas, and that what was once a curse might prove a blessing in Christian hands." Three years later Bishop Wilson wrote, "I cannot see how we are to get at Malanta [*sic*] except through Queensland and Fiji; yet as a rule returned labourers in these places are of no use to us." The bishops were late to the game, for by this time in Queensland it was said that roughly 75 percent of Melanesians were having some contact with Presbyterian, Anglican, or, especially, nondenominational teachings, mostly via small European evangelical groups or individuals, particularly women. Fewer Malaitans were proselytized in Fiji, most of them by Anglicans.[38]

Most important was the Queensland Kanaka Mission, a nondenominational evangelical mission founded in 1886 by Florence Young on her brothers' Fairymead sugar plantation in Bundaberg, where she had preached to laborers since 1882. The mission enjoyed phenomenal success and soon spread through the plantation districts; by 1904, 19 missionaries and 118 unpaid "native teachers" were at work. By its 1907 closing, 2,484 Islanders had been baptized in the area's rivers, 589 of them Malaitans. Up to 7,000 had attended Bible classes taught in Pijin at night or on Sundays, with more of them from Malaita than any other island. Teachers and students who had returned to Malaita besieged Young with requests for assistance, and in 1904 she took her mission there, where it became the South Sea Evangelical Mission (SSEM), later Malaita's largest and most politically active church.[39]

Relations in Queensland between missionaries and plantation owners could be symbiotic, and missions received money from businessmen who found Christian laborers more manageable. One donor, when told Young's mission did not ask for money, told her, "But it is *worth money* to me. My boys do better work, and I think we planters should contribute to the cost of the Mission." Other planters were less sympathetic, and Anglican Archdeacon Lonsdale Pritt said that some opposed missionary work "just for the reason that it makes the 'boys' 'know too much,' and sets them against their masters.... Boys have been known who were forward as leaders of others in school who were also leaders of sedition. The doctrine of all men's equality in the sight of Heaven may be so presented to untutored minds as to practically obliterate those relations of order and subordination without which no human society can exist. Care is needed."[40]

Florence Young's Bible schools became a centerpiece of her mission's structure. Other white Christians of various denominations set up similar ones, many taught by women. They offered Melanesians a sense of community abroad that bridged ethnic groups, a new or added source of spiritual protection, avenues for gaining prestige as church teachers, and interactions with Europeans who were friendly and sympathetic.[41] A promise of education remained the missions' most potent draw for decades, and Malaitan attendees acquired varying degrees of knowledge. The Kanaka Mission curriculum consisted of simple Bible classes with a modicum of elementary literacy taught by the Youngs and their colleagues—salvation, not education, was the overriding goal. Still, many Melanesians did learn to read; in 1892 it was claimed 45 percent of the men on one plantation were literate.[42] The most successful students were selected as teachers and many began holding small classes of their own. To this day Malaitans call church leaders *tisa* (teachers) and Christianity and Christian villages *sukulu* (school). Decades later, the missions' failure to fulfill Malaitan desires for serious education would lead many to reject white missionaries, but not their Christian faiths or the Malaita-wide organizational structures that Christians built.

Return from the White Man's Land

> A good house to live in, clothes of European cut, shops to spend
> money in, and alas! grog only too easily, albeit illegally acquired.
> This is the heritage of the kanaka, and he is happy in his new life,
> and, in some cases, all the better for it; for, possibly, a night-school
> is on or near his plantation and he goes there when the work of the
> day is done, and he learns to read and write, and to believe in God
> and his Savior.... Death carries off many and white men's vices are
> acquired, and all the misery that these vices bring: and it is a ragged
> regiment that returns after the three years' service in the white man's
> land.... All who are thus taken away, are, whether we like it or no,
> educated for evil if not for good by their contact with a white superior
> race; and the labour-vessel, in returning labourers, is really returning
> so many school-masters to teach their fellows the evil or the good that
> they themselves have learned in the distant, civilized land from which
> they have come. Thus it is that no ships have left their mark upon the
> islands, like these labour-vessels who deal in "souls of men."
> —Southern Cross Log *(August 1895, 12)*

> Beware of the non-Christian returned labourer; as a rule they are plau-
> sible, good-for-nothing fellows.
> —*Walter Ivens,* Hints to Missionaries to Melanesia *(1907, 26)*

Writers have often portrayed Malaitans who returned from abroad as having quickly blended back into their "closed," traditional societies, separated once again from Europeans and their influences, their lives little altered by the experience. Sometimes this expressed the notion that Melanesians were so deeply conservative that they could not truly change; changes that they seemed to undergo abroad were cast as superficial and ephemeral. This complements another image sometimes presented of Melanesians abroad as having fully shed their home cultures; likewise, on return they put aside the new and simply reverted to former ways and thinking.[43]

Part of the confusion stems from the assumption, deeply ingrained in the West, that change in the modern world inevitably means becoming more *like* the West. Malaitan innovations that develop Malaitan cultural themes, because they still appear exotic to Europeans, have often been misread as exemplifying unchanging "traditional" or "customary" ways. Few historians or anthropologists have conveyed the degree to which Malaitan societies— the local communities that returned laborers rejoined—were altered during these decades. Even before the labor trade ended, pre-1870 Malaitan life was a distant memory held by ever-fewer people, and long before Europeans gained any significant presence on Malaita, new tools, weapons, crops, and wealth changed every realm of life there. Just as important as material changes were the new ideas returned laborers shared out, including their familiarity with Europeans and recognition of dangers they presented. As the European presence on Malaita increased, so too did a defiant Malaitan insistence on autonomy that still infuses much Malaitan political thought today as an elemental basis of *kastom* ideologies. In these and other ways the labor period changed Malaitan worldviews and their conceptions of themselves and their societies, profoundly shaping the island's subsequent history. What follows will sketch out the close of the overseas labor trade, its impacts on Malaitans at home (particularly in terms of their political consciousness), and finally the imposition of British military control over the island.

As the new century began, the number of Melanesians in Queensland was still rising. Then, in December 1901, the Australian government passed the Pacific Islands Labourers Act to end the labor trade for good. No new Melanesian arrivals would be allowed after 1903, and those remaining would be deported en masse in 1906 and 1907. After Islanders, Christian missions, and others protested the bill's harshness, exemptions were granted to a few. Melanesians formed lobbying groups and thousands signed petitions, but to little avail. Some who had fled trouble on their islands and feared what might await them there pleaded to stay.[44] The Fiji trade carried on at one vessel per year until it too ended in 1911 under pressure from the Solomons, where a corporate plantation scene was developing. Resident Commissioner Woodford had attracted companies like Levers Pacific Plantations Ltd and Burns Philp to set up operations there so the fledgling Protectorate could support itself economically. Even were the Queensland trade to resume, he wrote, Australia would have to look elsewhere for laborers.[45]

The mass deportation from Queensland of so many Melanesians, including 3,000 Malaitans, was neither easy nor humane. About half had been there for long periods, and many had settled in Australia and adopted ways of life impossible on Malaita. Some of their offspring had never been to the islands and were ignorant of their people's languages and cultures. In some cases particular family members were expelled while others were eligible to stay. People who had run away from trouble at home begged to take their firearms back with them but were not allowed to, though many back on

Malaita were heavily armed, and the government had no presence there to protect deportees. In the Solomons, all had the option of being landed at the government center of Tulagi in the Gela group to seek work there or, from there, elsewhere in the Protectorate. About 250 Malaitans went straight to Fiji, and another 400 went there from Malaita. Others signed on for new Solomon Islands plantations, most on three-year indenture contracts.[46]

Some deportees did not know how different life would be on Malaita, and this ignorance of destination is further caution against overstating links

FIGURE 1.5. "On board a recruiting labour schooner, Malaita, Solomon Islands. A fortified island is visible in the distance," 1907. (Photo by George Rose, Thomas Edge-Partington collection, courtesy of the Edge-Partington family.)

Malaitans abroad maintained with home. Jack McClaren, captain of a boat carrying returnees, overheard Malaitans aboard happily anticipating their arrival: "I heard them talking of buying pieces of garden land and wives to work them, and of building houses with doors and windows and verandas all round, like white men's houses, and living down the years in ease and comfort. Wherefore they spent their wages-savings in trade-goods they thought would be acceptable to the people of their respective villages, who, dazzled by the number and utility of the things, would be ready to do anything for the wealthy home-comers." Ivens wrote of one ship's arrival: "Sewing-machines and gramophones might have been bought up cheaply a week or two after [the returnees] had landed. In some cases sewing machines were actually abandoned on the beach, for no one cared to carry them slung on a pole into the interior.... Brown boots and bowler hats and starched shirts and collars and ties were seen adorning the persons of all and sundry in the neighborhood when the trade boxes of the returns had been opened. Babies that were brought ashore in all the glory of woolen socks and bonnets and white clothes were rolling about naked by nightfall."[47]

There was scattered violence on Malaita, including killings, particularly during an initial wave of returnees before the deportation deadline arrived, but overall the main return took place without the bloodshed and upheaval many had predicted.[48] The event provided a splendid opening for missions, especially the SSEM. Everyone knew that many deportees were longtime Christians who had become alienated from mountain lifestyles and had badly wanted to stay in Australia. Missionaries made extensive preparations for their arrival, including establishing communities for them, and many Christians were landed at Maluʻu in Toʻabaita and other coastal mission settlements around the island. As some settled in areas not their own (most temporarily), churches cultivated social and political networks across linguistic and cultural boundaries.[49]

Some Malaitans saw larger church communities as dangerous, particularly if their members ignored ancestral taboos. In early years, many Christians followed some taboos, took part in bridewealth and other exchanges, and lived in relative harmony with neighbors. Many Christian returnees had faced intense pressure from relatives to come back to their ancestors and communities, and to the dismay of missionaries most did so. But as Christian settlements grew and church policies forbid following taboos or engaging in formal exchanges with the larger community, more people came to see the settlements as a threat. For protection, Christians formed larger villages and consolidated into united fronts, and while these provided some safety they also presented a more obvious challenge to the dominant social order.[50]

During the century's first decade, Christian life on Malaita became more perilous still. The growing enclaves that dotted the shore, and a few inland areas, were increasingly harried by neighbors. Some built forts, like one

Hopkins described at Malu'u: "They took us to their retreat. It was an amazing place. Built round the large men's hut, none too clean, dark and low, was a massive stockade. There was a first barrier of upright tree trunks some eight to ten feet high; then about two feet apart was a second barrier of tree trunks and the space in between was filled in with earth and soft stuff fastening the two together [with] the whole structure making an immensely strong stockade. In the hut at night forty people gathered, by day they gardened en masse."[51] Though Christians were often portrayed by Europeans as helpless victims of attacks, some fought back with their own deadly violence. Nonetheless, many continued to be killed right into the 1910s. They were further imperiled since they were attractive targets for blood bounties; they were less likely to retaliate, and government laws against guns more effectively disarmed coastal Christian communities.[52] These conflicts established religious divisions and rivalries that persisted until Maasina Rule and resumed after it.

Some returnees saw local leaders to be backward, and Hopkins observed them to "defy all authority tribal, governmental and Christian." A decade later, Malaita's District Officer William Bell commented that many of the men he chased as murderers had been to Fiji or Queensland. Still other returning laborers had simply lost all connection to their home communities or embraced Western notions of individualism and private property that clashed with local ethics. Hopkins pointed to new arrivals having to share out their goods to kin as motivating some to seek shelter in Christianity: "His raiment was divided waistcoat to one, coat to another, hat to a third, his tobacco distributed and soon smoked. No wonder that the picked ones among them who had led years of civilized life and become Christians, wanted a refuge."[53]

During and after the labor trade, Europeans debated its effects on Melanesians. Those with vested interest in the trade often painted it as a civilizing influence toward social and moral elevation. A former high commissioner, Everard im Thurn, wrote, "It is quite certain that the greater proportion of the natives who...were the subjects of this trade, benefited by it, in that they for the most part escaped from the 'rot' which is overwhelming most of such of their kindred owing to the hopelessly backward conditions in which they were born." Trade opponents took pains to counter this argument, particularly missionaries who also objected to aspects of the labor system being erected within the Protectorate. This is one reason why Ivens, Hopkins, and others accentuated returnees' rapid abandonment of Western clothing and other accoutrements—their seeming enlightenment was skin-deep. In Ivens's words: "The thousands of men who, throughout the years the trade was in existence, returned from civilization did nothing to better the conditions of life among their neighbors; they disseminated no knowledge, they started no spiritual movement for the uplifting of their people, they stirred up no divine discontent with the old-time conditions.

They brought back in a measure the outer trappings of civilization, but were ignorant of its power. While their axes lasted they made it easier for someone else to work; their purchases gave them for the time being a certain amount of importance; but once their stock was finished their influence was at an end."[54] This perspective coexisted with a common missionary narrative that savagery, too, was a veneer that could be removed by, and only by, Christianity, liberating a humanity that lay just beneath.

When white Protectorate residents did note shifts in Islander attitudes that they disliked, they often blamed the labor trade's corrupting influences and portrayed returned laborers as a menace to European and Melanesian alike.[55] European reactions to returnees provide some of our best historical evidence of how the labor experience molded Melanesians' attitudes toward the *waetman* who now began to occupy their region in greater numbers. Many whites had long despised returned laborers and feared their influence on their countrymen, though there were exceptions, most obviously the steadfast Christians beloved by missionaries. Many returned laborers did in fact threaten European agendas, and some, especially Queensland veterans, were thorns in the side of missionaries. For example, during 1882, one mission school on Makira lost pupils after a labor veteran told people they did not need to attend church since Australians did not, and others conveyed similar messages.[56]

More generally, Europeans were dismayed by their loss of prestige in the eyes of returned Islanders and those they influenced. As Ivens wrote: "There is no question that the Queensland return, except those who had been at some mission school, was as a rule a person to be avoided; he had learned something of the white man's ways and had a certain amount of the externals of civilization, but the old-time respect for authority had all vanished and its place was taken by a bold, rough style of address which did not differentiate between a high commissioner or a bishop and a recruiter of a labor vessel. All alike were hailed by him as mate and all would be asked for tobacco. In effect he had lost the charm of the natural state."[57]

Hopkins wrote of the non-Christian returnee, "He is self-important, vicious, a despiser of white man and of the old native rule too, and keen to stir up strife and to 'pooh pooh' the fears of his bushy friends of the white man's power. He landed yesterday in polished boots, starched shirt and collar, tie, etc.; to-morrow he is running about naked, or very nearly so, shell in hair, gun in hand on some bush feud which his return has perhaps restarted." Hopkins said leaders had no control over such men, who were involved in many disputes. The *Southern Cross Log* bewailed "these semi-Europeanised natives with their little knowledge, and, I am very sorry to say, their very poor opinion in most cases of the white people. You can plainly see, then, that one of the great difficulties at the present time that we have to face is the returned Kanaka. It is true, however, as Mr. Hopkins has told you, that many of them are splendid Christians, they start schools in different places—many of the schools that have been lately opened are entirely due to these Kanakas from Queensland. Yet, taking the Kanaka return altogether it has introduced things which are all against our work."[58]

Returnees also placed a higher value on their own labor, and on Gela some influenced Anglican teachers to stage a strike in 1908. Indentured Melanesians and whites could not legally strike in Queensland and the Solomons, but time-expired workers organized union-like groups that bargained for wages, and some would have known of 1906 strikes by Australia's unionized white sugar workers. Decades later, Malaita's Officer Michael Forster reported that many Australian-born Melanesians were "keenly interested in Labour activities and particularly strikes."[59] Thomas Edge-Partington, who in September 1909 became Malaita's first resident government officer, could at first find no Malaitans willing to work on his station for the 10 shillings a month he proffered, and he had to use convicts and men from the Western Solomons. He blamed Queensland veterans for the high prices that neighboring people asked for local foods, though he could sometimes "buy the food very cheap from bushmen who cannot talk any English and who are willing to take just what you can give them." Ivens expressed the indignation of many Europeans: "The returns expected to buy goods in traders' stores at Queensland prices; they demanded Queensland rates of pay, and both traders and missionaries were faced with labor troubles, and crude socialistic ideas circulated freely everywhere." Elsewhere he was more specific: his mission had difficulty finding ships crews on demand and people wanted to bargain for wages. William Bell, while working as a labor inspector, said many Malaitans refused to work for Solomon Islands plantations since the wage was lower than men had earned in Australia.[60]

Malaitans were already famous for their boldness toward Europeans, due not only to their independent behavior abroad but also to violent attacks and their tight control over recruiting on their island. Both were often organized by returned laborers and continued after the overseas trade ended. In Queensland there had been widespread resistance among indentured laborers, ranging from "everyday forms"—feigned ignorance, shirking, malingering—to desertion and violent retaliation for overseer violence, and these all carried on in the Protectorate.[61] The overall Malaitan approach to Europeans was more opportunistic than malevolent, but many of those forcibly repatriated, more sophisticated in European ways after longer residence abroad, worked out and disseminated political ideas as to how best to deal with whites, ideas that would develop and spread over the coming decades.

Returnees accentuated one particular worry about whites: that they would steal Malaitan land. This fear originated in part from observations of the plight of Aboriginal Australians whom Europeans had stripped of their lands, and also of alienated land in Fiji. Malaitans perceived in these cases a warning of what could happen if whites gained control of Malaita.[62] Fears intensified when men began to work in the Protectorate on land that white-owned companies had, with government help, taken from other Solomon Islanders.[63]

The forced eviction from Australia in itself contributed to resentment and more open postures of defiance. The Royal Commission on Sugar Industry Labour warned, "The persons to be affected are a race relatively helpless; but they include isolated individuals predisposed to foment amongst their fellows active hostility to action which, in their ignorance, they may deem oppressive. In case the hostility so aroused may have far reaching effects in some of the less civilized of the Pacific Islands, we deem it our duty to point out that the existence of this feeling has come under our notice." The anger reflected not just loss of livelihoods, properties, and communities in Australia, but also a hard-learned recognition that whites had a proclivity for exploiting and denigrating Islanders, whom they saw as inferior. Malaitans now saw their relations with whites more clearly and critically, and many called for a defense of Malaitan autonomy. Whites in the Solomons often heard the phrases "white man no good" and "country belong us."[64]

The Imposition of Pax Britannica

As I have said, little attempt was made to control Malaitan internal violence during the labor trade. Early retaliatory actions in the Solomons by warships were taken under the Pacific Islanders' Protection Acts of 1872 and 1875. The second of these contributed to establishment of the High Commission for the Western Pacific, "with instructions and authority, within such of the islands as were not subject to any Foreign Power, to protect the Islanders against aggression by British subjects, and, incidentally, to protect Europeans from attack by the Islanders, but without power to intervene in disputes in which natives alone were concerned."[65] With the Western Pacific Order in Council of 1877, the high commissioner was granted authority over British subjects in the Solomons but not over Islanders or other Europeans, and some attacks by warships were technically illegal. Various factors now forced Britain to try to assert more control. There was public outcry for more supervision of the labor trade and punishment of attacks on Europeans, and pressure came also from the international political arena since Britain feared falling behind Germany and France in a region being rapidly carved up.[66]

The Solomons were declared a protectorate in 1893 (expanded to included Santa Cruz, Rennell, Santa Isabel, and Choiseul in 1898–1899). Its people were "British protected persons" but not entitled to the rights of British subjects. This signaled the colonial approach that would typify coming decades. In the scramble for colonies, Great Britain shuffled into the Solomons; by proclaiming a protectorate, they "could lay effective claim to a territory without obligation to govern or develop it." When HMS *Curaçoa* sailed about the group declaring the new status, opposition was met only at Laulasi in Malaita's Langalanga Lagoon, where people declined to fly the Union Jack for fear their Kwaio and Kwara'ae neighbors would read it as a sign of war.[67]

The first government officer stationed in the Solomons was Charles Woodford, who as a naturalist had studied the area and published a book and articles about it, and had served in the Fiji Department of Immigration. He convinced High Commissioner John Thurston and the Colonial Office that the Solomons could be profitably administered and that his position should be made permanent and full time. He arrived in 1896 and with meager resources soon established his headquarters at Tulagi. As resident commissioner he remained answerable to the high commissioner in Fiji. This remained the command structure system until 1953, and we will see that it often hampered administration and placed key decisions in the hands of faraway men who knew next to nothing about the Solomons.

Woodford stressed opportunities for European-managed plantations: "As a locality for the growth of the coconut palm, I believe the British Protectorate of the Solomons presents advantages unequaled by any place that I have hitherto visited in the Western Pacific." He was convinced the Solomons could support a successful plantation economy, especially the prime coconut-growing areas of Guadalcanal and New Georgia.[68] This required the suppression of warfare and raiding there, which trade with Europeans had exacerbated, and Woodford set out to do this with a handful of Fijian policemen. He stationed a deputy, Arthur Mahaffy, in New Georgia to carry out punitive actions, and by the start of the century Woodford could report that raiding was "scotched for the present." Important trading areas of Guadalcanal were brought under control soon afterward.[69]

On Malaita different economic forces were at work, and punishments there were reserved mostly for violence against Europeans, though there were exceptions. Early government attempts to discipline Malaitans failed to impress inland dwellers, though some coastal areas were effectively subdued. Mahaffy knew the small coastal island communities were "completely at the mercy of a Man of War," and in 1902, to punish local killings, he orchestrated HMS *Sparrow*'s looting and destruction of offshore island settlements at Oru Island in Sio Bay in To'abaita, and at Kwai and Ngongosila off of east Kwara'ae.[70]

The government became a permanent presence on Malaita in 1909 with the establishment of a station at Rarasu on the central-west coast, which they named for the nearby island of 'Aoke (also known as Auki, Kwaibala). The station land, bought for £20, was surrounded by Kwara'ae speakers inland and Langalanga artificial-island dwellers seaward. The first European posted there was District Magistrate Thomas W Edge-Partington, a 25-year-old who had served in the Royal Navy and was the son of a famous scholar of Pacific artifacts. Since 1904 he had spent nearly three years posted at Gizo in the Western Solomons and he arrived on Malaita in command of twenty-some Western Solomons police.[71]

By December 1909, Edge-Partington began to realize the enormity of his task: "One whole village of about 60 or 100 fighting men came over from Quai [Kwai] and attacked a bush village at Langalanga. They expect me to have a lot of police here and have absolutely no fear of the Government.

FIGURE 1.6. Two men of 'Aoke Island visiting aboard a cutter, 1907. (Photo by George Rose, Rose Stereographs 12263, Thomas Edge-Partington collection, courtesy of the Edge-Partington family.)

They laughed at me the other day when I went down to Fiu about a murder and took 17 with me all I could spare, leaving 6 to guard the station.... This is going to be a very difficult island to tackle, and until the whitemen stop selling cartridges one cannot do much." The following May, Joe Maekali, son of the big man of Laulasi island in Langalanga, asked Edge-Partington for permission to kill a man from inland to avenge a killing, but when refused told him, "It did not matter whether I gave him permission or not he intended to kill a bushman." His reception was not wholly negative—that same month, while touring the mountains along the west Kwaio-Kwara'ae border, he was told that "they had done with fighting now that I had come here and they were very glad as now they could live in peace and attend to their gardens which they had not been able to do with safety in the past." Perhaps recalling his experience in the Western Solomons, he recorded, "Most of them want to be quiet but they want some one to tell them to be quiet first."[72]

I will not delve into Edge-Partington's frustrated tenure on Malaita. In the end he, and later his police officer, Frederick Campbell, had little impact except perhaps to embolden Malaitans for future resistance. In late 1911, Commander E C Carver of the warship *Torch* estimated what would be required to control Malaita: imposition of martial law with swift tribunals and punishment of men who killed, to circumvent the slow and ineffectual system of sending them to Fiji for trial; a prolonged presence by 150 soldiers and two naval vessels; and replacement of private labor recruiters with government ones to stop the inflow of cartridges.[73]

In December 1914, Edge-Partington resigned. History has unkindly portrayed him as a timid failure. Reading his reports, correspondence, and diaries, I find him no worse than his fellow officers and keener than many. He was assigned an impossible task, given his pitiful resources, and was held back from pursuing it by men in Tulagi and Suva who had no inkling of Malaitan realities and found him insolent because he was acutely aware of flaws in policy and unafraid to upbraid superiors.[74] Negative verdicts against him have come from those marking his accomplishments against the man who soon followed him on Malaita, a comparison that would tarnish most any district officer. Australian and Boer War veteran William Robert Bell arrived in 'Aoke in October 1915 after six years as a government agent on Fiji labor ships that mostly worked Malaita (1905–1911), and then four years more as a BSIP inspector of laborers.[75] Over the next 12 years Bell transformed Malaita to a degree few would have thought possible. How he brought nearly all of Malaita under his control, and his assassination at Sinalagu in October 1927, were explored in a 1980 book by Roger Keesing and Peter Corris. The following summary draws on that work as well as on archival and oral historical sources.

Bell faced the same daunting task as had Edge-Partington, made still harder by Malaitans' experiences to date of an impotent government. Bell

What about a Beer!

FIGURE 1.7. District Magistrate Thomas Edge-Partington and servant at 'Aoke, nd. (Thomas Edge-Partington collection, photographer unknown, courtesy of the Edge-Partington family.)

said his predecessors, hamstrung by superiors, had accomplished nothing: "The natives within a few miles of the Government Station are as little
under control as they were before the Station was established. If the Officer
goes a few hundred yards inland from the Government Station he has to
go prepared against an attack." Perusal of Bell's early reports reveals that
killing due to vendettas or to collect bounties was rife. He cited for Acting Resident Commissioner Frederick Barnett the example of Rohinari in
southwest 'Are'are, where the Marist priest Jean Coicaud told him that over
a three-year period there had been at least 60 to 70 murders, mostly of
women and children. Bell then listed for Barnett still unpunished killings
for bounties in the neighborhood of 'Aoke.[76]

Bell pushed his superiors even harder than had Edge-Partington for
aggressive pursuit of those who killed and was likewise held back by ignorant bosses, particularly Barnett, who had also stymied Edge-Partington
and did not think officers should punish Malaitans who killed Malaitans.[77]
When Bell protested directly and bluntly to High Commissioner Ernest
Sweet-Escott in Fiji, Barnett removed Bell as insubordinate. But he was
soon reinstated, and starting in 1917 a new acting resident commissioner,
Charles Workman, backed Bell on his proactive approach and many other
matters. The Protectorate's police headquarters had recently been shifted
from 'Aoke to Tulagi and Bell began with half the police force Edge-Partington had and no European police officer. By 1918, he said he had enough
police and lobbied to command them on his own. Unlike Edge-Partington,
he favored Malaitan police and formed a trusted force of 30, mostly men
from To'abaita and other parts of the north where he had made the most
progress.[78]

The new toughness Bell brought to the job is clear in the tone of his
early reports. After a patrol inland behind Kwai Harbour in 1917, he wrote:
"I told them that the Government knew that they had money and pigs on
offer for the killing of a white man, and advised them to eat the pigs and
make some other use of the money, to which they made no reply." Malaitans already knew Bell, and even in 1913, while he was still a labor inspector, Edge-Partington complained to Woodford, "There is too much 'Mr.
Bell' over here," and said Malaitans spoke of Bell as if he were the resident
commissioner.[79]

During his first year Bell conducted extensive inland tours. He knew that
patrolling merely to display his presence would be counterproductive if he
took no action, since that would imply the government did "not mind the
killings." He was noteworthy for his ability to analyze patterns of violence
and what was needed to stop it. He knew most Malaitans would not resist his
efforts to check killing—the key was to intimidate and subjugate assassins,
who drew wealth, prestige, and authority from bounties and feuding. Bounties of pigs and shell currencies were integral to the economic system, and
those who killed for them redistributed most of their rewards and invested

what remained in mortuary feasting, bridewealth, and other exchanges that augmented their strength. Bell was taking on men at the center of power.[80]

Bell recognized the unfairness of harshly prosecuting people in areas still outside government influence, of expecting people to lay down arms when enemies still held theirs, and of punishing only those who accepted his authority by turning themselves in. In the beginning he went so far as to give people permission to avenge killings of their relatives, for example when he met with a crowd of 400 people near Malu'u: "I told them that if the Government was not prepared to protect them that they were justified in taking any necessary steps for the preservation of their own lives....If any man killed the murderer of his relative I would take no action, but they must only retaliate on the actual murderer." Four years later, Bell reported that, while he was touring east 'Are'are, "Three men came down from the bush to see me who had taken part in the very recent killing of a man and a woman. [They] had committed adultery and the man's people killed him and the woman's people killed her. Under the circumstances as there are much worse men in the Takataka district whom I have not yet been able to deal with, I did not think it would be justice to charge these three men with murder. I explained to them the course they should have taken which, I am afraid, did not appear very satisfactory to them, and warned them against further killing under the same circumstances."[81]

Bell rejected as "repulsive" punitive expeditions aimed at "punishing natives as a community." The real problem was the men who killed for payment, most of whom lived in the rugged mountains, and he systematically applied several effective strategies aimed squarely at them. He did not need to overwhelm them all, but merely to force the strongest and most resistant to capitulate—weaker men would follow. Despite the relatively small fighting force at his disposal, the atomistic nature of Malaitan society made it possible to confront specific assassins from a position of strong advantage, forcing them one by one to submit. Actual fighting was rarely necessary. Bell demanded that such men "enter into recognizances for future good behavior" with shell money or cash. This strategy had been used in limited fashion by the missionary Hopkins, and by Officer Ralph Hill when he briefly served at 'Aoke in 1915, and Bell made it a regular practice after receiving such a deposit from Suina'o of Bita'ama in To'abaita, who had killed many people. Bell learned Suina'o and other strongmen had formed what they called a "company" to resist his police. But in 1916, after the police raided an associate's hamlet and killed four men, Suina'o came to 'Aoke in an enormous canoe and formally presented Bell with ten gold coins and shell money as a pledge that he would kill no more: "Me, Suina'o, me good fellow now." In April 1918, Bell extracted 178 strings of red money and 749 porpoise teeth from Irokwato, a Baegu man who many years before had shot a man on Hopkins's verandah and had frustrated Edge-Partington. Bell also offered cash bounties for specific fugitives. Another effective

tactic was to appoint former warriors or assassins to be government constables and make them responsible for peace in their areas. Key to Bell's
strategy was gun confiscation; arms and especially ammunition were still
being smuggled in.[82]

Bell unleashed his police on the uncooperative, as in a 1919 raid on
Na'oasi in east Kwara'ae that killed four. Though militarily disciplined,
thievery and gratuitous violence were standard practice among the police.
Their looting and shrine desecration continued previous government punitive tactics, and both had long been a part of Malaitan warfare.[83] I think
Keesing and Corris understate Bell's own ruthlessness and occasional brutality, at least as he acted through his police and some headmen, particularly
late in his tenure. Could someone so smart and informed remain unaware
of his underlings' cruelty? Yet Bell's empathy for law-abiding Malaitans was
extraordinary for his day. He agitated on their behalf on issues ranging
from taxes and fair returns for them in government services, to land alienation, their "unreasonable exploitation" as indentured labor, and their
need for medical care and education.[84]

In 1923, Bell began to develop a system of headmen and constables to
serve as his interlocutors with local populations, and another of "lines,"
groups said to share common descent, on which to base tax payments.
"Lines" often had little political cohesiveness outside the government system. It was hard to find suitable candidates for headmen since few men
wanted to be government representatives, and many were chosen not
because they were recognized leaders but only for their willingness and
sometimes for their knowledge of white ways (most had labored abroad).
Some headmen took advantage of their positions, a few wielding tyrannical
power, and this and bullying by Bell's police fed antigovernment bitterness
that grew among many inland people during the 1920s. Headmen wanted
guns for their own safety, and Bell agreed, writing, "I would not send an
unarmed Constable off the beach in a very great portion of Malaita, in
fact I would not send only one Constable." But High Commissioner Cecil
Rodwell (1918–1925) refused Bell's request because, his secretary said, "It
would be a most dangerous action to arm savages with rifles and invest
them a little brief authority so armed."[85]

Bell's early efforts concentrated on north Malaita, though as early as
1917 he began to extend his influence into the east Kwara'ae mountains
across the island from 'Aoke, and by 1920 Kwara'ae was fairly under his
sway. In that year Bell reported having gained sufficient control over the
northern third of the island, Small Malaita (also known as Maramasike) in
the far south, and in coastal areas to allow a census. His subsequent reports
were less optimistic, however, and four years later Bell acknowledged that
government constables still could not safely travel alone in most places.[86]

In 1921, the BSIP government had started to impose a "head tax" on
males from ages 16 to 60. The administration suffered ongoing revenue

problems, and Workman hoped taxation would "infuse new energy into the Solomon Islands and act incidentally as an incentive to recruiting." The latter was hardly incidental; the nascent copra industry faced a chronic labor shortage. As in other colonies, the administration used taxation, with jail time for defaulters, to coerce labor, particularly on Malaita. Other Europeans supposed that taxes would force needed "development" on the Islanders.[87]

Solomon Islander reaction to the new tax was often bewilderment. Anglican Bishop John Steward complained in 1921 that some were "inclined to regard the tax more as a fine inflicted on them for no ascertainable reason than as a contribution to imperial revenue." Adventist missionaries who witnessed the 1925 Kwaio collection recalled, "Many of the old men, finding they could not buy anything with their receipt, were disgusted. 'What name this government?' they muttered. 'He steal im money belong we fella. We fella no give more money along im-nothing!' " That year an old man in the north, fearing punishment because he could not pay, hanged himself, and Ivens wrote, "A terror of imprisonment for non-payment of the tax is very real." Though Malaitans came to understand the taxation concept, resentment would continue, as expressed by a man Hogbin overheard in the early 1930s: "I have to work for one week to earn five shillings. To the white man it is nothing. He gives it away for a drink of beer."[88] Taxation without return or representation was to be a key issue in Malaitan political resistance for decades.

Under Bell's influence the Malaitan tax was postponed until 1923 (as was Choiseul's), and then set at 5 shillings per annum, a quarter of the rate for some islands. Bell expressed strong reservations about the tax, questioning both Malaitans' ability to pay and his to collect it. Shortly before his death he complained, "I am unable to see what benefits the natives of Mala have already received from payment of the Native Tax," and, "It appears to me that the natives of Mala received less service after the Native Tax was imposed." He meant that due to his heavy tax-collection duties he could not properly tour or perform other work. Anglican missionary Albert Mason observed in 1925, "The two government officials are so busy most of the year collecting this money that little time is left for attending to court business, and the medical assistance rendered to the natives is practically nil." That year Bell told Resident Commissioner Richard Kane that extracting taxes without providing more services was a "despotic act."[89]

Bell taxed over 10,000 Malaitans in 1923–1924 and over 12,000 in 1925. Resentful, many refused orders to work on new communal tasks like maintaining tax houses and trails, and Bell came to believe the tax and the excessive time he spent collecting it were undermining his and the government's status. Yet government prestige was at stake: Bell and others worried that to exempt Malaitans from a tax demanded of other Islanders might be seen as an admission of government weakness. Indeed, Bell applied the tax as a way to demand and obtain submission, particularly from fighting men. For years to come, tax payment would represent for the British a vital acknowledgment of Crown authority, especially after World War II when many refused to pay. Bell also used the tax resourcefully as grounds to demand more logistical support from Tulagi.[90] He toured mostly in whaleboats or canoes, though at first he refused to travel in these, feeling they cost him not just time but also respect since traders and missionaries had larger boats. He did eventually use sailboats but for years superiors denied his requests for a better craft (except for a few months in 1918) and for an assistant "whose nerves are in good condition." In 1921 he was given a power-launch, and he began to get assistants at times, the last being Kenneth Lillies in 1925.[91]

Beginning in 1924, Bell determined to use the tax for the first time to force men of the east central mountains to submit to him. As early as 1921 he had visited the east Kwaio coast at Uru, Sinalagu, and 'Oloburi to confiscate guns, investigate crimes, and make arrests, but by the mid-1920s Kwaio was the last major area he did not control. During the first tax collections there in 1924 and 1925, he had been forced to back down from arresting defaulters at Sinalagu. But in 1926 Bell sent his police on a surprise raid inland behind Sinalagu to arrest a dozen defaulters on the 1925 tax, and they badly beat several men. This time, the Kwaio strongmen were forced to back down and pay fines for those arrested. During the 1926 collec-

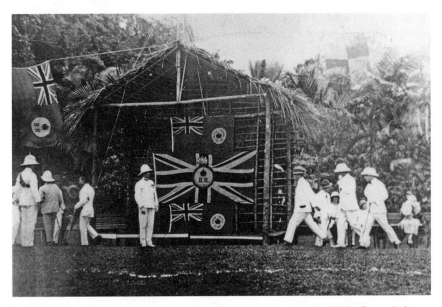

FIGURE 1.8. A 1927 event on Tulagi's golf course for a visit by High Commissioner Eyre Hutson. William Bell is last on right in foreground. (Photo collected by Commissioner of Lands Alexander "Spearline" Wilson, seen here walking two ahead of Bell. Courtesy of the Trustees of the British Museum, Oc,A56.1.)

tion, Kwaio offered no resistance to Bell and his police (though Kwara'ae men attacked them), but Bell had a personal encounter with Basiana, a renowned fighter, bounty hunter, and leader of the people of 'Ai'eda, and Bell cursed him as a "bastard." It was Basiana who in 1924 had forced Bell to withdraw from arresting tax defaulters by threatening to kill him and his men.[92]

By the 1927 tax collection, a personal animosity had developed between a group of Kwaio strongmen and Bell and his police. Several Kwaio whom Bell had arrested were hanged for murder, some of them relatives of these men, and he now demanded they hand over their guns, which were to them more than mere weapons; since the labor trade, guns had been symbols of power. To submit to further taxation and turn over their rifles would have publicly acknowledged capitulation, which was what Bell intended. Kwaio oral historians are fond of recalling how coastal Christians and head-men ridiculed the fighting leaders for having paid the 1926 tax, joking that they were "people of the *bisi*" (the menstrual area) instead of "people of the *busi*" (Pijin for "bush"). In the mountains, two *ramo*, Maenaafo'oa and Tagailamo, made curses with their ancestors' names, stating that Bell and his police were "shitting on their heads," which required them to seek puri-fication. The Kwaio warriors were backed into a corner with two choices: succumb to Bell's rule or confront him head-on.[93] Bell's options were simi-larly limited; by 1927 only Kwaio men had refused to submit to his control, and with the 1926 tax collected it appeared they would now yield as well. By forcing them to hand over their rifles and another tax, he could complete his domination of Malaita, to which he had dedicated 12 difficult years. On the other hand, if he failed to do so it would be widely noted and under-mine his hard-earned gains elsewhere.[94]

Kwaio men killed Bell and most of his party at the 4 October 1927 tax collection at Gwee'abe in Sinalagu. Details of this have been well docu-mented by Keesing and Corris and will not be recounted here. The attack was set in motion at the initiative of Basiana. Some Kwaio who had lived abroad warned that, if they killed Bell, government forces would come and crush them. But Basiana, who like many renowned Kwaio warriors had never left the area, belittled those who wavered, and he prevailed. By the time Bell and his party arrived at Sinalagu, detailed plans were in place and ancestors had received sacrificial pigs to clear the way for the attack. Even so, many Kwaio did not believe it would occur. Ri'ika of 'Ubuni, in his late twenties at the time, told me that on the way down to the coast many in the war party were in a jovial mood, thinking there would not really be a fight. He recalled his relief when they reached the coastal rim and saw three ships anchored in Sinalagu Harbour 600 meters below: "Oh, there are too many people. The fight is off!" But his father replied, "The fight cannot be off, we have sacrificed pigs for it."[95]

While collecting the tax at Uru, Bell had been amply warned of plans to attack him, but he believed he could finesse his way through. The action was executed primarily by fighting leaders of three kin groups from behind Sinalagu, and Basiana initiated it by caving in Bell's skull with a rifle barrel as Bell sat at the tax table. To defuse the confrontational atmosphere, Bell had unwisely ordered his police inside the tax house, where they were quickly overwhelmed. Bell, Lillies, and 13 of their party were killed, while the Kwaio attackers lost one of their leaders, Maenaafo'oa, and another man, both killed by a single shot from Lillies's pistol.

Much more bloodletting was to come. When word of the attack reached 'Aoke, the government quickly organized a punitive expedition. As detailed by Keesing and Corris, some two weeks later there assembled at Sinalagu a large government force consisting of the Australian ship HMAS *Adelaide* with a contingent of about 50 marines, 28 white civilians, 50 Malaitan police and volunteers, and 211 north Malaitan bearers. Bell had earned the esteem of many Malaitans, particularly in the north and on Small Malaita, and no love was lost between north Malaitans and the Kwaio. One Kwara'ae man named Dio told me in 1987 of being in an 'Aoke area church when news arrived of Bell's death, at which the entire congregation burst into tears and wailing. Some 3,500 north Malaitans visited the station to proclaim support for the government, and many volunteered to help punish the Kwaio.[96]

It soon became clear that only the Malaitans were capable of fighting

FIGURE 1.9. Members of the punitive expedition to Kwaio resting in an inland river, October 1927. (Courtesy of Jeff Wilmot, whose father Harvey Rosswell Wilmot was a crewmember of HMAS *Biloela*, a fuel supply ship; photographer unknown.)

in the mountains. Decades later, coastal Kwaio who had served as porters laughed when they recalled how the Europeans stumbled about and generally made fools of themselves in the jungle terrain. But the Malaitan constabulary was skilled in jungle warfare. Leading patrols were Maekali, Ba'etalua, and Timi Kakalu'ae, all of whom we will meet later as powerful government headmen. As described by Keesing and Corris: "[Shrine] desecration, garden destroying, shooting pigs and burning houses were diversions. The order of the day was people hunting....Whatever orders they received from above, their mission was to avenge Bell and, most of all, their own slain relatives."[97]

Women were gang-raped and shot, children were murdered, and prisoners routinely executed and their bodies mutilated. Gardens were sprayed with an arsenic mixture referred to as "Anti-Ant" donated by Levers. Even today, there are few Kwaio who cannot tell of atrocities committed against their kin. Most victims had played no part in the plot or the killings, and the constabulary attacked not only Sinalagu people but also those inland from 'Oloburi and Uru, and even in west Kwaio. Keesing estimated around 60 people were shot, while many children died of exposure and hunger while hiding in the jungle. Kwaio give much higher numbers. About 200 Kwaio men, most innocent of crime, were jailed in Tulagi, and 28 men, most of

FIGURE 1.10. A member of the punitive expedition with a Kwaio man, October 1927. (Courtesy of Jeff Wilmot; photographer unknown.)

them elderly, soon died during a dysentery epidemic there. Basiana and five others, who turned themselves in to stop the carnage, were hanged, and 17 were sentenced to prison terms.[98]

Kane determined to permanently deport the entire "Sinalagu tribe" to the island of Santa Isabel (he wildly underestimated the area's population at 500). Harry Moorhouse, sent from London to investigate the assassination, advised High Commissioner Eyre Hutson, who had originally deferred to Kane, against the deportation. Kane thought it necessary to "punish the evildoers" and that deportation would lead Kwaio to interbreed with the Isabel natives "and so bring to the natives of that island some of their undoubted and much-needed virility." His plan called for setting the deportees at forced labor to help pay for their own relocation. Finally, in mid-1928, the innocent "detainees" were taken back to Kwaio. The government had to provide rice rations for months until new gardens were established.[99]

The Bell assassination and its aftermath marked a key historical shift in the Solomons (coinciding with Charles Woodford's death in Sussex on the same day Bell was killed). Most obviously, it ended violent resistance to colonial rule. The punitive expedition dashed any Malaitan ideas that their mountains were impregnable or that they could challenge the government militarily. Many hoped opportunity, development, and other benefits to cooperation would now be forthcoming. Others continued to resist the government in subtler, nonviolent ways. Nearly six decades of dealing with Europeans as independent peoples had left Malaitans reluctant to fully surrender their political autonomy, and in the years that followed, reluctance turned to refusal as the government disregarded the island's development, failed to provide social services, and continued to treat its people as second-class citizens in their own land.

Chapter 2

Early Native Administration: Coping with Custom

The 1930s on Malaita are often perceived as a political lull between transformative events. As the decade began, the last violent resistance to British control had been put down, and 12 years would pass before World War II engulfed the Protectorate. The Great Depression brought economic malaise and hardship, and, for the few hundred Europeans in the group, Malaitans seemed hopelessly fragmented and resigned to, if not always content with, life and labor under their control. This was an illusion. Beneath the surface anger smoldered and deepened through the decade as Malaitans assessed the new colonial order and their status in it. While many have credited the war with arousing Melanesian desires for change, in the southeastern Solomons it was rather a catalyst for an eruption of resentments and aspirations already grown rife.

The decade is also crucial to this study because this was when officers on Malaita and elsewhere began to formulate and initiate native administration and social engineering projects inspired by models of "indirect rule" imported from African colonies and grounded importantly in the concept of "custom." After the war, Maasina Rule and kindred resistance movements built on Malaitans' critical appraisals of these projects, and *kastom* emerged when Malaitans appropriated the "custom" concept and took it in directions officers could never have foreseen.

The Idea of Indirect Rule

Conquered states that have been accustomed to liberty and government of their own laws can be held by the conqueror in three ways. The first is to ruin them; the second, for the conqueror to go and reside there in person; and the third is to allow them to continue to live under their own laws, subject to a regular tribute, and to create in them a government of a few, who will keep the country friendly to the conqueror. Such a government, having been established by such a new prince, knows that it cannot maintain itself without the support

of his power and friendship, and it becomes its interest therefore to
sustain him.
—*Niccolò Machiavelli*, The Prince

Repercussions from Bell's assassination were felt far beyond Kwaio, since
it compelled London to reassess standing "native policy" throughout the
Protectorate. In 1928 the Colonial Office under a special king's regulation dispatched Lieutenant-Colonel Sir Harry C Moorhouse, lately a high
official in southern Nigeria, to investigate the attack on Bell's party and
the killing a few months earlier of three policemen on Guadalcanal. The
scope of Moorhouse's recommendations exceeded those two events, and
his final report critiqued past administrative methods, especially how the
first Native Administration Regulation of 1922 (to be discussed presently)
had been applied. The government made little pretense of ruling by other
than direct means, and Moorhouse alleged that this had contributed to
not only the recent violence but also many other problems. He prescribed
gradual development of an indirect rule scheme such as he and others had
administered in Africa, starting with appointment of native headmen who
enjoyed genuine community followings. He acknowledged that the Solomons differed from Africa in important ways and that the approach would
face difficulties.[1]

It is significant that Moorhouse spent his career in Nigeria, where he had
been a key player in attempts to revitalize a moribund system of indirect
rule. In southern Nigeria he had enjoined new doctrines for "the resuscitation of indigenous forms of government, the consolidation of tribal units,
the selection of the rightful chief, his installation with appropriate ceremo-
nial, the re-establishment of the clan council together with the definition of
the jurisdiction and powers of the clan council and chief." The Protectorate's resident commissioners over the next 23 years all arrived having cut
their administrative teeth in colonial Africa. Like Moorhouse, they brought
with them African models of native administration, particularly indirect
rule, and so we must have a basic understanding of these.[2]

"Indirect rule" is a notoriously murky concept that has been used to label
diverse systems of rule applied by various colonial powers. For the British
Empire, it is most famously attributed to Lord Frederick Lugard, high commissioner of northern Nigeria from 1900 to 1906 and later Nigeria's first
governor-general, for whom indirect rule was "the cardinal principle upon
which the administration of northern Nigeria was based." Donald Cameron subsequently carried Lugard's approach to Tanganyika, and varia-
tions were extended to other colonies. The core idea was that Britain would
rule through indigenous political structures already in place, making "a
systematic use of the customary institutions of the people as agencies of
local rule."[3]

Indirect forms of rule were in part a response to stark necessity: London's colonial policy of the day strictly limited administrative spending, and the labor and resources of colonized peoples were expected to finance their own subjugation.[4] For example, as of 1906, Lugard had been receiving only £100,000 to £500,000 annually to administer 75 colonial officers and about 7,000,000 people belonging to diverse groups.[5] Manpower presented a special problem because there were not enough white officers to rule Africans directly. Use had to be made of "existing machinery." Mamdani pointed out that staff shortfalls in African colonies resulted largely from a refusal to fully employ talents of the many educated Africans. In the Solomons, too, manpower shortfalls were self-inflicted, but at a more basic level: the government failed to provide Solomon Islanders with any serious education at all.[6]

Colonizing powers throughout history have marshaled local political systems to their own purposes, as had the British in Nigeria before Lugard. His contribution was to systematize, formalize, and promote indirect rule as an ostensibly scientific administrative system with high moral goals. As Adiele Afigbo observed, historical study of indirect rule was long hindered by a preoccupation with the distinctive model Lugard devised for northern Nigeria and a tendency to define the approach in its terms.[7] I nonetheless highlight selected ideas from Lugard here, first because his basic model was an important influence on what the British tried to do in the Solomons, and second because Lugard laid out fundamental requirements for the success of indirect rule that clearly applied also to Malaita but that the administration there long neglected, contributing to many of its failures.

Lugard presented indirect rule as serving a "dual mandate" to facilitate both economic exploitation and the gradual moral and social advancement of African peoples. He asserted that indirect rule was in fact necessary to prevent a collapse of Nigerian societies in the face of European incursion. The alternative for Africans, he declared in a 1927 White Paper, was "disintegration into an undisciplined rabble of leaderless and ignorant individuals." Indirect rule would allow different African groups to develop along paths and at paces best suited to them, and at times it was claimed that its primary objective was didactic: "helping the African to become a better African." At the same time, administrators hoped that by sponsoring chiefly authority they could, in Cameron's words, build "a bulwark against future political agitation" by "Europeanised natives seeking to obtain political control."[8]

Lugard went far beyond merely maintaining indigenous Nigerian institutions. He shored up or broadened the power of local chiefs as required, and where no recognizable chiefs existed they were created.[9] Sometimes he found it necessary to "restore" to chiefs a real or supposed "prestige and authority which they had lost by the British conquest." Political institutions were similarly simplified, elaborated, standardized, or invented as needed, most notably "native courts" and "judicial councils of elders and chiefs," which were granted limited powers under close supervision. One should not assume that Africans were always passive recipients of these new models; in some cases they were active in their construction. John Iliffe was one of the first to argue this when he described how Tanganyikans met British expectations that they had tribes by creating them for their own strategic purposes within the colonial system. Many later historians have followed a similar approach by investigating the dynamic, dialogic, and emergent natures of political structures and identities in colonial settings, as I do here.[10]

Champions of indirect rule often downplayed British authority within it, as in Sir Anton Bertram's suggestion that, in northern Nigeria, British officers were "really only residing in a native jurisdiction" and "the District Officer is not dealing with a subject race, but with recognized communities under British Protection." Some Europeans complained that indirect rule gave too much autonomy to native populations or power to oppressive chiefs.[11]

Many students of African colonial history have questioned the claims for and political motives behind indirect rule there. Helen Lackner asserted that in practice Lugard presided over a government *through* chiefs rather than *by* them. John Bodley wrote, "Indirect rule was designed to preserve native political institutions only to the extent necessary to maintain order and to assure the availability of native labor." To colonial administrators, Lucy Mair said, "A 'progressive' chief or 'energetic headman' is one who is tireless in exhorting his people to obey [government laws] and not unwilling to prosecute them for failing to do so." As late as the 1960s, George Foster likewise observed in Northern Rhodesia, "The Native Authority system in no real sense of the word represents self-government. To a considerable extent it is a device to try to make a chief do some of the unpopular things Government feels must be done." Indirect rule, when it worked, typically did not so much give power to local leaders as it first limited their power and then drew on and channeled what was left. Immanuel Wallerstein traced the idea to "the responsive note it touched in British hearts," having emerged when the "romantics among the soldiers teamed up with the romantics among the anthropologists." Mamdani saw indirect rule's political aim as having been "to fracture the native population into ethnic groups" and said that it "signified a retreat from colonization's original project of civilization: the natives would remain natives, forever proscribed from the realm of civil law." Fulani bin Fulani similarly charged that indirect rule acted to "fasten down upon the African his own past," a way of life now dead or dying. Many of these same critiques could also be made of the indirect rule schemes later implemented in the Solomons.[12]

Indirect rule policies were applied with a good deal of variation and mixed success throughout the British Empire. Even within Nigeria, populations were graded according to their political systems, and those viewed as less advanced—mostly southern groups without powerful leaders or centralized institutions—were ruled more directly. Policies also shifted over time. Lord William Hailey, former governor of the Punjab and the United Provinces and himself once an enthusiast of indirect rule, later disparaged a gradual shift in attitude among its adherents: what had started as "a useful administrative device" became "a political doctrine," and finally "a religious dogma."[13]

Steven Pierce has employed data from Hausaland to argue that the indirect rule system in northern Nigeria never really worked as advertised, that it not only concealed and facilitated inequalities and injustices on the ground but also disguised the degree to which the colonial state failed in its modernist projects of classification, categorization, and organization of the sort James Scott has famously explored. Instead, the indirect rule model granted the system a façade of legitimacy to outsiders and let the colonial administration, in Pierce's phrase, "look like a state."[14] One could similarly criticize Solomon Islands native administration systems, but it is important to note that officers there did not see indirect rule as a façade or sham, and many trusted in and worked to promote its ideals and workability even when frustrated by its defects.

My interest here is not in scrutinizing the efficacy, sincerity, or morality of indirect rule in Africa or in general, but rather in understanding attempts to deploy it on Malaita. The basic social and economic pressures to institute it in the Solomons resembled those in Africa and, also as in Africa, indirect rule schemes were most problematic when imposed on societies that, like Malaitan ones, lacked the kinds of political leaders and institutions that colonial officials were prepared to recognize and work with. The British conceived "tribal" political legitimacy as based significantly on tradition and birthright, and they were stymied where leadership was not so ascribed, or where they encountered indigenous political structures that were fluid or unstable or appeared to have collapsed altogether. Roy Davies later wrote, "District officers transferred to the Solomons from African colonies usu-ally smiled pityingly at the prospect of administering a mere 40,000 people [Malaita's official population], used as they were to having to look after a quarter of a million. The smile did not last long." BSIP administrators right into the 1950s exhibited what now seems a persistent inability to grasp and adapt to unfamiliar or dynamic systems, as well as a dogged denial of cul-tural realities. Nowhere was this truer than on Malaita, where their attempts to apply indirect rule often appear in retrospect half-hearted and confused. Their efforts to apply indirect rule in the Protectorate came at a time—in the later 1930s and just after World War II—when the approach was being widely questioned and criticized in Africa and elsewhere in the empire, partly as a result of its failures during the Depression.[15]

Understanding how indirect rule unfolded and faltered on Malaita requires consideration of several key requirements that Lugard laid out for the approach to succeed. One was that district officers had to learn at least one native language, with their promotion dependent on it. Another, which Lugard deemed "paramount and essential," was continuity of administration—officers should be transferred as seldom as possible, since only through long residence in one area could they acquire knowledge of "native laws and customs" necessary to carry out their duties effectively, and since Africans would give full confidence to an officer "only after many years of personal contact." He also instructed officers to spend the least time possible in their offices and concentrate instead on "travel and work among the people." Lugard said that cultural knowledge was absolutely essential: "In order to develop a system suited to [the needs of the natives], the District Officer must study their customs and social organizations; for without a knowledge of their institutions the result must be failure." Regardless of one's view of indirect rule as idea or practice, it is hard to disagree with Lugard regarding these basic prerequisites for its workability. Malaita was to prove him correct when efforts to deploy indirect rule there were crippled by a failure to meet two of these provisos: no officers learned any Malaitan language, and most remained woefully ignorant of fundamental aspects of Malaitan societies.[16]

These failures made it difficult for an officer to gain effective authority, and they help explain why missionaries who stayed in one area for years and learned languages sometimes had more influence. Furthermore, with only two officers, and sometimes a cadet, working out of and maintaining 'Aoke station and overseeing thousands of hamlets scattered over rugged terrain, most Malaitan communities before the war received few or no government visits.[17] Relative to other islands, Malaita did enjoy an unusual continuity of senior officers from the 1930s into the later 1940s, but through the prewar years these officers rarely engaged socially with most Malaitans and this diluted the advantages Lugard believed long-term residence would bring. Lower-ranking officers were transferred often into and out of Malaita.

During the Depression, attempts to apply a formal system of indirect rule on Malaita remained piecemeal and desultory, until they intensified just prior to and immediately after the war. Yet even before that shift, officers had little choice but to employ elements of the indirect rule approach on a de facto basis due to shortages of funding and personnel and because they lacked the requisite knowledge to carry out core aspects of their duties without help from local people. I will return to how this system worked in practice.

Antecedents and Beginnings of Native Administration

Early endeavors at native administration in the Solomons can help us understand subsequent efforts to apply indirect rule as official policy. Prior to Moorhouse's 1929 report, a handful of colonial officials and other Euro-

peans had recognized the pressing need for more Islander participation
in administration, and there were attempts to effect this. The first was the
Anglican Melanesian Mission's establishment of a local "Parliament" on
Gela called the Vaukolu ("meeting"). Rev John Holford Plant and Bishop
John R Selwyn initiated Vaukolu gatherings in 1887 and 1888 to rebuild a
Gela leadership system badly undermined by labor recruitment and the
mission's own activities. The assembly devised a loose administrative structure dividing Gela into five districts, each headed by a "chief." At the early
Vaukolu, missionaries and local leaders fashioned laws relating to adultery,
pig trespass, and marriage (all said to be based on preexisting "native legislation") and instituted rules demarcating the powers of Melanesian church
teachers. Persons found to have broken the laws were to work on community and church projects and pay fines to the chiefs, despite problems determining who were "chiefs" and some displeasure with those selected. The
Vaukolu became an annual Gela event, sometimes attended by people from
other islands including Malaita.[18]

When Resident Commissioner Charles Woodford established the first
government station at nearby Tulagi in 1896, he disapproved of the church
having taken on secular powers and he soon began a campaign to transfer
those powers to his administration: "During January [1898] I invited the
chiefs and people of Gela to a meeting at Tulagi for the consideration of
a code of laws for the better government of the island. About a thousand
natives attended....District and village chiefs were appointed who were
to send offenders to Tulagi for punishment." The new code, modeled at
Woodford's suggestion on one from the Gilbert and Ellice Islands Protectorate, met with a positive response, and not only on Gela; his initiative
brought inquiries and some cooperation from nearby islands and even a
friendly Malaitan visit (probably Langalanga people calling on Gela trade
partners). He thought a broader formal code was "urgently wanted" and
hoped one could be quickly extended to Savo and to Guadalcanal's northern coast. Woodford supported enforcement of the 1898 laws until he left
the Solomons in 1915.[19]

Woodford attended subsequent Vaukolu "in full uniform—white duck,
fine helmet with enameled coat of arms, and dress sword—very imposing," but he remained concerned that the Anglicans stay out of what he
saw as government's exclusive domain. Worried that church teachers might
effectively become "chiefs," he excluded them and the clergy from his new
administration. Relations between the colonial government and the Christian missions remained generally amicable and cooperative, but tension
over their respective political authority and rivalries between government-
and church-appointed officials were to permeate BSIP politics for many
decades. In his 1929 report Moorhouse noted this continuing friction and
suggested that some synthesis of government and mission authority might
be wise and inevitable.[20]

FIGURE 2.1. Anglican Bishop Cecil Wilson speaking to the Vaukolu of 22 October 1906, at Honggo, on Gela. Resident Commissioner Charles Woodford is seated in helmet. (John Beattie photo 618, courtesy of the Trustees of the British Museum, Oc,B115.77.)

Through the following decades, many church leaders saw government appointees as threats to their power, and they impeded selection or recognition of some indigenous leaders and lobbied for installment of men of their own denominations. Anglican Bishop Steward instructed fellow missionaries to ignore local leaders: "Native Chiefs, may generally be divided into two categories, the Knave and the Fool. BUT THERE ARE CERTAIN OUTSTANDING EXCEPTIONS. Generally speaking, treat the Native Chief with outward courtesy but do not pay much attention to what he says. The exceptions are so rare that you are not likely to make a mistake. Since the arrival of the Government, the 'worth' of the Chief has decreased in the same degree as has his power." Steward likewise dismissed the native policeman as "nearly always a knave and an unmitigated nuisance. Lose no opportunity of putting him 'in his place.' "[21]

The annual Vaukolu outlasted the nineteenth century but became more social than administrative in nature and its political import declined. Nonetheless, in 1901 and 1903, despite strong opposition from local women, the Vaukolu chiefs set a limit on rising brideprices, with Woodford's promise to help them enforce it.[22] Subsequent Vaukolu addressed such issues as Christian converts "backsliding" to their ancestral religion, marriages without Christian rites, tattooing, and village cleanliness and maintenance of paths to link them—all concerns of Anglican missionaries.[23]

Despite these early initiatives, it would be decades before Islanders were allowed any real, formal role in government, due to a number of obstacles. Foremost was the common European conviction that Melanesians were far too "primitive," "savage," and "backward" to play any part. Officials argued further that rule had to be direct because local societies offered no political structures or mechanisms on which to build. They bemoaned the absence of discrete units by which to partition the landscape, particularly on Malaita. There, language zones contained innumerable (for officers) small groups with layered, nested identities, which often stressed their differences. Officers who had learned something of anthropological models of groups defined by unilineal kinship were confused by Malaita's cognatic systems, and in any case kinship there was only one of many bases for social relationships and identities. As in so many other colonies, officers demarcated and named groups arbitrarily across what were often ambiguous ethnic or linguistic borders. These hardened into "Kwaio," "To'abaita," "'Are'are," and so forth—ten language areas in all—divided for administrative purposes into 32 sub-districts based on the island's key anchorages (see map of Malaita, back endpaper). Despite their artificiality, over the years these units did acquire real political meanings for their residents, especially after World War II.[24]

The obstacle to Malaitans' participating in government most often cited by administrators was their leadership systems. Officers could not operate through political units that were small, atomistic, and fluid, and though they worked to consolidate them into larger, stable polities, they searched in vain for "customary" leaders to head such groups. As in many parts of Melanesia, few men fit European conceptions of a "chief." Most leaders in the southeastern Solomons had small followings that expanded or contracted contextually, and the basis of their authority was in most places only minimally inherited, if at all. Ritual organization linking clans through descent from common ancestors had some limited political coherence, but to colonial officers it was obscure and in many places it was disintegrating prior to Christian expansion, as were the more hierarchical leadership systems in the far south. Many men who did wield more power gained it, like past "passage masters," as brokers of European trade and labor recruitment, and some of them Europeans saw as scoundrels. Others were church teachers whom government officers and many Malaitans were unwilling to formally elevate as political leaders.

Sometimes it was supposed, by Malaitans as well as colonials, that "chiefs" (or even "chieftesses") had once existed but had disappeared due to the European impact or because of a progressive decadence of island cultures predating European presence. For example, Resident Commissioner Francis Ashley, soon after his arrival in the Solomons in 1929, insisted that there had been such leaders and proffered a list of powerful precolonial "chiefs," lifted (uncited) from an 1887 book by naturalist Henry Guppy. Most of these men were from the Western Solomons and, as Guppy described, had gained their stature by marshaling trade or labor networks involving Europeans. Nonetheless, Ashley lamented the absence of suitable leaders in 1929 and pressed for their resurrection: "It must be accepted, generally speaking, that any executive power the chief had, is lost, disintegration has taken place. As time goes on this complete emancipation from any kind of control will lead to trouble.... No education will instill the advantages of British rule, and advantages will be less and less realized by the increased security in which the people live.... With this in view, it may be advisable, if for no other reason, to reconstruct, as far as we are able, a native organization, upon which to build a native administration. A native authority responsible for law and order."[25]

Martha Kaplan has nicely analyzed the situation in colonial Fiji in which chiefly status was shored up and ordered according to British sensibilities of hierarchy, as an "aristocracy," all in the name of preserving Fijian ways. But in most of the Solomons this approach was too distant from reality to be feasible. Early drafts of the first Native Administration Regulation, like the Southern Rhodesia legislation on which it was modeled, made provision for appointing functionary "chiefs," but in the final version they had become "headmen," and, unlike its African precursor, the regulation made no reference to leaders with indigenous legitimacy. As one principal headman, Timi Kakalu'ae, testified approvingly even in the late 1940s, "The Government gave power only to the headmen. Not to anyone else."[26]

Prior to 1920, except for land law, the government directed no specific legislation at Solomon Islanders, and in 1918 Acting Resident Commissioner Charles Workman wrote candidly to High Commissioner Cecil Rodwell that Solomon Islanders were "in a backward state as a result of neglect of native administration in [the] past." Soon a native tax regulation and a labor regulation were introduced, and in 1922, almost 30 years after declaration of the Protectorate, the aforementioned Native Administration Regulation became law. It defined authority of different officers concerning native affairs; provided for creation of administrative divisions; authorized appointment and defined duties of "district headmen," "village headmen," and "village constables"; and "imposed upon natives generally the duty of respecting authority and complying with government orders." Rodwell, based in Fiji, and for many years before that (and again later) in southern Africa, personally prepared the final regulation. It was very different from a version proposed by Resident Commissioner Richard Kane, who had worked in Fiji and whom Rodwell plainly despised. Kane's version followed more closely the declared ideals of indirect rule, but Rodwell rejected it as "a hopeless jumble," and he was particularly critical of Kane for having tried to devise a system of administration in which Solomon Islanders would participate: "He has included provisions establishing native courts and conferring jurisdiction on natives which I consider altogether premature, the majority of Solomon Islanders being little better than raw savages." He rejected even Kane's suggestion that headmen organize and preside over local meetings.[27]

Kane defended his rejected proposal (modeled partly on Fijian regulations that Rodwell disdained), arguing, "The main idea is to inculcate in the native mind that he is having a share in the Government and that some at least of the Regulations governing his life emanate from him." Kane cited requests by people of Gela and the Western Solomons to participate in government as evidence that parts of the Protectorate were ready.[28] Nonetheless, under Rodwell's direction, the final 1922 regulation was designed to firmly maintain direct rule.

The only Islanders included in the resulting administrative structure were headmen, and their primary functions, especially early on, were to enforce government rules, help collect taxes, and act as the primary means through which officers communicated with the populations they stood over.[29] Kane issued them preposterous instructions to, among other duties, radically reorganize and police residence patterns, the division of labor, sanitation and burial practices, house building, gardening, pig raising, village interconnectivity, and treatment of the sick, and to report their success in these tasks to district officers on a quarterly basis.[30] Village headmen who failed to report a birth faced a fine of up to 5 shillings and up to seven days in jail. It is significant here that Kane came to the Solomons from Fiji; Nicholas Thomas has analyzed similar intrusive sanitary and other regulations imposed there, concluding their primary basis was not their substance, but rather, "the regulations were...ends in themselves, which constituted the ambit of state control." Few BSIP headmen were literate, and Acting Resident Commissioner Ralph Hill said they did not understand the regulation or the powers it did and did not grant them. Malaita's 1944 Annual Report recounted the duties of these early headmen as "little more than those of a common informer," though this was unfair to the better ones.[31]

Remarkably, given their critical importance to administration, headmen, of whom there were 47 on Malaita by late 1929, were paid the base wage of plantation laborers. Still, their position as middlemen gave them substantial power, which some abused. Most were appointed not due to their community status or in order to represent local views but instead for their ability to communicate with officers and their familiarity with European ways. They were meant to fully serve government policy and control, which officers saw to be synonymous with the peoples' interests. Some headmen effectively isolated officers from the populace.[32]

Implementation of Rodwell's watered-down version of the regulation proceeded fairly smoothly in some places, most notably on Santa Isabel (which was by then fully Anglican) and farther west, but Malaita was more problematic. We saw earlier that much of the island in the early 1920s remained outside government control and Bell found few men both suitable and willing to be headmen. As of 1924, he had appointed only a handful of village headmen and constables and just three sub-district headmen, but he predicted, "The application of the provisions of the Regulation will continue to increase and it will undoubtedly be of the greatest assistance in obtaining complete control of the native population." By 1926 Bell was recommending appointment of 22 sub-district headmen.[33]

The Moorhouse Report and Malaita Policy after Bell

Moorhouse's report on the Malaita and Guadalcanal murders was in part a critique of how the Native Administration Regulation of 1922 had been implemented. Many of his proposals echoed Workman's of a decade before. After initial dismay at the poor fit of African models with the Solomons, Moorhouse came to believe that a less direct method of rule was called for anyway, one that gave villagers some choice of their representatives in government. This could not be rushed, he stressed, and officers had to take into account difficulties specific to their areas and move at appropriate speed. Pulling a page from Lugard, he stressed that district officers had to tour more: "It is only by constantly visiting the natives in their villages and by taking an interest in their affairs that their confidence can be gained. I am afraid that at the present moment the majority of natives look on the District Officer merely as a tax gatherer or one who metes out punishment."[34]

The timing of Moorhouse's advice proved unfortunate, since the Protectorate was just heading into years of economic stagnation brought on by the global Depression and a precipitous plunge in copra prices. Many Europeans later blamed the failure to implement his ideas on the Depression, and certainly Moorhouse did specify that they could only succeed with a sizable increase in European staffing, particularly on Malaita, but matters other than financial woes contributed to the inaction that followed there. As will become evident, the policies, practices, and attitudes of colonial officials were fundamental obstacles to reform.[35]

Moorhouse's report did bring about certain changes. Some administrators tried harder to pick headmen who enjoyed popular support, though less so on Malaita. Kane's replacement Ashley supported Moorhouse on this matter, in procedure if not spirit: "With every confidence I believe that a native authority, under our guidance, can be formed from the existing chiefs of the native communities. . . . In ruling an illiterate community and a very scattered people, especially when for financial reasons, the European administrative staff has to be curtailed, we should rule through the natural leaders of the people. Even if the natural or elected head is not the best possible selection, the people will obey more readily one of their own choosing, than some person thrust upon them by an extraneous power; moreover their imaginary grievances will be more lightly tolerated." Ashley's tone here only hints at his demeaning views of Islander intellects and cultures. The next year he told High Commissioner Arthur Fletcher, "The Solomon Islands natives generally are of a low mentality and have the minds and understanding of children," and soon afterward he wrote regarding Malaitan land tenure that he saw "little object in sustaining, even in a protectorate, customs which are strange to our ideas."[36]

Ashley warned that government-appointed leaders might undermine the remaining power of traditional "chiefs." He issued instructions that where the leaders' customary and genealogical "credentials" were established, "We should support, by every means in our power, the building up of the authority of these natural rulers of the people," but he warned of chaos if more than one chief per village were appointed. As with the search for headmen, many indigenous leaders avoided government recognition; among other things, duties of a colonial appointee such as enforcing British laws and taxation could undercut their local standing.[37]

Officers on Malaita at the time received the new approach without enthusiasm. In charge of the district during the early 1930s was Jack C Barley (see figure 2.3), who staunchly opposed giving significant authority to local leaders. His response to his superior Ashley's vision of ruling through "chiefs" was lukewarm at best, and in Malaita's 1930 Annual Report he pointed out the Machiavellian advantage of maintaining headmen who lacked local standing and therefore had little choice but to be government loyalists:

> The great majority of the Headmen whom I found in office had been appointed on the principles of direct rather than indirect rule...and but few of them wielded any natural authority amongst their people as chiefs by hereditary right or personal prowess. Having, therefore, no individual "locus standi" outside their official status as Headmen, the appointees have naturally had to rely solely upon the prestige and power of Government to support and maintain them in the execution of their duties, and this factor has no doubt contributed toward keeping them loyal and also conscientious in the exercise of the authority entrusted to them. I am, however, strongly of the opinion that some effort should be made officially to recognize the position of the few surviving chiefs and natural leaders of the people by entrusting them with minor posts in the general scheme of Native Administration.

Not only had Malaitans not selected their own headmen, but also in Barley's day most headmen had minimal contact with most people since they rarely or never visited heavily populated mountain areas of their sub-districts. Barley said they did not know or even recognize most inland people under them. Moorhouse's recommendations notwithstanding, the system of headmen as instruments of direct rule was entrenched. Ten years after Bell's death, 70 percent of Malaita's district headmen were men he had appointed. Most of those stayed on at least until World War II and some of the most important ones were kept on into the early 1950s, including several who were hated by a large proportion of people in their sub-districts.[38]

Ashley drew from his experience administering native courts in Nigeria to raise the possibility of starting experimental ones in the Solomons. He soon proposed two on Malaita, presided over by "chiefs" and by district officers as vice presidents, with chiefs allowed to decide cases involving "native custom." High Commissioner Fletcher rejected this on the grounds that courts could not be adequately supervised and that customary laws had to be codified before such courts could properly function. But Ashley opposed codification; citing the diversity of rules on Malaita, he warned that it might "freeze" custom and leave it unable to adapt. Besides, he wrote, "No doubt in time the natives will adapt themselves to our laws."[39]

The issue of codification of custom and its real and potential impacts reappears later in this book, so let me digress to raise some basic considerations. Ashley was neither the first nor last to worry that codes of "customary" rules could rob colonized societies of flexibility; administrators and anthropologists in Melanesia, Africa, and India long voiced concerns that codes could "impose the grid of law on custom."[40] This issue is more complex than it appears. Efforts to codify unwritten rules can have two very different effects. One indeed would be to congeal once fluid and dynamic systems. Committing rules to formal codes can more tightly define offenses and clarify fuzzy categorical boundaries or other ambiguities, leaving rules less malleable. Administrators found this prospect troublesome in places like 1930s Malaita where rapid change was ongoing and inevitable, and, given European beliefs that Malaitans were inherently inflexible, they worried that codification would further hamper their ability to adjust.

Codes might also simplify or narrow disputes in terms of penalties or procedure, as Malaitan practices of dispute resolution illustrate. Outside of colonial and state law, disputes were and are profoundly embedded in broader social processes. Though disputes are vitally grounded in strong indigenous concepts of morality and justice as well as a Malaitan penchant for abstract rules and principles, their management is also intensely political. Compensation payments are typically subject to negotiations that incorporate a myriad of aggravating and mitigating factors—the personal status and reputations of disputants; their relative power and wealth (eg, people with lesser means to raise shell money and pigs can ideally pay smaller compensations); and their present and past social relations, including previous disputes or compensations and political rivalries between them or their groups that may reach across generations. Disputes commonly expand and escalate when parties raise other issues. These can at first appear tangential to the original complaint but then emerge as the true issues at stake, the complaint having been a pretext to broach them. Moreover, important men, and sometimes women, use disputes as occasions for political competition, either as disputants themselves or as explicit or tacit sponsors of those directly involved. As with all public presentations on Malaita, in compensation payments individuals and groups alike seek to earn prestige or at least to preserve face. Thus these payments transcend mere legal or economic calculation. If a code sets specific fines or compensations for particular offenses and procedurally demarcates and narrows admissible issues, then these dynamic aspects of dispute management can be constrained or eliminated, fundamentally altering the system. British officials desired this result, not only because these features of Malaitan disputes disturbed their conceptions of justice, but also because only if disputes were greatly simplified and extracted from the intricacies of social and political relations could officers ever hope to understand, regulate, and manage them.[41]

But this issue has another side. It is crucial to make an analytical distinction usually absent from discussions of codification's consequences, particularly of whether it freezes rules once fluid and dynamic. We must differentiate the deployment and enforcement of legal codes from the process of codification. This is especially important for colonial and postcolonial Malaita, where groups have invested tremendous energies in discussing, debating, and drafting *kastom* laws or similar codes, often over years or decades, with their efforts rarely or never culminating in working laws except during Maasina Rule. The codification process, far from hardening rules, can thrust what were once routine, mundane, or comfortably ambiguous rules into a volatile political realm where they take on new, extralegal meanings—objective, subjective, and metaphorical—and are thereby fundamentally transformed. Competing readings of particular rules can become political platforms for rival factions and, paradoxically, the codification process can thereby make rules more difficult to codify. Finally, especially in colonial situations, certain rules or bodies of rules may within this process become symbols of resistance to the state. This began to occur on Malaita during the 1930s, and Malaitans would later undertake intensive codification efforts in opposition to the government legal system. In a similar way, codification became a weapon in Malaitan religious conflicts.[42]

Administrators like Ashley, focused on codification as product rather than process, saw it as dangerous because it might lock down social change. If they had understood the more dynamic processual aspect of codification they likely would have opposed it still more, particularly as the 1930s progressed and officers began to fear that Malaitans were changing too fast, with, they believed, disastrous destabilizing and anomic consequences, including rapid depopulation (see chapter 3). This fear led them to try to stabilize local societies by restoring, preserving, and protecting selected customs, and custom codification became central to this effort. For example, Malaita's Officer George Sandars in his quarterly report for June 1937 called for speedy codification: "For much knowledge of things as they used to be is gradually being lost as the elders of the people die off." Later chapters explain how in the 1940s Malaitans themselves took up codification within their own social engineering projects aimed at radical change, which propelled to the fore the dynamic force of codification as process.

As noted earlier, Barley, who was Ashley's assistant during periods of the 1930s, opposed serious recognition of local leaders, and he counseled High Commissioner Fletcher against Ashley's native court ideas. He argued that codification was impossible, that Islanders were unqualified to serve on courts, and that Melanesians were inherently incapable of rendering fair and impartial decisions. In any case, he said, people wanted officers to handle their disputes for them. Ashley himself at times felt that there was little foundation on which to build a serious native court system; in 1933 he told Fletcher, "Owing to very rapid change of conditions I fear that the time has now unfortunately passed to attempt to revive any clan feeling or native customs. So damaged is it all in this short span of years. . . . Later, when the laws of these people have completely gone, as they must in time, and they have adapted the ideas of Western Europe, it will be possible and perhaps beneficial to have courts of Native Magistrates supervised by Europeans to administer laws we have made or adapted and codified for the benefit of the natives." Fletcher's successor, Arthur Richards, opined in 1937 that little was left of Solomon Islands cultures to preserve and that most of what did survive was obsolete and unsuitable as a basis for native administration.[43]

On the other side of the debate, anthropologist H Ian Hogbin became an advocate for building a native administration. In publications, popular articles, and reports to the government, written following his 1933 fieldwork in Guadalcanal and north Malaita, Hogbin lobbied heavily for indirect rule in the form of native courts and councils and custom codes, as well as for resuscitation of feasting to revive leaders' prestige. Later he helped compose an instruction booklet for councils and courts (eventually published in *Oceania*) that the government distributed to officers and these native bodies. Hogbin cautioned in *Pacific Islands Monthly*, "The scheme naturally presupposes that the district officers are trained in anthropology and are familiar with the customs of the area which they have to administer."[44]

Even in the early 1930s some BSIP officers saw a clear need for greater Islander participation in administration. As unofficial headmen had existed before the Native Administration Regulation allowed them, so too in places unofficial native councils and courts developed with officers' knowledge and even support. By 1934, for instance, native tribunals were hearing cases involving "native custom" on Guadalcanal. Fletcher did not challenge their existence but still insisted on codification as a precondition for official courts.[45]

Most officers involved in such projects seem to have been driven less by a desire to give Solomon Islanders a voice for its own sake than by a dire need for their help in administration, although these motives were not mutually exclusive. Throughout the 1930s, government, mission, and economic forces steadily eroded indigenous systems of dispute management, and the authority of local leaders further declined. Serious violence was no longer a viable response to offenses, and a growing number of cases were being brought before already overworked district officers. Legal work was just one of their many duties, as described by Martin Clemens, who worked for two years (1938–1940) as a cadet on Malaita: "The DO was responsible for practically everything. I learned what it meant to sit as a local magistrate; train police; keep prisoners' warrants; act as coroner; inspect labor on plantations, do accounts, and collect taxes; supervise medical work; captain the district schooner; and even, on occasion, serve as collector of customs.... The district officer was also, it seemed, the settler of disputes, not only between different groups within the native population but also between Solomon Islanders and Europeans." But though Malaita's officers bore pressures similar to or greater than those of other officers, they did little to encourage formal, unofficial courts in most places there until just before the war.[46] The rest of this chapter examines officers' relations with Malaitans during the 1930s as they grappled with expanding duties and court dockets, and as Malaitans sized up their new lives under British control. From these interactions, especially in courts, emerged aspects of later *kastom* ideologies that urged Malaitan control over the legal system.

District Officers, Law, and Custom Knowledge

Many Malaitans interacted with colonial officers most directly when officers presided over courts. Beginning in the early 1930s, new cadets received basic training in civil and criminal law during a year of Colonial Administrative Service Courses at Cambridge or Oxford.[47] To receive a commission they had to pass exams in criminal law, evidence, contracts, torts, indictable offenses, summary jurisdiction, and king's regulations and the Pacific Order in Council. Sandars described the Pacific Order in Council as "our real Bible" and said his 1932 law exams were his "great bugbear"; other officers who initially failed them would doubtless have agreed. Those who passed became "deputy commissioners of the Western Pacific" with magisterial powers to mandate prison sentences up to seven years and to hear criminal cases except for murder and rape.[48]

Officers handled all facets of a case, which, as former cadet Cyril Belshaw recalled, made legal work awkward: "The administrative officer has to act as judge, prosecutor, defense council and jury all at once, besides having conducted an enquiry as policeman a few moments before." Further, remembered Ronald Garvey, who served on Malaita in 1928 and 1930–1931, "You were also the Superintendent of Prisons to see that the accused were looked after, if you sentenced them." After the early 1920s, except for just after Bell's death, no police inspector lived on Malaita until the early 1950s. But even then Officer Jim Tedder followed "the convention that the District Officer or Commissioner always wore a tie" when hearing cases "to show he was not the officer from the district office but a magistrate."[49]

To manage most cases effectively an officer had to have, or have access to, local knowledge. His legal training was often of little use in disputes not justiciable under British law, the main source of government law except for specific BSIP regulations made under the Pacific Order in Council. Bell had quickly realized he had to adjudicate such cases if he was to claim authority. In one late-1919 report he detailed his criminal investigations, mostly of murders, on a Malaita tour, but then he told of other grievances: "Besides the above there were the usual number of complaints to try and settle which could not very well be brought under the category of crime, but which often cause considerable unrest among the natives of this island."[50] Disputes over ancestral oaths, sorcery accusations, and violations of local rules and taboos had to be dealt with to keep the peace, and to do so effectively required cultural sophistication.

Soon after arriving, Resident Commissioner Ashley, drawing on his Nigerian training, instructed, "An administrative officer's duty is to study the native customs of the people with whom he has to do." This was easier said than done since most districts had many language groups—ten on Malaita—with significant cultural variation between and within them. Gaining cultural and language fluency was made still more difficult when, against Lugard's prescription of continuity, officers were transferred frequently. For example, Cadet Clemens, posted to Wairokai in 'Are'are in the late 1930s, differed from most officers in compiling serious notes on local culture and a language word list, but he was soon transferred to Makira. He told me of being "furious" at having his work wasted: "One was just never left anywhere long enough to really get down to understanding the Solomon Islanders." His superior, Charles Bengough, had instructed, "Native custom should be carefully and exhaustively studied by the officer at Wairokai." Had Clemens been allowed to follow through, it would have been the first such study by a Malaitan officer.[51]

George Steinmetz has noted a common pattern in colonial settings of officials competing for "the cultural capital of ethnographic acuity or ethnographic discernment," and in the literature and archives of Malaita one occasionally finds claims to, or glowing attributions of, such expertise, sometimes presented as an essential tool of control. But in truth officers there before the war remained ignorant of crucial realms of local cultures, owing to the sheer complexity and variation, their segregation from Malaitan life, and prejudices of the day. Malaitans knew more about the daily lives of local whites, via servants for example, than whites did about Malaitans'.[52]

Though colonial policies would come to privilege and grant political power to local knowledge and practices—that is, to "custom"—officers lacked the resources and in many cases the serious desire to learn enough to adequately manage such policies. Some were conscious of what they did not know but confident that in the final tally it was not critical—local cultures were simply not worth the trouble for an already overworked officer to study in depth. The resulting misconceptions of local societies paved a treacherous road for colonial policy makers, from young cadets in the field to distant high commissioners in Fiji. There was also a pattern of more astute officers finding the local knowledge they did have and their decisions based on it overruled by resident or high commissioners who knew little and made decisions based on gross stereotypes or on their personal experiences in Africa or Fiji.

Raymond Firth, who was first in the Solomons in the late 1920s, remembered, "Only two officers in the Solomons administration at that time seemed to me to have any inkling of how the local societies operated." A major barrier on Malaita was that no officers there learned any local tongues, and Anglican missionary Albert Mason found them "rather afraid of the native languages and names." Into the 1910s, officers were told that to earn a salary increase they had to learn "at least one dialect spoken in the Solomons," or "the principal dialect of their district," but in the end they were required only to learn Pijin. By the mid-1920s, Officer Hector MacQuarrie found that, in the Protectorate generally, "The language problem, being beyond any workable solution, is ignored." Hogbin and his To'abaita informants alleged that Malaita's officers spoke even Pijin badly. As a mediocre linguist who managed to learn Pijin quickly I find this hard to believe, though Malaita's District Commissioner Sandars, whom we shall soon meet, did later recall it as "a queer sounding garbled business and not in any way satisfactory," and even after many years on Malaita he was not above using an interpreter to convey his words in Pijin. A common idea that Pijin was only a kind of broken English discouraged some English speakers from learning it as a language in its own right. The high commissioner and some others agreed with Acting Resident Commissioner F E Johnson's late-1930s call for rejection of "this bastard language," but officers used Pijin to interact with most Islanders until independence in 1978.[53]

Though the frequent transfer of officers was a problem across the Protectorate, prewar Malaita enjoyed unusual continuity of senior personnel. Bell had been so effective partly because he dealt closely with Malaitans for 22 years—as labor inspector from 1905 to 1911 on Fiji ships and from 1912 to 1915 in the Solomons, then for over ten years as a district officer—and thus understood many aspects of local life. He told Acting Resident Commissioner Frederick Barnett that during his three years as BSIP inspector, "I was probably more in touch with the doings of the greater portion of the island than were the District and Police Officers."[54]

Bell was followed by a succession of officers, including several on special short-term duty just after his death. For over a year in 1928–1929, Malaita was placed under Francis Filose, who had people flogged and was removed from his next posting on Santa Isabel for ordering Malaitans and others beaten and for pulling one behind his horse with a rope round his neck.[55] Filose was preceded and followed by Colin E J Wilson, who had been in the Solomons for many years. Three members of the Whitney South Sea Expedition, ornithologists traveling to the Kwaio interior in 1930, recorded in diaries their predeparture interview with Wilson, on 26 January. Walter Eyerdam wrote, "He told us a lot of awful stories about hostile and treacherous mountain bushmen but as he had never been farther than a day's march inland, he could not speak from personal experience"; William Coultas recorded, "He became so eloquent in his pessimism that he offered us one chance in a hundred of coming out of the mountains alive"; and Hannibal Hamlin noted, "He was almost alarmingly pessimistic about the Ari-Ari ['Are'are] natives in the vicinity of the big range in South Malaita.... These people live only for suspicious hatred and treachery which keeps them in constant fear of anything foreign. 'Why would they miss such an opportunity to destroy a few white men?' These sentiments do not jibe with what I have heard from more reliable sources." Lord Lugard would not have been pleased.[56]

Wilson's fears doubtless stemmed from Bell's assassination, and the fact that just before that Wilson had sent a police patrol to their deaths at the hands of people of Talise on Guadalcanal. He had been partly blamed for their deaths, having convicted one of the murderers of adultery with a woman who was in fact his wife, and he was reprimanded for dereliction of duty. Wilson had also been the officer in charge of the punitive expedition into Kwaio and, with Kane, had covered up its brutality in reports to High Commissioner Eyre Hutson. (Kane was also chastised behind the scenes for the Guadalcanal incident.) An American doctor, Sylvester Lambert, was told that it was Wilson who had decided to send the Malaitan constabulary into the Kwaio bush without escort. Now constant rumors circulated, all baseless, of Kwaio plots to again attack officers, and into the 1940s reports were regularly submitted to the resident commissioner about prospects of Kwaio unrest.[57] At this same time, Officer Garvey deployed constabulary in elaborate defensive positions at tax collections: "In order to protect myself I had the police in a V coming down towards my table, with the natives coming in single file down the center. And then at the back I had another V of police to prevent anybody coming from behind to obliterate me like they had poor Bell and Lillies."[58]

Soon after meeting the Whitney bird hunters, Wilson left Malaita, and the island came under the aforementioned Jack Barley, who had from 1912 served under Woodford as one of the Protectorate's first cadets and was now an experienced administrator. Barley was on Malaita for nearly two years from 1930 to 1932 and again briefly in 1933. Dr Lambert lauded Barley's

FIGURE 2.2. District Officer Ronald Garvey collecting the head tax at Uru, northeast Kwaio, in early October 1928, with soldiers in defensive formation. (Photo by Guinevere Anderson, courtesy of the Trustees of the British Museum, Oc,A61.42.)

"passion for ethnology and affectionate responsibility for the natives," and wrote admiringly of him as "Barley, who knew more about the customs, language and social traditions of the people than any white man who had ever lived in the Solomons. Barley, whose affection for the natives was fatherly, and who had devoted his splendid life to them." Lambert described him at his earlier "God-forsaken post at Kirakira" on Makira as "like something out of Kipling, dressing for the evening, having his spot of gin and bitters before dinner, and a sound cigar afterward." Barley held a bachelor's degree from St John's College at Oxford, and his reports from Malaita and Makira reveal him as in certain respects more sympathetic toward and knowledgeable of Melanesians than were his colleagues. He undertook some ethnographic study (which he later gave up), and before his posting to Malaita he had also gained, in his words, "a passing acquaintance with some six distinctive dialects." These included languages of Roviana, Ontong Java, Makira, and Fiji, although there is no record of his learning any on Malaita. But sympathy did not translate into confidence in Malaitan abilities or an appreciation of the moral moorings of their communities. Earlier in this chapter I noted Barley's opposition to the serious application of indirect rule in Malaita, and he held highly negative views of relevant aspects of Malaitan societies. In 1932, for example, he wrote that the authority and prestige of

FIGURE 2.3. Jack C Barley (seated with dog) picnicking with Stanley Annandale, on Gela, ca early 1910s. (Edge-Partington collection, courtesy of the Edge-Partington family.)

the island's leaders was based mostly on "exercise of traditional rights and privileges, totally repugnant to modern ideas of justice and humanity or calculated to retard social progress or vi et armis."[59]

Two officers who followed Barley—George Eustace Sandars (see figure 2.4) and Charles Bengough—were to have an enormous influence on Malaita and dominate its administration for years to come. Sandars, from Lincolnshire, spent over seven years on the island between 1928 and 1947 and is a key figure in this book. Londoner Bengough was in Malaita nearly as long, serving many terms between 1934 and 1943, when he died.[60] To understand how Malaitans developed their ideas about the colonial government before the war, it is important to know something of these two men and their dealings with local people. Sandars first arrived on Malaita in 1928 as a sub-inspector of the constabulary, a job he did not like but took in order to escape a weak Australian economy. He became a district officer on the island in November 1933 at the relatively late age of 38, serving under his close friend Barley and then replacing him when Barley left to become resident commissioner of the Gilbert and Ellis Islands. Bengough was first posted to Malaita in February 1934, while in his mid-twenties, to serve under Sandars, and for much of the next 13 years, one or the other presided there. Their reports show they saw eye-to-eye on most issues and

FIGURE 2.4. G E D Sandars with his staff at 'Aoke, ca 1934. L to R: (top) Sergeant Major Sale Vuza; Malakai Ravai (Fijian Medical Practitioner); Sandars; Gegi (domestic); Aliki Maena (clerk); unknown; seated is Vuza's wife Salome, from Kafusiisigi in east Kwaio. (Roger Keesing Papers, Tuzin Archive for Melanesian Anthropology, Mandeville Special Collections Library, University of California at San Diego, box 41, file 5, photographer unknown.)

closely coordinated policy, and Sandars later said they were "very firm friends." Dick Horton, on Malaita for eight months in 1938, thought that the two were much alike and that Bengough "had clearly modeled himself" on Sandars. SSEM missionary Norman Deck wrote of Bengough that Sandars had "taught him sound administration." Kwaio told me Bengough was quieter and physically smaller, and they and other Malaitans said that Sandars was the better-liked man.[61]

Junior officers who served under Sandars later described him as a stern taskmaster. One, Martin Clemens, recalled to me, "Bengough was very much under the eye of Sandars, his mentor and all that. It was always 'yes sir, three bags full' from Bengough to Sandars, you know." They were, Clemens said, "a most secretive mutual admiration society.... Neither ever encouraged us cadets to read up what they had written about Malaita." "They kept what they had written to themselves and never gave anyone else any credit." Sandars later expressed regret for not having spent more time in training his cadets but said he had been too busy.[62]

Sandars took pride in his knowledge of Malaitan cultures and in what he felt to be his resultant ability to minimize the need for official courts: "According to our Pacific Order in Council the native custom ran except where repugnant to British justice," he later wrote. "It was therefore most essential that any District Officer should thoroughly understand all native customs within his District. I suppose that of all the matters which came up before me I was able to deal with at least 75 percent of them according to native custom and if the people refused to accept the native custom then I had to deal with them in Court, but generally speaking if one knew one's job there was never any question of them not accepting the native custom as their true law." Sandars said he had started a "book of Native Custom" that he believed would be vitally important to administration, but that he never had time to compile it properly. "Native Custom," he wrote, "varies from zone to zone and it takes years before one can collect a good working knowledge of the whole. New customs, old to the people concerned, but new to me, keep coming to the fore entailing much lengthy discussion in order to get a grasp of the essentials."[63]

And yet, for a man so long on Malaita who claimed such ethnographic expertise, Sandars's apparent ignorance of many basic aspects of Malaitan life is startling. Take a trivial but revealing comment: describing the complex plaiting of Malaitan ornamental combs, he wrote, "How people who were quite incapable of counting could make up these very intricate designs always worried me but I could never find out how they managed it." In reality, many Malaitans display remarkable numerical abilities; their detailed memories and calculations of decades of marriage and feast exchanges, compensation payments, and commodity transactions often humbled me as their children's math teacher.[64] More consequential were Sandars's crude and sometimes ridiculous misreadings of Malaitan religion ("a thing of awful fear for everyone"; "of such terror that almost anything was preferable to it"); leadership systems ("They live in small family groups all thoroughly mistrustful of one and other and it was only through the ability of some family to slay more people than anybody else that they gradually gained an ascendancy over some family groups"); and social structures, exchanges, and concepts of liability. To Sandars, large swaths of Malaitan life were remote and morally indecipherable, and he therefore, like many other whites, judged them amoral or immoral.[65]

Some of Sandars's distorting statements just cited appear in a later autobiographical manuscript, which also contains surprising errors concerning Malaita's colonial history before his arrival. This calls for caution: colonial servant memoirs are peculiar in that some men who were erudite and impressive officers, as evinced by their reports, wrote memoirs mired in frivolity. They tended to curb discussion of serious topics in favor of humor, anecdote, and the chatty dinner-party tone characteristic of the genre (and often included mundane accounts of actual dinner parties). Sandars's presentation, which he dictated when he was old and unwell, falls squarely within this type. That aside, we will see that, although vital aspects of Malaitan societies obviously remained an enigma to him, his views of Malaitans did become more nuanced by the end of his tenure in the mid-1940s. This change arose not so much from a grasp of more ethnographic knowledge as from a deeper and more empathetic understanding of Malaitans' character and their grievances and aspirations.

That Sandars knew little about many basic aspects of Malaitan life was in part a result of the fact that he, like most prewar officers, remained socially distant from most Malaitans, due largely to an inability or unwillingness to see or reach beyond the colonial conventions and stereotypes of the day. This was exacerbated by the difficulty of learning about people so physically remote—at this time the majority lived in the mountains, and even many coastal communities could be visited only rarely. Sandars told Dr Ross Innes in 1938 that on Malaita "anything up to 8,000 people are beyond the ken of anyone, and not likely to be seen in the meantime by anyone." As Belshaw noted for the Solomons generally, inland villages "were seldom visited except by the most enthusiastic officials, and...none have ever been visited by the most senior officials of Government or Church." Sandars later said that he spent half of his time under Barley touring, but he did so mostly by boat and held his courts on the coast. Though notorious for breaking in new cadets by sending them on arduous mountain patrols—Cadet Alexander Waddell called him "the worst slave driver he ever knew"—Sandars himself strongly disliked bush walking. In his fifties by the time he left Malaita, he said he was bad at it, and anyway, "one saw very few people" and "it wasted too much time." Dr Innes, who from 1937–1938 conducted a leprosy survey with Sandars and other officers, recorded, probably advised by Sandars, that Malaitan officers *had* to tour by ship since there were so few trails in the mountains, but in fact there were countless footpaths. Davies, a cadet under Sandars in the mid-1940s, later acknowledged charges that Malaita had "a sea-borne administration, [which] had no roots on land and hence never got to know the people properly," resulting "in a less personal form of administration than if we had used Shanks' pony more often." But, he noted, "It was...a question of walking along the coast at three miles an hour (if one was very lucky) and being too exhausted to do much effective work, or traveling by sea at six miles an hour and being fresh enough do some work." Officers touring on ships usually slept on their boats rather than ashore. The upshot was that they spent little time in the milieus in which most Malaitans lived.[66]

To be sure, touring Malaita's mountains is no simple walkabout and it is no wonder so many of the thousands of hamlets before the war never saw an officer. Clemens described the logistics:

> We used to pad along in a long, silent column. A policeman, who knew the route, led the way, and I followed. Behind me came another constable, strong and sure-footed, who assisted me if the way was too slippery. We were followed by the carriers with our bedding and rations; they were supervised by the remaining police,

who also kept an eye on any felons who had been sentenced to a term of imprisonment at any court held during the tour. These had the privilege of carrying
the heaviest loads. The biggest burden was a heavy ironbound, padlocked box,
which contained court and Treasury forms, registers, and silver money collected
in payment of tax. We also had to carry tinned rations, to which were added
whatever fresh fruit and vegetables we could find in route. The farther away we
were from the coast, the less likely this was.... The work done was varied, and
very interesting, but the walking got monotonous—the shady jungle was always
the same, mile after mile—and I used to plan magnificent meals as I went along.

Mountain trails are not cut to European sensibilities. Routes often travel
as the crow flies, contours be damned, and a novice walker might guess
they had been blazed by someone traveling like an ant, climbing a blade
of grass to its tip and descending the other side rather than going around.
As Innes wrote, "One does not need to be very long here before one has
struggled through mangrove swamps, slipped and slithered over atrocious
bush paths, been sweated and reduced to exhaustion in crawling over the
surface of this roadless part of the earth." Touring was made still more difficult in that most mountain hamlets moved on a regular basis.[67]

Even when touring inland, officers could stay insulated from the people.
Ma'aanamae of Kwainaa'isi (a hamlet 900 meters above sea level), with
whom I lived in the 1990s, told me in 1987 how they at times played reluctant hosts to armed patrols that occasionally passed through Kwaio in the
1930s: "They would arrive on patrol and we would put them in a house:
'Here is the house for you to sleep in.' And we people who lived there, only
when it was time for them to give us orders would we gather together...and
then they would be on their way. [District officers could be kind] but their
kindness was selective, in that they only liked certain people. They liked
people like the headmen. But common people, they were not friendly to
us....When they were eating we could not go in to talk to them. If we did
they would say, 'Go on! Outside!' The white people on the plantations were
like that, and so were *gafamanu* [government officers]."[68]

The social distance enforced varied with the place and the officer, however, especially later in the decade. Some Kwaio told me that Sandars liked
to joke with elders and children when he came, and Dick Horton wrote
of a looser protocol he followed in 1938 when at age 23 he patrolled the
mountains of Kwara'ae and Kwaio: "The night would be enlivened with gos-
sip as all and sundry crowded into the huts to see the visitors, smoking and
spitting until I felt that I was floating on a miasma of the tuberculosis which
is prevalent in the islands. Then the police would drive out the crowd and
'Guberment' would go to sleep surrounded by his henchmen."[69]

Key for Malaitans was a European's willingness or refusal to eat with
them. Molaina'o of Nu'u accompanied officers Bengough and Brownlees
on a Kwaio tour in 1940 and 40 years later recalled to me vividly the people

at stops watching the two eat rice alone. I have heard other such stories and the important point is not that officers were selfish for not sharing out their rations to gatherings, but rather that those who pointedly did not eat with local people erected a high social barrier in the eyes of Malaitans, for whom food sharing is fundamental to human relationships. We will see that during the war Malaitan friendships with some American soldiers were cemented by the soldiers' readiness to share food and meals, and I have been given many heartfelt explanations of the symbolic import this had for Malaitans.[70]

In 1940, Officer Michael Forster, age 24, began impressing 'Are'are and Kwaio people by taking part in bridewealth exchanges and especially by eating with them. Decades later Malaitans still remembered him as a different sort of officer, who even invited Malaitans into his house to eat at his table. We will follow him through much of this book. Sandars wrote that Forster was "very fond" of the people of the southern half of Malaita and "was of very great assistance to me because these people were particularly hard to get on with but he managed particularly well." Forster gave lie to the maxim that firmness and distance, not kindness and familiarity, were the only safe and effective modes for dealing with Malaitans. He also toured more than other officers and not surprisingly his reports display more knowledge. Davies said Forster was "deeply in love with Malaita." When he was posted to the Western Solomons in early 1945, Forster wrote to Sandars pleading to return: "I find it extremely hard to contemplate settling down any where else." By June he was back in 'Aoke as assistant district commissioner.[71]

Headmen served as a filter between officers and most Malaitans, since legal or other problems were usually taken first to them and they might choose to settle things themselves. Jonathan Fifi'i told me, "The officers always worked through the headmen, and would not just talk to people.... If a man or woman had a problem or something bad happened to them, they couldn't go straight to the district officer; they would have to go through the headmen." Before the war, Sandars at 'Aoke used Sergeant Major Sale Vuza (see figure 2.4), an extraordinary Guadalcanal man who had joined the police in 1916, to screen even headmen who came to see him. Vuza later said Sandars disapproved of people casually visiting 'Aoke "because the station belonged to the government." The use of select individuals as a bulwark against general contact with other Melanesians was standard prewar practice. Hogbin and Camilla Wedgwood described this as part of "the prevailing attitude" and quoted a 1926 article in the *Rabaul Times* titled "How to Succeed as a Coconut Planter in New Guinea": "Never talk to the boys themselves under any circumstances; always do it through the boss boys. Apart from your house boys and boss boys never allow any native in your employ to approach you in the field or on the bungalow verandah." Most officers were not as exclusive as this, but many Malaitans, at times encouraged by headmen, perceived it to be the usual practice. When Dr Gideon Zoleveke of Choiseul was posted to Malaita in 1951, he found the officer living in "an enormous construction on top of the hill," and thought, "No wonder expatriate officers developed a colonial mentality, living alone in such huge structures, protected by policemen and served by prisoners." In this land of buffers, officers served as cushions between Melanesians and other Europeans, "standing," wrote Arthur Hopkins, "between the white men and the native, regulating their relations and intercourse in its every phase and complication." They also stood between Europeans in conflict, such as rival missionaries, who also sometimes clashed with planters.[72]

Encircled by selected underlings and intermediaries, Malaitan officers in the 1930s could fashion an enclave, shielded from the seeming chaos beyond, and this removed the need to learn more about the local scene in order to conduct one's daily life. On his 1929 arrival in the Solomons, Resident Commissioner Ashley had explained that, to succeed, the administration had to be accessible to the people, and he quoted Sir John Malcolm to instruct his officers "to live with four doors open, be of perfectly easy access to every native; for to listen to a man is sometimes as good as granting what he prays for." Perhaps Ashley had been thinking here of the people's "imaginary grievances," but in any case throughout his ten-year tenure this directive was trumped by black-white boundaries. Although individual officers on Malaita during this period exhibited varying attitudes and behaviors, older people I have known over the years have consistently maintained that there were few differences among them, excepting always Forster and sometimes also Sandars, and they remember prewar officers as aloof and unfriendly. I have heard more positive memories of some officers from elders who lived around 'Aoke, however.[73]

It was not only whites who cultivated separation. While headmen acted as gatekeepers to officers, they were also useful to Malaitans as buffers against unwanted contact with these same officers, blocking them out of local affairs—most Malaitans were not eager for extended interaction. Davies later said that officers touring by boat just after the war would have slept ashore more often but for a lack of rest houses, which government would not pay for, and "although it became fashionable in later years to criticize [officers] for living on board their ships, the people at the time certainly did not feel so strongly about it that they were prepared to build rest houses."[74]

One might wonder at this, in light of the idea some scholars have put forth that prewar officers were accepted as big men, filling roles once held by indigenous leaders. In the same vein, Forster portrayed the prewar head tax—sanctioned though it was by fines, jails, and at times bullying policemen—as analogous to a tribute to such leaders and thus not resented (though elsewhere he roundly contradicted this). This view of officers as substitute leaders receiving tax tribute may have had validity in parts of the Solomons, but one could scarcely be further off the mark insofar as how most Malaitan communities in the 1930s saw officers and the tax, or how officers performed their duties. J D A Germond, a senior officer who arrived

from Africa in the late 1940s, summed up the historical position of an officer on Malaita: "He has become, in the eyes of the people, a collector of
taxes, an investigator of crime and a judge and executioner who however
well disposed, cannot be regarded as impartial. He is in fact a man to be
feared and avoided as much as possible, whereas he should be a friend,
advisor and a protector." He added that tax houses were a prime symbol of
the people's resentment.[75] Some Malaitans did try to harness the power of
officers through real or feigned cooperation, but the social and logistical
distance separating officers from most communities by itself precluded their
approaching anything like the intensely social roles of local leaders. Viewing
particular government headmen in this light might be more fruitful, though
their close association with the government was as often a political handicap
for them (and with the worst headmen, for the government as well).

For many Malaitans, taxation without tangible returns, let alone representation, was a root of the problem. Shortly before his death, Bell warned
that the tax "appears to have caused a very pronounced decrease in the
faith of the natives in the good-will of the Government toward them and
consequently the confidence of the natives in the advice of the District Officer does not appear to be quite the same as in former times. Owing to the
amount of work and the time [spent collecting taxes] there is danger that
the natives have come to the conclusion that the principal duty of the District Officer is that of extracting money from them."[76] Five years later Barley
reported that taxation consumed more of his time than any other feature
of administration—in 1930 he traveled 3,800 kilometers in 167 days during
ten trips to 31 leaf "tax houses" around the island, up from 25 tax houses
in 1927. Most Malaitans came to see the tax with indignation as an onerous
levy bringing no return except incarceration for defaulters. Many before
the war perceived it much like Baegu people of the north did—in Officer
Tom Russell's words, as "an honorarium to government for the privilege of
being left alone." Colin Allan reported, "Fataleka like Eastern Kwara'ae and
parts of Kwaio before the war paid their taxes on the understanding that
the Govt. would leave them in peace."[77]

Malaitans commonly value leaders for their abilities to settle disputes
with erudition and to the satisfaction of all parties, but here especially, carrying out one of their primary duties, officers were often on shaky ground.
When trying to adjudicate "custom" matters, they could be made painfully aware that they lacked requisite cultural knowledge. In 1934, Officer
Leonard Wright of Guadalcanal gave this as a reason he allowed unofficial
native tribunals there based on unwritten native custom. And Wright was
no greenhorn; he had already spent some three years in charge of that
island, and before long published studies in *Oceania* and in *Journal of the
Royal Anthropological Institute,* for which he was a fellow and corresponding
secretary.[78]

Much more was at issue than an officer's familiarity with abstract rules.

FIGURE 2.5. Men queued up to pay the head tax at Maro'umasike, southeastern 'Are'are, ca 1936. (Photo by Robert A Lever, courtesy of the Trustees of the British Museum, Oc,B98.95.)

When Malaitans assess disputes they often draw on deep local knowledge of long-term, complex relationships of the disputants and their groups. Such sophistication comes only from enduring social engagement. I have often heard Kwaio declare their inability to properly evaluate particular disputes between Kwaio who live far away and whom they do not know well, citing their lack of social and historical knowledge about the case and its principals. In any Malaitan community certain individuals are known for their superior knowledge of social networks and legal and other histories and for having the brains, talent, and integrity to effectively apply it to skillfully managing disputes; they are called on when trouble cases arise. This is one realm in which "big men" earn that name—the same skills and some of the same information that allow one to navigate mazes of formal exchange networks can be brought to bear on disputes. The depth and breadth of knowledge of such men is formidable. I have studied a part of one Malaitan area, east central Kwaio, intensely over 30 years, at times with a specific focus on rules and disputes, and I have toiled to learn local networks and their histories, but many disputes there I would be loath to adjudicate. Officers were charged with doing so not in one area but across all of Malaita, sometimes after only brief residence on the island.[79]

Many Malaitans disdained the government preference for treating disputes as circumscribed and dyadic rather than as conflicts immersed in relations between groups or as episodes within complex histories. While Malaitans typically absorbed disputes within social networks, officers tried to isolate disputes from them. Malaitans commonly resented the government's emphasis on punishment over redress and on rights and liabilities of individuals over those of groups. For officers, settling disputes via compensations was a special challenge: lacking the knowledge to direct payments to multiple, appropriate parties, they often awarded them instead to individuals; they balked at ordering compensation paid by a party that seemed by their European sensibilities to bear no responsibility for a wrong or misfortune at issue; and they commonly disallowed demands for punitive compensations. British and Malaitan approaches to misdeeds and disputes were separated by more than different rules and procedures; at conflict, too, were basic moral principles regarding relationships between the individual and society, and between intent, responsibility, and liability. It is no surprise that law, or *loa,* and especially compensation, soon became key symbols of Malaitans' resistance to outsiders imposing foreign ways on them and of their demands that they be left to conduct their own affairs.

Other problems arose when officers presided over more formal courts. Strict rules of evidence could prove a handicap, and a common complaint was that officers ignored evidence Malaitans judged to be damning, such as sacred oaths made in ancestors' names (or refusal to utter them), while they granted weight to testimony Malaitans found implausible or irrelevant. Sandars had this in mind when he wrote regretfully concerning Kwaio thievery, "What they consider proof, and in many cases they are probably right, cannot be accepted as evidence in court." Observed Bishop Steward, "It must be a terribly difficult business for the Government official who is hampered by British Law and legal procedure and it is no wonder that his efforts are so little appreciated and that he is so often used as the unwitting instrument of revenge."[80]

Both Sandars and Bengough made extensive use of knowledgeable Malaitans when hearing disputes over "purely native affairs." Sandars felt that this both allowed him to make informed decisions and boosted community respect for "elders." At times the officers skirted British legal rules and procedure altogether. In adjudicating Kwara'ae land cases, Bengough sometimes admitted evidence in the form of 'aenimae, stylized historical chants about ancestral deeds sung in the Kwara'ae language that he did not know. In 'Are'are, Sandars went so far as to allow trial by ordeal, involving the handling of hot stones and swimming crocodile-infested waters, and he admitted evidence found through divination in cases there, in north Malaita, and probably elsewhere. He once tried the hot-stone test himself and, to the delight of spectators, burned his hands. Officers commonly employed ritual oaths of denial. After the war, Officer Wilfred Marquand explained how he let the local courts he presided over carry on in local language and afterward received a Pijin summary and the verdict to approve, modify, or reject.[81]

Sometimes officers hearing cases assessed local knowledge less formally. Officer John Brownlees—a barrister and eventually a chief justice in Tonga (1941–1947) and a judge in the New Hebrides (1956–1958)—later recounted his judicious assessment of catcalls in his Solomons courts, probably while he was on Malaita in the mid-1930s, or 1940: "I was always influenced to a certain extent, wrongly or rightly, by the audience. Their reactions to the proceedings were not put into so many words, but they were highly expressive: 'Waaahhh!' would mean 'You dirty liar!' This was often very helpful, and certainly did influence you. Above all, you had a strong sense of trying to get to the root of the matter, and seeing fair play. There was no finesse or nonsense about admissible evidence. That kind of thing never crossed my mind." Missionary Hopkins commented that officers were placed in a position where "a short, sharp settlement by guess work is very tempting." Sandars's rule for making difficult court decisions, which he taught to his cadets, was to "do something, even if it's wrong."[82]

Efforts to manage local disputes through indigenous mechanisms were admirable, but in the end officers had little choice, given that in many cases British law was unsuitable or irrelevant, or unacceptable to Malaitans involved. The predicament was, again, that properly applying such mechanisms required complex knowledge that officers often lacked. They could be left serving simply as referees, "seeing fair play" but basically ignorant of the rules of the game and sometimes even of what was really at stake in a dispute they were hearing.

The expertise required to properly apply indigenous mechanisms of dispute management could be daunting. Take as an example ancestral oaths of denial, just one of the types of oaths and curses routinely employed to settle Malaitan disputes. These generally take a conditional form: "I did X, and I also do Y," where X is the act the speaker is accused of, and Y some act of ancestral or personal defilement involving a polluting substance such as feces or afterbirth. If a man—let us call him Jimmy—is charged with stealing a pig belonging to Tom, Jimmy might utter the following oath of denial: "I stole Tom's pig, and I also defecate on the sacred shrine of my ancestor, Bighead." If Jimmy did in fact steal that pig, then his omniscient ancestor Bighead, knowing his guilt, becomes enraged since he has made the performative statement that by stealing said pig he has also defecated on the shrine. Bighead is certain to kill Jimmy or a relative in retribution. But if Jimmy did not steal the pig, then the second part of the oath is inconsequential.[83] While such oaths of denial may seem straightforward, they are often much more complicated than this example, and negotiations surrounding the precise wording an oath will take can be one of the most complex aspects of Malaitan disputing. They can drag on for hours or sometimes through recurring meetings over weeks. Accusers want the oath to be as deadly as possible and will try to eliminate potential loopholes. The accused—in our example Jimmy and his kin, collectively liable for any ancestral punishment that might result—will want to avoid the most dangerous oaths. They also want to tailor the oath's wording to eliminate ambiguity that might leave them open to ancestral wrath, or if Jimmy is guilty, perhaps finesse the wording to dodge an effective oath. For a simple illustration, Jimmy's oath will likely denote *this specific pig* rather than simply "Tom's pig," in case he has stolen another of Tom's pigs in the past, or has eaten pork, perhaps unknowingly, from a pig someone else stole from Tom.

To complicate matters further, secret counter-magics allow certain oaths to be made with impunity, and Tom's people will be suspicious these might be in play. Or someone in Jimmy's group—as variably defined—may have once made a prohibitive curse against anyone making certain types of oaths, or perhaps against any oath invoking a particular ancestor's name. Here, in negotiating oaths and their phrasing, Malaitans enter perhaps their most legalistic mode—each word may be weighed, worried over, and debated, with great attention to the subtlest shades of meaning. Oaths are deadly serious and their composition is not to be hurried. Sometimes the guilty will try to prolong negotiations as a stalling tactic. Keep in mind that all of this addresses only *formal* aspects of cursing. The proceedings are made much more complex when one superimposes on them the labyrinthine social relations and histories of the participants and their various ancestral spirits. Several Kwaio people complained to me that when Sandars and other officers allowed oaths there in the past they were often improperly worded, careless or even reckless, or invoked inappropriate spirits.[84]

Despite these complexities, there were several reasons why officers trying to settle trouble cases might find an oath an attractive solution. First, if the accused, in the end, refuses to utter an oath, and there are reasonable grounds for suspicion, their refusal is generally taken as an admission of guilt, they pay compensation, and the case is resolved. Further, once a person has made an oath of denial, henceforth no one can again publicly accuse that person of the same offense (at least in southern Malaita), and anyone who does so risks having to compensate the accused (in effect, they accuse them of "Y"). Oaths thus provide a singularly effective form of public closure. In reality the case is not over but has simply shifted to another tribunal, placed now in the hands of ancestors. People will note any death or other profound misfortune that befalls the accused or their kin as indicating a false oath that the spirits are now punishing. But even so, the original aggrieved party will usually make no further public claims on the accused for the offense (though they may stay alert for a reason to confront him or his people again).

Other aspects of Malaitan disputing can be just as bewildering to outsiders, one being how people manage compensations, especially who will contribute to and collect from them, how much, and why. I have already noted this as especially difficult for officers to manage. In some cases two sides may exchange compensations, perhaps even equal amounts, which indicates either that both concede to having committed an offense against the other (eg, one striking the other for an offense), or more basically that the dispute is less important than social relationships it might damage. This can occur under pressure to reconcile from the wider community that the conflict is disrupting. In cases involving taboo violations, such an equal transfer can mollify angry ancestors as well, as one or both sides use the money to buy sacrificial pigs. As one would expect, such mutual compensations are more common when disputants or their groups share significant, positive social ties in need of repair.

Government officers sometimes ordered matching compensations in an attempt to make peace, but because they and their courts were outside the community such directives had minimal moral force. For instance, in the mid-1930s in Kwaio, Sandars heard the case of Gwaruafane having during a land dispute mildly cursed Ma'aanamae, who then punched him in the face. Sandars ordered them to exchange equal compensations, but after Sandars left, the two men casually agreed it was pointless to do so. However, this same lack of moral force accorded to government officers and courts could make them *more* useful for certain purposes, most notably as circuit breakers to resolve deadlocked disputes that might otherwise spiral into violence. There was little shame in losing in government court, and parties ruled against by an officer could settle or withdraw from the case without public loss of face, having been "forced" to settle by the government. In this way the courts served as an expedient form of binding arbitration. This resembles in microcosm early twentieth century strategies when the government's having outlawed violence became for some a welcome pretext to end conflict that was interfering with new economic pursuits.[85]

Further complexity came from intricate notions of group and absolute liability, which can seem illogical or profoundly unfair to outsiders.[86] Litigants might also draw into disputes concerns that ancestral spirits have about a case as revealed through divination or possession. Land disputes demand still further erudition—they often involve multiple versions of boundaries, land histories, and deep genealogies. Woodford found early on in Gela land disputes, "Rules are subject to so many exceptions that it becomes difficult to formulate them with any certainty."[87]

One can only sympathize with district officers for the handicaps they faced, even beyond the language obstacle, in trying to deal competently with local disputes, let alone in managing formal courts simultaneously as investigator, judge, prosecutor, and defense council, in cases across hundreds of communities spread over multiple language and cultural zones. Despite Sandars's boasts, we must doubt that even a man who served as long as he "thoroughly understood all native customs" on Malaita, even those most pertinent to settling disputes and court cases, and indeed the evidence speaks loudly otherwise. The result was that officers were left heavily dependent on Malaitans, particularly on their headmen, to explain to them in simplified form what was happening around them. Their lack of knowledge and cultural sophistication was regularly and publicly on display to Malaitans.

Malaitans Consider Government Law

Despite ambivalence about government law, at the start of the 1930s some Malaitans were bringing disputes before touring officers. In 1930, Barley heard many cases from Kwai and points north along the coast to Fo'odo but reported a "deadness" of administration from Uru southeast. As the decade progressed, burgeoning caseloads made it impractical for officers to hear any but serious disputes. They did not respond by initiating native courts, but instead, in keeping with the inclination toward direct rule, they instructed government headmen to adjudicate more cases on their own, especially those involving "tabu and custom." Officer William Fowler observed that this was "a task for which they are infinitely better qualified than any District Officer." Headmen were already indispensable as informants and in taxation, censusing, and making arrests, but it was perhaps in settling disputes that they became most valuable and powerful.[88]

Hogbin detailed how this system worked in 1933 in and around Malu'u, in To'abaita. This area was distinctive due to the presence of the island's most powerful headman, Maekali. He had been a leader of Bell's constabulary and of the 1927 punitive expedition, and in 1928 he took over the subdistrict headman position from his uncle Stephen Gori'i, a former constable whom Bell credited for Malu'u's being the first Malaitan area brought under government control. On a 1929 visit, Ashley was so impressed with the Malu'u area's leaders that he advised they be given more responsibilities. Due largely to Maekali's presence, Maluʻu would years later be allowed to convene Malaita's first native council. In the early 1930s, Maekali often judged even serious and problematic disputes, and Hogbin said officers heard few cases there. Toʻabaita nonetheless shared an important feature with other parts of Malaita in that most disputes among non-Christians continued to be handled independently of the headman by communities and their leaders, and in Christian communities by mission teachers, particularly among SSEM people.[89]

Many in Toʻabaita strongly disliked Maekali and his administration, and in 1949 people there recalled why to District Officer Colin Allan, then stationed at Maluʻu: "A small faction of more or less insignificant men...enforced oppressive communal duties, dealt unskillfully in native custom matters, and misrepresented the true feelings of the people to successive Government officers. In this Council the men who carried with them the affection and esteem of their people had no place, and gradually the few who possessed that confidence, became disinterested and withdrew." In later years officers referred to the practice of domineering government headmen as "Maekalism."[90]

By 1936, Malaita's headmen were handling most conflicts brought to the government overall. Many had been resolving deadlocked disputes before officers began telling them to, and people sometimes welcomed adjudication by the better ones. They commonly ordered compensation payments and generally paid little heed to British legal formalities, something that troubled officers at times. Barley, for example, had this to say about Sinalagu Headman Sirifa, appointed by Bell in 1924: "The continued reports of 'All's well' in such a wide, thickly populated, and aggressive Sub-district are apt to arouse suspicion that either the [headman] is not carrying out inspectional visits and keeping in proper touch with his people, either through timidity or laziness, or that, on the other hand, he is fixing up rather too much, in the way of trouble and law-breaking, 'at his own bat,' with possible personal advantage to himself." Oral historical accounts portray Sirifa as guilty of both, depending on who was involved from which part of his sub-district. Wilfred Marquand, who became a cadet in north Malaita in mid-1947, was told that a typical prewar Malaitan headman had been "a stooge, who did what the people told him to do and told the District Officer what he wanted to tell him and what he knew the District Officer liked to hear. The cry of 'no any trouble, sir' became rather monotonous."[91]

Nevertheless, as the decade progressed government courts did hear more cases, for several reasons. First, officers rejected certain indigenous legal practices such as imposing absolute liability irrespective of intent, and sanctions such as compensations for theft far exceeding values of property stolen. Once Malaitans realized that colonial law had different ground rules, those who had lost their cases in indigenous proceedings, or who anticipated they would, might appeal their lost or weak cases to government courts in hopes of exploiting the different rules. This of course angered people who had already won their cases or thought they would have, without government interference.[92] In this and other ways, headmen's and officers' courts contributed to an ongoing erosion of the authority of local leaders, which left them less effective adjudicators, which in turn led people to take more troubles to the courts; leaders' clout decreased in a downward spiral. Hopkins wrote that as early as the 1910s in the north, "The common retort to a quarrel, to a disputed claim, was 'You no pay along me? Very well, me summons you along Governor.' 'Summons' became quite a current word with a hazy legal connection."[93]

In the early 1930s, Hogbin observed a related change in north Malaita that occurred to varying degrees in other areas—a decline in the importance of kinship and other social ties as factors within disputes. At Malu'u, with powerful Maekali settling cases single-handedly, one's kin were no longer as effective a support group. I noted earlier that many Malaitans resented officers in court ignoring group relations and liabilities, but Hogbin reported that some young people around Malu'u welcomed Maekali's doing so, as one explained: "In olden days each man helped his kinsmen and group quarreled with group. They used insults first. Then they remembered honour and fought. Honour caused the fight. Now Maekali listens to the talk of the two men only. It is settled by Maekali, and there is no fight." This must be read cautiously: Hogbin was a close friend and confidant of Maekali and all in To'abaita knew this; we do not know how deep or widespread such sentiments were in that area, and it is clear that many did not share them.[94]

Overall, most Malaitans developed mixed attitudes toward expanding government law during the 1930s, though, for many, ambivalence shifted toward resentment as the decade progressed. Most appreciated the end of fighting, and I have often heard elderly people express this with a worn cliché: "We sleep better at night." Others disliked government intrusion and wished to settle their disputes as they saw fit. There was also anger that when Europeans committed crimes such as murder, severe assault, or rape they were most always deported rather than punished in the Solomons (if at all) in order to avoid embarrassing the white community by a local trial and imprisonment. And when an Islander fought a European, it was always the Islander who went to jail. Such inequities made *gafamanu loa* a potent symbol of colonial injustice.[95]

Malaitans found irksome specific laws first imposed in the early 1920s: For instance, they were not to allow their pigs to forage but instead confine them in pens 50 yards from houses, or the pigs would be shot and the owners fined (and police charged them for the cartridges). To follow this law left both sacred and other pigs easy prey for thieves, which angered ancestors, and it hugely increased the labor and resources needed to feed them. Walter Ivens said that this regulation was one of three reasons Bell's party had been attacked, "as much a cause of the recent murders as the Poll Tax." This was untrue, but it does indicate the level of anger at pig laws that Ivens encountered during 11 months on Malaita in 1924. A 1929 king's regulation brought more onerous laws: villages were to be sanitized or structurally reorganized according to European sensibilities, births and deaths had to be reported, and even dogs would be registered and taxed. (Few mountain communities submitted to these.) Unauthorized, extended absence from one's village was forbidden.[96] Clumsy attempts at social engineering, imposed without regard to their impacts on people's lives, further stoked resentment of the government and its laws.

Many took special exception to a law that stipulated they labor, unpaid or to work off taxes, to clear and maintain government "roads"—bridle-path-width trails—through their territories. Each "line" was assigned the "communal service" of clearing and upkeep of a section, and men had to work on them one day each week. Noncompliance brought fines and jail. Russell later aptly conveyed Malaitan assessments of these roads as "a very labour-intensive way of preventing Europeans getting their feet wet," and said that northern people preferred to walk their own trails, which ran parallel to the roads. Roadwork at times during the 1930s was ordered partly to enhance authority of headmen, who oversaw compulsory labor.[97]

Farther south in Kwaio and parts of 'Are'are, some resented the government's prohibition of killing to punish serious moral transgressions, which people blamed for a rise in adultery. Others were bitter at officers' lack of consideration of and sometimes barring of compensation payments to aggrieved parties in certain disputes. Bita Saetana (Peter Satan) from Sinalagu, who served for a time under Sandars as a government "chief" (see chapter 3), recounted to me in 1981 how Kwaio had observed Sandars's courts with dismay: "Under the government before, if you discovered who had stolen your pig you wouldn't get any compensation: 'Take him to jail for two months.' Somebody committed adultery with your wife and it was found out? 'You go to jail for just a year, or six months. You can't compensate with shell money. No compensation for sexual offenses.' That was making our people very angry in those days."[98]

Yet we have seen that Malaita's officers, including Sandars, did recognize compensation payments as legitimate in some cases and, furthermore, employed them in their work. Officers from Bell onward realized that compensation was absolutely necessary to maintaining peace. But there were special difficulties: How should officers treat compensation demands for acts not criminal under British law? Should they let Malaitans address serious crimes with compensation alone? What was to be done when individuals bypassed the indigenous system by taking their cases to the government courts, where injured persons (or, via them, offended ancestral spirits) might receive no compensation? Was double jeopardy inflicted if a person was both sent to jail and ordered to pay compensation? Malaitans thought so, as did some officers who forbade compensation on top of jail terms they imposed. And, again, how could officers assure proper distribution of compensations awarded in their courts when they did not know the complex social networks, histories, or subtle principles involved?[99]

When government officers did allow or even order compensation payments in courts, they sometimes did so in ways that angered people. First, they commonly limited compensation in cases of theft or property destruction to restitution of the property's value. Compensations paid for thefts, particularly of pigs, are usually far more than the property's worth and address more the disrespect shown than the material loss. Malaitans are strongly motivated to negate any public humiliation they experience, something officers failed to fully appreciate—which, as we shall see, was to cause the government grave problems in realms far beyond native courts. Officers generally disallowed such punitive payments. At the matter's heart was unease with Solomon Islanders punishing each other for offenses; the right to punish was to be reserved for the state and its legal system. The state also of course reserved the right to employ force, and officers ordered return of compensations collected under a perceived threat of violence and even imprisoned those who threatened it. Like many Europeans today who understand and advocate compensation as a purely reconciliatory practice, the officers missed the point that such a threat is at least implicit in most major compensation demands. Officers almost always prosecuted serious offenses, especially murder and assault, via British criminal law, and in such cases courts often ignored or even disallowed compensation. As noted earlier, officers sometimes quashed compensations collected on the basis of indigenous principles of collective, strict, or absolute liability. Marquand later said that officers angered people by ordering compensations to be paid in state instead of local currencies, but this was not done on prewar Malaita, and indeed Sandars thought that only compensations in native currencies were legitimate custom.[100]

Many Malaitans resented British law more basically as an alien imposition. One of Hogbin's To'abaita informants, Aningari, who was once a fighting man but by 1933 a "pillar of the Evangelical Mission," explained, "You are familiar with the Law. It belongs to you: it comes from the place where you were born. For us the Law is different. In olden times we behaved as our fathers did before us. When you have asked me in our conversations together, why did I do that, have I not replied 'It is the custom; my fathers did it of old?' To-day that is changed. The white man has come and tells us we must behave like *his* father. Our own fathers, we must forget them. But we cannot forget them so soon." Another man complained, "In olden days we did this thing, we did that thing. We did not stop and say to ourselves first, 'This thing I want to do, is it right?' We always knew. Now we have to say, 'This thing I want to do, will the white man tell me it is wrong and punish me?'" Anthropologist Douglas Oliver summed a view of the prewar government as "that awesome institution whose agents collected taxes and put you in the calaboose if you acted like a Solomonese when you should have acted like a European."[101]

Hogbin said that he only heard To'abaita express resentment at specific issues like taxes or weak adultery laws, and that he rarely heard them condemn government as a whole; Hogbin also reported that everyone knew "rebellion was impossible." But this tells us only that dissident views were rarely voiced to Hogbin, with his close link to Headman Maekali. That people might conceal their views from Hogbin became clear a decade later when he returned to To'abaita on the eve of Maasina Rule to advise government on "native rehabilitation," and he, like other whites, was apparently kept in the dark as to the level of dissatisfaction then rife in that most rebellious of areas.[102]

People in Malu'u, Kwara'ae, Kwaio, and, it seems, Malaitans generally attached little stigma to conviction by government courts.[103] Older Kwaio friends have gleefully told me stories of "winning" in prewar government courts although they were guilty of the crimes charged, at times by their having employed magics that grant the ability to lie convincingly. Even today Malaitans sometimes see themselves as possessing a better understanding of what goes on in state courts than do the judges. That is, because they better comprehend human nature, they can see through the fallacies—or, as they see it, the naïveté—underlying European legal principles and rules of evidence. They believe their superior insights allow them to manipulate court proceedings and verdicts in the face of European social and cultural blindness.

Custom as a Basis for Colonial Law

As more Malaitans and other Islanders turned to the colonial courts, it became more incumbent on those courts to recognize "native custom" as a basis for settling cases. One reason some people liked Maekali's court in To'abaita was that he applied indigenous principles to cases and usually ordered disputes settled with shell money compensations, and other headmen pursued similar approaches to varying degrees.[104] We have seen that Malaita's district officers, too, often tried to adjudicate out-of-court proceedings according to local ways and to take those ways into account in formal courts. But as "custom" gained judicial importance, officers' lack of pertinent expertise became ever more problematic. More awkward still was the vague and problematic "custom" concept itself, which through the 1930s became more vital to policy.

Government had been obliged to design a few regulations directed at Islanders and their concerns, most notably the Native Adultery Punishment Regulation of 1924. Adultery was a grave offense on Malaita and had often led to killings (though not inevitably, as is often claimed), but it was not a crime under British law, leaving Malaitans no adequate way to punish offenders. Magistrate Edge-Partington in 1913 begged Resident Commissioner Woodford to let him punish adulterers, citing "local custom," and warned that otherwise he and the government would be "the laughing stock of Malaita," but he was refused. Bell said adultery was as disruptive to peace as murder, and that Malaitans' desire for tough penalties was nearly unanimous. Soon after arriving on Malaita, Bell began jailing male adulterers under a Pacific Order in Council rule (with Resident Commissioner Workman's approval) and urged criminalization, though he remarked, "The punishment most of them desire is, of course, greater than that which I am prepared to advocate."[105]

Anger over adultery and also mounting fornication became an early focal point of Malaitan resentments of government law, and many officers and missionaries shared their concern that enforced peace was undermining morality. Sexual promiscuity had become most problematic in Christian communities, and missionaries thrust themselves deeply into the adultery debate. SSEM leaders blamed the increase on "the disproportionate government penalty [dulling] their consciences as to the shame of sin." Norman Deck, now leading the SSEM in the Solomons, and other missionaries as well as anthropologist Hogbin called for floggings and other harsher punishments. But some colonial officers attributed adultery's rise to the missions themselves and blamed a perceived moral decline on church lifestyles and policies that removed severe sanctions. Particularly problematic were church policies that prohibited compensation and instead prescribed prayer and forgiveness. This was but one facet of a more general pattern: while missionaries typically presented Christians as having been saved from a degraded, dystopian indigenous condition, some officers saw Christians as more decadent, and increasingly as more politically dangerous, for having been freed from the social controls of "custom."[106]

The greatest pressures for adultery legislation came from angry Malaitans, who forced enactment of the 1924 law, which punished male or female adulterers with a £5 fine or up to three months imprisonment, and six months on second conviction. Malaitans' continuing complaints compelled a 1929 amendment that increased penalties, with an off-the-books understanding that its severity would be applied only on Malaita. (Where adultery was a lesser crime, as on Guadalcanal, people complained that penalties were too *high*.)[107] Even this failed to satisfy many Malaitans and missionaries, who, supported by Barley, demanded still heavier punishment.[108] In a partial tally of 225 cases heard by Malaita officers from 1931–1935, fully 20 percent were adultery cases (assault and theft trailed at 15 percent each).[109] Ashley seized on the growing problem to castigate High Commissioner Fletcher for barring official native courts that could punish adulterers by more effective means such as compensation.[110] The continuing ambiguous legal status of most indigenous rules and punishments, and of local bodies to apply them, was an ongoing problem for officers and Malaitans trying to keep the peace.

Malaitans also pressed the government to criminalize sorcery, and Edge-Partington had jailed men who were so charged. By the early 1930s, people were complaining sorcery was epidemic because the government would not punish it and had shut down alternative means of striking at enemies (though new magical counterattacks were invented). Ashley and Fletcher heard such grievances during a mid-1931 Malaita visit and, encouraged by Malaita officers Barley and John White, Ashley grudgingly tinkered with a sorcery regulation, targeted once again solely at Malaita, before declaring it unenforceable and unfeasible, writing, "I am not at all convinced that any measures for its repression are necessary, but if they are we must realize that natives are unbalanced in their beliefs in spirits [and] would be excessive in their punishments of anyone guilty or innocent whom they believed to be able to communicate with dwellers of the Styx."[111]

Such attempts to devise laws targeted at Islander sensibilities were few, and we have seen that through most of the 1930s local rules were not codified to augment the British laws in force. And yet, at the same time that Malaitans were pushing government to take more notice of indigenous concerns, pressures were emanating from Tulagi and farther abroad to preserve island "customs" and cultures. The next chapter details how as the decade progressed it became government policy, particularly on Malaita, to bestow a higher order of legitimacy on "good customs." These were contrasted with "bad customs" such as fighting or sorcery, which were deemed "repugnant to accepted principles of humanity" and required suppression.[112] Interference with good customs was to be avoided as far as possible, it was said, because their loss would contribute to "cultural fatigue," social degeneration, and depopulation; without "good customs" a society could become "a ship without a rudder drifting helplessly to destruction."[113] "True customs" were conceived in legal and other contexts as pre-European cultural features, and many newer practices were branded as spurious corruptions of custom, unnatural and even dangerous to natives.

These models of Melanesian cultures presented difficulties even if one assumed specific ideas and practices could be understood piecemeal, isolated from the wholes with which their meanings were intertwined. The approach expressed a widespread European belief that before European arrival local societies had been static, that the lives of their peoples were ruled by rigid customs, and that innovation and change were anathema to them. Like so many other societies classified as "traditional" in colonial settings, Malaitan ones were seen to be nonhistorical.[114] Those holding this view were ignorant of the fact that as the 1930s began Malaitan cultures had already undergone 60 years of radical social change, most of it before Europeans had even penetrated the island's interior. It was difficult if not impossible to know the antiquity of particular ideas, rules, or practices, especially for Europeans with their deeply flawed understandings of the societies in question. And of course one must ask: if Malaitans were so inherently conservative, then where had the plethora of new "spurious customs" come from? The implication was that the sweeping Malaitan innovations and adaptations of preceding decades had been illegitimate. The great irony was that colonial officials (like some much later anthropologists and historians) seemed oblivious to these realities, and while Malaitans were busily adapting and inventing, Europeans themselves were crippled by a remarkable inability to revise *their own* cultural models of timeless, custom-bound Malaitan societies capable only of prolongation or disintegration, not speedy change. Muddled as these ideas seem now, they generated or justified key colonial policies on Malaita.

Directives to bolster "good customs" pushed officers into a conflicted position: they were to be more attentive to valuing and preserving local cultures and their older ways, but at the same time they were assigned the task of bringing about great changes within them. As one would expect, the artificiality and vagueness of the "custom" concept led to its being selectively applied. When officers found an innovation acceptable, they either ignored its lack of pedigree or tried to show that it was actually a return to a practice once lost but now revived, as described earlier regarding the idea of "chiefs." On the other hand, government officers and sometimes missionaries (especially Norman Deck) deployed the same model to reject aspects of Malaitan life of which they disapproved—labeling something a modern corruption could strip it of the legitimacy it would enjoy as "custom." The custom concept's contrived nature, combined with the ignorance of those who applied it, made it what Kwara'ae call "a spear pointed at both ends," a two-edged sword that could be wielded to sustain or condemn as needed. Later, during Maasina Rule, officers came to label resistance leaders illegitimate because they lacked the "hereditary status" that officers considered the proper "custom" credentials of "true and traditional native authorities." Nicholas Thomas has described a similar situation in nineteenth-century Fiji, where "custom" was also "protected" to address depopulation, both disapproved practices and problematic leaders "were distanced from 'Custom' in order to be legitimately proscribed," and a "constant slippage" was evident "between interests in reducing mortality and other agendas."[115]

The contradictions involved in these selective applications of custom appear to have remained unconscious in the Solomons, with officials fully believing they were protecting, rehabilitating, and applying custom in a consistent manner. In thousands of pages of reports, correspondence, and classified documents across several decades I found no officer questioning the essential validity of the "custom" concept as Europeans were applying it. Instead, one often encounters a sympathetic, philanthropic belief that Malaitans had fallen out of touch with their own past, but that, through the help of white people, they could be reunited with it, albeit in more civilized forms. That most officers knew little of Malaita's pre-European past beyond crude stereotypes appears to have given no one discomfort or pause (and many knew shockingly little about even the more recent colonial past). In the final analysis, the custom concept as applied to Solomon Islanders was a legal fiction and a fantasy.

In the short run, the model of inherently static and endangered tribal cultures could serve colonial policy well, for it suggested that it was futile or even dangerous to educate such peoples or to try to develop their islands too quickly. The idea that Melanesians had to be protected from rapid change, again, denied decades of transformation that Malaitans had themselves brought about, recognition of which would have thrown into disarray not just the "custom" concept but also many justifications for the colonial project writ large. So far as the changes that could not be denied, particularly unwelcome ones, we will see that Europeans had a palatable reading: though it might appear Malaitans were changing and adapting like other human beings, these changes were so unnatural to them that they were killing them, as witnessed by a rapid depopulation that had occurred in many places. More European control and direction were absolutely essential, to help the Malaitans become better Malaitans and a viable population in the changing world.

In hindsight, this facet of colonial governance in the Solomons was dreadfully naive and became a wellspring of confusions and administrative woes. Government officers failed to grasp the fallacy in their approach and its basic conceptual underpinnings despite the glaring evidence before them. It did, however, become increasingly apparent to Malaitans, until eventually only the administration itself remained blind to it. As we will see, when opportunity presented itself, Malaitans would move to seize the political opening, and exploit the logical weaknesses of the "custom" concept itself.

Chapter 3

Colonial Experiments and Mounting Resentments

Limping through the Great Depression

The 1930s economic crisis, particularly the collapse of copra prices, cut deeply into government resources and hamstrung any plans for development or better administration. G Lennox Barrow called copra "the very stuff of life" in the Solomons, and the 1933 Annual Report lamented that copra comprised "the sole industry of the Group upon which the Administration relies...for its revenue; the European planters and the natives for their income; the commercial firms for their sales; and the shipping firms for cargo." Statistics are telling: in 1926–1927, 22,316 tons were produced annually, valued at £411,597; by 1934–1935 this fell to 18,093 tons worth £54,013. Total BSIP revenue that year was £55,687, against £61,319 in expenditures.[1]

Grim conditions through most of the decade constrained government spending and staffing, and as the Depression deepened, jobs available to Islanders fell by half. The number of Malaitan laborers recruited from 1931 through 1940 was 43 percent lower than the decade ending in 1922. Since the Queensland and Fiji days, most Malaitans had depended on indentured plantation work for money and trade goods; in 1930, Jack Barley guessed that 90 percent of the cash circulating the island came from wages earned by some 5,000 men, about 10 percent of the population, working on other islands.[2] The economic crash brought home to Malaitans their vulnerability within the colonial and capitalist order, and resentments grew.

During the 1920s plantation work conditions had become less severe, but to Islanders they remained demeaning, and Judith Bennett has described how, as the Depression set in, plantation interests cut corners in ways that made the labor scene again more harsh and exploitive. Many whites had always taken Melanesians' second-class status for granted as the good and proper order of things, and they wrote off workers' complaints as due to their ignorance of the economic process or the fruits of government mollycoddling (for examples, see any issue of the *Planters' Gazette*). For years there had been calls for laws to suppress the "cunning" organizer of resistance on plantations, the so-called "bush-lawyer," who "posed as a leader among his friends,...a confirmed instigator of discontent and trouble and an inflamer of the passions of his fellow labourers." Dismissals of Islanders' frustrations often displayed a peculiar blindness to social reality, expressed by Hector MacQuarrie, a relatively sympathetic district officer of the mid-1920s, when he wrote that his boat engineer was "the only Solomon Islander I ever met acutely aware of his colour and its disadvantages." Others, too, voiced this odd belief that Islanders were oblivious to or even happy with the discrimination and exploitation they suffered. This delusion was to cause Europeans no end of troubles. The discontents of workers and their communities, particularly as they grew during the Depression, are key to this book's project because, as Ian Frazer has observed but most studies have failed to stress, Maasina Rule was in important respects a labor movement, which voiced a shared "industrial consciousness" developed out of the plantation experience and indenture's negative impacts on workers' home communities. In what follows, I do not delve into 1930s plantation life but concentrate instead on impacts the labor scene and the Depression had on Malaita itself, particularly regarding Malaitans' growing unhappiness with the European establishment.[3]

The Malaitan labor picture dramatically worsened in mid-decade when, under pressure from planters, the Solomon Islands Labour (Amendment) Regulation halved the adult wage for indentured labor from 20 shillings a month back to the 1923 rate of 10, and also cut the wage advance—which had partly replaced the beach payments of old—from £6 to £3. Beach payments had ended with King's Regulation 7 of 1923, which outlawed them but hiked the minimum monthly wage to £1. District Officer William Bell at the time said that plantation interests wanted beach payments ended since they would recoup any wage increase by selling laborers goods in their stores at high profits.[4]

Now, many Malaitans refused to work for the halved wage, particularly from Kwaio southward through 'Are'are and Small Malaita. In places there was open hostility: in July 1935 a recruiter named Hill encountered complaints about taxes at 'Oloburi Harbour in southern Kwaio, and elders there blocked young men from signing on. Farther south at Maanawai, Hill was confronted by Headman Lilimae and a group of SSEM men who threatened him that "If [I] remained there they would bring down about 200 boys and clear us out as no natives would be allowed to sign out of Mana Kwoi." Adding to tensions was a surge in new recruits absconding with advance pay and trade goods. As during the Fiji-Queensland labor period, many Malaitans wanted to keep more men home because the absence of so many undermined their communities. In mid-1936, recruiting across the island's southern half remained "more or less at a standstill."[5]

The Depression brought a drastic reduction in jobs, even under the new terms. The 1934 Annual Report tallied only 3,578 indentured laborers, down from over 6,000 six years before. After mid-1936 more southern men again sought work, but that October District Officer Charles Bengough reported, "A very large proportion of the taxpaying population of Malaita is both able and willing to work, but there is no work," and men were having difficulty finding tax money.[6]

Malaitans' financial woes were exacerbated by the government's determination to keep collecting head taxes from men aged 16 to 60. When the tax was first introduced, High Commissioner Cecil Rodwell had bristled at charges that it was meant to compel indentured plantation work, but that intent was clear to all. Bishop John Steward had criticized the new tax for this reason and because money collected would not be spent on Islanders. Recruiter Ernie Palmer described to Roger Keesing how tax collections were the best times to get men: "This was very handy for us, the recruiters, because it meant that the boys came down and stayed until market....You heard the D.C. was going round to collect taxes at Auki or...Kwai. It was a race between us to see who got there first. Whoever got there first dropped his anchor, and he waited for the D.O. to come on the ship. And then after the boys came down to pay their taxes, you recruited them. So half the poor blokes hadn't got any money at all....We didn't pay in cash, of course, we paid in tobacco and parcels and axes and knives...and they got money for it from relatives ashore, and they paid their tax."[7]

Anglican missionary Albert Mason wrote from north Malaita, "In May [1924] some seventy people, or twenty per cent of the village of Bio, recruited on the *Mendana* on one day, the explanation being that they had no money for the tax. The village seemed quite depressed after such a general exodus." Some villages sent groups of men abroad expressly to earn tax money for the entire community.

Inland people, especially, had no saleable products, opportunities for casual work, or other means to earn cash, and so many faced a choice of indenture or jail. In 1933 Barley told Sylvester Lambert that he believed 75 percent of Malaitan workers left home for this reason and that the Protectorate was violating the international Forced Labour Convention enacted the year before. Colin Allan, writing as Malaita's district commissioner in 1951, largely blamed this prewar system for the great discontent during his time on Malaita, and he quoted a high commissioner's chief secretary who, just after the war, said the BSIP economy was based on, "in fact if not in theory, forced labour at very low rates of wages—forced by the imposition of a poll tax, by the desire for trade goods, and the total lack of other means of earning money, and organized on a system of two years indenture based on severe penal sanctions...the system is a vicious circle leading only to progressive impoverishment and discontent."[8]

The labor regulation aggravated the problem. By halving wages it reduced cash entering Malaita by more than half, for two reasons: Before, departing recruits had generally left their £6 wage advance with relatives.

But they now began taking all or most of the new £3 advance with them, for with the lower wage they now needed that money abroad. Second, because laborers now earned less, they spent a greater proportion of their wage on trade goods (prices of which did not fall) rather than bringing it home as cash. With less money coming in to families, inland people in particular had to pay taxes with savings that by 1936 were nearly exhausted. As in the past, some in desperation turned to opportunistic policemen who exchanged cash for shell money at dismal rates during tax collections, though officers at times tried to stop this.[9]

In the growing Christian communities, this situation was worsened by missions' reduction or elimination of brideprice, which left young men less dependent on seniors and thus less willing to distribute wages to their families or patrons for them to pay tax with. In some areas, too, control of brideprice and other exchanges was shifting as the shell currencies dominated by older men lost ground to the cash held by younger men.[10] Even in inland groups some young men were less attentive to seniors' directives as practical benefits of putting aside personal interests for community ones diminished. Similar processes were at work across Melanesia; Ian Hogbin and Camilla Wedgwood wrote that in places "the young men can—and do—snap their fingers at their seniors," and that on Malaita specifically, "The word *ara'i*, which originally meant 'old man' or 'person of importance,' has been degraded from a term of respect to a mild form of abuse."[11] However, today, one hears similar complaints from both old and young that many young men and women disrespect their elders, and these recall complaints made about rebellious nineteenth-century returned laborers. While big changes were certainly underway in the 1930s and 1940s, many indignant elders of that time had in their youth been impudent rebels, as many elderly complainers of later years were during the 1930s, and one must be cautious against perceiving intergenerational tensions as always marking a sea change; they have typified Malaita since the late nineteenth century and perhaps much longer.

Years later George Sandars recalled his sympathy for poverty-stricken Malaitans and claimed he had never penalized anyone for nonpayment of tax, and Barley gave extensions and accepted partial payments. Hogbin, though, said tax default was the second most common legal offense (after adultery) in 1933, during Barley's and, toward the end, Sandars's watch. At any rate, as the decade progressed, economic realities forced modifications of tax policy. First, Sandars on his own reduced or remitted some taxes. Resident Commissioner Francis Ashley, who before the 1934 wage cut had himself advised High Commissioner Arthur Fletcher that south Malaitan taxes should be cut by half, initially protested Sandars's move but after a visit to Malaita decided not to interfere. He rejected the idea that his having allowed a halving of the wage added to the tax difficulties; rather, he said, Malaitans should look within: "The real cause is the uneven distribution of wealth, that is due to the fact that cash does not circulate on Malaita and barter is still the form of exchange."[12]

Soon after, in March 1936, Ashley and Bengough visited Sinalagu to discuss taxation with a "large and comprehensive gathering" rounded up by a police patrol to meet them at Gwee'abe, where Bell was killed. Spokesmen from all three eastern Kwaio harbors explained that people were willing to pay if only they had money. Ashley told them, "The amount of wages paid a labourer under contract, had nothing whatever to do with the Government." But, as Bennett wrote, "In the eyes of the Solomon Islanders, the fact that the government set a wage meant it was a fixed, not merely a minimum, wage, a misconception planters fostered." Ashley then "proceeded to explain the objects of taxation and how every country was taxed and all free men had to pay as their contribution to government for the security of life and property that was provided." He gave as illustration "how a labourer under contract was protected from the time of his recruitment until his return home." Those who had been misused on plantations must have raised their eyebrows, and Charles Fox recounted one reaction to such "protection" justifications for the tax: After an officer had explained to people that without the government, "the Germans or the Japanese...would come in and treat you far worse than we do," one man said, "It's like this, a big boy is sitting on you and beating you, and you howl.—'What are you howling for?' he says. 'If I wasn't sitting on you, a bigger boy than I would be doing it, where's your gratitude?'" Ashley's civics lecture omitted something Malaita's Officer John Brownlees saw as fundamentally unfair: "Whereas we Europeans were not taxed, be we government or planters or commercial people in stores and so on, the natives were."[13]

Despite Ashley's distorted perception or at least presentation of the economic situation, he departed Sinalagu convinced that Kwaio could not pay 5 shillings and therefore lowered their tax to just 2 for 1936/1937. He "emphasized that it was not reduced for anyone else on Malaita and it was for one year only," though in truth 'Are'are taxes were also cut. But by year's end, Bengough reported that so little money was coming into Malaita that people could not pay even reduced rates.[14]

Temporary cash relief came in 1937 when numbers of men returned home from plantations, but by midyear, visiting High Commissioner Arthur Richards had to waive the tax entirely for mountain people with no known incomes. Sandars recommended that only bachelors be taxed because when married men left to labor for two years this caused hardships and conflicts at home as well as administrative problems. The next year Ashley reluctantly agreed to tax inland people only 1 shilling (with an option to work this off by laboring on government "roads"), a rate that stayed in place until the war, with the wealthier saltwater people still paying from 2 to 5 shillings.[15]

Disgruntled, Ashley asserted that Malaitans did not pay their fair share:

"It should be realized that there is no native in the Protectorate who pays less and gains more from the administration than the Malaitaman." To him, Malaitan poverty was a fallacy: "I am personally of the opinion that the native labourer is satisfied with 10/- per month.... It cannot be too often stressed that wages paid to the natives in the Protectorate are nothing more or less than so much pocket money. Apart from their tax obligation, no natives of the Protectorate have any financial responsibility in respect of either themselves or their families and very few natives have any idea of the value of money." Earlier in the decade, Ashley had been similarly pitiless toward Officer Ronald Garvey's pleas that Makirans had no money to pay taxes. Declaring Makira "quite the most fertile island in the protectorate," he directed that people should simply double their work.[16] Later, during Maasina Rule, Malaitans recalled these years to explain their refusal to pay taxes. In 1950 Officer Michael Forster reported why Naomani (who was from Waisisi in 'Are'are but a Maasina Rule leader at Guadalcanal's Marau Sound) said he "had no use for Government":

> In his opinion the Malaita people previously paid a great deal of money in taxes for which they received nothing. This allegation contains a large measure of truth. When the tax was first collected it appears that certain promises were made to the people. One was that they should receive medical services; the other was that they should receive pay for doing Government work. In the period during which tax was paid some £30,000 was contributed by Mala. During the same period the amount paid to headmen and their assistants never exceeded £318 per annum. Government medical services were not started until 1930 and by 1940 consisted of one [native medical practitioner] and four dressers and an extra [practitioner] and dresser seconded to 'Are'are to investigate an alarming decrease in the population. This question has been dealt with at some length because it forms a main plank in the MR [Maasina Rule] argument against paying taxes.[17]

Foreign commodities grew increasingly scarce on Malaita, particularly in the mountains. Besides the fact that returned workers were bringing back fewer goods, people in the south lost their other main source of supply: Australian and especially Chinese trading boats from Tulagi had long cruised the Malaita coast selling matches, tobacco, cloth, tinned meat, and clay pipes, with £1,400 in sales in 1930. As cash supplies dried up during the Depression, these boats declined in number and rarely visited the poorer south. In late 1936, Bengough reported an "unprecedented lack of new calicos and tobacco among bush natives during the past year."[18]

The injury was compounded when European trade stores charged Islanders higher prices for merchandise than whites paid, while paying them less than whites for identical produce. This practice was long-standing; Bell told Walter Ivens that Islanders often paid double what whites did in stores. In

1939 High Commissioner Harry Luke drew up legislation to criminalize
this practice but withdrew it in deference to plantation interests. When economic conditions improved a bit in the late 1930s, planters resisted raising
wages and warned that doing so would cause them great hardship. Bengough, knowing how difficult times were on Malaita, suspected planters
were exaggerating but could not prove it.[19]

The economy would not soon return to pre-Depression levels, and
laborers' prospects remained grim. Just when recovery seemed imminent,
the looming war contributed to a June 1940 collapse of copra prices and
further hiring slumps, and the trochus market was shattered as well. Most
smaller European plantations never recovered after the war.[20]

Throughout the 1930s, as before, plantations were sites of not just economic frustration but also the development and spread of political ideas
among Islanders who shared anger at the colonial system. New political
identities were forming that transcended old boundaries and enmities.
Lambert wrote: "Barley speaks of the nationalism of Malaita which Malaita
men show even from different parts of the island when opposing a common
enemy away from home. The island is divided into many tribes unrelated in
language or custom, but who are all proud of being Malaita men." Whites
had always dreaded the possibility Malaitans might unite against them, as
Caroline Mytinger described: "Malaitans were scattered all through the
islands; the houseboys were Malaitans, the boat boys were Malaitans, and
the labour lines on the plantations were made up almost entirely of these
sharp 'black fellows.' There were anywhere from fifty to eighty boys on each
tract under a single overseer, never more than two white men. And the
plantations were widely distant from one another, sometimes a matter of
two or three hours by launch—and that launch, paradoxically, in the hands
of a Malaitan boat boy, was the only means of escape from unexpected trouble." But Barley's observation was a counter to a comforting and widely
shared assumption that Solomon Islanders, and particularly Malaitans,
would never unite politically because of primordial intertribal hatreds.[21]

When this supposition was contradicted, whites were baffled and confused. Take an account given in 1980 by Bita Saetana of Kwaio of a 1930s
plantation fight: "Mister Birifi gave me a job with a young man from Guadalcanal named Rodo. He gave us eight hundred coconuts to plant in one
day. We started at 4:30 am and worked until 6:00 pm but we'd planted
just seven hundred. The white man cursed me for not finishing the job,
so I spun around and cursed him, and then he took a swing at me but
missed. He came at me with a shovel...and that man, Rodo, from Tatuve
[a mountain area of central Guadalcanal], jumped up and broke Birifi's
nose.... The white man asked him [painfully shocked tone], 'Why did you
hit me? You're not related to that man!' And Rodo answered, 'My color.
My skin. If you strike him, I strike you!'" We will see that when the Fallowes movement, and especially Maasina Rule, united diverse groups and

exploded the myth of Islanders helplessly divided by xenophobia, many whites were similarly astounded, disoriented, and dismayed.[22]

At this point in time, the broader of these plantation alliances were contextual and oppositional, and they faded from day-to-day relevance when men returned home and their active affiliations contracted to smaller communities (with the important exception of mission networks). But old divisions were also being countered by new, more inclusive identities emerging at home among groups loosely defined and structured by the administrative zones to which the government had assigned people. In many parts of Malaita, old factionalisms began to weaken and a broader community consciousness began to develop at political and judicial events organized by the government: tax collections, court hearings, and meetings with district officers. These proceedings drew together formerly atomized groups to interact as a body with the colonial state. In Malaita's Annual Report for 1931, Barley described a tax collection at Uru Harbour in Kwaio: "An altogether different spirit to that of previous years pervaded the atmosphere. Instead of the dour, suspicious crowd of bushmen, that one was in the habit of seeing at a tax-collection (and only then, for they kept well away at all other times), who sat around in small groups of their own particular kinsmen, only waiting for their tax-money to be taken before hastening back to their mountain fastness, the place was filled with sightseers." Four years later, Wilfrid Fowler reported from Kwaio tax collections and courts, "There have been large congregations of spectators which have remained until the last item of business has been transacted." In some places such government events were the first time people from across a language zone had interacted as a group with any regularity. Officers welcomed this change, feeling it would make their work easier, but such gatherings also planted seeds for the integrative networks and meetings of postwar Malaitan political actions.[23]

The Fallowes Movement

Two political movements in 1939 displayed growing discontent in the Protectorate with not just economic conditions but also peoples' general lot under colonial rule. Although both were quickly suppressed, they brought forward themes that resurfaced in more potent forms after the war. They were very different: the first was a thoroughly political movement initiated by an Anglican priest named Fallowes, and its impact was felt throughout the Solomons; the second was a politico-religious movement incited by an ancestress in central Malaita.

At the same time as Islanders were coming together as never before at government-staged events, other crosscutting political connections were developing via the churches. An expression of this was the Fallowes movement—sometimes called in the literature "Chair and Rule." It interests us for what it reveals about the growing politicization of church networks, as an articulation of and attempt to act to address Islander dissatisfactions and aspirations, and because Malaitan men who later helped start the Maasina Rule movement attended its final meeting.

A driving force was Richard Fallowes, who had arrived on the island of Santa Isabel—also known as Bugotu—in 1929 as a Melanesian Mission priest. Isabel's population was by then entirely Anglican, and church officials competed for power, quite successfully, with government officials. Fallowes feared that an ongoing decline of indigenous leadership and community cohesiveness would weaken the church, and he disapproved of the government's methods. Working with Lonsdale Gado, who later became Isabel's "paramount chief," Fallowes organized large meetings on Isabel to discuss a range of issues and grievances, and in 1931 they began to institute an island-wide system of church officials; "church chiefs" (or "mission headmen") were selected in each village and, in addition to their other duties, reported violations of church rules to Fallowes or his representatives. Fallowes offered some offenders, especially violators of sexual rules, a choice between excommunication and a severe cane thrashing. A weak government presence and Anglican dominance gave him considerable authority, and local people found it difficult to tell whether church or government was in charge. By early 1933, Sandars, sent to investigate, reported that the government had "almost handed over the administration of the island to the Mission." This state of affairs had been facilitated by the acquiescence of Isabel's District Officer Francis Filose. Filose was eventually removed for brutality, and Fallowes was probably the organizer of a petition to restore him to his position. Officers also investigated Fallowes for his thrashings, and in mid-1933 he was convicted on 3 of 13 charges of common assault and fined. In 1935 he suffered a mental collapse and returned to England.[24]

Fallowes returned to Isabel in October 1938, against Ashley's wishes and now unaffiliated, since Bishop Walter Baddeley had withdrawn his license to officiate. He talked to Islanders about government and the church having neglected their interests, and the dearth of economic, educational, and political avenues open to them. This came as no news to Islanders but struck a responsive chord. Fallowes later described this process in a letter to historian David Hilliard: "The Soga [Paramount Chief Gado] and other Bugotu chiefs would discuss their grievances with me rather than the district commissioner. In those days discussion with 'nigger' chiefs was not the policy of the colonial officials. At these informal discussions I pointed out that the grievances were not those of Bugotu alone but all the Solomons and that brought up the possibility or otherwise of meetings of chiefs from the other islands." With Fallowes's support, leaders from Isabel and other islands planned an interisland "Parliament" or "Assembly," reminiscent in some ways of the Vaukolu of decades before. A first meeting was convened in southern Isabel in early 1939, followed by a larger one from 28–29 April at Savo, and, largest of all, the Parliament itself from 12–13 June at Halavo on Gela, east of Tulagi.[25]

Hearing of the first meeting from Isabel's Officer John Brownlees, an unruffled Ashley wrote that Fallowes could do little harm: "The natives will soon get tired of attending meetings and getting nothing for it and it will do them good by teaching them a lesson." The crux of the meeting, he said, was "mythical grievances" of "an abnormal state of mind." But he sent Sergeant Major Steven Sipolo of east Malaita to attend the Savo meeting "in plain clothes."[26] As the movement grew, so did government concern. Soon after the June meeting, High Commissioner Luke visited Tulagi and received a list of the Parliament's proposals that Fallowes had helped prepare, along with two papers written by Gela headman John Pidoke, translated by Fallowes. Pidoke succinctly expressed the frustrations that energized the meetings: "In 1921 the Governor said that we shall pay taxes to help the King's realm of England here in Solomon Islands, and we have paid taxes for 18 years. We have only been taught the Gospel, but nothing yet about trade and commerce. We have been Christianized for 78 years now. The Church people are anxious for collections, and the Govt. for taxes, but where is the money? Here in the Islands wages and prices are very small, not enough for taxes and church collections. . . . In the year 1939 the Revd. Richard Fallowes explained the desires of the leading people in England. But we have been ready for many years. . . . I am writing down the words of all the people in the Solomon Islands."[27]

Pidoke said the group wanted a lawyer appointed to represent native interests, and movement proposals included the establishment of a technical school, improvements in medical care, better prices for copra and shell, changes in plantation labor regulations, and an increase in the standard wage for "those who work for white men and Chinamen" to £12 a month. Anthropologist Geoffrey White was told that the call for a £12 wage originated with Malaita representatives.[28] Both government and the missions were being challenged here, at a time when many Solomon Islanders were expressing similar disillusionment with church policies. In a subsequent letter attributed to Pidoke, the threat of a strike was clear: "Don't worry too much about the Europeans. If they can't take us to do any work they can't find any money either for tax or collections." Fallowes disavowed responsibility for the substance of the demands but acknowledged his role in organizing the meetings and promoting the idea of a more permanent native political body.[29]

Some of the changes being sought were also avowed aims of the colonial establishment, and Fallowes maintained that the participants did not expect government disapproval of their actions, or even believed officers would view them favorably. But the European response was predictable, as Fallowes later described: "The Govt. policy at that time was to divide and rule. A meeting of chiefs to express a common voice was viewed with indignation and alarm both by Govt. and missions. Hitherto Bugotu [had] thought of Malaita as foreigners if not enemies and consciously or unconsciously the colonial power fostered this. And then along comes a pestilential priest putting forth subversive ideas of a pan Solomon if not a pan Melanesian nationalism. It came as a shock to the 'whites' to discover that chiefs and others would travel hundreds of kilometers of open sea in their canoes to attend meetings to discuss matters of common concern." Shaken, the government and Bishop Baddeley united to condemn Fallowes and his followers as subversive. Fallowes said that Luke sent for him and "dressed me down for encouraging insubordination among the natives and putting pan-Melanesian ideas into their heads," and told him that his efforts were "mischievous, irresponsible and ignorant." Earlier, at a March meeting between Fallowes, Ashley, and Sandars, the latter recorded that Fallowes "appeared to me to be labouring under considerable mental excitement," and after the Parliament meeting, word was spread that he was crazy, to discredit him. With Baddeley's encouragement, Fallowes was deported in late July, defiant to the end. He vowed to return and to consult "influential people in England" and, "for conscience sake," disavowed the Melanesian Mission.[30]

In early 1940, a worried William Marchant, the new resident commissioner, sent officers a confidential circular asking them to ascertain the movement's influence on the people, whom he described as "particularly backward politically and are distinctly ingenuous." The upshot of the officers' responses was that the organization had dissolved after Fallowes's departure, although its ideas remained widely discussed.[31] Makira's Officer Alexander Waddell reported that Fallowes "had caused profound discontent throughout the Eastern Solomons for some months, and had aroused even in District Headmen an enthusiasm for a distorted Utopia that was incompatible with their loyalty to the Government." Makirans put forward men for the Parliament, though they apparently remained unsure about how to proceed. Waddell saw in all of this a need for more education, social services, and future "political advancement"—changes he continued to advocate after the war.[32]

Academic writers later portrayed the movement as mystical and cultic, and then as having been violent. "Chair and Rule" referred to a carved chair that speakers are said to have used. Cyril Belshaw wrote, "About 1939 a European missionary encouraged the Melanesians of Santa Ysabel, Gela, and Savo to agitate for a seat on the nominated Advisory Council. He emphasized the need for a chairman and rules of procedure. The movement got out of hand and was misinterpreted. The Melanesians elevated a flag, a wooden chair, and a wooden rule into positions of ritual importance." Vittorio Lanternari said the result was "an anti-European uprising," and A de Waal Malefijt wrote that it sparked "anti-European revolts."[33]

What these events revealed most profoundly were the growing political frustrations and ambitions of Solomon Islanders, and even Fallowes was surprised by the level and scale of their response. Several long-standing themes of resentment publicly crystallized, and although the Parliament itself soon faded, its grounding vision did not. Many Solomon Islanders were no longer willing to remain silent about their own governance, to tolerate the educational and economic limits imposed on them, or to quietly pay taxes for minimal returns. The Fallowes movement was not the first instance of Solomon Islanders questioning and protesting white dominance. For example, people of Gizo in the west had staged a nonviolent tax protest in 1934 over the lack of health and education services. This led the writer of a letter to the *Pacific Islands Monthly*, citing Malaitan discontent, to propose that hospitals and schools would be a more effective remedy than "a regiment of soldiers." Also in the mid-1930s, parishioners for several years boycotted the Catholic mission at Tangarare, on the west coast of Guadalcanal, after the departure of a priest, Rinaldo Pavese, who had pressured the bishop to give catechists better pay. Yet the Fallowes movement signaled something new: for the first time large numbers from across the Protectorate gathered formally to express shared grievances and ideas for change, and, most important, to attempt interisland organization.[34]

There is little evidence the movement had any great impact on Malaita, although many of its basic themes later reemerged during Maasina Rule. In 1939 a large proportion of Malaitans still worshipped their ancestors, and among them a missionary's message aroused less enthusiasm. For example, Tome Waleanisia in 1987 told me Fallowes had little effect in Langalanga, since "that one belonged to the Anglicans, not to the people." Allan later said the movement had caused excitement mostly at Lau and 'Ataa, while Brownlees, now transferred to Malaita, said it was having some impact at Malu'u and Su'u, and on Small Malaita generally. The next year Brownlees reported that even in those areas Fallowes was rarely discussed.[35] But officers were privy to only glimpses of local thoughts on such matters, and Malaitans did hear and talk about the Fallowes meetings. Several men who were to play key roles in Maasina Rule attended the Gela one—Nono'oohimae, Harisimae, and Hoasihau of 'Are'are; Anifelo of Kwaio; and Steven Sipolo from Kwai (none of whom were Anglican). The last three were at Tulagi with 12 other Malaitan policemen for preparation for possible war, and the police held their own meeting to discuss what had been said. Many postwar Malaitan resistance leaders were former policemen, and others of them were probably there.[36] The many Kwaio I asked about the Fallowes movement denied, some indignantly, that it inspired or shaped Maasina Rule. Some granted that both voiced common concerns but pointed out that these were widely shared well before 1939.

The Fallowes movement flustered the government and motivated attempts to finally start rudimentary native courts and councils, which some officers later credited with having pushed Fallowes's ideas into the background.[37] I will return to the courts and councils after examining a very different sort of movement that emerged in central Malaita at about this same time.

La'aka Speaks

One Malaitan area where the Fallowes events made the least impression was east Kwaio. The only politically important Kwaio man to attend the Gela meeting was 'Abaeata Anifelo, whom we will meet again as a headman and then a Maasina Rule leader. He carried word of the meeting back to Kwaio as instructed but sparked little interest. A dedicated SSEM man with missionary leanings, Anifelo was an ineffective messenger in the mountains where most Kwaio lived with their ancestors.[38] Also, people were still angry with Anifelo over the punitive expedition that his father Basiana had triggered by killing Bell.[39]

Shortly after Fallowes was deported, another vision for radical change did make a great impression in Kwaio. News spread that a powerful ancestress named La'aka was speaking through the medium of a priest of 'Atobala, within the Uogwari area in the central mountains, just on the west side of today's boundary between east and west Kwaio. As described by Bengough, La'aka alerted people to an upcoming invasion: "American warships and troops would shortly arrive and would kill all Government officials. The spirit entered into a detailed description of how he [she] had visited America, and arranged this with the King of the United States. Further instructions were given by the spirit to the effect that houses should be built to accommodate the soldiers and their stores."[40]

The priest, named Noto'i, was said to have met on Guadalcanal two American bird hunters traveling the islands on a sailing ship, who gave him La'aka's instructions to build special villages and palisades.[41] Later, back in Kwaio, word of La'aka's message spread, and small groups from across the area traveled to 'Atobala to hear Noto'i speak her words. In 1981, Tagii'au of Saua recalled his 1939 visit there with a delegation: "We said, 'Let's go and hear the words of our ancestress.'" They asked Noto'i to let them hear from La'aka:

Just after dusk Noto'i bespelled a betelnut for La'aka, and prayed to La'aka. Then a firefly entered the house and alighted on Noto'i's head.[42] The spirit asked, "Who wants to hear me?" and Feolate [Tagii'au's companion] replied, "I do. I've come to hear my ancestress speak, to hear what you have to say." Then La'aka spoke: "I am angry because I have been sitting at Tulagi for so many years with my descendants. And the government is killing my descendants at Tulagi. All I do is mourn. They hang my people at Tulagi and they persecute my people at Tulagi....I came back from Tulagi and I said, 'I have been grieving at Tulagi. Now I have come to you, Noto'i.' Tulagi, though life goes on there, Tulagi is mine.... The wireless at Tulagi, it is my wireless, La'aka. The flag there is my flag, La'aka. I am going to destroy it. One day you will all see!"

La'aka spoke to Tagii'au and his friends at length, venting her rage that her descendants had died on plantations and at government hands and that the Christian missions had desecrated "her land." The missions would be destroyed as well. Noto'i spoke in tongues, which he then translated for listeners. Men from the 'Ai'eda area returned home from a visit reporting that Noto'i spoke in American English.[43]

Noto'i was visited early on by a delegation of La'aka descendants related to him, from 'Airumu, several miles to the northeast toward Uru harbor. On their return home, La'aka began speaking through one of their number as well, a man named Nagwaafi (or 'Uia). By mid-August, La'aka had demarcated 'Atobala and 'Airumu as "safe areas" and warned that all who did not take up residence within them would be killed by the American invasion force. Palisaded villages were constructed at both places, enclosing men's houses and sacred pigs dedicated to La'aka, and some men there practiced military drilling and hand-to-hand combat techniques. The two, gated villages each hung a different calico flag in the trees in shrines above their men's houses. La'aka soon announced through Nagwaafi the day Americans would arrive at Uru and said they would also bring money and goods. Those who did not enter the safe areas by a given date would have to pay La'aka a shell money entry fee.[44]

Bengough estimated that by late August some 2,000 people—a large portion of the Kwaio inland population—had joined the movement, but this was based on faulty intelligence; in fact, primarily people from around 'Atobala and the 'Airumu people were fully involved. Various others visited to help build the villages or simply hear the two mediums speak La'aka's words, and many were merely curious.[45] Bengough later reported that many people who had not moved into the two areas carried out "wholesale killing of pigs and destruction of tabu gardens...so as to be able to enjoy them before dying," and that many houses were also destroyed. But most of this "destruction" was actually an upsurge in consumption through intensified feasting and pig sacrifices to La'aka.[46] Although this was not nearly so widespread as Bengough believed, it did occur in some places and, combined with neglect of gardening, resulted later in food shortages in the core areas.[47] This was neither the first nor the last episode of Malaitan destruction or unbridled consumption of property in expectation of calamitous events.[48]

In mid-September, Bengough dispatched Cadet Martin Clemens with several constables, headed by Diake Maenagwa and newly appointed Kwaio Assistant Headman Anifelo, to arrest Noto'i and six followers. As Noto'i was being led away, he vowed that La'aka would raze Tulagi. Clemens warned people that they would receive no help if they destroyed their property, though the government did later supply food to some. Following the arrests, the failure of Americans to appear, and several police patrols (the most important led by Sale Vuza, whose wife Irene was Kwaio), the movement's open manifestations ceased. According to Bengough, some people who had destroyed pigs and property expressed anger at having been misled.[49]

Bengough blamed enthusiasm for Noto'i's message on a crisis of confidence in government caused by rumors of impending war (England and France declared war on Germany in early September, and the news spread quickly) and a transfer of nearly half of Malaita's 25 police to Tulagi to prepare for it. He said the demonstration of government force and the failure of Americans to show up had restored people's faith in the establishment. But clearly more complex issues lay behind these activities, including a deep anger at the government and the Christian churches, as expressed so bluntly by La'aka. Contrary to Bengough's belief, there had been and remained little faith in the government. It is noteworthy that Noto'i's message was not a general rejection of foreign things or outsider involvement in Kwaio affairs—American liberators would replace the ousted British, and, some said, bring material wealth. The latter "cargo" aspect seems to have been of marginal if any interest to most Kwaio, and people recounting these events to me in the early 1980s—some who took part in and still celebrated the movement, and others who belittled it—did not mention the "cargo" element at all unless I asked about it.[50]

The story of Noto'i having received his instructions from two Americans on Guadalcanal will sound familiar to students of Maasina Rule. In a story still told throughout Malaita, one of Maasina Rule's 'Are'are founders, Nori, is said to have received his instructions on Guadalcanal from an American general who smoked a golden pipe, or, in many versions, from two American officers. The centrality of Americans to Noto'i's message, years before World War II introduced Solomon Islanders to thousands of US soldiers, is of obvious interest. Keesing and Bennett summarized several possible sources of the prewar American mystique on Malaita, and by at least the early 1900s Queensland returnees had brought word to their countrymen that Americans would someday come to the Solomons.[51]

Key to understanding the American inspiration for Noto'i's movement is a visit to Kwaio by three ornithologists of the Whitney South Sea Expedition from New York's Museum of Natural History, which collected specimens in the Solomons for several years beginning in the 1920s. In 1930, after six weeks working around Malaita's coasts, they arrived on the west coast at Su'u in the sailing ship *France* and ascended the Kwari'ekwa river valley to seek birds deep in the Kwaio interior. With no government escort, two of them, Walter Eyerdam and William Coultas, lived some six weeks in central Kwaio under the sponsorship of one Sale Babaamae, provisioned by his kin living in and around the village of 'Aulola, on the slopes of Mt Tolobusu, Malaita's highest peak at just over 4,000 feet above sea level. During the recent punitive expedition the government had designated 'Aulola a "safe area" where people could take refuge. The ornithologists first camped in west Kwaio along the Kwari'ekwa before Babaamae and his people guided them for two days up to Tolobusu's summit area, then a week later to Bobo'efuufuu at 300 meters lower elevation, and finally to 'Aulola itself. These camps, particularly Bobo'efuufuu, were near what would later be the Noto'i movement's initial focal area of Uogwari.[52] It is obviously significant that the men later said to have given La'aka's message to Noto'i on Guadal-canal were likewise two American bird hunters traveling the islands in a sail-ing ship. Moreover, both of La'aka's mediums—Noto'i and Nagwaafi—and at least three of the other five men arrested were Babaamae's close relatives; Nagwaafi and another, Wadoka, were his first cousins. Almost certainly, all had spent time with the Whitney Americans.[53]

When I first lived in Kwaio nearly 50 years later, people who knew Eyer-dam and Coultas still recalled their kindness with great enthusiasm. What was it about these American naturalists that so impressed the Kwaio who interacted with them, and how might memories of them have helped inspire, nine years later, an apocalyptic yet utopian vision of a Kwaio-Amer-ican future?

Fortunately, Eyerdam and Coultas left diaries of those weeks in Kwaio, as did Hannibal Hamlin, a third expedition member who was there with them for a shorter period. These diaries tell of behaviors and relations with local people that set these men fully apart from Europeans Kwaio had encoun-tered before, and it is no surprise that they "were a source of great wonder" to local people. Without realizing it, Eyerdam and Coultas managed to lay waste to some of the most basic rules of colonial white-black relations: "The natives are not used to the cold," wrote Eyerdam, "but come here in dozens and sleep on the ground and shiver all night. We never bother them and let them eat our potatoes and [skinned] bird bodies. They think this is a picnic and suffer exposure on the cold mountaintop because of the novelty of hunting and living with 2 white men in the bush. These boys like to work for us at small tasks, such as gathering wood, cooking, etc. We let them use all of our spare blankets and clothes at night and even let some of them occupy our bed with us so they won't freeze." The 90 kilograms of rice they had brought lasted just two weeks, after which they ate only local foods.[54]

These white men were friendly and curious, invited people to help themselves to their food, and ate with them. They enjoyed ancestral chants performed nights around the fires, one being the story of Bell's assassin Basiana, narrated by a second 'Aulola leader named Sale Suuburigeni, and Ofomauri of Tofu.[55] They did not order people about, and they negotiated payments that they thought fair for services rendered. They showed remark-able trust and routinely gave men rifles and 10–20 cartridges to hunt birds for them in the bush. This was soon after a government punitive expedi-tion had brutalized the area after Bell was killed, and Eyerdam noted dryly, "When government officers travel in the bush on Malaita nowadays, they have an armed guard of 25 police with modern rifles and plenty of ammunition." Decades later my friend Basiberi, who spent three nights with the birders at Tolobusu, told me how their sharing of food and clothing, and their trusting men with guns, greatly surprised and impressed everyone.[56]

Neither man's diary indicates whether or not they voiced any antigovernment or anti-mission sentiments to the Kwaio men and women who filled their camp each night—which would have violated the colonial prime directive to not criticize other whites in front of Islanders. They seem to have been focused on their collecting and on coping with the unfamiliar physical and social conditions. But Eyerdam did write critically of Christian missionaries, and both men expressed to Kwaio a respect for their religious beliefs. For example, though they badly wanted specimens of certain taboo birds, they did not pursue them, and they agreed, with deep regret, not to enter the bush by themselves to hunt, grasping without being told that Kwaio feared they might stumble into sacred shrines. Eyerdam and a senior local ancestral priest, in Coultas's words, "took to one another like ducks to water." This priest carried out rituals to protect their camp from dangerous spirits, and when he dramatically and successfully performed spells to keep away rain, "We repeatedly flattered and praised him before his countrymen as a powerful devil devil man that savvys too much along altogether something blong rain he no come."[57]

On their arrival in Kwaio, having talked to District Officer Colin Wilson and other Europeans, both men had already taken up some negative caricatures of mountain Malaitans. Eyerdam wrote, "There are many bad eggs amongst them" and "they are not to be trusted." At the start, Coultas referred to the people as "these imbeciles," and described "hordes of weird, naked savages who offer us as much interesting speculation as we give them in turn." But as time went on their tone changed, and their diaries comment repeatedly and—given warnings they had received about the dreadful "Malaitaman"—with no little surprise on their hosts' integrity and good natures: "These people are heathens and have not yet been contaminated by the efforts of missionaries to Christianize them. They do not wish to have their customs interfered with by missionaries and they are right." And on the eve of their departure: "Altho very shrewd and hard to deal with in business transactions, they need to take few lessons from missionaries in the 10 commandments." Eyerdam later wrote, "Although we had heard much of the treachery and cruelty of the mountain bushman, we learned to like them in many ways. They are a simple and industrious people, whose mode of living has not progressed much beyond the days before the white man's advent. Their wants are few and their code of morals strict. In driving a sharp bargain they are unexcelled, but like most warlike primitive people they possess a higher standard of honor than many civilized people. When once confidence and friendly relations are established there is not much danger as long as they are maintained. We never lost a penny's worth of anything by theft while with these people, and could leave an article unguarded no matter how valuable it might be in the eyes of the natives." At their trip's end, Eyerdam told the biological journal *Murrelet* that Babaamae "and the devil-devil man...were very sensible and quite decent chaps," and in contrast to the common European travelers' derision of Malaitan women, said that some were "real beauties."[58]

Kwaio nicknamed Coultas "Master Dio," the same moniker ("Joe") later given to American soldiers in the Solomons and elsewhere. At the end Coultas observed, "Although we have heard any number of stories regarding the maliciousness of these Malaita men, we found them quiet, peaceful and quite willing to cooperate with us throughout all of our stay." Contrary to the stereotype of the "always serious and sullen" bushman, the two birders found people's constant humor contagious, with Eyerdam writing, "We have won much favor by telling a few very simple jokes or bantering and playing tricks on some of the small boys or old men."[59]

Before long, the Americans became true guests of the 'Aulola people, Coultas recording: "[Babaamae] very kindly offered to supply all foodstuffs gratis [they had been buying yams and taro] and give us the house rent free [they stayed in his house]. Why I don't know; I have never experienced an act of gratitude of this kind." A few days later, after an earthquake, people came running to them, "for moral support I suppose," guessed Coultas, but they were likely concerned with the hunters' safety, since earthquakes are very dangerous in this area due to landslides.[60]

Sadly, Coultas, at least, left the mountains feeling that they had been a burden on the community. Shortly before their departure a feast was held in the area, which diverted their usual steady stream of visitors. Coultas, unaware that an important Kwaio feast must monopolize all of an area's socializing, perceived in their empty camp that people had wearied of them. Then, when their descent to the coast was imminent, he misread the joyous sendoff they were given as people celebrating because they were leaving: "The hotel Arola Reed [panpipe] orchestra entertained us with a number of selections to-night. The whole spirit of the place has changed since it has become known that we are leaving. Apparently we have been unwelcome guests all of these days." Two days later, they embarked on the *France* at 'Oloburi Harbour, but not before bringing their carriers out to visit the ship. Babaamae and Suuburigeni, and perhaps others, were rewarded with a trip to Tulagi in the ship.[61]

One scholar seemed to attribute Kwaio friendliness toward the Whitney Expedition to their paying high wages, but as above quotes suggest and numerous diary entries make clear, pay was the one continuous source of friction during their visit. Some men were unhappy when, despite "much haggling," the Americans followed to the end Sandars's directive to pay carriers (men or women) no more than government's daily wage of 1 shilling, although men demanded 3 shillings. A few walked off the job over wages.

Hunters they hired protested to no avail at being paid for most birds in
tobacco instead of money (despite a tobacco shortage), and carriers refused
to pack loads over 25 pounds (the later standard government weight was
40). These labor squabbles tell us that although Kwaio were fascinated by
the Americans they were not awed, and that what impressed them was not a
perceived largesse but rather how they interacted and socialized with people. (Eyerdam pointed out that a simple porter strike would have given the
people all of their goods, since they could not carry them out themselves.)[62]

Perhaps as an American writer I should stress that my point here is *not*
that these naturalists' behaviors can be attributed to some inherent fairness
or open-mindedness of Americans relative to the British or Australians. To
discard this notion, one need only peruse the many bigoted American writings about the Solomons, by Jack and Charmian London, Hermann Norden, Osa Johnson, and their ilk. Or a cursory glance through American
history will suffice. Even the Whitney men wrote things that most would
deplore today.[63] But how enlightened they were is beside my point, which
is Kwaio perceptions of their behavior and also how those might have fed
into people's later political aspirations. To be sure, being Americans gave
them an initial opening. When Babaamae and an armed party challenged
the third ornithologist, Hamlin, on his initial, separate arrival in their territory, he explained their purpose and Babaamae told him, "Because none
of our expedition belonged to the government and were not missionaries
and also because we belonged to another country he could see no reason
why we should not be welcome to his people"; Babaamae also said they were
anxious to trade. Eyerdam wrote, "Several have informed us that we have
nothing to fear from their country men, because we are Americans and do
not belong to the government." One old coastal man known as Queensland
Charlie told him, "Me savvy man blong this big fella country Merika. He
good fella. Me like um too much. Bushman he savvy him too. Bushman he
no like um England, no like um government."[64]

The key difference between these men and other whites Kwaio had met
was, in a nutshell, their unprecedented and disarming familiarity and their
treatment of Melanesians as fellow human beings. The power of this discov-
ery for Malaitans, perhaps difficult for readers to grasp today, can be appreciated from an anecdote told by American tourist John Vandercook about
his conversation with a coastal Kwaio man about two years after the Whitney
visit. While the two were chatting, the Kwaio man began to cry, and when
Vandercook asked him why, he shook his head and replied, "You first white
man, master, ever talk soft along boy."[65] Or take Xavier Herbert's account
of black-white relations while he worked as a hospital clerk and pharmacist
in Tulagi two years before the Whitney visit, in 1928:

> I did argue a bit at first about the treatment of natives; that is, they were treated
> like dirt. One man argued with me and said you've got no idea of how the Ger-

mans used to treat them in Bougainville.... They had sulkies, and no horses, and they used to put natives in the sulkies and then they used to whip them, and make them gallop and things like that. I remember my comment being that that was probably better treatment than the utter contempt that you people treat them with, as if they don't exist. I recall a situation where there was a Major [J C] Barley I think he was, the Government Secretary. There was a woman, a Mary as they called them, brought in. She had pneumonia, she was dying—probably had tuberculosis—but they brought her in and laid her on the floor, the steps outside the dispensary, a bit of an office and a surgery.... The doctor and I went to see her, she appeared to be dying, she was breathing very badly. And Major Barley turned up with his dog—he'd been on the golf course and his dog had fallen down or something and broken one of its front paws—and immediately the doctor drops the woman and went in to attend to the dog and put it on the operating table. So I became very angry about that. This woman was lying there dying, and her people were standing down respectfully and quietly. And I went in to the doctor and said 'Doctor, what are you going to do with the woman out there?' He said 'What woman?' And I said 'The woman out here, the Mary.' And they sort of looked at me, and I said, 'Surely a dog can wait.' And they just turned round and went on with it.... That would be the only protest I ever made. My sister shut me up and said you can't talk like that here.[66]

What most favored the ornithologists was what they did *not* know and follow: the strict prewar codes of black-white relations, particularly the imperatives of avoiding "familiarity" and preserving white separateness, prestige, and superiority—what BSIP geologist John Grover 20 years later referred to as "the supercilious isolationism which some Europeans call dignity," and Ralph Furse portrayed as a vital "attitude of aloofness" for colonial officers. We have seen and will again see the importance this had for so many Europeans. A cliché in accounts of the prewar Solomons is the "old hand" taking a new white arrival under his wing to instruct him on the "proper handling of the natives," particularly "Malaita boys." Walter Ivens early on included such directives in his *Hints to Missionaries to Melanesia* (in chapter 5, "Management of Natives," part 4, "Never Be Familiar"), and colonial officers in Melanesia later wrote guides on dealing with "the native" for distribution to incoming US troops.[67] The latter guides failed dismally in their purpose, and many soldiers made the same sorts of "mistakes" as the bird hunters, with predictable results. For some Kwaio men, working and socializing with Eyerdam and Coultas was a rehearsal of sorts for their future interactions with American soldiers.

As much as Malaitans resented the way Europeans treated them, by the 1930s most took it for granted. They had long come to believe, and taught their children, that most whites were hard-hearted and incapable of normal social relations, kindness, or proper modes of exchange, at least concerning Melanesians. This accurately captured how many Europeans viewed and interacted with Malaitans, not as fellows but as lesser beings, perhaps improvable, but only within sharp limits. A white axiom was that kindness toward Malaitans was counterproductive and dangerous. Thus a 1929 Labor Commission chaired by Barley pointed to "lawless and violent" Malaitans and warned, "Humaneness and consideration are apt to be misconstrued as signs of weakness or fear and the labourers consequently to grow increasingly arrogant and disobedient until a crisis occurs, resulting in a fracas and possibly loss of life." Former Burns Philp manager F Ashton "Snowy" Rhoades wrote, "The average Solomon Islander has no sense of gratefulness whatever and kindness is wasted on him." When medical worker Charles Gordon White was in 1929 presented with a generous gift by a community he had treated, he credited the act to a local missionary, since, he wrote, "The Malaitaman generally wants as much as he can get for anything he has to dispose of and giving things away he looks on as sheer madness."[68]

These social defects were all the more unfortunate in that whites seemed to possess immense riches. To Melanesians, a person of great wealth who refuses social engagement and exchange is grotesque, distressing, or even evil. Nevertheless, as abnormal as the colonial racial codes seemed to Malaitans, they had come to accept them as fixed. It should be noted that this was not only a Melanesian problem—some whites in the colonies also felt trapped by these codes, sanctioned as they were by severe social pressure and potential ostracism, not only from fellow colonials but at times from colonial subjects. In the words of one of novelist E M Forster's Indian characters, "They have no chance here.... They come out intending to be gentlemen, and are told it will not do."[69]

Eyerdam and Coultas did not know or follow the rules, and Kwaio found their behaviors surprising and refreshing. The experience must have suggested to them previously unimagined possibilities for productive social relations with a different kind of white person. It should come as no surprise, then, that a few years later, near the end of a long economic Depression and amidst dreadful rumors of a great war about to engulf the islands, Noto'i's utopian vision tied future hopes to a message of two American bird hunters under sail promising liberation from colonial subjugation and humiliation.

The Project to Counter 'Are'are Depopulation

> When asked for their opinion upon the probable causes of the
> diminution of the race, most Fijians attribute it to infectious diseases
> introduced among them by foreign ships.
> —*Colony of Fiji*, Report of the Commission Appointed to Inquire
>   into Decrease of the Native Population *(1896, 30)*

In these islands there are not enough people. There are 100,000
people in the Solomon Islands. There should be 10,000,000.
—*Officer Len Barrow, "The Work of Native Councils" (1946)*

The Fallowes movement, and to a lesser extent the Noto'i affair, startled
government officers and awoke them to the changing mood of Solomon
Islanders. Many concluded that a more serious attempt at native administration was imperative and overdue. Soon after the new resident commissioner, William Marchant, arrived in 1940, he decided to launch a concerted effort to establish native courts and councils based on those he had
helped administer in Kenya. They were initiated explicitly to help counter
Islanders' growing discontent with their situation under colonial rule.[70]

Councils and courts became part of a more general shift in administrative policy, especially on Malaita. The government had always depended
on Christian missions to carry out much of the social welfare work on the
island while its officers focused on law and order and taxation, but the
late 1930s saw a government rush to adopt a more active social agenda.
On Malaita, they had two core goals: to counter people's alienation from
government and to offset what they perceived to be a cultural decadence
haunting the island and depleting the population. The rest of this chapter
summarizes, first, a government project intended to halt inanition, anomie,
and depopulation through social engineering, and second, the early development of Malaita's native courts and councils. These overlapped considerably and both were seminal to the postwar Maasina Rule movement and its
kastom ideology.

Depopulation became a central concern of Malaita's officers during the
1930s. The idea that Melanesians were dying out was by no means a new
one. Anglican Bishop Cecil Wilson lamented of Solomon Islanders in 1905,
"They have but a short time to live, and all that can be done is done for
them, that their short lives may be brightened....We are placed then by
GOD in His infirmary, to work amongst a dying race; but a race which will
certainly die a Christian death." Resident Commissioner Charles Woodford
predicted Solomon Islanders' extinction, whatever Europeans might do,
and in 1910 expressed a common view that their demise was "as certain
as the rising and setting of the sun." Colin Allan later observed that this
justified early government land policies that "virtually disregarded native
interests."[71]

In the Protectorate's early years, some Europeans saw benefits to Melanesian extinction. Royal Navy Lieutenant Boyle Somerville wrote in an
anthropology journal that Solomon Islanders were doomed because of
their extreme violence and "the advancing oblivion of civilization," but he
was keen on the benefits this would have for whites: "Except from a scientific point of view, I think one might be almost reconciled to this dispen-
sation. The natives have their good points, certainly, but their bad are so

much more conspicuous that the elimination of the race would be no great loss to the world. Worst of all their bad points almost, is their incredible and incurable laziness—the heritage of all Pacific races." He went on to describe the economic potential the Solomons would have for Europeans once the Islanders died away. Burns Philp's 1899 *Handbook of Information* encouraged potential settlers: "It is, indeed surprising that such a magnificent country as this has been so long neglected. True, the natives have been, and still are, a troublesome factor to be reckoned with; but their claws are rapidly being cut, and every fresh settler furthers the work of civilization and reclamation." Upbeat anticipation of Islander-free islands usually did not include Malaita, for its people, the core of the Protectorate's labor force, were the island's great resource for Europeans. Hence the SSEM's Northcote Deck's warning in 1919: "If something radical is not done to check the excessive sums demanded for wives there can be no future for the race upon which the Protectorate depends for its development."[72]

The extent of depopulation in the Solomons and specifically on Malaita is hard to know because statistics from early decades of European contact are scarce and highly speculative, and even later figures are dubious. As late as 1916, Malaita population estimates ranged from 35,000 to 150,000 people. In 1924, Bell guessed Malaitans numbered 60,000 to 70,000, but a 1931 census estimated just over 40,000, and Barley reckoned there were 45,000. The latter numbers were likely undercounts. We do know that introduced diseases like influenza-pneumonia, whooping cough, and bacillary dysentery took awful tolls well into the twentieth century. The global influenza pandemic of the late 1910s and early 1920s wreaked havoc among Solomon Islanders, even though the Protectorate was sheltered from its most virulent early stages by an Australian maritime quarantine. Some 17 percent of Malu'u's population died then, but for other Malaitan areas data is slender or nonexistent. A medical officer guessed 3 percent of the Protectorate's people died overall, compared to 10 percent in bacillary dysentery outbreaks of 1913–1915. Ivens in 1924 estimated that numbers at Sa'a in the south had dropped by half since his arrival in the late 1890s, and he noted a dearth of children.[73]

Barley's 1930 Annual Report said nearly all new babies around Su'u in southern 'Are'are died in a whooping-cough outbreak that ravaged the island throughout the year, but how many people were stricken overall was impossible to ascertain because officers and most headmen had minimal contact with the inland communities where most people lived. The next year, Barley estimated, 2.8 percent of Malaitans died in a spate of influenza brought by the Anglican ship *Southern Cross*, which hit people of the north and elders hardest. These are just a few examples of appalling epidemics that continued into the 1930s. Even today, flu outbreaks kill Malaitans of all ages, and I write this having just learned that two close Kwaio friends have died in one, both of them young and strong when I last saw them a few months ago.[74]

For decades Europeans blamed depopulation on what they saw as the inherently decadent, unsanitary, or violent natures of Melanesian cultures, and it was often supposed that degeneration predated white arrival. Nicholas Thomas has detailed the application of this idea in neighboring Fiji, where extensive residence and sanitation rules were imposed in the interest of improving the health of Fijians and checking population decline. He observed that many of the regulations instituted—for house construction, village locations and layouts, pig penning—had no demonstrable link to improved health; rather, they reflected European values and privileged "an orderly and accessible village rather than because their consequences were known to be beneficial." The colonial projects for Fijian relocation and amalgamation that Thomas analyzed were in some ways similar to schemes in parts of the Solomons. Surprisingly, I have found no explicit references from Malaitan officers in the 1930s to Fiji's earlier reports about or efforts to address depopulation, though of course similar worries about subject populations being endangered by culture loss and too-rapid change were also found in other colonies, including in Africa.[75]

Missionaries at times asserted that Islanders were responsible for their own demise, which both downplayed their own destabilizing role—which officers and anthropologists sometimes stressed—and justified their pursuit of radical Christian transformation as Melanesians' only hope. Methodist Rev John Goldie wrote: "The advent of the white man, though a contributing cause, is not the principal cause of this decline, which has been going on for years. Going into a heathen village for the first time, seeing the filthy condition of the people, the wonder is not that they decrease, but that they are not extinct."[76] Bishop Wilson blamed declining numbers in south Malaita on a "refusal of women to bear the burdens of motherhood," something missionaries and others highlighted throughout Melanesia and elsewhere, often greatly exaggerating infanticide. Others portrayed mothers and infants as helpless victims of cruel ancestral birth taboos. Wilson further blamed decline of the Melanesian "child race" on antisocial impacts of native curses and high marriage payments, as well as on the labor trade. But he claimed that diseases brought by ships (like his church's *Southern Cross*) had minimal impact on the "hardy" Melanesian. When missionaries did link depopulation to Europeans, atop their list of culprits were usually the labor trade and the "unsuitable" things it brought, such as firearms, "excessive clothing," and "civilization's vices" more generally. Other Europeans blamed these also.[77]

On Malaita, mission activities could intensify the impact of diseases. Most Christians lived in relatively crowded coastal villages where they cast off many sanitary rules enforced in mountain hamlets because they were also ancestral taboos. For example, a myriad of taboos regulated food and water sharing, while others isolated feces from pigs and people. Scattered, tiny mountain hamlets and the lengthy segregation of groups observing mortuary taboos could impede the spread of illnesses. On the coast, people were more susceptible to malaria and tropical sores and had more contact with outsiders. For example, the SSEM reported this problem in 1921 as mountain Christians descended to the Langalanga Lagoon area: "Too often the site chosen is on the low-lying delta of a river, or even among mangrove swamps. We have tried to get the people to settle on the first line of hills for their own sakes, but they like being near the sea, and have often, in consequence, suffered much in health." The *Southern Cross* regularly collected and disembarked people throughout the islands and was notorious for spreading sickness; Norman Deck of the SSEM wrote with apparent satisfaction that it was known as "the death ship." In some places Christians' greater access to European medicines mitigated these factors. Still, statistics gathered in north Malaita from 1920 to 1922, and Bell's impression through his time, indicated higher mortality rates in Christian than in mountain villages. Bell correctly surmised that many who became Christian were less healthy to begin with—the chronically ill sometimes converted to escape ancestors believed to be causing their sickness, and invalids had an easier life in level coastal villages—and he also credited childbirth taboos that freed new mothers in the mountains from work. Later the imbalance in death rates disappeared.[78] While missionaries often blamed depopulation on perceived manifestations of moral decadence such as escalating brideprices or adultery, government officers more often highlighted secular and logistical factors like the isolation of hamlets, poor sanitation, "excessive feasting," and a breakdown of "custom law"—all said to be both symptoms and causes of malaise and societal decay.

Malaitans, too, worried about drops in their population. They typically, and correctly, cited introduced diseases as the main overt mechanism, though they often blamed alien spirits or angry ancestors for inflicting or failing to protect from them. Some north Malaitans, in particular, in the 1920 and 1930s attributed high disease mortality to sorcerers exploiting the government's forbidding execution of sorcerers while refusing to criminalize their predations.[79]

Here I am most interested in one European theory of depopulation: that it could be explained by "the psychological factor," that is, that Islanders were dying because they had lost interest in life or were otherwise emotionally exhausted because of cultural breakdown following the arrival of Europeans—that they were suffering from "premature civilization."[80] Melanesians, Stephen Roberts wrote in a widely read book, were bewildered without the "rule of custom" that had formerly "regulated every detail of existence" and had lost the will to live. Even after disease came to be recognized as the great cause of Melanesian depopulation, the psychological impact of change, of "modifications and interferences with native custom," was granted causal weight in influential quarters.[81] The mechanisms through which alleged confusion or depression led to higher mortality were generally left vague. Even so, for those following this line, a secret to combating depopulation was cultural stabilization, preservation, and revitalization. "The native, to be saved, must save himself," wrote Roberts. If Europeans charged with natives' welfare were to help them, said former High Commissioner Everard im Thurn, they were duty-bound to familiarize themselves with and protect "the habits, customs, and ideas natural to the Melanesian." We saw earlier in this book that many whites thought Melanesians innately incapable of adaptation and innovation, and this provided a basic premise for the belief that, for the natives, rapid social change could only mean social, psychological, and physical disintegration.[82]

When customs seemed already dead, many whites believed they might still be exhumed from beneath "the veneer of doubtfully genuine European culture which has been imposed." Some key aspects of Melanesian life, such as warfare, were abhorrent and intolerable to any civilized European, but they could be modified, or suitable, innocuous substitutes could be found. For example, competitive games might replace fighting. Some believed the best substitute of all was integration into the capitalist economy. Thus an 1893 commission on Fiji recommended several remedies for native depopulation that included "more steady work," "subversion of the communal system," and "creation of incentives to industry, stimulus to exertion, and motives for thrift." For decades to come, many whites would attribute Melanesian problems and discontents to idle hands.[83]

The Protectorate's resident commissioner, Ashley, was of the school that attributed population decline "not directly to the introduction of disease, but to the destruction of old native culture." When pressing High Commissioner Fletcher in 1930 to allow native courts, Ashley quoted a report by New Guinea Medical Officer Raphael Cilento: "Perhaps psychological causes, due to a consciousness that all that the primitive native held dear is being ignored and swamped by new ideas and customs, which at times leads to a species of melancholia, diminishing the activity of the seminal glands, may have an appreciable effect on population decline."[84] As the 1930s progressed, Malaita's officers, especially Bengough, based projects importantly on such theories, though by then most serious researchers dismissed them as, in Meyer Fortes's words, "mystical," and "pseudo-psychological."[85] Officers by then received some training in the anthropology of the day that analyzed different aspects of cultures as functionally interrelated, and functionalist models were at least implicit in many psychological depopulation theories. On Malaita, the remedies such theories suggested dovetailed nicely with indirect rule strategies and interventions and lent them a scientific and humanitarian cast as being necessary to save Malaitans.[86]

Much government activity on Malaita in the 1930s went forward against this background, and officers defended policies by citing a need to bolster cultures suffering "cultural fatigue." Take Bengough's argument against registration of native marriages: "It is maintained by authorities on population problems that the degree of social integration exhibited by a people is an index of their increase, or conversely of their decrease. A system of exchange of goods, such as that under the marriage customs, is a chief factor of social integration. I feel strongly that in administering a race whose tendency to decline has been so amply demonstrated, we should refrain from interference with any factor which helps to maintain social organization and structure."[87]

Worries about depopulation and the need to revitalize Malaitan cultures did not merely lead to policies of noninterference, but also provided both officers and missionaries with arguments for intervening in people's lives in ways each believed necessary. Ashley used them to advocate native courts, and in 1937, when urging importation of Chinese workers, he hypothesized that the indentured labor system might also be contributing to depopulation. The next year Sandars cited population problems in requesting legal powers to deal with marriage rules of Christian missions that he thought were too strict and an obstruction to matrimony.[88]

Population concerns combined with tenets of indirect rule motivated and justified native administration policies that had a great influence on subsequent Malaitan political ideas. It became government policy and a priority for several officers to approve and bolster "old native custom," as conceptualized by Europeans. Malaitans were told that officers would avoid interference with and shore up custom, "so long as it did not run counter to the dictates of humanity," and would accord them some power to administer it themselves.[89] Especially important in this respect was an ambitious government scheme to counteract depopulation in 'Are'are. It was pursued in the same area from which Maasina Rule emerged, and that movement later carried forward and expanded on most of its projects, in some cases under leaders who took part in the government endeavor.[90]

Malaitan officers had first discussed how to counter depopulation in the south of the island, in Kwaio and especially 'Are'are, in 1930. They believed north Malaitans had, in Barley's words, "the survival spark," and it was even predicted that population there would increase to the point where land shortages might emerge. Based on his 1933 fieldwork in To'abaita, Hogbin too wrote, "I feel the day of Melanesian depopulation is at last drawing to a close," and that the north, at least, was "showing signs of increase." But Barley in the early 1930s calculated that southern populations, who lacked the same "vitality," were in rapid decline and "already well on the road to extinction," and he felt that measures had to be taken to counter this.[91] Readers can better appreciate Barley's concerns if they consider that from 1919–1922 he was in charge of neighboring Makira during a drastic, disease-driven plunge in the population there.

While people across Malaita had clearly suffered greatly from introduced diseases, Barley used questionable methods, both subjective and objective, to determine the extent of population declines in specific areas and then set in motion targeted government interventions. First, he saw radical 'Are'are depopulation in "pathetic evidences in the shape of old gardens and deserted clearings of a one time thriving race." Though this may have indicated population loss or departure in places, he seems not to have realized that abandoned garden and hamlet sites were (and are) ubiquitous in mountain areas, where Malaitans maintained rapidly shifting horticulture and residence patterns. Barley further read declining tax rolls at face value as revealing a 30 percent population drop during the ten years prior to 1933, though he himself complained the tax rolls leading up to 1930 had "degenerated annually into an increasing welter of unconnected names and places, deletions, substitutions, and double entries." The government used its (male only) tax lists to estimate various populations into the 1950s.[92]

Barley in 1931 had gathered statistics through a census that he read to give a population of 45,000 (in 1930 he guessed 70,000, probably using Bell's gross estimate). What most concerned Barley was that the census indicated a stark imbalance in the southern area's sex ratio, which he said revealed a weak population. Ashley—who two years before had reported, based on information from Officer Wilson, that Malaitan men outnumbered women three to one—decided headmen would conduct censuses. Barley reported to Ashley that headmen were given "long rectangular tally sticks, painted at the four top corners to represent the two age-divisions of the male and female population," and that the method was serviceable and accurate. But in this same period Barley was telling Ashley that most headmen rarely or never visited the heavily populated inland areas of their districts, could not even recognize many of the people there, and indeed feared to venture into many places.[93]

Moreover, census zone boundaries were undetermined beyond the coast, and headmen argued over who should count whom. Eight years later, when Sandars sent Cadet Dick Horton into the mountains to collect census data, he told him, "It won't be accurate by a long chalk. . . . Most of it you'll have to do by adding up tallies on a stick—the headmen have to notch sticks in their villages for everyone in the village on a certain day—still, I suppose we'll have to do the bloody thing." Such crude methods yielded distorted data, as did many colonial Melanesian censuses of the day, particularly where, as on Malaita, many men (over 5,000 in 1931, with higher percentages from the south) labored abroad, and where many women avoided contact with Europeans.[94] Vital statistics were far less accurate for Malaita than for most islands, and Lambert was told their collection required "incredible toil." Sandars told Dr Ross Innes in 1937, "No complete register of births, marriages, and deaths is kept on Malaita; certain literate headmen keep registers of births and deaths, and in certain places do it well." But few headmen were literate, most of them in the north. Nonetheless, Ashley maintained an interest and required updates.[95]

In 1934, Bengough, working under Sandars, reported that ethnographic study and a detailed census in west 'Are'are revealed three primary causes of depopulation: courtship practices (*haruna*) through which unmarried men gained local money, a system of prohibitively expensive marriage payments (*toraana*), and an excessive number of *houraa* mortuary feasts that burdened married men while rewarding single men. He suggested these acted together to raise the average marriage age and thereby lower the birthrate. He also thought too many *houraa* feasts diverted people from gardening and left them more susceptible to disease: "People are continually going from Houra to Houra, at which they are inadequately housed in all weathers, which ill assists them to combat disease, and were it not for the fact that they ordinarily wear no clothes they would probably be even more unable to resist. The custom is not a true one, but has been grossly exaggerated by the increased freedom and greater safety of life in Ariari at the present time." Bengough also believed feasting led to "serious starvation" during taro and yam harvests from September to April, which increased the death rate and "induced an apathy into the people." He later imposed rules limiting feasting to certain periods.[96]

I know of no corroborative evidence of starvation in this period, but Bengough was correct that feasting on Malaita had expanded over the decades. As in many parts of Melanesia, the end of fighting and waning of aspects of religious leadership left feast giving as a more important avenue for earning prestige and status. Increases in garden production and the quantities of local and foreign currencies and pigs in circulation were democratizing exchange activities once dominated by senior men, and some enterprising young men converted cash they earned as laborers into local wealth used in feast exchanges, increasing their economic prowess. Over time, feast exchanges even began to open, more slowly, to women.[97]

It is significant that Bengough felt it important to assert that the "custom" of *houraa* feasting he described "was not a true one." He reported that "a number of the young men and a few old men" wanted to revise the *houraa* system, or as he put it, to "rationalize" it.[98] These points were later emphasized, and proposed limitations on both feasting and marriage exchanges were couched in terms of *restoring* "ancient custom" as opposed to meddling with it. Bengough also advocated codifying limits on compensation payments in similar terms.

Government concerns about population and cultural integrity aside, when Resident Commissioner Marchant toured 'Are'are in 1939, local debates over limitations were clearly about political and economic issues, with each side seeking government support for its position: "A certain number asked that the present limitation of period during which these feasts may be held should be lifted, while others, notably the headmen and richer old men considered that the present restriction should remain, in fact they sought to restrict the incidence of houra still further by limiting them to those held on the death of old men and women only." Marchant did not say who the "richer old men" were who favored restrictions, or what younger men thought, or what was at stake for whom, and he probably did not know. In any case, he favored letting 'Are'are find their own solutions.[99]

Though young men of Malaita were gaining more access to wealth and formal exchanges, many sought more independence. This goal clashed with the long-term debt and other relationships entailed in bridewealth finance, and feasting was a part of the same integrated exchange–social debt system. In the past, participation in exchange and other social projects had earned protection and support from one's group and its leaders, and the dependencies and networks of exchange helped keep young men in line—in community. But after more than a decade with no fighting and with growing opportunities for solo economic and other pursuits, community support seemed less vital. To some young men, large marriage debts no longer seemed worth the cost and sacrifice, and they looked more kindly on limiting brideprice and feasting. There were also older men and some headmen who were doing well for themselves and did not want a return to stronger social constraints. Justus Jimmy Ganifiri in the 1940s recalled a conversation with Kwara'ae Headman Tome Siru about Maasina Rule: "He said that he did not like collective but individual effort. I replied that we had been working individually for a long time with the result that we had not enough food or money and there were plenty of people who were sick and starving and had no one to care for them." Ganifiri remarked, "Those outside of the Marching Rule [ie, Maasina Rule] only think about themselves."[100] Though feasts can analytically can be seen as both individual and group endeavors, to Malaitans they are most importantly about community, as Jonathan Fifi'i explained to me in 1988, in criticizing a modern day effort to limit feasts: "Mortuary feasts are what tie us all together. If we gave them up then there would be no kinship. Mortuary feasts are what unites kin. They are what bring together reciprocity. They are what join together the people who look after each other. If there were not mortuary feasts, we would cease to be. If people are not kept together by mortuary feasting, then it will be every man for himself. Who will help us when there are problems?" Malaitan societies had always maintained a fundamental tension between individual and group interests, but mechanisms to balance these had eroded, resulting in a shift toward the former. Even many young people, however, saw this as problematic and, as we shall see, just after the war the balance was to swing radically in the other direction.

Missionaries had for years campaigned against brideprice, sometimes against government wishes; now government and the missions were allied in seeking limitations. However, though the SSEM's Norman Deck tried to pressure officers to enforce his mission's policies, when these incited disputes officers continued to overrule them.[101] Hogbin, noting claims by Deck (Hogbin's rival) that Kwara'ae men could not marry due to brideprice inflation, said he found no evidence of this in To'abaita in 1933. However, elderly Kwaio bachelors have told me that fear of brideprice indebtedness was a primary reason they did not marry before the war. As noted earlier, Sandars thought strict mission rules, too, blocked some marriages.[102]

Bengough's early reports stressed a need for detailed study, and in 1934 he advised against imposing restrictions on formal exchanges until more people's opinions could be ascertained. He cautioned that there might be significant variation in relevant practices even within 'Are'are, and that forced limits would probably fail. As the decade progressed, this advice was forgotten; officers increased the pressure to institute "reforms" and tried to restrict both 'Are'are and Kwaio feasting, with little understanding of relevant practices. In 'Are'are, feasts were limited to September–November, apparently with some local support. In the end, this restriction failed owing to noncompliance, feast congestion during the permitted season, and, ironically, a flu epidemic that killed hundreds of 'Are'are, which some people blamed on ancestral displeasure at the limitations. As for Kwaio, Bengough reported, "There was considerable agreement in principle for placing native custom in this area on a more stable footing, and for reducing the financial liabilities of marriage, but there is a hard core of diehard conservatism in this area, which sees in every variation suggested by either Government or their own headmen an attempt to break down what they consider to be their ancient rights. In actual fact, many of these so-called rights do not exist in ancient custom, but the Kwaio bushman is just as unable to follow a logical argument as are some people in an island much nearer to Great Britain."[103]

A 1938 'Are'are census indicated further decline, and in 1939, partly spurred by this, Bengough initiated a more formal repopulation project there. Its goals far exceeded mere limits on feasting and marriage payments; the stated ambition "was to check the depopulation of Ariari by improving the conditions, social, hygienic, medical and economic, under which the people live, and to attempt to give them a greater interest in life itself." In February 1940, the government opened an "administrative camp" at Haumatana, just inland from Wairokai on the west coast. It was staffed by cadet officers and a native medical practitioner to oversee multiple projects: "Roads were to be made, and the natives encouraged to live in larger, better sited villages. A permanent census record was to be started, and bride prices and the houra feast were to be stabilized if possible. The medical service was to be established in a dispensary at Wairokai, with a traveling Native Medical Practitioner in charge."[104]

Bengough stressed the need to inculcate 'Are'are with a spirit of "communal service" and "cooperative effort." He thought these had always been "conspicuously lacking" there, and by mid-1941 he reported progress in cultivating them.[105] In fact, 'Are'are always had undertaken enormous cooperative projects on their own in the massive group efforts necessary to carry off the very brideprice presentations and feasts that the government now wished to constrain. (A Pijin term for such teamwork is *kambani*—"to combine" or "to company.") The problem for the government had always been 'Are'are disinterest in cooperating on *government* projects, anchored in European conceptions of what a "community" ought to be and do.

The initial Haumatana efforts included construction of an extensive "road" system to integrate east and west 'Are'are. Locally made paths already crisscrossed the region, and most people showed little enthusiasm for making the new ones, but officers hoped the make-work of clearing the trails would itself foster greater community cooperation. More revolutionary was a project to persuade the 'Are'are to drastically change their residential patterns, as described by Bengough: "The old method of life of Ariari people was based upon small family settlements of one or two houses widely scattered through the bush. Such a distribution is obviously not conducive either to successful communal effort or to adequate public health control: nor does it assist the maintenance of public order. It was decided, therefore, that the Ariari people should be encouraged to build villages based on the patrilineal family groups ('lines') into which they are divided.... Concentrated in small villages, the Ariari people will find that companionship comes from living with others, and the old spirit of hostility will begin to disappear."[106]

This idea was not novel; Europeans before had instituted schemes to nucleate villages on Guadalcanal, Choiseul, Santa Isabel, and Makira, as well as in other places in Melanesia, usually justified as improving sanitation and community life but also making populations more visible and accessible to Europeans. As elsewhere, some Solomon Islanders inhabited these government-enjoined villages, with their houses arranged in neat rows, only when officers toured their areas, after which they returned home. On Malaita the strongest impetus to form larger villages had come not from government but from Christian leaders, both black and white. Like previous nucleation schemes, a key motivation behind the 'Are'are project was that people were easier to track and control when grouped into set villages. James Scott has observed that consolidated, permanent settlements allow rulers to "see" subjects better, but he found in a comparative study that the effort to impose settlement on mobile populations "seemed to be a perennial state project—perennial, in part, because it so seldom succeeded."[107] Many Malaitan Christian relocations had proved longer lasting because the people themselves desired them, or, earlier, because hostile mountain people forced them to congregate for protection. However, beyond managerial or defense motives, a growing number of Malaitans, like whites, shared a sensibility that stable villages, replacing scattered and shifting hamlets, were a prerequisite for forming proper Melanesian communities and identities for the future.

The speed with which 'Are'are took up the resettlement plan was remarkable; by mid-1941, close to half of them in the targeted sub-districts (Waisisi, Wairokai, Komunihaka, Tawana'oro, Takataka, and Maro'u) were said to be living in new villages, with most others in the process of building them, and Maanawai and Onepusu expected to follow suit. Officers hoped also to persuade people to abandon shifting horticulture and adopt large fixed farms near the new villages with the help of a "native agricultural instructor," and the staff worked to introduce terracing and new cash crops. Bengough wanted to convince 'Are'are their land would not be exhausted by several years of cropping in the same place. His conceit that he knew much more about gardening on Malaita than did Malaitan gardeners was indicative of the project's overall approach—that district officers could, with patience, educate Malaitans about complex aspects of their own lives in which 'Are'are were already experts but about which officers knew little.[108]

Another facet of the project was that a Malaitan clerk was to conduct a census and record all deaths, births, and marriages. Such data were needed since otherwise the population could not be efficiently monitored, controlled, and taxed, and as we have seen, previous census methods were highly unsatisfactory. Bell had anticipated that a crucial benefit of taxation would be that it would compel all men to register their names with the government (he often had to detain numbers of people until he could determine which one he had come to arrest), and Sandars, though he thought the tax "iniquitous" since most people had no money, said he found collections useful since they brought men to the coast annually for him to see them. But officers were unable to keep good track of identities in this way. For example, beyond the ongoing difficulty in hearing and properly recording native names, many names that men used, particularly with whites, were European nicknames—Tom, Biri, Dio—shared by hundreds of men, and most changed even their indigenous names at least once in their lifetimes; many used more than one. Men with four or more children under age 15 did not have to pay the head tax, so men would borrow others' children to take to tax collections as their own, and officers had no way to check familial authenticity. Ronald Garvey remembered similar problems with men claiming exemption for being over age 60: "A chap would get all his friends round saying they remembered old Jimmy, he was born eighty years ago, this sort of thing. Well, how could we know? If we were in a good mood we'd accept it, if we were in a bad mood, we wouldn't. So when it came to the [tax on] dogs, they'd try the same thing. But there was no exception for dogs of any age." A full census accurate for men, women, and children would be useful indeed.[109]

A loose-leaf record book of "native customs" was started at Haumatana, and Bengough envisioned a full reappraisal and restructuring of 'Are'are culture: "Native custom should be carefully and exhaustively studied by the officer at Wairokai with a view to the eventual elimination of all such features as have an adverse effect on the population, while upholding those which are beneficial." Efforts to limit brideprice and *houraa* feasts—as modern corruptions of custom—remained a key to the undertaking for its duration.[110] Throughout the project the two-edged colonial sword of "custom"—good and bad, genuine and fraudulent—was a tool of choice, always at hand to legitimize and promote, condemn and suppress practices according to whether they suited or hindered government ambitions and sensibilities. Again, it seems from most officers' writings that they applied "custom" sincerely, were blind to the concept's inconsistencies and contradictions, and did not try to manipulate it in any disingenuous way.

For us, the most important aspect of this 'Are'are scheme is the striking similarity between its projects and those of the Maasina Rule movement that emerged later. The scheme's main objectives all became central to the movement: large, permanent, and accessible villages; adoption of new gardening methods and cash cropping; censusing; and the creation of stronger, broader group identities. Further, a paramount Maasina Rule activity was the recording of *kastom* by Malaitan scribes with the goal of selectively adapting or discarding old societal rules and creating new ones, which would help the movement's leaders better guide the populace toward shared goals.

Moreover, Maasina Rule emerged from the same area in 'Are'are where the government repopulation project was centered, and three men central to the project—Harisimae, Hoasihau, and Nono'oohimae—were the key founders of Maasina Rule (and again, all three attended the Fallowes's meeting on Gela). Both Sandars and Roy Davies later credited Hoasihau, the Wairokai district headman, with having started Maasina Rule, while others said Harisimae had. Hoasihau was a key participant in Bengough's 'Are'are efforts from the start, and Officer Michael Forster said he had "displayed great interest and keenness" in them. Martin Clemens—the cadet assigned to oversee Haumatana's initiation and begin a "road" connecting Wairokai to Takataka—told me that it was Hoasihau who first explained to him the destructive effects of excessive brideprice in 'Are'are.[111]

When war came and officers left, the Haumatana camp continued for a time under a government clerk, Timeas Teioli from Abu village near 'Aoke, who Davies said was an able organizer despite his minimal education. But the camp was abandoned early in 1943, officers believed because Teioli and Hoasihau tracked and killed a local murderer and prison escapee. 'Are'are historian John Naitoro was told that the people were unhappy about being pressured to labor without pay on the roads, which as we have seen most Malaitans considered pointless. Everyone returned to their homes, and later in the year Sandars on his first postwar tour found Haumatana in "rack and ruin," with *houraa* again flourishing. He quickly imposed a seasonal ban on feasts—none while yams were in the ground—but the project was put on hold, partly due to lack of resources but also because Sandars thought its design needed serious modification. Also, heated disputes had emerged over who owned the Haumatana land, and the venture's original architect, Bengough, had perished in the war.[112] Thus died the 'Are'are repopulation project, its activities set aside until Sandars might give them his attentions. Or so thought Sandars.

Further Experiments: Councils and Courts

Partly in response to the Fallowes movement, before the war district officers on several islands began to initiate new, unofficial or "experimental" native councils and arbitration courts.[113] Like the repopulation project, Maasina Rule later absorbed these within its own social engineering schemes, and it is important to understand their development and how Malaitans perceived, employed, and at times rejected them. During the 1930s, a few areas had set up unofficial courts, but now there was a shift in government policy. In 1939, Bengough, with an eye to wider changes, initiated two "councils of elders" at Fo'odo and Malu'u, chaired by headmen and staffed where possible by "heads of lines." These councils were to "meet monthly, to discuss local affairs, and wherever possible, to settle disputes in native custom— a matter in which I consider they have far more authority than the District Officer." In 1940, Ashley's replacement Marchant strongly supported experiments in this direction, though he still had no authority from above to establish courts and those that started consequently lacked any legal status. But there were indications from London that their development would be supported.[114]

By 1941, new councils were operating in Lau (at Te), Baelelea, Baegu, and Langalanga, and a single one was charged to "co-ordinate custom etc. for all Kwara'ae" under Headman Tome Siru, whom Bell had appointed from the constabulary in 1925. Council boundaries did not in practice match those of sub-districts but instead followed more linguistic and cultural lines. The plan was that soon these bodies would arbitrate legal cases. Responses to councils in the north were almost wholly positive, and officers thought them popular and successful, though before long council members were reportedly "uneasy at having no legal sanction to back their authority." Bengough met with leaders in other areas to discuss local problems and lay groundwork for similar bodies. Within a year, four convened on Small Malaita, though with limited success due to problems "getting elders to take Councils seriously" and leaders' "indifference." At year's end there were still no official councils in Fataleka, Kwaio, or most of 'Are'are.[115]

Native courts proved more difficult to organize than councils. In 1941 they were still not legal, but most of the councils were arbitrating native custom cases and "proved of great assistance in administration." Most active in this respect was the north Malaita council operating a court under Headman Maekali, which was allowed to hear minor criminal cases and impose penalties up to a £5 fine or a month in jail, and civil disputes of values to £10, with its decisions appealable to district officers. However, "custom law" enjoyed a special, protected status, and no appeals were allowed in the "native customary cases," which predominated. Coupled with these courts was a push to codify and "regularize" custom law, linked to Bengough's ongoing concern to limit brideprices and compensations. The courts were mandated to maintain local language records of disputes that they heard and "rulings in native custom" they made.[116]

Unlike in some African colonies, and especially India, Malaita's officers did little to involve themselves in the nitty-gritty of custom codification and left it to Malaitans. They expected the codes to have minor legal importance, and in any case they lacked the requisite knowledge, time, and resources for such intensive work. Furthermore, there was a reluctance to officially interfere with "native custom," and, unlike India and parts of Africa, there were no classic texts of religious or other rules on which to build new codes.

With no legal sanctions to enforce their "custom" judgments, courts faced a growing problem that some men simply ignored a summons to appear. When such cases were referred to government courts, no means existed there for ordering compensations, and so offended parties were left unhappy. Clearly, if courts were to evolve as hoped they would require official powers, and in early 1941 Marchant instructed all officers to prepare outlines of planned native court procedures for their districts. On 30 April Sandars, acting as resident commissioner, submitted these to High Commissioner Luke, stating in his cover letter: "Establishment of native courts is fundamental to any system of native administration founded on principles generally accepted within the Empire. Moreover, the native peoples of the Protectorate have, for the most part, now reached a state of development where they are seeking some outlet for their political aspirations and there is little doubt that the best means of satisfying such a demand is to permit them to have a greater voice in the settlement of their own affairs."[117]

Bengough did not envision native courts as significantly empowering Malaitans. He made this clear in an outline proposal for their operation that specified government headmen would be in charge, with "elders" acting only in an advisory capacity. He noted, though, that the courts lacked qualified, literate headmen to lead them, and since officers only saw headmen a few times a year there was no way to train them. He therefore proposed starting a school for headmen at 'Aoke, but Marchant rejected the idea.[118]

Bengough regretted he could not allow Malaitans to select their own headmen or magistrates but fell back on an old justification: "I could wish that some form of native leadership existed which we could adapt for our purpose, but unfortunately on Malaita there is nothing of the kind. We cannot rule through chiefs, so we should, I consider, aim at ruling through Councils of Elders and Native Magistrates." He wanted to empower councils in each area to enforce settlement of "offenses against native custom which carry a penalty of monetary compensation," without any reference to the native courts. Thus, the only real authority Bengough intended to grant Malaitans who were not government servants was over matters of "native custom," which in practice they had already been allowed in the past. A key point here is that these and subsequent court and council policies generated "custom" as a category of practices—the only such category—over which Malaitans would be allowed full legal control, at least in the abstract.[119]

In early December 1942, with the war ongoing, Marchant sent officers copies of the Native Courts Regulation, approved by the secretary of state to the colonies, and modeled largely on past ordinances of the Gilbert and Ellice Colony, Fiji, and especially Tanganyika. This regulation finally legalized native courts and made headmen their presidents. Marchant ordered an end to all codification, however, citing the fear that it "stifled evolution." He emphasized that, unlike councils, the courts were not empowered to make new rules but only to administer the law and established native custom. Courts were to be "constituted in accordance with the native law or customs of the area," and their powers were limited to administration of "the native law and custom prevailing in the area of the jurisdiction." The regulation contained elements important for understanding later events: First, it said, "Nothing in this section contained shall be deemed to prohibit any person from adjudication as an arbitrator upon any civil matter in dispute when the parties have agreed to submit the dispute to his decision." This preserved community leaders' right to hear and judge civil disputes outside government-sanctioned courts. Further, "For offenses against native law or custom a native court may, subject to the provisions of this Ordinance, impose a fine or may order imprisonment or both...or may inflict any punishment authorized by native law or custom, provided that such punishment is not repugnant to natural justice and humanity." Courts were specifically allowed to order compensation settlements. When the war moved off to the Western Solomons, officers Bengough, Sandars, and Forster would work in south Malaita to draw 'Are'are *araha,* or chiefly leaders, into this system on a more organized basis.[120]

Also about this time Hogbin visited To'abaita. While in 1933 there had been dissatisfaction with the courts, he wrote: "Signs of a change were apparent on my return a decade later...although local government had then been in operation for only three and a half years. The councils and courts were still regarded as somewhat strange—these natives had had no corresponding organization which the Administration could adapt—but there was a growing realization that the rules of law are the natural outcome of social life."[121] Hogbin's optimistic assessment missed the essence of what was happening on Malaita. For many Malaitans, the government's stuttering attempts to erect a semblance of a native administration through the 1930s to the beginning of the war had been inadequate and too slow.

Colonial law and courts had become key symbols of discontent throughout the island, sometimes evoked to stand for all grievances against the colonial system. These grievances would soon come to the fore in organized fashion with the rise of Maasina Rule. A paramount purpose of this movement was to take up what the government had so tentatively started, and to transform the councils and courts into serious political and legal institutions run by and for Malaitans. The key event that energized Malaitans to act on their dissatisfactions with the government system and their aspirations for more self-rule was World War II, to which we now turn.

Chapter 4
The Wartime Opening

The Malaitan War Experience

World War II brought little actual fighting to Malaita but had profound social repercussions there.[1] As in the past, Malaitans were summoned to work on other islands, this time in the Solomon Islands Labour Corps (SILC) assisting US and allied forces on Guadalcanal and Gela, and later in the Western Solomons, under the command of district officers and plantation managers. Malaitans dominated the corps early on—in October 1943 over 2,000 Malaitans made up 85 percent of recruits—and for the war overall they made up more than half its members. Most were young, some under 16 years old. About 800 more Islanders, including many Malaitans, were with the Solomon Islands Defence Force. The wartime experiences of these men were to change Malaitans' worldviews and political aspirations forever. From among them arose leaders of political actions in years to come, men like Nono'oohimae, Nori, Ga'a, Sau, Fifi'i, and Irofiala. As elsewhere across the southwest Pacific, the war proved a demoralizing setback for those Europeans dedicated to tightly controlling Melanesians, and their attempts at war's end to reinstate the old social order were destined to fail.[2]

My focus in this chapter is the war's impact on the political ideas and actions of Malaitans and other Solomon Islanders rather than its military aspects.[3] In brief, the Japanese bombed the Tulagi area beginning in January 1942, took the town in early May, and in June began occupying Guadalcanal. By early February 1942, most white residents had been evacuated from the Solomons, although a handful of government officers and a few others bravely stayed to coordinate the Defence Force. Some worked with Islanders, many of them policemen, as guerilla fighters and "coastwatchers," using tele-radios to report on Japanese movements while on the run. Resident Commissioner William Marchant, with a radio operator and some constabulary, shifted his headquarters to Fulisango inland from 'Aoke until December, collecting and transmitting coded coastwatcher reports to Port Vila in the New Hebrides. Defence Force Captain Charles Bengough remained at 'Aoke with a police squad. Some missionaries also stayed on Malaita and other islands.[4]

Islanders closely noted the last panicked departure in February, as the final steamer slipped away from Tulagi jammed with frightened Europeans, their luggage abandoned on the wharves. Bishop Walter Baddeley lamented, "Many white men, I'm afraid, did not maintain 'the white man's prestige.'" Martin Clemens recalled the "appalling display of cowardice and irresponsibility" among Europeans: "Hundreds of laborers were left on the plantations to fend for themselves, unpaid, with only a few weeks rations. Most were Malaita men; they were confused and angry and had no means of returning home." A flotilla of government, missionary, and native-owned ships later collected some 3,000 workers and took them back to their islands.[5] In early August 1942, a US force invaded Guadalcanal, and serious combat continued for about six months before moving off to the west. Only dimly if at all aware of British campaigns on European and other fronts, most Malaitans perceived in these events British weakness and American strength: the former fled while the latter brought the fight to the Japanese.

During the evacuation and early fighting, widespread pillaging broke out, particularly among workers deserted by their employers. Cadet Clemens told of "over 1,000 smashing and looting," and wrote in his Guadalcanal diary, "There is much lawlessness afoot, and headmen finding it difficult to assert their influence"; he also reported "quite a lot of anarchy on the Weather Coast." Cyril Belshaw later said there was looting "on a grand scale" and hinted at political overtones to the mayhem in "the glee with which law books were burned" at Tulagi. Officer Donald Kennedy reported what Marchant called "wanton destruction" and ransacking of residences and the government store, and he advised Marchant of houses being built on Gela for storing stolen goods. Kennedy gave headmen and native courts powers to "deal drastically with defaulters" and offered special "tribal police" a reward of 5 percent of any loot produced in native court. Norman Deck, too, bemoaned a "wave of stealing that has spread through the group," but he was one of the few to mention that Europeans initiated the looting.[6]

Several hundred Guadalcanal people were employed by US forces early on, but in November 1942 they were dismissed after presenting written demands for work conditions and pay that were considered "most extravagant." It was decided to ship in Malaitans to replace them, on one-year stints. On 3 December, at the request of US Marine Corps Colonel Hunt, Bengough recruited the first 175 Malaitans, and by the following November, 2,740 Islanders had signed on. In 1942, the Americans pressed for 5,000 workers, but the government declined their request that labor be made compulsory. They did so because, first, they had insufficient records on which to base a conscription law, and second, if people resisted— and Ian Hogbin, now a government adviser, assured Marchant that they would—enforcement would expend more manpower than it gained. Further, resulting anger might lead to dissolution of the Labour Corps, and the government might lose face and perhaps control. So enlistment remained voluntary, although some headmen were heavily pressured to meet quotas.[7]

Various passages around Malaita initially supplied one or more "sections" of 25 men each, headed by a local sergeant, for example, 4 sections from east Kwaio, 2 from 'Are'are, and 6 from Kwara'ae. As during the nineteenth-century labor trade, subsequent SILC recruits enlisted after hearing returnees' stories of their experiences and seeing them distribute goods they had gotten. Ansene Wa'ii'a of Maka in west 'Are'are recalled his decision to join the Labour Corps in 1943: "After a year some of the men who went in the first group came home. Waopu and Houma'i, Sihiu, brought boxes of goods. I was watching them as they divided tobacco, tinned meat, clothes, matches, axes, and knives. Not one of them offered me a thing. This made me think and I had a strong desire to go on the next ship that came to take labor." Wa'ii'a had wanted to go in the first group, but found, "When they reached the number of men they wanted, they stopped calling. I was far behind in the line so I did not go."[8]

Most of the initial recruits, now recalled as the *fasimoorin* (first marines), had only vague ideas about what they were volunteering for, and many were apprehensive; rumors and anxieties about a coming war had been building for years, even before the Defence Force began to be organized in 1939.[9] Throughout non-Christian areas, pigs were now sacrificed in ancestral shrines to ask protection for the recruits and for Malaita itself (some feared Japanese would take their land). Such calls for ancestral help upset some Christians, and Wa'ii'a recounted Malaitan Sergeant Ilala lecturing their 'Are'are SILC section on arrival at Guadalcanal: "You people will not invoke your ancestors or worship them. Those who came here before did that and were killed by the bombs and their hands or legs were blown off. These [fox]holes they were hiding in had been blessed by the Bishop [Baddeley]." But many, including some Christians, prayed in foxholes to their ancestors nonetheless or asked non-Christian comrades to do so on their behalf, reasoning that ancestors knew more about warfare than God did. Some Melanesians later claimed that Americans bought local fighting magics for protection.[10]

Nothing could have prepared Islanders for what they found when they arrived on Gela and especially on Guadalcanal. They were set to constructing camps, unloading masses of cargo, building roads and an airfield, carrying supplies and ammunition, planting gardens, and burying the dead. Working from an inland camp on Guadalcanal's Tenaru river, just east of present-day Honiara, some were shelled by the Japanese, after which they asked to be returned to beach areas. In mid-December a Japanese plane bombed the same camp, and some sergeants requested that their sections be taken back to Malaita. Officers were sure this would blow over when they came "to see for themselves what little real danger exists," but on 26 January fears became reality when another bombing killed 11 laborers and wounded 9. This temporarily halted SILC recruiting, which by then had engaged 1,450 men—1,100 to Guadalcanal, 350 to Tulagi.[11]

This bombing catalyzed unhappiness among the corps and sparked a two-week mass walkout.[12] District Officer and Defence Force Lieutenant Lennox Barrow described the SILC "stampede" the next morning: "We met them on our way back from the range walking in an endless stream down the coast to the east piled high with junk of every description picked up from the Americans." Bishop Baddeley was brought in to ask men to pray together and return to work, and Norman Deck arrived to tell them to work on Sundays. Marchant sent over some senior Malaitan men, writing in his diary, "They want to tell the young men what they think of them."[13]

Eventually the men were convinced to return to work, but the bombing was only one source of their discontent, and resentments grew and more strikes followed. Among early demands were that they be given a raise to 3 shillings per day, that late wages be paid (a cash shipment had been delayed), that they receive better rations, that they be issued clothing, and that Sundays be holidays. According to Fifi'i, they also insisted they be allowed more freedom to fraternize with Americans. Jason Alaikona of Bokolo, To'abaita, a former policeman, in the defence force, and later a Maasina Rule and then Federal Council movement leader, recalled: "Two British men, named Mr. Clemens and Mr. Bengough,...wanted to pay us £1, or $2.00 a month. But some in my section, they didn't want £1, or $3.00, or $2.00, and asked to be taken back home. They did not want to fight for $2.00 a month because they thought their lives were worth more than that, [and they said], 'We don't think this fight has come here for we natives to fight; it belongs to you white people.'" Adequacy of food and tobacco rations had always been for laborers a crucial measure of a plantation employer's competence, and early SILC provisions were very poor. Men lived in dilapidated tents, and one camp was built on a Japanese burial site. Some Malaitans complained loudly when ordered to dig or clean latrines or to handle corpses unceremoniously, both religiously forbidden for many.[14]

Fifi'i told me in 1988 that he and other Kwaio, including sergeants Iriamae, John Te'efu, and 'Ui'aniaria (all three former policemen from Uru), were strike leaders. Government officers (and Fifi'i to a lesser extent) identified SILC Sergeant Major Jared Ramo'ifaka of Langalanga as a behind-the-scenes instigator, followed by sergeants Ata, Gwanoi, and Arnon Ngwadili. Ramo'ifaka was for years a trusted "boss boy" for Burns Philp, and Bengough had handpicked him to be in charge of Labour Corps workers. These men were organizers and were arrested, but the actions overall were loosely organized wildcat strikes with many leaders in the different sections, making them all the more difficult to repress. In response, "American overseers" were attached to the SILC in order, Marchant telegrammed the high commissioner, to "bring pressure on labourers." Fifi'i told of US officers gently pressing them to resume work, but he and others believed they were placed in the SILC camps because the Malaitans had demanded it as a condition for returning to their jobs—they wanted to work under American, not colonial officers. In the end, the fact that officers turned to Americans to help them control the Labour Corps amounted to an admission that they had lost authority. Charles Widdy, the SILC commander, complained to Marchant that US officers did not bother to even consult him when deploying laborers.[15]

Concerns to enforce strict discipline had dominated composition of the "Military Unit Regulation" of 1942 that established the corps—the government from the start had foreseen and feared losing its hold over Islanders in a volatile wartime setting. By the following February, Widdy reported to Marchant, "There is trouble throughout the Labour Corps," but now he recommended *against* strict enforcement of discipline, which might provoke "further trouble and defiance." Marchant recognized that more than wages was at issue and wrote enigmatically to Widdy, "They may have some other grouse at the back of their minds which they are reluctant to mention." But he clearly did not comprehend the degree to which government control was fading. While the formal launching of Maasina Rule as a movement remained more than a year away, it started here with the loosely organized but open defiance in the SILC strikes, and with the emerging Malaitan idea that Americans might act as their allies against the colonial government.[16]

Government officers quickly attributed discontents to American influences and thereby avoided confronting problems of or complaints about the colonial system of black-white relations. Still, there was a degree of validity to their suspicions, in that some Americans openly counseled Islanders to rebel and shared their own anti-British sentiments. ("You should throw them out like we Americans did.") Many soldiers would have been union veterans of the ongoing labor battles back home, and in some of them the Melanesian strikers stirred unexpected feelings of camaraderie. Arnon Ngwadili of west Kwara'ae remembered Americans asking them, "Why is it that you all came and joined the war and are doing the same kind of work that we are doing, but your government is not paying you well?" I have heard many similar stories. But beyond American instigation, what Islanders were seeing on their own was enough to raise their expectations and encourage them to demand change.[17]

Decades later, SILC veterans vividly described their shock on arrival at Guadalcanal. The ships, thousands of troops, airplanes, and weaponry initially frightened many, while the sheer scale of organization amazed all. Most accounts note the abundance of material goods and Islanders' easy access to them. US soldiers casually gave men what seemed extravagant gifts—military clothing, tools, and sometimes even guns. Ma'aanamae of Kwaio, a former plantation carpenter, and his friend Gwauni were kept busy building false-bottom boxes in which men smuggled their guns back to Malaita, a trick passed down from nineteenth-century laborers. Belshaw later wrote, "Every one of the 6,000 people of Gela...acquired a stretcher bed and mosquito net in this period. In the Russell Islands...so I am told, the villagers acquired their own telephones and electric lighting system, and rebuilt their houses entirely of timber."[18] The end of significant fighting on Guadalcanal in early 1943 brought a surge of wealth still more impressive. On Guadalcanal, between 1942 and early 1944 US construction battalions erected a huge transit camp to push soldiers and supplies north. They laid 217 kilometers of roads to connect camps and built airfields, fuel depots, and cemeteries. Islanders contributed their labor and their skills in working with local building materials. Farms of over 800 hectares were planted to supply troops with vegetables, which Islanders, supervised by US Army officers, weeded, transplanted, and harvested.[19]

Many Malaitans now took stock of their prewar poverty and blamed it on British selfishness. Americans amplified resentment by paying higher wages. While most SILC recruits received £1 per month, this was greatly supplemented by salvaging and American gifts. Men working for Americans as casual labor could earn £15 or more per month doing cooking, laundry, and odd jobs and selling art and curios. Marine Corps Lieutenant Colonel

FIGURE 4.1. Islanders bartering local products with American Seabees off Gela, September 1943. (US Government unnumbered photo, Naval Construction Battalion Center, Port Hueneme, California, photographer unknown.)

Alex Sharpe was on Guadalcanal in 1944 and told me in a 1988 letter of buying carvings: "I got a jeep and drove up in the hills looking for a native village and found one. The price of the clubs was US$5.00 each and he had change for a twenty... his hut had a sliding door." Malaitans today believe Americans gave the government money to pay higher wages but that it diverted the lion's share for such purposes as buying ships after the war. In 1992, I attended a Honiara meeting of SILC veterans, mostly Malaitans, on the 50th anniversary of the marines' landing, and listened to speaker after speaker demand the government seek British repayment of American wages still owed. The administration did in fact insist on lower wages with an eye to checking postwar expectations and American influence.[20]

Given the high moral, social, and prestige value of food exchange in their societies, Solomon Islanders were enormously impressed by American food gifts. More important still was some soldiers' willingness to share meals with them, something taboo among most whites before the war. This was the first thing many Malaitan veterans highlighted years later when telling about the soldiers. Fifi'i remembered: "They asked us to come inside their tents... and when we were inside, we could sit on their beds. They gave us their glasses so we could drink out of them. They gave us plates and we ate with their own spoons. That was the first we had seen of that kind of thing. We talked about it like this: 'Those people like the British and the whites before, it was terrible because they were not kind to us! These people here are very kind. We can all sit on one bed, and we all eat together.'" Isaac Gafu of Kwara'ae described a fatalism among soldiers that diluted racial and cultural boundaries: "When the boxes would break open and food would fall out all over the place we wouldn't take any because we were afraid as we never stole before. But the Americans said, 'You all eat these things. This is our food. Let's all eat while we are still alive.'" Government officers later cited Islanders' appreciation of the novel American cuisine to rebut an old company excuse for poor plantation rations: that laborers would reject new foods.[21]

In these and other ways, some Americans shared with Malaitans a black-white camaraderie hitherto forbidden. To Malaitans, that there were white people not obviously concerned with protecting a superior status was a profound revelation. Said Gafu, "We all stayed together as if we were of one race. They were very loving toward us.... They did not fight with us. They were really good friends. We all ate together." Ariel Sisili, in a 1949 political manifesto formally presented to the government, described the perceived contrast with characteristic Malaitan flair (this very bright man's poor grammar speaks to the lack of education available to Malaitans, addressed later in this chapter):

Since the white people and B. P. Govt arrived and settled in the S.I. we've the native realized and have noticed is a great distinction between them and us:

They have never shown any sign of real friendship, Love, nor sympathy, therefore it is quite obvious that there will never be any equality between them and our coloured race....

At last a new dawn breaks upon the Sol. Is. The U.S.A. Navy Army Air Force arrives and bravely plunges into war against the advancing enemy eventually beat, and drives them back from the ground. Which as a result has freed us from our fears, our hearts burst forth every day, and gratitude in excess from men women and children both young and old great and small to God and to that Country who with grace and mercy of God, and their hearts of sympathy, guided by them to safety us poor and helpless people of these islands. Ever before they came here true love we've never known or even had we any dealings one with the other. The Americans and us were quite strangers one to another, we even have never worked for these in the past but we can about three years American was in the Sol Is. during the war. We never know nor ever did we realized before they came here the true love and friendship mentioned in the bible and ignorant peoples to become better as one should say, that all men were created equal and that man is a trinity consisting of both spirit soul and body and that from common sense man can distinguish without being educated what was true right and not right fair and not fair.[22]

Anthropologist Kenneth Read suggested Melanesians could readily accept that there were different sorts of white people because their own societies were made up of people who looked alike but were in many ways dissimilar. But after the impressive wealth, generosity, and intimacy of these white Americans came a more shocking encounter: with black Americans. Islanders had heard of them; some had even learned songs about them from missionaries, as one veteran later demonstrated with a rendition of "Swanee River." Kwalafaneiʻa of Kwaio told Keesing in 1962 that before the war they were told that *all* Americans were black, "*olsem yumi*" (just like us), and this belief existed elsewhere on Malaita. When black troops of the 93rd Army Infantry Division began to arrive on Guadalcanal in early 1944, they seemed to many in the Labour Corps to have overcome the inequalities they themselves suffered. This was far from true, of course—the US military was not even fully integrated until the 1950s, and the marines would admit no blacks until President Franklin Roosevelt ordered them to in 1942. Most black soldiers in the Solomons were given labor or security duties.[23]

Racism would have been common among US troops of the time, but on many Malaitans it made little impression. Racism is fundamentally about fear and boundary maintenance, and while the Protectorate's white residents saw uncontrolled Islanders as dangerous, for Americans they presented little threat to their jobs or status in the way black soldiers might. As to segregation, some Malaitans thought black Americans were a separate nationality with their own country in the southern United States. As SILC veteran Sulafanamae explained in 1980: "The British had their own sections, as did Australians, Fijians, and white Americans, and so did the black Americans." Misconstrued in this way, segregation could raise the status of black troops. Islanders misinterpreted other American expressions of racial bigotry, and into the early 1980s some thought *niga* an acceptable term for black Americans. Others did recognize racism among some Americans, and some Islanders resented it when Americans made fun of them. Some recalled for me confrontations between black and white soldiers. And yet most saw American racism to be different from the ordered, colonial racial discrimination they knew so well. Tom Titiuru of Ulawa told me in 1987 that one thing that struck Islanders was how black soldiers were quick to stand up for themselves and fought back when insulted: "The MPs had to keep the blacks and whites separate because the Negros, even though they were black like we Melanesians, they were different—they had a very tough, aggressive way of thinking.... It was taboo to call them *niga* because they would shoot you very quick. They called them 'colored boys.'" Malaitans were impressed that these "Black Joes" appeared to wear the same uniforms and have the same rations, equipment, and freedom of movement as white soldiers. Fifi'i recalled working with them: "We saw the black soldiers there, and they all wore shirts, and they wore trousers. And their job was to work just like the white soldiers.... and we saw them and they were better than we black people here in the Solomons... they were really fine people! Any kind of thing that the whites did, they could do it too. They knew how to do carpentry, and they knew how to write. And they were the people who we worked together with." Some Malaitans read prestige into the relegation of blacks to labor battalions, or carpentry or cargo work, since, they reasoned (or perhaps rationalized), such work required more skill than did fighting.[24]

Some told me of fearing black soldiers and socializing more with whites, while others strongly denied this and recalled working with blacks as close friends. Edgar Vaea, a scout and carrier from Temotu Province, later recounted, "We liked the black Americans, but sometimes we were afraid of them, because they were bigger and taller than us from the Solomons.... They told us, 'If you go to school, you can be like us, and do the jobs we do.'" Titiuru said they told him and others, "You are low down and not good, and you have to raise yourselves up. We had to struggle, and even though some of us died, you can see that now we are doing well." Fifi'i, later east Kwaio's Maasina Rule leader, recounted long talks with one black American overseer, a Sergeant Jackson, as inspirational for that movement.[25]

Whether individual Islanders fully recognized or overlooked American racism, or disregarded it as enigmatic, variable, or relatively mild, few highlighted it in later war accounts or in stories they took back to Malaita. Generic oral histories of the war have often obscured subtleties and ranges of interactions with foreigners in service of narrative or political themes.

Thus colonial officers may be presented as uniformly mean in contrast to always-magnanimous Americans. Japanese, too, are stereotyped; Islanders sometimes tell of deceiving them by exploiting crude images that some Japanese held about "primitive natives."[26] Relative to broad-brush depictions of the war, personal accounts of specific events tend to distort less and distinguish individuals and their characters, be they colonials or Americans. Publicly constructed histories and personal reminiscences influence each other in complex ways. For one, there is a "survivor effect" in that, as witnesses to an event die away, the accounts of those who remain become more influential in their community's ongoing construction of its historical memory. This has occurred in oral histories of the war.

The 15 colonial officers managing the Labour Corps observed Islander-American amity. Several were former plantation managers selected for their experience overseeing native labor, and Malaitans already despised some of them, most notably SILC Commander Widdy, infamous as "Mista Wiri" for his bullying. These and more benign officers alike recognized in the wartime scene a dire threat to white authority. The prewar code of white-black relations, with its directive "familiarity is disastrous to one's prestige," was being swept aside before their eyes, and they acted to reassert control.[27]

In early 1943, US Major General Alexander Patch was influenced to write a memorandum on "Native Labour" to put a stop to "certain practices on the part of military personnel prejudicial to the full utilization of native labor and the control of natives by the British authorities." In addition to "over-payment for services or commodities" and "employment of casual labour without adequate supervision or control," he ordered soldiers to cease "permitting casual natives to wander through camps and military areas and encouraging this latter bad practice by feeding or making gifts to these casual natives." The memorandum upended reality and warned, "By the native's own standards, over-payment and the making of gifts is interpreted as weakness on the part of the giver." He attached a "schedule of prices for native labour and commodities" including food and curios, and daily wages were not to exceed 1 shilling.[28]

US troops were issued a booklet written by one or more colonial officers for New Guinea and titled *You and the Native*, which advised, "The native is nearly, if not quite, as good a man as you are," but warned, "Always…maintain your position or pose of superiority, even if you sometimes have doubts about it. It is flattering to the vanity and in the circumstances must pay us well. As for the native, he will not resent it, because he has brought it about himself and he is used to it.…Always, without overdoing it, be the master." For another counter-weapon, Ian Hogbin considered it "of profound importance" that British journals such as *Illustrated London News* be imported and circulated to counter *Life Magazine* and the other American periodicals to which Solomon Islanders were being exposed that glorified the American war effort.[29]

This situation is interesting viewed within a larger context. The US military had faced similar threats to its own racial status quo during World War I, when General John Pershing issued to the French a 1918 directive similar to Patch's, regarding his black troops: "We must prevent the rise of any pronounced degree of intimacy between French officers and black officers....Make a point of keeping the native cantonment population from 'spoiling' the Negroes." A popular American saying after that war was, "How do you keep them down on the farm after they've seen Paris?" Now, while Protectorate officers fretted over Americans spoiling Solomon Islanders, white American officers and many enlisted men stationed in Britain, along with the British government, worried over British civilians socializing with, and especially British women dating, black American troops, and how this would raise the latter's postwar expectations back in the States and influence Britain's nonwhite populations.[30]

Just as French and British people widely ignored directives to discriminate, so too did many Americans in the Solomons. Hogbin said "officers of the military Administration were so few and the soldiers so numerous" that rules were unenforceable. SILC officers lectured Islanders not to eat or fraternize with Americans, and eventually these activities were made illegal, but such efforts were futile. Some Islanders went so far as to don uniforms to impersonate black soldiers to sneak into the service clubs, movies, or PXs, which the US War Department in early 1943 ordered desegregated (although the American Red Cross clubs and canteens remained segregated, as did their blood supply). Fifi'i described the strangeness: "During the day we lived in one world [working under Americans], and at night and in the morning, in our Labour Corps Camps, we lived in a different world where our officers tried to treat us as if we were plantation labourers."[31]

There were other indignities. In 1942, SILC men were told not to wear shirts, or trousers instead of wrap-around *kabilato* cloths, and violators were threatened with a week in jail. Fifi'i remembered carrying his sergeant's stripes around in his hand because he had no sleeve to pin them to and he found instructions to tie them to his bare arm humiliating. Those who earned medals had to hang them from their necks. After the war Titiuru visited New Zealand, and he recalled to me the grim irony of seeing dogs there wearing "nice coats" while SILC men had been restricted to *kabilato*: "I thought, 'those dogs have a higher status than I.'"[32]

Colonial officers took more drastic steps to reassert their authority. In the SILC camps men amassed items given them by Americans or salvaged from camps as troops left for other islands. While they were away at work, officers with police repeatedly ransacked their tents and seized clothing and equipment or formally burned their goods in a heap in front of them when they returned in the evening. Some of this property they had received not as gifts but as payment for working for Americans, but officers labeled their property "loot," lumping it with goods stolen during the evacuation.

More items were taken when recruits returning home had their boxes searched and plundered. Some men began asking Americans to write notes with gifts or payments, to produce if they were accused of theft. On Gela in August 1945, SILC Lieutenant R Hosie and Captain "Viv" Hodgess (owner of a Guadalcanal plantation) carried out heavy-handed property confiscation, in which US officers refused to participate. This led workers to down tools, and in an ensuing confrontation Hosie and Hodgess were beaten.[33]

Such shortsighted bullying inflamed resentments, and even decades later Malaitans evoked these events to highlight what they saw as British desires to keep them poor and powerless and to selfishly prevent their partaking of the wealth Americans seemed so willing to share. Confiscations made subsequent SILC recruitment more difficult, and William Davenport believed that Santa Cruz people did not take up Maasina Rule partly because their Labour Corps men had been allowed to return home with all of their collected goods. Judith Bennett suggested that the planter-officers were worried that men taking goods home might hamper getting laborers in the future. Gülbün Çoker O'Connor noted that insult was added to injury when after the war Solomon Islanders "saw European residents making small fortunes on surplus and salvage materials left behind and, what is more, employing natives to do the salvaging." Americans and others destroyed much surplus, often in highly irresponsible ways. Even in places like the Western Solomons where fighting had wrecked gardens and villages, men who had risked their lives fighting the Japanese watched as badly needed food, goods, and building materials, forbidden to them, were burned or buried.[34]

American political influence went beyond simple kindness. Again, some US soldiers openly incited Malaitans to rebel. This was sometimes spontaneous; veterans fondly narrated to me episodes of Americans castigating SILC officers with streams of obscenities for ordering Islanders about. They particularly remember Bengough's confrontations with Americans when he tried to segregate them from Solomon Islanders, and especially in mid-1943 when he accused some of giving Malaitans guns: "They were shouting at each other," remembered Molaina'o, "and the American said we might need the guns to fight the Japanese if the war went badly. Later Bengough left and said he would be back in two weeks, but he never returned and we heard that he died. We figured the Americans had killed him and blamed it on the Japanese." Although Bengough in fact died when the Japanese shot down a plane in which he was a passenger, the supposition indicates the degree of antagonism that Islanders sensed between some Americans and Protectorate officers.[35]

Other Americans spent long hours talking with Malaitans about their low status. In 1987 Fifi'i told me of weekly Sunday meetings where he and others, including future Maasina Rule leaders Nori and Nono'oohimae, were "taught" by American friends, who advised them to stand up for themselves, put forward leaders, strike, collect their own taxes, and make demands on the British or even eject them. "The way the government is," they were told, "if you just sit and do nothing, if they see that you are weak, they'll just look at you as if you were one of their knives, or one of their axes." Dehumanizing images of Islanders used as tools or treated like dogs would become a mainstay of Maasina Rule oratory. Waʻiiʻa worked with Nori and Nonoʻoohimae at "Matanikoa No. 3" on Guadalcanal and recalled long hours conversing with an American named "Mr. Gemo," who told them: "Your villages are not in good health, you are sleeping with pigs and dogs.... We were like you people [ie, before US independence]; whatever development we wanted to do the government would put us in prison. But we did not give up.... If we Americans had come here first, your country would be well off these days, your towns would be like ours today." Some soldiers told Islanders that the United States might retain its new island bases after the war.[36]

Most of these Americans were of low rank, and many Europeans attributed their criticisms of the colonial system to their being bounders, or ignorant, illiterate hillbillies; as missionary Charles Fox put it, they "naively imagined that if you gave a race of head-hunters immediate independence they would at once become a good and democratic people." Belshaw, however, concluded "from personal experience" that the American influence was part of a conspiracy by officers hoping to "prepare the way" for military control after the war. In actual fact, the US Command tried to stop troops from fraternizing with locals. This mostly failed on Guadalcanal and Gela, but later camps elsewhere were fenced, and several American veterans told me these kept them from meeting any Islanders. The US Command also supplied BSIP authorities with intelligence on Islanders' political contacts with Americans.[37]

Previously, few Malaitans had ever been allowed to approach whites casually, ask them personal questions, or investigate what they were really like. Many took advantage of this novel familiarity to become ethnographers, interviewing American informants about their beliefs, homes, and lives, and many stereotypes about whites were exploded. Non-Christians took heart in finding that many Americans made no pretension of religiosity, while both Catholics and Protestants were pleased to meet Americans with like affiliations—in some churches, US soldiers were the first whites ever to participate in services. Garrett notes that soldiers socialized across denominations in ways uncommon on Malaita.[38]

The net result of the American presence was a general undermining of the prewar racial status quo; the average soldier did not know about it and many were unconcerned with maintaining it, and this doomed attempts by SILC officers to sustain it. In many ways, then, for Malaitans among the troops, and those who heard their stories back home, Americans suggested new possibilities, which were widely discussed in meetings held to plan for action after the war.

We Must Be Willing to Die for the Red Cross

After the strikes, the first organized resistance activity to emerge from the war formed around collections of funds to present to the American Red Cross. This interests us as a nascent form of more effective political actions soon to follow. Islanders had already heard of the Red Cross. In 1917, Santa Isabel people "donated" over £200 to the war effort, which was given to the British Red Cross, and William Bell and other officers were pressured to collect Red Cross donations during that war. Whether Isabel donations were voluntary I do not know, but Acting Resident Commissioner Frederick Barnett the year before commanded Shortland Islanders to contribute. The International Red Cross was only established in the Solomons in 1951, but in 1939 European women there had formed a branch, which soon received nearly 300 donations from a north Malaita collection organized by headmen Maekali and Ba'etalua.[39]

Beginning in early 1943, former headman Oliver Alogobu of Gela and George Kabini of Kwarade in Lau separately gathered "Red Cross donations" from SILC members on Gela and Savo. Kabini, a former constable and a survivor of the 1927 attack on Bell's party, had a Gela wife and lived in the east of that island by the Sandfly Passage. Riufaa of Kwaio told me in 1996 that about this time he and other Malaitans made similar collections on Gela, giving each contributor a receipt. The government had tangled with Alogobu before: Sandars had dismissed him as Big Gela's headman, for adultery. Hogbin and Malaitan Sergeant Major Steven Sipolo investigated the Red Cross matter for the government, and Hogbin reported that Alogobu had been "the popular choice for the office and had an immense following," and that locals told him that but for the dismissal "there would have been no thought of approaching the Americans." Hogbin recommended that Alogobu be either reappointed or banished to another island to stifle his activities. Around this time Islanders gave food, money, and curios to US officers at Tulagi, and Hogbin told the new resident commissioner, Owen Noel, that these were meant as "evidence of goodwill" or as a "bribe," and were part of a general movement, the thrust of which he said was: "We don't want the government back at Tulagi," and "The Americans must stay." This was more than crude bribery; people wanted to institute an exchange relationship with Americans, one that would indeed entail their replacing the British. Hogbin suspected, rightly, that similar activities were underway on Savo, and there were also connections to Isabel, Guadalcanal, and Malaita. Exactly which Red Cross collections were linked, and how, is unknown, but several proceeded independently. Police raids on Gela confiscated documents and American flags, and Sipolo arrested Alogobu, who was released with a warning. Officers forced him to redistribute funds and apparently asked the US Command to do so as well, which caused unhappiness among donors. Sipolo later testified, "The Nggela natives were never the same again. The movement had changed them. Henceforward they never welcomed Government Officers as before when on tour." Collection efforts continued, and in December 1945 Belshaw discovered on Gela a list of 3,318 north Malaitan names "in support of American Red Cross," and the next month Kabini, now back home in Lau, was arrested for "spreading false reports and bringing government authority into contempt."[40]

It is clear that "Red Cross" labeled political ideas more complex than simply giving money to Americans. We do not know how people came to link the Red Cross with American intentions, and the connection was also obscure to the many Malaitan contributors. Malaitan Officer Wilfred Marquand was told that the misunderstanding originated when gifts were proffered to an American officer, and he, missing their political significance, told contributors that he would forward them to the Red Cross. Many contributors did grasp that the money was to help children of Americans killed or others in need, but they also hoped for reciprocity after the war, and even decades later some wondered what became of their donations. To Malaitans, sincere charity and expectation of reciprocity are not incongruous—that those you help will later help you is a basic moral precept of gift exchange. We will see in chapter 7 that during Maasina Rule many Malaitans nurtured hopes that Americans would help them by replacing or driving out the British and becoming their benefactors, sometimes stoked by rumors that they were about to arrive. As Lamont Lindstrom wrote of Tannese similarly seeking American help in the New Hebrides, Malaitans were "a group of clients in search of a patron," and based on their wartime experiences, Americans seemed the obvious choice. Such hopes became an important motivator for some and helped to energize movement activities.[41]

During 1944 and 1945, Maasina Rule activities were being organized in 'Are'are and starting to spread, and though it seems Red Cross activities never challenged the movement in the south, in other places they were stronger and sometimes in direct opposition to it.[42] For example, Tome Waleanisia of 'Aoke Island in Langalanga recounted to me how John Toliole—later arrested for Federal Council movement actions—had collected £1 per man and told them that joining the Red Cross "means you can't join this Maasina Rule. Everyone must belong to the Red Cross now. We must be committed to it, all around Malaita, we must be willing to die for it." As late as mid-1946, a Red Cross faction rivaled Maasina Rule in Langalanga, but in most places Red Cross activities had by late 1945 been absorbed into the larger movement.[43]

The War Years on Malaita: Government Control Slips Away

Though Malaita was spared most horrors of battle, the war's impact was nonetheless profound across the island. Officers instructed many coastal people to relocate into the mountains, while others went on their own, abandoning villages, pigs (or killing and eating the pigs), and often gardens. Many spent miserable months living in makeshift jungle houses without fires at night. Today, people recall acute shortages of store goods, and Fifiʻi cited this as a reason SILC men hoarded clothing. While Widdy and colleagues were burning confiscated garments on Guadalcanal, Sandars worried that Malaitans were "desperately short of clothing."[44]

In some areas, SILC over-recruiting caused suffering. The government tried to limit recruits to 7 percent of the total population, based on a shaky precedent from New Guinea labor rules, but they calculated this by entire islands, not individual communities. Overall, the number absent from Malaita was said to be less than half of those employed on prewar plantations, but the burden was distributed unequally, especially in the north. Hogbin, serving as a "temporary district officer" and Defence Force captain, spent September and October of 1943 there, assisted by Headman Maekali, conducting a government study on reestablishing native courts and councils. He reported that recruiting had left only 5 to 10 percent of young men at home, and many older men were also gone because prewar restrictions on married men departing alone were not now enforced. Local men working on a radar base near Maluʻu further depleted that area's food when they received insufficient rations. With few men left to clear new gardens, a dismal sweet potato harvest, and a severe influenza epidemic, people went hungry. The government had to issue rations to some families, but these were inadequate. Things got so bad that women marched on ʻAoke to demand that their men be returned. Such hardships began to undermine SILC recruiting, as Sandars discovered while circumnavigating Malaita in mid-1943, reporting, "I have made numerous inquiries as to whether anyone wishes to sign on for the Labour Corps—and I do not think that I could have recruited a section anywhere."[45] On Guadalcanal, too, where Bennett told of similar privations, and many people had suffered from the fighting, men refused Viv Hodgess's attempts to recruit them to the SILC when he circled the island that December. They said they were needed at home to work family gardens. Reporting to Noel, Hodgess derided their "feeble excuses," an ironic word choice given his own estimates that Guadalcanal's population was "65% emaciated, and 10% sick or maimed." Headman and war hero Sale Vuza forbade people from Tasimboko, east of today's Honiara, to join the SILC without higher wages.[46]

Some groups on Malaita enjoyed intermittent economic benefits from war-related projects in their areas. On Cape Astrolabe near Maluʻu, a New Zealand radar base was built using local labor, and 50 local men guarded it. Locals also sold thatch and other items for American use on Guadalcanal, as did people in ʻAreʻare and Small Malaita, who sold an estimated 400,000 thatch slats in all. Government officials, partly in hopes of limiting American contact and influence, coordinated on Malaita several schemes in which they acted as middlemen to sell curios, vegetables, or thatch to the troops. By the time the war moved north and most Malaitans had returned home, many thousands of American dollars were held on the island.[47]

Officers later told of how the government kept control of Islanders during the war, albeit at times only through headmen. In places like Isabel and parts of Makira problems were few, but the war seriously damaged the government's position on Gela, Savo, Santa Cruz, and areas of Guadalcanal, and especially on Malaita.[48] Throughout the war there was a relatively large European presence in parts of Malaita; during the Guadalcanal fighting Marchant and his party hid in the Kwara'ae mountains, Bengough was at 'Aoke, Bishop Baddeley toured the north, and other missionaries were in west 'Are'are, and at Fauaabu, Kwai, and around the Tae Passage in Lau Lagoon. Yet for the government all was not well on the island; just as it had lost its hold over Malaitans in the Labour Corps, it no longer controlled much of Malaita, most strikingly in parts of 'Are'are and Kwaio that of necessity had been ignored for well over a year. After his first postwar Malaita tour in September 1943, Sandars gave a grim assessment: "In Ariari, where intensive administration was attempted, by means of stationing a Cadet officer at the bush camp of Haumatana, things have gone to rack and ruin. The 'Houra' or burial feast custom has flourished.... The whole social structure, always flimsy, appears to be even more so than before. I had to deal with an astonishing number of cases of men who had cast aside their wives and taken others."[49]

Sandars saw similar if less severe problems on Small Malaita, but he found the greatest changes farther north: "Eastern Kwaio, with the exception of Uru, is in a bad and dangerous condition. I recently spent a week working at Uru, Sinarago and Oloburi. The last two named sub-districts are in a very bad way. In fact I was told on two occasions that they want no more 'Government Law.' And on many occasions in the past couple of years they have taken the law into their own hands. Murders are the order of the day. These disturbances are chiefly due to two causes. Robbery with violence ending in death and then the demanding of a native fine (totona) by the injured party which, if not paid to great excess leads to further murder or fighting.... These last two years have put Koio back where it was when I knew it in 1929." Sandars described Sinalagu District Headman Sirifa as "useless," condoning violence, and "afraid of the people," and urged that he be dismissed and replaced with Assistant District Headman Anifelo, but this was not done. Of other Malaita headmen, Hogbin wrote, "All are dissatisfied and [some are] contemplating resignation." He attributed this to their wage, which was still on par with plantation labor despite tremendous demands on their time. Sandars blamed the state of affairs on "contact with the more irresponsible elements of the U.S. forces" and pervasive rumors that Americans intended to take over the islands.[50]

Kwaio I have spoken with at length do not remember this period as one of anarchy, though there were several murders there. Kwaio leader 'Elota in his autobiography recalled the lack of options most Malaitans faced in such cases, illustrating this with the killing of an old man by a lunatic named Meke 'Ala'ota: "Headman Sirifa wanted to arrest 'Ala'ota for murder. But that was the time the Japanese had invaded Guadalcanal and destroyed the government capital at Tulagi. If Sirifa had arrested 'Ala'ota, what would he have been able to do with him? What court would he have taken him to?"[51]

Charles Fox later recalled the tense atmosphere around the Tae Lagoon in Lau: "It was all a time of confusion, with wild rumors flying about, and the truth impossible to discover. For the first time for years I saw every Melanesian armed again as in the old days. People went about in companies, as it was not safe to go alone; in two weeks there were half a dozen murders near where I was, people cut up on the roads just because everyone's nerves were on edge." There were obviously reasons beyond "edgy nerves" for the four killings in the north by mid-1944—three in To'abaita, one in Langalanga (none in Lau)—and Fox may have suffered from nerves more than Malaitans, but in all 13 people were killed on Malaita in 1943. Sandars deemed the situation serious enough that he asked for and was granted special judicial powers, and he quickly tried and hanged four men, the Protectorate's first executions since 1935.[52]

Some missionaries reported that their Malaitan work slowed (to a full stop in places) and also noted a growing "attitude problem." The SSEM's K E Griffiths lamented, "It is going to take time and effort to get control of the natives and get them back to where they were," and quoted the Pacific Islands Native Welfare Association publication "The Pacific Islander—After the War What?": "Now into their life there has come the soldier who is more happy-go-lucky, and in whom the Islanders sense an irresponsibility and familiarity such as they have not hitherto known. There is a real danger lurking in this newfound semi-equality and irresponsibility. To the Islanders it will appear as the birth of a new era and it seems reasonably certain that they will not again willingly submit to the same European dominance."[53]

To add to government problems, district officers, recently unhappy at the dearth of SILC recruits, were soon worried more about the flood of SILC returnees—more than 1,000 in the second quarter of 1945 alone— many of whom were spreading messages of discontent. Almost a year after Sandars's first postwar tour, District Officer David Trench visited Kwaio and found there was still "not a good atmosphere" and concluded: "Undoubtedly recent lack of control has put the place back a lot and there seems to be no authority left in the bush."[54] One should read such reports cautiously, especially those depicting leaderless decadence and fighting, since most Europeans expected to find chaos after a period without their supervision. But the government was indeed losing control and would not regain it for many years, and Europeans would never get Malaitans "back to where they were." What would emerge in the postwar environment was not anarchy but a great Malaita-wide political movement determined to bring about radical social change.

The Promotion and Refusal of Postwar Native Administration

The war left the Protectorate in shambles. A Western Pacific High Commission press release later summarized the situation: "Administration buildings had been wrecked, coconut plantations were derelict; plantation owners and the trading community had left the country, and the shipping link with Australia had disappeared. The native population was unsettled, little evidence of the British administration remained.... The problem was thus not to start from scratch, but considerably below it." At the same time, important changes were taking place in London, expressed in postwar policies and objectives emanating from the Colonial Office. A critical notion put to the fore was that of trusteeship: "dependent peoples" had a right to eventual self-government (though not necessarily independence), and colonial administrations were obligated to guide and financially support them toward that goal. This shift had begun just before the war reached the Solomons with enactment of the Colonial Development and Welfare Act of 1940, which directed that colonized territories no longer had to fully support themselves. In the postwar Solomons this meant there would be money for reconstruction and development, though the Protectorate stood near the end of the line to receive funds.[55]

Even so, a policy of gradualism envisioned very long periods of tutelage as essential in some cases, particularly in Melanesia.[56] Julian Huxley and Phyllis Deane summarized the model: "The British Colonies have often been described as a constitutional procession, each advancing in its own way and at its own pace toward the goal of responsible self-government to which it is the avowed policy of the United Kingdom Government to guide them. The position of each colony in the procession is determined by a number of factors in its political framework." Other factors ran deeper than politics, as a former high commissioner, Harry Luke, explained by pointing to Gilbertese who could "lead full, communal and happy lives on their sunny, open, breeze-swept strips of coral, speaking the same language as their neighbors and free from the isolation, the fears and the depressing *tabus* that darken the lot of so many Melanesians."[57]

Solomon Islanders were to find their political aspirations stymied by such crude stereotypes, remarkably unchanged since the nineteenth century. In the chapters that follow, we will examine in detail the Maasina Rule movement that began its rise in 1944 and 1945, within which Malaitans set out to pursue their own course. But first we need to look at the efforts of BSIP officers to initiate these gradualist policies at the same time that the movement was forming, and how Malaitan responded to them.

Government Social Services: Education and Medicine

By the 1940s, the Solomons was an obvious straggler in the great constitutional procession and was becoming an embarrassment to the British. Recognition that the government had badly neglected social development was evident in the circulation of an anecdote later related by Malaita's District Commissioner Stanley Masterman: "Just before the first Munich, Hitler, when told that he could not have the Cameroons back because he was not fit to govern backward people, retorted 'What have you done about education in the Solomons?'" The most glaring failure was indeed in education, followed closely by medical services. They are important to this history because, for Malaitans, by the 1940s both had become highly politicized. Like the Fallowes movement, Maasina Rule would soon be demanding schools and doctors, and Malaitans would often cite their absence when refusing to cooperate with the government.[58] "They wanted their freedom," said Titiuru, "to be equal with the whites, and they wanted schools—the government didn't provide any, only the missions, and that was mostly religious schools, just the Bible." As in many colonies, impoverished prewar administrations delegated both medical and educational services primarily to the staffs and budgets of the Christian missions. Moorhouse's 1929 report had advised against upgrading education, and anyway the Great Depression dashed any inclinations to do so.[59]

The conditions of mission schools varied widely into the 1940s; many on Malaita were of poor quality and their curricula excluded whole realms of knowledge thought unsuitable or dangerous for Melanesians. Bell thought the schools offered little education, and Bengough in 1938 could still write, "Enrollment in school cannot be regarded as a criterion for literacy. Many natives enrolled in Mission schools are unable to read or write." Moreover, most offered nothing to the majority of Malaitans who were not Christian. Still, during the 1930s the government, while recognizing that mission schools were "from an educational point of view...quite inadequate," relied on them to "satisfy the craving of the natives to learn." During Maasina Rule Allan wrote, "Natives have become disillusioned with mission education and this has been one of the reasons for the break with the European missionaries who are now regarded to have hoodwinked the people and withheld the 'proper' education or in the pidgin expression 'skul b'long world.'" Many Europeans openly opposed serious schooling for Islanders because, in Fox's words: "They think it will make the native more sophisticated, spoil him, as they say." As Ariel Sisili put it in a 1949 political manifesto, "We have never had the Whiteman's best or ever taught or shown anything above the ordinary. These has always been holding back from the native in case he may see his position."[60]

By the early 1940s, the craving for schooling had only intensified, and the postwar period brought "bitter native demands for education," which

Solomon Islanders saw to be "the key to future well-being." Sandars wrote of Malaitans, "The whole population feels the need for [education of the young], and the elders feel that if necessary, they must make large sacrifices to obtain it." After touring neighboring Makira in early 1946, one officer reported that the people were "Fanatics about education and accuse government of lack of help, since they help the government by paying taxes." Some whites demeaned or brushed aside Islanders' desire to learn as based on a superstition that European knowledge was magical. In the meanwhile, the resident commissioner sought permission to bring in Fijians to serve as government clerks, typists, and cashiers.[61]

Beyond infuriating Malaitans, failure to provide education meant the government had never cultivated an institutional domain within which to instill colonial ideology in young people. Resident Commissioner Francis Ashley had explicitly rejected the idea that education could achieve this. While there was no medium for fostering effective European hegemony, by the 1940s channels for the spread of rebellious ideas were flowing fast, and as resistance heated up officers yearned for a way to impart their plans and promises to an alienated and mostly illiterate populace.[62]

Officers knew they lacked the expertise to create a school system. At the end of 1945, Sandars worried that if no government educational expert was immediately provided, officers might be forced to turn to the missions for advice, which he felt "should be avoided at all costs." Yet not until 1947, at the height of Maasina Rule, did the Protectorate employ a director of education, and he soon resigned.[63] In 1945, Sandars and colleagues busily tried to divert frustrations with the government into "reasonable channels" by counseling Malaitans to focus on education and erecting hospitals and dispensaries. Sandars expected these could and should be paid for not by the government but by local taxes, and in December 1945 Sandars told Kwara'ae to use money that Maasina Rule had collected to build a school to teach farming, carpentry, and other crafts, and Roy Davies later called their failure to do so "a great tragedy." Two days later Sandars told Malu'u people they should use their Maasina Rule money to build a hospital. There is no indication that either man suggested to Malaitans where trained teachers or hospital staff, or school supplies, or medicine would come from. In any case, Malaitans, who for two decades had complained at receiving nothing for their taxes, balked at this suggestion, as later expressed in a Maasina Rule communication: "They say medicine is something for the work of the people but we have paid for it already in the taxes." No doubt some remembered when the head tax was first imposed in the 1920s and officers followed High Commissioner Cecil Rodwell's instructions on how to explain its necessity: "The resulting benefit to the natives of law and order, development and education, should be brought home to them on every opportunity. They should be made to feel that by paying this tax they are taking a share in a great work for their own ultimate benefit." Just after

Bell was assassinated, missionary Walter Ivens wrote to Secretary of State to the Colonies Leopold Amery, "When first imposed it was stated that the purpose of the tax was to provide money for the proper medical care of the natives," and he counseled that erection of a hospital on Malaita would "go far to remove the grievance felt in the matter of the Poll Tax." The year before, Ivens had urged the secretary to direct that all head tax money be spent on health services, to help reverse population declines, and Bell himself argued for appointment of a medical officer (and for education). Rodwell's successor, Eyre Hutson, privately blamed Bell's death on these broken promises. He was wrong, but his supposition exposes higher-up knowledge of Malaitan aspirations and their betrayal.[64]

BSIP medical services had always been feeble, and what little Malaitans did get came, again, mostly from missions, particularly the Anglicans and Adventists. The government at times contributed help with money and drugs, though sometimes reluctantly and resentfully due to a fear of being outshone. They also worried that missionaries might treat only their own flocks or demand donations for care. In 1928, the Anglicans had received a £2,000 donation to found the Hospital of the Epiphany at Fauaabu, 24 kilometers north of 'Aoke, and, soon after, a 50-hectare leper colony nearby, which received small government subsidies and donations from New Zealand and Australia and was apparently run well until the war and after.[65]

Adventists had long deployed medical services as an "entering wedge" for evangelization: "Missionaries would also be health workers and the connection between health and salvation remained inextricably linked." They maintained this strategy in the Solomons, and on Malaita they opened a hospital at Kwailabesi in Lau in 1936, but the mission had only a small presence on the island before the war. The SSEM's minimal medical services were, in Hilliard's words, "mere palliative measures." Medical policy was also stymied by church rivalries. Ross Innes, designing an anti-leprosy plan for Malaita in 1937, was dismayed when Anglican doctor Clifford James told him, "One mission is not likely to co-operate with another, or with the Government, or with the Mission to lepers in any united anti-leprosy work."[66]

No government medical system was instituted on Malaita before 1930, though doctors at times toured with officers and most officers treated people when and as they could. One senior medical officer told Sandars, "You can't make bricks without straw and you can't run a medical service without funds." We have seen that the prewar government blamed many health problems on local cultures and therefore tried to impose hygienic rules for penning pigs, to consolidate hamlets into ordered villages, and to suppress cultural practices deemed unhealthy. In 1931, the Protectorate's first native medical practitioner, George Bogese, was posted to 'Aoke to open a leaf-house "hospital" for people of that area. It provided outpatient dressings and injections for yaws and later admitted some inpatients (eg, 268 in 1938). But this did little for Malaitans elsewhere, and in 1940 the medical staff for well over 40,000 Malaitans consisted of four "dressers" (minimally trained medical workers) and a native medical practitioner, with another practitioner and a dresser seconded to the 'Are'are population project.[67]

Malaitans had valued European medicines since the labor trade, but from 1928 until the war their potential was demonstrated dramatically by the stunning success of campaigns against yaws (perhaps 60 percent of Malaitans were or had been infected) and hookworm (85 percent of Solomon Islanders infected), which were funded by Levers and then by the Rockefeller Foundation. In 1928 alone, some 36,000 people received injections for yaws, many from medical officer Charles Gordon White. Barley called this campaign "one of the greatest returns which the British Administration has found itself able to give to the native people of the Protectorate in justification of its having assumed control of their destiny and welfare." Lambert worked with the project and wrote of Malaitans: "The news had spread to them that the white doctors jabbed them with a needle. They were all crazy for the treatment." He also recollected, "Our needles wore out and our fingers grew stiff from puncturing the skin of hundreds who applied, clamoring for 'neela.'" Elsewhere some feared and fled injections, but "Malaita men loved the needle—sick or well, they demanded it." Women, too, flocked to touring doctors. Ellen Wilson recounted, "Patients with feet half eaten away crawled miles to receive an injection. Mothers brought their babies with their little faces disfigured and repulsive, and, lo! The sores healed and disappeared, and the tiny children recovered their roundness of limb and childish beauty."[68]

During Maasina Rule, Norman Deck, ostracized by his flock, advised withholding medicine as an excellent way to blackmail movement followers: "I again suggest that if the Government, and all the Missions, were to withhold all medical amenities from members of the Marching Rule, but make them available to those outside the movement this would have a deep effect, and would probably bring the offenders to heel quicker than any other administrative act. I think all missions would agree to this if asked, but I am not sure about the Roman Mission. The people would probably say 'no matter,' but this would only be a pose; they would really feel it very much, for they greatly value medicines." Even at the height of Maasina Rule hostility toward government, Malaitans at times welcomed touring native medical workers, despite their police escorts, though at other times they were rebuffed.[69]

In 1947 the British government reported to the United Nations that, in Linden Mander's summation, "the Protectorate, with a population of 94,965 had only two medical officers [one fewer than in the 1920s] and eleven Native Medical Practitioners trained in Fiji. The government doctors per thousand of population amounted to .02, hospital beds per thousand 6.31; no staff and no organizations existed to promote social welfare." Many Malaita areas would enjoy no regular health services until the Malaita

Council began to take action in the 1950s, and some populous mountain regions have none to this day.[70]

In October 1945, district commissioners Alexander Waddell, David Trench, and Frederick Bentley, all Malaita veterans, drafted a relatively progressive five-year plan to start developing the Protectorate's infrastructure and its educational and medical services, as well as a more advanced and participatory native administration. Their assessment of education's near future was bleak: because there were no teachers, people would have to remain dependent on mission schools. They suggested that over the five years a maximum of 60 Solomon Islanders be sent to Fiji for education. They hoped an education department and teacher training might then be started, followed later by general education, hopefully "in one generation." They also proposed that the government give more money to mission schools on the condition that they include "a minimum amount of secular teaching."[71]

The latter point raised its own problems. Missions and government had skirmished for years over the proper balance of worldly and religious content in curricula, and this conflict now escalated as the postwar government began showing more interest in education. Missionaries, Belshaw argued, were "well aware that it is through education that they retain such hold on the native people as they have." Deck had warned in the early 1930s that nonreligious education would produce "men of the agitator class, disobedient to authority," and he explained to Ashley that his evangelical mission's "aim was not to give education with a spiritual appendix as it were, but to teach the Word of God, incidentally teaching reading and writing in the process." A decade later, the SSEM was asking its Australian "Prayer Partners" to pray for Solomon Islanders, "That Satan with his devices may not be able to create a desire for education instead of the desire for spiritual things." Others worried that government promotion of secular knowledge would, in Anglican Bishop Sydney Caulton's words, create "a race of 'clever devils' to whom God is fiction or at best unnecessary." Caulton objected to a 1949 education regulation draft on the grounds that "a mature legislation is being proposed for an immature people." Reading such pronouncements one senses that, apart from rival missions, many missionaries saw education as the greatest menace to God's work. As Maasina Rule gained force, these same missionaries and many government officers, without hint of self-reflection, belittled its adherents as appallingly ignorant of the ways of the world.[72]

The Protectorate's 1946 "Ten Year Plan of Reconstruction and Development and Welfare" called for better social services but most important as a means to sustain an adequate workforce. The first goal was to improve diets with farming development: "The long-term results of this policy, lowering of infant mortality, increasing of adult efficiency and working capacity, and economy of effort deriving from improved methods and tools, would all tend to increase the quantity and improve the quality of labour available for purposes other than subsistence farming. Education and Medical Policy will be directed to the same ends." Four years later Malaita's Officer Marquand wrote, "The government also intends to carry out a programme of education, but here they are thinking of the education of more clerks and tradesmen who can keep their machine running." During Maasina Rule, particularly after mass arrests began, education would come to a halt as Malaitans rebuffed both missionary and government help and most schools ceased to operate.[73]

Given the years of unfulfilled government promises of education and medicine, and the determination of many Europeans to obstruct practical schooling, it is little wonder Belshaw observed from his exposure to Maasina Rule in its formative stages a widespread belief, particularly among Malaitans, that "The European is with-holding advance from the native.... This means that European ends are conceived as being necessarily incompatible with native ends, the basis of mutual confidence is removed, and it is difficult for policy to be effected."[74]

Councils and Courts Revisited

As the war moved off to the north, discussions of the need for social services continued, but the government, unsettled by discontent on Malaita and elsewhere, was preoccupied with quickly establishing native political structures and its own presence in the new capital of Honiara. On 17 May 1944, Acting High Commissioner Philip Mitchell presided over a conference of district commissioners at Tenaru Camp on Guadalcanal, and in what Hogbin called "a momentous step" they decided to revive and accelerate Ashley's and especially Marchant's prewar plans to develop native councils and courts, the beginnings of which had mostly collapsed during the fighting. This led to a 1945 Native Courts Regulation and eventually a new Native Administration Regulation. Seven nascent councils were already operating on Malaita (at Malu'u, Fo'odo, Makwanu, Kwarade, Anoano, Lau, and Langalanga), and by year's end seven more were established or being organized (at Fiu, 'Aoke, Kwaimela, 'Ataa, Bina, Onepusu, and Su'u). Areas with no councils continued to be administered as before, through headmen.[75]

A first order of business for these councils was to resolve "what is and what is not true native custom, and how much of it should be retained or modified or discarded as no longer applicable." Councils around Malaita were instructed to discuss this and record the results in drafted codes. As before the war, the plan was that these codes would form a substantive basis for native court rulings.[76] Just a few months earlier, Sandars had declared establishment of courts on Malaita "out of the question" and, according to Hogbin, he reduced the powers of even the existing Malu'u court. But in September 1943 Sandars fell ill and left again, and under Trench, Bentley, and then Michael Forster, experimental courts were initiated in areas with councils; the plan was to establish them under the new regulations. The system was devised so that "[t]he Government, through its administrative officers, will be able to keep a strict control, if required, on the activities of Native Administration, and at the same time encourage the development of the idea of self-government."[77]

In practice, both the officers and Malaitans saw courts and councils as tightly linked and at times synonymous—both were led by headmen, subject to overrule by the district commissioner, and usually made up of some of the same men. A native clerk was to keep court records, collect fines, and record births, deaths, and marriages, though finding suitably educated clerks was a persistent problem. Marquand noted that all native court cases were subject to review by the officer in charge "when he had time to do so, but, in most cases, the records were so badly kept by the nearly illiterate clerks that it was difficult for him to criticize." In an innovation already standard practice in parts of Africa, councils were told they would soon be allowed small treasuries to hold court fees and fines for local use, to be spent under "careful supervision." Treasuries would also receive as "fines" any compensations native courts awarded to Christians whose churches forbade their accepting them. In February 1945, the government drafted a new policy, modeled partly on the 1934 Tanganyika Native Tax Ordinance, that would, in future, allow some councils—starting as ever with Malu'u—to fix a local tax, collect it, and decide how to spend it, subject to the resident commissioner's approval. Further, defaulters would no longer be imprisoned.[78]

Native courts were now granted powers not only to decide "native customary offenses, and award any native customary punishment [thought reasonable]," but also to hear minor criminal cases and impose fines up to £25 and sentences up to six-months' hard labor, and small civil suits with a £50 award limit. Despite growing resentment of government institutions, Malaitans needed no urging to settle their own cases; the 1945 Annual Report says their courts dealt with 405 people in civil cases (only six land disputes) and more than 600 on criminal charges (with a 95 percent conviction rate), against just 207 criminal cases heard by government courts.[79]

Notwithstanding the new powers being granted to courts and councils, district officers now faced men returning from the Labour Corps who looked on these bodies with scorn because they were government entities. As Forster later lamented, "The Government suffered a very serious loss of prestige. Its material resources, which prior to the war appeared to be not inconsiderable, by comparison with those of the armed forces, became microscopic. The Protectorate capital disappeared from Tulagi and, as far as the majority of natives is concerned, has been lost in the jungles of Guadalcanal ever since. . . . The war set new criteria as to what constituted power and, by these criteria, the Government appeared to have little or none at all. The loss of prestige suffered by the Government was shared by all white people whom they knew before the war." The poll tax, officially suspended in early 1943, had not been reimposed, and Forster believed that Malaitans' disdain could be traced to its absence and to the wartime absence of officers. Government remoteness was only accentuated as native courts and councils began to take on duties formerly carried out by touring officers.[80]

Malaitans were reacting to much more than the government's policies, actions, and inaction—the war set new standards of dignity in their relations with white people and inspired new aspirations. Like other colonial subjects after World War II, Solomon Islanders felt that, having suffered and sacrificed to defend the empire, they now had an indisputable moral claim to higher status within it, and they refused to slip quietly back into their former demeaning roles. The power of humiliation to motivate political action is almost always underappreciated by those who inflict it, and Malaita was to prove a case in point. The collective war experience intensified and roiled shared resentments of prewar exploitation and degradation, and diverse groups who were once divided or even antagonistic now found common political ground. The colonists were seen to offer little toward meeting people's raised expectations, and indeed it was presumed they would try to frustrate pursuit of them, as already manifest in, for example, government attempts to restrict their access to Americans and seizures of their gifts. Malaita's new district commissioner, David Trench, reported a relentless theme: "The government does not do enough for us," and said that even "amongst the more responsible natives" he met "some rather nebulous dissatisfaction." At this time a particular metaphor for government became popular on the island: the banyan tree, which slowly encases another tree as if to care for and nurture it but eventually kills it.[81]

A further difficulty was that the two pillars of Malaita's administration, Sandars and Bengough, were gone. Their replacements, Trench and Forster, had before the war served on Malaita for only four and nine months, respectively, and their relative inexperience handicapped their efforts to manage new courts and councils and monitor and counter growing discontent. In their favor, Trench had started courts on Guadalcanal and the Shortlands, and Forster in 1940 and 1941 toured 'Are'are to teach court procedures—some there later called him "the father of the 'Are'are Council." As described in chapter 2, Forster was already popular in the south for his kindness and displays of respect for local people and practices.[82]

The first SILC sections were returned to 'Ataa in February 1944 under Kelebeti (or Gilbert, Giribiti, Fugui), an associate of Kabini of Red Cross fame, and the men brought "disturbing ideas" to an already unsettled situation. In June, European government workers were reportedly threatened with violence at Walande on Small Malaita, with an 'Ataa man among the instigators.[83] By the end of 1945, only 317 men were still in the Labour Corps, but most plantations were still not operating. This meant there were more men living on Malaita than in many decades, and officers found this "over-dose of young men with too much money and no desire to work...decid-edly troublesome." Many declared they would only return to plantations for £12 per month, a figure voiced in Fallowes's meetings six years before. Returnees berated those who had dutifully maintained government "roads" during the war, and that work ceased.[84]

Officers were still finding little success in starting councils in most of southern Malaita, where people remained "somewhat unresponsive." Of 15 courts established by 1945, only three were in the south—at Anoano in west Kwaio and Su'u and Onepusu in west 'Are'are—though two more were soon started, named "Western 'Are'are" and "Southern 'Are'are."[85] Enthu-siasm in the south, and elsewhere on Malaita, was in fact declining, partly because most headmen were finding their close association with the gov-ernment and its particular council plans a liability and became supporters of Maasina Rule, which by the end of 1945 had already spread throughout the island. There were still loyalists. Malaitans most loyal to the govern-ment tended to be followers of headmen who had been relatively privileged under the prewar regime and whom officers allowed more power over their communities, such as Maekali at Malu'u and Timi Kakalu'ae in Lau (both former Bell constables). As Maasina Rule expanded, such men would find their power being wrested away by new and often younger leaders beyond their control. Fifi'i later opined that these headmen opposed Maasina Rule because "[t]hey wanted only themselves to have power over the people, and put their interests above the people's." But headmen whom the govern-ment had so favored were few; the archives are rife with officers' comments about the perceived stupidity, incompetence, or disrepute of various head-men, and many enjoyed little respect from either officers or the people. Thus most headmen had little to lose by working with or in some cases becoming leaders in Maasina Rule. Many did not see joining it to be a nec-essarily antigovernment move. Later, in May 1948, Forster compiled a list of Malaita's 52 headmen that identified all but eight as present or former Maasina Rule members, and Germond in February of that year estimated 75 percent of headmen were still movement leaders or active supporters.[86]

But as I will explain in chapter 6, through 1944 and most of 1945 district officers carried on largely unaware of Maasina Rule's early emergence and spread, and they blamed people's lack of participation in the government's native administration plans on either apathy or foolish contrariness. We have seen how much they depended on headmen for intelligence, and the fact that so many headmen joined the movement goes far toward explain-ing government's ignorance of it. The degree of officers' isolation at this time is painfully clear in Forster's reports advising that, with patience, coun-cils might be gradually developed in the southern areas. These were written while that region's people were busily organizing the very activities councils were expected to perform and much more, but within Maasina Rule.[87]

Overall, Malaita's revived native councils were weathering postwar changes poorly. Dissatisfaction with them even at the end of 1943 was "almost universal" among the "chiefs" that officers had appointed to councils and later placed on courts, and many headmen, too, were soon expressing unhappiness with both. Headmen who genuinely tried to lead obedient councils and courts, such as Maekali and Kakalu'ae, Nat Salaimanu at Tae in Lau, and Tome Siru at Kwai, were widely resented, though even Maekali and Kakalu'ae and later Siru dabbled in political activities outside of government auspices for a time, as we will see. Still, officers were determined to firmly educate Malaitans in participatory government and proper civic life. They instructed councils to report anyone who made trouble for them, and in November 1944 Trench asked permission to issue guns to assistant headmen to keep order during meetings, arguing, "In their present state of development, the courts and councils are liable occasionally to be somewhat turbulent and the presence of a man with a rifle might well have a sedative effect."[88]

Like Ashley two decades before, officers hoped courts and councils would foster a Malaitan idea that they were now part of a government from which they had hitherto been excluded. But years of alienation were not so easily reversed, and despite their assigned emphasis on "custom" matters, Malaitans saw the bodies as British made and run. As Marquand later wrote, councils "enforced the wants of the Government which were not necessarily, and not often, the perceived wants of the people." Even Maekali expressed this to Hogbin about the Malu'u court he presided over: "The Court *doesn't* belong to us: we never had Courts before: it's a Government affair."[89]

Bita Saetana (also called Falasi) of Kwao, near Sinalagu, in 1981 recalled an argument he had with Sandars a few months after Cadet Roy Davies appointed him a "chief" in February 1945: "I got to 'Aoke and I said to 'Abaeata [Assistant Headman Anifelo], 'Let's the two of us ask the government one thing: Why is it that we chiefs are only given tobacco and biscuits? When the district officers come that's what they give us. How about a little cash for us, to go along with it?' [When we asked] Mister Sandars he replied, 'But you're a leader of your community! Who is going to pay you for that?' I answered him like this: 'If a headman goes to court, or he goes to break up a fight, we chiefs go along with him. If they kill him they are going to kill us too. Let's have us some shillings.' But Sandars said, 'No. We don't pay wages for you chiefs.' So my chiefing finished right then and there at 'Aoke." Such complaints highlight a dissonance between government and Malaitan views as to what "chiefs" and headmen could be or ought to be. Officers envisioned them as the people's representatives, but as they came to understand, Malaitans, for so long barred from governance, considered most native officials, especially certain headmen, as at best government employees and at worst informants, stooges, or lackeys, and unsuitable leaders. This was still more palpable where headmen had made enemies by abusing their power.[90]

Among the loudest critics of courts and councils were mission teachers, especially of the SSEM, who had for so long been rivals of the government and its servants. The new "native" institutions threatened to take away the administrative and judicial powers they had attained in Christian communities, especially after the wartime European exodus. SSEM teachers as a group were among the most powerful Malaitans, often wielding more authority than headmen. They objected to many of the "chiefs" and "elders," especially the non-Christian ones, being appointed to the new bodies.[91]

Many white missionaries, too, saw courts and councils as a threat, just as before the war they had instructed teachers to avoid taking disputes to the government. When Hogbin visited the north just after the war to study the state of native administration, he reported that white missionaries unanimously opposed native courts because, they argued, Malaitans were too ignorant and inexperienced to run them. At Malu'u, which Bengough had called home to "some of the most vigorous and politically argumentative people on Malaita," and where the Christian-government rivalry was oldest and most bitter, Headman Maekali, though an SSEM member, had prevented appointment of teachers as council "elders." In particular, he shut out an old enemy, Shem Irofa'alu, who had succeeded Peter Abu'ofa, one of the first Christian leaders on Malaita, as the area's SSEM head. We will encounter Irofa'alu again in chapter 7. Forster believed the root of problems at Malu'u was SSEM teachers' jealousy of Maekali's power and anger that "he would not kow tow to their wishes." While it seems church hostility to courts and councils was most fervent at Malu'u, similar tensions were evident elsewhere, and some headmen who belonged to the SSEM, especially, found their positions awkward.[92]

Despite sharing Malaitan church teachers' dislike for courts and councils, white missionaries returning to postwar Malaita, like colonial officers, found their positions much weakened. Partly this was due to teachers' resolve not to surrender their wartime independence to either missionaries or government schemes. But even before 1942, teachers' resentment of their white bosses had been growing. Most important were complaints that missionaries—again, particularly those of the SSEM—refused to interact with Islanders as equals, provide them opportunity for advancement, or pay them enough (or sometimes anything) for their work. These were not trivial complaints; decades later Norman Deck, asked to cite a mistake the SSEM had made, responded, "Not paying teachers sufficiently. We were a faith mission and I thought that principle should be applied throughout. But sometimes the teachers hadn't enough to live on." This was a reason Maasina Rule adherents gave for boycotting SSEM missionaries along the east coast in 1948.[93]

Through 1945, then, many Malaitans, Christian and not, showed little deference to the new councils or courts. Courts had no police (Trench's rifles were not issued) and increasingly their rulings were being flouted. Their biggest handicap was that many people saw them as mere government fronts. Sandars, who returned to replace Trench as district commissioner in late 1945, misread the problem and vowed to "enhance their prestige and authority by applying full weight of Government authority to back up proper decisions," but he would soon change his tactics.[94]

Many Malaitans remained unsure as to how much autonomy native courts were being granted and, later, of the courts' relationship to Maasina Rule. As the movement spread, people in a few places rejected headmen outright, and rival assemblies challenged their councils and courts. Other councils appeared to be functioning as instructed but had been absorbed into Maasina Rule as forums for Malaitans to plan their own administration.[95] It often was unclear to either officers or Malaitans whether a particular council or court was the government's or Maasina Rule's, especially where headmen and members belonged to the movement. We shall see that officers gave ambiguous instructions as to how these various bodies should proceed.

Some headmen who had been effectively deposed pleaded explicitly or in effect for stern government counteraction, but their complaints were not acted on until later, when the government needed justification to repress the movement. Officers recognized that some unpopular headmen were inept, corrupt, or autocratic, but feared their removal might lead people to say the government had capitulated to Malaitan demands. So rather than lose apparent face they left them in place as the government's primary representatives among the people.[96]

Elsewhere in the southeast Solomons, efforts to set up councils were finding mixed success. Len Barrow recounted how, at the end of 1945, big men of Arosi on Makira greeted councils with suspicion, while on Guadalcanal, Gela, and elsewhere on Makira, "The councils continued to develop with varying degrees of ambition, enthusiasm, muddle-headedness and downright indifference." These were areas that quickly embraced Maasina Rule in 1945 and 1946.[97]

We will see that later, when officials grew more aware of Maasina Rule and its scope, they still hoped courts and councils would facilitate their agenda and at the same time diffuse growing discontent: "Not only is the immediate initiation of Native Authorities, however rudimentary, a prerequisite to social and political progress," said the Protectorate's "Ten Year Plan" in 1946, "but it is urgently necessary to provide this legitimate outlet for the aspirations aroused by the sudden and large scale contact with European and Negro troops of the United States Forces." In August of that year, Resident Commissioner Noel spoke to native council representatives in 'Aoke: "Councils have been established by the Government so that you can express your opinions and hear the views of the Government. It is therefore through these Councils that the views of the Marching Rule or any other movement should be expressed. The opinions of the council are considered by the District Commissioner, who will give a decision." Noel also vowed, as did other officers, to take legal action against anyone obstructing government orders.[98]

Noel's speech corroborated Maasina Rule critiques of the councils at this time, that they would neither allow communities any real control over their own affairs nor change the status quo. Perhaps for some it supported rumors then circulating that Americans, "hearing of the founding of Native Councils had told natives that this was merely a trick on the part of the British and that, as soon as the Americans had left, the British would destroy these Councils and act as they did before the war." At all events, Noel warned High Commissioner Alexander Grantham, "I do not believe and I cannot advise that that which is now occurring is but a passing phase inevitable after war and will vanish sooner or later. The demands of the people are too genuine.... The Solomon Islander is bent on securing more benefits from Government than he was granted before the war." Whatever the government now intended to offer, for most Malaitans it was much too little and far too late, and the government's native administration plan was soon to become a dead letter.[99]

Chapter 5
The Rise of Maasina Rule

Genesis and Spread

By late 1943, much of the southeast Solomons was rumbling with discontent and political groups were forming. Although they shared many grievances, their actions were as yet uncoordinated except as men interacted within the crucial setting of the Labour Corps, and in some places rival factions emerged. The need for a unifying leadership and platform was soon met by men from west 'Are'are, particularly Aliki Nono'oohimae and Nori, who had been sergeant and corporal, respectively, of a Waisisi SILC section. They had formed definite ideas about how Malaitans should proceed. Both spent a good deal of time talking with Americans, and Kwalafanai'a of Kwaio later told Roger Keesing how Nori had gone around Camp Guadalcanal telling people of his plans to organize politically back home, though many were skeptical.[1]

In September 1943 Nono'oohimae began working to establish a council for southwest 'Are'are. He allied with Harisimae—who had been a feared strongman and passage master, and then, until 1934, a headman—and with Harisimae's nephew Hoasihau (or Houasi'au). Hoasihau had been a corporal in the armed constabulary and succeeded Harisimae as headman; he was a favorite of Sandars, who called him "a lion hearted fellow." Older but still vigorous, Harisimae proved key in convincing senior men to join the new political work, and Nori and others later spoke of him as Maasina Rule's founder. Years afterward, Nono'oohimae dated Maasina Rule's beginning to a January 1944 meeting at his own village of Arairau. On 25 January, the work was also taken up in east 'Are'are, at Takataka under big men Waiparo and Puahanikeni and Headman Aruhane. The earliest 'Are'are activities bore several names: "Level Meeting" (or "Leveling Meeting"), "Native Union Council," and "Maasina Law," and to the north people used "Council Union" (in Kwaio), or "Congress Union" (Langalanga). The Level Meeting name was said to indicate either a desire to establish equality with whites and Chinese or that all participants were to be as of a single mind.[2]

As 1944 progressed, "Maasina Rule" was adopted. Much ink has been spent on a marvelous diversity of explanations of the name. Its pronunciation varies across languages—"Maasing Rul" in Kwara'ae, "Maasina Ruru"

FIGURE 5.1. Harisimae of Rohinari as a younger man, ca 1922. (Courtesy of the SSEM Archive, photographer unknown.)

in 'Are'are and Kwaio, "Marching Rule" in British—and movement scribes fashioned their own variants (eg, "Mercy Rule" or "Marcy Rule"). Among Europeans the name was to become a chameleon to various fantasies about the movement: "Marxian" or "Marx's Rule," or "Marxist Law," with communist agitators imagined lurking in Malaita's mountains; eponymously as "Marchant's Rule," after that resident commissioner's native administration scheme on Gela; or even "Basiana Rule" in honor of Bell's assassin. Some said it derived from "martial law." Most Europeans settled on "Marching Rule," which Roy Davies said was derived from Forster's mishearing of "Maasina." It nicely conveyed the image of mindless regimentation and fanaticism that many attributed to the movement. Malaitans with their proclivity for wordplay have also enjoyed naming games. Some say *ruru* meant "children," expressing adherents' newborn social status. Others have told me the movement was named after John Martin (at times pronounced "Maatina"), who commanded US troops as they prepared to depart the Solomons, but he arrived years after the name was coined. What is clear is that the name originated in 'Are'are, where *maasina* can be translated as "sibling," "cousin," or more broadly "relative" or "close friend" (To'abaita *thaasina*, Kwaio *waasina*, Kwara'ae and Makwanu *saasina*, Sa'a *mwaasine*), and *ruru*, as in many Malaitan languages, is a word for a gathering or work party. Either *ruru* or the English "rule," or both, could be the correct etymon—as Keesing noted, Malaitans have a penchant for cross-language puns. Many 'Are'are would have known "rule" as a term denoting rules of daily life in Catholic and Anglican monastic communities like the Melanesian Brotherhood. Many movement documents use the English spelling.[3] Nori credited the name to Harisimae and said that Sandars told them they needed a name, though the name predated Sandars's knowledge of the movement. Today, Solomon Islands scholars and political organizers at times use an alternative 'Are'are spelling, Ma'asina. For simplicity, in this book I use the familiar "Maasina Rule."[4]

For many months, into early 1945, organizational activities remained within southern 'Are'are and Small Malaita, where Nono'oohimae, his "messenger" Sale Namohani'ai, Harisimae, a local headman named Ho'ogisau, and others toured to tell out its ideas.[5] It is significant that the movement began here, because this is where the government's prewar repopulation project, detailed in chapter 3, carried on until 1942, headquartered inland from Wairokai. We saw that Hoasihau was a key local participant in that, and Nono'oohimae and Harisimae were also involved.[6] The blueprint these men eventually drew up for Maasina Rule stressed many of the same goals as that project had: to build a broader ethnic unity, construct centralized villages, plant communal gardens, codify "native customs" and abandon "bad customs," and reverse perceived population declines. As noted in chapter 3, Harisimae, Nono'oohimae, and Hoasihau had all attended the 1939 Fallowes meeting on Gela, but how that might have influenced them is unclear.[7]

Surviving documents from the early meetings highlight the importance of "custom" as a foundation of the movement but do not elaborate on the term's meaning for 'Are'are people at that time.[8] Nono'oohimae later testified in court that they were motivated to act partly by depopulation fears and that he had voiced these concerns during his early proselytizing; other testimony supported this claim.[9] Kwaio oral histories, too, say depopulation was an early movement concern. To this day, inland Kwaio worry their numbers are shrinking, even though, as elsewhere on Malaita, the overall population is booming. The tangible source of their worry is a steady fall of interior numbers as people move to coastal Christian villages; that is, their population is relocating, not shrinking. People nonetheless blame the shrinking inland population partly on decreasing longevity and increasing mortality, and they nurture a powerful metaphorical linkage between Kwaio dying off and what they see as progressive societal decay. I note this here because similar ideas likely inflected 'Are'are perceptions of their population in the 1940s, particularly given that government officers had gone to such lengths to persuade them of a causal link between cultural decadence and population decline.[10]

The early 'Are'are activities were seminal to the form the movement eventually took across Malaita, yet one should avoid the common mistake of seeing 'Are'are as the sole source of the Maasina Rule movement and its ideology or of its challenge to the government. The image of a wave of resistance sweeping out of 'Are'are across political waters vaguely troubled by World War II is a false one; in fact southern 'Are'are emerged from the war as one of the politically calmer areas of Malaita. More to the point, as 'Are'are held their leveling meetings, nascent movements were also emerging in the northern Lau Lagoon and at its southern end around 'Ataa, where the first SILC returnees were landed in February 1944. Many of these returnees disparaged the embryonic government councils and courts, and soon after they arrived, the district's senior headman, Salaimanu, was openly rejected and the Tae Native Council effectively dissolved. North Malaitan antagonism toward the government was from the start more open and confrontational than in the south, a difference that, as we will see, continued through Maasina Rule's various phases.[11]

At this same time, grievances were being discussed at central Malaita "tract meetings" (*talake mitini*). Clement O'ogau, from New Valley along the Kwaiba'ita river in southeastern Kwara'ae, told Ben Burt of attending these across the river, in Kwaio, and the complaints discussed: "We make the paddock for them, then it bears fruit, they make copra, they take the money; they don't give us good money or good wages. So it means the white men are robbing us....We are like dogs. They make a dog go into the scrub to attack a wild pig; well, they eat the good parts of it and throw the bones away for the dog....We get everything to give them a good living but we don't do anything for our own living." Similar meetings were being held through east Kwaio and Kwara'ae and over to the west coast and Langalanga. Some political activities, especially in the north and in Langalanga, were permutations of the "Red Cross" ventures described in chapter 4. The essential point here is that in almost every part of Malaita political actions were being organized outside of and in opposition to government channels and purview. When Maasina Rule rolled out from 'Are'are, it meshed with these activities and synchronized them for a time into an island-wide movement that rejected the prewar status quo and pursued a new vision of a liberated and prosperous future.[12]

In early 1945 the movement began to extend; at a Takataka meeting in January, 40 'Are'are leaders agreed to transmit its ideas across Small Malaita and then northward. Also about this time, emissaries from 'Ataa, northern Lau, and the adjacent mainland began canoeing to southern Lau villages near Walade and 'Are'are, seeking information about the movement. Throughout Maasina Rule, this northern-southern Lau social and trade network facilitated linkage between the two ends of the island. Before long, men from Kwaio and points north were traveling to consult organizers at Takataka, Wairokai, and Kiu in 'Are'are, and on Small Malaita. In early November, the movement was carried to the 'Are'are community at Marau in east Guadalcanal from whence it spread westward, and soon men were paddling trading canoes from there and other islands to 'Are'are for discussion and advice. These contacts paved the way for rapid expansion through and outward from Malaita, though for the movement's duration Malaitan leaders remained concerned mostly with their own island and with Malaitans working elsewhere.[13]

Word of mouth and rumors often distorted Malaitan leaders' ideas and words. William Davenport told me that when he spoke to former Makiran movement leaders in the mid-1960s he found "great variation in their beliefs and goals" from those on Malaita, yet "in every case there was an insistence that the 'word' they proclaimed had come directly from one or another of the movement leaders: Timothy George, Nori, Aliki Nono'oohimae." Elsewhere, too, there were often differences between what leaders said and messages attributed to them, which confused government officers trying to fathom the movement. Later, District Commissioner Central Ken Crass was told George was refusing to meet with anyone from Makira but leaders, because "M.R.M. sections in the latter island are mis-interpreting higher policy and bringing the whole movement into disrepute."[14] Tomasi Leo of Small Malaita testified during the 1947 trial of the Maasina Rule head chiefs: "All the small chiefs in the MR and the people use...your name [Nori], Aliki Nono'oohimae's and Timothy George's as justification for everything."

Nori had rejoined the Labour Corps after a short visit home in February and March of 1944 and so was away for most of the earliest activity, but in March 1945 he returned to 'Are'are and quickly joined Nono'oohimae as a leader and organizer. In April some ideas of the movement—now conceived explicitly as a Malaita-wide organization—were put forward in a "council" document likely written at Nono'oohimae's village. It declared the movement's primary purpose to be to talk about and oversee "custom." It named as leaders Nori, Nono'oohimae, and Hoasihau and called for appointment of a single "chief" to oversee the political organization of Malaita, with four other chiefs to serve under him—two each for northern and southern Malaita.[15] It said that when the main chief was selected the government would be informed and that cooperation had already been secured from all headmen as far north as Sinalagu. Though this document was not given to government officers, like many produced over the months to come it forswore opposition to either the government or the Christian missions (in this context meaning missionaries and their activities). Soon after, the government appointed Headman Hoasihau president of west 'Are'are's new native council and Nori to its court.[16]

A turning point came in mid-1945 when Nori led his first extended tour or "patrol" (*patalolo*) north from 'Are'are along the east coast as far as southern Kwara'ae, stopping at passages to speak to large waiting crowds over a three-week period. Sale Kaakalade from 'Oloburi, on the Kwaio-'Are'are border, in 1982 described to me Nori's visit there: "When Nori came [in a large 'Are'are composite canoe], we had an honor guard perform for him and prepared a big feast and all sorts of festivities. The men who ran the meeting were 'Unuamae of 'Oloburi, Balaone Porohiano, who was Nori's older 'brother,' and Nori.[17] Everywhere they went we duties [movement police] escorted them." In his speeches Nori stressed that Malaitans had failed to achieve their goals under European guidance and that instead they had to follow Malaitan leaders in pursuit of Malaitan ambitions—success would come only in this way. He spoke of the need to plan educational and medical programs that Malaitans would administer. Some have told me that he talked at this time about Americans helping the movement, but others say not.[18]

I am inclined to believe that Nori did not on these tours tell people that Americans would help the movement. But on this point evidence is poor, and it is well to caution here that oral historical overviews of Maasina Rule, like European accounts, often collapse the movement's diverse ideas and phases into a single historical moment. One manifestation of this is that Nori is at times recalled as having laid out the complete Maasina Rule program during his early patrols, even aspects that emerged only later, sometimes conceived by others. It is also apparent that aspects of Nori's message were opaque, heard by different people in different ways as filtered through their own political views. Finally, many statements were later attributed to Nori and other Maasina Rule leaders that they never made. In any case, it is clear that many Malaitans were at this time motivated partly by hopes that Americans would come to their aid, something I delve into in chapter 7.

In June 1946, at invitation from northern leaders, Nori led a second east coast patrol, this time continuing north through Lau and as far as Suu'aba in northern To'abaita, at one point addressing an audience of several thousand. Meetings about Maasina Rule had been held across the north since November 1945, and people were already preparing to plant large coastal villages and gardens. SSEM leader Mariko of Malu'u took diary notes on Nori's visit to Kwai on 10 June 1946, which more than 900 attended. There Nori received a fanfare similar to that Kaakalade described from 'Oloburi, with songs performed by a band and several prayers said by Christians present. Nori spoke of "staying together in one village either in the bush or along the coast. Feeding pigs, making farms of rice or potatoes, collecting and putting money in one house." He told the people, "Those who do not believe what Masine Rule says will stay out side of Masine Rule. Don't listen to what they said. But you must listen to what we say." Mariko's summary says nothing of Americans.[19]

Many along these tours met Nori's request for "pound-head" (£1 per person) contributions to the movement, often proffered in the US currency in wide circulation. (Malaitans called US dollars "pounds.") Some gave less, and in places senior men gave on behalf of their extended families, a mode of feast presentation of the period. These and later contributions were held by local leaders in each district and were intended to fund movement programs, including hiring foreign specialists such as medical personnel and agricultural advisers. Forster heard that by June 1945, £3,000 had already been raised.[20] People contributed enthusiastically and contrasted this with paying government taxes and mission tithes—not only was it voluntary, but Malaitans would decide how this money was to be spent, exclusively on projects for them. Donations, and in places public displays of shell money, harnessed indigenous meanings of wealth displays to symbolically raise leaders' status and show allegiance to them. Government officers initially suspected fund collectors were grifters but later discarded that idea. As David Trench later wrote (within one of the most negative appraisals of Maasina Rule ever written), movement funds "were carefully preserved."[21]

Nori's patrols won the movement enthusiastic followers over a wide area. Soon after his second such tour, the SSEM's R J McBride toured Malaita in the mission ship *Evangel* and found that everyone on the east coast belonged to it. Malaitans across the island were carrying out patrols of their own, and movement ideas also spread by other means. A structure was developed of "messenger duties" that manned a relay system reminiscent of the "Pony Express" to swiftly carry directives and other communications around the island. Kaakalade, one of two messengers for 'Oloburi Full Chief Geni'iria, described the system: "Suppose there was an announcement for a meeting at Kiu [Nono'oohimae's home in west 'Are'are] and the message was sent today. By tomorrow it would have reached north Malaita already. A man would carry the message from Kiu south to Maro'u [Takataka] and then up to Maro'upaina, and another duty there would bring it to Maanawai, and then to 'Oloburi and put it in my hand. Then I would take it to the Sinalagu duty Mai'a, and he would carry it on to Uru and their clerk Jason Frankie." Tome Waleanisia, a Maasina Rule leader and scribe on 'Aoke Island in Langalanga, told me of his astonishment when he sent a message to a distant place early one morning and received a written answer that evening. Messages also moved north and south on Lau and Langalanga native-owned cutters. Teams of scribes wrote multiple copies of documents to facilitate their wide and rapid dissemination.[22]

District officers' movements were also tracked in this way with help from Malaitans working for the government, and word of their impending visits reached their destinations ahead of them. Buloli of Laulasi, near 'Aoke in the northern Langalanga Lagoon, described this to anthropologist Guo Pei-yi in 1997: "If the D.C. [district commissioner] from 'Aoke was touring from 'Aoke to Kwaio, on the other side, when the D.C. went into the ship, the message would be passed. The person from 'Aoke would run to the village and tell them that the D.C. was moving to Kwaio....A person from here would run to the next village and tell them, 'the D.C. is coming tomorrow,' and then come back. And then a person would run to the next village and tell. The news would go around the island just like that." There were precedents for this: in 1919 Bell reported that people across Kwara'ae were closely tracking his movements from 'Aoke, and he thought intelligence was being passed from nearby mission villages: "These people know everything about the police on this Station and I have had proof that when I have left here in the *Mala* they have known right across Malaita within twenty-four hours." Regarding the speed at which news of Bell's death had spread through north Malaita, Sandars concluded, "Mental telepathy possibly."[23] Later in the 1940s, officers began composing many messages in code.

Movement Structure and Unity

By 1946 an island-wide structure was coalescing. Malaita was divided into nine districts based loosely on languages. These and lower-level divisions borrowed elements of the administrative structure Bell designed in the 1920s, based on vaguely demarcated sub-districts defined around government tax houses, and subsequently refined by Jack Barley with coastal but only sketchy inland boundaries. (Later the government copied Maasina Rule's model to revise its own administrative divisions.)[24] By mid-1946, each district had appointed its own "head chief." They (and their religious affiliations) were as follows: Timothy George Marata (SSEM) of Ro'one for Small Malaita; Aliki Nono'oohimae (ancestral) of Airairau, Kiu, for 'Are'are and west Kwaio; Jonathan Fifi'i (Adventist) of 'Ilemi, Sinalagu, for east Kwaio; Justus Jimmy Ganifiri (SSEM) of Naafinua for east Kwara'ae; Aliki Basia (ancestral) of Makwanu for Baelelea; Hedley Heber (SSEM) of Rerede for Fataleka; Arnon 'Atoomea (SSEM) of Aniuke, near Malu'u, for To'abaita; and Shadrach Diote'e (SSEM) of Okwala for west Kwara'ae. Timi Kakalu'ae (ancestral) of 'Adagege, a sometimes headman, was head chief for Lau for a time, but in July 1946 he withdrew and became a staunch loyalist. His replacement was Loea (ancestral) of Funafou, who was jailed at 'Aoke in March 1947 and was replaced in turn by Timoti Bobongi (ancestral) of Kwalo'ai (between Makwanu and Takwa). Nori (ancestral, later nominal Catholic) held a pan-Malaita position. Kwara'ae had two chiefs because it was the most populous Malaitan region and because of historical differences between east and west stemming from 'Aoke's location in the latter. Nono'oohimae led both 'Are'are and west Kwaio, and the Kwarekwareo area between them, because of deep cultural and historical ties between these areas and because he already had standing in both.[25]

Under the head chiefs was a nested hierarchy of lesser chiefs over each passage, territory, and descent group, called "full chiefs," "leader chiefs," and "line chiefs" (or "headlines").[26] Some places, like Malu'u, also had "ground chiefs," and below them, "privates." There was variation in lower and, to some degree, higher titles in different times and places, and distinctions sometimes got messy. Formalized hierarchies existed in tension with deeply rooted egalitarian sensibilities, and the leadership structure was more horizontal than vertical—most every senior man could be a chief of some kind. Some held named offices with specific functions: "*kastom* chiefs" (or simply "*kastoms*") oversaw movement rules and regulations and their codification, and "farmer chiefs" supervised communal gardens. "Women's chiefs" (usually men) directed women's labor and other activities, delegating through female leaders who sometimes held titles as well. For example, at Sinalagu in Kwaio, the woman Falaori was chosen *alafanigeni* (women's chief) for inland people, and another, Sula'au, stood for Christian women. Under these chiefs, women held their own meetings, particularly to inculcate rules of sexual behavior, violations of which were presented to the male chiefs by the *alafanigeni* standing with and for the woman involved. A force of movement police called "duties" were led by "strife chiefs," also called "stripe chiefs" for their armbands, which bore the letters NCD, for "Native Council Duty." Duties were to become a special worry for district officers, who accused them of a plethora of abuses.[27]

Although Maasina Rule was remarkable for integrating Malaita politically, its island-wide structural cohesion has often been overstated. Political authority was fragmented, and most "head chiefs" had clout only in their own districts. All embraced basic tenets of movement ideology, and chiefs from across the island met together several times, but in practice the different areas never surrendered autonomy to overarching leaders like Nori or Timothy George. Under a regime of coordination and guidance, even lower-level chiefs could retain significant independence, their authority grounded largely in preexisting personal networks. Few Malaitans envisioned or desired concentrated, centralized control. One source of exaggerations of the movement's unity in academic work has been the writings of colonial officers charged with suppressing it. Even after it became obvious that the movement was a popular one unified more by shared grievances, goals, and ideology than by an integrative leadership structure, many senior officers continued to understand and write about it as a centralized conspiracy orchestrated by a chiefly cabal, who, in Roy Davies's words, "reduced the people nearly to a state of serfdom."[28]

The authority of higher-level chiefs could be fragile even within their own areas. This was a common trait of Malaitan political leadership before Maasina Rule, but now these men were challenged to lead constituencies of unprecedented size and diversity in undertaking extraordinary projects at enormous sacrifice, including mass relocations to the coast, with few sanctions at their disposal other than social pressure. There is little evidence of chiefs using outright coercion to control followers, yet as Maasina Rule took shape, the vast majority of Malaitans threw themselves wholly into the endeavor. To truly understand the movement's success and accomplishments we must look not to chiefly authority but to the solidarity and determination of the rank and file—the real power of Maasina Rule flowed upward from them. This, as I have said, many officers failed to recognize, which led them to make critical tactical blunders in dealing with the movement, as chapters 6–8 detail.

Though Maasina Rule across Malaita shared much in terms of ideology, symbols, rhetoric, and practice, it displayed considerable geographical variation there, and still more on other islands, and it also changed a great deal over time. Differences were starkest between southern Malaita, where the movement developed more in the mold of its founding social engineering projects, and the north, where opposition to government was more bellicose from the start. Furthermore, divides remained everywhere between ancestral and Christian communities and between different Christian denominations, and their relative populations and centrality to the movement varied from place to place. One of Maasina Rule's great achievements was that, for a time, it melded these culturally and religiously diverse groups into a cohesive movement pursuing common goals, and much credit for bringing about this unexpected unity must go to the leaders the people elevated to guide them.

New Leaders

> On one occasion that Nori went and asked for his pipe from the big man of the USA.
> Nori now is the big man for our place. He and Timothy are big men for our place.
> Malaita this time are nearly getting on well, with good things which Nori fight for.
> Nori and Timothy, you two look after our place well because you two are big men for us this time.
> Name of Nori came from USA and it reach England and many other places.
> —Song of the Maasina Rule[29]

What may be the first written government political reference to Nori is a note that Cadet Roy Davies jotted in his east Kwaio tour book for 13 June 1945: "[Uru Headman Maenaa'adi] states that one Lori has been picking up money in Sinerago having worked Wairokai, & Areare. He has little idea of what it's for, but thinks L will be coming to Uru soon. Told him to run him out if he comes." To Europeans, with their stereotypes of classic Melanesian elders and big men, the organizers of postwar movements throughout the region often seemed unlikely leaders and hard to take seriously, and young Nori proved no exception. Sandars later remembered him as "a nice lad and very polite" but "of no particular presence" and not "anything very out of the ordinary." He was described by Resident Commissioner Noel as "a glib-tongued orator," and by Davies as "a flabby, unprepossessing little man," but later as "a born politician and a wonderful orator" who could "charm the birds out of the trees for a Melanesian audience," "but no policy-maker." "To the natives," Davies wrote, "his name was magic." To Colin Allan he was "short, slight and somewhat timid" but "something of an extrovert" and "single-minded, obstinate and determined." Trench saw in him "an insignificant specimen, with the obstinacy of foolishness, a codger at heart." Michael Forster in 1946 gave a more detailed and less disparaging depiction: "Nono'oohimae appears to have given place to Nori who is a more colorful figure. This man has a small stocky well-knit figure with a light skin and black wavey hair. He has a pleasant personality and good manners. His knowledge of English is limited to pidgin. He comes from a part of Malaita where the people are above the average in intelligence and general ability. His previous dealings with whites have convinced him that they were making large profits out of the natives. There is no doubt that he is a clever orator and has been known to address an audience of some thousands of natives for a whole night. Nevertheless it is unlikely that his is the brain behind the movement. Generally speaking primitive peoples keep their leaders in the background and Nori is more likely to be a scapegoat." In reality, Nori was a creative thinker and renowned as a gifted speaker, no small compliment coming from Malaitans. His official position in Maasina Rule's hierarchy was ambiguous at times, but most came to see him as the leader, and he is generally remembered as such today.[30]

Ma'aanamae of Kwaio was a close friend of young Nori and bunked with him on Levers's Russell Islands plantation until the Japanese invasion. During the evacuation to Malaita their ship ran aground on Nu'ula'a reef, miles from the coast, and young Nori impressed fellow passengers by grabbing a canoe, paddling to 'Aoke, and bringing the *Tulagi* to tow them off. Ma'aanamae remembered the 20-year-old as kind and articulate, but, like others I talked to who knew Nori before the war, said that at that time he was notably apolitical. Nori is often recalled as expert in 'Are'are *sahu* divination, in which answers are read in patterns in lime sprinkled on the diviner's arm. Men who had been with Nori on Guadalcanal told me how, after the January 1943 bombing that killed several Malaitans, he correctly divined that the rest of them would survive the war. Crack Malaitan diviners I know are socially highly astute, and in addition to his other traits Nori had a reputation for social acumen. He was "in practice a pagan," though he was later baptized as a Catholic.[31]

A now-famous story tells how, in a Guadalcanal bunker, Nori met with an American officer who instructed him to carry out Maasina Rule. A version circulating in 1945 said that Nori, along with Ratu (Fifi'i's uncle and later an 'Oloburi full chief) and Sukulu (later a west Kwara'ae chief), had met an American general who told them to organize a Malaita-wide council to administer the island on behalf of the coming American government. Later renderings became still more mythologized, and the general has a golden pipe, inspired perhaps by Douglas MacArthur's famous corncob, while much later adaptations say Nori met John F Kennedy. Excerpts from one version capture the main themes: "Nori met with an American lieutenant who was in a foxhole. He gave Nori a pipe. The American told him, 'The government is blocking the higher wages and the things we Americans want to give to you. You must work apart from the British government. They are treating you badly. We have died to protect you, and the British would not have done that. You must go and collect a pound-tax from each person.'...Nori was a bushman and unsophisticated...but after this meeting he came back to Malaita and launched the work." Still other versions share elements with the 1939 story of the priest Noto'i being given instructions by two American bird hunters, also on Guadalcanal. In these, Nori is given the word by two US captains named "Dio Wao" (Joe War) and "George Masin" or "Maasina." The latter may be a spin on US General George Marshall, or perhaps on Captain John E Martin, who in 1950 commanded the few Americans still in the Solomons and received unsolicited letters and money from Malaitans seeking American help in removing the colonial government. Whether Nori ever met any Americans of significant rank is unknown. To my knowledge, he never claimed to have received direct instructions from specific Americans to organize Maasina Rule, though he did discuss his and others' many political conversations with Americans, and this would have been interpreted and distorted in various ways by word of mouth.[32]

A key visionary for Maasina Rule, and a primary leader in its formative stages, was Aliki Nono'oohimae (also known as Erehau), head chief for 'Are'are, west Kwaio, and Kwarekwareo. His founding role has already been described, and he was a major force in the movement until his 1947 arrest and then again later. In many places, especially in the southern half of Malaita, he is recalled as Nori's equal or second-in-command and sometimes as his superior in social stature. Labor recruiter Ernie Palmer, who knew Malaitans well, especially 'Are'are and Kwaio, thought Nono'oohimae was "the real brain behind the Movement."[33] There is less in government archives from this period about Nono'oohimae than about Nori or Timothy George, probably due to his more reserved countenance around officers and Europeans generally. Forster, for example, wrote, "Not much can be said of Nonohimae who is quiet and gives the impression of being a thinker." Colin Allan, not given to praising resistant Malaitans, later recalled him as "a man with piercing eyes, grave, thoughtful, dignified, sensitive, a charismatic leader and an orator," and in 1950, when the head chiefs were released from prison, amidst Allan's demeaning caricatures of each of the other head chiefs he wrote, "Undoubtedly he gives the impression of having depth of character, capacity for thought, and fixity of purpose. One feels he has bourne his imprisonment and release with detached dignity." (Allan wrote these words after Nono'oohimae agreed to work with the government; see chapter 8.)[34] Davies found Nono'oohimae "inflexible" and wrote, "Above all else he was a traditionalist and probably more responsible than anyone else for the emphasis on 'custom.'" Malaitans accorded Nono'oohimae high respect, and alone among the head chiefs he brought to the movement a chiefly status, from within the 'Are'are leadership system. One of his key confederates in the south was Takataka Full Chief Waiparo who, as we will see, became the most influential figure in Malaitan post–Maasina Rule *kastom* politics.[35]

Another principal Maasina Rule leader to emerge from the south was Small Malaita's Head Chief Timothy George Marata, of Ro'one, Port Adam. At a meeting at Waisisi on 1 November 1945, he was formally elevated as the movement chief over 'Are'are and Small Malaita (though he had been selected some time before), and each local group presented him with shell money to hold. He later became for a time the formal head of Maasina Rule as a whole, with Nori named as his second-in-command. Over the longer term, George was less important than Nono'oohimae and especially Nori in the movement's advance, but he nonetheless stands as a key leader, particularly in the early stages.[36]

George's background was unusual, having been born about 1892 in Queensland and raised there by his Langalanga father and Small Malaita mother, with whom he first arrived on Small Malaita around 1906. His father leased a small Queensland cane farm and could have been exempted from deportation but chose to return home to work as an SSEM teacher. George completed several years of education in Queensland, and he wrote and spoke English well enough to serve Norman Deck as a mission text translator. In 1913 he traveled to Australia and New Zealand where, Corris wrote, "he witnessed dock strikes and may have picked up some pointers on industrial action." Forster observed of George, "Like many Australian-born people he is keenly interested in Labour activities and particularly strikes." George had been a senior headman for Small Malaita beginning in mid-1923, one of the few early appointees in whom Bell expressed confidence and expectations. At the end of 1925, however, Bell suspended him, citing allegations of sexual impropriety and assault, though George was already preparing to quit. He taught briefly at a school at the SSEM station at Onepusu and then turned to crewing on mission and plantation ships. During the war, George organized the supply of Small Malaitan thatch leaf to US forces and made several visits to their camps on Guadalcanal.[37]

In early 1944, Forster appointed George an assistant district headman and also charged him with running a trade store scheme from his village of Ro'one. Forster said he was "thoroughly reliable and trustworthy, and very well educated." When he learned George was to be the head chief for the south, Forster opined that he was "much too fond of his five pounds a month as storekeeper to be a serious nuisance." These assessments soon changed when George did become an active leader, after which Forster wrote that he had been dismissed from earlier headman and SSEM positions because he was *not* reliable. Forster described him then as "an energetic man among a moribund people.... He has a smooth and hypocritical manner and is clever at saying what he thinks his hearers wish to hear.... It is doubtful if he has any great intellectual power. He enjoys his position on account of his knowledge of English and his experience of the outside world. It was felt [by Maasina Rule adherents] he would be able to supply knowledge formerly obtained from white people and would know best how to deal with them." George resented the low status and wages that, despite his education, were his lot as a Solomon Islander, and, as Corris observed, it is no surprise that he became involved in Maasina Rule. Equally unsurprising is that many Europeans despised him. Trench thought him "mercenary minded" and "mostly in it for what he could get," and others expressed similar contempt.[38]

Head Chief Jonathan Fifi'i was not as prominent as Nori, Nono'oohimae, or George in Maasina Rule as an island-wide movement, and his influence was limited primarily to east and central Kwaio. Still, Fifi'i would attain a different sort of importance: his vision of the movement has significantly influenced the written history of Maasina Rule through his work, starting in 1962, with anthropologist Roger Keesing, and through the publication of his 1989 autobiography and other papers that give lively accounts of the movement as he experienced it.[39]

Fifi'i returned from his first stint as the Sinalagu SILC section's sergeant in mid-1944, hoping to organize political activities he had discussed with Nono'oohimae, Nori, and others on Guadalcanal. He presented these ideas to people around Sinalagu, including his uncles Headman Sirifa and Assistant Headman Balaone Kwarialaena (or Brown, Faana'o), but they vetoed the plans, warning they might provoke government punitive actions like those of 1927. Sirifa, slowly dying of tuberculosis, pressured Fifi'i to assume his position as headman, but Fifi'i instead rejoined the corps. He returned to Kwaio in August 1945 at age 24 to find the political scene dramatically changed and Maasina Rule well underway. Sirifa, who died three months later, had become a movement supporter and had invited Nori to Sinalagu to tell people about the 'Are'are work. Though Fifi'i had spent much of his adult life away from home, in mid-1946 Kwaio selected him as their head chief. By then Kwaio had told Sandars about their Maasina Rule activities, including the choice of Fifi'i, whom Sandars met and approved. Shortly after, Fifi'i led a large Kwaio patrol to 'Aoke, where Sandars again endorsed his appointment but warned him to work with the headmen. Fifi'i also led several patrols to 'Are'are and Small Malaita to meet with Nono'oohimae, Nori, and others.[40]

FIGURE 5.2. Jonathan Fifi'i campaign poster, ca early 1970s. Pictures of a house, canoe, or pipe cue voters to the correct candidate's box in which to place their ballot. (Author's collection.)

Fifi'i was the only Adventist head chief, but he was not particularly religious. Throughout the movement and his life he nurtured staunch ties with Kwaio inland groups. During Maasina Rule, Christians were still a small coastal minority in east Kwaio, and many important movement leaders there came from the mountains, though others were SSEM men, like Full Chief Jason Frankie and 'Abaeata Anifelo at Uru, and Fifi'i's Strife Chief Tome Toloasi Teeboo, a former policeman from Naanakinimae on the Sinalagu-'Oloburi mountain border. For SSEM leaders, these men all maintained unusually good relations with the non-Christian community. The 1947 Malaita Annual Report of Roy Davies, by then district commissioner, singled out Fifi'i among the head chiefs as "perhaps the most fanatical of them all. Obsessed by religion and what he thought was his own mission in life, he was exactly the stuff of which martyrs and fanatics are made."[41] If so, Fifi'i fully altered his personality by the time Keesing met him 15 years later, and Kwaio oral histories contradict this portrayal as well and depict him as having been a moderating influence (see chapter 8). On what Davies based his opinion is unknown—Fifi'i got on well with Sandars and Forster, and until his arrest had not met Davies or his cadet Peter Cameron, although Cameron, based on secondhand information, believed Fifi'i's politics were more "extreme" than leaders of nearby Kwai. East Kwaio was perhaps Malaita's most fully Maasina Rule area, though the following was near 100 percent in the east from Kwara'ae south through at least Takataka. Fifi'i spoke the truth when he testified at his trial, "I do not know of anyone in my district outside Marching Rule." Some months after Fifi'i's 1947 arrest, three people were outside the movement at Sinalagu, and none at Uru.[42]

Farther north, in Lau, after Loea's early-1947 arrest, the head chief was Timoti Bobongi, age 26, of Kwalo'ai. He had left Lau in his early teens, in 1934, to work as a cook for Carpenter's and then on Choiseul, and he later became captain of the BSIP Medical Department launch. This prepared him for wartime work driving an American barge. Davies, who denigrated the character of nearly every chief, later described Bobongi as "easily led by the wrong people, and almost completely lacking in moral fiber," and Allan, who followed Davies's example, said he had "no character, no personality." Sixteen years later, anthropologist and folklorist Elli Maranda worked closely with Bobongi, an expert storyteller, singer, and carver. She wrote that he was intelligent and subtle, and noted, "Whatever the task at hand, Bobongi is a very ambitious man and sets himself high standards." The head chief in adjacent Baelelea was Basi (or Basia, Basi'a, Basi'i, Basini), a former crewmember of the Melanesian Mission ship *Gwen*. Fifi'i recalled Basi for his generosity and prowess as a feast giver. Davies wrote of him, "A pagan with no education but many years of experience of the ways of Europeans; emotional and unpredictable, he was an exhibitionist with admittedly considerable personal magnetism; the complete bully— but of no consequence and social standing in the community according to former native standards," and later said that "he had no brains." I present these officers' comments on the chiefs to introduce readers to the deep disrespect many paid to Malaitans who dared to challenge white rule, not only in writing but also to their faces. Such attitudes purged Malaitans of any regard for these same officers and led to grave problems for the government.[43]

Christian Leadership and the Missions

Maasina Rule was not a religious movement in the usual sense, but that is not to say it was nonreligious, any more than almost anything important on Malaita was or is. Catholic priests said mass for chiefs, people who followed ancestors sacrificed and prayed to secure their support, SSEM members virtually melded their church with the movement, and Anglican laymen (though few clergy) prayed and sang hymns for its success. Even Adventists formed their own towns. In other words, everyone marshaled their various spiritual forces to the service of Maasina Rule, and a miraculous aspect of the movement is how they all worked together.

The other four northern head chiefs (Ganifiri, Hedley, 'Atoomea, and Diote'e) were SSEM mission teachers. SSEM leaders were well represented in Maasina Rule's hierarchy overall, making up half of the original head chiefs. Even in Kwaio, 'Are'are, and other places where Christians were a minority, mission teachers were key participants. There were many reasons for this. First, teachers around Malaita had for years gathered regularly for training at SSEM conventions and schools such as Onepusu, and they held weekly sub-district meetings. Teachers had maintained letter-writing networks since the Queensland days. For Maasina Rule, such church networks offered ready integrative structures. Teachers also had the relatively high levels of European knowledge the movement was expected to need, and many were already experienced managers of larger coastal communities, much like those Maasina Rule was now creating. Teachers, like inland leaders, had always dealt with many disputes outside of government courts, as Maasina Rule proponents now planned to do.[44]

There was a more fundamental reason for Christian enthusiasms for Maasina Rule, both among leaders and within the rank and file. In becoming Christians, most had staked their faith not only on one version or another of the Christian God, but also on a brighter future that would follow if they took up other European ways and gave up valued Malaitan ones. White missionaries encouraged this expectation, though most envisaged tight constraints on Melanesian secular advancement. To the degree Malaitans accepted church rules against participating in local economies—bridewealth, compensation, mortuary exchanges, and sometimes even shell money use—they were left more dependent on the cash economy and vulnerable to its vagaries. For them, too, the need for education was more pressing and the dearth of medical services more glaring. Furthermore, Christians, particularly the large majority living near the coast, had little choice but to interact much more with Europeans and their surrogates and to allow their interventions in their affairs—not just missionaries but also colonial officers and police who frequented coastal areas, as well as the government headmen who lived there. In contrast, most inland people, except when laboring, could for the most part avoid such entanglements so long as they paid their tax and did not commit serious crimes. Many Christians felt they had given up and taken on much by breaking with their ancestors, kin groups, and past ways, and they expected to enjoy benefits in return. When these were not forthcoming, Christians had more reason to feel betrayed by the colonial system as they came to realize that it would continue to humiliate them and stymie their aspirations.[45]

For Christians, too, shared religious beliefs provided an ideological base that helped the movement transcend other divisions. Christians often cited biblical concepts of human equality and brotherhood as corroborating movement goals, and even non-Christians could relate to these and appreciate basic Christian messages about liberation from oppression. As forewarned by Archdeacon Pritt at the century's turn, Islanders' "untutored minds" had taken literally "the doctrine of all men's equality in the sight of Heaven," and they were now determined to demand its fulfillment. In sum, it is little wonder the vast majority of Christians enthusiastically embraced Maasina Rule and its message. The movement over time also changed aspects of Christian ideologies and permanently redistributed power within the churches, particularly the SSEM.[46]

The SSEM's power in the movement increased from Kwara'ae northward. The head chief in east Kwara'ae was 40-year-old Justus Jimmy Ganifiri, a teacher headquartered at the settlement of Naafinua on the Bulia river (missionary McBride dismissed him as a teacher in early 1947 due to his movement activities). His father, Jimmy Fiuloa, who had been forced to go to Queensland by his family in punishment for misdeeds, returned years later as a Christian. Naafinua was founded (at a place named Rade) in 1916 and grew into east Kwara'ae's main SSEM center. In 1938 Ganifiri started a school there and the site later became Maasina Rule's base of operations. Overall, he was a moderating force within the movement, opposed to some of the antigovernment policies that eventually emerged in the north. Davies described him as "a shrewd and determined man, with many years of experience of exercising authority, and with a firm belief in his own inspiration and essential rightness," and Cameron thought highly enough of him to recommend his appointment as a headman even though he was a Maasina Rule leader. Ganifiri's intellect is apparent from reading his testimony at the trial of the head chiefs, the most impressive statement made there.[47]

The SSEM's centrality to Maasina Rule peaked in To'abaita. We have seen in earlier chapters that the mission there, particularly at Malu'u, had often crossed swords with Headman Maekali and his native council, and Maekali soon became a movement enemy. Cadet Wilfred Marquand wrote from his Malu'u post in 1947, "The Marching Rule appears to be based around S.S.E.M. teaching tied up with religion." There were many non-Christian members—Frazer estimated that about half the To'abaita were Christians in 1939, including many Anglicans, though Christian numbers likely had, as in most places, risen by 1946 (see note 93). The head chief there was SSEM teacher Arnon 'Atoomea (or Anoni, Rinalu) from near Malu'u. A former student at the mission's Malu'u school, he began teaching at its Onepusu center in 1938, and during the war he administered Onepusu while white missionaries were away. In 1945 he returned home to start a new school and soon became a community leader. In April 1946, at age 26, he was selected as To'abaita's head chief. Davies called him "proud and arrogant," and later "a zealot," while in 1951 Resident Commissioner Gregory-Smith was struck by 'Atoomea's "presence and dignity."[48]

To'abaita's key leader over a longer term, with a strong following also in nearby Baegu, was Full Chief Shem Irofa'alu of Kalemane, 'Airade. He was 'Atoomea's uncle and held great influence over him. Successor to the famous Peter Abu'ofa as the area's SSEM leader, Irofa'alu had long been a bitter rival of Maekali—he pointedly reminded Marquand that he had always been excluded from Maekali's government council "because he was not a proper chief." During the early Maasina Rule period Irofa'alu and his followers competed for power with Maekali, leading in June 1946 to the latter's resignation for a time. One officer described Irofa'alu as "a man of outstanding personality, tremendous egotism and ambition," and Marquand believed that Irofa'alu, not 'Atoomea, was the effective Maasina Rule leader in To'abaita.[49]

Fataleka's head chief was another SSEM teacher, Hedley Heber (or I'amaea). Davies wrote that he was "a well-educated and highly intelligent man…quiet and intensely sincere, but embittered by imagined wrongs, and with a streak of fanaticism in him," while Officer Tom Russell thought him "a personable man with intelligence." A few years later District Officer James Tedder found him "intelligent and interesting" and running a medical aid post, and Hedley later earned high praise as a teacher at a Rerede elementary school. The head chief across the island in west Kwara'ae was SSEM teacher Shadrach Diote'e Kalani ("Shadrach Dio," or "Joe"), from Okwala. Sandars had in late 1945 appointed Diote'e head of the Kwaimela Native Council because he was not then a Maasina Rule member, and he was also headman for Kwaimela Sub-district. Davies later wrote that Diote'e was "intelligent, able, and sincere, but with a deep conviction that he was leading his people away from an unrighteous bondage," and in 1948 Forster said he was "a man of ability and influence and to be trusted," but "suffering from a conflict of loyalties." By then he had broken with Maasina Rule, and Fifi'i disparaged him to me as the only head chief who "gave up to the government." As 1947 progressed, Diote'e was pushed aside by Full Chief Nelson Kifo (or Kefu [SSEM]) of Fulisango, whom we will meet in the next chapter.[50]

As described earlier, many SSEM teachers had established themselves as political leaders and led sustained opposition to particular headmen and government policies. Many had also come to resent their church's Australian missionaries, whom, as Maasina Rule grew, Malaitans began to disparage as "church government." The missionaries' standing had declined during the war and now began to slip away completely, especially in the north. The Decks and their colleagues were beside themselves when Irofa'alu, 'Atoomea, Ganifiri, and other teachers thought to be steadfastly loyal rejected their authority, and the movement ordered men working for the SSEM at Onepusu to return home. At first the SSEM missionaries tried to maintain an outwardly neutral position toward the movement, but when they found themselves rejected outright by rebellious teachers and congregations they became staunchly anti–Maasina Rule and labeled its people philistines. The church's Wilbur Clark lamented, "The Devil has deceived the people into believing that their Movement is of God," and Deck wrote, "The people have refused to hear us in their churches," and then, "There can be no question I think of the Satanic deception of the movement, but the teachers don't see it yet." A popular Christian song was "Jesus He Say 'Yes' for Maasina Rule."[51]

The independence that Malaitan church leaders had enjoyed during the war continued to varying degrees, especially in the SSEM. In July 1947, citing Justus Ganifiri and Irofa'alu as examples, Sandars argued that many government troubles were "directly traceable to these SSEM native leaders who have gone wrong through lack of supervision," and he complained that SSEM missionaries would not visit their flocks: "Since 1943 they have done no fieldwork. The few European missionaries remain at Onepusu stating that they are hampered by lack of transport. This is true but so are others who still get around amongst their people. The missionaries are now looked upon with scorn by many of their adherents—who have joined the Melanesian Mission." Deck had left in late 1944, and Sandars hoped that his return that July would help matters, but an informant warned him that things had gone too far for that.[52]

Anglican missionaries were scarcely more successful in controlling their flocks; many people resented the church's links to the government and thought some of its missionaries arrogant. The latter were not the compassionate freethinkers some of their predecessors had been. Bishop Baddeley, in particular, still saw Melanesians as his inferiors: "an infant race, they are loveable—like children," and he described the non-Christian life as one of "darkness, dirt, disease, devils." (His more progressive successor, Bishop Caulton, promoted them in 1950 to "adolescents.") Though most lay Anglicans joined Maasina Rule, few of the church's 80 native priests and deacons on Malaita did so, and for this they were shunned. Archdeacon of the Central Solomons Harry Reynolds in early 1948 issued a pastoral directive—"To all the Faithful of the Church of Melanesia. I command...you all to leave Marching Rule at once"—to be read out in every church. Caulton claimed that Anglican Maasina Rule adherents had "without exception" remained loyal to the church, though he noted difficult personal relations between priests and laity. But in truth many Anglicans in the south and some in the north defected to the Catholic Church—some because of Reynolds's directive—and others went over to the SSEM (though in places SSEM members became Anglican). Despite these troubles, most Anglican missionaries did not experience the degree of personal rejection the SSEM missionaries did.[53]

To the disgust of government officers, the Catholic Church was for a time sympathetic toward Maasina Rule. Father Bernard Van de Walle in 'Are'are wrote to Bishop Jean-Marie Aubin in March 1947, "The Marching Rule has done only good for the advancement of our religion. The lagoon is ripe. There are fine villages of sixty to eighty people where formerly there were only one or two families." Catholic numbers on Malaita grew from 5,410 in 1946 to 7,694 in 1950. Hugh Laracy, who has detailed Marist–Maasina Rule relationships, particularly in 'Are'are, pointed out that, relative to other missionaries, Catholic clergy tended to have closer, more social contacts with Malaitans, and in the south in particular the movement was friendly toward priests. The priests were also more distant from the government, particularly compared with Anglican and even SSEM missionaries, who were committed to imperial rule. One priest in particular, Jean Tiggler, is said to have advised the movement early on at Rokera in 'Are'are, and after he died of blackwater fever in 1945 some thought the government had poisoned him, perhaps for contacting the US Command on Maasina Rule's behalf. It was later rumored on Guadalcanal that Tiggler's skull was exhumed and taken back to Malaita. In places, Catholic prayers were offered before Maasina Rule meetings and, later, masses were reportedly said for release of jailed chiefs. In early 1949, however, some Catholic priests turned against the movement since, said one officer, they "decided, rightly or wrongly, that the movement is communistic."[54]

Maasina Rule dismayed most white missionaries and they spoke against it. Noel later told the high commission, "They have not failed to observe the religious note in Marching Rule propaganda, and the danger that it may result in the founding of some new amalgam of the various Christian faiths." In April 1947, District Commissioner Central Crass was concerned that a "bastard religion" might be forming. Missionaries also worried that they would cease to be integral to Malaitan Christianities, and it was said that Shem Irofa'alu and other SSEM teachers were already saying, "The day of the independent Malaita Church has dawned." Charles Fox seems to have been alone in admiring how Maasina Rule united people across denominations.[55]

Later, after the government began trying to suppress the movement, the SSEM would come still more to the visible fore, especially from the European perspective, because many non-Christians relocated their towns into the interior where whites rarely ventured. But the SSEM position also became more difficult to gauge because, in parts of the north at least, some movement settlements, even some with multidenominational and large non-Christian populations, began to be called "Mission Towns," and Maasina Rule council houses were, Cadet Marquand reported, "converted into schools and decorated with religious pictures"; he also said, "The teachers, although often unqualified as such by any recognized mission, are actually the Marching Rule leaders of the town and state that the pagans are 'learners' in the mission." Some officers came to associate Maasina Rule exclusively with the SSEM, to an exaggerated degree. Colin Allan's misstatement that all but one head chief (or at times *all* of them) were SSEM men has, as Keesing noted, been much repeated. Allan despised the mission, which he thought was, "in the native mind," a cargo cult, and at times he blamed Maasina Rule largely on its sins. The literature is infused with distortions drawn from Allan's misstatements from this perspective. The SSEM's role in Maasina Rule was also exaggerated when, as we will see, officers Marquand, Cameron, Davies, Allan, and Russell spent almost all of their time in the north, especially at Kwai and Malu'u, where SSEM leadership was strongest, and extrapolated the situations there to the entire island, including many places they had rarely or never visited.[56]

None of these cautions are meant to downplay or deny the major role of the evangelicals in the movement—they were key in many places, as other churches, or ancestors, were elsewhere. This presented a problem for the government: colonial policy had long been to defer to religious practices so long as they did not deeply offend European sensibilities. Marquand, for example, worried about the religious trappings he observed in Maasina Rule because, he wrote, "Owing to the necessity for allowing the people religious freedom this might make it very difficult in future to proclaim this a subversive organization." Malaitans were well aware that officers were averse to interfering with things they perceived to be religious, from having long observed this in practice and having officers explain it to them. Though most Christians were sincere when wrapping what Marquand called a "religious cloak" around their political pursuits, this did not preclude them and others from also doing so as a savvy political tactic. Later, when officers worked tirelessly to destroy Maasina Rule, particularly after 1948, some came to believe that the SSEM, run by teachers free of white missionaries, had become a religious veneer deceitfully covering secular, criminal political activities. Marquand said meetinghouses were falsely labeled as "churches" so officers would not destroy them, and some officers thought the SSEM in particular was no longer a legitimate religion or deserving of protection as such. They greatly overstated this, but years later I myself watched Malaitans plan and execute manipulations of government noninterference policies. In 1951, Allan declared the SSEM teacher community was "an enemy of the state" and that the church was a "pathetic relic of Victorian evangelism" that should not be let to "once more fasten its stifling tentacles on the island of Malaita." He also loathed the Catholic Church, however, and blamed Maasina Rule on its "endeavouring and succeeding to roll its purple carpet across the length and breadth of Malaita."[57]

Better Homes and Gardens: Maasina Rule Social Engineering

Beginning in November 1945, Nori spent two or three months with Timothy George at Ro'one to gain his counsel. On 15 December they composed Maasina Rule's "First Order for the Island" for circulation. Labeled "made up by Nori, under Chief Timothy George," it directed that no one should volunteer to labor for Europeans, for all would be needed for new works at home, and it gave the first indication as to what those works would be: everyone was to consolidate in large villages and select chiefs for their areas. At this time also, plans were broadcast to plant large gardens all round the island.[58] The First Order formally launched a massive project of social revision soon taken up by most Malaitans, which entailed radical changes in leadership structures, residential and subsistence patterns, substantive and procedural law, and social relations generally. What follows examines these undertakings and some of their successes and failures.

Key aspects of these endeavors were partly inspired by and closely resembled colonial projects described in previous chapters, most obviously the division of the fluid cultural landscape into circumscribed zones for administration, taxation, and the appointment of chiefs; the organization of native courts and councils; and aforementioned elements of the 'Are'are repopulation project. Yet it is a mistake to see these, as some have, as naive imitations of colonial ventures or crude mimicry of US military practices. As leaders set out to organize the diverse and atomistic Malaitan populations, many of which were dispersed in hamlets that shifted often across rugged country, they faced some of the same problems as had the colonial state, and in many cases they borrowed and adapted similar solutions: concentrating people into coastal settlements to better monitor and organize them and to sustain cooperative projects, devising rules by which the new society would be governed, conducting a comprehensive census including vital statistics, and even reviving the formerly hated maintenance of "roads" from place to place with groups responsible for specified segments. But now, because these endeavors were undertaken by and for Malaitans, the populace took them up with enthusiasm.[59]

Towns and Farms

Following Nori and George's First Order, Malaitans began planning large villages they called "towns" (*taoni,* or occasionally "communities," *komunima*) on or near the coast, building them most intensively from later 1946 into early 1947. Towns became central to Maasina Rule's development and, later, to its challenge to the government. Their nature and meanings changed through phases of the movement, but here I focus mostly on the initial towns in 1946 and 1947.[60]

People iterated many reasons for building towns. Most often stressed by leaders in the movement's formative years was that concentrated communities would allow organization of projects through which Malaitans could attain development and earn money, impossible if many lived in scattered hamlets. Kwaio have portrayed the radical and difficult relocation to me as having expressed their shared commitment to work together for change. In the same vein, Fifi'i later attributed to Nori the idea that towns would communicate to the government just how serious Malaitans were about the work. At a deeper level, relocation to the sea had over the decades come to symbolize a shift, sometimes a radical one, toward adoption of new ways and other kinds of changes, and this harmonized with Maasina Rule's transformative aspirations.[61]

Some hoped that coastal towns would protect their land from theft by foreigners. This threat was sometimes glossed as *kolonia,* "the colony," inspired by conceptions of early land alienation in Fiji, encounters with dispossessed Australian Aborigines recalled from Queensland days, and probably also by US soldiers telling Islanders about the conditions that had led American colonies to rebel against England. *Kolonia* also referred more broadly to a dreaded situation of government control over every aspect of people's lives.[62] *Kastom* rhetoricians today still employ the Maasina Rule trope of rejecting "99 years" of oppression, inspired by land leases of that duration granted to Europeans in the Protectorate's early years. Relatively little Malaitan land had been alienated, the key exception being a large plantation and several smaller ones run by the Young family (brothers of SSEM founder Florence Young) around Baunani on the west coast. Resentment lingered over how that land was purchased, shrine desecration on the estates, and the violence once inflicted on Malaitans who ventured onto the land. We have seen that Malaitans had feared land theft for decades, not just because of what they saw in Fiji and Australia but also from their experiences working on plantation land alienated from other Solomon Islanders.[63] Worry was only heightened by the Japanese and American invasions. Some officers tried to exploit these fears to further government goals: they warned Islanders that without Her Majesty's protection they might lose their land to foreigners poised to invade. This tactic was ill advised, given that people credited Americans and not the British with turning back the Japanese, and a government propaganda imperative was to quash hopes for American return, liberation, sponsorship, or protection. But before long, officers began to charge Maasina Rule's leaders with cynically fostering worries over invasion and highlighted this as an example of Malaitan delusion.[64]

Michael Scott has explored still greater fears of land-stealing invaders on nearby Makira, though, like Malaita, relatively little land there had been taken. On Makira, protecting land appears to have been the overriding concern of many Maasina Rule followers. Officer Len Barrow suggested in a 1946 circular to Makirans that foreigners would like to come and take their land and the government would not be able to stop them if their population did not radically increase, and Makirans subsequently massed their villages on the coast—permanently, as it turned out.[65] On Malaita in the early years of Maasina Rule, worries over land loss were only one of many motivational ideas in circulation. We will see that, for some Malaitans, anxieties about possible renewed war or invasion and the land alienation these might bring became more overt on Malaita during several years of severe government oppression, as hopes for American assistance faded, and apocalyptic fears at times were rife.[66]

By early 1947, towns encircled the island and thousands of Malaitans were living in them full or part-time, including people who descended from their mountain hamlets. At first, in 1946, many mountain people built towns not on the coast but on upper reaches of coastal slopes. Ancestral spirits had long restricted their descendants' movements within the coastal Christian villages because their taboos were openly flouted there, and these restrictions were still in force. During late 1946 and into mid-1947, however, many mountain people spent much or most of their time in coastal towns, sometimes alternating between residing there and in inland towns or hamlets. After government arrests began in the second half of 1947, many inland people went to the coastal towns primarily for extended meetings. At their peak, some town populations on the east coast topped 600 people, while others had only a few dozen. Overall, north Malaitan towns were smaller than those along the east coast, most having 100–300 people. The smallest of all were in Baegu, where people continued to prefer more hamlet-like settlements. Some towns, especially in the north, remained primarily meeting places.[67]

Much of what happened in these communities was hidden from or misconstrued by Europeans, and so here we depend on Malaitans for much of our information. Most of the oral accounts I have collected on this topic are from Kwaio, and, drawing also on material gathered by Burt in east Kwara'ae, the picture presented here is to some degree biased toward the towns in east-central Malaita. However, there is enough information in government and mission sources, and in oral accounts collected from elsewhere by others and myself, to piece together aspects of town life around the island. I hope Malaitan or other researchers will fill the many gaps.

Written accounts by officers and missionaries about Maasina Rule towns in 1947 display their limited and distorted understandings of life in them, and some constructed highly negative portraits of repression and social calamity that were later cited to help justify repression. They were generated partly through ignorance and partly as calculated political propaganda, and even officers' tour reports contradict the most disparaging claims. Europeans got a good deal of their information on Maasina Rule activities from loyalists ostracized by the movement and keen to discredit it, or sycophants looking to please listeners already convinced that it was wrongheaded. At other times movement adherents knowingly misled Europeans.[68] None of this is to say that town life was idyllic; there were many problems and difficulties. Indeed, in many areas most people eventually wearied of these (and later, of government raids on towns) and returned to their hamlets, smaller villages, or inland towns, and visited coastal or other towns only for communal work and to attend codification and other meetings, which could last for many days. (In the north, it seems more people who moved to the coast during Maasina Rule stayed there after.) Nevertheless, most Malaitans were excited over and proud of what they did accomplish in the towns in 1946 and 1947, and rightly so.

Europeans recorded few first-person observations of town life at this time. The SSEM's Clark published one of the most detailed in the mission's newsletter *Not in Vain* in 1947, after he toured towns along the east coast from 'Oloburi in southern Kwaio north into Kwara'ae. Clark did not say exactly when he was there, but it was in later 1946 or early 1947. He counted three large coastal towns at Uru and five in Kwara'ae, each occupied, he said, by 500–600 people. Kwaio today say these towns were not arranged in any formal hierarchy, though Kwara'ae told Burt that Head Chief Ganifiri's town of Naafinua was the effective center of operations for the Kwai harbor area.[69]

Although Maasina Rule delineated the island roughly into language groups (excepting west Kwaio and Langalanga), towns often had residents from more than one language zone. For example, there were Kwaio speakers living at A'arai and Age towns in Kwara'ae, and at Farisi in 'Are'are, and people from both Fataleka and Kwara'ae lived at 'Ofakwasi town on the 'Auluta river that separates those two areas. Burt suggested that Age and 'Ofakwasi aligned themselves more with the Kwaio and Fataleka Maasina Rule districts, respectively, than with Kwara'ae. Dense trade and marriage relationships have always crisscrossed language divisions. Malaitans living near linguistic borders typically know both languages, and most people can at least understand neighboring languages; one often hears Malaitans conversing in two tongues, each person speaking their own. Thus it is no surprise that language groups mixed in some towns. This reflected an indigenous flexibility and fluidity that Maasina Rule's structure allowed but that the government administrative system and its formal divisions could not countenance. A frustrated Barley had written in 1930, "The natives themselves unfortunately have no clear ideas as to the geographical extent of the different recognized bush regions into which the interior of the island is divided and regard them each rather as the tribal homes and sphere of influence of some particular 'line' than as a definite territorial unit." Dr Gideon Zoleveke described still more diversity at Abu near 'Aoke, with residents from Kwara'ae, Kwaio, 'Are'are, To'abaita, and even Makira and Guadalcanal.[70]

Clark was informed that the chiefs told people to "make im town alsame white man, long saltwater." He was taken aback by the flurry of construction taking place, and something that struck him at Naafinua reveals Malaitan attitudes toward this work as opposed to laboring for Europeans: "I saw men, women, girls and boys carting stones, breaking them and making a road to the water place. The bell rings for midday rest. Then bell and work again. And do they work? They DO. I was amazed yesterday to see men carrying huge logs for a community house. Two men would carry what would take six hired men."[71]

From A'arai, Clark described a residential pattern found in towns around the island, in which religious denominations formed distinct neighborhoods: "The S.S.E.M. has about a dozen houses at one end...then a small gap before seven Seventh Day Adventist houses, then ten Melanesian Mission houses, and finally about forty or more S.S.E.M. buildings." Non-Christians, too, had their own neighborhoods, or in some cases separate, adjacent towns. For example, at Sinalagu they built their main town of Koontalake ("Contract") just above Christian Kafulagelebasi, thereby preserving a fundamental Malaitan symbolic spatial scheme of ancestral: uphill :: Christian: downhill.[72]

In September 1947, Cadet Marquand, working in and around Malu'u, where the SSEM was especially strong, described seven smaller towns there: "All these villages have been built in the last year, they are all of a standard type except for the ones with the council house and office. They are based around SSEM 'Church Houses' and are laid out as regularly as the land permits. They are all one-roomed houses about 12ft x 8ft. In every village is at least one larger house for the full chief or leader chief....At the entrance of the village is a guardhouse containing four or six beds and in some villages a raised lookout has been built in the trees....Separate from the Christian villages but only a short distance away are the heathen houses, these are built on exactly the same lines. The council house is built on the same style as the Government Council House except for the office attached." Many towns were arranged in similar patterns, sometimes with neat rows of houses separated by graveled paths, reproducing a previous government and mission ideal and also resembling US military camps. Kwara'ae at Faumaamanu used a tape measure to space their houses with exactitude. Many coastal towns, especially in later 1948 and 1949, as well as some inland ones, were enclosed by fences, and some had watchtowers (Pijin *haetaoa*), which people have told me were modeled after a particular American military radio tower at Lunga. Towns were often entered via gatehouses manned by "sentries" (*sentirii*), inspired by American ones. A few fences resembled stockades made by early Christians, but most were mere symbolic rails (see chapter 7).[73]

People also initiated enormous gardening projects they called "farms" (or sometimes "union farms" or *kabani gaden*). These were inspired partly by the 'Are'are repopulation project, and several officers before the war had advised people to replace indigenous shifting horticulture with large permanent plots. Another model was the vast vegetable gardens Malaitans helped Americans work at Ilu Farm on Guadalcanal to feed troops and workers (later taken over by the Protectorate). Maasina Rule people planned to fund projects by selling farm produce on a large scale. In Malu'u, Kwaio, Kwara'ae, and elsewhere it was sold at local markets, though in some places a dearth of regular markets led to waste. Davies later charged that some chiefs in the north (but not the south) had sold farm yields for personal gain, and Dr Zoleveke hinted at this also, though neither offered evidence.[74] Farms were not just important for fund-raising; town residents also had to be fed, especially after mountain people moved to the coast far from their inland gardens. With this in mind, in most areas farms were planted before towns were built and occupied, the people staying in small, temporary structures whenever on the coast to do garden work. Communal farms were also planted near inland towns during early and later phases of Maasina Rule.[75]

In some places, smaller kith and kin groups cultivated separate gardens, or plots within larger farms, but many farms and other Maasina Rule projects, particularly in the beginning, demanded broader cooperative effort. This concept was not new to Malaitans, and for many Christians group work was already routinized. For example, SSEM members had long labored for a week or fortnight per year to maintain their churches' and teachers' houses and gardens, and they supplied food to teachers. Other missions had similar policies, "collections," and, at times, tithing. Mission teachers also received first fruits from gardens, which in the past had gone to ancestors through their priests, and some food from Maasina Rule gardens was supplied to the higher-level chiefs and sometimes to the duties.[76] Mountain people, too, had often worked in teams, although except for massive feast preparations their groups were usually smaller. We have seen that the government had had only mixed success in trying to compel regular community work. Now, towns and gardens required everyone to undertake much more cooperative labor than ever before, of a qualitatively different kind, and on behalf of much larger communities.

Male "farmer chiefs" or "gardener chiefs" officially directed the farms, though in most if not all places women supervised much of the labor.[77]

Farming followed varying schedules and fees in different areas. Clark, who visited the east when many farms were not yet producing, was told that people who were still living in the mountains had to descend every second week to garden and bring their own food for that week, and he commented, "It is no joke for them. No wonder they readily agree to come down and live at the sea." At Faumaamanu town in east Kwara'ae, everyone worked for three days each week and also brought to town produce from inland gardens. Those who missed work more than once were fined 5 shillings. A similar system operated in Kwaio, and in both places and elsewhere "farmer clerks" kept detailed records of work done and produce contributed. Some people hoped for reimbursement later, perhaps from Americans who would come to help. Leaders told Noel in March 1947 that people gardened two to three days a week, and in some places paid an annual fee of 2 to 5 shillings to access produce. Other towns charged a onetime fee, or no fee, and later Noel was told those who gardened paid nothing for food—by then almost every family was contributing labor, and gardens were producing their own stocks for replanting. In Fataleka and Baegu, and probably elsewhere in the north, at least, couples with more than one child were excused from communal farm work.[78]

The coastal farm staple was sweet potato, but most people also grew other subsistence and cash crops such as pineapples, sugarcane, yams, and corn—and around Malu'u and Langalanga, rice, which the government had introduced without much success just before the war. Some living inland experimented with cocoa, and people continued to maintain taro gardens there.[79] Davies tried to persuade people that their large coastal gardens were folly because soils there were already overworked and taro grew poorly (and Malaitans were well aware that soil degradation would become a problem in the longer term). He predicted that soil exhaustion would force mountain people to return home, but by early 1948 many communities, even those that still maintained towns, had given up coastal farms for other reasons, to work smaller plots inland.[80] Davies said there were food shortages in some places, but did not say where, and blamed them on young men he said worked as duties but not in gardens. Later in 1947 he reported, "The mass of the people are hungry," but this, at least, was untrue.[81] In fact farms did well in many places, and, after touring the east coast, both Cameron and Davies, in July and December 1947, respectively, reported ample food, vegetables in good supply, and regular markets. Marquand, based farther north, said farms were "very well run, neat and tidy, and it may well be that the production per unit area is greater." In January 1947, there were 18 farms around Malu'u alone. People had also planted farms inland where soils are far better and officers did not tour. Malaitans I have spoken with uniformly emphasize the abundance of food during this period. The government later claimed farm labor was forced, citing this as a reason to outlaw Maasina Rule, and Peter Worsley wrote, "Numbers of people had died...through being obliged to work long hours exposed to the heat of the sun in communal gardens." He cited no source for this claim and I know nothing that backs it; surely officers eager for anti-movement propaganda would have reported such deaths.[82]

Many towns also started piggeries with large communal pens set away from the residences, particularly when and where the bulk of the population lived on the coast. Sandars was told pig breeds had been brought from 'Aoke to the east to improve local herds, and likewise ducks and chickens. Both mission rules and government laws dictated the penning of swine, but most inland people had always flouted these, penning their pigs inside houses only at night and releasing them each morning to forage (some in the north fenced villages instead of pigs). In 1947 many people, even in the mountains, began to keep their beasts in communal pens. The first reason a Malaitan will give you for penning pigs in or near their house is theft protection—pig stealing had been a popular, nocturnal, ancestrally supported pursuit among young men—but there was less chance of theft in the towns. Some in 'Are'are and probably elsewhere instituted a system in which pigs were still loosed to forage, but each week a different man acted as swineherd.[83]

Roaming, marauding pigs had often caused disputes, and confining them removed a source of divisive conflict, but the shift to communal pigpens was also part of a larger Maasina Rule effort to implement sanitary practices in towns. Sweeping missionary and government statements that towns were "filthy" are contradicted by many tour reports and oral accounts. For instance, Cameron in mid-1947 reported that people on the Sinalagu and 'Oloburi coast were healthy, and in mid-1948 Forster was impressed as he led a patrol through about a dozen Sinalagu and 'Oloburi mountain towns: "The area presents a marked contrast to its prewar state. The people are living in large well-planned and maintained villages. All of them occupy attractive sites and it is pleasing to see how well these people have managed to organize themselves. They appear to have succeeded in adjusting themselves to community life." Dr Zoleveke, writing years later, after he had served as Solomon Islands minister of health, wrote that in the north Malaitan coastal towns he visited in 1951, "everything was kept clean and tidy." Kwaio told me of their great attentions to keeping towns hygienic and ordered. This had always been an ideal for both Christian villages and inland hamlets, though of course not everyone kept to the ideal and different rules and standards prevailed in the crowded towns. Allan wrote that when Langalanga and Lau island people moved to towns on the adjacent coasts they had little choice of location and building materials, and thus their towns were poorly sited and built, and most specific government complaints of poor sanitation concerned these towns. Later, during the years of government raids and mass arrests, some towns suffered more sanitary problems.[84]

Townspeople tried to establish schools. Justus Ganifiri and Sadius Oge taught classes in the Kwai area, and Headman Futaiasi had 50 students at 'Oloburi. David Ridley, later a district headman, tried organizing a Sinalagu school, but told Cameron that he was being hampered by his rival Fifi'i's attempts to control it. From the information available, it seems these and other schools around the island had little success—most teachers had inadequate knowledge, training, and supplies. Like Sandars just after the war, Maasina Rule leaders were loath to ask white missionaries for educational advice or assistance, and after the government began trying to suppress the movement, most shunned government assistance as well.[85]

The Social Life of *Kastom*

When Malaitans took up residence in coastal towns, their lives were altered not only spatially and organizationally but also socially. Inland people had always controlled their own territories and affairs, and those living close together propitiated mostly common ancestral spirits and strictly regulated contacts with the defilement of Christians, who ignored ancestral taboos. Most Christians already lived in relatively large coastal settlements, but the towns were much bigger and they now had to adjust to residing with not only inland people and their ancestral rules but also Christians from rival denominations. From the movement's start, its founders Harisimae, Nono'oohimae, and colleagues stressed the need to transcend religious divisions in order to work together.[86]

These distinctions and rivalries were imposing obstacles to movement cohesion. Students of Maasina Rule have always highlighted its achievement of an unprecedented Malaita-wide political unity that Europeans had always assumed impossible, but impressive as this was, more remarkable was its success in surmounting deep local-level divisions not only of long-term factionalism at every level but also of newer modernist versus traditionalist identities and, most daunting of all, religious faiths. Whereas Maasina Rule's loose pan-Malaitan alliance had little impact on people's everyday lives, overcoming local divisions between and especially within towns was a challenge that required constant innovation and negotiation of new rules, policies, and practices to allow coresidence and cooperation. A most fascinating aspect of town life is how these rival groups did manage to live and work together as a community.

The mass relocations to towns could have bred chaos, and clearly leaders saw this danger. When Malaitans today describe town life, they often recall first the regimented routines and restrictions on personal movement. At times, duties manned gates to check comings and goings, and people needed written passes for specific errands or moves. In the north, some people carried passes in small bamboo tubes to move freely in and out of their towns. Zoleveke wrote of life in SSEM-dominated Abu town near 'Aoke: "Its leaders were elders of the church and attendance at services compulsory [for Christians]. The village itself was fenced and everybody passing in or out was checked. Strict rules governed the times of working and rest, and a bell was rung to remind people of the schedule. The late night bell rang at nine o'clock, by which time everybody had to be in bed." Schedules and mobility were similarly managed in towns throughout the island. Some early *kastom* codes stipulated that young people's movements be kept in check, and in May 1946 Noel told the high commissioner, "A few natives from Malaita who preferred to be demobilised from the Labour Corps on Guadalcanal still refuse to return to their villages, fearful lest once back in their villages they will not be free to move about as they wish but come under the orders of the Marching Rule."[87]

Coastal town residents who also maintained mountain towns or hamlets, or smaller Christian villages, considered restrictions on coming and going and vigilance by duties necessary to protect unattended properties. Ma'aanamae of Kwaio recounted to me in 1996, "During the time of the Maasina Rule towns there was little theft. One reason is that people's movements were tightly controlled. You could not just go and casually visit people. If you walked off without a reason people would suspect that you were going to steal. The chiefs would tell you where to go and when, to work in the gardens and so forth. You did not just walk about as you pleased."

The most obvious reason for tighter regulations was that many conventional mechanisms of social control were incompatible with communal town life, based as they were on complicated alliances and rivalries between small flexible groups anchored in distinct territories, each liable for its own members' actions and for settling disputes within and between themselves. Adding to the difficulty was that different groups brought to towns different rules and conventions. While individuals and groups did not discard their old identities and social networks, the system was in disarray with all of them thrown together, and the strict rules shaped a new sort of stability.

Rules and obedience of them served more than practical needs; they embodied the new social order, and by following rules people displayed shared commitment to that order. Malaitans are famously, aggressively protective of their personal freedoms and independence, and I have always been surprised at how Maasina Rule veterans, men and women, recall town restrictions not as oppressive or invasive but with high approval, as exemplifying how well the people organized themselves. Today, it is said that people followed the rules without complaint, and Maasina Rule is recalled with nostalgia as a time when all conducted themselves as good citizens, obeyed their leaders, and bettered their communities. Ian Frazer wrote in the 1970s that To'abaita people similarly evoked the period as one when "everyone was of 'one mind'" about the tasks at hand.[88]

Kwaio elders, too, have often painted Maasina Rule for me as a period of almost utopian social responsibility, especially when criticizing today's young people as footloose and inattentive. I know for a fact that some of these same seniors were so criticized when *they* were young—such cross-generational affectations are hardly unique to Malaitans—and readers will forgive younger Malaitans (and the anthropologist) for hearing such high-minded, moralistic recollections with more than a little skepticism. But archival records do support claims that Maasina Rule's rules were widely and freely obeyed. Read, for instance, from Forster's report of a September 1945 tour behind 'Oloburi and Sinalagu, where he visited early Maasina Rule villages: "Influence of the activity in Ariari has spread to the bush but seems to have taken the right direction and chiefs were actively supporting law and order and admonishing their followers to refrain from stealing and killing. Telling the truth is not a strong factor among Koio people and statements as above should be accepted with a certain amount of reserve. The facts did however appear to bear it out." And three years later he wrote: "This area was formerly noted for crimes of violence which seem to have ceased now that they live in bigger communities."[89] Even Malaitans today inclined to reassess Maasina Rule critically attest to the lawfulness. Further evidence of a civil society is the scarcity, despite the turmoil of the period, of nonpolitical crimes even in the reports of officers and informants eager to show the social project was failing. To manage problems that did arise, people convened their own "*kastom* courts" that applied "*kastom* law."

Kastom Loa *and* Kastom Kouti

Issues of legal jurisdiction and judicial power proved critically important to both Malaitans and the government and became their most explicit sphere of conflict. We have seen that, although most Malaitans welcomed the end of fighting, through the 1930s and early 1940s colonial law had become a crux of general dissatisfaction with government rule—its presence always had been most conspicuous and intrusive in its courts and in its attempts to stop communities and congregations settling serious disputes on their own. Thus there was great symbolic as well as practical import to Maasina Rule's move to reassert Malaitan-controlled legal mechanisms, not only for "custom" cases and minor offenses, as the government allowed, but for most crimes and disputes. Here again, leaders stressed that Malaitans needed to follow rules made by Malaitans. Movement codes, called *kastom loa* (law), were put forward as supplanting British law and certain mission rules, though many codes included rules derived from both of those sources. Many conceived of *kastom* codes as, in part, declarations of legal independence to be presented to the government. Even after wide adoption of the name "Maasina Rule," both Malaitans and district officers often called the movement "Maasina Loa" and "Marching Law."

An exception to demands for legal autonomy centered on murder cases.

Most people wanted to retain the option of handing murderers over to the government, and it was usually said that all would be. Some colonial officers saw this as evidence of movement weakness, an indication that people expected the government to keep doing the heavy lifting of law and order. For Malaitans the subject was more complicated. They had long used government jails as a partial solution to the strife that inevitably followed a murder, and murderers themselves sometimes opted for prison rather than face the danger that they or their kin might be killed in revenge. Murder compensations had to be to delicately negotiated; the victim's living relatives and, in non-Christian communities, each of the victim's ancestral spirits and the victim's own spirit, had to be compensated with costly sacrificial pigs before the relatives of the killer and the victim could again interact socially. But if a murderer was imprisoned and thereby "disappeared" from the social scene, this reduced compensation costs, including to ancestors, and also likelihood of strife. Christians and mountain people alike knew the Maasina Rule project would fail if feuding capsized their new, fragile unity. Better to put murderers in a government jail.[90]

As Maasina Rule grew, communities throughout Malaita discussed and drafted codes of *kastom loa* that often went beyond what the government was instructing native councils to compile. They also collected genealogies in order to record descent group land rights, quash divisive property disputes, and protect land from possible theft by foreigners. Maasina Rule code-smiths were prolific, and codification meetings that often stretched over days became a regular feature of town life, key performative events demonstrating Malaitans' determination and ability to work together for strong communities, social stability, and collective goals.[91]

Some early codification projects, both within and outside of government channels, bred tension between Christians and mountain peoples and between different churches. Justus Ganifiri, paraphrased in a 1945 story in *Not in Vain*, declared that government native councils were (as translated by the editors) "taking advantage of their authority and reviving old heathen customs and…causing enmity in the Mission." Some Christians, including Ganifiri, felt compelled to compose their own codes, not to repudiate *kastom* per se but to counter *kastom* codes that seemed to dictate ancestral taboos, compensation, and brideprice rules for all, and to explicitly deny their applicability to Christians. In east Kwaio, Assistant Headman Anifelo had attempted this as early as 1940, likely with Norman Deck's encouragement, in response to district officers ordering Christians to pay compensation for having violated ancestral taboos. When I first stayed with Anifelo in 1980, he was at work on a *kastom* codification project with much the same thrust, incorporating both ancestral taboos and biblical commandments but clearly differentiating them and to whom they applied. Early codes illustrate these Christian-ancestral tensions: some were written by Christians and contested ancestral rules, others sought compromise and

listed both ancestral and Christian versions of many rules, while still others contained explicitly anti-Christian passages. Ganifiri himself compiled a
book of laws that sought to encompass both Christian and ancestral rules.[92]

Despite these initial conflicts, most Christians and non-Christians soon
joined political forces and began to cooperate on codification, though disputes over content still flared up from time to time, and in places Christians
declined to participate in writing codes that highlighted ancestral taboos.
Some codes, again, were conceived primarily as manifestos to present to the
government, and Christians in Kwaio and likely elsewhere rationalized that
for such purposes it was primarily ancestral rules that needed codification,
since "the government already knew Christian law."[93]

When Maasina Rule began, something more than one-third of Malaitans
self-identified as Christians, with more in the north than in the south.[94] In
most areas, Christian communities and those following ancestors had for
decades been intense political rivals, typically fighting their battles over and
through conflicting religious and other societal rules. For this reason, and
because government had always worked to impose its idea of proper laws
on Malaitans, by the mid-1940s rules, codes, and law generally were already
conceived in highly political terms.[95]

The great emphasis Christian missions had always placed on behavioral
rules, including many with no biblical grounding, contributed to the recep-
tiveness of both Christian and non-Christian Malaitans to the codification of
kastom, and this linkage is made explicit in many later *kastom* movements.[96]
Nonetheless, it is well to caution here against attributing to Christianity
a determinative influence on the Malaitan concern with rules and their
codification.[97] We have seen that detailed systems of rules had long been
fundamental to Malaitan ancestral religions. They were markers of identity,
modes of interaction with ancestors, and mechanisms of cultural creativity. This deeply rooted attentiveness to rules intensified their importance
within Malaitan Christianities, particularly as oppositional identity markers. One reason the SSEM was popular was its stern social regulations, and
some Malaitans rejected (and still reject) Catholicism because it was seen to
impose too few rules; they reasoned that a religion so "easy" could scarcely
be powerful. More to the point here, concerns to codify *kastom* rules can
also be traced directly and explicitly to the prodding of colonial officers
from the 1930s onward to produce "custom" codes to help resuscitate
Malaitan societies—officers linked the two tasks and framed them under
the colonial rubric of "custom," as Malaitans now pursued codification for
societal renewal under that of *kastom*.[98]

Malaitan communities around the island convened proceedings, called
kouti (courts), which varied in composition and style from place to place.
Though there was less crime relative to the past, offenses and disputes did
occur, the most remembered today being pig thefts and illicit sexual affairs
in towns. Persons who committed such offenses or violated other movement

rules were sometimes fined or ordered to perform community labor, and many *kastom* codes listed specific sanctions for particular offenses. Leaders, including some head chiefs, mediated or arbitrated serious disputes, though lower-level chiefs and their communities handled most troubles, particularly in mountain towns. Fifi'i told me that he and the other head chiefs all agreed that one thing they liked best about the concentration of people in towns was that it facilitated dispute management. In Kwaio, as in many and perhaps all places, courts were held regularly, during some periods every second week, others every month. Fifi'i presided over some, usually at Sinalagu, often with a government headman in attendance. A few times he toured to all three east Kwaio harbors (where no government native councils or courts had ever been implemented) with duties and his first cousin and clerk 'Adifaka, who later became a high-ranking police officer. Similar courts toured in at least some other districts. As time passed, Malaitans' deployment of their own legal system became their most overt rejection of government control of their affairs. Many *kastom* "courts" were legal, while the status of others was ambiguous, and a few were clearly illegal under colonial law; officers had long allowed chiefs to handle voluntary arbitrations but not crimes like serious assault. We will see that Maasina Rule's system of dispute resolution and its purported abuses later became the government's prime justification for arresting leaders and trying to forcefully suppress the movement.[99]

There is little reliable archival data on Maasina Rule courts because until mid-1947 they were mostly hidden from officers, except as sometimes presented as regular native courts. Malaitans suspected of being government informants were at times barred from court, council, and other meetings, and in areas that had anti-Maasina Rule factions, many recall being on watch for spies trying to attend or overhear. There were in fact spies in places, often acting for loyalist headmen, but officers' knowledge of most courts was partial or based on rumor, and it was often unclear to them, and sometimes to Malaitans, whether a body was acting as a Maasina Rule court or a government native court, and whether it was adjudicating cases or rather arbitrating or mediating them.[100]

In October 1946, Forster likened the Maasina Rule courts that he had heard about to what he called "kangaroo courts" convened on prewar plantations and more recently within the Labour Corps. Some officers, particularly higher-ups, later charged that the courts had been highly abusive and coercive. Some appear to have believed this, but others promulgated the claim in order to discredit the movement and justify its suppression. I have found no evidence of abuse in central Malaitan courts, and clearly it was not the norm elsewhere. Fifi'i, in an undated personal letter to Nono'oohimae and Nori that was later seized by the government, complained that Maasina Rule courts had no real power because they wielded no sanctions and thus people had no fear of them. All of the Malaitans I have talked with, including some who lost cases in the courts, recalled them as fair, and of east Kwara'ae Burt wrote, "The courts seemed to operate to the satisfaction of all concerned." The vast majority of people appear to have viewed them in similarly positive ways, and as better than government courts. This is as one would expect, considering the difficulties officers had always had in delivering verdicts that fully satisfied Malaitans, and given the political and symbolic importance the *kastom* courts had for Maasina Rule adherents.[101]

People brought most disputes to the courts voluntarily, where they were dealt with through mediation or consensual arbitration of compensation payments. This is important because, again, such proceedings were not illegal, and officers had even encouraged them just prior to and after the war. In June 1947, Cameron was sent for a month to Kwai, which was Justus Ganifiri's sphere of influence and was, along with Malu'u, one of the two most difficult places for the government. Cameron thought that nearly 100 percent of the Kwai people were Maasina Rule followers. One of his assignments from Sandars was to investigate reports of illegal courts. The government native court had not convened for at least a year, and before that it had been a Maasina Rule court in practice. Cameron looked into proceedings that local chiefs had presided over and found them "arbitration committees rather than courts," settled by compensation and based on "custom law." "The standard of justice in the so-called courts must have been high," he wrote, "In spite of the widest publicity I was unable to find any dis-satisfied 'customers.' Personally I do not think that this lack of complaint was due to intimidation." Though he found gathering evidence difficult, he believed these were legal out-of-court proceedings, similar to those government had always allowed Christian missions and to those convened by churches, clubs, and other bodies in England. In criminal cases he found "ready acceptance of authority of Government," and "no concealment of crime." From 'Oloburi, on the Kwaio-'Are'are border, he reported the people thought the government sanctioned their court, and, "I believe the court is being operated correctly and fairly." His colleague Marquand, posted to Malu'u in 1947, and then as the district officer at 'Aoke, later wrote of Malaita's "alleged illegal courts" that they "operated satisfactorily in opposition to the unsatisfactory Government courts." He could find nobody willing to give incriminating evidence about them, "either from witnesses or from persons who have been convicted in them, none of whom voluntarily complained."[102]

Still, as officers became more aware of the extent to which Malaitans were settling their own disputes, they grew increasingly concerned about what they were up to and how to respond: Were their courts coercive and illegal, or were they lawful mediation and arbitration, or something in-between? Might court actions of Maasina Rule adherents be prosecutable offenses, perhaps grounds for arresting even movement leaders not directly involved in any court so charged? Officers were unsure, but we will see that many Malaitans were later prosecuted retroactively and jailed based on the hard-line answers a legal adviser gave to these questions.

Officers later worried over news that the courts were putting people in locally run jails, but here there was much confusion. There were some offenses for which people were sentenced to terms in "jail." But this typically meant lax internment and performance of communal work—usually cutting grass or farmwork—for a specified number of days, often with the "prisoner" each night returning home or being restricted to a regular house. Some European critics decried this as slave labor, but it continued a long-standing government practice of punishing lesser offenses with a stay in the "calaboose belong headman" and "extra-mural imprisonment"— community labor supervised by native authorities—in the government system up to nine hours a day, six days a week, which guidelines Maasina Rule also followed. The Protectorate had borrowed this concept of "gaol" from colonial native courts in Africa. The underlying problem for the government seems to have been not that the system was unjust but rather that Malaitans were in charge of it. In August 1947, a few north Malaitan courts did in several cases impose something closer to imprisonment, as will be examined in chapter 7.[103]

Making Kastom *Fit*

While it is clear that Maasina Rule developed competent mechanisms for settling disputes and enforcing community rules, achieving agreement as to exactly what those rules were to be posed a thornier challenge. The diverse groups that came together in towns each brought with them various rules and conventions of proper social interactions and boundaries, and these were often at odds. The most obvious divides were religious. In decades of interdenominational battles a weapon of choice had always been rules, about everything from marriage transactions to ancestral taboos, to principles of dispute resolution, to biblical interpretation. The most daunting internal challenge to the Maasina Rule project was to work out these differences in ways that preserved social harmony and order. To illustrate, I will focus on the broadest division with the most obvious potential for conflict: that between Christians and those who worshipped ancestors.

Mountain people and their ancestral spirits had to make the most radical adjustments in relocating to towns. To begin with, Malaitan ancestral religions are firmly grounded in physical space that is highly charged as social and sacred space. It is imperative that communities maintain control over everything from who and what enters their gardens and taboo areas—shrines, men's houses, and women's areas—to the relative location of spaces and houses within hamlets—most basically, areas demarcated as ancestral shrines, men's areas, family clearings, menstrual zones, toilets, and childbirth clearings.[104]

The majority of mountain men had lived most of their lives within one home territory, excepting, importantly, their labor travels, and most of their key life experiences had taken place there. Married women identified with two areas—natal and affinal. A territory's social essence transcended the lives of living people to encompass ancestors who had spent their mortal lives there and remained there in spirit, and whose deeds were preserved in myths, histories, and stories that stressed the import of specific places. The best way to grasp the theography of the mountains, even now, is to stroll with Malaitans through their home territory and ask them to narrate the terrain as you move along. What seems "natural" jungle will come alive with shrines and other spots of power and danger, and countless tales of people and spirits once and still attached to the land. It was these territories, saturated with social, religious, and historical meanings, that mountain people left to take up residence in coastal towns. Clark was told, correctly, that many of them were less than happy in the towns because "[t]heir animistic faith decrees that any pig offered as a propitiatory sacrifice MUST be slain on the worshippers' ancestral, tabu ground....They naturally wish to remain near such sacred places." The system is more complex than Clark knew: ancestors can receive pigs in satellite shrines founded far from their home territories. But his point holds since, to my knowledge, no new shrines were established on the coast during Maasina Rule. Such concerns, which of course cannot be reduced to practical logistics, later contributed to most mountain people abandoning the coast for towns they built closer to home.[105]

In the mid-1940s some Christians lived inland, usually in or near home territories, and for them the move to crowded coastal towns was nearly as drastic. But Clark said they were the first to follow movement directives to descend, in defiance of missionaries, who were crestfallen to lose hard-won mountain footholds. He wrote: "Once we abandon the bush Mission places it is going to be very difficult to start them again....The Devil is behind this removal of Christian witness from among the bush heathen." Most Christians did in fact stay on the coast after Maasina Rule.[106] Many Christians who already lived by the sea in 1946 had once lived in the mountains, recalled their own past experience, and empathized with those now forsaking their homelands.

The potential for different Malaitan social structures to be carried into the crowded coastal settlements varied. In parts of the north, a limited number of clans, each consisting of many nested groups, were hierarchically arranged over wide areas, and these integrative structures might be adapted more readily to town organization. By contrast, Kwaio and northern 'Are'are descent groups were relatively atomized and acephalous, even if crosscut by extensive, complex webs of ancestral sacrifice, marriage, and exchange. Farther south, remnants of the former chiefly system lent themselves to movement organization, and indeed an 'Are'are word for "chief," *alaha,* was soon adapted to title movement leaders throughout the island (see chapter 6).

Although these organizational structures were sometimes muddled within the towns, one sort of social disintegration was being reversed. Over the preceding decades, many kin groups and even nuclear families had split up when members left to join rival Christian denominations, while others remained devoted to their ancestors. In the towns, broken families were now rejoined within a single community, pursuing common rather than antagonistic goals. Some of these rejuvenated ties were maintained long after inland people returned to the mountains and even after Maasina Rule. Here again, the movement not only established a remarkable island-wide unity of purpose but also reunited individuals and local communities that had become estranged, fractured by religious and other factionalisms. This is one striking sense in which Maasina Rule was what Laracy aptly termed a "reintegrative movement."[107]

Grasping Maasina Rule's integrative accomplishments is essential to understanding its intensity. Malaitans place tremendous importance in and put great efforts into the creation and activation of social ties. Success in doing so represents more than a logistical accomplishment—on an aesthetic level it is for Malaitans morally and emotionally fulfilling. The fundamental reason big men are "big" is that they excel at doing this by means of exchange, feasting, and other activities they organize; their bigness is measured by the quantity and quality of social interaction and integration that they and their groups create. The word *alaha* (or *alafa*) can be translated as wide or expansive, referencing the reach of such leaders' social agency, their ability to merge people across social and geographic distance. Their challenge is that they must constantly fight the countervailing fissiparous tendencies of Malaitan societies. Likewise, the "biggest" ancestral spirits are those that link together the largest numbers of people who maintain relationships with and sacrifice to them in shrines dispersed across multiple, large territories. As with mortal big men, the bigness of Malaitan ancestors is highly relational, grounded in their position as a nexus of social relationships and actions.[108]

I have written elsewhere, regarding contemporary Kwaio, of how *kastom* political activities can be understood in terms of creating and restoring sociality. Kwaio today fear their society is coming undone. Their *kastom* meetings have long been the principal events that bring together people from throughout the Kwaio area. These meetings are themselves performative acts, which, by their very occurrence, effectively deny the disintegration of their community. The same anxiety over ongoing social dissolution and breakdown was at the center of Maasina Rule's *kastom* ideology (and today's Kwaio *kastom* activities have their roots in the movement). But Maasina Rule was more than reintegrative; it created an unprecedented, unified social group consisting of the whole of Malaita. As Charles Fox recounted,

"I talked to a native of North Mala and asked him why he had joined and why he liked Marching Rule. He said, 'Because it has made us Melanesians all one. We are all brothers now.'...And so it was too in the other islands. British rule had not united them, Christianity had not united them, and here they were suddenly swept into a unity never dreamed of before by this new movement for independence and self government. It amazed us all." It astounded Malaitans as well and stimulated them to undertake projects and achieve goals together in a way that had been thought impossible.[109]

Many difficulties of integrating town communities were specific and immediate. Most ancestors had long imposed strict rules concerning their descendants' contacts with Christians and their villages and especially with their houses, where menstrual and birth taboos were not observed. Also problematic were ancestral restrictions on food sharing between women and ritually mature men, which most Christians ignored. These taboos were most numerous and exacting for ancestral priests, many of whom were important in the Maasina Rule organization and now lived near and had to spend time among Christian men and women. Some communities responded by building separate towns or neighborhoods, and others erected men's houses in the towns' upper reaches where, as in the mountains, stricter taboos applied and Christians and women could not enter. Priests living on the coast still ascended to inland shrines, sometimes many hours away, to perform rituals and sacrifices.

Christians had to compromise too. They consented to observe some important ancestral rules—or at least to breach them only discreetly—in deference to their new neighbors, although observance deemed less than adequate could still cause tensions. Malaitans already had well-developed systems for managing the great diversity of ancestral rules followed by different individuals and groups, and a cardinal principal was that one should show respect for another's taboos while in their presence or their territory. Before Maasina Rule, the degree to which Christians had followed this tenet varied widely. Some, especially those who lived in the mountains, avoided openly violating neighbors' taboos, and some even gave first fruits of their gardens to ancestral priests. At the opposite extreme were Christians who intentionally desecrated shrines and violated taboos in order to anger spirits so much that their descendants would have to flee to the churches for refuge; at times this had caused open conflicts. During Maasina Rule the former approach became the norm.[110]

For some Christians this required shifts in religious practice and attitude as drastic as those demanded of mountain people. Their teachers, both European and Melanesian, had taught that ancestral rules were Satan's rules and that to honor them was sinful. The SSEM, in particular, had insisted on separation from and restricted social interactions with "heathens" and their wickedness (and sometimes with people from other missions). Practices and symbols exalted in some Maasina Rule rhetoric and

codes had been anathema to local Christian theologies. As interdenominational town life took shape, reactionary policies had to give way to flexibility
and compromise. For example, in Takataka, 'Are'are, a small percentage
of movement donations was earmarked as "*kastom* money" to be used for
religious activities forbidden to Christians. Because Christians could not
utter ancestral oaths of denial to settle disputes, they were allowed to use
other sorts of oaths that did not invoke ancestors. To the consternation
of some missionaries, members of rival Christian churches, too, began to
collaborate.[111]

Though people made concessions all around, some ancestral taboos
were impossible to follow rigorously in the close-quarter towns. Consequently, these taboos were modified, relaxed, or waived. Priests in shrines
carefully explained to ancestral spirits the necessity of cooperation and
religious adjustment.[112] Since the nineteenth century, Malaitans had been
creatively tailoring and modifying ancestral rules to make them compatible
with life on plantations and in urban centers (as Christians had with some
church rules), and this equipped them now to better negotiate the novel
town conditions using already established principles.

Tensions did arise, though, and women in particular sometimes criticized
what they perceived as men's growing laxity in following ancestral taboos in
the Maasina Rule towns. In Kwaio, the flip side of today's idealistic remem-
brances of the movement is that many men and women, including some
who evoke the period as a golden age, also recall it as a time when people
in the service of working together let down their guard against Christian
and other incursions. They now credit the town scene with initiating a long
slide into religious decadence that they see as ongoing. I have been told this
many times, but have never heard it expressed more clearly than by Oloi'a,
a woman from the mountains above Sinalagu, when in 1977 she explained
to Keesing how people discarded food and related taboos. She highlighted
personal bags, and fire hearths and coals, because ancestors pay special
attention to them, and they are thus prime conductants of tabooness:

> When Maasina Rule came, the men said, "We have to work close to the coast now,
> mixing up with the mission people. And those mission people have to mix up
> with us non-Christians."...And so bags were taken back and forth, people asked
> for tobacco back and forth, and for fire. Even men ate things from the bags of
> the mission people. And we women started to kindle our pipes from the coals
> of mission people. "The Rule governs you." That's the way they talked about
> Maasina Rule. "It has come. The Rule governs you." And we looked around us
> and said, "Oh, the men are taking their bags into the [mission] clearing,"...and
> they were the ones who ate [sacred] consecrated pigs. "Let's us women do it too.
> When we go down to the mission, let's take our bags into the clearing. Let's leave
> our bags outside and peep inside the church. Let's kindle our pipes with their
> coals. The men who consecrate pigs, the 'custom people,' are doing it."...The

important men saw us do it and they said, "Oh, that's all right." That was the beginning of things turning in a different way.[113]

Many Kwaio women were troubled by these new behaviors. I have no information on such apprehensions elsewhere, though they were likely widespread given that antagonisms and stark divisions between Christians and non-Christians had been ubiquitous on Malaita long before Maasina Rule. These and other anxieties among women found curious expression in Kwaio towns, which I will address only briefly here since I have analyzed it elsewhere. The women's concerns exemplify subtle but deep ramifications Maasina Rule had for Malaitan societies that are invisible in archival sources. In east Kwaio, an epidemic of aberrant behaviors broke out among mountain women in one Sinalagu town due to extraordinary, unprecedented spirit possessions. These sparked suicides and a rash of women openly committing or confessing to violations of menstrual and related taboos, and the phenomenon proliferated "like the wind" (*mala iru*) to other Kwaio towns. Most people came to blame this on foreign sorceries, perhaps brought by 'Are'are Maasina Rule emissaries, or else on imported *buru* spirits.[114]

In-depth exploration of this would take us astray, but a major factor was that many women were unhappy in the towns, and the possessions can be seen as a form of protest of the sort famously described by I M Lewis. Most women were active Maasina Rule supporters (see chapter 7), but men dominated most public movement activities and women worked hard on the farms and piggeries. Europeans often perceived Malaitan women as docile and subservient, but most display a very different persona in their own hamlets, neighborhoods, and gardens, where they take pride in their knowledge and work and can have significant authority. They often play important roles in community decision making. Senior women exercise substantial control over younger women by overseeing their observance of taboos and managing their labor, and young women gain status as "good women" through participating in reciprocal exchange, being hard workers, and conscientiously observing taboos. Removed from their homes to the towns, with taboos relaxed, women lost the social and spatial context in which they enjoyed the most status and power. Like the rest of the populace, they at times needed permission to even visit their hamlets or home gardens. Very few had shared men's experiences of working away from home under the disciplinary regimes of plantations or US military farms. The explosion of women's real and supposed taboo breaking during Maasina Rule initiated a steady escalation of such violations that continues in parts of Kwaio today and has transformed the ancestral religion.[115]

There were other sources of religious tension. When Malaitans determined they would settle their own disputes, this laid bare old conflicts over compensation. As discussed in previous chapters, compensation had before the war become a core symbol of Malaitan social life and dispute management, as juxtaposed to the government and its laws, while at the same time Christian churches, particularly the SSEM, had long directed their members not to participate in compensation settlements if they could avoid it. Some Christians vigorously opposed compensation while others remained highly ambivalent about it, and still others paid and even received it, in at least some contexts. Now, as compensation became central to Maasina Rule's ideology and practice of dispute resolution, many Christians found their positions awkward.

European and, initially, some Melanesian missionaries urged their flocks to resist: Clark wrote of how SSEM teachers had always taught people who were "at variance" to address their problems through talk and prayer, "But now the heathen custom of asking for money as damages...to settle grievances and 'make im belly (heart) belong man goodfella,' is being pressed upon the Christians. Pray that, even if it means persecution, the believers will not disobey God's Word." Some areas managed the problem as the Naafinua court in Kwara'ae did, with Justus Ganifiri presiding: most cases were settled through compensation, but Christians unwilling to compensate could instead pay a fine. This followed a government plan to allow Christians the option of paying compensations into native courts treasuries, which was probably first suggested to government officers by Malaitan Christians.[116]

Before the war, apart from annual tax collections, large gatherings inland had taken place primarily at mortuary, marriage, and other feasts, and around the coast at multi-community Christian church events. These usually took on a festive atmosphere, as they still do, and after a short time on Malaita one notices that any sizable gathering usually means high socializing. This carried over to the unprecedented concentrations of people in Maasina Rule towns, with music sometimes played until dawn. Naturally this worried puritanical missionaries like Clark, who bemoaned "the ukulele and guitar menace" among young people in the towns he visited, "with its heathen singing and dancing." He had more reason for concern than he knew: large gatherings are also prime settings for young people to "date" and court. One former chief told me women acted fortuitously as "bait" to keep the young men working in towns. The upshot in towns was that romantic relationships and sexual scandals were fairly common, leading when exposed to demands for compensation or marriage. Perusal of Kwaio marriage histories of a certain generation reveals many took place during residence in Maasina Rule towns.[117]

The unprecedented mixing of Christian and non-Christian men and women in towns made another problem inevitable: brideprice disputes. Most missions imposed a drastic limit on brideprice payments, whereas non-Christians not only had no such limits but saw them as emblematic of Christian decadence and church warfare against their ways. What were people to do, then, when a couple wanted to marry across these religious lines? The same problem faced Christian couples from different churches with different marriage rules. Even marriages within one church could bring controversy: many Christians themselves had long chafed at church brideprice rules, and their enforcement was and remains today a challenge for missionaries and more orthodox church leaders. Before Maasina Rule, when Christians buckled under pressures or their own desires to pay or receive higher brideprice, or when they participated because they felt that giving a woman "for free" was immoral or shameful for both the couple and their families, they were condemned by more pious church members as deviant "backsliders." In the turbulent times of Maasina Rule, with white missionaries mostly out of the picture, these issues came to the fore and ideas about brideprice were in flux. For example, the SSEM brideprice limit was soon raised from three to five large shell valuables—*tafuli'ae* ten-string shell valuables in the north, or *baani'au* six-string valuables made of the smaller shell beads used in the south.[118]

The problem was further met with an innovation in brideprice calculation: shell money denominations were redefined, with standard shell unit terms adapted to label longer-than-standard money bead strings. This was analogous to declaring, say, "A dollar now means 1,000 cents." These semantic adjustments allowed Christians to pay higher brideprices while technically staying within the letter of church limits on the number of valuables given. The strategy originated in the north and spread south throughout Malaita, and it was taken to great lengths: people exchanged only the maximum of five multi-stringed shell valuables, but the individual strings could be over 30 meters long. Each valuable thus contained shell beads equal to many valuables of normal size.[119]

This innovation, like the redefinitions of ancestral taboos and Christian compromises with other faiths, represented more than just a practical solution to religious squabbles. This is clear in that, for a time, mountain people, too, adopted the five-valuable limit and elongated valuables for even marriages among themselves—I have known several non-Christian couples that were married in this way during Maasina Rule. People agreed to adopt these and other new practices because they saw them as part of forging a new social order, of replacing division with unity, conflict with "one-mindedness." The dynamics of this surely varied in different parts of Malaita according to the religious makeup of communities. My case data on these brideprice compromises comes mostly from east Kwaio, but it is all the more striking for that, because nowhere else on prewar Malaita were divisions between Christians and non-Christians deeper, and Christians were still a relatively small minority. That people nonetheless worked through their differences in such remarkable ways underscores their commitment to pursuing Maasina Rule's social project together.[120]

Beyond religious divisions, people saw certain aspects of Malaitan life as catalysts for conflict more generally, and they were banned as incompatible with movement solidarity and goals. This resembled government and mission attempts over the years to suppress "bad customs." A few examples will suffice. Foremost were practices associated with fighting and stealing. Ancestors confer powers for these (including to Christian young men who appeal to them secretly), and some "fighting ancestors" (Kwara'ae *akaloramo'a,* Lau *agalimae,* Kwaio *adalonimae,* 'Are'are *hi'onaniramo*) will pressure descendants to make use of those powers. Resulting success in fighting and stealing both pleases those spirits and brings renown to individuals and communities— what appear to outsiders as starkly antisocial acts can have a profoundly social aspect. With the imposition of British law in the 1920s, groups devised innovative ways to stop ancestral demands for killing by magically shutting down relevant shrines or modifying them to support only theft or, sometimes, only mortuary ritual. Now, with Maasina Rule's new orders against both killing and stealing, this process intensified. In 1946, on chiefly orders and wide public agreement, priests magically constrained, muted, or disengaged from many of their more problematic ancestors.[121]

The movement also banned or altered certain compensation types, some of which Christians objected to but more basically those that commonly led to quarrels. For example, a man could no longer demand compensation from another if he discovered that the man had once secretly (but celibately) courted his wife. Disallowed, too, were demands that a widow pay money to her late spouse's family when she remarried (ostensibly in case she had killed him by sorcery or violating taboos), and the exacting of compensation from women who walked near (but not into) shrines or from feast givers for property stolen or injuries occurring at their events. Trees or other property had sometimes been destroyed when demanding certain compensations, but this was now forbidden. Specific kinds of curses were prohibited.[122]

Also barred were certain marriage transaction types, the joyful destruction of property that sometimes occurred at marriage feasts, and a popular type of saturnalian men's feast called *totora* in 'Are'are (Kwaio *tootola*). *Totora* attendees were expected to be rowdy, and there was much sexual joking and boasting of carnal exploits, which sometimes led to compensation demands or fights. Chiefs from Kwaio southward also stopped enchained competitive feasts (Kwaio *di'iriu*) that gradually escalated in size, since they diverted labor and resources from Maasina Rule work, and even standard feasts had to be scheduled away from movement activities. Many practices abandoned were never revived, and my Kwaio field notes are sprinkled with descriptions of older ways that end, "but that finished with Maasina Rule."[123]

Kastom *in Maasina Rule*

Starting very early in Maasina Rule, Malaitans began working to reinstate or strengthen selected indigenous principles and practices, as well as to institute many new and novel ones. They compiled codes that included older rules, others that were older in form but new in meaning, and still others that were fully innovative. As they were made part of movement platforms and working codes all of these were labeled *kastom,* and the term soon became the overarching label for Maasina Rule's entire program and ideology, for everything from towns and farms, to chiefs and courts, plans for education and development, and the drive to escape British domination. Some of the things highlighted—for example, compensation—were powerful symbols of opposition to colonial policy. These exemplify Nicholas Thomas's point that some aspects of colonized societies labeled as "traditional"—particularly those highlighting "ethics or cultural predispositions"—are "substantivized" in opposition to perceived European ways. Thus compensation paid by and to groups was contrasted with the European emphasis (once imposed on Malaitans in serious cases) on punishment of individuals. This was particularly so among some Christians, who held their own ambivalent views of compensation and other practices emphasized in the codes. But these elements of *kastom* codes cannot be reduced to the process Thomas described. Compensation, for example, was not "invented" for this purpose; it had long been a deeply rooted, broad-spectrum means of dispute resolution for many Malaitans, above and beyond the oppositional, political meanings it acquired under colonial rule, and it continued to be so used during Maasina Rule (and after). More important, it is crucial to recognize that many elements of codes that were labeled as *kastom* were not attributed any "traditional pedigree"; rather, they were recognized as wholly new or as adaptations of European practices. Nonetheless, the entire enterprise was framed as moving forward in a Malaitan way, as opposed to the European way, which had failed Malaitans.[124]

We have seen that officers were confused by *kastom* since they thought it was, or should be, synonymous with their own concept of "custom," meaning enduring native ways from the past, from before European arrival in the Solomons. For them, it followed that because Maasina Rule grounded itself in *kastom* it was anachronistic. Officers writing of "custom" often perfunctorily added "old" or "ancient" to it (including when quoting Malaitans), as in, "The movement seeks a return to ancient native custom." On one hand this was an innocent muddling of *kastom* and "custom," neither of which district officers understood. But it was also politically useful to depict Maasina Rule as a desperate flight from the modern world rather than a progressive movement, and as an ignorant and dangerous mass retreat into "ancient native custom" that had to be blocked.[125]

Malaitans did pine for the past in the sense of a return to controlling their own affairs, and particularly to recovering the dignity that colonial rule had taken from them. As in most human societies in flux, there were tensions within the movement between aspirations for change and desires to maintain some valued, established ways. To be sure, certain explicit practices from the past could symbolically encapsulate what had been lost. But the indigenous ways Malaitans wanted most to maintain were not specific practices but fundamental and threatened moral principles and rules that provided frameworks and direction for proper social relationships, and these, too, could be marshaled for revolutionary reform. They saw the colonial system as having both undermined Malaitan ways and blocked Malaitan progress; Maasina Rule adherents sought to counter both, and they worked to resolve conflicts inherent in this dual undertaking. Those who joined together to create codes worked not merely to recover but also to discover, to find the essence of what it meant to be Malaitan in a time of new hopes and possibilities. *Kastom* was declared to be the basis for a new civil society, and it soon became the label not simply for specific practices or even guiding principles, but for the entire Maasina Rule project for self-determination in all of its features, including, as necessary, determined resistance to colonial efforts to hold them back.

A key ideological theme of Maasina Rule—which still runs through Malaitan *kastom* thought today, though often in competition with other ideas—was the principle that "foreign" ways, while not inherently bad in and of themselves, are ineffective or inappropriate for those to whom they do not belong, and that reckless adoption of them can lead to anomie or social collapse.[126] This relativistic precept very likely predates the colonial era, but it took on new resonance, first, with the growing awareness that Europeans and their ways threatened or had already devastated key aspects of Malaitan life, and later, with colonial officers' admonitions that only by following their true "custom," albeit in modified form, could Malaitans survive as a people. Malaitans had previously applied this precept most importantly to regulate proper relations between different localized groups and their various ancestors with their diverse taboos, but by the time of Maasina Rule it had expanded in meaning, scale, and scope, and it was now evoked to critique the imposition of European ways on Malaitans and to censure Malaitans who embraced those ways to the detriment of their fellows. Malaitans believed that for as long as they had worked under European direction they had been in decline, and progress would come only if pursued in the Malaitan way under Malaitan leaders—according to *kastom*.

When Nori spoke during his first east coast patrol, a central theme was the necessity of being guided by Malaitan sensibilities and leaders. Sale Kaakalade recalled his words at 'Oloburi:

> When Nori spoke this is what he told us: "We have held meetings with the white men, and you have seen all of those laws they have brought. They don't belong to us Solomon Islanders. They are their laws from *their* country. They came and gave us *their* laws, and we didn't understand them and we just followed them. But now, under this Maasina Rule we are organizing, you will no longer follow another man's laws. You will follow your own *kastom*. You must select a leader for yourselves and for all of your affairs. Your leader must be a man whose body

is like yours. If he is like you, then when he tells you something you can believe him. But if you follow some other man whose body is different, eventually you yourself will be different. You'll be different from your own place. He will turn you in another direction with his talk and eventually will lead you astray. No. You must follow a man whose body is black like yours and who speaks your language. Then you will be following something true."[127]

From the beginning, the movement framed *kastom* as "Malaitan ways of doing things," though we will see that it was soon given additional meanings, particularly that of political self-determination, which distanced it still further from European notions of "custom" (and also from classic anthropological concepts of "culture"). Nori and other leaders emphasized the need to analyze *kastom,* modify it, codify it, and apply it, a process sometimes referred to as "straightening out *kastom*" (Pijin, *steretem kastom*). This included forsaking older practices that might disrupt the social cohesiveness Maasina Rule required and fashioning new rules and practices that would help Malaitans reach their objectives. In contrast to European conceptions of "custom," to qualify as *kastom* something required no real or contrived pre-European pedigree. *Kastom* did not denote old ways in any exclusive sense but rather labeled a revisionist and forward-looking package of rules, institutions, and goals. Also developing at this time were specific concepts of "Christian *kastom.*"[128]

In chapters 2 and 3, readers were introduced to the colonial usage of "custom" in some detail. To briefly review, the government had since the early 1930s espoused a policy of selective preservation of "native custom." It was believed that tribal cultures were rigid and incapable of adapting to rapid change. If customs were undermined too much or too fast the result would be anomie or depopulation, even extinction. "Good customs" were to be protected as possible, but there also were "bad customs" that had to be suppressed. Because customs were by definition old and unchanging, to label any new innovation as "custom" was a corruption.

The European "custom" idea was deeply flawed in that Malaitan societies never had been static and, particularly over the previous 70 years, had been thoroughly transformed by colonization and by Malaitans themselves. By the mid-1940s, few Malaitans remembered pre-European life, and in any case many older ways were now irrelevant to their contemporary lives. Furthermore, officers were largely ignorant of Malaitan cultures and had to depend on Malaitans to tell them what "proper custom" was. Despite the concept's artificiality and officer ignorance, custom emerged as a keystone of administrative policy. "Custom chiefs" were granted powers to settle disputes via "customary laws." Just before and after the war, Malaitans were told that where their custom was concerned they would be given more rights and control in councils and courts. Custom was the one realm within which "the natives" would be granted a say in their own affairs.

To Malaitans, "custom" as officers were using it must have seemed a nebulous and puzzling concept. It had no direct counterpart in local languages, and it would have been difficult for people to fully understand what officers meant by it.[129] They knew full well that what officers seemed to denote with that term—precontact culture—no longer existed. They also observed officers reifying as "custom" things that were obviously modern innovations—"chiefs," "lines," limits on feasting, written codes, and the like. But if custom was understood more broadly to mean doing things in a Malaitan fashion, according to what were believed to be enduring principles and perspectives, this was more in line with Malaitans' own more flexible outlooks on their traditions, unfettered by a need for rigid conformity with the past. If taken in this way, then when Malaitans were told to codify their custom, they could be creative in good faith.

At the same time, Maasina Rule leaders did take advantage of the vague and confused nature of government custom policy and of officers' dearth of cultural knowledge. In 1988, Fifi'i told me how, especially during early phases of the movement, leaders strategically employed *kastom* as a gloss for movement activities, including those that harmonized with government policies. They knew officers would be less inclined to suppress custom than Malaitan innovations. When officers delegated to Malaitans more control over custom matters, Malaitans marshaled them as *kastom,* an expansive, predatory category that came to encompass more and more aspects of Malaitan life that Malaitans *wanted* control over. As Makira's Officer Len Barrow wrote: "Native Custom was always a safe card to play since it was Government policy to protect it so long as it did not run counter to the dictates of humanity, but it could be used to cover a multitude of sins." Other officers similarly portrayed Malaitan use of *kastom* as cynical and fraudulent, but the reality was more complex; while there was political manipulation, *kastom* was also a useful mediating category for interacting with Europeans. It could be used to translate Malaitan ideas into a category that officers found accessible and palatable. Some officers saw Malaitan presentations of *kastom* as simply ignorant, based on crude misunderstandings of what "custom" really meant. But it was not Malaitans who were confused.[130]

Chapter 6

Maasina Rule and the Government

In early 1947 Maasina Rule was at its zenith. Towns were in full flower, Malaitans were settling most of their troubles by *kastom,* and for most people the government seemed a distant entity. This historical moment was short-lived. As the year progressed, some officers came to believe that negotiation and compromise with Malaitans were undesirable or impossible and that a forceful crackdown was essential. This and the next two chapters examine in succession how the government learned of Maasina Rule, beginning in 1945, then the path to confrontation, government attempts to destroy the movement, and Malaitan responses. After several years this culminated in an end to both British efforts at gendarme suppression and overt Malaita-wide resistance. What emerged was a new relationship between the government and Malaitans quite different from that before the war, as well as new *kastom* political ideologies and practices.

The Government Becomes Aware

> Will you kindly, indicate briefly the nature of the "Marching Law"?
> —*Secretary to government to District Commissioner Malaita Sandars, 29 Dec 1945*

In describing Maasina Rule's programs and actions, I have come out ahead of my story, and readers are surely asking how the government reacted to the movement's meteoric ascent. One answer is that it was an organized and powerful force across much of Malaita before officers were fully aware of its existence. Their isolation from Malaitan life was at no time clearer, with such grim consequences for the government, than during the period dealt with here. As detailed earlier, movement meetings began in early 1944 and by year's end the name Maasina Rule had been adopted and the work was tooled up and running. As 1945 progressed, emissaries carried the movement over the island, it melded with other new political groups, and an overarching structure emerged. Nori led his first patrol north that July, and District Officer Forster later wrote that, by October, the movement "was firmly established throughout the whole district" and "very little opposition to it remained." Resident Commissioner Noel later told High Commissioner Grantham that officers had not heard of the movement or of the names "Marching Rule or Mercy Rule" until 1946, and that there were no open manifestations of it until May of that year. This was untrue and suggests that he was chagrined at having ignored the movement and at being so tardy reporting it. In reality, officers Forster and David Trench had been trying to monitor Maasina Rule since mid-1945, and Sandars's 1945 Annual Report notified Noel, based largely on Forster's tours, that "Mercy Rule" was everywhere.[1]

In early May 1945, a group of 'Are'are chiefs at Wairokai shocked Officer Fred Bentley and Cadet Roy Davies by announcing that all the people would soon move to the coast "so that government's task would be made easier." The officers did not object but cautioned them about problems that would result. Forster, who readers will recall was close to southern Malaitans, first got wind of Maasina Rule as a movement that June. He and Davies heard that Nori and Nono'oohimae were collecting money, but Hoasihau, the southern region's most important and trusted headman, and Onepusu's Headman Joe Tepi both said this was untrue. Then, while Forster and Davies toured west 'Are'are in July, Hoasihau told them that he himself was behind a plan to install a chief for all of south Malaita. He said his ambition was "to see Ariari with one Council, one custom, one Paramount chief." The officers departed believing that they had persuaded him to drop the plan. The administration's view, Davies later wrote, was that Malaitans "did not have the innate organizing ability" to run such regional councils and should therefore form sub-district councils and worry about larger ones later. The Malaitan view was that government was trying to thwart their organization and advancement. Soon after, the two officers found the movement had extended throughout east Kwaio, where, as in 'Are'are, large meetings were being held. They authorized chiefs at various places to continue meeting and to convene courts "to try routine native customary offences" and advised them to codify their "true and correct native custom." Still, they were perplexed; they knew something big was in the works, but what exactly it was remained a mystery.[2]

As Malaita's officers learned more about Maasina Rule, they could not settle on how to regard its activities. After a late–August 1945 'Are'are tour, and another inland in Kwaio, Forster worried about the movement's evident secrecy, possible misgovernment by unqualified chiefs, and the difficulties they might cause for government relations with the people. He lamented "the apparent lack of confidence in the Government," which in 'Are'are he blamed on the collapse of the prewar repopulation project. Still, he asserted that, all things considered, the movement was "a good thing," citing cleaner villages, a drop in crime, and new enthusiasm for communal work and improvement.[3] In early September, Forster brought Nori and Nono'oohimae to 'Aoke for discussion, where they spent several weeks waiting for an absent District Commissioner Trench to return and, Davies later guessed, imparting their message to west Kwara'ae villages.[4]

In November, Sandars arrived to replace Trench and sent Nori and Nono'oohimae home with, Davies said, "the mildest of lectures." Nono'oohimae later testified that Sandars at this time gave them permission to appoint chiefs and build farms and villages but forbade them from carrying the movement elsewhere unless invited, and other Malaitans from traveling to visit them in 'Are'are without Sandars's permission.[5] Sandars's initial reaction to the movement was more negative than Forster's, and he told Noel that Shadrach Diote'e (who later became a head chief) should replace Amasia as head of the Kwaimela Native Council in west Kwara'ae—partly because Amasia had "undoubtedly been mixed up with a subversive movement known as the 'Marching Law'" and had lied about it. Soon after, Sandars's 1945 Annual Report described "a semi-political and pseudo-religious movement known as the 'Mercy Rule,'" which in its 'Are'are beginnings had been laudable but as it spread had been corrupted by "disciples fascinated by their own eloquence" and "grandiose and foolish schemes." His examples of the latter were plans to shift residence from hamlets to larger villages and put aside family gardens for community ones. Both were bad ideas, Sandars thought, especially because "the naturally contentious and extremely parochial nature of the Malaita man would make constant strife and bickering inevitable."[6] But he was not overly concerned; he thought that the troubles were due mostly to recent contact with Americans, particularly "Negro troops," and that once men went back to work things would return to normal and native administration plans could move forward. "Mercy Rule" seemed "fairly under control."[7]

Sandars's remarks exemplify a dual vocabulary found in government writings about Maasina Rule: Here, what was formerly a pioneering government "project" had become in Malaitan hands a "grandiose and foolish scheme." In many officers' writings, crowds summoned by the government or its supporters were "gatherings" or "meetings" but Maasina Rule assemblies were "mobs" or "hordes." (For Davies, the entire movement was "a mob."[8]) Government constabularies were "police," while Maasina Rule ones were "thugs." The government sponsored "native courts," but Maasina Rule held "secret tribunals." Loyalist headmen were "confident," but uncooperative chiefs "swaggered" or "strutted." I call attention to such loaded terms not to argue that there were never ill-advised undertakings (on both sides), unruly crowds, thuggish duties (or police), or swaggering chiefs (or headmen), and some legal proceedings were indeed kept secret from white people (though many were not), but rather to note that the negatives were often default terms applied indiscriminately to Maasina Rule and its people. This language was heartfelt and displayed deep prejudice against the movement and indeed any Malaitans who undertook political actions outside government auspices. When this attitude met with Malaitan prejudices against the government, cooperation was difficult.

By early 1946, officers recognized the breadth but not the depth of discontent. Sandars and others for a time downplayed it as a problem of young Labour Corps returnees, thankfully frowned on by older, "more responsible" men. Against growing counterevidence, officers viewed the returnees much as Europeans once had regarded men back from Queensland—as scallywags corrupted by naive misunderstandings of their experiences abroad and as outside the mainstream of Malaitan society.

Yet Sandars soon tempered his derision of the movement, and over the following months he and Forster met most of the main Maasina Rule chiefs around the island and approved their selection (Sandars was on leave June–October 1946). At Wairokai in January 1946, Sandars rejected calls for a single chief to represent Malaita as well as requests that chiefs be allowed to judge all legal matters "according to custom," but he did give Nori and others suggestions on setting up their chiefly structure and other movement matters. He had determined to take up a more salutatory policy of constructive engagement to try to steer Malaitans' new enthusiasm toward goals he approved of. Officers on other islands were instructed to follow his lead; in District Commissioner Central Ken Crass's words: "Every effort should be made to direct the movement into Government channels where it may be observed controlled and assisted."[9]

Early Altercations

The first half of 1946 was fairly uneventful, and officers remained much in the dark while the movement further consolidated. Tensions persisted, and Forster later wrote that by June "the movement had attained dangerous proportions," and "the natives were excitable and truculent." He was undoubtedly referring to three mid-1946 incidents of open defiance. The first involved Officer Cyril Belshaw during his May tour of Ngorangora village at the northern end of Ulawa. Belshaw had first visited there the previous December, at which time he had declared five houses unsanitary and ordered them axed and burned. In the 1920s Solomons, "unsanitary" dwellings had sometimes been destroyed, but it was no longer common practice even though a regulation that allowed it remained on the books. After Belshaw departed, angry villagers met and talked of challenging him the next time he came.[10]

On his next visit, 23 May, Belshaw ordered the village cleaned in preparation for another sanitary inspection, and the community decided that the first man he confronted should protest. Belshaw entered each house in turn, while his wife and a constable named Matanigabu waited outside. Near one house he saw betel nut husks and leaves on the ground and ordered its owner, Taheolo, to clean them up. Proceeding to the next house, he glanced back to see the constable sweeping them up. He shouted at him to give the broom to Taheolo, who sat down and untied it, he claimed in order to tighten it (palm-bristle brooms require this often). Belshaw, probably correctly, interpreted this as defiance and berated both Taheolo and the constable, at which Taheolo vigorously challenged the entire surprise inspection as illegal—cleaning days were always scheduled, and only on Tuesdays and Saturdays—and refused the command. A large and noisy but not violent crowd gathered, encouraging Taheolo "not to be frightened and go ahead." Afterward, Belshaw called a village meeting and determined that the episode was, in the words of his superior, District Commissioner Kenneth Crass, "entirely due to the subversive influences connected with the Mercy Rule Movement." According to Belshaw, people said that Timothy George, who was expected to visit soon, had advised civil resistance (though not resistance to Belshaw specifically), and that they wanted George as their headman. The Ulawans themselves ended the meeting, Belshaw reported, "saying further talk would lead to losing of tempers." He was told by some that they did not want the government anymore, but he was also told that Sandars supported Maasina Rule, and that "they wanted T. George and D.C. Malaita."[11]

Belshaw urged his superiors to punish the "premeditated insolence unconcealed hostility and resistance." He telegrammed Crass a list of Ulawa rumors (including that George was arming and fomenting violent revolution), advised "time for action soon," and warned, "Unless I have strong police backing [to arrest Ulawans] there will be resistance which will set ablaze movement in Malaita." He urged restriction of George's movements. Crass ordered Belshaw to take no action and to apply "care and reasonableness" so as not to interfere with Sandars's Malaita policy of working with the movement; he also asked Makira and Malaita officers to investigate the rumors. Forster, who had just toured Small Malaita, telegrammed a reply: "Timothy George elected chief Small Malaita by General consent of people to which Sandars raised no objections....Movement is generally for betterment social conditions people," and Maasina Rule was "anti-European exploitation." Forster thought George "highly unlikely to start any actual resistance against Government." Still, planter Henry Kuper, a bitter Maasina Rule opponent on Makira, reported that Ulawans were "elated" at having stopped Belshaw, and David Trench, now acting as resident commissioner, ordered Crass to arrest "ringleaders" at Ulawa and to detain George if he visited.[12]

Crass's early June investigation on Ulawa concluded that Maasina Rule there (where everyone was a supporter) was not obviously anti-government. One organizer "stressed the need to use Government backing and assistance in getting the aims of the movement," and those who had visited Malaita for George's guidance, he was told, brought back instructions to follow the government.[13] He noted anger at Belshaw's house burning and believed subsequent discussion "centered round the Mercy Rule as the only hope of a permanent relief from such interference" in their private affairs.

He concluded that the trouble had been caused by Belshaw's actions both previously and that morning: "Such actions would probably not of themselves have produced the disturbance had it not been for the radical ideas and feelings of self assertion which are in existence throughout the Solomons....But at the same time such ideas and feelings would probably not have produced such an incident but for the lack of confidence resulting from such actions." Still, Taheolo was sentenced to two months of hard labor since he "failed to make his complaint in a manner through his Headman." For the next few months Maasina Rule seemed tranquil on Makira and Ulawa. No more houses were burned.[14]

I present this incident at length because it so well displays a new attitude that had emerged among southeast Solomon Islanders: many were willing to cooperate with government, and at least some Maasina Rule leaders were disseminating instructions to do so, but they would not tolerate bullying. Further, the government's speedy dismissal of Belshaw's call for soldiers and suppression highlights the sincerity of its policy of positive engagement, with which Belshaw's actions were out of step. (It seems he then knew little of either Maasina Rule or the policy.) Nonetheless, the episode was later excavated as evidence that the movement was dangerous, and Noel (and later Colin Allan) identified it as perhaps the point at which "Marching Rule first showed its hand" as anti-government. Belshaw soon published his reading of the Ulawa situation, concluding: "There was no question here as to the aims and desires of the natives; concern with economic rights and benefits, basic as it may have been, did not appear to be uppermost in their minds. Instead, there was envy and hatred of the white man—hatred so irrational as to resemble religious hysteria."[15]

Two other "truculent" events to which Forster referred took place concurrently at 'Aoke in mid-June just after Sandars departed on leave. First, people of 'Aoke Island in Langalanga staged an honor guard of 48 men to greet visiting Maasina Rule dignitaries, much as government police formations had always greeted visiting colonial bigwigs. Such guards were being formed everywhere and greeted Nori at stops on his patrols. The 'Aoke Island guard wore homemade white uniforms with red sashes and carried mock rifles of coconut boughs, bugles made of leaves, and drums of kerosene tins and paper. Their Maasina Rule leader then was Sale "One-Arm" Fotarafa, who had once served as a police sergeant under Bell. Forster had already arrested men of a guard farther north for drilling and, he said, for coercing a bush hamlet to move to the coast. He later charged that such "bands" pressured people to join Maasina Rule. Drilling itself was illegal and would soon become a government worry if not a preoccupation. Inspired partly by US soldiers and parades in the Labour Corps and Defence Force, it had a much longer history. Malaitans drilled on some Queensland plantations; Rev Arthur Hopkins in 1904 watched a former policeman direct hundreds of north Malaitans in drilling; and Edge-Partington held twice-

FIGURE 6.1. Schoolboys drilling at the SSEM's Onepusu center, ca 1922. (Photo by Norman Deck, courtesy of the SSEM Archive, 55P160~1.)

daily police parades and drills at 'Aoke. Drill was also routine for students at some of Malaita's mission schools, and aspects of it were adapted by SSEM "young people's bands" (later called "marching bands") in performing religious songs. Police touring the east coast with medical officer Gordon White in 1929 were asked by local people to entertain them with bayonet drill, or "dance belong soldier." White said the drilling looked "for all the world like a bushman's dance." Lambert described public drills by police escorting his 1933 medical tour, which left a Malaitan crowd "speechless with awe, wonder, and a high degree of jealousy among the young men who envy the smart short lavalava and belt and especially the rifle."[16]

At this time Maasina Rule was gaining strength in Langalanga, from whence men had paddled south to meet with 'Are'are leaders. But a rival Red Cross movement was still active, and some of its followers informed Forster about the guard. Forster later said the headman complained to him that Maasina Rule used the drills to "overawe" the local council and interfered with native court decisions. On 12 June, Forster arrested Fotarafa and 38 others, "tried" them on the spot, and sentenced them to four months of hard labor for drilling (Fotarafa, later, to six months). One of those arrested, Tome Waleanisia, insisted to me in 1987 that they were summarily sentenced with no inquiry or trial after they affirmed that they had formed the guard (but only an honor guard, which they had thought legal). The prisoners and their community hotly protested and several hundred Langalanga in a fleet of canoes accompanied the district boat as it took their men to 'Aoke, escorted them to the prison gates, and announced that they all wanted to be jailed.[17]

The resident commissioner later approved Forster's arrests and reported that, while touring in August, "The leading Elder from the Langa Langa Lagoon...thanked the Government for the action taken to relieve his area of intimidation by some foolish people." Later reports highlighted this same unnamed "leading Elder" (Red Cross member or not), typifying a future pattern of officials pointing to anti–Maasina Rule individuals or small anti–Maasina Rule minorities and declaring that to protect their interests the movement and the vast majority who belonged had to be brought to heel.[18]

At this same time Forster received word from west Kwara'ae headmen Ngwangwaki of Fiu and Amasia of Kwaimela that two Maasina Rule chiefs, Nelson Kifo and Sukulu, had formed what Forster loosely called a "private army" to the north of 'Aoke. The next day he walked to Fiu and, after a meeting during which Kifo and Sukulu told him that Maasina Rule was not subject to government councils, he ordered the two to 'Aoke. But they summoned a "mob" of 200–300 to come with them, which, Forster wrote to Trench, they did "in good humor." Once at 'Aoke the others refused to leave, and Forster recorded all their names and "locked them up" in groups of 25 in leaf houses (from which they could wander if they wished). That night, Norman Deck later wrote, each policeman slept surrounded by many Kwara'ae, Agricultural Officer Jock Beveridge and a Chinese shopkeeper fled south to Buma, and Forster and Davies were "marooned" in Forster's house. The next morning hundreds more Kwara'ae arrived, having gathered at neighboring Abu village, saying they too wanted to go to jail. Forster feared trouble, but all left when Sukulu and Kifo "exercised a quieting influence on the crowd" and Forster announced that the two men could go home, evoking cheers. Forster was bluffing and had always intended to release the two (he had no grounds to charge them, let alone the hundreds of others), but in Davies's view, "There was no doubt that that particular round had been won by the Marching Rule." Further, Davies wrote, "This was all done without incident and the self-discipline of the Kwara'aes was even more thought-provoking in its implications than a bit of turbulence would have been." Kifo was a particular worry, since "he was quite clearly not going to be bluffed or overawed."[19]

The next morning another Langalanga fleet arrived carrying several hundreds to demand their men be released or that they be arrested, too. Unlike the Kwara'ae, this group was disorderly, and Davies said a virtual riot ensued as the crowd pushed Sergeant Major Steven Sipolo and several other policemen off the wharf into the sea and rushed the prison, while Davies struggled to prevent frightened clerk Alec Maena and police from shooting into the crowd. Once the police were settled and the crowd had surrounded the jail, Forster suggested to Davies that, given they could do nothing, they go and enjoy a beer at his house. In the end the crowd did not break into the prison and, after failed bargaining with Forster, they gave up and went home. Forster afterward told Trench he "had to be quite rude" to get rid of them and begged Trench to send over footballs and cricket balls so young men could "let off steam."[20]

These were important events because, in Malaitan eyes, civil resistance in the form of the well-disciplined Kwara'ae group lining up to be jailed and peacefully refusing to back down had forced the government to yield, while the unruly Langalanga had won nothing. The former was to become a basic Malaitan resistance tactic in years to come. The first incident was also significant as the first successful action led by Kifo, who the next year was to become a key north Malaitan figure in Maasina Rule's conflict with the government. Further, the Langalanga considered their men unjustly jailed, and while Forster believed their harsh sentences had frightened the Langalanga and given them "a well-deserved kick in the pants," Waleanisia told me that they instead incensed many Langalanga outside Maasina Rule, who now joined the movement. Finally, it was whispered on the station that Sipolo, the Malaitan there whom Europeans trusted most, had prior knowledge of the Langalanga action and had incited the rowdiness.[21]

"Things are of course fizzing at Kwai, Kwarade (bush) and Malu'u," Forster wrote on 17 June in one of a series of personal letters to Trench. From these it is clear he was both amused and exhilarated by these events, but for the moment they altered his view of Maasina Rule. He told Trench, "Finally figured out that Mercy Law's object is Malaita for the Malaitans and no Government" and on 15 June had noted, "Now the fact of its anti-government aspect is revealed it should be easier to deal with." Two weeks later he wrote, "The Marching Law is a political party run on Nazi or Communistic lines and is tending to create a state within a state.... The time has come to wind up the Marching Law." But Forster still thought any show of force inadvisable. "It would appear that natives have been going round with a chip on their shoulders," he told the government secretary, "and care should be exercised in choosing the time to knock it off." Soon he weighed whether to arrest Nori and George, though he had little grounds on which to charge them with anything. In June or July he visited 'Are'are, and, Nori later testified, told them their work was permitted, but he ordered a halt to any drilling or honor guards. He took Nori and his wife and Timothy George to 'Aoke and persuaded Nori to join the 'Aoke police as a third-class constable—Davies claimed by offering an alternative of arrest. Nori agreed, went home for five weeks, and returned to 'Aoke to don his uniform. He wore it till the end of 1946, when he left under pressure from other movement leaders, who said he should not work as Sandars's "cook boy."[22]

Provisional Cooperation

Despite Forster's strong words, 1946 saw no more altercations, and both movement leaders and government officers sustained a less confrontational atmosphere. Sandars earlier in the year had consulted with and advised various chiefs on how to pursue Maasina Rule's agenda, as he understood it, in tandem with the government's, and when in mid-October he returned from leave, things calmed further. He resumed his previous strategy of trying to canalize the movement, now working especially closely with Nori, whom he sent about wearing his police uniform to advise councils on Maasina Rule and government working together. The two men subsequently took trips together around the island on a district vessel, carrying the same message. Sandars later testified that Nori "went out of his way on more than one occasion to assist Government and in preaching moderation," and Divisional Officer Germond wrote that Nori "was used to solve knotty problems which the local headmen had failed to settle."[23]

Davies later claimed that Forster fully opposed Sandars's friendly tactics. Decades later, in a book manuscript on Maasina Rule to be discussed presently, he was at pains to portray Forster at this time as despising the movement and as trying to stamp it out, and Sandars as having on his October return ruined Forster's tough approach by reinstating appeasement. Forster's writings contradict this claim, at least in the blunt terms in which Davies presented it. To believe Davies, one would have to suppose that by reporting his more nuanced and shifting approaches and views Forster had intentionally deceived his superiors, and explain why. Forster's assessments oscillated between positive and negative in reaction to events at hand. In August 1947, soon after taking over Malaita from Sandars (while Forster was away on leave), Davies was to launch a crackdown on Maasina Rule that wrecked government administration on Malaita for years. A central goal of Davies's manuscript was to justify this action despite its disastrous consequences, and in service of this he attempted to portray Sandars as a dupe of mendacious Maasina Rule leaders, to discredit his more placatory approach, and to isolate him by depicting Forster and other officers as having been firmly in Davies's own camp.[24]

In 1946, Forster had opposed using force against the movement, writing to Trench on 1 July, "I know Sandars more or less said it could be done...but he was about to go on leave and would not have to cope with the aftermath." Then, just before Sandars's return that October, Forster, in a comprehensive report on Maasina Rule, again called attention to the movement's positive gains in law and order, "custom" codification, better villages and gardens, health and sanitation, and, especially, a "revival in natives' interest in their own affairs." Since June he had seen "a great increase in frankness and willingness to co-operate with Government." He hoped this could be sustained, since "failure to win and maintain the confidence of the Malaita people...may seriously prejudice the future of the Protectorate." Forster was optimistic, for he believed Nori's influence was waning, headmen's confidence in the government had been restored, and white SSEM missionaries were now reining in their flocks. Disappointment awaited him on all three fronts, and, as Davies bemoaned, "The Marching Rule proved a plant of sturdy growth."[25]

Beyond trying to reroute Maasina Rule, Forster and Sandars had a wily aim in bringing Nori into the police and working with him publicly: they hoped that by appearing to co-opt Nori they could undercut his reputation and thereby weaken the movement. Readers should remember this when appraising later, pious government complaints that movement leaders manipulated or deceived officers. The two officers succeeded to the extent that Nori suffered criticism, most notably from some southern leaders, that he was now government's man, or had "turned the movement over to the government," and he was for a time abandoned as an overarching leader. But the officers were too clever by half—Nori was relatively moderate and progressive and was the leader with the strongest working influence throughout the island. In the end, to the degree they deflated him, they undermined government's ability to deal with Maasina Rule. Contrary to their assumption, the movement had not hitched its wagon to Nori's star. More important, their tactic had the unintended consequence of adding to Malaitan confusion about Sandars's own position on Maasina Rule. The spreading idea that he fully supported the movement caused the government serious problems. Already the previous May, Ulawans had told Belshaw that Sandars supported the movement, and while Sandars was on leave in September, letters circulated saying he had gone to England to secure for Solomon Islanders a £12 monthly wage. Davies said that clerk Maena told him in October that people from Laulasi, in Langalanga near 'Aoke, saw Sandars as Maasina Rule's leader, and Davies claimed that even loyal headmen suspected Sandars really was "the Father of Marching Rule." This confusion extended upward; after Noel later met with movement leaders, letters circulated saying that he, too, had approved the movement's programs, except for demands for a £12 monthly wage. Years later Allan wrote that leaders respected Sandars and had asked him to be the movement's secretary: "His tongue in cheek response was that they could not afford to pay him the wages; to which, they asked how much did he earn, adding that they would pay him £100 more." When the head chiefs were later arrested and tried, multiple defendants, including Nori, told of Sandars's, Forster's, and Noel's authorizations of various Maasina Rule activities, citing or quoting multiple, specific talks with them.[26]

A final defect in the strategy to undercut Nori was that he was no fool and likely spotted their game; it was probably due at least partly to his influence in 'Aoke that the entire police force joined the movement, and not long after he returned home they temporarily resigned en masse (see below). Still, as Sandars had instructed, Nori did hold discussions at various places—by all accounts in earnest and good faith—about how Maasina Rule should work together with government councils.[27]

By late 1946 most Europeans in the Solomons had awoken to Maasina Rule's magnitude. Initial disbelief gave way to shock. Fears of a violent Malaitan uprising had always lurked, but it had been taken for granted that Malaitans were too fragmented, xenophobic, and backward ever to unite as a serious political threat. A divided Malaita was controllable, but all knew that, as Sandars later wrote, "Malaita would be extremely difficult to run if all the people were good friends together." While the 'Are'are were constructing a multi-tiered Malaitan leadership structure, legal codes, and social programs, Trench had bemoaned the difficulties of native administration in the face of "the general backwardness of the population, to whom the conception of Government as we know it in any form is still rather strange." And how could officers have anticipated that Malaita would produce powerful political organizers? Most had long believed Malaitan leaders, including many headmen, to be weak, incompetent, or corrupt, and a tour report cliché was the notation that an area visited had "no suitable leaders or outstanding personalities."[28]

Charles Fox recalled European distress at the movement's impressive organization and the fact that Islanders had hidden it from them: "Men you had known from their childhood, who you expected would tell you anything, would not tell you a word about it.... It astonished those of us who knew them best." Many Europeans began criticizing the government for not cracking down, for they saw officers' attempts to work with Maasina Rule as condoning the intolerable.[29]

A turning point came on Boxing Day, 26 December 1946, when by arrangement Sandars and the head chiefs held the first of several public meetings at 'Aoke station. In an orderly and cordial atmosphere, nearly 6,000 men attended what was at that time the largest gathering ever held on Malaita. Just beforehand, Sandars was handed a list of policies titled "The Heads of the M.R. Council Decision," which stated, in sum: Maasina Rule would work together with the native courts and leave "big" cases to Sandars; communities would have at least 100 residents; the movement would not oppose mission or other training and would send young men for agricultural instruction; anyone could join Maasina Rule who agreed to follow its rules; the movement did not oppose the government or the missions; and finally, chiefs across Malaita were to set their people to work on economic development.[30]

Sandars responded to each point: he approved larger villages and seconded the calls for training, cooperation with the government and missions, and economic development (especially production to market to outsiders), but he said that the movement must not put "moral pressure" on people to join. He also stressed "the need for loyalty to our King by all" and warned against drilling. More problematic was the court issue, on which Sandars vacillated. He told the gathering that "matters of Native Custom, small criminal and civil cases were already dealt with by the existing Native Courts and Councils; that many of the men present at the meeting were both Councilors and Justices and that the system seemed to work well when all the people pulled together." This tiptoed around the call for Maasina Rule's direct participation in the legal system. Soon after, Forster observed and publicly approved of a court at 'Ataa run by the headman and movement chiefs together, with the verdict decided by the local Maasina Rule council. When the chiefs later told Sandars of this he was, according to Head Chief Heber, "very pleased." A few months later "Maasina Rule courts," some presided over by the same "councilors and justices" who had received Sandars's approving nod, became government's main grounds for attacking the movement.[31]

At the 'Aoke meeting, Sandars formally received the names of the nine head chiefs. Nori, despite Sandars and Forster's efforts to weaken him, was again presented as an overarching chief. Sandars wrote afterward: "These men [except Loia of Funafou in Lau] are of good character and known to the District Commissioner [Sandars] personally. It is the District Commissioner's opinion that these men have the well-being of the people at heart and if they can be guided by friendly advice they may assist the Government in its aims." Sandars was also informed that people thought a fair wage would be £12 per month.[32]

Cadet Davies's experience of this meeting was strikingly different from that of Sandars and also of the several Malaitan attendees I have known, and it betrayed a visceral fear that would mark his dealings with Malaitans in the coming year. He had awaited the meeting with trepidation: "Perhaps the District Commissioner was at last to be given his orders and told what he could and could not do on Malaita henceforth. I wondered whether the leaders would produce a large mob and whether they got around to considering violence....There was no longer any doubt in my mind that the Marching Rule was going to stage some sort of coup." He described Sandars at the meeting as "being harangued and haranguing." "The men were disciplined and orderly, but the naked menace was there; weapons or no weapons, 5,600 adult male Malaitamen gathered together was a dangerous event....The multitude was quiet but emanated curiously disturbing wavelengths and I formed the impression that it could quickly become an excited mob."[33]

Wavelengths notwithstanding, other officers and many Malaitans saw the meeting as a breakthrough, and it ushered in a high point in relations that lasted into the following spring. Sandars still worried that northern areas—especially To'abaita and around Kwai harbor, and excepting west Kwara'ae—might be developing "along quite different and less desirable lines" than the south, but he hoped that was "largely a matter of political growing pains." Government options were in any case limited. The great majority of Malaitans now belonged to Maasina Rule. It could no longer be spoken of as a commotion by a recalcitrant minority; the 1946 Annual Report acknowledged that 95 percent might, as claimed, be adherents, and officers reported unanimity in many areas.[34]

A few days after the 'Aoke meeting, Davies left for a post on Makira, happy to leave behind "Marching Rule with its truculent bloody-mindedness; its perverse obstruction of everything the Government tried to do even when this patently meant cutting off their noses to spite their faces; the lies, the threats, the distortions, and all that pathetic wasted energy," and rumors of foreign invasion. "I was sick of the bloody lot of them."[35]

In January, High Commissioner Grantham visited the Protectorate and met with Noel and district commissioners. Afterward, he penned a report to the secretary of state for the Colonies: "[Maasina Rule] is not primarily subversive or disloyal in intent. On the contrary, the fundamental aim is the development and welfare of the people, who, the leaders consider, should have a greater control over their own affairs, at any rate in minor matters. These are admirable aims, and are in fact the policy of Government. In a primitive community, such as the Solomons Islands, it is only to be expected that there should be some undesirable manifestations. But these on the whole have not been the result of deliberate malice or wickedness, but are rather the result of wild rumours coupled with the general unsettlement consequent on the war, and an insufficiency of females as wives for the young men. . . . If we can keep the movement along these lines and not drive it underground, good will come of it."[36]

Much credit for this upbeat assessment must go to Sandars, who by 1947 was the Protectorate's most senior officer under Noel and highly respected by other officers (excepting Davies), especially regarding Malaitan affairs. He had spent over seven years on Malaita since his arrival just after the assassination of Bell, the only officer to serve there longer. For Maasina Rule's younger leaders, Sandars had from their childhood been the most important government officer and, except for Forster in some quarters, he was the best known and liked. Sandars now knew more about Malaitans than he had in the mid-1930s, knew more of them personally, and, most important, clearly held them in higher regard. He knew the chiefs were not evil or reckless and respected them and many of their goals, some of which he himself had promoted for years. In many of Sandars's reports of 1947 one finds a palpable excitement at the rush of activity and people's eagerness for change. Now in his fifties, he approached the end of his career, having seen many a well-meaning project falter along or fail outright, often for lack of Malaitan enthusiasm or for, as District Officer Bengough had put it, a dearth of "natural leadership, sense of public responsibility and communal co-operation." Now Malaitans had grabbed the reins to undertake some of these same projects, with impressive leaders, solidarity, and intense initiative. It is no surprise that Sandars viewed Maasina Rule more positively than did most Europeans, particularly after the affable Boxing Day meeting. Perhaps he recalled his stint attached to the British "Black and Tans" in Ireland during the 1920s, when he had been sympathetic to the cause he was tasked to suppress, which he termed "Ireland for the Irish," as he now expressed sympathy toward Maasina Rule and its desire for what he called "Malaita for the Malaitans" (though he certainly would have opposed Malaitan independence). Davies wrote that Sandars saw Maasina Rule "as a heaven-sent opportunity to get things done after years of fighting the deadweight of conservatism," and Norman Deck said Sandars told SSEM missionaries that it was "the very thing that he had been hoping for, and that he was going to foster and guide it into right channels." For the next six months Noel would follow Sandars's advice and back his efforts to tame the movement. But when the following July Sandars left Malaita for the last time, so did the government's strategy of cooperation.[37]

The Path to Conflict

Initial and later European impressions that Maasina Rule was subversive were, from a colonial perspective, accurate in the sense that a central tenet held that Malaitans should control their own affairs with minimal interference, to a degree that the government had no intention of allowing. The movement did conceal some of its initial organizing activities, though later movement leaders became quite candid, and as Cadet Wilfred Marquand observed, they held many meetings "within a stone's throw" of 'Aoke station. One often gets the impression that some of the secrecy stemmed not from hostility or a fear of suppression but rather from a belief that government was no longer terribly relevant to Maasina Rule's project. During the war, Malaitans had, in Forster's words, "seen white people in a new light," and their perception of the colonials' place in the wider world had changed accordingly: "From being 'masters' they had become a minor party of a vast machine." Reading the archives, too, one realizes that many officers considered "secret" almost any idea or activity that they had not pre-approved and were not supervising.[38]

Then again, to say that Maasina Rule was fully subversive is inaccurate in that many leaders and members were not unequivocally anti-government. As we have seen, some movement courts and councils separated from their government counterparts, particularly where headmen were antagonistic, but they more often absorbed or melded with them, sometimes with headmen as members, their status left ambiguous to Malaitans and Europeans alike. Leaders, particularly in the south, often denied that the movement was anti-government—they welcomed and even urged the government to help with medical, agricultural, and other services, and they consulted often with colonial officers. For many leaders and followers this cooperative stance was clearly genuine, if fragile and at times tentative, into early months of 1947 and, for some, after that. Even Davies, who usually portrayed Maasina Rule as a disingenuous conspiracy, acknowledged that Maasina Rule chiefs did not see their dispute resolution proceedings as illegal.[39]

Some of the ambiguity came from similarities of movement goals to those promoted by the postwar colonial administration: new councils and courts, codifying "custom" and shedding "bad customs," law and order, larger and cleaner villages and gardens, and medical services and education. Ambiguity increased when officers began to openly encourage these and other aspects of the movement and worked to integrate them with government programs. Because many Malaitans perceived officers as supporting many Maasina Rule projects—as indeed Sandars, Forster, and even Noel at times professed to—they did not see joining the movement as a seditious move, and a steady flow of letters and rumors fostered that view. In the midst of this, Sandars hoped to shepherd Malaitan ambivalence into full collaboration between government and the people. It is important to remember when talking of Maasina Rule as a "resistance movement" that, though adherents were keen to resist a return to the prewar colonial system, many at this time did not agitate for outright rejection of the government, and even those that did so sought not just to resist but also to create new, forward-looking programs to improve Malaitan life.

We will see that when relations later collapsed, some officers declared retrospectively that Maasina Rule statements of cooperation with government had always been a massive charade. To explain events in this way requires belief in a fantastic conspiracy reaching far beyond secreting aspects of the movement, one that thousands of Malaitans acted out for years—not only in their actions toward government but also among themselves—and even maintained for decades after. The reality was far more complicated and presented awkward problems for those who later determined to bluntly vilify and crush Maasina Rule. Officer Marquand later wrote that many Malaitans had said, "They joined because they did not believe that the movement was against the Government. Often they held responsible positions in the movement, and it seems hard to believe that they did not understand what they were joining.... It makes one wonder if the theory that the movement was subversive is really correct. Undoubtedly the natives demonstrated avoidance after the end of the war, but this in itself is hardly subversive."[40]

Shortly after the Boxing Day meeting, in January 1947, a new Native Administration Regulation was adopted. It authorized native councils, but communities could only nominate their members for appointment at the resident commissioner's pleasure. Headmen were automatically council presidents and assistant headmen vice presidents, and all council resolutions required the resident commissioner's approval. Marquand wrote, "A resolution passed by the council through the District Officer to the Resident Commissioner and to the Legal Adviser and back again, usually returned so long after the event, that it had either been put into effect regardless, or forgotten. It had also usually been rewritten by the Legal Adviser so as to be completely meaningless to the people who had passed it in the first place." The regulation assigned to councils a range of responsibilities: to define and regulate "non-repugnant" native customs; to pursue development, public health, and education; and to preserve law and order. It set rules for native council funds into which native court fines and fees would be paid. Headmen would control these funds, for use, again, only with the resident commissioner's consent.[41]

Aspects of this and the 1945 Native Courts Regulation potentially gave considerably more leeway to councils and courts to run their own affairs. However, Marquand lamented the BSIP administration's insertion of sections, such as one requiring high official approval of their resolutions, that undermined the basic principles of "community development" toward the self-government that the secretary of state had declared were to guide British colonial policy worldwide. Their insertion showed "a lack of understanding and knowledge of these principles, or an unwillingness to put them into effect."[42]

In the first months of 1947, two new cadets were assigned to Malaita who over the next two years became central figures in government dealings with the movement. Peter Cameron, age 27, spent much of 1947 working on the island's northeast coast, at times based in the Kwai area in east Kwara'ae. In March, Forster took extended leave due to "nervous exhaustion,"[43] and in early June his replacement, the earlier-quoted Wilfred Marquand, age 29, began working in Malu'u and other areas farther north. Cameron and Marquand wrote some of the most detailed accounts of events during this period. Cameron was to remain committed to the government program until his departure at the end of 1948, while Marquand later became disillusioned and authored a scathing critique of the government's Maasina Rule policies for a 1950 London Devonshire Course for colonial officers.[44] Davies wrote in his manuscript that both Cameron and Marquand "had only recently left the Armed Forces after spending all the war years in them, during which time both were badly wounded, and they saw things in largely military terms—people who broke the law should be dealt with firmly and promptly. There was no question of compromise for them." But this portrayal, like Davies's depiction of Forster as reactionary, was a concoction, and we shall see it starkly contradicted in their reports and, for Marquand, in Davies's own writings.[45]

While the two cadets worked in the north, Sandars also toured, visiting most passages around Malaita, including the most difficult areas of Kwai and To'abaita: "At every center I was well received," he recorded, "and the people were very willing to hear what I had to say." He believed that the southern people would cooperate with government councils, but about the north he remained less confident. The only complaints he heard in east 'Are'are, in areas that were 100 percent Maasina Rule, were that he should visit more often. He discussed with people everything from the tax that a king's regulation would soon reimpose, to how to base a council's future laws on "the best of native customs together with a certain amount of 'white men's' laws," to the meaning of "freedom." He even arranged for the government to buy produce from movement farms.[46]

Cracks did appear in the amity. In February Sandars recruited 50 northern men to work in Honiara, breaching movement policy and broad Malaitan consensus that men were to stay home. Then, in March, Loea of Lau, the only head chief Sandars disapproved of, was given five months in jail for nonpolitical "sundry misdemeanors." In early March, also, Sandars found out that his two top policemen, Sergeant Major Stephen Sipolo of Ngongosila in the Kwai area and Sergeant Eban Sau (full name Funusau) of Fokanakafo in Fataleka, were involved in plans for a constabulary walkout set for 30 June. Forster had the previous year jailed Sau for participating in and probably leading a police strike for better food, but Sau later returned to duty. People had whispered their suspicions about Sipolo's loyalty for months, including to Sandars, but Sandars had known both men for as long as he had been in the Solomons, so when matters came to a head he was astounded. Sipolo had been an exemplary officer since the 1920s (he refused to take part in the 1927 attack on Kwaio) and had helped to suppress the Fallowes and Red Cross activities, but then he retired in 1939, only to return to duty during the war. Trench said that for the first half of 1946 Sipolo had "acted, in effect, as District Officer" at Kirakira on Makira. After the previous strike Sipolo had replaced Sau as 'Aoke's commanding officer. In late 1945 Sandars had told Sipolo to stay with Maasina Rule, "to help me to keep this as a good movement which it was when it started." Other police looked up to Sipolo and Sau, and now Sandars wrongly blamed them for ongoing problems in Kwai and To'abaita since they had trained many police from there. He threatened to cancel their pensions unless they renounced Maasina Rule, but they refused and were dismissed. We will encounter both men again. After a short walkout, Sandars reported, the other police reenlisted and seemed happy, but they remained "Marching Rule almost to a man."[47]

Rejecting Indentured Labor

On 17 March, Sandars and Noel met at 'Aoke, first with headmen and then with several of the head chiefs. The chiefs told them an island-wide strike for a £12 monthly wage was planned for 30 June, exempting at Sandars's suggestion hospitals and missions. Further, they said people had no money to pay the impending tax. After the meeting, Noel wrote that Maasina Rule "manifests an irresistible, blind urge, illogical and unyielding," which could not be suppressed but only "guided," and once again he stressed the movement's positive potential to develop into "a naturally evolved form of indirect rule."[48]

For Malaitans to strike seems redundant insofar as the vast majority had turned down outside work throughout 1946, in remarkable solidarity. Of the diverse expressions of Maasina Rule across the island, this was the most consistent and unifying.[49] Why then were strike plans announced to Noel and Sandars? Malaitans had bandied about calls for a £12 wage since the 1930s, as had movement leaders for some time, but a formal strike and refusal to pay taxes would be a new, open challenge. Trench, Davies, and Colin Allan later supposed the chiefs knew that £12 was unrealistic and were merely underscoring the determination not to labor. There is truth in this, and Nori later testified that Timothy George had told him in mid-1946 that he did not think a strike could win that wage. The timing may have been prompted by Sandars's recent recruiting in the north, which might have tempted some young men to break ranks, and indeed Noel hoped so. Some officers portrayed the strike as a cynical political maneuver by chiefs aimed at defying the government or a crass attempt to control the populace and, particularly, impetuous young men.[50]

Chiefs were conscious of the political import of keeping young men in line with movement policy, but most of the rank and file also wanted men to stay home for other reasons. The previous October Forster had written, "In telling the natives not to work for the white people the Masina Law is mainly preaching to the converted." Because Malaitans' refusal to labor was a core aspect of their conflict with the government, readers need to understand their motivations. First, the refusals to labor and to pay tax were inextricably linked. Noel addressed long-standing criticism that people were taxed to force them to labor. He argued that, unlike the prewar poll tax, the new "Native Administration Tax" about to be imposed would be kept and spent by native councils (under his supervision) and was not an income tax, so the critique was now invalid. However, even if Malaitans had trusted this explanation—and Marquand wrote that in fact the primary reason for the new tax was, as in the past, to compel labor—the tax would still be compulsory, which, since few Malaitans could earn money at home, meant that many would have to enlist for extended periods as indentured plantation workers. I note this to argue not that the tax was unjust per se but that Noel's dismissal of a tax-labor linkage was disingenuous. Or perhaps Malaitans, from long experience, simply understood that linkage and its implications for their communities better than he did.[51]

The Native Tax Regulation of January 1947 imposed a 5-shilling tax on Malaitans (and a tax on employers for each person hired), though as it turned out no taxes were collected there until late 1949. The regulation said the money would be deposited into sub-district native council funds;

internal documents said it would go into the general revenue, and district commissioners would have the *option* of so depositing some or all of the money. Sandars assured unhappy Malaitans that he would do so, but he met with complaints that since councils could not hold their own funds the government would earn interest from them. More to the real point, they saw paying the tax as a submissive act, and indeed Tom Russell later recalled that there was extreme reluctance to allow Islanders to collect their own tax because "the tax was symbolic of fealty." Some officers still held Ashley's old view that Malaitans had no use for money *except* to pay tax.[52]

To begin to grasp the enduring impacts of taxation and circular labor migration on Malaitan communities, we can turn to District Officer William Bell. With his experience as a labor official on Fiji vessels, and then as a BSIP labor inspector in the 1910s, Bell recognized how the plantation system fundamentally exploited not just laborers but also their families at home: "Many employers of native labor in the Solomon Islands appear to think that they should receive all their money back from the labourer forthwith [by selling them goods in company stores at 100 percent profit], and also the labourer back, unless he has become useless and then he can be dumped onto his people. They appear to think that the natives should be treated as cattle, and they do not for one moment consider the people who have suffered pain, and years of worry and toil, in order to bring the natives, who become labourers for the white man, into the world and to provide for them until they reach a state of usefulness." As Judith Bennett has noted in relation to this same Bell statement, his critique anticipated neo-Marxist models of the 1970s, most famously that of anthropologist Claude Meillassoux, who argued that self-sufficient rural communities subsidize the capitalist sphere of production when they supply it with workers "fed and bred" in their own domestic economies. They thereby bear the costs of reproducing its labor force—nurturing boys to working age and later caring for them when they are too old to work. Further, the community loses the fruits of the labor of its fittest men to the productive endeavors of outsiders (Solomon Islands men aged 16 to 60 were to be taxed). Another cost of the system on Malaita was that, with so many men away, the burden of women's work grew. Work conditions had improved since Bell's time, but indenture's negative social impacts remained.[53]

Colonial policy had exacerbated these impacts when, long before the war and at the behest of plantation interests, beach payments were banned and the wage advance cut. Before this, kin typically shared in recruits' trade goods, and the recruits gave them some of their advances to pay their own taxes. Jack Barley and others argued the changes were needed to "protect" the recruit "from being duly imposed upon by relatives, friends, and others who remain at home and for whose sake under present conditions he is virtually compelled to labour for six months without remuneration." One intention, then, was explicitly to reduce the benefits that families and communities received in return for their men going abroad. This forced more local men to the plantations to earn money for taxes.[54]

Malaitans were attuned to the socioeconomic costs of raising workers to adulthood. Short- and longer-term adoptions were common, and if bride-wealth was later paid for an adoptee as an adult, adopters could claim a share by citing their expense and effort in having "fed" the woman who would now labor for her husband's family. Malaitans also recognized the opportunity costs the labor system imposed on them. Noomae, an elderly 'Oloburi man, in 1982 explained to me the reasoning: "Thousands of Malaitan men have worked in other places. If they had worked here on Malaita for their own people, Malaita today would be like Honiara town." Since Maasina Rule's 1945 "First Order of the Island," leaders had said men could not go abroad because they were needed to work on and for Malaita, but officers rarely took this argument as legitimate or sincere. For example, when Ken Crass was visiting the London Colonial Office, an official suggested to him that ongoing labor problems were due to continuance of the indentured labor system. Crass replied the issue was not that, but rather "the politically active M.R.M. with its 'apparently' nationalistic aims was largely responsible," along with people having been spoiled by the high wartime wages. In August 1948, as Malaitans still refused to work, Noel told the new high commissioner, Leslie Freeston, "There is, I can assure Your Excellency, nothing in the rights or wrongs of the present system of indenture which is relevant to the present political ills. Men who volunteer on Malaita for work on plantations 'overseas,' realize that there is advantage in securing a contracted period of service, and do not object to a period of one year."[55]

The years of no plantation work or taxes had removed any doubt that the indenture system was parasitic on Malaitan societies. Take Forster's observations from an April 1948 tour of Malaita, by which time shortages of cash and foreign goods were even more acute. In a section on labor he wrote: "Although a number of scattered young men would like to work almost the entire population is opposed to working away from their homes. Most of the chiefs absolutely refuse to discuss this question at all. The effect of having the former labour force at home has been extremely beneficial to the District. Areas which before the war were notoriously poverty-stricken and with declining populations are now prosperous and vigorous communities."[56]

Noel's comments on Forster's report ignored this section, although, or because, labor was a prime concern of Noel's, and this perhaps motivated Forster's extended commentary on the topic two months later: "The native condemnation of the plantation system is that the man power is better employed at home. The returns from plantation work were too small to justify the absence of the men." Forster granted this argument's validity, and wrote, "The changes that have occurred since the war with the cessation of outside work have been remarkable." He proceeded to blame the indenture system for past malnutrition; poor living conditions and especially poor housing; marriages deferred until a later age, which led to more orphans and widows with higher mortality rates and too many spinsters; fewer men at home, who therefore "were hard pressed to keep their dependants alive and had little energy to spare in improvements"; and wealth concentration in young men's hands, emasculating elders' authority. Chiefs at their trial (see chapter 7) stated, "Our work was to help the poor, orphans and widows," which sounds maudlin until considered against this background; whites portrayed it as laughably disingenuous. This was also a basis for Malaitan complaints that white people were "robbing" Malaitans and assertions that Maasina Rule would stop this. Forster sketched possible solutions of hiring fewer men and for just six-month terms, concentrating workers and maintaining their links to their homes via government ships, a more flexible wage, and even profit-sharing tenancies.[57]

Readers will recall that Bengough had blamed 'Are'are depopulation partly on late marriages, which he credited to the marriage system he hoped to change; overall he blamed feasting and other 'Are'are practices for the problems Forster now laid at the labor system's door. This highlights the contradiction in the British approach of the 1930s, when the putative goal of protecting Malaitan cultures from a harsh European impact clashed with the government's dependence on locking Malaitans into the indentured labor system, the institution that most damaged local societies. This was in contrast to Fiji, where under the justification of protecting Fijian village life, partly by restricting Fijian movements, South Asian laborers were brought in to work plantations beginning in the late 1870s.[58]

There were international pressures to end indenture globally, and eventually laboring would resume under a system that incorporated some changes like those Forster suggested, while others came later (including a free labor system). But in early 1947 the government and planters were determined to reinstitute, and Malaitans to resist, a system much like that of before the war, and there was little serious negotiation for comprehensive labor reform. It was clear that indenture would once again sap the strength of communities, but it was thought utterly necessary if the copra-based economy was to recover. If the government had instituted a freer labor system at this juncture it might well have both undermined Maasina Rule unity and eased the labor shortage.[59]

Again, officers sometimes depicted the labor strike as a means chiefs used to oppress the Malaitan people, who really wanted to work, but there are further indications that on this matter the chiefs were indeed "preaching to the converted." In April 1947, Nori negotiated with Levers recruiter Ernie Palmer at Waisisi and told him to come on 25 July when he would have 50 men for him. This led Noel to tell the high commissioner in early July that Levers had started to recruit Malaita at Nori's invitation, and that he, Noel, had issued a permit to sign 1,000 men. But when Palmer arrived only nine men were waiting, and Nono'oohimae told him, "He could not possibly agree to boys leaving Malaita, as they were urgently required there for the purpose of rehabilitating their village and gardens." In a bizarre turn, Nori told Palmer he feared being killed and begged for protection. Both men told Palmer privately that if they allowed recruiting the people would be angry with them and tribal strife might result. "Therefore," in Palmer's words, "the ten leaders of the Marching Rule were forced to hang together." The three agreed to later organize a Malaita tour by Palmer and the ten chiefs, to talk to the people about laboring, a plan Noel approved. Nono'oohimae wanted and received Palmer's assurance that if another war broke out laborers would not again be left stranded on plantations, as both he and Nori had been.[60]

Declarations of economic noncooperation dismayed officers counting on Malaitan labor to put the Protectorate back on its economic feet—early the next year Trench warned Noel that they faced £340,000 in projected expenditures, with an estimated revenue of just £65,000. Only if the economy was resuscitated could government improve—and native councils fund—social services, and only in that way could the government begin to reclaim ground lost to Maasina Rule. Malaitans made up an estimated 80 percent of the potential labor force, and people of other islands were watching for Malaita's lead on both laboring and taxation.[61]

To return to the order of events, these looming concerns, combined with Maasina Rule's growing co-optation of courts and councils, provoked a notable shift in Noel's attitude toward the movement after the March meeting. While acknowledging that leaders might be unconscious of the degree they were challenging authority, he said, "The situation must...be faced up to at once, and appropriate action must be taken forthwith to prevent deterioration of the position—obviously the Government cannot allow itself to drift helplessly."[62]

Noel began exploring the legality of a strike. The head chiefs, too, via Sandars, asked for legal guidance, but in April the Protectorate's legal adviser and judicial commissioner, William T Charles, refused to counsel them, because it was "potentially controversial"; he also said, "The Legal Adviser must always have regard to the false and embarrassing position in which he may be placed as a Judicial Commissioner should a matter upon which he had previously advised come before him for decision in the latter capacity." Over the next months Charles gave Noel and other officers close legal advice on how to construct charges against the chiefs, including regarding a strike, and indeed he became a vital architect of a crackdown. Yet he later cast aside concerns about falsity and embarrassment to sit in judgment of the chiefs on these same charges. With an eye to a possible strike, Charles in May advised Noel that any organization demanding an oath or affirmation was illegal unless specifically exempted by law. Noel opined that the "drastic powers" this legal reading gave the Crown could be used only if the safety of the realm was imperiled. He believed that a strike for an "uneconomical" wage of £12 would so imperil the Protector-ate, but that if leaders called a strike they should be advised to form a labor union (dubbed by the Australian press "a jungle trade union"), and only if they refused would prosecution be warranted. Yet he asked Sandars to tell leaders that a strike before there was a registered trade union would be an offense unaffected by subsequent registration. Due to Nori's negotiations with Palmer, Noel was optimistic that things would not come to that. Noel made no mention of Solomon Islanders who lived on other islands and had never worked as plantation labor, or whether by not doing so they too imperiled the Protectorate—to labor had been and always would be Malai-tans' role and obligation.[63]

Regarding other issues at stake, Noel said that even a boycott of govern-ment councils might be seen as legitimate, but, "We cannot tolerate under any pretext whatsoever the usurpation of the powers of the Judiciary by a political organization." This suggested that the grounds on which leaders might be prosecuted lay in movement members settling Malaitan disputes.[64]

Alaha'ou'ou *and the North-South Split*

Sandars continued to assure Noel that, in Noel's words, there was "still nothing subversive in the activities of the Marching Rule" on Malaita, and in mid-May Noel wrote, "It is not so material to the issue that the present leaders may be hostile; it is more material that they are the leaders." He now believed that the movement was not merely a reaction to the war and that it could not "be expected to vanish under the pressure of so-called instant 'strong' action; for example something dramatic, a coup in the form of spectacular arrests of leaders and the show of the glitter of bayonets of the Armed Constabulary." But, citing reports submitted by Crass and Davies from Makira, he suggested that the time for repressive action on that island might be near.[65]

Sandars had been employing Cameron to keep an eye on the Kwai area and in early June he sent him to spend a month there to investigate pos-sible illegal courts. When Cameron and his police arrived and tried to draw water from a well the people had constructed, an angry (but not threaten-ing) crowd demanded a fee. He warned them that they would take water by force and ordered his police to fix bayonets, but the people would not back down. He finally agreed to deposit a sum with Stephen Sipolo to hold, after which he found "real friendliness," and people brought him coconuts and a chair. Cameron realized that his rude demeanor and bringing armed police had been mistakes, and he told Sandars the episode "taught me a valuable lesson." He quickly proposed major changes: the area's Maasina Rule leaders were "capable and sincere in their willingness to work with the Government," and he suggested that Head Chief Justus Jimmy Ganifiri or Chief Sadius Oge be appointed to replace the reviled headman there,

Tome Siru, or at least that they be allowed to convene native courts. Kwai island people favored Ganifiri but wanted to pay him themselves, while nearby Ngongosila island people said Ganifiri should receive only room and board so that he would not grow arrogant toward the people. Cameron said that the area was too far from 'Aoke to administer directly, and since it was "99.9%" Maasina Rule, "any form of indirect rule based on an anti-Marching Rule policy is impossible.... Nothing will be more harmful to the orderly administration of this island than a suggestion that the Government is raising 'black and tans' and the creation of little Ulsters."[66]

Strike day, 30 June 1947, proved a redefining moment. Sandars had arranged to meet alone in 'Aoke with Cameron, Marquand, and the head chiefs, after they had held discussions with their people on taxation, finances, and wages. While 'Are'are followed that plan, "the North came to the meeting almost to a man." Some 7,000 attended in all, including a sizable Kwaio contingent. Sandars was notified that all the people wanted to hear the discussion. Nono'oohimae and Shadrach Diote'e told him privately this "was far from their wish but it was the business of the north."[67]

For weeks, northern people had talked of the coming event, and word was, Waleanisia later told me, "The egg is going to break at 'Aoke." Marquand described the impressive orderliness he witnessed at this and other 'Aoke assemblies: "No arms were carried at these meetings, not even sticks, and the people marched on to the station in three ranks, and formed up on the parade ground. There was no talking, except by the leaders when addressing the District Officer, and except where the people were requested by a leader to show their approval."[68] After a 45-minute entrance procession, discussion began with the strike—it had been called off because, Nori (who was not at this meeting) later said, Sandars had told him, following Noel, that it would be illegal. But they wanted laborers off-island to return home as their contracts finished. Sandars praised the decision and on request explained the basics of a trade union, translated by Timothy George in what Sandars called "the finest display of pidgin English I have ever heard." Jonathan Fifi'i told me that Sandars said he would help them to form a union. Sandars had just recruited 52 'Aoke-area men to work in Honiara, and Baelelea Head Chief Basi demanded that they be returned and that the government help punish them for breaking Maasina Rule's order. Expulsion from the movement was an insufficient penalty, he said; "In Malaita everybody must obey the native custom."[69]

Here Basi used *kastom* to label not ancient "custom" but Maasina Rule policies, and this meaning, which by now was standard on Malaita, is crucial to understanding the next item discussed. On 30 May the head chiefs had met at Nono'oohimae's village of Arairau and decided to defer the strike and instead present Sandars with a different topic. After the strike cancellation was declared, speakers from the north told Sandars "in no uncertain terms" of the people's unhappiness with government councils and courts, and Maasina Rule's desire to take over their functions and control council money and court fines and fees. Toward this end the chiefs announced the institution of a new office, the *alaha'ou'ou* (which Sandars wrote "alaha-ohu"). This was an old concept on Small Malaita and in southern 'Are'are, where *alaha* (or *araha*) is a word for hereditary leaders, and *'ou'ou* an honorific suffix. Sandars was told that each district would appoint an *alaha'ou'ou* to determine and oversee *kastom* law, on which henceforth the island's courts would be based.[70]

This plan did not spring from nowhere, and its history is important because so many would soon be arrested for participating in it. As described in earlier chapters, officers before the war depended on "elders"—some of them not in fact elderly—for guidance in settling the local disputes that so sapped officers' time and resources.[71] In 1939, Bengough began bringing them into the legal apparatus and told Malaitans he would allow "councils of elders" powers, under headmen, to adjudicate custom matters in native courts and to impose fines and even jail time. In the south in 1940 and 1941, the men who he indicated would exercise these new powers were the *alaha*. Moreover, Bengough encouraged *alaha* (and in the north, "elders") to arbitrate cases *outside* of courts with compensation when possible, and Davies wrote that leaders in the mid-1940s received further permission to so settle "customary offense" cases as practice for eventual official courts. Within this same framework, Bengough, Forster, and Sandars urged Malaitans to codify their "custom laws." Thus *alaha*, custom law, codification, and self-directed courts had for some years been bundled in a single, ongoing government initiative. The prewar southern Malaitan response to Bengough's initiative had been tepid, though *alaha* did settle disputes, but just after the war the people quickly appropriated the model for their own *kastom* project. For example, in late 1944 the Takataka Council told Nono'oohimae that they had appointed leader Waiparo "head *alaha*" over 12 other *alaha* to oversee the area's "native custom." Kwaio soon adopted the Kwaio cognate term *alafa* to similar purpose. *Alaha* throughout the south, like Malaitans everywhere, continued to participate in *kastom* codification efforts into 1947, which Sandars encouraged so that, he said, government could learn "exactly what the people desire."[72]

The approach of letting local leaders hear cases had been applied in a mostly informal manner, without official authorization from above, and later officers were often unaware that it had been employed. For example, though these policies were enacted during Noel's tenure, he seemed unaware of them in August 1947 when he told High Commissioner John F Nicoll that, despite his plans to arrest Maasina Rule chiefs for court offenses, he would meet with other leaders, because, he said, "Their proposal for Native Custom Courts may have much to commend it and it may prove particularly suitable in the southern areas of Malaita where formerly some such courts are believed to have existed prior to the advent of Marching Rule."

Either Noel had not read reports over the years, or else he muddied the history to conceal from Nicoll that he had allowed informal courts or that he was about to arrest Malaitans for acts that officers on his watch had permitted and even instructed them to carry out. The next year, in May 1948, Divisional Officer J D A Germond lectured "line chiefs" and "alahas" from the 'Aoke and Fiu areas regarding their claims that Sandars had said they could "try minor cases in accordance with Native Custom," telling them, "I do not believe that he ever made such a statement," and that Sandars must have meant "arbitration." At the same time, Forster was telling chiefs and *alaha* around Malaita that they could adjudicate, but when Germond upbraided him he recanted and said he only told them they could arbitrate.[73] In other words, in 1947 and for some time after, the government could not settle on its own policy or its history, but Malaitans who misunderstood (or understood) the very points on which officers were confused would be jailed for it, including for settling cases by what was clearly arbitration.

Over the months before the June 1947 'Aoke meeting, the desire to settle disputes according to Malaitan sensibilities and methods rather than "white man's law" had moved ever more to the fore across the island. Northerners also adopted the *alaha* title, though some applied it to different ends than southerners. In early June, Nori, Nono'oohimae, and other 'Are'are chiefs had presented Sandars with the plan to appoint *alaha'ou'ou* and, not grasping their full meaning, Sandars had casually supported their selection as, in his mind, "experts on Native Customs and Compensations to sit with the Headmen in court and expound the true native law."[74]

Now, at the 'Aoke meeting, Nono'oohimae told Sandars that headmen knew little of *kastom* law and asked him to again approve their selecting *alaha'ou'ou*. When Sandars replied they could be chosen to serve as advisers or assessors on the headmen's courts, "the assembly" objected. (An unknown man shouted, "We don't want the headmen!") Northern spokesmen Head Chief Basi and especially Full Chief Nelson Kifo explicitly rejected future government involvement in legal matters except for murder and rape cases. Malaita's legal system would be built on *kastom* law, as determined by *alaha'ou'ou,* and applied in *kastom* courts presided over by chiefs, with compensation as the primary means of resolution and punishment.

Sandars told the 'Aoke gathering that it was illegal to hear cases outside a "legal native court," but his request that native councils compile codes joining custom law with European law met no favor. When pressed—not wishing, he said, to argue with 7,000 people—he promised to convey their wishes to Noel and report back with his answer. The next morning, he met alone with chiefs in the 'Aoke courthouse to clarify the meaning of *alaha'ou'ou,* and he told them to proceed to select them around Malaita and submit their names, and that they should set the laws. But he said that the headmen should give judgments in courts when required, and he insisted that he could not by himself approve *alaha'ou'ou* hearing cases on their own. Finally, he asked them "whether they were against the King and the British," and their reply was "definitely NO."[75]

Despite the boldness of Kifo, Basi, and others at the main ʻAoke meeting, the *alahaʻouʻou* system remained only vaguely worked out. None had been appointed, and many northerners conceived of them differently than did Kwaio people and especially ʻAreʻare. Southern leaders had throughout Maasina Rule deftly maneuvered between government "custom" policies and their own *kastom* ones, exploiting overlap and ambiguities and marshaling and expanding elements of government policy that delegated to them more control. This was again the case with their presentation of *alahaʻouʻou*, and it was a savvy course for negotiating with Sandars. Nonoʻoohimae later testified that Sandars told them he thought *alahaʻouʻou* were a good idea, a claim supported by what Sandars wrote to Noel soon after the meeting: "Provided bad native custom is not revived their scheme of evolution has a certain amount to recommend it and the creation of Alaha-ohu is a basis upon which society might work....From all I can gather the people will be very careful in the selection of the Alaha-ohu and will choose the best men possible."[76]

The *alahaʻouʻou* concept, especially in the southern half of Malaita, was more than a political tactic for dealing with government. As explained in chapter 5, *kastom* ideology encompassed twin goals: the expansive transformation and advance of Malaitan society and a reassertion of valued indigenous ways, many of them relatively new and many Christian. The government was perceived to have stifled the former and, along with missionaries and the labor system, undermined the latter. The Maasina Rule project pursued both goals and the resolution of conflicts between them toward a single blueprint for the future. Within the movement, differing outlooks on the relative emphasis that each of these should receive were an ongoing source of tension. This was not a simple factional issue; most people were dedicated to both objectives and their integration and they were sometimes torn between them. One expression of this was strain between people's desires for leaders knowledgeable in European ways and for leaders whose power was grounded in their local knowledge and networks. Most of the head chiefs and many lesser chiefs were young and had spent significant periods of their lives abroad. Many were not recognized experts in indigenous legal principles or dispute management, or local ways generally, and they had been chosen in large part for their knowledge of and ability to negotiate foreign ones. Most people did not want Maasina Rule to relegate established local leaders and the social principles they represented to a secondary or mere advisory role, as officers and headmen had always done. The plan for *alahaʻouʻou*, particularly in the south, was in part an attempt to allocate powers to these leaders both symbolically and practically, and one realm in which they were seen to have superior qualifications was the determination of proper rules for and means of dispute management. Significantly, many Malaitans said neither *alaha'ou'ou* nor head chiefs would outrank the other.[77]

We have seen that there had long been generational tensions throughout Malaita, especially when the end of warfare and economic shifts favored young men's growing independence, but it is a mistake to understand the *alaha'ou'ou* idea as speaking simply to a generational divide, a rivalry between old and young. Many younger people were erudite in indigenous rules, had been dismayed at the prewar decline in community authority, and ardently supported creation of *alaha'ou'ou*, just as elders backed the younger chiefs. The distinction between *alaha'ou'ou* and head chiefs was grounded more in ideological than generational matters, and the move to elevate both together followed a model for balancing the movement's dual and sometimes conflicting aims within a cohesive leadership structure. Even today Malaitan *kastom* groups sometimes select such dual leaders and, as in the past, refuse to declare one to be of higher status than the other.[78]

All that said, at the June 1947 'Aoke meeting some northern chiefs like Kifo and Basi presented the *alaha'ou'ou* plan to Sandars most immediately as a move to absorb courts openly into Maasina Rule, and before and after the meeting, especially in parts of the north, there was considerable public pressure on leaders to pursue this agenda.[79] The meeting exposed another fundamental tension within Maasina Rule: the old division between north and south was quickly reemerging and was soon to fracture the movement for a time. Many north Malaitans, particularly just before and after this meeting, followed a very different course from the south. They marshaled *kastom*, and more specifically the *alaha'ou'ou* position, as bases for wholesale rejection of the government's role in courts and sometimes in Malaitan affairs generally. Led by Basi and especially by the audacious Kifo, their approach was less negotiation than declaration. At the June meeting the rift was obvious to Sandars, who reported to Noel regarding the hard-line demands of these speakers, "I fancy the South do not agree with the North.... There is no doubt that the north will not have much to do with government councils and want to run their own business according to native custom.... It seems to me that the Marching Rule party are beginning to split into the moderates (who would be willing to evolve along the lines of the Government Council) and the young hot-heads who wish to run before they can walk and desire a policy of non-co-operation with Government. I should have liked an opportunity of visiting the South before writing this report but it has not been possible." There were northern moderates, and some southerners opposed compromise, particularly on labor issues, but that more northerners wanted more of a break from the government became evident in several places over the following weeks. Kwaio, which the government mostly ignored, sat somewhere in the middle, but except for parts of the Uru area people there looked more to the southern lead.[80]

A most revealing expression of north-south differences was how the *alaha'ou'ou* idea was put into action. Southern areas, in line with Sandars's directive, did not formally appoint them. The three who were eventually appointed were all in the northeast, and their qualities contrasted sharply with southern conceptions of the office.[81] Two—Belo and Basi, for the Lau sea and bush areas, respectively—were young with no special legal knowledge and were already important Maasina Rule chiefs (Basi retained his head chief status). The third appointee, Steven Sipolo, chosen for Kwai along with three "assistant *alaha'ou'ou*," was different: he was older, had more legal expertise from two decades of police work, and did not want the position. He had never been a chief and was nominated in absentia at a meeting of about a thousand people at Naafinua on 31 July during a visit by Kifo. Only in mid-August did he reluctantly agree, under great pressure. Sipolo knew Sandars had approved selecting *alaha'ou'ou,* and Kwai people told him that he was chosen because he knew both government and *kastom* ways and that they all wanted him to work with the headman to "straighten the custom with the Government." He later testified that Sandars told him to do that same thing, for which he was highly qualified from having traveled Malaita with Trench to explain courts and councils. Yet Sipolo clearly knew more was at stake, and he glumly told people that taking the *alaha'ou'ou* position would be his downfall.[82]

In late July and early August, Kifo "appointed" these three *alaha'ou'ou* with varying levels of community input during patrols of the northeast with a group of Kwara'ae. He was the most openly radical of the major Maasina Rule leaders, and one must be cautious of sweeping readings of "the north" based on his actions. But the appointments were part of a broader shift in northern stances toward the government. People now misconstrued Sandars's statements more than ever. Both sincerely and not, many read into them more than he intended or heard distorted accounts from others. For example, five days after the 30 June meeting, To'abaita's Head Chief 'Atoomea wrote from Malu'u to his ally and uncle Shem Irofa'alu: "We have face our Government for the Custom, and he well bright agreed to let the Malaita Island hold his own. 'I am quite agreed to let the Alaha oo to hold the Law for this Island of Malaita.'...Then afterward he try to make Excuse for the R. Commissioner he said...I cannot make any program to this Island without [the high commissioner and the resident commissioner]. But he is already agreed to us." Later 'Atoomea, and then his lieutenant, Chief Jason Alaikona, surprised Marquand by telling *him* that Sandars had, in his private 1 July meeting with chiefs, agreed that *alaha* could try cases by *kastom.* At 'Ataa, also, word was passed that Sandars had approved *alaha'ou'ou* selection (which was true) and said they could "start holding trials in accordance with our custom" (which was not). Some Kwara'ae and Kwaio said that not only had Sandars ceded the courts, he had acquiesced or even given his blessing to self-rule. Ma'aanamae remembered that some speakers at the 30 June meeting told Sandars that they wanted the government to leave and that Sandars "did not answer," which in a Malaitan debate is taken as ceding the issue. In the south similar news was circulated, but to a lesser degree, and not, it seems, by head chiefs.[83]

That many had both desired and anticipated this outcome from the meeting was clear in Cameron's report to Sandars from Kwai two days after, telling him how opinion had congealed:

> The people want...to appoint their own Headman and pay him themselves. To have their own Council and rule in its name according to their own custom. They seem unable and unwilling to see that the Native Council as under the 1947 Regulation was their "own" and that it offered them practically all the freedom and independence that they wanted. The implication was that they did not want the Native Council as established, neither did they want a Headman. They wanted something completely free from any part or sign of Government, symbolical or actual.... [Their position since the 'Aoke meeting] seems to have crystallized into a request for a system of Malaita-wide independence based on a combination of Custom Law and Marching Rule. In wider issues, apart from a certain minority, they are not disloyal. The more educated appreciate the need for Government but rather on a Protectorate level. As far as their own affairs are concerned they are adamant and I fear are becoming increasingly intransigent....However, I consider there is still a chance for a satisfactory settlement. They have some intelligent leaders and although these people's demands are great and in some cases impossible they are made with good will and a genuine desire for settlement. At the same time it must not be forgotten that there exist less moderate spirits in the movement. It is difficult to assess their influence but it is potentially harmful and flourishes on un-certainty.[84]

Roy Davies Takes Charge

At this critical juncture, on 17 July, Sandars stepped down as district commissioner, nearly twenty years after his first posting there. He needed a hernia operation and the plan was for another officer to replace him briefly, but in fact he would never again serve on the island. The timing was unlucky, because with Forster on leave there were no district officers with suitable Malaitan experience to take over (Cameron and Marquand were still cadets). Moreover, government–Maasina Rule relations had to date oscillated with Sandars's presence or absence: They had warmed after his return in late 1945, but when he took leave in May 1946, Davies recorded, "immediately we found ourselves in a state of crisis," referring to the June episodes at 'Aoke. Things improved again on his return that October, Davies writing: "It was as if the Marching Rule was happy again now that Sandars had returned to take charge again from its arch-enemy Forster."[85] Davies wrote this within his account dedicated to portraying and isolating Sandars as a lone fool, and Forster and other officers as sharing Davies's opposition to any compromise with Maasina Rule, and we know that in reality many Malaitans liked Forster. All the same, the archives confirm that these shifts did occur, and their timing indicates Sandars's importance to sustaining workable relations with the movement.

Noel tapped Davies to stand in as acting district commissioner. Davies had been a cadet on Malaita from February 1945 to January 1947, from whence he was posted to Makira as district officer and then assistant district commissioner Central District under Crass, and he was soon to have succeeded Crass. Though he had spent nearly two years on Malaita, Davies by his own account had mostly been anchored at 'Aoke while Sandars and Forster toured, and even when he convinced Forster to take him along on tour Forster routinely slipped away from him when there were delicate matters to discuss with Malaitans. Davies now returned with limited knowledge of most Malaitans, and they of him.[86]

Davies in the late 1970s penned a remembrance of his experiences with Maasina Rule, the longest work written about the movement. The typescript is available only as a poor quality microfilm and has scarcely been cited by historians. Before proceeding, it requires comment. When I obtained the microfilm it was quickly apparent that it had great value to me for its first-person accounts of several events I had already written about for the present book, and for details found nowhere else in writing. Davies's manuscript is unified by one unstated but patent goal: to justify his decision to suppress Maasina Rule by force. An unwary reader will finish it convinced that Davies inherited with the district commissionership an unholy mess left by his incompetent predecessor, Sandars. Sandars did make mistakes—and it would have been an extraordinary man who did not—but what Davies inherited seems tidy compared to what he left his own successors.[87]

As I began reading Davies's work, my enthusiasm turned to disappointment as it became clear that he was misrepresenting events to push his case, often by distortion or omission of information damaging to it. Blatant contradictions abound. Then again, the manuscript starkly reveals his attitudes toward Malaitans and Maasina Rule, and I was buoyed by the prospect that it might shed light on what had motivated his decisions as district commissioner. And so it does.

A case in point is Davies's accounts of Malaitans, and also Makirans, which display disdain and a nimbus of fear that verges on paranoia. He seems to have perceived looming violence in almost any political gathering or complaint, regardless of the people's demeanor: "Solomon Islanders who have worked themselves up to the point of making a mass protest are usually in a sullen and obstinate mood which does not acknowledge logic." We have seen that for Davies even the affable Boxing Day meeting had threatened riot, palpable to him in "curiously disturbing wavelengths." His manuscript tells episodes of his publicly humiliating communities, which angered people but provoked no violence, and yet afterward he believed that he had narrowly escaped with his and his party's lives. After one such incident in a small village on Makira in early June, where he browbeat people into finding money to pay the dog tax after they had pleaded poverty, he concluded: "It was clear to me at last that there lay within the Marching Rule much stronger seeds of potential violence than I had hitherto believed, or indeed wanted to believe. As far as I was concerned now we needed to review our entire policy towards Marching Rule urgently for it could no longer be based on the belief that it was non-violent in intent." Davies was convinced that barbarity lurked "deep down inside" Maasina Rule. He was uneasy even outside of political contexts. For example, the killing of pigs at a friendly feast had, for Davies, "an air of unrestrained savagery about it which I found disturbing," and Makira Harbour, on that island's western coast, had "an eerie and sinister atmosphere, and I wondered how much of it was due to the memory of the murder of a Roman Catholic bishop there in 1846." Other officers of the period, even the few who clearly despised Solomon Islanders, evinced no such dread of them.[88]

And yet, while Davies's fears may provide insight into his actions, one might also read them as a sham. His prime justification for his crackdown, both at the time and later, was that Maasina Rule was innately violent, and thus arrests were necessary to avert "the threat of violence which hung so heavily over the island in August 1947…which a sudden spark could have changed into a bloody rampage through the Mission stations." In his manuscript Davies had to amplify the peril in order to justify his actions, and the impression that he was obsessed by it may in fact derive from Davies the author having overplayed his hand. Regarding this and many other matters, one is never sure the degree to which his words convey his real views or are instead contrived to persuade readers that his response to Maasina Rule was the only possible or responsible one. The same holds for his reports of the period, which later officers and some scholars accepted and cited as true, objective accounts. Readers of the present book will see that Davies was often untruthful when working to advance his position, and they may already have noticed my frequent use of cautionary qualifiers to bracket information drawn from him alone.[89]

Davies's understandings of Maasina Rule were crude. Consciously or not, he filled vast gaps in his knowledge with conjecture that he presented as fact to superiors and, later, to readers of his manuscript. He had left Malaita for Makira already highly antagonistic toward the movement and its leaders and dismayed at Sandars's attempts to work with them. For him, Maasina Rule had absolutely no political legitimacy, and of its followers he believed "perhaps one per cent had any real idea of what was going on and why." He saw Malaitans' noncooperation as despicable, irrational, and dangerous, and yet over and again when they showed willingness to discuss, negotiate, or even cooperate, he dismissed this as subterfuge to conceal Maasina Rule's diabolical plans. While at times he allowed that a few Malaitans were sincere, he wrote that they "were a small minority in the midst of a mob of uneducated people of primitive instincts, to whose inherent and historical love of anarchy and destruction the movement appealed greatly."[90]

Most damaging to the government in 1947 was Davies's inability to grasp or cope with the complexity or diversity of the movement and its relationship to the government: "What it boiled down to was that one either believed the Marching Rule was subversive and potentially dangerous or one believed it was not subversive and was susceptible to guidance."[91] He consequently reduced Maasina Rule to a caricature of a homogeneous scourge that had to be smashed. In his final analysis, he saw little difference between north and south Malaita, or at base even Malaita and Makira. Any untoward action by a single village or individual, however minor or singular, real or imagined, he conceived as embodying Maasina Rule throughout the southeastern Solomons, and presented it as such to his superiors to convey the dire need to put down the entire movement without delay.

Even before returning to Malaita he had determined, "The whole policy of Marching Rule was so patently fraudulent: join us and live a life of luxury and idleness or desert us and die; so poverty-stricken in real ideas; and so capable of degenerating into primitive reaction, that I had progressively moved to the view that we had no real alternative but to put an end to Marching Rule, and I was beginning to urge this view strongly on my superiors." Davies's reports from Makira that I have read contain no such urgings, but if he was pushing this view, perhaps verbally, this gives pause to ponder why Noel chose him to spell Sandars.[92] Be that as it may, Davies was now poised to orchestrate a drastic change in policy that had dismal and enduring consequences for Malaitan relations with and perceptions of the government, and vice versa. How the government decided to try to destroy Maasina Rule has been subject to debate, often grounded in limited or erroneous information concerning the events I will now summarize.

Just before leaving 'Aoke, Sandars, likely mindful of Davies's views, briefed him and urged caution. Davies wrote of this briefing: "Malaita was now in a very tricky state, he said, and precipitate action on my part could upset the apple cart completely. Sandars made it quite clear that he only expected to be away six weeks and hoped to find on his return that I had not stirred up any hornets' nests; in fact, it would be best if I took no action at all." For a confluence of reasons this was not to be. Davies wrote, "Sandars had no sooner departed for Honiara than things started to fall apart," and indeed the timing of Sandars's illness was fateful in terms of the rush of events in parts of the north where a harder line was emerging.[93]

Less than a week after Sandars's departure, Cameron reported that a "so-called illegal court" had fined three Malu'u people over a curse. The court's three "victims"—two women and a nine-year-old boy—had complained to the loyalist Fo'odo Headman Ba'etalua. Cameron and Marquand investigated and recommended charging five "pseudo-justices" from villages along the northwest coast around and south of Bita'ama with holding an illegal court and To'abaita's Head Chief 'Atoomea with instigating it.[94] Marquand warned that to turn a blind eye would leave the government open to ridicule, but he and Cameron, perhaps with Davies's outlook in mind, counseled a low-key approach of serving summonses for the men to attend a preliminary hearing at 'Aoke. They expected no disturbance and Cameron urged against "any abnormal or spectacular police action," for "the object of this action is to restore respect for law and order not to maintain the rule of an occupying power." He advised that a prosecution would serve to frighten leaders at Kwai. On 26 July Davies issued the summonses, for 6 August, on charges formulated by Legal Adviser Charles. If the men failed to show up, Davies said, "extraordinary measures should then be taken."[95]

Davies later contended that he felt pressured by Cameron and Marquand and was himself reluctant to take any such measures, fearing they would lead to large-scale confrontation, until Marquand convinced him the area was "plunging into anarchy" and, in Davies's words, the people "babbled about having at last obtained their 'freedom' from the Government." He said Cameron told him, "Our Police detachment, properly organized and deployed would suffice to make the arrests, if it came to that. [Cameron] had worked out an Operation Order, which he gaily called 'Operation Delouse.'" Davies said he now decided to "take the plunge," later recalling "a desire on my part to commit us all to positive action and have an end to the years of temporization which had landed us in such a sorry mess. Certainly I had crossed my personal watershed: from then on I was to press whole-heartedly for action to break up the Marching Rule."[96]

Three days after issuing the summons, and twelve days after taking over Malaita from Sandars, Davies went to Honiara to tell Noel of his plan and convinced him that a hard-line approach was now imperative. During their conversation, Davies said, Noel decided to back him and told him "he had always had grave misgivings about the intentions of Marching Rule and was not overly surprised at my news." He asked Davies, before returning to Malaita, to prepare a report for him to send to Suva "so that he could justify a reversal of Government policy to the High Commissioner." Davies's 31 July report, "Illegal Courts on Malaita," said that in the north government courts were defunct and Maasina Rule courts were proliferating, and that people were intransigent, obstructive, and refusing to meet with Marquand and Cameron. (The last was only true at Malu'u, and not completely so there.) Davies rejected Noel's suggestion of a week earlier that *alaha'ou'ou* might be adaptable to native administration, because, Davies said, in the north they had "no historical basis, nor any roots in the social structure," and in any case they had already assumed jurisdiction that the government could not tolerate. In fact, at that point people had followed Sandars's instructions and no *alaha'ou'ou* had heard any cases. Davies represented a handful of worrisome events in parts of the north as "Marching Rule policy."[97]

Noel still saw the refusal to labor as the crux of Maasina Rule's political challenge and believed that if men gradually returned to work, "solution of the present political impasse would be in sight." But the court issue had now become the rudder of government policy. Legal Adviser Charles, assessing Davies's report, told Noel what he saw to be the fundamental issue: "A tribunal which purports to exercise compulsory power is illegal, offending against one of the elementary principles of British law, dating at least from Magna Carta, that no person shall be condemned in his liberty or property without due process of law." Charles opined that the justices in the courts were also guilty of assault, false imprisonment, theft, robbery, and perhaps, he suggested, sedition. He declared the courts "inherently instruments of oppression and extortion and their existence is a challenge to Government and the Court which cannot be ignored.... All means at Government's disposal" should be used to suppress them.[98]

Noel's commentary to Davies on his report was more measured, indicating that he was not yet so fully swayed by their conversation as Davies later claimed. He said he was "not, of course, disposed to act in this transitional stage of native thought against institutions which are freely accepted, merely because so far they have not been recognized by Government." He expressed doubts that it was fair to prosecute the courts given Sandars's past talks with chiefs, and referred to Cameron's report from Kwai that courts there were voluntary (though a confused Noel thought Cameron had been living in Kwaio—"Koio"—rather than at Kwai in Kwara'ae). Correctly surmising that Malaitans had not worked out details of what they wanted their courts to be, he proposed to meet with the chiefs in October to discuss and clarify court issues. Noel said Davies's summons of the "justices" had been proper because it was not clear that the courts in question had been freely accepted, but he ordered that if they did come to 'Aoke on 6 August, the preliminary exam be postponed until 4 September, when Sandars would be well.[99]

Into early August, Cameron still found Kwai area people courteous, respectful, friendly, and also confident that the government would grant them the right to hold courts. Ganifiri made no claim to have that right yet, but Cameron wrote, "The people genuinely believe that the Government has ceded its jurisdiction to Marching Rule, in particular since the 30th of June. In a way, I suppose this means that they submit themselves to the jurisdiction of these tribunals of their own free will," though he thought, "The moral pressure is so great as to be equivalent to compulsion." Still, he said at Kwai there was no atmosphere of intimidation such as there seemed to be at Malu'u, where Marquand had found "an obstructionist attitude." Cameron thought that the movement was neither disloyal nor subversive but that both qualities were latent and that the people were "started on a path that can have only one ending." Nonetheless he felt that attitudes had improved slightly, that with the planned arrests of the "pseudo-justices" things would improve further, and that in general Kwai gave "grounds for optimism."[100]

But Malaitan officers could not assess the island-wide situation. While Cameron and Marquand saw so far as they were able what was happening from To'abaita down the east coast to Kwai, and some information was coming in from the northwest, little was known from the southern half of Malaita, where no officers had been for some time. Cameron did briefly visit as far south as 'Oloburi in Kwaio and came away guessing that the area was "progressing satisfactorily," having gotten his limited information from Kwaio headmen who belonged to Maasina Rule but were, he said, "loyal and enlightened." Davies told Noel that his 31 July report "Illegal Courts on Malaita" applied only to the north, and in it he made no mention of the south. But this distinction was soon lost in his reports and, consequently, in his superiors' understanding of the movement. Thus officers pursued a policy based predominantly on the situation in the two most volatile parts of the north, which, notwithstanding Sandars's belief that there were fundamental north-south differences, they soon extrapolated to the entire island. The particular came to represent the whole in guiding Davies's course due to his inability to fathom, or a desire not to see, the larger and many-sided Malaita picture.[101]

In early August, the Malu'u justices, probably steered by 'Atoomea, indicated they would refuse the summonses, and the government issued warrants for them all to be arrested on 4 September. Soon after, officers heard reports of five additional courts in the area. But even in the north it was difficult to determine what was really going on. Unlike in the south, in the north there were minority but significant and bitter anti–Maasina Rule factions grouped loosely around Timi Kakalu'ae in Lau and Ba'etalua at Fo'odo. Most historians have labeled these factions "loyalist," and while probably accurate for the headmen, the term is a misnomer for many of Maasina Rule's foes. Noel himself warned the high commissioner that these factions were not necessarily pro-government and that some disdained Maasina Rule's aim of more independence because they remained hopeful of getting help from Americans. Complaints about courts had come from these groups, and Marquand had already concluded that both pro–and anti–Maasina Rule factions, including the headmen, were lying to him. One of the government's stated reasons for not accepting Maasina Rule–dominated councils was that they did not represent everyone. Maasina Rule leaders in the areas in question told officers that they had not formed fully representative councils, as the government had urged for many months, because headmen and opposition factions refused to participate and instead threatened them. This was true, but the hostility was, or at least became, mutual. By early 1947, when Sandars, speaking through Nori, told people that the Maasina Rule and government councils had to join into one, people answered, "They would join with any headman other than Kakalu'ae."[102]

Many in the opposition expressed anger at being steadily pressured to join the movement, and they were sometimes harassed. As Cameron guessed from Kwai, "The life of such a person in a wholly Marching Rule area would be made very unpleasant." One way to understand the harassment of those outside the movement is by analogy with a striking union's hostility to scab workers, particularly since some opposition members were acting as informants for the government, sometimes untruthfully. Noel had suggested this perspective in July: "Another instance could also be considered, before we condemn what is apparently an attempt to force on the people a one party autocracy, and that is the Trades Union outlook. Malaita has little wealth to expect other than labour, hence their approach to political problems may well be on the familiar lines of unity amongst workers." But, he said, Maasina Rule had to learn that "Trade Union Congresses do not aim at controlling affairs outside their own particular interests."[103]

The northern opposition groups are a key to understanding why Maasina Rule evolved differently in the north and south. Nearly all of the southern headmen were movement members, which made it possible to sustain a more ambiguous status for courts and councils and for overall positions toward the government. Overt resistance was unnecessary. In parts of the north, by contrast, headmen like Kakalu'ae, Ba'etalua, and Maekali determined to sever any cooperative links with Maasina Rule, despite appeals from movement leaders (and some of their own relatives). Hard lines were drawn between Maasina Rule and these headmen—who, as Cameron observed, were "the outward and visible symbol of the Government"—and thus in effect between the people and the government as a whole. Readers will remember that Bell had drawn heavily from particular northern groups for his constabulary, and headmen there had always been granted more power; the interdependence of certain headmen and the government was now well over two decades old. This situation led Marquand to assure 'Atoomea in July that the government was not taking sides. But antagonism escalated when the aforesaid headmen publicly declared themselves to be movement enemies and acted as government agents against it, even dispatching spies to falsely join. It was in their areas—Malu'u and particularly Lau—that Maasina Rule opposition to government was growing more strident. Sandars's proposal to Maasina Rule followers was that they place themselves under government courts and councils, but this meant recognizing the authority of the headmen who were automatically heads of both bodies. In the north, that meant people would have to submit to the power of their bitterest enemies. This was a nonstarter, particularly since some of the headmen had previously ruled their councils and courts in doctrinaire fashion (ie, "Maekalism," as described in chapter 2). It is a puzzle why so few officers seem to have grasped this; a common refrain for years was that foolish Malaitans could not see that government courts and councils offered them everything they said they wanted.[104]

Kifo, though still only a full chief, had unofficially eclipsed the more moderate Head Chief Shadrach Diote'e in west Kwara'ae and, as we have seen, starting in late July he patrolled areas of the north and helped appoint three *alaha'ou'ou*. Some people had heard about Kifo's defiant 30 June speech to Sandars that people would hold their own courts, and on this tour he confirmed this with exaggeration. He told them not only that Sandars had agreed to *alaha'ou'ou* hearing cases independently, but also that throughout the south they had already been appointed and were hearing cases. At this time several courts had already been held in the north and, over the next two weeks, two of the appointed *alaha'ou'ou* and others there heard several more cases and even sentenced a few people to imprisonment.[105]

Noel waited ten days to send Davies's 31 July report to High Commissioner Nicoll and inform him that things had "very suddenly deteriorated" and that he had decided to reverse his Maasina Rule policy. He vouched for Davies's reliability by pointing to his success in having turned the political situation around in parts of Makira (although he surely knew this was phony) and asserted the promise of his methods for Malaita. He described the troubles with courts—Noel thought Maasina Rule courts were called "alaha-ohu"—and minor incidents (eg, Malu'u people having delayed gathering for a church service until Marquand had departed the area) and quoted Cameron: "Barring natural differences of climate, economic and geographical this (ie, Maalu [Malu'u]) district bears an astounding resemblance to a National Socialistic Gau during the heyday of that party's power in the Third Reich." Noel added, "The mystic appeal of this movement makes a further parallel with the strange fervour that swiftly swept over Germany and resulted in the promotion of the Third Reich." Noel nonetheless said he planned to meet with chiefs in October about the courts. Nicoll's cool response asked why it had not been made clear to the chiefs that "no parallel system of [courts] could be contemplated."[106]

In a series of August cables, Noel pressed Nicoll to find warships to attend the planned 4 September arrests of 'Atoomea and associates and to remain in the Protectorate for a time, as "good will ambassadors." He argued that the root problem was a belief that the government was impotent, and that warships would counter this, which would in turn facilitate negotiation with the Maasina Rule chiefs in a "less tense atmosphere." Most important, it would reduce chances of violence, which he said he feared not from Maasina Rule but rather from the anti–Maasina Rule factions. Noel worried that where leaders were arrested their followers would face vengeance attacks from these factions, setting off tribal strife that would spread to other islands. And yet, he also planned to have the loyalist headmen personally make the arrests. An unnamed headman had told Davies that "the bodies of the police belong to the Government but their hearts to the Marching Rule," and Davies recommended that Western Solomons police be deployed to Malaita. Nicoll for a time resisted sending warships but in the end secured visits by several. He also sent to Noel Malaita's former district commissioner, David Trench, now Nicoll's assistant secretary, to serve as "secretary for development and native affairs" and assist in "the restoration of authority." Noel promptly sent Trench to 'Aoke to take charge of the upcoming arrest operations.[107]

Meanwhile, Head Chief Bobongi and Belo announced that on 18 August a court would be held at Sulione, in Lau. Headman Kakalu'ae told Cameron and they arrived at Sulione together. Cameron warned a line of duties carrying truncheons and a large crowd that the court would be illegal and that Maasina Rule must end. In front of all, he argued with Bobongi, and with Belo, who the week before had been appointed an *alaha'ou'ou*. Belo declared that on 30 April Noel had granted Malaita "freedom," and on 30 June Sandars had given permission to run their own courts. Cameron said Belo lectured him with "a spate of demagogic nonsense concerning freedom," which was Belo reading a list of 15 "freedoms" that the people had compiled. Belo and Bobongi, parroting Kifo, declared (in Cameron's words), "Marching Rule was holding courts and imprisoning people all over Malaita," and Bobongi added, "If the Government wanted to try and stop this business the Government would have to fight all Malaita, many thousands." Another man shouted that Cameron would have to "bring back plenty of ships to arrest us all." There were claps, cheers, and shouts that people did not want "the headman," referring to Kakalu'ae, but there were no physical threats. After Cameron repaired to his vessel, a court was held near the beach, which a new assistant headman, Molea of Funafou, observed and reported on.[108]

Cameron's understanding of Bobongi's threat became important. Later, at the chiefs' trial, Molea testified that Bobongi had actually said that to stop Maasina Rule "The Government should go round and *arrest* every man all round Malaita, and after that it would have to arrest all the people in Lau" (my emphasis). Confusion as to what Bobongi (who did not attend the 30 June meeting) said to Cameron was likely due to multiple meanings of the Pijin word *faetem;* although it can refer to physical fighting, it as often means nonviolent conflict or competition or even effort in the pursuit of a goal (eg, *hemi faetem seleni* = "he is trying to earn money"). When Bobongi told Cameron the government would have to *faetem* all Malaita, especially in the context Molea placed it in, it was likely threat not of violence but of resistance that would lead to thousands of arrests, and thus Molea's more benign translation was accurate. The latter also matches the reality of what did in fact happen.[109]

Davies wired Noel about the Sulione incident, with Cameron's quote of Bobongi, and told him, "Marching Rule saying same thing everywhere and if Government wishes to stop Marching Rule Courts they must fight all Malaita." This had the perhaps-intended effect of panicking Noel, who forwarded the quote to Fiji, but it nearly sparked disaster. Noel, expressly in response to the wire, ordered Secretary to Government Stanley Masterman, who was visiting 'Aoke, to recruit 20 police and 70 "special constables" from among the northern anti–Maasina Rule factions. He warned Nicoll that from this, "We must expect immediate armed repercussion Malaita and elsewhere," and he pleaded again for a warship. Davies was appalled, knowing that to enlist such constables would lead to catastrophe, but Nicoll saved him: doubtless recalling that Noel in arguing for a warship had just warned of attacks by these same factions, he quashed the "dangerously provocative" plan. Noel quickly wired Davies to disregard his order and told Nicoll: "Did not intend actually recruit North Malaita if by then situation improved by unanticipated success in other measures also in hand."[110]

I have noted the pattern of officers over the years being overruled and stymied by men in Tulagi or Fiji who were ignorant of Malaitan realities. During 1947 a reverse pattern emerges, of Davies, knowingly or not, misleading Noel as to the Malaitan situation, and Noel in turn, at least sometimes knowingly, distorting reality in his exchanges with Nicoll in Fiji. Noel, in particular, continued this practice until he left the Solomons, and we will see in the next chapter that, even after his departure, high commissioners were often kept in the dark about much that was happening. During this crisis on Malaita, when having correct information was so crucial for deciding how to proceed, Fiji was fully dependent on news passed on by resident commissioners, who in turn relied on intelligence from their district commissioners. The result was policy tragically misconceived from below and approved from above.

While Cameron was at Lau, Davies was in the midst of his first tour of the south as district commissioner, along with Marquand, who had never been there before. Hoasihau on 18 August told Davies that no courts or councils had operated since well before the 30 June 'Aoke meeting, and that Nono'oohimae had put both on hold "until custom had been codified" (and people still had no answer from Noel regarding Sandars's inquiry as to whether they could manage their own courts). Meanwhile, Davies wrote that, though there had been no move to usurp government courts, "matters were being settled quietly according to native custom. . . . In other words the South was in much the same state as the North, but without its turbulence and excitement." As we know, much the same situation had long held in the south, with people settling most disputes by "custom," sometimes with officers' (including Davies's) approval or encouragement. On 20 August, Davies held two meetings with Nono'oohimae and other southern leaders at Onepusu. Given his vilification of the entire movement and its leaders in reports to Noel, his account, written decades later, is striking: "For people who were supposed to have thrown off the hated Government yoke they were very civil, and we were able to argue sensibly if inconclusively. I had the feeling, not for the first time, that if we could have dealt with the Ariaris in isolation from the rest of Malaita, we might have been able to work out some sort of acceptable compromise. They were not out to throw down any gauntlets: they simply wanted to go their own way and for the Government to leave quietly; and I was not out to rock any boats with the day for the arrests coming closer. In a way it was all rather unreal, and I was fooling only myself in half-believing that they could be won over, because from the first to last the Ariaris were quite immovable on the subject of Marching Rule."[111] Some have written that by this point leadership of Maasina Rule had passed to northern leaders. This reflects the government's attentions: As parts of the north became more confrontational in mid-1947, the government mostly ignored the southern half of the island in terms of its officer postings, touring, and written record. Southern people certainly did not see northern chiefs as their leaders, and indeed many saw them as distorting, endangering, and ruining the movement.

Two days after, as arrest day approached, Davies ratcheted up pressure not merely to arrest the summoned north Malaitan "justices" but to begin on 4 September a crackdown on Maasina Rule across the island. On 22 August, he reported to Noel that the south was basically the same as the north, and "the entire movement is subversive." He told Noel, "In the past Malaita was pacified and remained peaceful because the Government was feared and respected—synonymous terms to the Malaitaman.... There will be no real respect for the British Government henceforth unless and until the Government has demonstrated its own power to impose its will." "The Marching Rule is in fact an organization controlled by a vicious clique," he wrote, which along with local "committees" was oppressing the people, forcing them to buy food from them ("the mass of the people are hungry"), and ransacking their houses and stealing their belongings. In sum, "The people must now be protected from themselves and the power of the clique broken before it has succeeded in destroying completely the progress of a quarter of a century." That same day Davies, Trench, Masterman, Allan, Legal Adviser Charles, and Noel met in Honiara and, Davies later wrote, "It was a far cry from the situation a month previously, with the Resident Commissioner now fully prepared to take a good crack at the Marching Rule." On their return to 'Aoke on 24 August, Davies and Cameron began planning a new "Phase III" of "Operation Delouse," entailing widespread arrests of Maasina Rule's leaders.[112]

On that day also, Norman Deck brought to 'Aoke *alaha'ou'ou* Belo, who wanted to apologize to Cameron for their argument at Sulione, as well as a prisoner, Oliga, who had been sentenced in a court held immediately after that argument to six months for getting a woman pregnant. Deck and fellow missionary Robert Vance met with officers and told them they thought the SSEM teachers would now cooperate with government. Furthermore, at this time Nori and Timothy George, visiting 'Aoke, became alarmed by developments in the north. They called a meeting for 3 September at nearby Abu for all of the higher and lower Maasina Rule chiefs to quell tensions, and George borrowed Deck's boat to visit the north for preliminary talks. For Davies, "This was the worst thing which could have happened." He did not want the meeting to take place because it would complicate his plan to begin arrests on 4 September. He apprehended Belo on the spot and convinced Noel to move up the arrest date to preempt the Abu meeting.[113]

Nicoll visited Honiara from 28 to 30 August to determine for himself what actions to take. He arrived thinking that the serious problems were limited to north Malaita; by the time he left, Noel could write to Sandars, "His Excellency has made up his mind that Marching Rule is an illegal body and that there can be no temporizing with its adherents." Noel had likely asked Davies to write the incendiary 22 August report to convince Nicoll that Malaita-wide suppression was essential, much as he had with Davies's provocative 31 July report.[114]

Readers are probably wondering where the convalescent Sandars had been over the six weeks Davies substituted for him, while these decisions were being made. Given that Davies's policies so contradicted and shattered those of Sandars, I searched the archives for answers, but in vain. After July they are mute on the question, almost as if Sandars, his policies, and reports had never existed. I have already warned that Davies's accounts are highly suspect concerning Sandars, but his is the only account of what happened, and for basic facts it rings true:

> [Sandars] and the Resident Commissioner had quarreled bitterly over handling of the Marching Rule. Noel reproached Sandars for not telling him the real truth about the movement; Sandars retorted that he had told him the truth as he understood it and could not help it if other, inexperienced people (i.e., me) saw the situation in more highly coloured terms; if a policy of repression was to be followed he washed his hands of Malaita and gave the required six months' notice of his intention to retire, which he was perfectly entitled to do. The basis of Sandars' refusal to have anything to do with a policy of repression stemmed not from moral revulsion, but from a belief that it would (1) spark off God only knew what strife and (2) that it would fail. His first belief proved absolutely correct; the second—in the long run anyway—was wrong. The weakness in his position was that he would not face up to the fact that the alternative to repression had been tried, and tried very hard, but had failed dismally.

Davies went on to recount a drinking session in 'Aoke with Sandars, who had come to collect his belongings: "He certainly told me what he thought of us all but curiously enough appeared to exonerate me personally of all blame for everything except bloody stupidity, and that I could scarcely help anyway. It was all the Resident Commissioner's fault for listening to me." That Sandars fell out with Noel is clear in that since at least 31 July he had been cut out of strategy discussions. Noel on 30 August in a personal letter instructed Sandars that if he talked to any Malaitans in 'Aoke while gathering his things he was to voice only the government's firm line and informed him, "As doubtless you know, arrests are now to be made in North Malaita." He told him nothing of the plans to arrest Maasina Rule's leaders throughout the island.[115]

During the high commissioner's visit, on 29 August, Legal Adviser Charles drew up a new king's regulation, the "Public Order (Recognizance) Regulation," which provides a window into the legal mind of the man who, though the chief architect of the sometimes contorted legal grounds for arresting Maasina Rule's leaders, would before long judge them. It declared that anyone merely suspected of doing "or being about to do any act" that would "occasion grave danger to public order" could be arrested and ordered to enter a "recognizance," to include monetary payment, restrictions on where they could reside, and orders to report to officials at specified times for up to two years, with violation punished by two years with or without hard labor. Charles cited for legal precedence Article 56 of the Pacific Order in Council 1893, under which such recognizance might be imposed on persons who had actually committed such acts. But that law, he argued, was inadequate, for, "It is well known that certain partially educated natives have been spreading false reports which are likely to have a very dangerous effect on their more primitive and excitable fellows, and lead them to actual rebellion and civil war."[116] Unfortunately for the government, it had proved impossible to obtain real evidence of most leaders having done this—thus the regulation. Charles admitted that it involved "a departure from English law" but justified it for Solomon Islanders due to "the requirements of preserving law and order in the future amongst a primitive people susceptible to rumours and mass hysteria." He noted that a regulation that so departed from "accepted principles of law" would normally require prior secretary of state approval, but he opined that in this case Nicoll could "properly assent in the name and on behalf of His Majesty."[117]

With this and other unusual legal opinions in hand, and the momentum toward Malaita-wide suppression now unstoppable, on 31 August Noel put the arrest plans in motion. He informed the Protectorate with the following radio address:

> The Government has arrested certain alleged leaders of Marching Rule or, as commonly known, "Massina Rule," against whom complaints have been made by natives of the Protectorate. Other arrests are pending. The complaints which have been made are to the effect that the persons who have been or will be arrested have sought to establish an organized terrorism and robbery of the native people by a system of illegal police spies and courts, and have even threatened death to those who do not obey their dictates. It is alleged that the illegal courts have usurped the functions of the properly constituted native courts which have been

established, and even of the superior Court, in the Protectorate. The complaints, if true, would indicate that the individual liberty of the native people has been endangered by a military despotism like those of Nazi Germany and Japan which recently threatened the world....

People of this Protectorate, do not listen to rumours. If you are in doubt about what some people are telling you, consult your District Officer, missionary, nearest planter, all those in fact who share your lives, have looked after you and whom you so often consulted in the past. Remember that you have with you District Officers, missionaries and planters who shared with you the horrors of war and of the Japanese invasion, as they had shared with you the fortunes of peace. Your welfare and their welfare are one, for welfare is indivisible.

Let us all remember that war and strife lead to havoc and that peace and work alone lead to a better life. I would like this opportunity to congratulate the native producers of copra in the West Solomons on their efforts and commend their example to all.[118]

"Operation Delouse" was now under way.

Chapter 7
Suppression and Resistance

Operation Delouse

Early on the morning of 31 August 1947, three forces commanded by Cameron, Marquand, and Trench staged surprise raids in north Malaita. They came on ships with squads of police from the Western Solomons. High Commissioner Nicoll had offered Fijian police, which Noel badly wanted but declined when Nicoll warned that they would draw press attention.[1] What was now officially "Operation Delouse" began arresting head chiefs and some lesser chiefs, men charged with holding illegal courts, and various duties or others perceived to be interfering in the arrests (in Trench's case, even by wearing an armband). Houses were searched for incriminating documents. The next day Davies jailed Nori on minor charges in 'Aoke, where Kifo and Basi were also picked up and Belo was already in custody. Arrests had started earlier on Makira, Isabel, Gela, and Guadalcanal, and over the next two months operations would move south across Malaita. Most chiefs could have escaped inland but chose not to. Noel reported to Nicoll that in the first month they made 190 arrests, all "as a result of complaints preferred by natives."[2]

The government worried about violence, and the 31 August forces carried several thousand .303 cartridges for their Enfield rifles. But not a shot was fired, and though officers met angry crowds in places, they suffered only verbal hostility. Cameron told Davies he believed that, but for the police, there would have been clashes at Malu'u, but Marquand wrote that of all the arrests he made, he never used more than three policemen, and usually just one, and was never resisted: "There have been reports that had a large force not been available there might have been unrest but in my opinion a large force only aggravates." Special Constable Charles Lamond later testified, "On the day of ['Atoomea's arrest at Malu'u] I saw no indication that the people were against the Government." Noel assured Nicoll that violence would have been certain without the warships he had sent, though they arrived after the opening arrests in the most difficult areas: ships *Warramunga*, *Contest*, and *Shoalhaven* visited Malaita between 4 and 15 September, and soon after that, destroyers *Cockade* and *Aeneas* called at various harbors and escorted the aircraft carrier *Theseus,* which launched 14 fighter planes to soar around the island's coastline. Marquand gave a Pijin message to headmen to read out to their publics, telling people not to fear or flee: "They are coming to show all the people the British airplanes and warships that are working with us for the people to keep any enemy from stealing their land and to see that no native tries to stop government work." Marquand later wrote, "The natives...realize that the appearance of destroyers and other war-like materials is only show."[3]

As Cameron made arrests he proclaimed to spectators that "Marching Rule was finished, and its leaders would be tried and if found guilty of breaking the law would be punished. The Government was doing this because these men had lied to the people, robbed the people, and oppressed the people." Knowing what we do about Maasina Rule's levels of popular support, to depict chiefs to the people in this way seems absurd, but the portrayal of chiefs as tyrants, and the notion that with strong action the people might come over to government's side were not subterfuge—officers shared and took comfort from these ideas. Cameron would have known from his time at Kwai that his caricature was false there, but it did match the image he had formed of Malu'u, and officers possessed little or no reliable information about most areas.[4]

Cameron's arrest of Kwaio Head Chief Fifi'i at Sinalagu on 18 September is instructive. Cameron knew next to nothing of Kwaio and had never seen Fifi'i, but he berated the crowd of several hundred who had awaited him: "I told them of the lies and extortions of the Marching Rule leaders. I told them how these men had grown proud, how they had broken the law and oppressed the people. When I felt that these points had been appreciated and understood I announced the Resident Commissioner's order that Marching Rule must finish. I told them of the action in the North and of the arrests that had been made. I told them that all the evil men who had broken the law and deluded the people would be arrested." He also declared that Americans had lied to them and the British were their real protectors. His Kwaio audience knew all about the previous arrests, and Ganifiri and Sipolo had visited to warn of the pending ones. What Cameron did not know was that many men hid in the surrounding jungle armed with rifles and other arms, and a few had been trying to convince Fifi'i to agree to their wrestling down the police, but Fifi'i hotly forbade any defiance. "We could have killed them all easily," one of them told me years later. When the people refused Cameron's demand that they identify him, Fifi'i stepped forward. As Cameron led him away, the crowd raised a *tongatonga,* or war cry, of anger and defiance. Cameron's party knew the danger but Cameron did not, reporting to Davies, "There was a moment of silence then a burst of cheering and shouting. I may be wrong but my impression is that the cheers were for the Government and not against it." Facing a real threat of violent resistance, the officer imagined himself hailed as a liberator. On this day Cameron also arrested Ganifiri, Sipolo, and Heber, and the next week Nono'oohimae and George.[5]

Where did officers' profound misreading of chiefs' standings in their communities come from? Dynamic as well as areally and ideologically diverse, Maasina Rule posed a complex challenge for the government. Sandars, for all the gaps in his knowledge, grasped this and the necessity of dealing with the movement gingerly, flexibly, patiently, and with a degree of respect and humility. We have seen that, by contrast, his successor Davies's conception of Maasina Rule was crude: to him, its dealings with the government had been wholly fraudulent, a sham masking a Malaita-wide conspiracy with a nefarious agenda to oppress gullible or helpless Malaitans:

> The Marching Rule is in fact an organization controlled by a vicious clique, who have secured the allegiance of the vast bulk of the population by methods running the whole gamut from mild persuasion to dire threats. Vast as is the power of the big leaders they can be deposed by the sinister "committees" in the background as easily as the Jacobins removed their leaders when they failed to please. This hard and vigorous minority inside the Marching Rule has oppressed the mass of the population and curtailed its liberties to an alarming degree....When the people are lined up in the mornings in the villages and marched off under escort to work in the gardens all day, in order to feed the hordes who trek from meeting to meeting and the numerous "duties" who strut amongst them with their uniforms and truncheons; when after all their labour on communal farms the people are told that they can only obtain food from them by purchasing it from the chief; when after all the propaganda about the big farms that were being made, the mass of the people are hungry; when the people are unable to leave or enter a village until they have obtained permission of a "duty," and submit to a rigorous cross-examination; when they are liable to have their houses searched by duties and have anything purchased from a trade store confiscated by them, when their every movement is watched and controlled un-til they are frightened of mentioning the words "Marching Rule" to an outsider, it is clear that an organization has grown up which is wholly repugnant to our conception of liberty.[6]

Noel, knowing little of Malaitan realities and thus fully dependent on the counsel of his district commissioners, had abandoned that of Sandars, whose more nuanced, cautionary approach had failed to resolve the situation or induce sufficient Malaitan cooperation, particularly in providing laborers. Clearly frustrated, Noel embraced Davies's twisted perspective and the clarity of the response it demanded from him as resident commissioner. "Marching Rule must finish" became the official line, which over the following weeks officers delivered everywhere they went. The key to finishing Maasina Rule was to remove the "vicious clique" of leaders and to display government power in order to overawe the "sinister committees."

Surely the people, liberated from the oppression, bullying, and cruelty that Davies described, and given the Malaita scene's "astounding resemblance" to Nazi Germany reported by Cameron, would welcome rescue, and yes, perhaps even cheer the arrest of chiefs. Government officers, though they knew little about the situation in most places and possessed ample counterevidence from areas they did know something about, had become convinced by their own propaganda. Their reports, particularly Davies's, also served to mislead their successors, who would read them as factual and thus misconstrue the movement they were struggling against and the roots of Malaitan anger and resolve.

Officer confusion regarding the position of head chiefs was a critical element in the government's misunderstandings of the movement overall. Chiefs had told officers all along that it was not they but the people who held the real power; they had been selected and approved by popular opinion, and many accepted warily under community pressure. They often told officers, "It's not my fault I'm a Marching Rule chief, the people made me one," which, as Marquand came to realize, "was perfectly true." Malaitans openly worried their chiefs might become *bikihedi* (proud, or arrogant) in their positions, and several times when officers and chiefs had tried to meet in private, the public had objected, saying that they, too, wanted to hear what was said. Ganifiri testified that the head chiefs never met together alone but always had many other chiefs present. In 1946 Noel had reported of Nori and Timothy George, "Both deny that they are the leaders and admit only that they are the mouth-piece of people," and we saw in chapter 6 that Nori and Nono'oohimae told Palmer that they feared people's anger if they tried to allow labor recruiting. Even 'Atoomea, often depicted as the most dictatorial chief (excepting perhaps Fifi'i), repeatedly told Marquand he could not tell To'abaita people what to do. In July, Marquand had watched people ignore 'Atoomea's instructions to boycott a medical clinic, and when 'Atoomea, having been bitten by a snake, was eager to go with Marquand to the hospital, the people had stopped his going. Nori later testified, "My appointment was as head of the Marching Rule. This did not mean that I controlled Marching Rule policy but I was only there to carry out the people's wishes; we natives differ from Europeans in respect of powers given to a leader."[7]

Officers had dismissed chiefs' assertions that their positions were constrained as a conspiratorial deception, as their deploying a fatuous popular will as a smokescreen for personal machinations. Leaders, Noel warned, would try to "bluff the Government that [their programs are] what the people want." Trench said chiefs "pushed themselves forward and were accepted by a people who did not really know what it was all about," while Cameron wrote of them as "misguided men" who "under the intoxication of power...became perverted and evil." Some officers soon realized their mistake, however. The chiefs, Marquand later wrote, "were careful not to incur the displeasure of the people upon whom they depended for their position," and officers "were convinced that the movement was controlled by a minority who were bullying the people and therefore, if the leaders could be arrested, the movement would collapse. But the Marching Rule did not collapse. There was no minority of bullying leaders. The whole of the Marching Rule members were the leaders; it was controlled by the people." In mid-October, Cameron told Davies that the "evils and vices" of the leaders "were only the sublimation of the evils and vices of the mob, therefore understandable to the mob." "Since it was a people's movement," he said, "it is to the people that we must appeal."[8]

Marquand came to see that fundamental to the people's lasting enthusiasm for the movement was the fact that the "direction of control" in their lives was upward from them, in contrast to the top-down control of the government system: "The chiefs of the Marching Rule were always careful to ensure that a contemplated move was popular before submitting it to the [Maasina Rule] Council. The Government headmen on the other hand, with the District Officer on his tail, forced any required move through his council regardless of popular opinion." Malaitans were resolved not to resubmit to this structure of government authority imposed via headman, especially now that Kakalu'ae, Siru, Maekali, and Ba'etalua and some other headmen had helped to imprison their leaders. Their resolve would only deepen over time as these headmen urged and assisted in the arrests and jailing of more and more Malaitans.[9]

For a brief period, Operation Delouse put Malaitans in disarray, and colonial officers, flush with apparent triumph, began speaking of a mission accomplished. The chiefs had been seized and Maasina Rule crushed with speed and panache. On 10 September, Davies told Noel that operations in the north had been "a great success and...have demonstrated most effectively that disobedience to Government orders and lawlessness will not be tolerated." Even at formerly unyielding Malu'u, Marquand reported, "They are too afraid of the Government now to be anti-Government." Noel was particularly exultant, assuring Nicoll in early October, "It is generally believed...that the threat of further disorders is not likely to occur for some time if at all." In early November he read the Advisory Council a message from Nicoll saying of Maasina Rule, "Happily the outbreak was of short duration and dislocation to public business caused by it was not of serious proportions," and praising officers who had dealt "so expeditiously and efficiently with the situation caused by the Marching Rule leaders." Noel, like Nicoll, knew by then that things were not nearly so rosy as that, but he nonetheless reassured the council, "Respect for Government authority has now been restored, except in certain remote areas where it has not yet been possible to deal with the recalcitrant leaders." The press, too, carried stories of movement collapse and a government back in control, citing Colonial Office statements from London. With smug optimism, Adventist Pastor J

FIGURE 7.1. On Santa Ana, trader Henry Kuper at left and Major H S N Robinson, general secretary of the Melanesian Mission, displaying a "captured flag" of the Native Union Council, an early name for Maasina Rule, ca 1947. (Anglican Church of Melanesia Archive, Box 5-45-1, photo album of Archdeacon Harry Reynolds, Solomon Islands National Archive.)

H Newman told readers of his mission's magazine, *Australian Record:* "The natives have once more learned a lesson."[10]

In the glow of perceived victory, officers of every rank failed to grasp the profound discontents that had brought about the movement. They could not fathom the depth of Malaitan anger at being second-class citizens of their own country, disdained and belittled by aliens who controlled them with the arrogance of taken-for-granted superiority. We have seen that various officers through the years had spoken of Islanders' "imaginary" or "mythical grievances," and in the months after arrests began, this view came to the fore as officials endeavored to quell any idea that Maasina Rule was incited by legitimate complaints, especially about inept British rule. Key to this propaganda was a revisionist history that dismissed Malaitan criticisms as concoctions or fantasies. The movement's wide following, Nicoll reported, had been due to "ignorance and dissatisfaction with the existing economic conditions" that lay beyond government control. Noel instructed officers to remind Malaitans they had no grounds to complain about prewar labor conditions, since they should have reported problems to an officer or court at the time. Davies was soon singing praises of the old native councils, citing Maekali's at Malu'u as most outstanding, while Cameron said the problem with previous councils had been that "people mistook them for expressions of the Government's will rather than as a means of expressing their own will." The courts "failed for the same reason as councils: courts were misunderstood and were regarded as an attempt to force an alien code on the people by means of the Government through the headman. That this was not true we know but it was one of the Marching Rule's most successful lies." The chiefs, Noel concluded, copied courts and councils since they were so popular, and the only problem with these government bodies had been that "Their leaders lacked the political and legal experience necessary to operate these institutions without the guidance of trained District Officers." Trench quipped, "Surely imitation on this scale is flattery," and dismissed the Maasina Rule legal apparatus as having been simply "a mischievous copy of existing law."[11]

Trench went farthest in dismissing the idea that Malaitans might have had sound reasons for their unhappiness: "The question now arises as to why this rebellion—for such it was—broke out. My conclusion...is that there were no specific grievances which gave rise to the movement....The ordinary villager is remote from Government and does not have sufficient contact with Government to make any serious specific grievances possible." He further observed that there were in New Guinea "cults astonishingly similar" to Maasina Rule, and he reasoned that because government policies there were different, BSIP policies could only be blameless. Nor would concrete changes address the problem—which was, though policy had been sound, that "Government has failed to give the *appearance* of good government." Therefore, he argued, "The first aim must be to convince Solomon Islanders that they have a better government than they think." From claims that Malaitans had no rational basis for complaint, it was but a short step to judging Malaitans irrational, and we will see that some officers and other Europeans came to explain Maasina Rule as a mass delusion of "the native mind." What choice did a responsible government have, then, but to destroy it?[12]

Noel and his officers hoped to reach a quick "reconciliation" with Malaitans, perhaps even as they were arresting their leaders. On 6 September, Noel spoke to 300 people at Malu'u with this in mind but encountered hecklers, including one who "pointed out that I could not always return with a warship," and another who shouted, "Marching Rule is not finished." The north, Noel concluded, was "unrepentant." Touring the south six weeks later, Davies could find nobody there interested in giving up Marching Rule. Waleanisia told me that, after the arrests, most of the remaining anti–Maasina Rule people in Langalanga joined the movement. Malaitans soon began to reoccupy coastal towns, and, toward the end of 1947, to build new towns there and inland.[13]

By the end of 1947, with the chiefs long jailed and Malaitans still openly defiant, officers realized they were dealing with a ground-up movement, now a rebellion. They increasingly and perhaps unconsciously began evoking "the Marching Rule" as a euphemism for "Malaitans" but as if it were an ethereal entity with a single mind: "the Marching Rule says," "the Marching Rule expects," "the Marching Rule believes." It was more palatable to talk of suppressing "the Marching Rule" than "the Malaitan populace," and some officers, even years after, could not acknowledge that they had battled the people, so wedded were they to the notion of Maasina Rule tyranny and the moral justification that perspective had afforded the government's own.

Colonial Justice: *Rex v Bobongi and Others*

As officers went round Malaita to seek out the mood of the people, the word they heard everywhere was that all were awaiting the verdict on their chiefs. But the people's wait was to be a long one. Despite consultations with Legal Adviser William T Charles, Trench was finding it difficult to construct a case against many of the prisoners. Charles had first advised what charges to file based partly on Davies's assertions of widespread oppression and abuse by Maasina Rule's chiefs, evidence for which had not been forthcoming. By September's end, Trench told the district commissioners that prisoners would be separated into three groups and each group tried for "conspiring to effect a public mischief on the grounds that Marching Rule agreed that illegal courts should be set up and agreed on certain other aims contrary to law." By early November, Nicoll in Fiji was pressuring Noel to try the chiefs quickly. Noel telegrammed in reply that delays had been unavoidable and told him for the first time that the leaders would be tried jointly for conspiracy. Nicoll was displeased: "In your memorandum of 4th October...you stated that all persons had been arrested as a result of complaints preferred by natives, and charges were either making illegal arrests or being members of an illegal court that sentenced people either to fines or imprisonment. I now observe that it is proposed to prosecute jointly on conspiracy charges. I shall be grateful if you will confirm this is really necessary, and that there is not some more straight-forward manner in which the bulk of the persons arrested could be brought to swift and substantial justice." Noel rejoined that a "greater number of serious offenses have been committed than was [previously] expected," but that "sifting evidence reveals that possibly 10 major leaders could not be charged with holding illegal courts having only advocated others to do so as part of general Marching Rule policy and illegal activities. In these circumstances and in light of evidence Legal Adviser [Charles] advises conspiracy is sole charge." Otherwise, he added, playing to Nicoll's concern for speed, the "legal calendar might have been filled with [an] unnecessary number of separate trials." Three days before, Trench had told Davies there was "no evidence at all" against 15 of the prisoners, including Head Chief Fifi'i, and insufficient evidence against four others, and he asked, "Could any of [these] be let off with flea in ear after sentence of leaders or dealt with summarily?"[14]

The chiefs had in early October formally asked for legal council. Nori said movement funds had been put aside in case of arrests and that they had £1,000 to hire a lawyer. Noel wired Nicoll that this was refused because no lawyer was available, because one was "unnecessary as no injustice would result since there was no legally qualified prosecutor," and because the chiefs "would be assured trial before Judicial Commissioner." The prosecution would begin with a preliminary examination to decide if there was sufficient evidence to proceed to trial. David Trench chose as magistrate for this examination none other than Roy Davies. Trench, reasonably seeing that stage as a mere formality, said that he would act as prosecutor at both the exam and the trial. As Noel had assured Nicoll, the trial judge would be a judicial commissioner—William T Charles, who for months had worked closely with Noel, Davies, and prosecutor Trench to construct charges against the defendants. There would be no assessors, "there being no indifferent persons to act in that capacity." With the deck thus stacked, the head chiefs never had a chance of acquittal; this was an exercise not in considered justice but in calculated suppression.[15]

The head chiefs and several lesser leaders (33 men in all) were indicted and tried together in *Rex v Bobongi*. The preliminary examination was held from 17 November to 6 December, the trial from 15 December to 14 February. The indictments, exam and trial transcripts, defendant statements, and verdicts total 280 single-spaced legal pages, including testimony by 31 prosecution and 13 defense witnesses and their cross-examinations by defendants and the prosecution.[16] The government also entered ten exhibits selected from documents seized.[17] A detailed study of the trial is impossible here, and I will just summarize some key points.

Given the minimal amount or absence of evidence against so many, the government's case had to be that Maasina Rule was a massive orchestrated conspiracy, involving all of the defendants, to depose the government. The charges were worded such that the great majority of Malaitans, including most of the government witnesses, could have been convicted under them:

He the said [defendant's name] on diverse dates between the 1st day of January 1944 [changed after testimony to 15 August 1947] and 1st October 1947 at diverse places in the Protectorate did in company with others unlawfully combine and confederate c.s. 2 Unlawful Societies Act 1799, s. 25 of the Seditious Meetings Act 1817, in that they did become members of an unlawful society or club known as the "Marching Rule" or did act as members thereof or did directly or indirectly maintain correspondence or intercourse with the said society or club ["on Malaita" later added] or with a committee or delegate, representative or missionary, or with officers or members thereof as such or by contribution of money or otherwise did aid, abet or support said society or club or the members or officers thereof.[18]

The only head chief not so charged was Shadrach Dioteʻe, who alone now renounced Maasina Rule, and against whom the government therefore judged there was insufficient evidence. Fifiʻi told me that Charles explained the sedition charge to them by analogy with Judas having betrayed Jesus. All pled not guilty.[19]

A large portion of the prosecution testimony came from witnesses who had stood before or had observed 15 purportedly illegal courts. All but two of these courts had been held in the north after 30 June. The witnesses told of proceedings that were generally just, and almost all who had been tried admitted their guilt, both in the proceedings themselves and again in their testimony at this trial. Few declared they had been treated unfairly, and some said they were still Maasina Rule members. Just two said they attended the courts because they were afraid not to (and how many would not have said this about government courts?), while one man had bargained successfully with those hearing his case to halve his penalty. Some found guilty were "jailed" in the sense described in earlier chapters, held under minimal restraint and working for the same hours as in government custody, some because they could or would not pay compensation. All but four had faced charges of sexual trespass or assaulting women, and some agreed that they were placed in custody for their own protection from angry relatives of the offended women.

Several of these courts were, technically, probably legal, since officers had allowed chiefs to conduct arbitrations.[20] Government headmen were usually present at the proceedings, but in most cases they merely observed. Not in evidence at the trial were reminders of Nazi Germany, Gestapo-like "secret tribunals," or the originally planned charges of assault and robbery.[21] The courts' fundamental offense was not injustice or maltreatment, but that they were held outside of government auspices. These were the cases the prosecution chose to present, and clearly they were unable to find any evidence of the sorts of abuses earlier alleged. The government gave much attention to the presence of duties in most courts, often carrying truncheons, since this implied involuntary arbitration, but they were also there when the accused clearly attended voluntarily, more as performance than menace, and no evidence was presented of any duty inflicting or even threatening violence.[22]

All of this aside, the evidence about courts was most important to establish that *some* people in the movement, even a few, had conducted them, and it was presented to assert that the entire movement was seditious. Only two of the head chiefs, Bobongi and Heber, were charged with actually convening illegal courts, but all the others were judged guilty on this score since they were leaders of Maasina Rule and thus said to have conspired to overthrow the government court system.[23]

Proving that Maasina Rule was unambiguously conspiratorial and seditious was a challenge. It was imperative to refute defendants' repeated, detailed testimonies of how they had, in many ways, worked with and been guided by the government. The cooperation, advice, and at times open support of officers—particularly Sandars and Forster—could mar the government's case, and it was important to show that the chiefs' cooperation had been a charade to conceal their conspiracy. The government for this critical point depended heavily on its opening and star witness: Lau Headman Timi Kakalu'ae. Though he had briefly been Lau's Maasina Rule head chief, Kakalu'ae subsequently stepped down—or more likely was pushed out—and became the bitterest Malaitan enemy of the movement. His testimony centered on his detailed account of a private talk he said he had with Nori, when Nori's second patrol visited Lau in June 1946:

> [Nori said] we must start to make gardens, big gardens, farms. We must make big towns. We must make this work strong. The Government has been on Malaita a long time now, and it has done nothing but rob us. The Marching Rule must work hard to take everything from the Government's hands. We must stop the Government holding courts on the people, from putting us in prison, from fining us. No-one must work for any other white man either. No-one must pay tax— we must collect this ourselves. We must block everything that the Government wants to do to us, and we must do everything ourselves. He said that we must make the big gardens and big towns so that we could point to them when the Government came round and say that we were too busy with this work to do anything that the Government wanted us to do. He said that the headman must lie to the Government, and hide what was going on.[24]

Kakalu'ae also attributed earlier and strikingly similar statements about Maasina Rule's secret plan to a Lau man named England Kwaisulia, which he said England made in 1945 after he visited 'Are'are and returned to Lau a movement supporter. Nori and several others challenged Kakalu'ae's testimony (and that of his assistant Saeni, which was the same), not only his claims that Nori had said Maasina Rule's mission was "to finish the government on Malaita" and that the towns were phony, but that the private meeting that Kakalu'ae recounted even took place. Years later Fifi'i emotionally told me of Kakalu'ae's "lies" that sent them to prison, and it did always seem to me bizarre that Nori would have chosen to reveal a secret, seditious master plan to Kakalu'ae, of all people.[25] And it appears that Kakalu'ae did concoct the conversation. Davies, in a part of his manuscript unconnected to the trial, quoted from his field diary of a stop in Lau the month after Nori's visit there:

On the 14th [July 1946] I had Kakaluae hammering away at me all day on the
subject of Marching Rule, mostly about Nori's tour of the North in [June].[26]
He said that at the big meeting Nori called, attended by some 7,000 people, he
Kakaluae grew hot under the collar and told the assembled multitude that if the
Marching Rule was in any way anti-Government he wanted nothing to do with
it. Nori had denied publicly that the movement was anti-Government, but he
[Kakalu'ae] suspected that Nori would have spoken differently to him had he
proved more susceptible to his blandishments. He said that others had given
him vastly different versions of what Nori said at his meetings. Just what Nori
did or did not say at his meetings was always the subject of flat contradiction:
he preached subversion; he preached cooperation with Government. Here was
Kakaluae saying he knew he was subversive, but admitting that Nori's public
utterances in his presence were not.[27]

Kakalu'ae, eager to convince Davies of Nori's subversive intent, was frustrated that he had heard Nori say nothing subversive, and so had no first-
hand evidence to offer against him. Nor did Davies say that Kakalu'ae had
mentioned England Kwaisulia's reputed earlier seditious statements. This
indicates not only that, as Nori and others charged, Kakalu'ae made up
his courtroom story, but also that Davies should have known he was lying
when he presided over his preliminary exam testimony, yet said nothing.
Several explanations are possible. Davies might have suborned Kakalu'ae,
and in support of this, his testimony was just the evidence the government
required but could not otherwise find. Or Davies might have known his
testimony was false but kept silent about it. Or he may have forgotten the
conversations with Kakalu'ae that contradicted his testimony. That Davies
included this diary excerpt in his manuscript favors the last interpretation,
though there he said nothing of Kakalu'ae's testimony before him. Against
this interpretation, one would think that Kakalu'ae, if he had not planned
or cleared his testimony beforehand with Davies, would have feared, after
having "hammered away all day on the subject" during Davies's visit to Lau
the year before, that Davies would now recognize that he was lying under
oath in his court. In any case, officers afterward cited and even quoted
Kakalu'ae's testimony as conclusive proof that Maasina Rule's more moderate platforms had always been a conspiratorial fraud, and that its towns
were a "complete sham"—a "bogus" contrivance to avoid working on government projects. This became a common government narrative that subsequent district officers learned as historical truth.[28]
    Kakalu'ae's is but one example of prosecution testimony that any
defense lawyer would have demolished, and it is no wonder the chiefs were
denied one. Several witnesses significantly changed their testimony under
defendant cross-examination. Kakalu'ae had particular trouble explaining
under such questioning why he had agreed to become Lau's head chief
just two weeks after, he said, England Kwaisulia had told him that Maasina

Rule was highly seditious. He testified that he did have strong suspicions, yet he voiced these to no one, including men he subsequently appointed to high movement positions, such as Shem Irofa'alu and defendants Basi and Ramo'oli. He had instructed these men to make the very towns and farms that he claimed England and then Nori had told him were fakes to fool the government. Kakalu'ae, moreover, had retained the head chief position for some time after Nori's visit. None of these contradictions appear to have troubled Commissioner Charles.[29]

In delivering the guilty verdict, Charles began his summary of evidence with a page-long synopsis of Kakalu'ae's testimony, stating that both he and Saeni "impressed me as truthful witnesses and Nori impressed me as a liar, particularly in respect of this conversation." And toward the end of the verdict he wrote, "The unavoidable conclusion from the above findings is that England and Nori correctly told Kakaluae of the real aims of the Marching Rule and that at least from the time of that conversation the secret aims of those controlling Marching Rule policy were intended to bring into hatred and contempt the administration of justice and the Government. In other words, the real and secret policy of Marching Rule, as directed by its leaders, was a seditious one." He acknowledged that the leaders had canceled the strike when Sandars told Nori it was illegal, but he wrote, "The significant feature was...that it was not brought to Government's notice until at least six months after Nori had disclosed the aims of Marching Rule to Kakaluae." Thus did Charles make Kakalu'ae's story the centerpiece of the government's case. This required a sweeping dismissal of contradicting testimonies of defendants and witnesses, which, given the dearth of evidence against so many, left Charles only a subjective justification: "I am confirmed in my conclusions as to the real aim of Marching Rule by my observation of the accused who gave evidence...their demeanour as witnesses was most unconvincing, particularly in denial of alleged advocacy of anti-Government policy." Like Nori, they all impressed him as liars.[30]

On 13 February, Charles sentenced all the head chiefs and Nori to six years penal servitude, and other defendants to terms ranging from several months to five years. Six less important men were acquitted. Noel lamented that more did not receive maximum sentences, but noted that "Charles could not have done anything else in the light of such evidence as was available," the lack of which Noel credited to Malaita's officers having been too busy to collect it.[31] Seven months later, High Commissioner Freeston's legal adviser, J H Vaughan, took Charles to task:

> In view of the amount of "illegal" advice the Marching Rulers have clearly been receiving during the last year or two it is unfortunate that some attempt was not made to enable them to obtain legal advice when they asked for it. Furthermore, no class of case is more likely to lead to injustice than a "political" trial. The prosecution have to rely almost entirely upon the truthfulness of their witnesses

uncorroborated by "material" evidence. Unless their veracity is tested by expert cross examination injustice is likely to result. I do not think it is proper, particularly in this type of case, for the Legal Adviser to advise the prosecution and then try the case as Judicial Commissioner. . . . Such procedure is quite contrary to the principles upon which criminal trials in British courts are conducted, and gives the Marching Rulers just the sort of ammunition they are looking for.

Charles responded: "I think it may be safely said that until I received the proceedings of the preliminary examination I knew very little more of the nature of the case for the Prosecution than would normally and unavoidably be known to any member of the public in a very small community with a daily newspaper." The advisory opinions he gave to government officers, he said, he had regarded as "being upon hypothetical cases." As to the absence of a defense lawyer, "The accused . . . consisted of some educated and intelligent natives who were able to guide their fellows, as in its essentials their defences were the same."[32]

The Peaceful Wars of Savages

Malaitans mostly marked time during the trial, and officers worried about how they would react to the verdicts. After all, Davies's and Noel's most urgent rationale for the crackdown had been the looming threat of violence, and the government still did not control much of Malaita. But even before the judgment, Malaitans initiated a different sort of response. In early November, Headman Siru had ordered people of Faumaamanu and A'arai towns in east Kwara'ae to repair a dilapidated tax house. People tore most of it down. This may have been a dismantling before rebuilding and thus not political, but Davies had heard talk that it was the latter, and he arrived with Cameron and 25 police and ordered that 50 men be assembled the next morning to repair it. In the morning he found the 50 on the beach with their bags packed for prison. Davies had 64 arrested, and afterward he mustered a "surly" crowd of 700 in order to tell them "they were a disgrace to themselves and to the District, and that as they had shown they did not wish for anything but anarchy, the area would now be taken under direct rule again." When he departed, the tax house was torched. One prisoner, David Kosionami, told Ben Burt that they were abused en route and some were displayed at Malu'u in hopes of frightening people there.[33]

Readers will recollect that Kwara'ae had done something like this before, when in June 1946 hundreds challenged Forster to imprison them all at 'Aoke, forcing him to back down. This would soon become the foremost resistance tactic across the island. In December 1947, Marquand submitted a prescient forecast: "I consider that the collection of tax from these people is essential even though it may be more difficult to collect than in Mr. Bell's time. There is no doubt that when the time comes to collect tax there will be mass refusals to pay in some districts, to which the only reply can be mass imprisonment. The collection of tax will undoubtedly require a considerable force of police when villages will have to be rounded up one by one."[34]

As Davis lamented in the Annual Report at year's end, Operation Delouse had been a great disappointment, and Maasina Rule was now an outright revolt. Officers thought it imperative to force obedience, to compel Malaitans to accept government's absolute authority in the land. For several years they and their successors would chase after this paramount goal by ordering Malaitan men to perform a series of actions that would signify their capitulation, the three main ones being, in general order of appearance, that they remove fences from around their villages, that they provide census data about themselves and their families, and that they pay the tax. These were important not so much in themselves but rather as acts of surrender to British suzerainty.[35] Men or communities that refused were subjected to familiar tools of a repressive regime: mass arrests and imprisonments, catchall sedition laws, and collective punishments, all imposed by partisan courts, often with contempt and derision. A common historical narrative has been that these tactics eventually succeeded in forcing defeated Malaitans to abandon resistance and resubmit to British rule on British terms. We shall see that this is in error.

Late in 1947, J D A Germond arrived from Africa to fill a new post of "divisional officer," ranked above district commissioners and based in 'Aoke.[36] It was an awful time to put in charge a man so green, particularly with a tutor like Davies, who claimed that Germond soon adopted his views, vowing, said Davies, "No offence was to be too unimportant to be pursued and pressure must be remorseless." Like so many before him, Germond arrived brandishing Africa models for ruling the natives (he liked to quote Lugard). Knowing little of Malaita or its history, he straightaway criticized previous administrations and called for sweeping changes, including abandonment of indirect rule plans for which "backward" Malaitans had never been ready, and bringing in more police to implement an intense, direct approach. This earned him a rebuke and lecture from Noel, who (with his eye as always on the labor problem), warned, "Militant administration will never balance a budget," though he did agree that more police might be useful "to facilitate production of copra," that is, to get labor. Noel clearly detected Davies's influence on Germond (Cameron was away November–May) and told him, "If your District Officers have told you otherwise, leading you accordingly to believe that Government policy must be varied out of recognition, then their error is due to their lack of experience and understanding of administration and the Malaitaman." Noel also corrected criticisms that Germond, misinformed, made of how Sandars had dealt with Maasina Rule.[37]

Davies's manuscript says that just after the verdict on the chiefs Noel sent

Germond a dispatch to tell him that Maasina Rule would now cease to be a threat and that police action would be unnecessary. I have not found this dispatch in the archives, and Davies's assertion does not match Noel's views at this time. Davies wrote in his manuscript that Noel blamed him for Maasina Rule's failure to dissolve, and he depicted Noel as, like Sandars, naive and soft on the movement. He blamed the failure on Noel for having given him insufficient resources to crush the movement and for having agreed to Davies being taken away to judge the preliminary examination. But if Noel was angry with Davies for having advised him to attack Maasina Rule, and for the dismal results, he did not commit it to writing; to do so would have exposed his own blunders, and he had presented some of Davies's flawed analyses to the high commissioner as his own. Be that as it may, two weeks after Germond's report, in early March, Noel replaced Davies with Michael Forster, who had just returned from leave.[38]

Soon after Germond arrived, he, with Davies and a police detachment, had made a three-week tour around the southern half of the island, just before the verdicts were announced. They visited nearly 100 places, and whereas before the arrests many southern people had met officers courteously, now Germond reported everywhere only "studied indifference and insolence" and a state of "suppressed revolt." Wherever Germond suggested native councils might be restarted, "I was told bluntly that there could be no question of this until the return of their leaders from Honiara and that in any case the councils would have to be run 'in accordance with Native Custom' which means that they must be free to run them their own way and not the Government way. The high sounding phrase 'in accordance with Native Custom' is just so much nonsense. Very few of the men who babble about 'Native Custom' know anything about Custom." Germond found the usage of *kastom* absurd: "This island has no administrative background—there never was any native judicial and administrative system as was the case in Africa and in some of the territories in the far East; therefore, to talk about Native Custom in so far as Courts and Councils are concerned does not make sense. In this respect it may be of interest to mention that at one of the District Centres I paraded all the 'Alahas' of the area who I was informed were the experts on Native Custom, they were almost to a man young Marching Rule adherents who, I am convinced, know almost as much as I do of 'Malaita Custom.'"[39]

Germond criticized the government's approach, without naming Davies: "The present mode of administration...can best be described as armed forays into a hostile country with no attempt at sustained or sympathetic contact with the people."[40] Yet for the rest of the decade this would remain most officers' primary mode of interaction with most Malaitans. Most wanted the sympathetic contact Germond called for, but on government terms—policy soon became that *all* Malaitans had to fully capitulate before government would deal with the island in any positive way. Most refused, concluding from the gendarme rule, oppression, and harassment that, despite timeworn promises of schools, medicine, and development if they cooperated, *gafamanu*'s (the government's) character and policies had changed little or had even deteriorated since the prewar years. Officers who knew little of the history of Malaita-government relations, or, like Germond, had been taught a distorted history by others, saw this attitude as ignorant and unreasonable.

Fences, Operation Jericho, and Civil Resistance

When the verdicts were announced on 15 February 1948, most Malaitans displayed little reaction—though, when Marquand toured 57 northern coastal towns soon after, many showed him their backs as he passed. Others told him that they would continue Maasina Rule and were ready to be arrested. Norman Deck, in the same area when people heard the judgments, found hostility and tried to convince people he was blameless. About two weeks later Forster returned as district commissioner, placed in charge, under Germond, of implementing government's program to break the back of Maasina Rule. He soon reported being shunned on Small Malaita and said that in west 'Are'are the convictions had been "a severe blow to their pride." He felt the south was less confident than the north, where he said the movement was dominant and people gave no thought to compromise, while in west Kwara'ae and Langalanga public opinion had hardened. Most defiant was the Kwai area, where police were barred from towns, and Assistant Headman Dausabea's house was reportedly burned. Davies later recalled more broadly that though Malaitans were dismayed by the chiefs' heavy sentences, they were "completely unbowed and, if anything, even more determined to hang on to Marching Rule than before."[41]

At this time many towns were rebuilt or newly built. Particularly in the south, but also in parts of the north, many non-Christians had after the arrests returned to the mountains to build towns or villages there, visiting the coast mostly for meetings. Christians urged them to stay, and some complained they were deserting the cause. Officers showed little inclination to bother inland towns. The week before Christmas of 1947, people had started to erect light fences around towns, first in the north and then everywhere.[42] Marquand described the fences in the north as a single rail, 4 feet high, with posts every 8 feet, decorated with cross-sticks and gates. They prevented no one from entering or leaving; some people, like Headman Siru, told Marquand that they were mere decoration, and others said they were to facilitate cleaning. Still others—Marquand does not say if they were Maasina Rule followers—said the fences would signal to any Americans who might come that the village was friendly. He thought the fences were harmless, intended merely to keep the people interested in Maasina Rule. He also met complaints from men outside Maasina Rule who said this town or that stood on their land and demanded eviction. Forster soon asked, seconded by Germond, that new ordinances be instituted under the 1947 Native Administration Regulation to forbid building any village for more than 40 people without an officer's approval, and to allow officers to order any villages built after 1944 removed if the majority of occupants were not landowners, on grounds that they might cause quarrels or be unsanitary.[43]

The government was as yet in no position to widely enforce such measures; police numbers were too low—Germond said he needed at least 80—and ships were under repair. "It is no good showing our hand until we are strong enough," Noel told Germond. He counseled him to be patient and plan for collecting taxes when they were ready, "For it is the collection of tax which will convince all except the fanatical amongst the Marching Rulers that not only can we rule, and intend to rule, but that we are ruling. 1948 must be a year of change." "By May," wrote a later resident commissioner, "the Divisional Officer and the Administrative Officers were ready to apply themselves to the imposition of the will of Government on the people."[44]

As it happened, the tax was not the first issue to be prosecuted. In June Noel issued an "Order" to people of Malu'u to remove all fences, for which they would be "held jointly and severally responsible." Forster and Germond proposed to Charles that if people reerected fences after they had been torn down they would be guilty of sedition, and that they as well as anyone suspected of "contemplating action likely to disturb the peace of Malaita" would be liable to deportation to Vanikolo in the distant eastern Solomons for up to two years. Charles feared other judicial commissioners would reject deportation under Article II of Pacific Order in Council (instituted to expel undesirable Europeans); to avoid this he advised that they exploit a rule whereby Noel could declare any location in the BSIP a "prison" and send people there. Charles also detailed how officers could tear down fences and other structures in people's private villages without being technically guilty of "trespass" or "forcible entry," and he suggested a Native Administration Regulation amendment to allow officers to destroy the fences without seeking an injunction from him. Later, in August 1949, he advised that fences and towers could be destroyed on sight without warrant because they were "seditious publications" and thus legally forfeited to the state, but Germond told officers to stick to established procedure, which "is more correct." Charles decreed that fences could be legally categorized as dangerous: "The enclosures are not in themselves dangerous. Their danger lies in their symbolism to the native mind of successful defiance of Government." Initiating what was to become a pattern for government decrees, the definition of fences as symbols of overt resistance was self-fulfilling.[45]

The anti-fence program was named "Operation Jericho," and Malu'u was picked to assault first since its people were believed to be leading the rest of Malaita, or at least the north. Also, it had been decided at Germond's urging to build a government station there, which Cameron, just back from leave, would open in June. Cameron wrote that the northern people reacted to Noel's order as he had expected: they built more fences. A deadline of 1 July was announced when arrests would begin wherever fences stood, but Cameron told Forster that since the "Maasina Rule must finish" order had gone unenforced, people were saying "Government 'im 'e talk no more." When Cameron spoke with leaders of the first villages scheduled for raids, they agreed that the fences should be removed but said they were powerless to make people take them down—an argument Cameron called an "old Marching Rule gambit."[46]

Officers could only wonder who were the real leaders, though they knew that 'Atoomea's uncle, Shem Irofa'alu, was one. In fact, excepting Irofa'alu, no overarching leaders had replaced the head chiefs. Nonetheless, Noel conjured up leaders for High Commissioner Freeston, "fanatical in their dislike of British rule," who "appreciate that they are beginning to lose that vicious omnipotent grip they had over all and sundry." This he said was behind their orders to make fences in "defiance to Government authority," so as to prevent young men leaving towns or villages to work on plantations. (Forster had just reported that across Malaita perhaps only 50 men might be willing to sign on as indentured labor.) The government, Noel argued, had to show the many "waverers" that it had the power to "free them from fenced in villages," from which, he wrote, many "desire to escape and secure once more their personal liberty." This elusive mass of "waverers" became a perpetual government hope. From this point forward, Noel would credit almost every action taken and rumor heard on Malaita to vicious, omnipotent Marching Rule leaders.[47]

On 1 July 1948, Operation Jericho was launched with the arrest of all of Malu'u's 28 men, including Irofa'alu. They were tried before Charles, and most were sentenced to two months at hard labor. Over the following days Cameron and his police arrested a total of 99 men from three other villages. They waited for him, lined up for arrest with kits packed, and pleaded guilty. He opined that they employed civil resistance because, as Europeans had said since the nineteenth century, Malaitans had "no physical courage."[48]

After a ten-day "truce," the people still held firm, and Cameron proposed arresting all of the estimated 600 men in Malu'u Sub-district—but in shifts, so that no more than 400 would be in jail at once. "Except for the Headmen and their friends," he said, "the whole sub-district is enthusiastically pro Marching Rule." But Germond predicted that Malu'u people would get so tired of it all that they would stand down in two or three months, and he hoped this would frighten all other Malaitans into doing so as well. However, Cameron warned, if people did not give in, the government had to be prepared to jail most of the adult male population of the entire island. He found this prospect "alarming and it may be considered that in the long run the MR civil disobedience campaign is bound to succeed. However, Malaita is not India and from a purely technical point of view there is no reason why we should not be able to organise ourselves to cope with the problem. From an administrative point of view we should be able to do it without serious harm to the community; we may even do a certain amount of good." Still, Cameron worried about lasting effects of such "a full scale attack": "Over an entire generation is going to pass through our prisons. Their experience during the next two months is going to influence their attitude toward us, hence Malaita politics, for the next 30 years, possibly permanently." Meanwhile, Germond pondered whether Shem Irofa'alu had Gandhi's moral courage and intelligence.[49]

Over the first eight months of the campaign, only three places tore down their fences, and a prisoner cap of 400 proved unrealistic. In August, Noel told Freeston there were 25,000 people in the northern towns and that they had to arrest every man there since they did not know who the leaders were—and if tactics changed and leaders stepped up "for martyrdom" such that only they were arrested, Malaitans would detect a "government admission of weakness." He offered a domino theory: if rule was not imposed in the north, a militant form of Maasina Rule might engulf the Protectorate. He expected that a limited number of operations would convince Malaitans "that the British Government is not impotent and that Marching Rule is a tragic farce." This letter is a prime example of Noel's pattern of hoodwinking high commissioners into allowing his oppressive tactics; unless one takes him for an utter fool, it is an exercise in distortion and deception. It worked; Freeston responded with blanket agreement.[50]

In mid-August, Cameron laid out plans for Operation Jericho Phase II, which would expand raids into Lau and selected major towns elsewhere in the north, into early October. Forster now reported Maasina Rule's influence waning in the north, even in Kwara'ae, and that it was completely finished in Baegu, but he warned, "Disaffections from the Marching Rule are no cause for complacency because they mean no more than that the people are tired of it and it by no means follows that they become pro-Government." Cameron, too, now submitted an upbeat report from To'abaita saying that people had made no new fences, were friendlier, and were ready to obey government orders. But just three days later, Marquand, now in charge of 'Aoke, reported that women and children at nearby Abu had rebuilt fences as soon as they were torn down, directed by an old man named 'Akote'e. Soon Cameron conceded that his To'abaita report had been "over-optimistic"; people were queuing up for prison again, this time for resisting his attempts to census them, or for refusing to pay fines he tried to impose in lieu of jail. He and Forster blamed the setback on Shem Irofa'alu's recent return from prison, and they urged Germond to deport him. Irofa'alu's influence could not be countered, Forster said, since it was religious. Norman Deck tried to turn Shem: "I have again stressed the Christian principle, enunciated in Romans 13:1–7, of non-resistance against properly constituted authority, as I think this will appeal to his conscience."[51]

This scenario was to be replayed over and again: Officers reported Maasina Rule to be on its last legs and resistance in decline, with the news relayed up to the resident, the high commissioner, and even to London. The pattern was that the higher the position held by a report's intended recipient, the more upbeat the report was.[52] But in each case these hopes were soon dashed by renewed defiance, often in reaction to officers trying to consolidate a perceived advantage by intensified suppression. This unremitting cycle of illusion and disillusion bred a frustration that soon became palpable in reports, yet officers at every level were to prove unable to reassess and revise their approach. They became trapped in a mindset in which the only way forward was to pursue a still harder line. Any conciliatory move, however reasonable, had to be scrupulously avoided for fear that it would be taken as a government admission of weakness. Cameron's warning about permanently poisoning the Malaitan political well was forgotten in a dogged quest to force submission.

This was not simply a matter of muddled strategy. In 1950 Marquand wrote, "The machine for implementing the policy of arrest had started and could not now stop without loss of face." Officers' "determination to show that they were the masters" was "aggravated by the lack of respect shown by the people," and thinking in the terms of the past, the officers "still consider that they have sufficient force to impose their will as their grandfathers did," and "do not think, or perhaps do not realize, their force is rather weak." To resolve the situation, he advised, the government had to sacrifice face and accept people's right to have their own leaders.[53]

On the other side, Malaitans were just as loath to surrender, not only in the immediate sense of abandoning Maasina Rule resistance, but also in the larger one of resubmitting to a system of alien rule that they believed would continue to be humiliating and unjust. Increasingly, this became the overriding motivation for resistance, and government oppression and demeaning actions simply reinforced the widespread belief that colonial attitudes and actions would never change without a determined struggle.[54]

In late August 1948, Forster reported that in some places on the east central coast, particularly at Uru in Kwaio, people were building not just fences but virtual stockades. One at Ilanunu at Uru had a gate, and the local headman Maenaa'adi was refused entry and treated "generally rudely." Others were being built at Sinalagu, 'Oloburi, and in adjacent east Kwara'ae. Like some towns elsewhere around Malaita at this time (but not in 'Are'are), these had watchtowers 50 and more feet tall. Lookouts manned these crow's nests with conch horns to blow an alarm if government ships approached. Forster called for a surprise attack on Uru to arrest the men in the towns and force them to tear down the structures, and Germond concurred. Forster proposed also to demolish the local SSEM chapel, "as it has undoubtedly been used as a center of sedition"; he reasoned, "As Deck has described the M.R. as damned I don't see that he would have any objections." If at the same time they destroyed structures at Kwai and Ngongosila, Forster said, "I think the M.R. would just about be done." At his request warship HMS *Shoalhaven* passed through the area. He sought warrants to arrest Anifelo, Jason Frankie, 'Adifaka, and other Kwaio for instigating the building, but only 'Adifaka was arrested.[55]

Uru was raided on 21 October 1948, and 'Ilemi (Fifi'i's home) and Laalalo towns at Sinalagu soon after. Ganifiri's former base of Naafinua, a town with 600–700 inhabitants, was attacked on 6 December. A letter from 'Adifaka in jail had been smuggled out, warning of the impending raids, so Kwaio and Kwara'ae people met to decide who should stay to be arrested while leaders repaired to the bush. Mountain people had been summoned to the coast, but after a brief stay and no sign of police they went home. When the police did come, 61 Kwaio were arrested, and the next day 20 men were ordered to raze the Ilanunu stockade. They declined until they were threatened with bayonets, at which they began to work. When women berated the men to stop, Forster had 21 of *them* arrested, prompting the men to sit down and refuse orders. The women were jailed in the 'Aoke lunatic asylum to separate them from male prisoners.[56]

Women's roles in the resistance have been missed or even denied in previous accounts of Maasina Rule. Most of the exceptions have been mentions of their pressuring men to end their resistance, but as Fox wrote, "The Government hoped that the women, left to do all the heavy garden work the men usually did, would persuade their men-folk to give in; it was not realized that the women were in the movement as strongly as the men." Later, in places in the north, some women did so pressure men, but many communities appointed specific men to comply with tax or census demands, or to evade arrest, so as to be able to stay home and help them. Men also intensified their work before pending arrests; when the government announced a plan to tax and census Malaitans in late 1949, a Catholic priest at Buma wrote, "All the natives are now feverishly working their gardens in preparation to go to gaol for five months." Women sometimes pressed men *not* to capitulate, as in the Uru episode just described. The absence of women in writings about Maasina Rule is partly a result of officers' keenness to discount and expunge their role, especially Germond, who in October 1948 replaced Noel in an acting capacity until early 1950. The report on the Kwaio raids that he sent to Freeston, who requested one in advance, omitted the 21 women from both the report and prisoner count. Trench, writing for Germond from Honiara, ordered Forster not to proceed further against the women he had jailed until Germond arrived, and I have found no subsequent mention of them.[57]

In November, Germond issued officers formal orders on Maasina Rule policy, which stated, "The female population do not and must not come into the picture at all. We have no quarrel with the women folk for this is a 'game' which does not fall within their province. The native understands and appreciates this as he has shown time after time in our recent operations on Malaita." He no doubt feared, and rightly so, that to drop this fiction and arrest women across Malaita would both further inflame the situation and jeopardize the support he required from his superiors for the campaign to continue. It would also have undercut the claim that one reason the movement had to be repressed was that it oppressed women. Europeans had long depicted Malaitan women as docile drudges who toiled under men, and portrayals of them having no part in Maasina Rule played to this stereotype. Women's exclusion from the Maasina Rule record is but one facet of the invisibility of women and their perspectives in the colonial archive concerning Malaita, though it stands out in its calculation.[58]

Women sometimes took even more active roles in the resistance. In his mid-twenties, Tom Titiuru of Ulawa was a member of the constabulary charged with raiding towns. In 1987 he recounted to me how the men in the watchtowers would see them approaching, and sometimes women and children would leave: "By the time we got there only the men would be left.... Sometimes they would all be standing in a line ready to go to prison. Most people behaved very well, especially in Small Malaita and in 'Are'are, and Makira.... But in the north everyone would be in the villages when we came, even the women would be there throwing stones at us while we were tearing down the fences [the men by then having been arrested]. And they would all be cursing us." Germond's instructions that women "must not come into the picture at all" is probably why such episodes are invisible in most reports and thus have been mostly hidden from the purview of historians. After Germond's orders, one finds few mentions of women at all, though Peter Hughes did note in an early 1949 telegram, "Allan reports women taking more active part at arrests." And that May, Allan said the women in one Makwanu town "massed to cheer their men folk as they were marched off" to jail, and at 'Ofakwasi town at Fokanakafo, "as the prisoners were marched off, the women burst into hysterical shouting and crying and made to follow the men through the gateway. Imprecations and oaths were shouted to the [Western Solomons] police who fortunately did not understand and for a moment the atmosphere was unpleasant." Any Malaitan man would have been speedily arrested for such behavior. Shortly after, some women in the north were found to have started rumors that all Maasina Rule opponents were to be exiled from Malaita, and they were warned that if they repeated those rumors they would be arrested.[59]

Even putting aside that women were watching husbands, fathers, brothers, and sons jailed for standing up to the government, they had shared men's humiliations and suffered hardships under the indenture system that Maasina Rule was repudiating. Recall that women had marched on 'Aoke in 1943 to demand return of their men from the Labour Corps. Women were not apolitical, and the idea that they were expressed not only a dismissal (or fear) of their agency but also the view that Maasina Rule was an abstract, male ideological cause, "a game," rather than an earnest protest against real privations and degradations shared by all Malaitans.

Resistance was not always fully passive even among the 'Are'are, despite their more benign reputation with officers and police. Titiuru described another incident in which he and other police landed on a beach in the southeast: "We were ordered not to shoot anyone except in self-defense. I remember during one raid at Takataka a crowd came down and slowly walked toward us and backed us up until we were knee-deep in the ocean, and then waist-deep, neck-deep, and finally we were out there floating and swimming. [Akin: "What did they say?"] No, no! They didn't *say* anything! They just came down, and they were having fun with us. Maybe a thousand people, or two thousand. And we only fifty soldiers. We were very frightened."[60]

Such actions were not the norm, and the dominant Malaitan mode of response to Operation Jericho was a well-ordered civil resistance campaign, carried out mostly in the north where officers focused their attentions and actions. A puzzling feature of the literature on Maasina Rule is how little attention it pays to this, given that it was for so long the movement's key strategy and the principal target of government's attempts to end it—civil resistance was the crux of the matter, yet many writers seem unaware that there was any, and no one has stressed its intensity and central importance. Some state only that thousands were arrested, suggesting either pervasive Malaitan disorder or that the government simply rounded up and jailed people.

Other writers have not just omitted the civil resistance but have told of violence by Malaitans or officers that never took place. Many merely implied this with references to unspecified "Maasina Rule militants" or "terrorism." Others went farther, like William Davenport and Gülbün Çoker, who said that the government only resorted to suppression after "tax collectors had been attacked." (No postwar tax was instituted until late 1949, and the officers and headmen collecting it were not attacked.) Gideon Zoleveke recalled, "Inevitably the police were brought in to maintain order, violence broke out and lives were lost." Belshaw credited the establishment of native courts and councils on Gela in early 1948 with the fact that there, "political discontent did not reach the peak of violence that it has reached in other areas." Remo Guidieri wrote, "For the first time, violent political conflict between colonized and colonizer became inevitable. The chronicle of the Maasina Rule that ended in the violent suppression of the movement around 1948 was marked by deaths, by military expeditions on the part of the colonial administration, by bloody suppressions and prison." In Allan's 1950 anthropology thesis, an entire section titled "Terrorist Tactics" alleges, "Flags were being carried from village to village, drilling was increasing,

open threats to British life and property were being offered and mass meetings, accompanied by mass-hysteria were becoming more popular." But
beyond this sentence of crass distortion, the thesis mentions nothing that
could be construed as "terrorist." A section called "Passive Resistance" tells
merely of refusals to destroy fences and says nothing of the thousands he
and others had arrested for civil resistance. Later Allan said that the head
chiefs were arrested due to "evidence of bodily injury sustained by a number
of people" and that at every 'Aoke Maasina Rule meeting from 1946 onward
"rioting had narrowly been avoided." None of these authors cite sources for
these statements, even each other, and the statements are false. Most writers
were ignorant of the facts; others, like Allan, distorted intentionally. The
Maasina Rule years saw just one anomalous, tragic death, when a policeman
shot a man in self-defense in a confused situation, an incident to which
I will return. The truth is, there was an extraordinary dearth of violence
despite the years of intense repression and resistance and high emotions on
both sides—something for which both Malaitans and government officers
deserve high praise.[61]

To be jailed for the cause was honorable, and especially during Operation Jericho people went to prison with enthusiasm, under sardonic mottos
like "Eat government rice," or "Work free for government."[62] As described
by Marquand, who was in charge of many arrests, they believed "they had
done nothing to justify this treatment by the Government and determined
to show their disapproval with dignified passive resistance." Malaita's 1949–
1950 Annual Report recorded, "Impatient ones crossed the island to a village that was to be arrested rather than wait for their turn. Adolescents
and young boys, mere children, entered the line with their fathers, uncles
and brothers and sometimes had to be forcibly ejected, as tears of disappointment streamed down their faces." Marquand observed the "faultless
discipline," excepting such young men and old ones unhappy at being
pulled from the arrest lines. "Courts were convened on the spot," wrote
Tom Russell, " 'Rex v Alabaia and ninety-nine others,' and off they went."
Allan reported that Baelelea men resented having been ignored in favor of
Fataleka and that they eagerly awaited the soldiers; and after arrest operations were carried out there, he believed, "The single month gaol term has
given every man in Baelelea a personal stake in the Marching Rule."[63]

Once men were jailed, security was easy. As Marquand wrote, "The prison
facilities being inadequate for such numbers [at times well over 1,000 at
'Aoke alone, with others in Honiara], the overflow were often billeted in
ordinary houses, and sometimes unguarded; and yet they made no attempt
to escape. They worked, armed with picks and shovels, in gangs of up to
fifty and sometimes more, guarded by one warder, generally insufficiently
trained, armed with a truncheon. They worked hard and conscientiously
without complaint, and once released and return home, they are treated
very well by their own folk as soldiers are who return from the wars." Russell

gave a similar account of some 1,500 prisoners who toiled on an 'Aoke to Malu'u road in 1949, when each warder oversaw 100 men. In this peculiar symbolic struggle, Malaitan prisoners experienced the government's power to impose its will as embodied in isolated, untrained guards carrying sticks. In March 1949, Germond told High Commissioner Freeston that prison labor had built 24 kilometers of road; a Fiu river bridge; a police camp, barracks, and school at 'Aoke; and the Malu'u station. These accomplishments he hoped would help to defray the extra £10,000 cost of operations on Malaita for the 1948–1949 fiscal year and the £10,000 more projected for the coming year. Allan, however, said in mid-1949 that ration costs for those arrested for fences and census refusals in To'abaita alone had been £10,000, "or about £62 per Marching Rule adherent censused." The government that had for decades suffered a lack of money from London to develop Malaita was now given ample funding to jail its populace.[64]

Germond's November 1948 directive said that his anti-Maasina policy was one of simple direct rule. Officers were to announce: "Government will not tolerate Marching Rule *in any shape or form* and is determined to stamp it out and obtain the submission of the people to its authority and to that of its approved native officers [ie, headmen]." They were not to discriminate: "What is sauce for the goose is sauce for the gander, in other words what is good for Malu'u is good for Ari Ari." They were strictly forbidden to vary from this policy, since Malaitans had to know it was that of the government and not of an individual officer. The goal was "to impose the will of Government over the people" through destruction of fences, forced compliance with a census, and "the reimposition of taxation on the *whole* island." These steps would be pursued in that order, he said, since each required the completion of the previous stage: fences prevented access for censusing (in truth, few did), which was necessary to compile rolls for the taxation, expected to begin on 1 April. Germond's resolve to avoid all nuance bred a simplistic, hard-line approach with no flexibility. As with the unremitting decree of 1947 that "Marching Rule must end," the government placed itself in a position from which it feared that any policy modification, negotiation, or gesture of reconciliation would lead Malaitans to think that it was backing down—which indeed it would be by the terms of its own proclamations.[65]

The Census and the Tax, 1949

With Noel's "year of change" now over, in early 1949 Malaita's officers met in 'Aoke to set new strategy for the coming months. They estimated that more than 150 fenced towns and villages remained on Malaita, and, unlike the biblical Jericho, once destroyed these could quickly be rebuilt. Forster, under Germond's November plan, expected to arrest 300 men a month, while Colin Allan, who had just taken over Malu'u from Cameron, would arrest 200. But at Forster's lead it was decided that pulling down fences would be unproductive—they had lost much of their symbolic significance and did not restrict movement, and while people still made or repaired some of them, many were simply rotting away. "The real symbol of Marching Rule power and principles was in the town itself," said Forster, and the fence policy "slowly applied would, and in fact was, raising a nagging resentment and not the respect for authority which was necessary if Government were to prevail." He tabled a new approach in which officers would inspect towns and, if they were deemed unsanitary—and Forster clearly thought most could be—condemn and destroy them, "if necessary by fire." For speed's sake officers would arrest only those who resisted. However, when Germond received their plan he rejected it and insisted his policy as previously stated be followed to the letter.[66]

Readers know that Forster, before taking leave in March 1947 for "nervous exhaustion," was devoted to Malaita and close to southern people. Perhaps this was a factor in what now proved to be his inability to maintain composure in the face of defiance and disrespect. He suffered this more than other officers because, as in the past, he toured almost continuously (now with a large police contingent); Cameron in January asked that routine Malu'u matters be administered separately because Forster was so rarely at 'Aoke. Forster's assessment of Maasina Rule had always been capricious, reacting to events at hand. Even now he was more openly sympathetic to Malaitan grievances than were other officers, but with the people in full, if civil, rebellion, Forster proposed the most drastic tactics, such as destroying Uru's SSEM church and burning towns. Matters came to a head on 26 February when he arrested 51 'Are'are men at Takataka—essentially because he was offended by their demeanor—and charged them with rioting. When all but four refused his attempt to, in effect, extort shell money deposits from them for future good behavior, he sentenced them to six months in prison. A headman protested, and Germond asked for a report and sent it to Charles, who declared Forster's actions "inexcusable," "a serious dereliction of duty," and "a mere travesty of a trial," which gave an impression that Forster was "actuated by anger and a desire for revenge and not a desire to do justice." Charles saw no evidence that most of the men, who had by now been in jail for six weeks, had broken any law, and he said they should be released. Germond conceded the injustice but urged Freeston not to order their release pending review since to do so would undermine government authority.[67]

As 1949 began, more than 2,000 Malaitans had been arrested, and many more soon would be. This is a fitting place to pause and note how unhappy most officers were as they carried out these actions. None had come to the Solomons seeking this sort of job. In Russell's words, "Those of us who went out into the colonial service after the War, we'd had a year's academic study at Cambridge or Oxford with three months at London University, doing regional anthropology, languages, if they could teach you one, under Evans-

Pritchard and Raymond Firth. And we really believed that our mission, the career we'd chosen, was decolonization." Further, the staff "profoundly disliked the imprisonment policy which they were directed to implement, and had a sneaking feeling of regret when it undoubtedly paid off." That some officers did not share Russell's perspective is evident from their writings, but we have seen that Marquand came to see the suppression he took part in as ineffectual and unjust, and Forster was obviously a troubled man. How many of them came to think as Marquand or Russell did I cannot say; most were in no position to write critiques of policy, and few recorded their candid views after. In mid-1954, District Commissioner Val Andersen wrote that due to "strenuous and exacting" conditions, since the start of 1947 only one Malaita officer had finished his full term there.[68]

What is clear is that mass arrests wrecked officer-Malaitan relations and scuttled government objectives—above all its two declared, essential goals of securing respect and acceptance of its legitimacy and Malaitans' cooperation toward advancing its plans. Well-intentioned officers arrived to find themselves pegged as the enemy; a handful of young men bore the brunt of Malaitan resentments built up across decades of misrule, neglect, and degradation. Colonial officers typically lived under less than luxurious conditions with a heavy workload, and few would call them overpaid (they joked that they were "the cheapest form of labor in the colonies"), but a mitigating factor for many had been that in their jurisdictions they held positions of status, responsibility, and power, in the sense of an ability to make things happen. Now they found themselves among a population who refused to grant them either respect or authority, with their principal duty being to punish them for this. Without proper briefing in even recent Malaitan history, let alone training in local cultures or languages, most officers could not fully fathom the anger they met, which therefore seemed to them unreasonable, offensive, bigoted, or irrational.[69] It is little wonder that through their time on Malaita some officers came to dislike the people with increasing intensity, as expressed in their reports. The atmosphere was noxious and, in terms of strategizing, debilitating. During 1948 and 1949, in particular, when policy did change it was generally in the direction of still further repression, with public humiliation the weapon of choice. Later shifts toward conciliation were to be instituted by officers who had spent little time on Malaita and were not caught up in this crippling cycle.

Readers may think it misplaced to highlight the plight and unhappiness of a handful of officers in a period when thousands of Malaitans were being imprisoned away from their homes and families for what they felt were acts of conscience. Yet it is critical to be aware of the subjective factors that contributed to officers' actions and shaped government policy. It is also important to keep sight of the fact that most of Malaita's officers during this period were charged with carrying out policy rather than making it, particularly once Germond took charge.

The officer who bore the bulk of the work and strain of mass arrests in the near term was Colin Allan. As his predecessor Cameron had recommended, Germond in mid-March designated a new "Malu'u Sub-district" that included the area north of Kwara'ae, to be administered largely apart from the rest of the island. At the same time, Germond ordered an intensification of anti-fence enforcement and census taking in that area, particularly along the eastern coast. This escalation, titled "Operation Orestes," ran from 12 April to 16 May. As Orestes began, Operation Jericho by itself had resulted in the arrest of more than 2,000 Malaitans, the large majority of whom served at least a month in jail for refusing to destroy fences. Malu'u's police, under Choiseulese Sergeant Frank Taburi, had torn down 41 fences, though by early 1949 many were so rotted that they were hard to find and even loyal headmen puzzled over why Allan arrested people for them.[70]

Allan reported that fences now meant nothing to people except as symbols of defiance; he said, "If Government were, for instance, to ban the wearing of grass hats popularized by some members of Marching Rule, that order, too, would be resisted and all who wished to sacrifice themselves to the Marching Rule by going to gaol, would automatically wear grass hats."[71] In fact, Germond's approach was no different than the Malaitan one Allan described—at issue were symbols, not substance. Germond's goal was not simply to make people obey the law, as officers often flatly stated, but rather to make new laws to ban whatever symbols of resistance they employed and force them to either capitulate and be humbled or go to jail. This was an aggressive policy of mass humiliation.

In just over a month, Orestes arrested 1,060 more people, and Allan calculated that over 76 percent of the men in Malu'u Sub-district had been given jail sentences of 2–16 weeks. In places, 80–99 percent were imprisoned, most not for the first time. Not arrested were the old and infirm, the 5 percent who quietly agreed to be censused in private (almost never publicly), and men who ran away. Some of the latter two groups had been chosen by their communities to stay home to work. Several area headmen refused to be censused and went to jail. At saltwater villages, people readied for the police by decorating their decomposing towers with flowers and bunting, and men put on dancing regalia. An overarching goal of Orestes had been to prove to people that the government had the ability to "arrest the entire population of Malaita desiring to go to gaol for the Marching Rule." After it was over, Allan worried it had done no good and had actually harmed census plans. People had started to bring some legal and other problems to Malu'u station for help, but Orestes ended that. Intelligence also dried up as Allan's primary function became to arrest people. This made Malu'u administrative work "impossible," and Allan reported his situation as "unfortunate and unhappy." In a summary report to Germond, however, he conveyed Headman Kakalu'ae's worry that police actions had been too weak and jail sentences too short, and that in consequence the government might lose the respect of even the few loyalists. Germond highlighted this concern in the report's margin and wrote one large, underscored word: "Tax."[72]

Taxation indeed was to be the new focus of arrests, though census and fence prosecutions would continue. This was all to proceed under a new district commissioner. Though Forster remained through 30 May 1949, Germond had in February decided to replace him, even before the Takataka false arrest fiasco. Germond felt that Malaita's staff was not working together, that his officers held varied views of his approach, and that this might lead Malaitans to think that policy depended on officers' individual notions. Rev Arthur Devlin said Maasina Rule leaders in the area around Buma were happy when Forster was removed because he undermined their claims that the government was uninterested in people's welfare. Germond sent Forster to Guadalcanal and replaced him with Stanley "Monty" Masterman. A later resident commissioner called Masterman's appointment "not a very desirable move but necessary and unavoidable in view of the absence of experienced Administrative Officers." Even granting the staff shortage, the choice of Masterman for this most critical assignment in the Protectorate is baffling. His only qualification cited was that he had been in the Solomons for a long time. A likely explanation is that Germond expected Masterman to pursue his rigid policy without question and with gusto. If so, he was not disappointed.[73]

Except for serving in Europe during World War II, the 50-year-old Masterman had been in the Solomons since 1922, working mostly as a clerk or labor inspector. He had acted as secretary to the government from 1946 to 1948 but had no formal training in administration. Russell wrote, "He had two negative attributes.... He had no political antennae and was about the worst Pidgin English speaker in the service." More than one person described him as "old school." As a labor inspector in the 1930s, he had complained for years about not being promoted. This angered Resident Commissioner Ashley, who communicated to him in 1938, "The correspondence shows little evidence of your fitness for promotion, even were a suitable vacancy available." In 1935, Masterman was investigated for brutally beating a prisoner because, he told Ashley, the man "grinned in the manner that is objectionable in a certain type of native," and, "I think very few of us are willing to tolerate direct impertinence from natives."[74]

Many Malaitans would have heard in these remarks a fair indication of Masterman's attitude toward them. Today he stands alone among officers in his historical reputation as a churlish thug, and he is still cited as the epitome of a reviled type of European, even by young people who have only heard elders tell of him. His actions as district commissioner further worsened his standing. Policeman P V Collins, reporting on shots fired near Masterman's house at 'Aoke toward the end of his service in May 1950, wrote, "It is common knowledge here in Malaita that Major Masterman is utterly disliked by the majority of Malaitans, and from information received, people have sworn by native custom to kill him. Their dislike for him goes back to the time when he led a party into Sinarago District to suppress riots after the Bell murder." Masterman had to be placed under 24-hour police protection. To Malaitans, his selection to administer their island spoke loudly of the government's outlook and intentions, and for this alone it was a long stride backward. Fifiʻi told me in 1987 he thought Masterman was sent specifically to try to frighten people.[75] A keystone of Malaitan resentment and resistance was the disrespect Europeans had always paid them, and now a man who personified that attitude was being placed in charge.

As Masterman took office, Germond told him that while "the dogged resistance of the Malaitamen has not been broken," the government had achieved much—in having earned "the respect, if not the regard, of the people" in showing they could conduct mass arrests, in people no longer building fences, and in a few young men signing on as labor. "This being the position," Germond continued, "it is now time, not to relax, but to press on!" He promised more police and directed harsher sentences for fence and census offenses. When the 1950–1951 tax came due, Germond told Masterman, he should meet refusals to pay that, or the 1949–1950 tax, with further imprisonment.[76]

Masterman soon did increase sentences and proposed building "a holding cage at Sinerango on the site of the one I set up there in 1927." He destroyed a building identified as a church at Kwai and raided an Ulawa church service. The latter raid provoked charges that his men had stolen from houses and defecated in a Catholic church, and that one had exposed himself to women. Charles Fox wrote to W J Durrad of "police surrounding the [Ulawan] churches when the people were at prayers, and going in with fixed bayonets, telling the people not to bother about God, and arresting and taking to gaol every man on Ulawa except at [one] village." In early July, Masterman reported to Germond the first of what would become regular rumors of planned attacks against the government. Though these never developed beyond hot talk and rumor, they did indicate a general shift in mood.[77]

Two months after Masterman's appointment, Tom Russell arrived to take over Maluʻu from Allan. During the war he had been a parachutist and then a prisoner in Italy. He quickly began intensive touring of the north (Masterman even told him to make his tours shorter) and soon reported that Maasina Rule had become "an integral part of the social structure of Malaita" and was "likely to remain for some years." He said that eliminating it as a political force would be a long and slow process and that for the time being officers could only try to keep its adherents within the law.[78] Russell found that officer relations with the people had been "severely damaged" by the arrest policy and warned that the few links that remained might be destroyed: "That children should run screaming from an approaching Government officer on an Administrative tour is a serious indication of the present divorcement between people and the administration." He noted, too, the "coloring" of officers' and headmen's attitudes brought about by the people's "studied insolence, by the snubbing and ignoring of genuine efforts towards the common weal." Russell's own reports are notably free of slurs, and perhaps his attitude is one reason that some people soon grew friendlier toward him. He gave the example of people of one Fataleka town who offered up their Maasina Rule *kastom* (meeting) house for his party to sleep in. Masterman's comment on this captures his and Russell's dissimilar approaches: Masterman said he always occupied such houses "in any event as being the best in the place. That is one reason why I do not destroy them." The other reason was that he expected to soon put *kastom* houses to government use, after Maasina Rule had surrendered.[79]

Rumors, Hopes, and Fears

> There are always ten stories about a fight; the tenth and last is the one to believe.
> —*Lau proverb*[80]

As officers toiled to defeat Maasina Rule, Malaita was thick with rumors of still more drastic government actions to come, pending arrivals of foreign ships or troops, or looming apocalyptic wars. The rumors' frequency peaked in 1949 at the height of the arrest campaign, but they were not limited to that period. The stories proved impossible for either officers or Malaitan leaders to control and hampered the efforts of both to communicate their messages. Some Malaitans were motivated by these rumors to prepare for the events they warned of or promised.

People have disagreed as to the relationship of such ideas and actions to Maasina Rule. Some Europeans, particularly certain officers of the period, saw in them the movement's essence as a millennial movement or mystical "cargo cult," and for years anthropologists studied Maasina Rule within the cargo cult literature. In a historical study of the concept, Lamont Lindstrom described how "cargo cult" first surfaced in print in 1945, in a New Guinea resident's political diatribe in *Pacific Islands Monthly*. The basic idea in its crude form was that Melanesians, envying the wealth of whites but having only distorted understandings of how they got it, decided that it could be obtained magically, usually from the spirit world—the performance of proper rituals would summon goods in staggering quantities. This was said to express their primitive, magical worldview and cupidity. The phenomenon was at times portrayed in the singular as "the cargo cult," attributing sameness to diverse movements across time and the region, and even beyond. From this idea administrators and soon anthropologists constructed models for understanding Melanesians and their movements. In time, some anthropologists developed theories of cargo cults that were far more complex, nuanced, and varied, but the concept as applied by key colonial officers during Maasina Rule generally was not.[81]

The first BSIP officer to mark Maasina Rule as an instance of a broader Melanesian phenomenon was Noel in March 1947, just after the head chiefs told him of their strike plans. Reporting this to his officers and the high commissioner, he likened the movement to "strange transgressions from common sense" found in "Fiji, New Hebrides, Papua and New Guinea." We have seen how Trench equated Maasina Rule with "cults astonishingly similar" in New Guinea and thereby absolved BSIP policies of any blame for it. Belshaw later cited the Ulawa incident described in chapter 6 as having sparked his interest in "messianic movements," and in 1950, in an *Australian Intelligence Digest* article that was distributed to officers, he submitted Maasina Rule as "a strange native cult," representative (along with the Fallowes movement) of a general type.[82] Colin Allan's 1950 anthropology master's thesis at Cambridge, supervised by Reo Fortune and finished just before Allan became Malaita's district commissioner, portrayed Maasina Rule as most importantly an irrational cult seeking magical cargo delivery. According to anthropologist Davenport, whom the government consulted on various matters during the 1960s, Allan's thesis "became sort of the official version of the movement to subsequent administrators in the Protectorate." Allan later donated a copy to the Malaita District Office for his successors, suggesting that they read it along with "Mr R Davies' excellent political section in the 1947 Annual Report."[83]

For officers who could not understand Malaitans or why they were so unhappy, the cargo cult model was simplifying and liberating. It explained Maasina Rule, obscured political and ethical grievances, and morally validated repression as saving Malaitans from their own folly. More specifically, the government's most fundamental problem with the movement was, as Noel so often emphasized and as Allan put it in the opening paragraph of his thesis, "the stranglehold which it has had on the Protectorate's economy." The cargo cult portrayal suggested that Maasina Rule could not be dealt with as a labor movement because Malaitan economic thought was delusional. Europeans often stressed the idea that Melanesians thought wealth could be "free." Officers lectured them that prosperity came not from cargo but hard work, and the BSIP Annual Report for 1948 scolded, "Marching Rule leaders must learn that the world does not owe Solomon Islanders a living." Noel and other key officers were confident this argument would soon win the day since they believed Malaitans judged power and most everything else in materialistic terms, and cargo cultism would not deliver the goods. In other words, the materialist core of the cargo cult model was central to its meaning and usage and to how officers subscribing to it tried to combat Maasina Rule. It diverted some officers from considering or addressing practical Malaitan concerns and thus severely undermined their effectiveness.[84]

As occurred with other Melanesian movements, traits of "the cargo cult" absent from Maasina Rule were at times attributed to it, sometimes taken from New Guinea anecdotes, and minor features were inflated to fit the type. Among other things, this was good propaganda for checking criticisms that might surface abroad that officers were repressing legitimate labor or political actions. An excerpt from a story from the *Sydney Herald* will illustrate:

> Marching rule is similar to the New Guinea cargo cult. The natives believe that ships laden with goods and food are due to arrive shortly, and that they will then enjoy a Utopian life with everything free and no work. The difference is that in New Guinea they think the ships will be manned by their own dead ancestors, while the marching rule adherents expect them to be manned by Americans—they regard the shipments as a magic form of Marshall Aid.... British officials in the Solomons have found marching rule a great nuisance. Thousands of natives, at times, have refused to work or co-operate with the Administration.... There were a number of similar cults among the North American Indians when the palefaces moved into their territory.

I know of no organized conspiracy to spread such portrayals, but officers did give them to the press. For example, the high commission's chief secretary, G D Chamberlain, told the same newspaper about movement promises: "In September 1947 Liberty ships crammed with goods would appear off the Solomons; The skin of all the natives would change from black to white; European houses, complete with refrigerators and bathrooms, would be distributed free to the natives; and never-ending supplies of food, drink, and comforts would be handed to the natives," and "when these things did not materialise 'Marching Rule' suffered a setback."[85]

While some officers highlighted cargo beliefs as the mainstay of Maasina Rule, others in their writings minimized their significance or do not mention them at all.[86] This second view was more in line with that of later historians and anthropologists, who challenged the cargo cult portrayal as a misrepresentation of what was actually a movement for social advancement or liberation. Most allowed that some cargo-like ideas were in circulation but discounted their importance. Keesing wrote, "Cargo doctrines were peripheral in Maasina Rule, if they occurred at all," and Laracy later said, "The expectation of the arrival of 'cargo' was never a major influence on Maasina Rule thinking or behavior." Peter Worsley claimed that cargo ideas were "lingering myths" and unimportant on Malaita.[87] These writers all provided vital corrections to past distortions. That said, in rectifying cargo cult distortions one must be careful not to obscure less practical ideas and activities that did motivate many Malaitans, ideas that could be just as political in spirit as strikes or civil resistance but were based on misconceptions of global political realities.

Some Malaitans did suppose that Americans could bring goods—and not only in later stages of the movement, as is sometimes asserted. Sandars wrote in Malaita's 1946 Annual Report that over the preceding year some Malaitans had thought Americans might bring "boatloads of free supplies...and free issues of cutter boats and all the good things in life," and the next July he noted, "The hopes of free cargoes from the Americans still persists although I feel sure that in their hearts they know it is false." There is ample archival and oral evidence that such ideas circulated widely, evoking Malaitan reactions ranging from belief, to skepticism, to laughter.[88] An episode at Uru in Kwaio shows how they could coexist with other very different expectations and actions. In 1982, Saelasi Lounga of Uru told me what happened there in 1948 when people learned Forster and his soldiers planned to raid their town of Ilanunu, and rumors spread:

> The Americans are out there at sea watching everything we do. If the government tears down our fences, then Americans will come and defeat them, and kill off all of their soldiers. They are waiting off to the side. And cargo [Pijin *kago*] will come. The Americans will bring it for all of you. When you move down to the sea don't worry about going hungry there; Americans will be bringing cargo for you all, and we will eat what they bring. There is a big submarine [Pijin *daefasifi*, or "diver ship"] out at sea. Everyone go down to the sea, and when the submarine comes...all of you will go inside until it is full, and it will take all of you to America. And there will be plenty of cargo left for those who stay behind. Those are the lies they told.[89]

As described earlier, the soldiers destroyed Ilanunu in October, and Lounga said this left some people disillusioned: "The government said, 'Who told you to build these things for war?' And they chopped down every tower at Uru, and every fence....We thought, 'Hey! The Americans they said would come, the Americans to fight with us, what's taking them so long?'" Lounga did not identify the "they" who spread the stories, but Kwaio generally blamed people to the north.[90]

Several Kwaio have told me of participating in this event, and some talked of hopes that Americans might come. Yet only Lounga stressed "cargo" (or mentioned submarine trips), and most said nothing about it unless I asked, at which they responded with something like, "Oh yes, some people said Americans would bring *kago*." This resembled accounts of Noto'i's 1939 movement, in which the idea that Americans would bring wealth was mentioned only as an afterthought, when Keesing or I asked about it. People did not omit mention of cargo due to embarrassment; a common theme was chagrin for thinking Americans might come at all, and people laugh at their gullibility. No one ever hesitated to discuss cargo ideas when I broached them.

Forster's reports mention no Americans; he saw Kwaio fenced towns as a political challenge to the government. That leaders were not behind the rumors seems clear in that, on learning of the coming raid, they called a meeting to decide who would stay to be arrested. Further, mountain people—and the large majority of Kwaio then lived inland—told me they went to the coast reluctantly, under pressure from people there to show solidarity against the raid, and that they heard rumors about Americans but few believed them. Forster's account supports this: "All bush people were induced to come down to the shore on Saturday but when the Government did not appear that day they went back to the bush next morning. A similar attempt to induce the bush people at Sinalagu to support the people of Lalalo [Laalalo town] and Ileni ['Ilemi] was frustrated by [Headman David Ridley,] who told the bushmen that the notice only applied to the Lalalo and Ileni people. The bush people seemed pleased to hear this and went away." In fact, at Sinalagu some mocked Christians angry at their departure: "It's good for them to arrest you, to protect us all! It will leave we bush people strong to carry on the work. You should not be angry!"[91]

Here leaders prepared people for a civil resistance action, which, as described earlier, is what did happen, but rumors that Americans would come, with and without goods, piggybacked on the event, and different participants held varied expectations. This was likely true of similar episodes around Malaita, though sadly we currently have no reliable, multiperspective accounts of events elsewhere. Lounga truthfully told of cargo hopes, just as officers and informants did at times, but obviously this event cannot be reduced to those. Yet desires for American goods should not be dismissed as trivial, since they did inspire some people, and others thought it possible they might turn up. Remember that Americans had recently expelled the Japanese and, by local standards, bestowed great wealth. In Keesing's words, "Solomon Islanders had been up to their ears in real cargo." Furthermore, some US soldiers advertised their dislike for the British (even to their faces), counseled Islanders to rebel, and said America might keep its new bases. To many Malaitans it seemed feasible that the United States might come to their aid and perhaps, as before, also bring good things. They built hopes on the interpersonal politics they knew and had pursued with US soldiers, not realizing its irrelevance to global politics.[92]

Speculating on how "cargo" beliefs got to Malaita, Keesing focused on diffusion through plantation networks. Malaitans also at times had access to *Pacific Islands Monthly*. Tim Fulbright has suggested that officers' denunciations of cargo ideas may have piqued Malaitan interest in them. That could also be true for other ideas about American help, since officers lectured people on their absurdity, as they had to Labour Corps men.[93] Still more likely is that such derision led anti–Maasina Rule informants to stress cargo ideas in their reports—most news of them in archives came from informants. Many Malaitans came to believe that loyalists were trying to undermine the movement by inflating cargo beliefs in their statements to officers or even by starting the rumors; Waleanisia told me that Langalanga people accused loyalist Lau headman Tome Wate with initiating them, and Fifiʻi made the same charge. Tricksters were certainly at work; Aliki, once a duty at Kwai in Kwaraʻae, in 1992 told me of an incident, notorious across Malaita, in which two men littered a beach with boot tracks, cigarette butts, and tin cans scavenged at ʻAoke, and the next morning called them to everyone's attention as evidence a submarine had come, causing great excitement.[94]

My oral historical data from the east coast indicates that for most but not all people, "cargo" expectations were secondary, fleeting, or nonexistent. More common and enduring were hopes that Americans would drive out the British and become political benefactors (sometimes with grim consequences for loyalists). One can consider these ideas separately, but note that while those seeking liberation were often blasé or dismissive toward cargo ideas, rumors of cargo always predicted that liberation would arrive with it. The distinction is, I think, not as significant as has sometimes been implied. The concern to separate the two, and then to minimize cargo while recognizing the hopes for liberation, reflects a distracting preoccupation with a flawed European taxonomy. Because some colonial officers used the cargo cult label to impute mysticism and deny political legitimacy (and some anthropologists and other writers perpetuated this), some scholars have countered by playing down or denying hopes for American wealth, as if such hopes would in themselves mark the movement as "a cargo cult" with everything that label implied. This bolsters a simplistic cargo cult concept by arguing in its terms. The fact is, to anyone who understood global political realities of the later 1940s—which few Malaitans did—expecting Americans to liberate Malaita from colonial rule was no more realistic than waiting for them to arrive bearing gifts. Yet neither fallacy was inherently irrational or mystical, and most Malaitans expected that any American arrival would herald this-worldly, political-economic reform.[95]

It is often hard to distinguish cargo from liberation hopes in the written record since, although some officers stressed Malaitan wishes for American intervention, others simply presumed that hopes for Americans were largely about cargo. Just as those who misconstrued *kastom* automatically added "old" or "ancient" to "native custom," so too "Americans" were perfunctorily coupled with "cargo." Moreover, these two misunderstandings were linked: Maasina Rule adherents were seen to seek both a return to an ancient past and benefits of modernity, to be isolated yet enjoy foreign wealth or conveniences. This perceived discrepancy did not lead officers to reassess their own understandings; rather, they believed it expressed a fully contradictory Maasina Rule ideology, which in turn showed that Malaitans were confused, or to use a favored term, "bewildered," and did not really know what they wanted. The BSIP Annual Report for 1948 explained this:

> Marching Rule [fostered] ridiculous rumours of a paradise to come—the most persistent and firmly believed...being that American ships would soon come to the Solomon Islands and hand out free gifts of rice, meat, cotton materials and everything else that the Solomon Island heart could desire in unlimited quantities, all free. It is difficult to write clearly of what Marching Rule aims are, since they vary from time to time and from area to area; no one seems able to give any precise account of them. Nevertheless, the general trend has been similar everywhere. The Marching Rule advocated, firstly, a return to the ancient way of life, a revival of all old customs, even those which had been dropped by mutual consent for many years, strong leadership by the few and discipline for the many, and a decidedly anti-foreign attitude generally. Coupled with this reactionary attitude, however, was a marked desire to obtain the material advantages which Western civilization had to offer—hospitals, schools, imported goods and so on. No attempt was made to reconcile the two desires, and, if the matter was given any thought at all, the common feeling seemed to be that the foreigners, whose friendship was shunned, had a duty to provide these material blessings....They cannot withdraw into a shell of ancient customs and exclusive systems of self-government and yet expect others to aid them in their search for a higher material standard of living.[96]

Malaitans did want a return to the past—to *kastom*—but in the sense that they wanted to again control their own affairs and organize and advance their lives according to their own principles and ideas rather than European ones. The desire for American benefactors, far from contradicting this, gave lie to presumptions that *kastom* ideologies articulated an archaic agenda; that Malaitans, as officers commonly said, were deeply anti-white or anti-foreign; or, as officers often asserted, that they simply "wanted to be left alone." Though hopes for American help were unrealistic, they also expressed an important realism: Malaitans well knew they were unprepared to go it alone in the larger world. Keen awareness of this is what made gaining American help so important to so many. Malaitans hoped Americans would not only free them from what they saw as the fetters of colonialism but would also help them transform their lives toward a more progressive future such as Maasina Rule had sought from the start. Some thought they had to first liberate themselves from the British, after which Americans would come. They did not want separation from the world but liberation from a particular type of connection to it, which they thought would keep them an oppressed people not only in the Solomons but also on the global stage.

Throughout the Solomons, particularly in the southeast, there had since the war been ideas that Americans might end British rule. Even though the numbers of Americans in the Solomons fell steadily from early 1945, rumors that they would intervene intensified in 1946 and 1947 and persisted in various forms into the early 1950s. In east Kwara'ae (but not Kwaio), some men practiced drilling and training with wooden rifles—divided into "scouts" and "enemies"—to perhaps fight alongside Americans, though it is unclear if this was in earnest. This took place even though, as Burt has detailed, their Head Chief Justus Jimmy spoke out against pursuing American help.[97]

Actual vigils for American arrival were episodic, and in Kwaio at least, many took part just once and dismissed later rumors as hoaxes. The first such event on a large scale occurred in 1947, before the arrests began. Fifi'i recounted how Nelson Kifo, just after an 'Aoke meeting, spoke to the chiefs and brashly rejected working with Sandars: "Are you all afraid of Mr. Sandars? Come January we will carry him to the ship *Nancy* and push him out to sea. You are all afraid, and he wants to tell you all sorts of things, but he is a rubbish man." No others present voiced support for this. But later Kifo called a meeting at Naafinua, which people from Sinalagu and northward attended. He said an American force was on Guadalcanal and would evict the government, and he initiated a collection of $2,000 that was apparently taken and offered to the small US contingent still at Lunga.[98] Soon Kifo circulated letters reporting that submarines and ships had been sighted, that Americans would soon land, and that people were to gather on shore. In Kwaio, duties one night scoured the area to summon people. There was no coercion, but most everyone came, including those far in the mountains. After three days and no Americans, people said the stories were lies and gave up the wait, but not necessarily their hopes for future American help.[99]

For many Malaitans, anticipation of American assistance had been and remained an important motivator to carry on with Maasina Rule. Years later, Fifi'i told Keesing of this event: "We heard [Kifo's message] and we wanted to believe it. We thought it was true, and we pushed on with more confidence. This time we didn't want to give in to the government—our heads were strong because we thought the Americans were really going to help us." And he later recalled, "We'd seen some pretty amazing things during the war, so it wasn't impossible."[100]

Ma'aanamae of Kwaio credited Malaitans' diligence to prospects of American help: "During Maasina Rule...everyone worked very hard, every man and every woman was so willing. The reason things went so well is that at that time people were still ignorant. When those lies came from Kwara'ae, and Lau, they led people to work hard and that made Maasina Rule strong." Toloasi Teoboo, a key Kwaio leader after Fifi'i's arrest who openly disparaged such ideas at the time, told me years later that he thought, on balance, hopes for Americans had been a good thing since they sustained people's will. Said Tom Titiuru, "The hope for Americans made the people thoughtful and unafraid of the British: 'Don't be afraid, the Americans will come, with gunpowder, and food, and to help us. We must keep on with the struggle.' It boosted their spirits; encouraged them. They worked hard because in this they had trust, faith, and great hope." Though rumors of Americans at times caused problems for Maasina Rule leaders who could not control them, they also stymied the administration. Forster, after an early-1949 tour of the north, urged that strategy "must include complete disillusionment on the American Question. There is little doubt that the attitude of these people is largely being sustained by the hopes of deliverance by the Americans." These hopes should not divert us from understanding Malaitans' pragmatic grievances and actions, which persevered long after most people realized Americans would never come, but neither were they marginal to Maasina Rule, especially during certain periods.[101]

Many government officers routinely blamed such ideas on a cynical conspiracy devised by the head chiefs, or sometimes a vague Maasina Rule "intelligentsia," to keep people engaged. They offered no real evidence and appear to have simply assumed this was true.[102] Except for Kifo, I have found little to show that senior leaders falsely manipulated such hopes, and Fifi'i, likely 'Atoomea, and probably some others were themselves susceptible to them, at least initially. On the other hand, there is little to indicate that senior leaders other than Teoboo and Ganifiri spoke strongly *against* such ideas before their arrests, though they may have, and it seems that 'Are'are people sat out Kifo's call to action. A lack of evidence of either manipulation or critique cannot resolve this question, but it is highly unlikely the head chiefs, or any group of high-level chiefs, conspired to fool the people; the realities regarding different places and times were more complex than that. Rumors swelled rather than declined after the head chiefs were jailed, and when they heard of rumor-generated actions after their arrests, they conveyed their disapproval back to Malaita.[103]

Starting in late 1948, some rumors became more apocalyptic, warning of vicious government punitive plans or of cataclysmic battles that would follow invasion by Americans—or, in a few cases, Japanese or Russians.[104] Many responded to these not by gathering at the coast but by retreating inland. Some (and only some) communities dug holes or trenches like the wartime foxholes, and, in parts of Kwaio at least, people made long tunnels for cover from government bombings or battles that might come. Some in the north built hidden mountain villages, just as officers had instructed in 1942 when the Japanese were invading. Many communities collected huge stacks of firewood, said from Kwaio south to be stockpiles for the war's duration or to be lit as beacons for American ships. In the north Russell said that he was told the wood was to cook food that would arrive, but he did not say who told him this. Stockpiling of firewood is symbolically important for intensive social events such as mortuary feasts. In 1950, some in the north retreated to hidden villages in response to rumors that Maasina Rule men were going to attack the government. These sorts of activities, which peaked in 1949 into early 1950, were varied and sporadic, and the lack of island-wide coordination at this time is obvious in the diversity of purpose and actions in different times and places.[105]

These more fearful rumors rose with falling hopes for American emancipation, a disappointment that led some to reject Maasina Rule or at least its original leaders. As officers came to realize, this did not mean that such people had decided to capitulate to or work with the government, or that they would not follow different leaders and messages. The government's true challenge was not to disassemble Maasina Rule as a movement but rather to counter Malaitans' deep alienation from the government, which was more fundamental than any particular movement following specific chiefs, and which repressive policies were only exacerbating. As 1949 drew toward its end, new leaders appeared on the scene with different anti-government agendas. Officers, already weary and frustrated, were dismayed.

Chapter 8
Attrition and Compromise

As 1949 drew to a close, operations to suppress Maasina Rule had been ongoing for nearly two and a half years. The results could only have disappointed officers. Some tried to boost morale by tallying successes: most fences were destroyed or rotting, a few men had agreed to labor on shorter-term contracts, and if many Malaitans now saw the government as their worst enemy, it was said that they "respected" it for having shown that it could arrest thousands. Yet officers on the ground knew that most Malaitans remained resolute. Russell wrote that attitudes, especially in the north, had "hardened" into an "unbroken front of defiance." Masterman said the census had been "a complete failure" due to refusals, and the enumerators were dismissed in April 1950. He laid plans for more arrests and longer sentences and asked for a new boat to transport the many prisoners he expected to take. Those in jail were given harder labor, and plans were made to reduce their food rations.[1]

Russell in September had suggested a new "constructive approach" for when taxes came due on 1 November 1949: to prosecute only leaders for census and tax refusals and to target followers with propaganda to alienate them from those leaders. He guessed there were 250 "chiefs" in Malu'u Sub-District alone, with several heading smaller groups in each town. By Allan's estimate of the adult male population the previous May, this would mean that about one in five men was a "chief." Officers, Russell proposed, should not again pursue the rank and file until April. He feared that mass arrests were failing as a political weapon and that to continue them "would merely aggravate the situation." Masterman agreed and offered the new approach as his own to Germond, who approved. If this failed, Russell said, the choices would be to either arrest—in most cases rearrest—the entire male population of north Malaita, or perhaps begin seizing property in lieu of the tax. If that renewed crackdown failed, he advised, a "neutral commission" might then be brought in "to arrive at a solution to the impasse." It would include a mediator—he suggested anthropologist Ian Hogbin— "with semi-mandatory powers" recognized by Malaitans, who could offer compromises the government could not, even if they harmonized with its own plans, since to do so "would be regarded as weakness and might have serious repercussions."[2] No commission was ever formed, but Russell's proposals represented the first time an officer had suggested that full-blown suppression was failing and that less-confrontational alternatives might be required.

These suggestions stemmed in part from a growing awareness that, though there had been and would be progress in getting some Malaitans to be censused, pay tax, or labor, this did not at all mean that they had given up Maasina Rule or resistance in some other form. Thus Allan had reported the previous May that a minority of To'abaita people had agreed to be censused, but only "for reasons of family, health, private interests, or Marching Rule policy"; he also noted, "that they will not join the battle on some subsequent issue is extremely unlikely." As for laborers—who would sign only shorter-term, non-indenture contracts—Russell wrote in November, "Headmen report that labourers employed outside the District for short periods are merely replenishing diminishing stocks of trade goods and return to Marching Rule with renewed zest." Later he warned that tax payments were a poor measure of movement decline: "Young men in Marching Rule are allowed to tax to go out to plantations; to draw their Labour Corps and Defence Force gratuities; in hardship cases to avoid imprisonment; to maintain skeleton caretaker staffs in Marching Rule towns. There is no guarantee that these people will tax next year and whereas payment of tax once was the badge of loyalty it may now represent no more than a temporary relief from imprisonment."[3]

Thus, just as destroyed towns could be rebuilt, officers were beginning to recognize that apparent acquiescence was fleeting. They, not Malaitans, had long and often declared that people paying tax, censusing, or laboring would spell the death of Maasina Rule, but the officers' preoccupation with these specific issues had blinded them to Malaitans' enthusiasm for the movement's core ideology, which could be expressed in any number of ways. So long as there was serious resistance, or even widespread, passive refusal to interact or cooperate, the government was trapped, unable to pursue any projects but expensive repression, except for those that harnessed the copious prison labor. Starting in early 1950, the administration slowly and haltingly began to shift from confrontation to conciliation. Over time it would grant a series of concessions that—although at times publicly framed as seizing an advantage or even as conciliatory gestures to a defeated foe—were in fact pressed on it. This would culminate in later 1952 in a government-sponsored Malaita Council dominated by leaders of the resistance and an end to both overt suppression and acute resistance. This chapter explains how this shift occurred.

Hardened attitudes toward the government at the end of 1949 were displayed at two meetings in 'Aoke. At the first, on 22 November, about 500 mostly Kwara'ae people presented Masterman, 'Aoke's Officer John Bartle, and clerk Timeas Teioli with demands "To raise our custom, but not to despise the King's Rule," and that the government recognize the local councils that Malaitans were already running and give them better wages and "freedom." Afterward, Masterman distributed a curt reply—"All People Read these Words and Know This Is the Truth"—approved by Germond, declaring that Maasina Rule would not be tolerated since it oppressed the people, that headmen were the only proper representatives of the people, that councils would not be revived until Malaitans "recovered their senses" and obeyed the law, and that they had to learn to work for what they wanted. He added that the English people were short of money from helping starving people in India and China, and Malaitans needed to do their part. While his letter circulated, Malaitans were also consuming a rousing nine-page manifesto that laid out historical and current grievances, written by Ariel Sisili of West Kwara'ae and distributed to dozens of towns. Sisili was a principal organizer of and the key speaker at the 'Aoke meeting, but officers would not grasp his importance until later 1950.[4]

On 22 December, over 2,000 men from as far away as Small Malaita and Ulawa met the same officers and Russell. Sisili's manifesto was read out by Ariel Billy of Ngongosila, and Sisili then stated more specific demands, including for the release of the chiefs, for locally run councils and courts and election of a leader over Malaita, and for the division of Malaita between Maasina Rule followers and opponents. Unlike previous 'Aoke meetings, many men carried their everyday weaponry, and Russell described an ugly mood and expressions of anger when Masterman dismissed their points. Masterman himself called the situation "tense" but said the group was "excellently organized" and "very well behaved." His circular in reply to this meeting told people that the chiefs would *not* be released and that nothing else they wanted would be allowed until every last man on the island had paid the head tax and every person had provided the information required for the census. If they did this, he said, a Malaitan could be chosen to sit on the BSIP Advisory Council, an enticement that officers held out over the months to come. Though officers put great stock in this offer, few Malaitans knew what the Advisory Council was, and even if they had it would have carried little weight; they sought more than an advisory role in government. They would also have assumed that a staunch loyalist would be chosen, and indeed Masterman later proposed that the symbolic position be used to reward headmen, with Ba'etalua, Kakalu'ae, and Tome Siru atop his list. In his insistence that these headmen should and would act as Malaitans' primary representatives in governance, we see Masterman's political antennae at its weakest.[5]

Relations worsened markedly after these meetings. Some who had been outside the movement now joined or rejoined it. Northern headmen called for a prohibition on further meetings since they encouraged Maasina Rule, and Russell agreed that meetings should be banned until Malaitans had submitted to taxation and the census. Compliance, he said, was an issue between individuals and the government and did not merit discussion: "The proper redress for grievances was by reference to the Headmen for submission to an Administrative Officer."[6]

This period also saw a shift in Malaitan tactics from waiting for the police, to fleeing them, which stymied Masterman's plans to step up arrests. In early December he tried to stage raids along the northeast coast from Fokanakafo to Malu'u; as Russell reported, "Every effort was made by day and night patrols to apprehend offenders but an elaborate warning system coupled with the density of the Malaita bush made Marching Rule avoidance tactics highly successful from their point of view." Bartle described a smoke signal warning system to track patrols, and Russell told of alerts being spread by torch, drum, and runner systems. Farther south, Kwara'ae and Kwaio soon adopted the same tactics. More prisoners, whom officers had once counted on to stay put, began to escape, and by early 1952 Allan said they had to be jailed in Honiara since "It is the determination of all recalcitrants to endeavour to escape from prison."[7]

As 1950 began, officers worried over rumors of plots to violently confront the government, perhaps at a third 'Aoke meeting. Many north Malaitans, in reaction to this "coconut news" or simply to evade arrest, moved to hidden mountain villages. It was impossible for officers to know what truths the stories might hold, as Russell wrote years later: "What credence were we to give to rumours that government and mission stations were to be sacked, an open confrontation with the Government was being organized, and individual government officers attacked? The killing of Bell and Lillies...twenty one years before was a reality."[8]

On 8 February, Russell and 20 police set out on an all-night march to the Suu'aba peninsula to attempt dawn tax arrests. At dusk, the patrol heard the chop of an axe nearby, and Russell sent Sergeant Taburi and two policemen to see if there was a hidden village. They surprised an older man, who shouted, "The army have come to kill me!" Men came to his aid and threw spears at the policemen, wounding one in the wrist. The police fired on them and killed a man named Ramositau. The next day, four men involved in the attack turned themselves in. At their trial, Russell pleaded for leniency since they had thought they were defending their kinsman, and they received three-year sentences.[9]

Two days after this clash, an emergency meeting was held in the resident commissioner's office, at which some argued for removing European women from 'Aoke since "the natives" did so with their women before fights and, Germond said, it would show that the government "meant business." Police Superintendent E J H Colchester-Wemyss (whom Tedder later described as "a Col. blimp") disagreed, because an evacuation would show "weakness and fear." He argued also that guns should be taken away from the Malaitan headmen, who might use them against the government. Masterman thought that possible but unlikely since northern headmen in particular "were too deeply involved to turn against Government now." In the end, the resident commissioner ordered 'Aoke's white women brought to Honiara, let headmen keep their rifles, and sent more police to Malaita armed with

10,000 extra rounds of ammunition. Malaitans, however, reacted to the shooting with calm, and some, though antigovernment, expressed anger at the men who had attacked the police. It was said that in Ramositau's area there was talk of revenge but that his relatives vetoed it. Rumors circulated in the north predicting that Americans would come now, in reprisal.[10]

Gregory-Smith and the Release of the Head Chiefs

Ramositau's tragic death had an immediate impact on the government's approach to Maasina Rule. As Russell readied for his patrol, a new resident commissioner, Henry Graham Gregory-Smith, had just arrived to replace Germond. Gregory-Smith had spent years as an officer in the Kikuyu area of Kenya where he had dealt with anticolonial movements, and he was sent to the Solomons in the hope that he could make a change. The high commissioner had wired Germond the week before that Gregory-Smith would seek "a rapprochement with Marching Rule," since its aims were the same as government, and noted, "It may well be that the people are as tired as we are of the present stalemate." Now, at the emergency meeting following the Malaita shooting, Gregory-Smith ordered that 'Are'are Head Chief Nono'oohimae be brought to him from Gizo prison in the Western District so that he could ask him if he would be "willing to talk to his people and use his influence to restore peace and order," possibly in return for a remission of his sentence. Colchester-Wemyss objected to the "awful gamble" of letting the prisoner address his people and said that if they pardoned Nono'oohimae they would be obliged to do the same for all of the chiefs, to which Gregory-Smith replied, "If resistance broke down this would certainly be considered."[11]

As Gregory-Smith already knew, the chiefs themselves had suggested a similar approach in January. Through Justus Jimmy as their spokesman, they had told Davies—now district commissioner of the Western District—that the ongoing arrests distressed them, and, in Davies's words: "They themselves have been in prison for two and a half years and have made no comments because Government had chosen not to believe them," but "they knew that there would be continued resistance to Government on Malaita unless they, the leaders, told the people to obey orders and remain quiet." They asked to meet with Germond, but Davies reported that he thought most of them just wanted out of jail and that Ganifiri was still "fanatically pro-Marching Rule," and Germond did nothing. Steven Sipolo, on his own, had in November offered to go with Germond to Malaita to talk to the people, but this had been rejected as "unwise."[12]

Gregory-Smith met a week later with Nono'oohimae, who much impressed him. Gregory-Smith had been misled into believing that Nono-'oohimae had the power to make all Malaitans be censused, pay tax, and behave. If they did all of these things, he told Nono'oohimae, he would meet with them to discuss their grievances. A week later they met again, but Gregory-Smith had now dropped his preconditions for a meeting—he just wanted to be sure that if he called one, people would attend. Nono'oohimae told him that he had influence only in 'Are'are, but that he would ask the other head chiefs about writing letters to their people. He did soon write one that told 'Are'are to meet with Gregory-Smith, but it was not disseminated because he labeled it an "order," and officers feared it would appear they acknowledged his legitimacy. But Gregory-Smith, during a mid-March round-Malaita tour with Masterman, Germond, and Russell, read parts of the letter to a meeting at Onepusu in 'Are'are. When the people asked if he would let Nono'oohimae visit them, he told them no, but that if, and only if, they all paid taxes, he would let three 'Are'are men visit Nono'oohimae in Gizo and would institute a Malaita-wide council, with half its members elected and the district commissioner as its president. But they turned him down. 'Are'are leaders had already told Masterman in January that, although they disapproved of the north's confrontational mode, the people thought they should all disobey and go to prison anyway, at least once, since they had started Maasina Rule and owed it to the suffering north, where the vast majority of arrests had been made.[13]

Gregory-Smith was now convinced Nono'oohimae was the key to all of Malaita. Though his tour had little impact and most of his meetings drew few people, he returned to Honiara believing Malaitans were sick of the conflict and that they sought only a way to save face. Masterman afterward circulated a letter, titled "Read and Remember My Words Again You People of Malaita," saying the king had sent Gregory-Smith since he had heard "there is much foolishness and badness in the island of Malaita." He declared it illegal for adults to miss any meetings called by government officers or headmen.[14]

While Gregory-Smith pondered new approaches to Maasina Rule he continued the suppression campaign and instructed Russell to step up arrests along the northeast coast. This was easier ordered than done, since people were still fleeing officers, with the motto "Let's jail in the bush, not with the government," and they were warned of some raids even before policemen got their orders. Allan said evasion "presented Government with one of the greatest problems in dealing with the movement." Others promised to pay the tax—later. "The Malaitans," Russell said, "are deliberately playing for time in the hope that they can avert decisions on policy until the release of the 'Nine Chiefs.'" Masterman guessed that up to half of Malaitans had now paid the tax, but this was a considerable overcount, and many payees were To'abaita and Lau who could not evade police.[15]

By mid-April, Gregory-Smith had decided that he would probably let Nono'oohimae out, though, citing Masterman, he still said it was contingent on people paying taxes first. But on the 30th he traveled with Masterman to Gizo to meet with the nine chiefs with an eye to releasing them all, with no taxation proviso. Fifi'i later told me how Gregory-Smith asked them what their grievances were, what changes they wanted, and how they would pursue them, and informed them of his plans to start a Malaita-wide council and to let people manage their taxes for their own benefit. Fifi'i said the chiefs all liked him because he listened to them and because he made Masterman treat them with dignity. Each signed an agreement to work at convincing people to cooperate and to "deplore law-breaking." They were instructed to announce that if everyone paid their tax then a Malaita council would be formed, consisting of ten members chosen by the people and ten by the government, and that a Malaitan would be placed on the Advisory Council. All, with Steven Sipolo, were released at 'Aoke on 8 June at a flag parade for the King's Birthday, right after Masterman formally turned the district over to Colin Allan, who had just returned from England. Few people attended, and against expectations there was no visible excitement at the chiefs' return.[16]

The released northern chiefs spent a week at Malu'u so that Russell could assess their sincerity, which most northern headmen doubted. Russell had opposed their release, particularly because Masterman had assured December's 'Aoke meeting that the chiefs would stay in jail until every Malaitan stood down. The government had now conceded a key demand that Malaitans had been making for nearly three years, and Russell feared the reaction: would they expect other demands to be met, for "freedom," "recognition of a single popular leader for Malaita," and "Marching Rule councils"? He warned that the chiefs might revive a strike for higher wages.[17]

Arrests were now suspended to see what the chiefs could and would do, and as Masterman departed he recommended that if they did cooperate and all Malaitans paid the tax and submitted to the census, then his successor should release all political prisoners, including tax and census offenders. However, he said, under Charles's advice, if chiefs failed to bring about change, then any civil resistance should be proceeded against as a criminal conspiracy with two years in prison for each offense. But he hoped "that a fresh start can be made through the medium of the District Council and the native Member of the Advisory Council." This proved unduly optimistic; most of the chiefs were sincere, but officers, as so often in the past, greatly overestimated the chiefs' power to control the populace. Most Malaitans had wanted the chiefs back as leaders in their struggle, not as advocates for government policy. It may be that the chiefs did not fully realize just how much people had suffered while they were away and failed to foresee how many would reject their message and themselves as leaders. It seems the only officer who anticipated this was Russell, the one closest to Malaitans on a daily basis. He warned, "Should the nine chiefs have a genuine change of heart they may find that popular feeling supports the radical element who controlled Malaita in their absence.... The position of the nine chiefs is not an enviable one." Their release did ease the situation in certain places but not in the more difficult ones, and most of the chiefs found themselves in no position to bring about the sort of rapprochement Gregory-Smith desired. As Ben Burt noted for Kwara'ae, "The government had effectively destroyed the moderate faction."[18]

Reactions to the chiefs' return differed from place to place. In the north the welcome was muted. Some prepared by cleaning towns and rebuilding meetinghouses, but at 'Ataa notices of their pending release were defaced, and many elsewhere declared they would refuse to pay the tax regardless of what the chiefs might say. Some in To'abaita said they would pay, but only later, and the previous trickle of payments in other sub-districts stopped altogether. By mid-June, most in the north were boycotting meetings the chiefs called. In east Kwara'ae, Justus Jimmy Ganifiri was fully spurned, and Sipolo found himself berated by even his wife and children. Allan described Sipolo's humiliation as "a thousand times worse punishment than any he had undergone in prison." Only 'Atoomea, who ruthlessly spurned his uncle Irofa'alu's approaches, regained influence, and To'abaita was the only northern area besides Lau from which substantial taxes were paid that summer. Elsewhere, wrote Allan, "The mere asking of a man about his tax obligations was tantamount to arresting him." By mid-August, most of the northern chiefs had been rejected as "yesterday's men" and "turncoats," and talk of a government Malaita-wide council fell on deaf ears. "They won't tax and they won't go to gaol," wrote Allan, "so they remain in the fastness of the bush." Russell said that those who did pay in no way renounced Maasina Rule and, in September, that even To'abaita remained strongly anti-British and "vindictive." After Gregory-Smith presided over a meeting there, Allan warned him that the only candid question he had been asked was, "How long does the government intend to remain at Malu'u?"[19]

The situation in the south was brighter for the government. In vulnerable Langalanga, most people paid their taxes in June. In 'Are'are, Allan reported, people would no longer listen to anything Nori said; he became a scapegoat for many, including northern head chiefs who ironically now blamed him for their arrests. Nono'oohimae fared much better. On arrival he told a meeting that he "had never advocated resistance to Government authority and he never would." Many 'Are'are still saw him as their leader, and at amicable meetings that he and Allan held in later June most paid their tax or said they would soon. Small Malaita attitudes were mixed, but by September many there had paid tax as well, largely due to Timothy George having reestablished his influence. It is instructive that, across Malaita, only in these two places, the parts of the island that had suffered the least government oppression (other than loyalist Lau), did officers find a genuine willingness to cooperate. However, Allan cautioned that they paid the tax "because they think that Nono'oohimae, Timothy George, and maybe Fifi'i, want it. They are looking to their chiefs, not the government." But not all 'Are'are liked Nono'oohimae's stance, and more resistance would soon coalesce there under his former ally, Waiparo of Takataka. Also at this time priests in 'Are'are were forming "the Catholic Welfare Society" as a church-based organizational alternative to Maasina Rule, but Allan and Gregory-Smith believed it to be subversive and convinced Bishop Aubin to shut it down.[20]

Kwaio is of interest because it was there that Malaita's political attitudes divided. Fifi'i met a mixed reception. Although like some other chiefs he told people their failure to pay tax might land him back in prison, many initially vowed not to pay, citing the lack of returns for their prewar taxes and the government's refusal to allow a single leader for Malaita. Some who had hoped Americans would intervene blamed Fifi'i for the letdown. Few east Kwaio people came to July meetings Allan called, and he said their attitude resembled that he found in east Kwara'ae: "coldly insolent, truculent and contemptuous." Kwaio had long had split affinities, looking both north and south for political direction. Now in the Uru area, Anifelo effectively promoted an antigovernment ideology emanating from Kwara'ae, while at Sinalagu and 'Oloburi more people began to pay the tax after Fifi'i on 13 July read out a letter from Nono'oohimae urging them to do so. Otherwise, most Kwaio wanted no contact with the government, and a year later Allan reported that they "were still wild and refuse to obey the headman." East Kwaio people today remember this period as marked by rivalry between Fifi'i and Anifelo. West Kwaio was similar; when Fifi'i called meetings there, he was welcomed nearer the 'Are'are border but could hardly raise an audience north to Kwara'ae, and the area as a whole remained "thoroughly disaffected."[21]

Fifi'i was further weakened at Uru when headmen there publicly demeaned him, for which Allan reprimanded them. This, too, evinced a Malaitan split, in that northern senior headmen disliked the chiefs and tried to surveil them, while from Sinalagu south friendly chief-headman relations were reestablished, and the conditions of the chiefs' release—including that they report to headmen every two weeks—were interpreted liberally. The northern tensions presaged a dilemma that officers were to face when they tried to cultivate popular leaders but met with resentful headmen accustomed to being the people's only legal representatives.[22]

The Federal Council

Even before the chiefs' release, Kwara'ae had become a new center of resistance, with its influence first and most strongly felt in Fataleka, Baegu, Baelelea, northern Kwaio, and parts of To'abaita, and eventually reaching everywhere on the island. Its leaders were a group known variously as "the Nine New Chiefs," "West Council Malaita Property Owners," "the Kwara'ae Council," or "the Malaita Council." In 1951, some leaders settled on "the

Federal Council," the name the literature uses to label this group and, at times, all resistance of this period. Starting in late 1950, Sisili and some other leaders said, "Maasina Rule is finished." Some of them were keen to distance their project from certain discredited aspects of Maasina Rule, and a new name served this purpose. Those who rejected the old name also underscored their break from head chiefs who were urging cooperation. People in Kwaio and throughout the south, however, continued to use "Maasina Rule," or sometimes "New Maasina Rule," as did some farther north. Sinalagu and 'Oloburi resistance veterans I have asked—even some related to men like Anifelo who were said to be its key leaders—have never recognized the name "Federal Council," though district officers in 1951 reported that "the Federal Council" had permeated those areas. Officers used it as a generic label for diverse antigovernment ideas and activities that were hard to pin down in their dynamism, complexity, and interconnections. I stress this here not to discount the name, which was important to many, but rather because the different appellation, and disavowals by some Federal Council leaders of "the old Maasina Rule," can obscure fundamental continuities in the leaders, adherents, grievances, and goals of Malaitan resistance, and the fact that Maasina Rule and the Federal Council were different phases of a single, evolving movement.[23]

Some of the continuity is clear in the leadership, which like the structure was far less formal than during Maasina Rule before the 1947 arrests. Officers found both the leadership and structure enigmatic since both changed through time, and depending on whom they talked to. Some of the men whom others said were leaders denied or rebuffed the status. But there was a core of men who anchored the northern activity over time. Most feared by the government was Eban Funusau, or Sau, of Fokanakafo, the sergeant Sandars had jailed for organizing a 1946 police strike for better food and then dismissed, with Sipolo, for involvement in the 1947 police walkout. Sau had been a wanted man since Operation Delouse, living armed in the jungle with a varying band of companions and wielding influence far beyond his native Fataleka. He was said to hate the government bitterly, and for some time officers blamed Sau more than anyone for their unending political problems. Another key leader, Jasper (or Josepa) Irofiala of Fo'odo in Baelelea, had also been a sergeant under Sandars, who had known him since he was a boy. He was with Marchant on Malaita during the war, and for that and his role in a 1942 attack on Japanese in north Malaita he had earned a British Empire Medal. To punish his Maasina Rule activities, in 1947 Irofiala was given two years at hard labor and his medal was canceled. When released, he joined Sau. Allan called Irofiala "proud" and "resolute."[24]

Jason Alaikona of Bokolo in To'abaita had been a constabulary corporal, and during the war he had led dangerous patrols hunting Japanese. He had been a Maasina Rule full chief under 'Atoomea at Malu'u, and after arrest and prison he returned to the movement. Readers already know 'Abaeata Anifelo of east Kwaio as another former corporal, headman, the designated president of Kwaio's native council, and a Maasina Rule leader from the movement's beginnings. Beni Ramoalafa of Agia in Baegu had as a corporal in 1942 led a police squad to capture downed Japanese pilots, but in 1947 he was tried with the head chiefs, convicted of sedition, and jailed for two years. Takanakwao of west Kwara'ae had also been a constable, whom Sandars called "very bright and a great talker." From 1938 he was headman for the 'Aoke area, and from 1945 president of 'Aoke's native council, but he was jailed over fences in 1948.[25] Salana Ga'a (full name Maega'asia) of Areo, north of 'Aoke in Kwara'ae, had from age 12 worked for several years for Charles White on his yaws-eradication tours and on a trip White took to Rennell and Bellona with the Whitney Expedition ornithologists. Ga'a had been in the police for many years, rising to the rank of corporal. He had acted as a scout during the war and was also the senior orderly for Resident Commissioner Marchant from 1940 through the war's end, and then for his successor Noel. In 1947 Ga'a was charged with stealing china from the resident commissioner's house and imprisoned. On release he joined Maasina Rule and had been a wanted man ever since. In 1950 he was named the Federal Council's "vice president" under Ariel Sisili. Dr Gideon Zoleveke described Ga'a as "a man of real integrity"; Colin Allan called him "a supreme liar."[26]

Nearly every leader, then, had once belonged to the loyalist elite and had subsequently joined Maasina Rule. Each had been forced to choose between devotion to colonial benefactors and relinquishing his position to stand with his own people.[27] For making the second choice, they were, despite having served the government well and long, condemned as traitors of weak moral fiber and punished or hunted. Assistant High Commissioner G D Chamberlain explained the official view when stripping Irofiala of his war medal: "Irofiala had an exemplary character and was one of the outstanding natural leaders in the Solomon Islands. His loyalty had never previously been questioned and there is little doubt he joined the 'Marching Rule' under considerable pressure. Nevertheless...he should have had sufficient strength of character to withstand pressure as had many other Solomon Islanders of similar experience." It is easy to understand the determination of these men not to again submit to the colonial system, as well as the resolve of their followers who had gone to jail and undergone great hardships, only to hear their views dismissed by Davies, then Germond, and then Masterman as illegitimate, ignorant, and unworthy of consideration or even discussion until they bowed down before them.[28]

An exception in background was Ariel (Eluele) Sisili, who had been an SSEM teacher at Bina in west Kwara'ae and a clerk for that area's government council. He now lived inland, and in 1950 most northerners saw him as the resistance leader. He had not at first joined Maasina Rule and became a political organizer only in early 1948. Sisili had written the 1949 manifesto read at 'Aoke, but officers, focused on Sau and others, did not begin to realize his importance until September 1950; that August Allan still called him "one of Sau's runners." When his status was finally grasped, Allan reinvented Sisili as cursed with "a marked inferiority complex" and displaying "schizophrenic characteristics...so typical of Christian Malaitans" and "the driving force behind much of the terroristic behaviour in Western Kwara'ae and the Langa Langa in 1946 and 1947." When Allan had earlier met with Sisili at 'Aoke, he described him as "quiet and reserved" and "obviously intelligent." Sisili was certainly smart and determined and, like many northern leaders at this time, not the sort of man to quietly queue up for arrest and imprisonment.[29]

Since early 1948, this loose-knit group of northern leaders had kept links to an 'Are'are "Kiu Council" based near Nono'oohimae's village of Arairau and to Waiparo's activities at Takataka. But their leaders had not met together since 1949, and after Nono'oohimae's release the Kiu activity subsided for a time. Russell was told that these two groups had disseminated instructions across Malaita, such as to refuse to pay taxes and to flee from government parties.[30]

Beginning in later 1949 and increasing through 1951, the government and the resistance carried on a running propaganda battle via dueling written documents, each posting its messages in villages and destroying the other's. Several written or inspired by Sisili highlighted "the Four Freedoms"—of speech and expression, of religion, from want, and from fear. President Franklin Roosevelt's famous 1941 speech proposing these rights to be universal had been found in a book given by a US soldier during the war, and many documents circulated at this time were copied directly from this and other books.[31] The Four Freedoms had been much discussed within Maasina Rule for years, most importantly as embodying the idea that there were universal human rights not dependent on one's race or culture. Nelson Fo'ogau had read them aloud to Noel at 'Aoke in March 1947. Decades later, older Malaitans could still rattle them off for me. Other documents produced included a "Malaita Declaration of Independence" copied largely from the American one, as well as many original statements stressing rejection of the government and noncooperation regarding its taxation, census, and other demands. In July 1950, the "Kwara'ae Council" sent an unsigned dispatch to Fataleka's Headman 'Itea, warning that people would reject the tax and the census until the government compensated them for past costs of Maasina Rule and listing losses sustained. To my knowledge, this was the first of many instances of Malaitans demanding that the government pay compensation to Malaitans as a group. After the released head chiefs had spread government's message, some proposed suing them for movement costs, and in 1953 there was much talk of exacting compensation from loyalists.[32]

From 1949 into 1950, couriers for the "West Council Malaita Property Owners" hand-delivered a series of letters intended for the United States. The first letters were given to John Martin, commander of a small US Topographic Battalion still on Guadalcanal. One laid out Malaitan grievances, but Martin wrote back saying he was uninterested in Malaitan affairs. These last Americans left Guadalcanal on 25 May 1950, but in June a bundle of documents targeted at Americans was delivered to New Zealander salvagers working there. One asked to buy guns to drive out the British. Russell thought these letters were in earnest and that they indicated a changing mood captured in a popular slogan, "I will die for Malaita." Allan, always fond of conspiracy theories, was not sure but that they might be a ruse to confuse officers.[33]

Some of the letters were in Sisili's handwriting, and it seems clear he was behind most of them. Yet some contradicted parts of his revolutionary message, as least as it developed subsequently. Sisili rejected aspects of Maasina Rule that had led some astray, specifically ideas about "cargo and lies, and Americans," and he later told Allan the movement was being retooled on a sounder basis. American and even some British documents and ideas would remain important, but by later 1950 most Malaitans seem to have discarded serious hopes of direct American help. Allan came to see this new approach as more dangerous than "the old Maasina Rule," which he understood as a cargo cult, since this-worldly ideas of Malaitan independence would be harder to discredit and suppress. Still, he understood Federal Council's leaders and adherents, like those of Maasina Rule, to be "irrational," "pathetic," "mystical," and "messianic." Meanwhile, Malaitans were beginning to explicitly liken government's perennial, unfulfilled promises of development projects to the rumors of cargo en route that never arrived.[34]

By September, government relations with Malaitans in the north had further deteriorated. Most people still refused to pay tax and more had moved inland, where they ignored officers' orders and coastal visits. When Gregory-Smith toured the north that month, taxpayers and defaulters alike snubbed him, and turnouts at his meetings were "insultingly bad." Russell urged withholding the promised district council and Advisory Council position until all of Malaita "capitulated to taxation."[35] This followed a policy meeting Gregory-Smith held with Malaita's officers at Sinalagu. They devised a strategy to intensify pressure where people refused to pay tax, and grant rewards where most had paid up, namely 'Are'are, Small Malaita, and To'abaita. In the latter places, Allan warned, "The initiative had passed to the Marching Rule. They had done all that Government had asked. Government must therefore do something tangible and quickly." Unfortunately, focused for so long on suppression, "Government had been caught without a plan": no cash crop was ready, scarce medical resources were overstretched, and there was no machinery to start education. Gregory-Smith said he would ask Fiji for £10,000 for education and medical projects and would argue that this would be less expensive than if London had to send troops later. In the meantime, it was suggested, in the north they "must cover up" the lack of readiness to provide promised services "by saying that this was deliberate policy on account of the recalcitrance of other parts of the island." The island's southern half would be easier since, as one officer remarked, "The present situation in South seemed to be much the same as at the beginning of the M.R. movement when Major Sandars was working through Nori." Gregory-Smith soon did convince High Commissioner Freeston that development funding was essential, warning him, "A pistol is being shown at our heads and we would be unwise to take no heed." He also urged Freeston to permit initiation of graded administrative positions that Solomon Islanders would fill.[36]

In the uncontrolled areas, officers and their police had toiled without success to capture leaders, whom Gregory-Smith called "bandits...ensconced in a veritable Edinburgh Castle." Russell, about to go on leave, said that it was imperative to arrest them and resume arresting tax defaulters, and he proposed what now seem desperate measures. One was to form a special armed constabulary of loyalists to hunt leaders down, which might also frighten others into paying the tax. With such constables, sweeps could be conducted and gardens guarded to catch people forced to come out of hiding for food. A difficulty, Russell warned, was that everyone would try to help fugitives. He said officers also needed a law that would allow them to make "lump sum assessment of tax by villages" and seize an equivalent amount of property. Gregory-Smith did not at first take these suggestions, but he later presented to Freeston the idea of a loyalist constabulary—"a few platoons of young indigenous natives"—and added that the inhabitants, whether they had paid their own tax or not, could be forced to pay for the constables themselves, which he thought would turn the populace against the rebels. Allan had himself suggested in August that Fijian commandos might be required to hunt down leaders, but he also pointed to the 1947 arrests of the head chiefs to forewarn that even if all leaders were so arrested, resistance would continue.[37]

Allan now thought they should try a succession of approaches, in the following order if each failed in turn: further persuasion, "fully fledged police action," still more police, deployment of "tribal police," and if these all failed, bringing in foreign troops, by which time "the island would be in a state of bloody rebellion" and it would be years before "the remotest confidence" in government could be regained. Beyond some targeted police actions, these plans were never implemented. As Allan intimated, the more repressive ones surely would have brought about political disaster and probably worse. He also said that even if "persuasion" did end outright resistance, the government was unlikely to be left in a position to "put into operation plans for Malaita's political and economic rehabilitation," which was, after all, Gregory-Smith's assigned mission. Allan felt persuasion had to be tried anyway, with a focus on separating "recalcitrants" from leaders.[38] Nonetheless, plans were soon laid for more large arrest operations.

Despite the grim political situation, Gregory-Smith thought it essential to set up a Malaita District council and sub-district bodies as rapidly as possible. Officers debated which of these should come first, but in late 1950 it was clear that only 'Are'are and Small Malaita would cooperate. When Gregory-Smith toured Malaita in September, people in those places told him they had elevated Nono'oohimae and George as their "chiefs." He officially recognized them (he saw them as "similar to Members of Parliament") and explained how their duties had to be balanced with those of headmen. He hoped people would later choose such chiefs across Malaita to, in Allan's words, be "the ultimate authority in the district on matters of native custom," tell the government "what actually is custom," and convey to the government people's wishes regarding land, labor, the economy, and agriculture. Behind the scenes, Allan told Gregory-Smith that he feared people would see his recognition of the two chiefs as another Maasina Rule victory.[39]

Officers worried over how northern headmen would react if chiefs were recognized there and if a Malaita-wide and local councils were started—all of which would require headmen to share power. That their concern was justified became clear at a headmen's conference held soon after. Malaitan headmen were shocked and dismayed when Gregory-Smith told them, in Allan's rendering (in a letter to Gregory-Smith), "Headmen must not worry about money or wages but must work for the people and for the love of the people." Allan said they interpreted this "as being an instruction to join the Marching Rule and cease to work for the Government.... The headmen believe and have been taught to believe for forty years that they are working for the Government. Such an abstract idea that the Government is the servant of the people is almost impossible for the Malaitaman to understand in his present stage of development. That anyone should ever work for nothing for an institution or even for an abstract idea is entirely foreign to their philosophy." Beyond the facts that Malaitans' understandings of the colonial government were based not on backwardness but on long experience, and that most had for years been working for Maasina Rule and its ideas without pay, officers like Allan seemed oblivious also to the headmen's unhappy position—reviled by their people for urging and helping the government to stifle and punish them, and now told to go and earn their love. These headmen were wedded, for better or worse, to direct colonial rule and domination, and their fellow Malaitans recognized that. To understand this is to better appreciate people's blunt rejections of government orders to obey headmen as their proper representatives.[40]

Allan also advised Gregory-Smith, "The Malaita people are highly suspicious and very conservative," and their headmen "extremely imaginative like all primitive people." The headmen were angry, too, at the overbearing manner of Sale Vuza, who, Allan said, acted at the headmen's conference as if he were the Protectorate's "paramount headman," and especially at Vuza's open criticism of High Commissioner Freeston in front of everyone. Officer Frederick Bentley added that the latter anger might reflect "that the essentially magic-believing Malaita people have a faith in a semi-mystic, powerful being in the back-ground" (ie, Freeston). In any case, Allan told Gregory-Smith, the conference had so dashed headmen's confidence in the government that widespread police actions they had been planning against north Malaita had to be shelved.[41]

Meanwhile, Russell and Allan had been offering selected resistance leaders amnesty if they would surrender, comply with the census, and pay taxes, but most refused. Allan asked Sisili to come to 'Aoke and tried to "negotiate" with him, reporting after, "I told him he was a liar. He accepted the rebuke gravely." He thought he had convinced him to pay the tax, but Sisili reneged.[42] In December, Malaitans tried to hold another 'Aoke meeting, but Allan forbade it, posted notices to that effect, and had police patrol the station's perimeter to block anyone who came. He told Gregory-Smith why: "The Government had permitted or had been forced into permitting or had called massed meetings in connection with Marching rule in June 1946, June 1947, December 1946, and December 1949. At all of these meetings, rioting had narrowly been avoided, no advantage had accrued to Government, all speeches had been deliberately misconstrued, anti-Government activity had been stimulated by them, and at the last previously held meeting on the 22 December 1949, Ariel Sisili who was the main speaker and who had called the meeting, had deliberately insulted the District Commissioner by walking off the assembly field before the District Commissioner had finished speaking." He cited also rumors that Sisili and Sau had threatened violence and noted that unlike the other meetings, organizers had not sought his permission, so allowing it would lower government's prestige. No meeting was held, and another planned for January was also forbidden and therefore canceled.[43]

Afterward, leaders rebuffed Allan's invitation to meet with him alone. Kwara'ae headmen Dausabea and Shadrach Diote'e did meet with Sisili, Ga'a, and Takanakwao, who gave them papers for Allan, including the "Declaration of Independence," parts of the United Nations Charter, and Roosevelt and Churchill statements on "peace aims." Sisili said these would explain why people disobeyed the government.[44] Allan decided it was pointless and perhaps dangerous to try to talk to Sisili, and on 27 January 1951, 'Aoke's Officer Alexander MacKeith and Police Officer Frank Moore led a raid of Sisili's village of Namogisu, arrested him, and seized a "bank" of US$1,185. They expected to find guns but did not. Sisili, who had been quite sick, resisted mildly (his convictions for assault and resisting arrest were soon quashed). On their descent to the coast the patrol was harassed, but not attacked, by large groups of angry men, some from Kwaio.[45] In

September Sisili was tried under the 1848 Treason Felony Act, contrary to which he did "intend to deprive Our Most Gracious Lord the King, from the Style, honour and royal name under which His Majesty holds, exercises and enjoys jurisdiction within the British Solomon Islands Protectorate." The specific offenses were "writing" the "Declaration of Independence" that he had sent to Allan and planning to read it out at the blocked 'Aoke meeting. In September he was sentenced to 12 years in prison.[46]

In his 1951 Annual Report, Allan said that evidence seized in the raid showed that disaster had been narrowly averted and that if he had allowed Sisili to read the Declaration of Independence at the blocked 'Aoke meeting, it "would have set the political fires of Malaita blazing from one end of the island to the other." But in a confidential report to Honiara written at the time, he said that the raid revealed they had overestimated both the threat Sisili posed to security and the sophistication of the Federal Council "intelligence service."[47]

In mid-April 1951, ten weeks after Sisili's arrest, northern people as far south as Uru posted notices in every village, much like those Allan had posted to forbid Malaitans entering 'Aoke, but these barred entrance to loyalists, police, and officers. Other notices presented aspects of Federal Council propaganda. Officers, particularly Allan, were deeply frustrated at how effective these seemed to be in stiffening resistance across the north, though in fact how much they incited rather than simply expressed hostility is unclear. Officers had no means to strongly repress them—it would have been impossible to catch those who posted them at night, Malu'u's officer Bartle was ill, and Charles advised that people could not be prosecuted for notices in their villages if they did not block officers from removing them. Furthermore, 'Aoke's Officer MacKeith and 12 police were kept busy through much of April guarding geologist Frank Rickwood as he prospected across Malaita for a Colonial Development and Welfare project. People almost everywhere forbade Rickwood's team to enter their land, fearing it might lead to its alienation, but MacKeith and his police forced him through, and this likely sparked the growing defiance more than Allan realized. In any case, Allan told police to merely tear down the notices when they found them and to order people not to put up any more. People soon stopped posting them in the north, and Allan later said that the government should have handled the fences and towers in this way in 1948 and 1949, rather than responding with severe repression. He had inadvertently discovered—though he later recalled it as thoughtful strategy—that ignoring civil disobedience could be more effective than attacking it, though, as usual, he explained the outcome as due to primitive Malaitan notions of magical causality: when notices did not keep police out of villages, he said, people ceased to believe in them. In fact, the notices had made their point.[48]

On 30 August 1951, Minister of State for the Colonies John Dugdale visited 'Aoke and spoke to a large crowd of Malaitans, loyalist and not. One of the latter was Salana Ga'a, whom Allan thought had replaced Sisili as the Federal Council's head but in fact had resisted pressure to do so. Beforehand, Anifelo gave Dugdale an unsigned letter that asked, among other things, that Malaitans be allowed to choose a "president" of the island; that a Malaita "capital" be established inland; that an eagle (a sacred bird across Malaita) be on the district seal (the government wanted a turtle); and that headmen who "caused enmity or division [between] the people and the Government" be replaced with "trusty, faithful persons." It complained that people had been "chased...in the forest as dogs hunting animals," that they had been prevented from meeting with the government at 'Aoke, and that Malaitans had never known how government spent their tax money, which they now wanted their own "president" to collect and oversee. Dugdale's prepared speech focused on Americans, and he told the audience that some of their "colonies" were worse off than British ones. He gave the now-standard lecture that if they wanted good things Malaitans had to work rather than wait for Americans, and that they had to start cooperating with England. He responded to the Federal Council letter, bluntly rejecting some points and refusing to address others. Allan later cited this as a high point for the quarter: "The people have heard a Minister of the Crown berate their idiocy."[49]

Though the posted notices heralded intensified northern resistance, the real tragedy for the government was emerging in the hitherto cooperative south. At first the notices were stopped from spreading past Sinalagu in Kwaio, when in April Fifi'i and Headman David Ridley led a group of men to block a patrol Anifelo tried to lead from Uru to post them there. But in May and June, notices flowed from the west coast into southern Kwaio and across 'Are'are and Small Malaita. This coincided with a rapid turn of 'Are'are's *alaha* chiefs and most of the people against Nono'oohimae and his message of cooperation, to the point where he threatened to resign his "chief" position if it continued. Their leader was Waiparo (also named Haiware) of Takataka, a Maasina Rule founder who had never been arrested, whom Allan called "the second most influential man in Ariari, Waeparo, hypocrite, liar and leading subversive agent of the South." Waiparo had started challenging Nono'oohimae's efforts earlier in the year and now restored links with activists in the north. By August, he was touring 'Are'are and Small Malaita, telling people not to pay the 1951 tax until they received something for their 1949 and 1950 payments. Headman Hoasihau told Allan that Federal Council ideas had spread throughout 'Are'are, and in much of Small Malaita George was in a bind similar to Nono'oohimae's. Allan promised to respond by taking stern measures to collect taxes there and by encouraging recruiters to take laborers without consulting their *alaha*. By December the *alaha* had announced that no 'Are'are taxes would be paid until they were allowed a "president" of Malaita, selected by Malaitans in congress. Allan wired Honiara to report that the *alaha* "asserted that just as Government conceded to demands for release of Nine Chiefs so it would in time concede on this one. It is only a matter of time states Alaha Council." People expressed regret that Nono'oohimae had sided with the government, and in early 1952 Allan reported that Waiparo had "successfully annulled Nono'oohimae's authority."[50]

In the north, in December, the situation remained little changed, or in places had grown slightly worse, though things were relatively quiet. The government now faced noncooperation or open opposition across the length of Malaita. The deadline for 1951 taxes was 17 December, after which Allan vowed to begin "prosecutions and large scale police operations" with six-month penalties for nonpayment. He said Malaitans had to learn that "This Government would not tolerate the open flouting of the law and that whether passive resistance to authority continued for twenty years, nothing would persuade it from adhering to the course of its policy."[51]

Resolution

Ten weeks after the tax deadline, some 4,000 of the 8,000 Malaitans liable for the 1951 tax, and almost all of those in 'Are'are, had refused to pay. But Allan imposed no stern measures in the south or sweeping police actions in the north, or any punitive measures at all.[52] He was leaving. He recalled later that he was sick and "exhausted and had run out of steam." A former officer told me that he was informed Allan was removed because he was succumbing to the job's pressures, something I had already guessed from his writings of the time. Even by the end of 1950 they reveal a deepening hatred of Malaitans, particularly those in the SSEM, Catholics, or anyone else he thought was interfering with his administration. His frustrations are evident in some of his formal reports, which boil over into rants or seethe with bitter sarcasm. Readers will have noticed his fondness for faux psychological analyses of Malaitans, sometimes joined with crude anthropological ones, an approach that anchored his master's thesis but became progressively harsher back on the island: He declared Malaitans "paranoid," "schizophrenic," "fanatics," and to be suffering "fear complexes" ("like other primitive people") and displaying "extraordinary" levels of "neurasthenia, obsession, mania and deranged behavior." Malaita was "a festering sore," a condition Allan seemed desperate to blame on anything but government actions—Christian missions, Americans, white malcontents, and above all psychotic Malaitans.[53]

A late 1951 report reveals Allan's awareness of one key to his and the government's problems. In describing the singular success of a unique community development project administered by Sandy Peebles at Hauhui, just south of Su'u in 'Are'are, he wrote: "I have not yet observed among a Malaita

community a better spirit of goodwill and a genuine desire for self improvement than that which now pertains at Hauhui. . . . There is little doubt that
[Peebles's] own particular friendly and optimistic approach, untainted by
the haranguing approach, that the very character of the Malaita people
inculcates into its administrative officers—a most unfortunate tendency
which has to be deliberately and consistently avoided—has been largely
responsible for this most hopeful attitude." He added, in a rare positive
statement about Malaitans, "The Hauhui Survey has shown . . . something
of the drive and mainspring of the Malaita people." Even if one declines
to read between these lines, Allan must have recognized that he had suc-
cumbed to the very unfortunate tendency he lamented, and that this
approach, in which, as he wrote, he was not alone, had played a significant
role in the colonial failure. A great barrier to the government achieving its
objectives, particularly the central one of gaining Malaitans' respect, had
been the deep pattern of officers publicly and relentlessly disrespecting
Malaitans.[54]

In late February 1952, Allan was replaced by Valdemar (Val) Jens Andersen, a New Zealander, who from 1947 into 1948 had been district commissioner of the Eastern District, and more recently Gregory-Smith's secretary
to government. After Davies, the angry Forster, Masterman, and then Allan,
Andersen brought to Malaita's administration a desperately needed change
in attitude. James Tedder, who from 1952 to 1954 served under Andersen as
'Aoke's and then Malu'u's district officer, remembered, "Perhaps his best
trait was the way he could talk to the Islanders as equals and gain their
confidence," and this portrayal is borne out by his actions and successes.[55]

Andersen was hampered by his Malu'u officer, John Wrightson, who had
been posted there in late 1951, and the contrast between them highlights
the broader change that 1952 would bring in the government's approach.
From Wrightson's writings it appears he saw Malaitans much as Allan did,
and his attitudes and actions were distinctly prewar in tone. He sent his
superior, Andersen, condescending lectures arguing that the only thing
Malaitans understood was force and that "more strong and bold acts [like
mass arrests] will be necessary before Government ideals are irrevocably
implanted in the minds of the bush people here." Before leaving, Allan
had ordered reimposition of prewar pig-penning laws, and in protest some
To'abaita people loosed all of their swine. Wrightson had his police shoot
pigs at Rerede and force their owners to carry the carcasses to Malu'u, which
led loyal Headman Ba'etalua to visit Andersen at 'Aoke to complain and
even suggest that he might join the people against the government. Andersen told Wrightson his actions were obviously illegal, ordered restitution to
be paid to the pig owners, and informed him that their overall policy had
to be directed at "gaining the confidence of and the friendship of the main
body of the people." He continued more broadly, "While I agree that the
Government of Malaita largely rests on force we cannot hope to develop

a sound indirect administration based on it and administrative ends must be obtained without the use of force as far as possible even to the extent of accepting an inferior result." Andersen also thought it time to reign in Tamburi and his Western Solomons police, whom Ba'etalua said were frightening people. Wrightson responded that it was impossible to follow the law under Malaita's circumstances, and that his action had "served its purpose and generally I think that it went within an ace of hoisting the people here onto another rung of the ladder that reaches to social and political enlightenment." "There are times," he wrote, "when the Law is a damned nuisance in my opinion." He also pushed to be allowed to destroy birth huts, a step he argued, citing decades-old texts, was necessary to reverse population decline, avoid "committing sick primitives to the grave," and overcome "the evils of indigenous culture," which was "rotten to the core." Andersen, who forbade such actions, had reached different conclusions, including that the Federal Council or an equivalent would be around for some time to come and that it therefore had to be brought into the system of legal authority by incorporation into a district council. If its adherents would follow the law, the Federal Council could become a political party and "a power for good on Malaita." For this reason, he minimized police raids and met with Anifelo and other leaders who were willing.[56]

Andersen was also convinced that Maasina Rule and the Federal Council had deep roots in economic disparities, and that in the longer term only development would change the Malaita political scene. His motivations clearly went beyond political ones, and Tedder recalled his great concern with "providing opportunities for people to earn cash without leaving the island." Development was now becoming a more tangible possibility because Gregory-Smith, who left for good on 1 April, had kept his promise to find funding for education, medicine, and cash crop schemes. He had proposed each project specifically as a means to address Malaita's political crisis. Colonial Development and Welfare money had now been approved for several elementary schools; a central school at 'Aoke (King George VI); a hospital at Rerede and the rebuilding of the 'Aoke one; and a major cocoa-planting scheme. These projects were now coming on line and lacked only the broad Malaitan support without which they could not effectively move forward. An added difficulty was that a census, needed to properly allocate services, could not be conducted on Malaita due to its previous use as a coercive weapon.[57]

Malaita's officers devoted much of the first half of 1952 to holding meetings around the island to urge people to select delegates for a district council and to try to discredit Federal Council ideas. But though they were no longer demanding that people pay tax as a prerequisite for a council, Malaitans were a poor audience. They boycotted meetings northern headmen called on the topic (even in Lau), and even after officers told headmen to stay away from meetings most people still refused to attend. Malaitans argued that they had chosen leaders before and the government had put them in jail, and some leaders now feared being chosen for a council. Sometimes when a leader did show interest, his followers quickly reined him in. In June, Andersen decided to minimize tax arrests so as to improve the atmosphere for discussions of the council.[58]

However, by late July things were worsening in the north; still more people were relocating to the bush, and even former loyalists fled from Wrightson, who described "a great surge forward in Federal Council activities." In the south, people were vowing not to pay tax or put forward council delegates until they received what they called "four signs": education, medical help, agricultural help, and councils and courts. Despite this, officers pushed ahead, and on 29 July managed to inaugurate a four-day District Council meeting. The 29 members, most of them loyalists, chose 'Atoomea as "the native leader of the Council and of Malaita," meaning he was to be the vice president under Andersen. So strong was northern feeling against 'Atoomea for this that his village of Aniuke was largely abandoned. Still, though the bulk of Malaitans did not accept the District Council, delegates told people at home about the meeting, and it was said that some Federal Council leaders and adherents showed interest.[59]

The difficulty was that the Federal Council was perfectly capable of crippling or derailing the District Council. As Allan had written in mid-1951, "Only in two or three areas is it possible to detect among the people as a whole that essential good will without which a constituted local authority can fail to work....The Council will fail ignominiously if it is established on an artificial basis—that is the basis of lip service paid by a passive, platitudinous, and patronizing minority." The body could only function as a popular one.[60]

The legal deadlines for prosecuting nonpayment of taxes from 1949, 1950, or 1951 had passed, and thus there was now little pretext for arresting most Federal Council leaders or followers. But on 30 August officers would be able to jail people for not paying the 1952 tax. Andersen decided that because officers' intensive efforts and eight months without major government raids had failed to improve the situation, on that date they would have to "revert to a policy of force." Police would conduct "massive raids" using "maximum force" over a four-month period, striking various locations from Kwara'ae and Fataleka in the north, to Uru in Kwaio, and south into 'Are'are. He said he wanted the operation "to be a force tempered with kindness," and that when police confronted people, be they leaders or followers, they were to be allowed to pay up and avoid arrest. He thought that if leaders did so that would weaken them politically more than would jail terms, which had always proved ineffective. Andersen did not want officers to be directly involved in the raids but rather to continue to tour, writing: "The Malaita man has by centuries of family vendettas developed an unforgiving nature and the less he has to forgive the better." At the campaign's end people would be told they did not need to pay the 1949–1951 taxes, and the Federal Council would be offered the nine open seats on the District Council. If that did not work, then another period of raids would commence.[61]

When the 30th of August came, very few Malaitans contravened Federal Council instructions by paying tax. Andersen thought they were waiting to see "whether the District Council was really going to do anything." Wright-son told Andersen that after six years of conflict, north Malaitans were tired of resisting, and that the more they pressured them, the faster they would give up. Again and again he pressed Andersen to launch a broad crackdown.[62]

This was not to be. Andersen submitted his attack plan to Honiara on 11 August, but the next day Acting Resident Commissioner Philip "Pip" Rich-ardson asked him to put it on hold while he consulted the new high com-missioner, Robert Stanley, though he said this would mean only brief delay. Then, while Andersen was patrolling east Kwara'ae in late August, he was met by Kifo with a message from Takanakwao saying that he and the other main Federal Council leaders wanted to meet with the high commissioner, who was soon to visit. Four days later, Stanley telegrammed Richardson and Andersen that he wanted to discuss in Honiara "the Malaita situation in light of the latest information available." Further, he wanted to meet Fed-eral Council leaders at 'Aoke in September. The 50-year-old Stanley would be visiting in preparation for the relocation of the Western Pacific High Commission from Fiji to Honiara at year's end. Stanley was a veteran of over 20 years in the colonial service, most recently as chief secretary and sometimes acting governor of Northern Rhodesia.[63]

Once in Honiara, Stanley forbade further tax arrests, a decision that Andersen later praised as "wise." Stanley explained his reasoning in a let-ter to London months later: "I had decided on a conciliatory approach as the only one likely to succeed and if there was to be any chance of success I had to reduce any conditions I felt it necessary to impose on the accep-tance of the Federal Council's representations...to what I considered to be the minimum essential to ensure recognition of my own authority as well as obedience to the laws of the Protectorate." He also hoped to chan-nel Malaitans' political energies toward constructive ends. Gregory-Smith had departed holding a very different view. In front of an 'Aoke meeting with Federal Council representatives in mid-November, he had torn up a document they gave him, writing afterward, "I believe that we are making a mistake in admitting even the existence of this 'Federal Council.'...I think from all I have seen of the members of this 'Council' that they are just a band of otherwise unknown and unimportant local scalawags, and my impression is that we are placing them on an unwarranted high pinnacle by recognizing them and talking about this Council."[64]

The Federal Council leadership was now said to be "the big four": Takanakwao, Sau, Anifelo, and Irofiala. Salana Ga'a had decided to support the council and was urging the others to do the same. Through Ga'a and Dausabea, Andersen sent them and other leaders ground rules for the meeting and told them that Stanley had important announcements to make. Takanakwao said they also wanted to meet with the District Council members about a possible amalgamation with the Federal Council, though this was not raised again until Stanley suggested it. Andersen proffered several explanations for the shift: the government's nonaggressive policy had made people appreciate quiet, the government had started real development projects rather than just talking about them, and people had learned more about the council due to the constant touring. He believed Federal Council leaders had come to recognize that the District Council gave Malaitans what they wanted and that the government now genuinely sought to help them.[65]

From 25 through 27 September, Stanley, with Richardson and Andersen, met at 'Aoke with 12 Federal Council and District Council representatives, with Ga'a acting as spokesman for the Federal Council. Stanley told them he wanted to forget the past, and what he proposed went far beyond what government had offered Malaitans over the past two years: (1) Council members would not be evenly divided between government appointees and popular choices but would instead consist of 30 members selected by the people, and just ten, one from each sub-district, by the government; (2) the Malaita Council would elect a president, who would be the "big man" for Malaita; (3) a new name, "the Malaita Council," would mark the transformation; (4) after a year, delegates from each sub-district would be elected, with representation to be worked out by the council and Andersen; (5) there would be no more arrests for taxes, and those from before 1952 were now waived; (6) the council's president could become a member of the Advisory Council; and (7) they could choose their own flag "emblematic of Malaita." The new name was Andersen's idea, and attendees said they would discuss this, since many wanted the name Federal Council. Malaitans had demanded a Malaitan president for years, and Andersen had told Stanley the leaders were unlikely to concede this. Stanley did not specify that the "big man" had to be a council member, and the possibility was raised that they might pick Sisili, still in jail. Stanley said that if they did so he might have Sisili released if he would agree to cooperate.[66]

Federal Council representatives for their part agreed tentatively: (1) to accept the high commissioner's formal authority (he would eventually retain the power to veto their actions) and to work with Andersen as their adviser; (2) to later let the Malaita Council's president be chosen by all Malaitans (something Malaitans had demanded for some time); and (3) to have the Malaita Council collect taxes and pay them into a council fund to be used for the Malaitan people. The leaders said that they wanted no taxes collected until November since they wanted October to explain everything to the people, obtain their agreement, and let them choose representatives.[67]

This was the major turning point. Afterward, following Stanley's instructions, Andersen ordered that no officer was to tour with more than two police, and that no police would patrol except in extreme circumstance. There would be no further tax arrests, no tax would be collected for previous years, and people would not be pressed for the 1952 tax. Every effort was to be made to befriend Federal Council people.[68] Andersen welcomed the meeting's results with "sober optimism" but said the agreement could only be preserved by quickly developing economic projects. One reason for his caution was that Takanakwao, Irofiala, and Sau (who was ill) did not attend the meeting, and people of the northern sub-districts other than Kwara'ae had few representatives there. However, it was said and later confirmed that the three absent leaders approved of what had been done.[69]

Just after the 'Aoke meeting, Andersen undertook a round-Malaita tour, traveling in the south with Anifelo, Dausabea, and two other speakers, and in the north with Ga'a, Ba'etalua, and two others (mission representatives accompanied them also). These men explained the agreement to waiting crowds. Responses were enthusiastic throughout Kwaio and the south. In the north there was suspicion in many places but no open opposition. "There was a general feeling of jubilation," wrote Andersen, "because it appeared that the long drawn out struggle between the pro- and anti-Government factions was coming to an end." There was also a general belief across the island "that the Federal Council had won a great victory and was now in charge of the district." Andersen noted this "misconception," but after the tour he dropped the "sober" from his declaration of optimism. Not everyone was so pleased. Wrightson at Malu'u, dismayed, called the agreement "a political coup d'etat" and all but predicted its failure. Six days after the 'Aoke meetings, he received orders to transfer to Guadalcanal and not to wait for his replacement, Bartle. Wrightson's views were obviously out of step with and a threat to the new agenda.[70]

The Malaita Council's first meeting was held on 6 November, which today is a public holiday on Malaita called "Maasina Rule Day." There were 35 delegates in attendance, including 23 Federal Council men, 3 former Maasina Rule leaders, and 6 senior headmen. The council voted Salana Ga'a its first president by secret ballot with 26 votes. Justus Ganifiri was a distant runner-up; some delegates had argued that one of Maasina Rule's original head chiefs should be chosen "because they had started this work." This idea lost favor after Takanakwao arrived and said at one of many informal meetings held nearby that the main Federal Council leaders should choose the president, which in essence they did. Andersen told the council that their work would be to help people make money, to improve medical and educational services on the island, to see that all people obeyed the law, and "to make good laws about Customs for the people." He emphasized, "The Council did not belong to the Government it belonged to the people of Malaita." The council decided that when the high commissioner gave

Ga'a formal authority in January, each "line chief" on Malaita would give him strings of shell money, much as Timothy George had received in 1945. It would be his not to keep but to pass on to his successor. It was "to make him the biggest chief on Malaita."[71]

Once the council began and police action and threats ceased, relations between the people and the government, including headmen, dramatically improved. Andersen reported a "friendlier spirit" in Kwara'ae and the south. Tedder recalled how "a notable change occurred," and while touring Kwara'ae near the end of 1952 he wrote, "Previously when we entered a village people had turned their back or walked away and did not return a greeting. Now they were staying to talk." The north, where suppression had been most severe, was less accepting of the council at first due to its association with the government, though this varied by place. There, some saw delegates as government agents and would not attend meetings they called to discuss the council. Some wanted loyalists to be punished with fines or a special tax for their role in past suffering. Things improved over time, however, and by January Andersen—whom Stanley called "by nature a bit of a pessimist"—guessed that 75 percent of Malaitans supported the council. Then, on 27 January, Sau, Takanakwao, and Irofiala met with Stanley,

Figure 8.1. Delegates to the first Malaita Council, 'Aoke, 28 January 1953. Ga'a wears the beaded vest. (Photo by and courtesy of former District Officer James Tedder, the only person on scene with a camera.)

Andersen, and Ga'a in 'Aoke. They had come, Takanakwao said, "to shake hands with the high commissioner." The next day they attended the inauguration of Ga'a and the Malaita Council. Three to four thousand people came from across Malaita, including northern leaders who had opposed the body. Ga'a wore a waistcoat and hat decorated with shell money. A Malaitan choir sang "God Save the Queen."[72]

This was a hopeful moment, especially after the hard years since August 1947. Malaitans and officers alike were relieved at the apparent end of conflict and at the chance to return to a semblance of routine. Malaitans had by no means become lovers of government, and many troubles lay ahead, some of which are touched on in my final chapter. Nonetheless, Andersen could write in his next Annual Report, "By the end of 1953 Malaita contained no major political problems and the District was as quiet as it has ever been." The year 1954 was also calm, and that April Andersen reported, "Of the original Marching Rule leaders all except T. George have accepted some form of appointment in the Native Administration organization.... Only Irofiala of the important Federal Party leaders has not accepted any appointment and he remains in seclusion near Auki." Sisili had just become the council's vice president, and the next year he was elected as its president and Irofiala its vice president. The years of overt repression and resistance were over.[73]

Chapter 9
Gains and Losses

The general consensus in writings about Maasina Rule has been that it was largely a failure and that Malaitans in the end resubmitted to government rule. Many authors have credited Gregory-Smith's mid-1950 release of the head chiefs—conceived as a conciliatory gesture to a movement already dying—with ending serious resistance. Some have presented the Federal Council phase as a localized resurgence or as—to use a favorite government euphemism—"remaining pockets of resistance" quickly put down in humbling fashion.[1] No one to my knowledge has told of the full breadth and perseverance of Malaitans' refusal to be dominated and dictated to by the government, of colonial officers' despair at their inability to reimpose control or find resolution, or of the pressure Stanley, Andersen, and others felt in the last half of 1952 to compromise and finally accede to Malaitan demands that the government had rejected for so long. Sometimes these omissions appear to reflect reliance on BSIP Annual Reports, which concealed the extent of the government's difficulties, confusions, frustrations, and ultimate concessions, and later, through 1974, portrayed Maasina Rule as a cargo cult that "needed a show of force to control it." Other authors have simply repeated distortions found in the secondary sources, passing them along.[2]

As relieved as most officers were when overt conflict ended, those serving at the time saw no government victory over the movement. We see this in Acting Resident Commissioner Peter Hughes's observation, "The Federal Council requests...are suspiciously like the demands made of Mr Sandars in 1946," and in Wrightson's condemnation of the settlement as a Malaitan "political coup d'etat." In his Malaita Annual Report for 1953, District Commissioner Andersen wrote, "Apart from the wish to be independent the only major aim of the Marching Rule and Federal Party movements which has not been achieved is an increase in the basic wage."[3] This was an overstatement, but these comments indicate officers' perceptions of the agreement.

To ask if Maasina Rule was a success or a failure poses a simplistic question about a long and complex process. We have seen that movement followers had multiple, diverse, and often-subtle goals that changed over time, particularly in reaction to shifts in government policies. Some have judged Maasina Rule a failure for not having won formal Malaitan independence.[4]

That was never in the cards in the mid-twentieth century, and by such a measure the movement was doomed from the start (those who reduced it to a "cargo cult" would say the same). But few Maasina Rule adherents wanted independence in the sense of Malaita being left on its own in the world with no benefactor, and most who held hopes for American assistance eventually gave them up. Before arrests began, many Malaitans foresaw an abiding if diminished role for the colonial government in their lives, and during the years of suppression many more accepted this as likely, inevitable, or even desirable.[5] This was clearly expressed in the ongoing demands for fundamental changes in the state's relationship with the people, toward one in which they would be allowed more self-determination and participation in governance, be offered economic options beyond poorly paid and socially destructive plantation indenture, receive education and medical care, and be treated with respect rather than as backward, inferior "natives."

While Maasina Rule's outcome can be evaluated partly in terms of formal political and economic gains or failures, other fundamental issues at stake were critical for Malaitans, and I want to highlight those here since most writers have overlooked them. In addition to Malaitans' positive goals, this was a movement of defiance, anchored, particularly during its last five years, in a resolve to resist a return to the colonial status quo. Therefore, we must also consider the government's objectives and the degree to which Malaitans successfully thwarted those to which they objected. Most studies have given little attention to the state's aims, which they appear to have taken for granted. But the government's agendas changed considerably in dynamic relationship with Maasina Rule in its various configurations. Twice, new district commissioners—Davies, and later, Andersen—critically altered government objectives and approaches.

A common assertion has been that changes Malaitans sought and felt they won through Maasina Rule would have occurred anyway, because the colonial outlook had already changed. From this view, Maasina Rule accomplished nothing but only obstructed progress. It is true that there were plans for gradual administrative and economic development on Malaita as well as on other islands. Most officers seem to have been sincere about implementing these, though they came to see them as urgent on Malaita only in response to rising discontent.[6] But arguments that attitudes had fundamentally shifted are difficult to sustain in the face of the government's Malaita policies and actions and the writings of many officers from mid-1947 into 1952. Davies, Germond, Forster, Masterman, and Allan—to mention only senior Malaitan officers—all thought and acted in ways that would have played well in the 1930s. If one does argue that the Maasina Rule period hindered progress, then a goodly portion of blame must be placed on the government itself, especially its decision to try to destroy the movement across the length of Malaita and its futile campaign to discipline Malaitans into becoming obedient colonial subjects. These were expressions of an antiquated mindset, and one of Maasina Rule's major accomplishments was that it ended suppression as a viable state response to political dissent and resistance.

An appraisal of the impacts of Maasina Rule must consider not just the outcome of 1953 but also its longer-term legacy. The period transformed Malaitan-government relations in enduring ways. This was foreseen, at least by junior officers in regular contact with the people; we have read Cameron's warning to Noel in mid-1948 that the mass arrests were "going to influence their attitude toward us, hence Malaita politics, for the next 30 years, possibly permanently," and a year later Russell reported that Maasina Rule had become "an integral part of the social structure of Malaita" and was "likely to remain for some years."[7] They were correct, and even after Malaitans suspended overt resistance, key features of Maasina Rule ideology and practice persevered, including the importance of *kastom* as a political ideology and organizational framework.

Malaitans at the beginnings of Maasina Rule had two basic sets of objectives: the first was to reject the low status and position Europeans imposed on them and end unwanted government interference in their lives; the second was to reorganize their societies and work for social change and development in harmony with Malaitan sensibilities. Many saw these to be inseparable, since they thought that officers and headmen were dedicated to maintaining prewar policies of discrimination and white control and to thwarting Malaitan efforts to raise themselves up—as indeed some were.

Yet, for a time, Malaitans and key government officers partially shared certain goals. That is, these officers, too, sought social reorganization and political, social, and economic development, and from 1945 into 1947 many of them, especially Sandars, recognized positive aspects of the movement and tried to varying degrees to work with Malaitans to find common ground and direction. Sandars was willing to significantly sacrifice control in order to harness Malaitan energies toward developing the island. While he would not allow fully independent courts or councils, both he and Forster experimented with allowing people much more say over them, and Sandars even offered to help Malaitans form a labor union.

The main disputes during this period were over the degree and pace of change and the extent to which Malaitans would be in charge of it. The government planned to reinstitute and gradually expand the embryonic prewar model of native councils and courts under close regulation by officers and headmen. Malaitans wanted rapid institution of both, with popularly chosen rather than government-appointed leaders, so they would be free of the unpopular appointed headmen and could make decisions and settle most disputes according to indigenous ideas and methods. They also wanted a popularly selected Malaita-wide council headed by a man of their own choosing. In the island's southern half, most leaders and people were willing to work with officers, while in the north, where people were contending with powerful and hostile headmen and their followers, some were more aggressive in seeking separation from the colonial apparatus. That many northern headmen forcefully opposed any cooperation with Maasina Rule followers as dangerous appeasement greatly contributed to the more confrontational atmosphere there. Nonetheless, Sandars expressed faith in Maasina Rule's leaders and believed progressive compromise was possible if the situation was managed with tact and care. He saw in Malaitan enthusiasm and mobilization not just a challenge but also an opportunity.

Though Sandars verbally supported Malaitans in some of their goals and activities, he offered little of the financial or logistical help that only a government could access; he suggested that they pay for building and running schools and hospitals themselves. Given the lack of state funds, plans, or personnel for significant near-term expansion of educational or medical services, one cannot blame Sandars personally for this lost opportunity to actively work with Maasina Rule—he could not single-handedly catch the Solomons up from decades of neglect. Three years later, though, in 1950, the government did hurriedly develop such plans and obtain money for them when it was realized, as Gregory-Smith put it, "A pistol is being shown at our heads."[8]

Roy Davies was the most obstinate critic of working with the movement, and once he replaced Sandars his misunderstanding and hatred of it radically changed the government's approach and aims. Noel adopted Davies's portrayal of sinister chiefs oppressing a clueless and helpless populace; both of them were determined to eradicate the movement and free Malaitans from its clutches. Many Malaitans continued to live in towns and tend farms, settle their own disputes, and organize politically, but sustained mass arrests over the years that followed crippled their ability to pursue Maasina Rule's grander programs of social transformation. Thus the state successfully destroyed this aspect of Maasina Rule, and many Malaitans would never again work collectively for such goals, even when urged to by their own leaders or subsequent governments.

This left Malaitans to concentrate on their other objective: to avoid a return to their previous relationships with the government and whites or otherwise submit to them. In 1949 Allan reported in the north a view widely held on Malaita. He said To'abaita people were no longer resisting due to "positive goals" of Maasina Rule, "but rather on the negative principles, directed against previous misrule, Maekaleism, Government-native courts, enforced communal work on the road, bad plantation conditions, bogus councillors, misunderstanding of native custom, and the rule of petty Government chiefs, tax gatherers and pimps....The people seem to believe that to comply with the census is to accept all the old irritations." Many Kwaio have explained to me their resolve at that time in similar ways. Simply to be left alone would have satisfied some; others still sought a role in governance, but on new terms that would end such "irritations."[9]

From 1948 into early 1952 this remained the main grounds for confrontation. Most officers by the end of 1947 realized the movement was
a popular one, and most must have recognized that the decision to carry
out Operation Delouse had been disastrous. But it was thought too late to
turn back without losing face, and the government's overriding mission for
the next four years became to reassert government power and legitimacy
and restore "the respect for authority...necessary if Government were to
prevail." Officers doggedly pursued the chimera of forcing Malaitans to
cease all resistance and fully submit—failing, as Marquand observed, to recognize that officers no longer possessed the capacity to accomplish this.
The government, they believed, would become "feared and respected," by
displaying the "power to impose its will." Malaitans had to accept that the
government would "not tolerate Marching Rule *in any shape or form*," and
the state had to show that it was "determined to stamp it out and obtain the
submission of the people to its authority and to that of its approved native
officers." Any sign of willingness to negotiate or compromise, even toward
goals that the government and Malaitans still shared, had to be vigorously
avoided since it might be taken as a display of weakness. If enough punishment and humiliation were dished out, Malaitans would fully surrender.[10]

Officers underrated the will of Malaitans, and their endeavor was doomed
to failure as surely as any Malaitan pursuit of formal independence. Only
when it was abandoned did a settlement become possible. Though the government could intimidate some people into being censused or paying the
tax to avoid prison, this meant little if they remained hostile and unwilling
to cooperate in any other way. As Marquand put it, "Everything to do with
the Government and every plan put forward was very successfully boycotted. The District Officer's hands were completely tied."[11] At the heart of
the matter was a contradiction between trying to force Malaitans to bend
before the government's uncompromising will, while also trying to convince them that the government was a friend and partner with which they
could collaborate toward political and economic advancement. The latter
agenda transcended local officers, since senior colonial officials abroad
began to apply pressure to move forward. The Protectorate's methods of
administration had been anachronistic even before the war, and by 1950
direct rule through unending suppression was an unacceptable and embarrassing mode of governance. Early that year Gregory-Smith was sent out to
resolve the crisis, and then in 1952, more emphatically, Stanley.

The Malaitan triumph over the government's efforts to break them
through gendarme suppression was an important victory for Maasina Rule.
Though officers hoped to coerce "respect" from Malaitans by instilling in
them a fear of government punishments, what emerged was a government
respect for Malaitans in the same sense—a fear of their reaction if repressive measures were again applied. One reason that many have seen Maasina
Rule as a failure is that they have missed the degree to which Malaitans

forced the government to stand down in this matter. Again, some might respond that the old methods of rule were antiquated and would have disappeared eventually even if Malaitans had capitulated. But one could say the same thing about colonial rule in India, or racial segregation in the United States, or the targets of any number of other resistance movements—yet few would dismiss the movements that fought them as irrelevant to the historical turns they forced through. Episodes of liberation often appear preordained in the hindsight of more liberal times.

This victory had long-lasting consequences for how the government dealt with Islander political actions in the years to come, and not just on Malaita. For example, in 1988 William Davenport, who advised the government on the Moro movement on Guadalcanal in 1964, told me that he learned that "The High Commissioner [Robert Foster] was considering whether or not to send a police contingent over to the weather coast to jail everyone connected. He was being urged to do so by a group of hard-case veterans from Maasina Rule days. In the end he decided against it, citing early mistakes made during Maasina Rule, and instead he directed Honiara administrators to invite Moro and his aides to come to Honiara and set up a sort of 'headquarters' Custom House." Two years later, anthropologist Francis Harwood wrote that the government had "acted very reasonably" toward the Christian Fellowship Church she was studying in the Western Solomons, "and cooperation between government and the CFC grows progressively closer for two reasons: A. CFC leadership are as shrewd a bunch as one can find.... B. Government has learned from Marching Rule to avoid direct confrontation."[12]

The change was clearest on Malaita itself. Time and again older Malaitans have told me about past, aggressive government rules and actions they found humiliating and then added: "This was before Maasina Rule." I thought at first they were using Maasina Rule as a chronological marker, but I soon realized that they meant Maasina Rule itself had put an end to such things. Beginning in 1952, officers replaced harangues with negotiation, force with persuasion. They also abandoned the most resented intrusions into people's lives, such as compulsory labor projects, domineering headmen, bullying soldiers, the shooting of pigs, and arrests for census refusal or tax default. Maasina Rule did not win Malaitans control over the government, but it did cast off a good measure of the government's control over Malaitans. The significance of this is perhaps hard for some European readers to fully appreciate, as it is now for many Solomon Islanders who never had to suffer an oppressive and demeaning colonial rule.

Once people realized that the new Malaita Council was to be part of the colonial government, many did not fully support it or refused to cooperate with it. How district officers responded to their contrary actions displayed the shift in their attitudes and policies toward the island's people. More broadly, this was a critical period for the emergence of a new Malaitan relationship with the government that was typified by selective cooperation, ambivalence, and avoidance of overt discord, and the development of a new politics of *kastom* as a basis for autonomy and self-direction. For most Malaitans, the government remained an alien entity rather than a cooperative partner in collective endeavors.

It soon became apparent that many Malaitans had misunderstood the 1952 agreement, particularly regarding what the Malaita Council and its powers would be. When officers and delegates alike told them that the council "belonged to them," they took this to mean that it was in no way a part of the colonial government, which, not surprisingly given recent history, many still regarded with varying degrees of suspicion or hostility. In December 1952, Andersen wrote that, among Malaitans, "It is now generally accepted that the Federal Council is in the process of obtaining all that it has sought for Malaita and that it has virtually won its long struggle," and he later said that after the Malaita Council's formal inauguration in 1953, "Many people thought that the District had been given 'Freedom' and were surprised to find Government Officers still on Malaita."[13]

Some council delegates found themselves caught between officers initially wary of their political pasts and followers who suspected they were now puppets of those same officers. Over the next election cycles, various delegates were turned out by their people in favor of men expected to challenge the government more. Andersen believed this was a key reason the council elected Sisili to replace Ga'a as its president in 1955, though officers were relieved, and many supporters disappointed, when Sisili was dutiful and cooperative. Fearful that Malaitans would fully reject the council, officers tried to disguise their direct connections with it. Andersen had Ga'a and Sisili tour without him for this reason, and Allan wrote that actions taken by the central government (in which he now served) had to be falsely credited to the council if they were to be accepted. A later district commissioner, W St G Anderson, advocated giving the council control over headmen in order to help remove "suspicion that Government is interfering with the politics of the Malaita people.... It may be argued," he said, "that by this move Government will lose its last remaining hold on the people. This is far from being the case, insomuch as the council in its short history has given adequate evidence of its loyalty and ability to cooperate with Central Government."[14]

It was a tricky balancing act for the government to try to persuade Malaitans that the council was their own and was running Malaita, but at the same time show them that the government was still in charge and claimed authority. Likewise, delegates had to convince constituents that they were carrying out their wishes, while they also worked with government officers to keep the council viable. The Malaita Council has sometimes been portrayed as powerless and unrepresentative or as a sort of political spackle intended merely to quiet resistance.[15] This can seem the case if one only reads the formal rules by which it was established, under which the high commissioner appointed delegates and could veto any of their decisions. In practice, though, the government dreaded the consequences of council collapse and was loath to either antagonize its members or undermine its status in the eyes of Malaitans. In practice, the people selected their own council members—sometimes, as I have said, because they openly hoped that they would oppose the government—and I know of no high commissioner having rejected their choices. Moreover, officers tried to choose for some of the government's few appointed seats men who would not antagonize their constituencies, some of them former resistance leaders. Even before the council was created, Russell warned that if the government was forced to quash its decisions it would be rendered "inefficacious" and that this would lead Malaitans to set up their own alternatives. The government thus wanted to avoid bluntly negating council decisions it disliked or thought impracticable, and preferred for the district commissioner to try to convince members of their inadvisability when those matters were considered. More often than not, the problem was a lack of money. This is likely what Andersen meant when he said he sometimes interfered in discussions when members "developed fantasies of their own." Members and their constituents had big ideas and plans, but the council had to work with a tiny budget and feeble infrastructure.[16]

Most members of the Malaita Council did try hard to make it work, but few possessed the know-how or training to administer the complex financial and other aspects of governing the island. Andersen recorded that, by the end of 1953, "President Ga'a and some members realised Council could not stand on its own two feet, but they had difficulty in convincing their followers of this." Few delegates wanted to estrange their people by telling them of the council's limitations and dependence on government officers, and some did not properly consult with their communities or report to them on their work. This left the people feeling shut out of the governing process, as Malaitans always had been. Malaitans still sometimes complain that their representatives do not keep them properly informed.[17]

Council delegates soon became more sophisticated in the fiscal aspects of their work, though a few were embittered by financial and other limitations and blamed them on government paternalism or interference. Nonetheless, in September 1954, when Russell returned to Malaita, now in a more benign role, to replace Andersen as district commissioner, he found the council a "power-house" that was, he said, more dynamic, imaginative, and efficient than those of other districts.[18] Many Malaitans were developing a different perspective, however. Though officers like Andersen and Russell clearly wanted the council to succeed and worked hard for it, they wished it to do so as part of the state, and the central government was anxious to keep control. Dissimulation could not for long conceal this truth from suspicious Malaitans, and many did not like it. As time passed, disappointment grew over the council's nonrevolutionary nature and its failure to provide development to the degree hoped for. A large proportion of its tax-supported budgets during the 1950s was spent not on the Malaitan people but on council salaries and its operation.[19]

Officers believed that the council was fulfilling Malaitans' political ambitions. There was truth to that belief with regard to former resistance leaders and others who belonged to it, but it repeated the old mistake of focusing on the views of leaders instead of the populace. District Commissioner Anderson observed astutely in 1957, after six months on Malaita, "Undoubtedly the council has gone far towards satisfying the political aspirations, but one wonders at times, whether it has only satisfied the more vociferous inhabitants of the island, and the more backward look upon the council as just another Government institution foisted upon them."[20]

Many of those deemed "more backward" were in the southern half of the island, where fewer government projects were put in place. John Naitoro described the perspective from 'Are'are: "In reality, there were few real advantages from the Council. It marked the restoration of central government power on the island. The Council came to be used, with headmen and assistant headmen, as another means of maintaining order and stability, with only limited scope for promoting development. It hadn't been operating long before people were expressing their dissatisfaction with it. They looked for other ways to satisfy local level aspirations and interests. Attempts at more independent local organization continued. Some of this activity was a continuation of things that were started during Maasina Rule."[21] In Kwaio, with the largest proportion of people living inland, even less help had been forthcoming and anti-council feelings were rife.

Not all Malaitans were so unhappy with the council. Some areas benefited more from its work; a few schools were quickly established, and some medical services were provided and these increased over time. Some Malaitans successfully pursued business endeavors, particularly in Lau, To'abaita, Langalanga, and parts of Kwara'ae. In other places, however, such as the south, Baelelea, Baegu, Fataleka, and almost all bush areas, many people increasingly saw the council as doing little for them. Even in these areas, though, few were openly hostile in their interactions with government officials, who were no longer harassing or arresting people. Face-to-face relations were more amiable than they had ever been, and for the most part they remained so for years after. Neither officers nor Malaitans wanted a return to open hostility, and most Malaitans saw little to gain by kicking up a serious fuss.[22]

Officers worked hard to help businesses, start people growing cash crops (particularly cocoa and copra), and further develop the council. But in addition to a shortage of funds and an inadequate infrastructure, they and the council remained hampered by a deep Malaitan distrust of government that had not dissipated. Some feared government schemes would leave them dependent upon or indebted to the state or would otherwise cost them their independence so were unenthusiastic about or shunned them.[23] Another problem was that many basic tools of governance had so recently been used as weapons to punish and discipline Malaitans or as tools of European domination—headmen, taxation, censusing, sanitary regulations, labor on government-sponsored projects (on which thousands had recently worked as prisoners), and, of course, government courts. For many Malaitans during the 1950s and even after, these remained evocative symbols of government as something done not *for* the people but *to* them.

As Andersen handed over to Russell in September 1954, he told him that disillusionment with the council had produced "a slight resurgence of past malpractices in some of the poorer areas" and that "the present form of militant political thinking on Malaita will persist until more wealth brings higher living standards." But he warned, "Punitive measures or threats of them for political purposes would be a very retrograde step until the general outlook changes considerably."[24]

Tensions were most notable around taxation and native courts, and a brief look at how these developed will illuminate broader patterns in post– Maasina Rule Malaitan-government relations. The council quickly realized that it needed more money to pursue any real agenda, and one of its early acts was to increase the tax rate. Andersen had decided to give a low priority to tax enforcement so as to focus on the economic development that he saw as so crucial to both social and political progress. He did urge Malaitans to pay, telling them, "Tax is the blood of the Council," but over the years that followed, many did not.[25] Few refused outright or declared political reasons for defaulting; most instead pleaded poverty. How officers reacted to this during the 1950s displays the new, softer approach toward those who disobeyed them. One area where few paid was inland Kwaio, which received virtually no government services (as has remained the case ever since). Sub- Inspector Allan Lindley, in charge of Malaita's police, patrolled the area in May 1958, at a time when a tax hike to £2 was planned. In meetings with the community and council delegates about the tax, he found himself pitted against masters of friendly resistance. His report captures the frustrations of tax collection in parts of Malaita during the decade:

> There is and has been a great deal of talk about the new tax. The general atti-
> tude as far as I could make out, and was told, was that there is not any outright
> refusal to pay out but they say they just do not have the money in the bush. I was
> told at both meetings that they would try hard to pay *but* only if all the saltwater
> and the remainder of the bush people of Malaita had paid. It was told to me that
> Delegate [Toloasi Teoboo] was only elected to the council last year because he
> went around saying he had worked the custom not to pay the higher tax.... It is
> said that a large number of people have not paid their tax (5/-) for last year, not
> because they have not got it but that Delegate Anifelo does not collect it or go

round but only fishes.... Koio [Kwaio] is crawling with rumors about tax such as: if they pay the new tax the B.S.I.P. will become a Colony; that Guadalcanal is £5 and Malaita will also be that and pigs and gardens will be taxed; all women will have to pay tax; that Waiparo and Alic Nonohinimai said they must not pay (a statement without foundation to the best of my knowledge). When I asked the bush people if they had tried to find work I was met with the answer that the wives of married men did not trust them out of Malaita alone (laughter at the meeting) and that the single men spent their money on rubbish at stores. I suggested the Baunani Plantation [in west Kwaio] but was told the boss-boy would not employ bush people but only saltwater, also that the recruiting ships did not stay long enough in one place to allow time for news to come up and them to get down. When I suggested that they could "pay" for their tax by working on roads, council buildings and so on it was not met with enthusiasm, in other words I was met with all manner of excuses.... At Fa'agania... the people were troubled by the tax saying that they had paid certain monies to [Maasina Rule] and that they now wanted that money back to pay the tax.... When it was suggested that they grow rice it was put to me how could they get it out to the coast.[26]

Lindley left unsatisfied, but he did not berate the people, and he could not have arrested anyone even had he wished to, since there was now no law for prosecuting tax violations. Shortly before this, Anderson, disturbed by the many defaulters on Malaita, had asked Colin Allan, still in Honiara, what he might do about it. Allan assured him that he could arrest them under a law that he had used for this purpose during Maasina Rule, and an acting legal adviser seemed to concur. Anderson's doubts were confirmed, however, when, in 1958, the first four convictions he obtained were quashed. It appeared that the government's tax arrests during Maasina Rule had been illegal all along. Anderson feared this legal decision might be "sufficient to destroy the slender thread of administrative authority on Malaita."[27] The next year a new law was instituted that allowed local councils to take civil action against those who flouted the new £2 tax and officers to file criminal charges if they could show that the defaulter had had the money. But the legal procedure involved proved cumbersome for officers, who in any case did not have sufficient manpower to chase violators down, particularly through the mountains, and the law was too complex for native courts to prosecute. Tax collection would remain problematic in the years to come.[28]

The government also encountered problems with the courts, of a nature that will by now be all too familiar to readers. Officers had quickly reinstituted them across the island. The courts were supposed to apply certain government laws and also, under section 12 of the 1953 Native Courts Regulation, "native custom" and to handle both using English legal procedure and rules of evidence.[29] Permitting courts to highlight "custom" was crucial to gaining Malaitan acceptance of them. Officers' conception of custom, however, was the same as in the past: to be legitimate, a custom had to be pre-European in origin. Forewarned by, but still not fully grasping Maasina Rule usages of *kastom,* the government in 1953 tried to shore up the custom concept, and a "Native Court Book," issued under the name of the Malaita Council, gave courts guidance for determining whether or not a practice qualified: "When Native Courts judge these troubles they must make quite sure that they are against a proper native custom and not against a new custom that has not been going for a long time. The Court can always ask some of the old men to come into Court and tell them all about the old customs but these old men cannot help to judge cases." The booklet also warned, "Do not let anybody start new customs."[30] The same message was stressed in a 1957 instructional book issued to the courts: "The custom which is broken must be an old one from before the time Government came to the Solomons. It would be no use a Council Member saying that a man who did not do what he said was breaking the native custom: Council members are a very new thing. Also be careful not to mix up what is in the Bible with law and custom.... It would be a good thing for Presidents [of courts] to write down wrongs in their sub-districts against which there were tabus long ago, and to show these to the D.C. or D.O. These should be read out in the Council and possibly passed as Resolutions so that they would not be forgotten."[31] We have seen the past artificiality and unworkability of this custom concept, and the idea that there were living authorities on details of pre-European ways was even more fictional in the 1950s. As before, officers knew little of indigenous rules or their newness or antiquity.

The results were predictable, again. In many places by mid-1953 few disputes were being brought to headmen or the police, and instead they were taken to what one government officer referred to as "custom men" to settle. Only when one party was dissatisfied did people turn to the government—colonial justice was utilized primarily when it suited litigants, drawn on more as a power of convenience rather than one to be reckoned with. In 1954, Russell found only two courts (and "possibly" two others) on Malaita were "working within the bounds of natural justice. One cannot say more. It is quite certain that not a single case in the other courts and only the exceptional case in the better courts would pass the scrutiny of a legal officer on review." By the next year there were 13 courts in operation, but Russell said that reporting crimes to the police was "the exception rather than the rule." Most of the southern half of the island, moreover, was "totally unpatrolled." In other words, most native courts were operating much as had most of the Maasina Rule legal bodies. But this time no "Operation Delouse" was launched. In the realm of law, many Malaitans were getting much of what they had wanted.[32]

The courts were not supposed to judge as custom any crime also covered by a British law, and they were allowed to impose only limited punishments for custom offenses, which Russell called "petty native affairs."[33] But by 1958, Anderson complained the courts were awarding "fabulous compensations" for violations of "minor 'custom' laws," and Attorney General J N Glover bemoaned the "vague and almost unlimited jurisdiction" they enjoyed under the Native Courts Regulation. Glover thought their jurisdiction over customs should be limited to customs made into resolutions and approved by the high commissioner. This was not done, and a decade later "custom offences," handled mostly as torts, continued to dominate native courts. Officers by then believed the courts had much improved, at least in their procedures. District Commissioner Richard Turpin in 1967 reported Malaita's 14 native courts heard 1,000 cases annually. He supposed custom might "cease to be applicable as the people grow away from old ideas although judging from many indications received a 'reversion to custom' may well be possible as a reaction from too much westernization....I consider Government should now accept that native courts should be given a full and proper part in the administration of justice and not be regarded as a necessary evil until custom, pagans and District Commissioners have died out."[34]

During the 1950s, the government's biggest court problems were in 'Are'are. As the Malaita Council absorbed most of the major Maasina Rule and Federal Council leaders, Waiparo of Takataka emerged as the key resistance leader across the southern half of the island. His activities set a style that would be followed by many other *kastom* movements across Malaita in years that followed. Waiparo was introduced earlier in this book as a founding figure of Maasina Rule, and then as an 'Are'are leader with links to the Federal Council and a rival of Nono'oohimae and his attempts to work with the government.[35] Now, under Waiparo's leadership, 'Are'are, parts of Small Malaita, and later Kwaio set up a structure of "sub-district committees," conceived as a political and administrative alternative to the Malaita Council and to the government generally. These comprised smaller committees designated by functions (eg, "Farm Committee," "Shell Money Committee") similar to those in Maasina Rule. Waiparo was head of his area's "Kastom Committee." At the center of the committees were *alaha*, and a key part of Waiparo's message was that they were 'Are'are's legitimate leaders and that the Malaita Council should not be allowed to undermine their authority. Areas without traditions of *alaha* appointed them (eg, Kwaio *alafa*), or "chiefs," to lead *kastom* political activities.[36]

There had been talk of Waiparo, too, becoming a Malaita Council member, but as Russell reported in 1955, it was thought that "By association with Europeans or the Malaita Council he is likely to have his knowledge contaminated by what is not pure Ariari custom." A trope in *kastom* discourse is that foreign and indigenous knowledges and behaviors are to some degree incompatible. This stems partly from Malaitans' experiences with people who gain sophistication or education in foreign ways and thereafter disparage local ones and become alienated from home communities. Some have kept their children from schools for this reason. More to the political point here, the fear was that the government might absorb Waiparo as it had other resistance leaders, undermining the entire thrust of his *kastom* message advocating autonomy from it. At the same time, a headman informed Russell that Waiparo had to approve any Malaita Council plans before people would cooperate. "The inference," Russell concluded, "is that only measures consonant with local custom will be given the full publicity that the Malaita Council hopes for."[37] The degree to which this activity opposed or contested government agendas was left unsaid or explicitly denied, but Andersen worried that the committees might try to "usurp the powers of the Council," which, as indicated by Naitoro's remarks earlier, lacked support in the south. Waiparo, however, presented the 'Are'are movement as in no way opposed to the council—it was qualitatively different from and parallel to it. He and his people would work on *kastom,* and the government would do its work; there was no reason for argument.[38]

Kastom was even more prominent in the 'Are'are movement's ideology than it had been in Maasina Rule, but now it was couched more in terms of preserving "old custom." Waiparo warned that if *kastom* was not "straightened out" and codified it would be lost forever. His own sweeping knowledge of Malaitan traditions was widely asserted. Years later many recalled him simply as "a man who knew all about *kastom*" or "the man who woke up *kastom*" after Maasina Rule ended. But although some officers at times took this at face value and worried that Waiparo was leading 'Are'are backward to an obsolete past, the political thrust of his message was unmistakable. He and his followers pursued fundamental goals that were also central to Maasina Rule: autonomy, self-determination, and freedom from interference in their affairs. Also like Maasina Rule, *kastom* was particularly important in the legal realm, where it was juxtaposed with and unabashedly given priority over "government law."[39]

Waiparo deftly played to the European conception of *kastom* as "old Malaitan custom" and manipulated the ambiguity of the movement's political position when dealing with officers, leaving them unsure of his intentions and without grounds for accusing him of subversive intent. In this way he extended the subtle political strategy of 'Are'are leaders during the early years of Maasina Rule. At an 'Are'are meeting in 1955, when Russell and Malaita Council President Sisili pushed attendees to participate in council-run development initiatives, Waiparo responded, "The committees were not opposed in principle to progress or new things. But they were concentrating on codifying their custom, writing down their genealogies, and listing land boundaries. When this work was complete they would decide what new things could be admitted without danger to their social structure. They were not against planting of cocoa but the older generation were in favour of concentrating on subsistence crops. If the younger generation wanted new crops let them go ahead."[40] Waiparo's message here, framed in terms of "old custom" and "the older generation" obscured the facts that many of his followers were young; that he was a savvy, modern political operator; and that many of the "customs" at issue were fully recognized to be contemporary in origin.

When Andersen toured southern Malaita to instruct people on running native courts, he thought the 'Are'are bodies were "a little dominated by thoughts of 'Custom'" and so persuaded Waiparo and his *alaha* to sit in on his training session. Wrote Andersen, "He had the idea that I should give the Court members training about 'law' and that he should then give them training about 'Custom.' My insistence on his being present was something of a boomerang as Waeparo produced a parallel in custom for everything but dynamiting fish and licensing a firearm." Though Waiparo late in life voiced some approval of the Malaita Council, the 'Are'are committees during most of the 1950s became in essence its rivals, as did similar groups elsewhere on Malaita. Waiparo later talked of generating a united *kastom* that would amalgamate all of Malaita, but, though his influence was widespread, this never eventuated in any formal sense, and since Maasina Rule, *kastom* movements have been mostly local or regional in scale. Nonetheless, *kastom* remains an idea that can at times unite Malaitans as a single people with a common outlook, particularly when they interact with non-Malaitans. The bonds that formed during Maasina Rule have never fully disappeared.[41]

This was the template for much of the *kastom* political activity on Malaita over the decades to come as movements came and went, some existing briefly, others for decades, still others from time to time changing their names but little else. I will not address these later movements in this book, but to take just one moment in time, in 1968 a Honiara conference discussed "custom movements on Malaita," attended by a representative of the "Special Branch," which was investigating them. Their brief listed ongoing movements as the "Political Condition Movement" in Baegu, Baelelea, Fataleka, and Lau; the "Gwanataru Bush Landowners Custom Committees" in west Baegu and west Fataleka; the "Fataleka Bush Landowners"; the "Fifi'i Custom Movement" in east Kwaio; "Olofimae's Custom Committee" in Kwarekwareo; Timothy Bobongi and Sade Maeli's movement on Kwaloai island in Lau; "Dausabea's Malaita Landowners" in Kwara'ae; and the "Maroupaina Committee" in east 'Are'are. There were others as well, and officers worried they might coalesce and noted that several Malaita Council members were prominent in them.[42] In some cases, the movements were a means for council members to mediate their relationships with the government and their people. Most *kastom* movements, like Waiparo's, have not portrayed themselves as against the government, but all have to some degree been presented as alternatives to it and as a means to interact with it from a position of autonomy and equality. All have been at pains to contrast their *kastom* platforms with the policies of the government, though they have sometimes urged the government to adopt their agendas as being more fitting for Malaitans.

In this way, many rural Malaitans distinguish their polities from a government they continue to view as an external entity that cares little about their welfare. This feeling of separation in some ways deepened after Maasina Rule, both during and after the colonial period, as money, development, and investment were concentrated in Honiara, and as endless official discussions of and plans for decentralization or devolution of power came to naught. The state was not prepared to allow "chiefs" or other rural leaders a significant role in governance. In the decades since Solomon Islands' independence in 1978, rural alienation has been further and increasingly aggravated by the corruption widespread among elected and other government officials. I once watched a politician's representative carefully oversee distribution of small bribes to each of a community's men before a parliamentary election, and afterward I listened to recipients bemoan the lack of a "real government" that would offer them something more. When I asked why they took the money, one man quickly answered, to general agreement, "What else will we ever get from government?" I have heard elderly Maasina Rule veterans observe that, whatever their faults, at least colonial officers were honest and hard working, unlike government men today.

The ongoing estrangement many Malaitans feel from the state, for better and worse, is in part a legacy of Maasina Rule. Just as Cameron and Russell more than six decades ago warned might happen, the years of suppression forever altered Malaitan attitudes toward politics and the state, and the clock cannot be turned back. During those years, Maasina Rule's political ideology congealed as an integral feature of rural Malaitans' worldviews, particularly the refusal to surrender autonomy and direction of their affairs to the state and its laws, programs, and "foreign" ways of thinking.[43] Many young people have told me that they still follow this creed because "It is what our fathers taught us," often accompanied by descriptions of dangers that government presents to society. Today this perspective permeates political thought and activity in much of rural Malaita, and many Malaitan communities in Honiara, though it often competes with or is contextually overridden by desires for "development" and opportunity, or for the individualism of the capitalist economy. The ideology itself is referred to as *kastom*. *Kastom* in this usage is not an anachronistic longing for the past, or an attempt to preserve or revive lost traditions per se, but rather a modern and evolving political philosophy born from the colonial and postcolonial experience. *Kastom* on Malaita is deeply rooted in a long, common history of resistance to domination and exploitation, and shared recognition of the social costs of wholesale embrace of "modern" ethics and behaviors.

I have in this book given considerable attention to colonial conflations of *kastom* and "custom," and how these so often confused Europeans as to what Malaitans were saying and seeking. During the 1980s and 1990s, anthropologists and historians established a large and productive body of work on "custom" in Melanesia. It generated many insights and greatly influenced my own thinking. But despite this literature's contributions, readers familiar with it cannot but have noticed similarities between the colonial confusions of custom and *kastom* and the way many scholars conflated *kastom* and "culture." Anthropologists often relied on a commonsensical understanding of the term and its origins, frequently expressed in a simple etymological aside: "*kastom* (from the English 'custom')," prefacing an ahistorical analysis. Not only did this oversimplify but, left by itself, it could also distort the concept's history and meanings. Anthropologists writing on "custom movements" generally saw "culture," or "custom," as the focal meaning of *kastom,* and they were understandably interested in exploring how "culture" was politicized. This is a legitimate question, but for Malaitans, the focal meanings of *kastom* have always been modern, political ones, which they sometimes—and sometimes not—"culturize" by linking them to specific Malaitan traditions. Even when Malaitans use *kastom* in ways that seem to more closely resemble "custom" or "culture" (including sometimes in recent years with a usage of *kalsa* or "culture"), it almost always carries a contemporary political subtext or framing.

This false conflation prompted anthropologists to sometimes ask questions that led to analytical dead ends: Was this or that aspect of *kastom* "real culture," or was it a "spurious," "manipulated," or "invented tradition"? Why did Christians who openly renounced ancestral ways still organize themselves around *kastom*, sometimes allied with non-Christians, who were "still living *kastom*"? How, given the tremendous cultural diversity of Melanesians, could they possibly use *kastom* as a shared symbol for overarching identities, and did this not mean that for such purposes *kastom* had to remain semantically empty?[44] For Malaita, these questions become moot, or at least simplistic, with the understanding of *kastom* as a political ideology rooted more in shared historical experiences and ongoing political realities than in any common commitment to specific past cultural ways. *Kastom* was not a synonym for or often even about "culture" in the anthropological sense of the concept at that time.

This is not to argue, of course, that *kastom* is never used as a gloss for "traditions" in the European sense (particularly moral values attributed to the past), that it is somehow acultural, or that it does not become intertwined with and shaped by local cultures. I have elsewhere published detailed analyses of how the latter can occur, and how *kastom* ideology is significantly changing religious practice in the Kwaio area on Malaita where I work, and I would be surprised if broadly similar processes are not ongoing elsewhere. In places where *kastom* has for decades been a central aspect of local life, it has become part of what Marshall Sahlins called people's "culturally specific modes of change." I also do not wish to be reductionist; *kastom* is an extremely polysemic and dynamic term, and Melanesians have employed nearly as many usages of it as anthropologists have of "culture." Not only are its meanings contextual, but they also vary greatly from place to place and over time. For example, *kastom*'s meanings on Malaita differ in many ways from those found in Vanuatu, where it has a very different political history and where the government has more successfully brought *kastom* within its outlook and policies than has the Solomons state. Even in other parts of the Solomons, *kastom* can mean very different things than it does on Malaita, particularly in places where Maasina Rule never took hold. One weaker aspect of the anthropological *kastom* literature was that its overarching analyses of "*kastom* in Melanesia" were often insufficiently attentive to the great diversity in the concept's meanings across the region.[45]

Today many Solomon Islanders besides Malaitans express hostility toward their government, but it is on Malaita that alienation has been most steady and enduring. There, in recent years, some *kastom* groups have loudly critiqued the government's shortcomings such as its corruption and disregard for rural areas, the hoarding of power and resources in Honiara, and the obvious declines in the country's economy and infrastructure. Their message to the state today is often a complaint of abandonment and malfeasance rather than a vow to defy its control—gross neglect is difficult to "resist."[46] But enduring anger and resentment toward government is always close to the surface. This facet of Malaitan *kastom* ideology differentiates it from *kastom* applied as a less contentious mediation of old and new ways or as a more subtle form of politico-economic enclavement (though *kastom* has also played those roles on Malaita).[47]

For most Malaitans, *kastom* has never lost its grounding as a challenge to the government, and this theme has in recent years moved to the fore as anger at the Solomon Islands state has grown. Shared discontent in the late 1980s and 1990s inspired normally rival Malaitan groups to undertake coordinated actions on Honiara's streets to demand compensation from the central state, and then more tragically during the political crisis at the century's turn to intimidate the government and drain its coffers with militant actions and compensation claims.[48] It is within these scenarios of dissatisfaction and rebellion that various government officials have most blatantly attempted to harness *kastom* sentiments to their own interests, particularly through the historically and politically evocative act of compensation claims. In doing so, they try to tap into not indigenous "culture" in the older anthropological sense but rather *kastom*'s political, ideological force. Because most politicians are unwilling to delegate real political power to rural peoples and many hold them in low regard or even contempt as political actors, it should surprise no one that their evocations of *kastom* are often manipulative and trivializing—they are, after all, self-serving politicians. The militant actions of the late 1990s and early 2000s were in some cases thuggery and extortion, but many militants had political motivations. To frame these events merely as state representatives attempting to manipulate "culture" or "custom" obscures the political meanings *kastom* has acquired over the past 60-plus years (particularly regarding law and compensation).

Furthermore, as Matthew G Allen has shown in a recent study, if we perceive politicians as simply stage-managing these activities, as manipulating ignorant, rank-and-file Malaitans, we make the same fundamental error as did British officers who analyzed Maasina Rule in the same terms. Many Malaitan (and Guadalcanal) former militants gave Allen heartfelt *kastom*-linked explanations for why they acted as they did, sometimes while disparaging their leaders. Of course many other Malaitans, and even some of the militants, viewed the tragic aspects of these events with as much dismay as did other Solomon Islanders.[49]

Despite the perseverance of *kastom* ideas and anger at politicians, few Malaitans want to bring down "the government" per se (as opposed to particular politicians), and *kastom* movements since Maasina Rule have typically not sought this. Like so many Solomon Islanders, most just want a better government, though few are optimistic for the future. My late friend Ma'aanamae, who grew up in the hamlet of Basiana, the man who bludgeoned Officer William Bell's skull with a rifle barrel, was a veteran of more than a half century of *kastom* political actions. When my father visited me in Kwaio many years ago, friends performed for him a five-hour ancestral chant about the killing of Bell and its aftermath, and in the middle of the concert Ma'aanamae made a formal speech and asked me to translate it for my father. In it he employed the events of 1927 as a metaphor to express how many Malaitans view the enduring relationship between *kastom* and *gafamanu*:

> Officer Bell was killed because he tried to bring his own law here and use it to put an end to *kastom* law. Then government came again and arrested Basiana and others who killed and took them away and hanged them. The government wanted *kastom* to be finished. And Basiana, he wanted the government to be finished. That is what the two of them were thinking, and that is why they killed each other, why they took Basiana and hanged him. But how is *kastom* going to be finished? It is still here today. And the law, even though they killed Mister Bell, how is it going to be finished? It's still here. So although the law stands today, so, too, does *kastom* stand today. They wanted to finish it. But no!

Abbreviations

The following are confined to citations and references, except for BSIP, SILC, and SSEM.

AR   British Solomon Islands Protectorate Annual Report

BSIP   British Solomon Islands Protectorate. Unless otherwise noted, "BSIP" file numbers refer to files in the Solomon Islands National Archive, Honiara.

C, CF   Confidential File, as coded in BSIP file numbers or on documents

corr   Correspondence

DC   District Commissioner

DH   District Headman

DO   District Officer

HC   High Commissioner of the Western Pacific

IR   Intelligence Report

MAR   Malaita District Annual Report

MQR   Malaita District Quarterly Report, for quarters ending on date cited

NIV   *Not in Vain* (South Sea Evangelical Mission journal)

PC   Project Canterbury. At http://anglicanhistory.org/oceania/ can be found many Anglican Church documents related to the Solomons. The acronym "PC" after a reference indicates the document is there. All accessed 9 Nov 2011.

PIM   *Pacific Islands Monthly*

RC   Resident Commissioner

S, SF   Secret File, as coded in BSIP file numbers or on documents

SCL   *Southern Cross Log* (Anglican Melanesian Mission journal)

SDNA   Secretary for Development and Native Affairs

SG   Secretary to the Government

SILC   Solomon Islands Labour Corps

SSEM   South Sea Evangelical Mission

WPHC   Western Pacific High Commission

WPHC IC   Western Pacific High Commission, Incoming Correspondence

Notes

Introduction

1. My oral historical accounts and knowledge of Malaitan cultures are biased toward Malaita's midsection because I have spent most of my time in the Solomons (something over five years) in the Kwaio area, and anthropologist Roger Keesing also produced a body of work on Kwaio that is relevant to this book. Furthermore, the best data I have from elsewhere were collected in neighboring Kwara'ae by anthropologist Ben Burt, who has generously made material available to me. To balance this somewhat, there is less archival material about Kwaio than other parts of Malaita, particularly about the inland areas where most Kwaio lived during the years covered here. I am writing another book that is a more cultural analysis of *kastom* ideas, practices, and history, particularly with regard to Kwaio women (Akin nd).

2. In places I include with Malaita the island of Ulawa, which, partly due to close cultural and historical links with south Malaita, in late 1947 was for a time made part of Malaita District. Naitoro discussed a conception in 'Are'are in southern Malaita of "greater 'Are'are" as including western Makira, east Guadalcanal, Ulawa, and the Three Sisters islands to Ulawa's south (1993, 26–28). Readers seeking historical information on the Solomons as a whole can start with fine studies such as Bennett 1987 for socioeconomic history; Laracy 1976, Hilliard 1969 and 1978, and O'Brien 1995 on Christian missions; and Lindstrom and White 1990 on World War II. On the Queensland and Fiji labor trades, see Corris 1973b and Moore 1985, among many other detailed analyses.

3. Said 1979; Cohn 1996; Dirks 1996, ix, passim; Ballantyne and Burton 2005. For a good overview of debates over colonial knowledge, see Ballantyne 2008. Banivanua-Mar has coined the term "Melanesianism" for the distinctive Orientalism applied to the Western Pacific, which emphasized Islander savagery, violence, cannibalism, and the like (2007); Malaitan peoples were often portrayed as epitomizing these traits.

4. Cohn 1996, 16; Dirks 2001, chap 3, passim.

5. Guha 1989; Irschick 1994; Thomas 1994, 15–16; Cohn 1996, 21–22, passim; Trautmann 1997, 135–136, 217–222; 1999, 44, passim; 2009; Peabody 2001; Wagoner 2003; Newbury 2003; Pierce 2006; see also Breckenridge and van der Veer 1993; Mir 2010.

6. Thomas 1994, x; see also Thomas 1992a.

7. From 1921–1928, the resident commissioner was Richard Kane, who arrived from Fiji, where schemes of indirect rule had been in place since the nineteenth century (see Kaplan 1989, 1995; Thomas 1990, 1994). We will see that Kane wanted to develop similar policies in the Solomons but was frustrated, particularly on Malaita. On broad imperial models applied to colonized people, especially those who resisted, see Stoler and Cooper 1997, 13–14, and Goh 2007. For the conveyance of administrative models and legal codes from India to African and other colonies, including as carried by transferred officials, see Metcalf 2007, chap 1. Influences of these models and codes are perceptible in the Solomons, but they came indirectly, filtered through African colonies.

8. Steinmetz 2003, 42.

9. Hogbin was the only professionally trained anthropologist to work on Malaita until the 1960s. Ivens published excellent linguistic (1918, 1921, 1929, 1932/1934) and ethnographic studies (1928a, and esp 1972; see also Fox 1925; Hopkins 1928; Codrington 1969). Hogbin in 1933 began advocating establishment of native courts and councils, and after the war he advised the government on reinstituting them and on how to contend with rising political discontent (see this book, chapters 3 and 4). Later, Officer Tom Russell published a good paper in *Oceania* (1950a). Cadet Cyril Belshaw (who did not work on Malaita) became a well-known anthropologist. I discuss aspects of Belshaw's work and writings by Officer Colin Allan later in this book.

10. See Stoler and Cooper 1997, 7–8.

11. For the broader context of this confusion, including interconnections between anthropological and colonial modes of analysis, see Johannes Fabian's seminal critique of anthropology made at the time much of the literature on *kastom* was being published (1983).

12. Im Thurn 1922: xvii; Roberts 1927, 154; Barrow nd, part 3, 55.

Chapter 1: The Half Century Before

1. For studies of the labor trade, begin with Scarr 1967, 1970; Corris 1973b; Saunders 1980, 1982; Bennett 1987; Shineberg 1999; Banivanua-Mar 2007; re Malaita, see esp Moore 1985. For recruiting voyage accounts, see Rannie 1912; Dickinson 1927; Cromar 1935; Giles 1968; Melvin 1977; Palmer 1973; Philp 1978; Wawn 1973.

2. Corris 1973b, 24, 38–43; Price and Baker 1976, 115; Meleisea 1980; Saunders 1984, 225–227; Shineberg 1999; Moore 2007. Siegel said that more than 80 percent of Islanders who arrived in Fiji in the last years of its labor trade were Malaitans (1987, 53).

3. See Patteson 1871; Allan 1958, 2; Scarr 1967, 143–145, 160; 1968, 5–6; Corris 1973b, 55; Sankoff 1985; Moore 1985, 337–343; Fifiʻi 1988a, 220–221; Maʻaanamae quoted in Akin 1993, 79–80; Burt 1994, 87–89. To cut length I deleted a section of this book on the complexities of defining "voluntary" recruitment, but for a discussion of some of these, see Banivanua-Mar 2007, chap 2. Her book also details violent aspects of life on Queensland plantations.

4. Mahaffy nd, 23; Moore 1985, 52–55; Keesing 1992a, 199–206.

5. Woodford 1897a; Mahaffy 1902; Edge-Partington 1910a; Northam 1913, 6; Barnett 1914; Ramoi 1928, 62–63; Ivens 1928a, 43; Ashley 1929b, 6; Hopkins 1934,

35, 36; Cromar 1935, 114; Scarr 1967, 281–282; Melvin 1977, 48; Keesing and Corris 1980, 42; Moore 1985, 79; D'Arcy 1987; Grant 2007, 16; see Shineberg 1999, 52; Banivanua-Mar 2007. The cartridge shortage is evident in Bell's report of a fight with a large group of Malaitans who shot only arrows (1918f).

6. See Hopkins 1934, 35; Ivens 1928a, 153, 184–185; 1972, chap 14, esp page 296; Fox 1925, 305; personal communications from Arugeni, To'oni, Folofo'u, Ri'ika, and Larikeni, all 1982.

7. On passage masters and other middlemen, see Cromar 1935, 217–221, 299; Ivens 1928a, 190–191, 199; Corris 1970; 1973b, 60–67; Keesing 1992b.

8. Cromar 1935, 151; Hopkins 1930, 21; Ivens 1928a, 65; Corris 1970, 257–259; Wawn 1973, 405, 414; Melvin 1977, 54.

9. Melvin 1977, 50 (1st quote); Wilson 1899, 7 (2nd); Malaita District 1909 (3rd). See also Wilson 1932, 197.

10. Guppy 1887, 5; Wilson 1899, 4; see Ivens 1918, 184, 225; Burt and Kwa'ioloa 2001, 96. Re tobacco as a recruiting motivation, see Bell quoted in Keesing and Corris 1980, 75.

11. See Woodford 1888, 356–357; 1890b, 16; 1903; AR 1897–1898, 4; Mahaffy 1902, 9; Bell 1917, 2; Higginson 1928; Ivens 1928a, 72; Hopkins 1928, 30; 1934, 17; Marwick 1935, 38–39; Philp 1978, 183; Boutilier 1982, 52–53; Moore 1985, 348. On Malaitan attacks on ships and European retaliation, see Keesing 1986b; Burt 1994, 91–94; Akin 2000. Inexplicably, Malaita's Officer George Sandars (nd, 86), and anthropologist Ian Hogbin (1935, 19) said women were rarely killed for bounties. See Montgomery 1892 for one example of a more positive missionary appraisal of the labor trade.

12. Hopkins 1934, 13, 31, 34. See, eg, Great Britain Colonial Office 1863, 48–49; Bruce 1881; Wilson 1883, 56–57; Lewes 1908; Scarr 1967, 172–175.

13. Woodford 1890b, 15, 23; Goodrich 1894, 7, 17; Mahaffy 1902, 12; *SCL* 12 Dec 1910, 97; Murray 1916, 12–15; Norden 1925, 34–35; Scheffler 1964a, 399–400; Corris 1973b, 55–56; McKinnon 1975, 305; Zelenietz 1979, 36; Rodman 1983, 7; Bennett 1987, 122.

14. Corris 1973b, 97–98; Saunders 1980, 31–32; Shlomowitz 1989, 592.

15. Bita Saetana 1981 pers comm; see Bolton 1963, 240; Corris 1973b, 69.

16. Parnaby 1964; Corris 1973b, 83; Saunders 1982, 73–95; Moore 1985; Shlomowitz 1989. Banivanua-Mar described the hard work regimens of Queensland laborers (2007, passim).

17. Scarr 1967, 147–154; Saunders 1982, 72–95; Moore 1985, 254–263.

18. Thomas 1886, 356; Sinker 1907, 27; Wawn 1973, 442; Corris 1973b, 80, 123, 151; Sayes 1976, 139; Melvin 1977, 55; Shineberg 1999, 88–89.

19. *SCL* Jan 1898, 37; 15 Sept 1899, 6; Montgomery 1904, 203; Parnaby 1964, 144; Scarr 1970, 232; Corris 1973b, 87; Moore 1985, 170–188; Megarrity 2006, 2; Banivanua-Mar 2007, 59–60, 113.

20. *SCL* Jan 1898, 37–38; Mamdani 1996.

21. See Pritt 1901, 182; Raucaz 1928, 57–58; Wilson 1938, 26; Steward 1939, 134–135; Luke 1945a, 20; Wolfers 1972, 76–83; Deringil 2003, 37. On white fears of Melanesians in Queensland, see Banivanua-Mar 2007, chap 3, passim.

22. Woodford 1896; Hopkins 1928, 223; 1934, 37; Scarr 1968, 13–14; Corris 1973b, 89; Mercer and Moore 1976, 85; Saunders 1980, 34; Moore 1985, 63, 321; Banivanua-Mar 2007, 106–107, 110.

23. *SCL* 15 June 1900, 19; Ivens 1972, 348; Larikeni 1981 pers comm; Molaina'o 1996 pers comm; Akin 1993, 82; Gwa'italafa quoted in Burt and Kwa'ioloa 2001, 87.

24. See, eg, Corris 1973b, 96; Kuva [1974?], 10; Moore 1985, 68.

25. See Corris 1973b, 96–97; Mercer and Moore 1976; Moore 1985, 67–68, 215–217, 272–273; Shineberg 1999, 87–88.

26. See Akin 2004.

27. Pritt 1901, 184; Bolton 1963, 246; Corris 1973b, 95–96; Saunders 1980, 35–36; Moore 1985, 215–216, 323; Clacy Fotanowa 2006 pers comm; Brian Kissier 2006 pers comm; see Maranda 1974; Akin 1993, chap 7; 2003.

28. Wilson 1932, 150; Woodford 1897a, 29, 31; AR 1898–1899, 26; Ivens 1918, 228; 1928a, 44; Wawn 1973, 122; Corris 1973b, 84, 97–98, 171–172; Shlomowitz 1989, 592, 609; Kuva [1974?], 14–15. Woodford, the first resident commissioner, spoke Fijian. On "Solomon-Fijian," a pidgin version of Fijian that most Solomon Islanders probably spoke, see Siegel 1987.

29. Kuva [1974?], 10, see also 13–15; Corris 1973b, 83, 88–89.

30. *SCL* Sept 1899; Corris 1973b, 88; Kuva [1974?], 10; Moore 1985, 292–297; Saunders 1984, 231.

31. See Lambert 1934b 8; Laracy 1983, 8–11, 44–49; Banivanua-Mar 2007, 47, 108–109.

32. Schwartz 1962, 224–226; Keesing 1982a, 300; 1986a; Bennett 1987, 297.

33. *SCL* Jan 1898, 37 (quote); Hopkins 1934, 28; Thomas 1992a, 382–384; see Raucaz 1928, 58; Hilliard 1978, 102–103.

34. Young 1925, 163; see Pritt 1901, 182.

35. *SCL* Oct 1895, 3. Mission statistics for 1901 show 649 converts to date for southeast Malaita, 30 for northern Malaita.

36. *SCL* Jan 1898, 36; see Pritt 1901, 183; Ganifiri 1956, 5.

37. Redwood [1890] quoted in O'Brien 1995, 94; Brittain 1894; *SCL* Oct 1895, 4; Ivens 1918, 230–231; Hilliard 1969, 41; 1974, 105–106.

38. *SCL* Aug 1895, 12 (see also Oct 1895, 3–4; 15 Oct 1898, 4); Wilson 1894–1896, Dec 1895, 5; Montgomery 1904, 203; Ivens 1918, 230–231; Kuva [1974?], 15–17; Aston 1948, 39–47; Corris 1973b, 92–96; Moore 1985, 306–320; O'Brien 1995, 92–95; Macdonald-Milne 2003, 67–69. A few Methodist converts did return to Malaita, such as Alfred Amasia (see Burt 2002).

39. Young 1925, 181; *NIV* Dec 1971; Hilliard 1969; Corris 1973b, 96. For a detailed study of the Queensland Kanaka Mission's early years, see Moore 2009.

40. Pritt 1901, 183; Young 1925, 45–46. See *SCL* Oct 1885, 4; Corris 1973b, 93–94; Nolan 1978, 134; Saunders 1980, 42. The Young family later bought land tracts on Malaita's west coast and used converts as workers (Young 1925, 194; Vandercook 1937, 346–347; Allan 1951b, 3; Hilliard 1969, 53; see Hill 1915; Kirke 1917; Bennett 1987, 145–146; and 1911 papers re their land buys in BSIP 14/40/1909–11).

41. Young 1925, 38–42; see Hogbin 1970, 179.

42. Young 1925, 39–40; see Moore 1985, 320–325.

43. See Corris 1973b, 96–97; Keesing and Corris 1980, 7, 12; Boutilier 1984, 26; Moore 1985, 137–138; Bennett 1987, 121–122. Some of the same writers who presented this perspective at other times pointed to changes that did take place.

44. Commonwealth Parliament of Australia 1901; Royal Commission 1906; Hopkins 1934, 58; see Laracy 1979, 100; Megarrity 2006; Banivanua-Mar 2007, chap 4; Lake and Reynolds 2008, 160.

45. Woodford in AR 1903–1905, 26; Scarr 1967, chap 9; see Bennett 1987, chap 8, passim; Moore 2007, 221. Supporters of the 1901 act cited the US government's mistake in having ignored calls for deportation of its entire black population to Africa (Lake and Reynolds 2008, 150–157).

46. Hopkins 1928, 219–220; Ivens 1928a, 93–94; Young 1925, 176; Corris 1973b, 87; Banivanua-Mar 2007, 101–103. By March 1909, 2,284 laborers were working on Solomons plantations; by March 1911, 3,940; and by late 1911, 4,500. Some two-thirds to three-quarters of them were Malaitans (BSIP 1911, 46–47; AR 1912–1913, 15; Murray 1916, 6, 11). The largest employer was Levers Pacific Plantations Ltd (later Unilever), directed from the headquarters of Levers Pacific Proprietary Ltd (LPPL, nicknamed "Levers Poorly Paid Laborers"), which acquired 120,000 hectares of land on 99- and 999-year leases. Levers eventually held some twenty plantations. Burns Philp too obtained expansive plantation lands. By 1916, over 12,000 hectares of coconuts were under cultivation (Murray 1916, 17), mostly on Guadalcanal, New Georgia, and the Russell Islands. Taxes these companies paid alone nearly met government budgetary needs, and Islanders' interests became secondary (Scarr 1967, 266, 269–270, 291–297; Lever [1990?]). For studies of plantations and associated land alienation, see Bennett 1987, esp chap 6; 1993.

47. Ivens 1918, 232 (and see 1905); McClaren 1928, 158; Hopkins 1928, 218; 1934, 35, 41.

48. *SCL* 6 July 1907; Hopkins 1907; 1934, 58; Ivens 1918, 231; 1928a, 161; Scarr 1970, 251; Corris 1973b, 132–133; Moore 1985, 276–279.

49. *SCL* 6 March 1906, 3–4; May 1906, 3; Ivens 1918, 230; Hilliard 1978, 178–180; Moore 2009.

50. Ivens 1903, 23–24; Hopkins 1905, 23; Wilson 1932, 202.

51. Hopkins 1934, 27. On Christian fortifications, see Wilson 1895–1897, Dec 1895; Ivens 1899; 1902, 79; 1928, 191–193, 240; Hopkins 1903, 6; 1904a; 1904b, 20; 1905; 1906; 1908a; 1928, 180; 1934, 17, 36, 52; *SCL* March 1905, 8; Dec 1905, 9–12; 1 Sept 1913, 214; Coombe 1911, 268–269; Simmons 1917; Cromar 1935, 218; Hilliard 1978, 109; Burt 1990, 152–155.

52. See, eg, Ivens 1905–1906, 9 Dec 1905, 9–10; Deck 1910b, 3. See a photo by John Beattie of an armed Christian guard at Anglican Fiu, in *SCL* 24 May 1910, first page (np).

53. Bell 1916g, 10; Hopkins 1934, 28, 37; re changes on Malaita, see Hopkins 1928, 84–85; Corris 1973b, 137–142.

54. Im Thurn 1913, 159; Ivens 1918, 190–191; see Hopkins 1927, 9; Raucaz 1928, 57–58; Scarr 1967, 160.

55. See, eg, Miklouho-Maclay 1883, 84; Meek 1913, 195; Ivens 1918, 226–232; Hopkins 1928, 224; MAR 1936; Bolton 1963, 79; Hogbin 1970, 160; Wawn 1973, 17, 123–124; Corris 1973b, 118. On the idea of the childlike savage transformed by Christianity, particularly among Methodists in the Western Solomons, see Thomas 1994, 128–142.

56. *SCL* Jan 1898, 37; Wawn 1973, 17–19; Sayes 1976, 115; Hilliard 1978, 107.

57. Ivens 1918, 228; see Hopkins 1908b.

58. Hopkins 1907, 97; 1908b, 369; *SCL* Dec 1908, 369.

59. Forster 1946b, 7; Hilliard 1978, 179–180; see Saunders 1984, 234, 237; Bennett 1987, 274; Banivanua-Mar 2007, 111. By 1924 two strikes had won Tulagi stevedores higher wages (Ivens 1924).

60. Bell 1908–1909, 12 Dec 1908, 5 Jan 1909; Edge-Partington 1909a; Ivens 1918, 232; see Deck 1910a; Bennett 1993, 135; Moore 2007, 222.

61. Saunders 1979; Scott 1985; Frazer 1990, 194; see esp Bennett 1993.

62. Hopkins 1905, 25; Young 1925, 152; Corris 1973b, 172; Burt 1994, 180. See Akin 1993, appendix 1, for a poignant story of the influence the Aboriginals' plight had on Malaitans.

63. See D.R.D.V. [1947?]; Allan 1957a, v; Heath 1981; Bennett 1987, chap 6; Fifi'i 1989, 64.

64. Royal Commission 1906, 234–235; im Thurn 1922, xii; Hilliard 1978, 179–180; see Laracy 1979, 100; quoted phrases in *SCL* Dec 1980, 366.

65. Rivers, editor 1922, xii–xiii; see Scarr 1967.

66. Belshaw 1950a, 50; Scarr 1967, 30, chap 9; Boutilier 1984, 6; Bennett 1987, 104–105.

67. Comins 1893; Welchman 1894; Labour Party 1933, 16; Healy 1966, 196; see Bertram 1930, chap 8; Bennett 1987, 104–106.

68. Woodford 1888; 1890a; 1890b; 1897a, 15–16; Scarr 1967, chap 9; Heath 1978, 200–202.

69. Mahaffy quoted in Heath 1978, 205; see Scarr 1967, 266; McKinnon 1975; Jackson 1975; White 1983, 118; Bennett 1987, 107–109.

70. Mahaffy 1902; see Burt 2002.

71. Edge-Partington 1910i; 1911d. "District magistrate" was used from the end of 1911 until "district officer" was adopted in 1914.

72. Edge-Partington 1909b; 1910b, 2; 1910c (and see 1910i; cf 1914d); Scarr 1967, 243; Hogbin 1970, 157; see Carver 1911, 8.

73. Carver 1911, 6–7; May 1911a, 1911b; Campbell 1913; see Keesing and Corris 1980, 41–44; Burt 1994, 123–126.

74. See, eg, Keesing and Corris 1980, 41–44. A detailed account of Edge-Partington's time on Malaita was excised from this book, but I will send it to anyone interested.

75. For a good discussion of the work of Bell and other BSIP labor inspectors in the 1910s and 1920s, and improvements they brought about in plantation conditions, see Bennett 1993. Bell told the high commissioner, "I put the Native Labour Department on a working basis in accordance with the Regulation, single-handed, and in the face of the most strenuous opposition, of which [acting resident commissioner] Mr. Barnett's opposition was not the least" (1916g, 1).

76. Bell 1915a, 2; see also Bell 1916a, 1916b, 1916e.

77. Bell 1915a, 2, 3; 1916a; 1916b; 1916f; 1916g; 1917; Barnett 1915a; 1915b; 1915c; 1916b; 1917, 3; MAR 1916; see Woodford 1918b; Keesing and Corris 1980, 55, 57.

78. Bell 1916a, 1916f, 1916g, 1918a; Barnett 1917; *Argus* 1919; Workman 1918b; Keesing and Corris 1980, 54–59, 67; see Gilchrist 1927, 265.

79. Edge-Partington 1913a; MAR 1916; Bell 1916g, 4; 1917.

80. Bell 1916, 1916g, 1917, 1920a; Keesing and Corris 1980, 57–58; see MAR 1916. *Ramo* (Kwaio *lamo;* 'Are'are *namo*) in various parts of Malaita denotes an important fighter, a group's war leaders, and also those who killed for bounties. In the far south it was a more formal office of a chief's enforcer. See Hopkins 1928, chap 12; Ivens 1928a, 199–201; 1972, 224–225; Hogbin 1970, 91; Ross 1973, 190–

191; de Coppet 1977, 1981; Keesing 1978b, 90–105; 1985; Keesing and Corris 1980, chap 2; Akin 1993, 62–65; Burt 1994, 73–76.

81. Bell 1915b; 1919c, 2; see also Bell 1916a; Rodwell 1921a; Mann 1948, 290–292; Keesing and Corris 1980, 55–58. Keesing and Corris identified Bell's Malu'u audience as "a delegation of Christians" (1980, 38), but Bell reported half were SSEM and the rest bush people. All had been gathered by the resident constable, Stephen Gori'i, for Bell's visit (Bell 1915b). Bell sympathized with Christian victims of violence, but no more than with non-Christian ones. He "held no brief for the Missions" but liked their ban on murder, and to the high commissioner he defended the missionaries and their impact when Barnett disparaged them. Christians often served Bell as informants and guides (Bell 1916a, 6, passim; see also Bell 1916b; 1916e; 1916f; 1916g, 6–8; MAR 1916).

82. *NIV* 1918 (nd); Hopkins 1908a, 1909; Edge-Partington 1910f; Bell 1916c, 1916d, 1916g, 1918d, 1919b, 1919c, 1920a, 1921a; Workman 1918a, 1918d; Ivens 1928a, 200; Mander 1954, 218; Keesing and Corris 1980, 56–57, 68, passim; Burt and Kwa'ioloa 1991, 96–97; Suina'o quoted in Mann 1948, 294–295. On Irokwato, see also Sandars, who knew him (nd, 83, 87). Receipts for several "good behavior" deposits to Bell are in BSIP 14/46. Bell was criticized for seizing guns in the mid-1920s, since it was assumed most were inoperative and without cartridges, and some blamed his assassination in 1927 on this. R F Thompson, chief inspector of labor at Tulagi, told the *Sydney Herald* in 1927 of Malaitan proficiency with firearms: "The natives love them, and seem to have a natural facility for bringing old blunderbusses up to date with hair-triggers and other attachments they fashion. They are expert at converting cartridges belonging to modern arms into ammunition for the most old-fashioned weapons imaginable" (11 Oct, page 11). Revolver and other cartridges were modified for Sniders; on a 1929 visit RC Francis Ashley saw homemade ammunition ranging from refills to shells made of copper from ship bottoms with locally melted lead bullets, and he banned import of wax phosphorous matches used to fabricate percussion caps. A Kwaio friend of mine in the early 1980s still fashioned scavenged World War II ammunition into bamboo-point cartridges for his 1870s Snider (Northam 1913; Moorhouse 1929, 13; Ashley 1929b, 6–7; Ivens [1928b?]; Ta'ika 1982 pers comm; see Forster 1946c, 10; Sandars nd, 170–172).

83. See, eg, Edge-Partington 1910c, 2; 1910–1911, 9 Sept, 8 Nov; F May 1911c; Workman 1918f; Fowler 1959, 62–63; Scarr 1967, 174; Heath 1978, 205; Burt 1994, 141–142, Burt and Kwa'ioloa 2001, 112–117.

84. Bell 1918e, 1921b, 1922c; McGown 1920; Keesing and Corris 1980, 68–72, 119; see Burt and Kwa'ioloa 2001, 116. Examples of Bell's correspondence re land sales to Europeans and his advocacy for Malaitans on other matters can be found in BSIP file 14/46.

85. Bell 1922a; 1924, 1; Hill 1924a, 4; Pilling 1924b; Keesing and Corris 1980, 78–79, 92.

86. Bell 1917, 1920a, 1922a, 1924; see Burt 1990, 174–177.

87. *SCL* 12 Dec 1910, 97; Workman 1918g; Mason 1925, 134; Keesing and Corris 1980, 31–32, 74–78; Bodley 1982, 128–130; Bennett 1987, 162; Frazer 1990, 194–196.

88. Steward 1921; Mason 1925, 134; Ivens [1928b?], 2; Hogbin 1970, 155; Anderson and Anderson 1980, 6.

89. Bell 1918c; 1920a; 1922a; 1925b; 1925c; 1927, 12; Mason 1925, 134; see Bell

1915a, 3; 1923b, 1925a; 1927, 13; MAR 1925; Hilliard 1974, 108; Keesing and Corris 1980, 75–80. Charles Fox wrote of colleague Mason, "It was largely through his influence that the people accepted the first poll tax without any trouble" (1958, 174; cf Seymour 1928, 10).

90. Bell 1927. Bell did not prosecute tax defaulters whom he believed genuinely unable to find cash. In 1925 he wrote, "There have been 179 convictions for willful neglect to pay the Tax…only five of the offenders failed to pay the fine" (1925c). In 1926 he granted 1,384 exemptions, 562 of them due to indigence and inability to work (Seymour 1928, 7).

91. Bell 1915a, 2; 1916b; 1920a; 1922a; 1925a; 1925b; 1925c; MAR 1916; Kane 1922b; Keesing and Corris 1980, 78, 106–107.

92. Bell 1921a; Fifi'i 1989, 5–7; Keesing and Corris 1980, 76–77, 108–116. Fifi'i's story here of Basiana having given Bell a tax shilling he had made from a sacred shell *dafi* ornament is apocryphal. The 'Ai'eda area surrounds Kwainaa'isi on this book's Malaita map. Later, District Officer Sandars wrote that the 1925 beatings were the reason Bell was killed, but he wrongly thought the police had killed one of the men (nd, 100). On the 1926 attack on Bell in Kwara'ae, see Burt 1994, 153.

93. Higginson 1928, 3; Ivens [1928b?], 3; Keesing and Corris 1980, 116, passim. I draw here also on widely known Kwaio oral histories. According to Judicial Commissioner Robert Higginson, who presided over the 1928 murder trial, Basiana cited these curses and a particular hanging as motivations (1928, 9). Before he was hanged he told his son Anifelo that he killed Bell "to get my purification" (Keesing and Corris 1980, 187; Anifelo 1981 pers comm). Also tempting an attack were bounties posted for the death of Bell or another European. For speculation on Basiana's motives, see Keesing and Corris 1980, 122–124; and Fifi'i 1989, 6–9. Malaitans sustain fictional explanations for why Bell was killed, such as his having slept with Kwaio women (as, it is often told, half-jokingly, he did with SSEM founder Florence Young).

94. See Keesing and Corris 1980, chapters 8, 9. Tome, from the coast, made the *bisi* remark when inland people refused to help build a tax house (Fifi'i 1987 pers comm).

95. Ri'ika was not prosecuted partly because he and kinsmen shielded one of Bell's police, a relative from west Kwaio named Sibeamae (or Forikea), and protected him in the bush for several days (pers comm 1981).

96. Mason 1927, 29; Thomson 1927. Five hundred volunteered under Suina'o of To'abaita (Keesing and Corris 1980, 158), the same man who in 1916 gave Bell his first recognizance.

97. Maeluma, also from the north, led a further patrol. Innocent Kwaio tried to surrender to another patrol of 25 non-Malaitans led by Sale Vuza (also called Jacob Vouza) of Guadalcanal, the only one that did not shoot prisoners or commit other flagrant abuses (Keesing and Corris 1980, 166, chap 11, passim; Vuza 1970). A photo of volunteers Bill Adams, Jack Clift, and J A Johnstone (MBE) with looted skulls appeared in *PIM* (Feb 1953, 78). See also photos in Keesing and Corris 1980.

98. Deck 1927b; Palmer 1970, 21; Ross 1973, 190–191; Keesing and Corris 1980, chap 11.

99. Kane 1928; BSIP 1928; AR 1928, 4; Moorhouse 1929, 14–16; Keesing and Corris 1980, chap 12. District Commissioner Eustace Sandars wrote that he later found those Kwaio sentenced to jail terms to be "fine men and fine workers" (nd, 16).

Chapter 2: Early Native Administration

1. Moorhouse 1929, 21.

2. Rodwell 1921b; Allan 1945; Gregory-Smith 1951c, 4–5; Trench 1956, 186; Chilver 1963, 108 (quote); Malaita District 1958; Beckett 1989, 26; and see Lambert 1934b, 21; Bennett 1987, 320. Francis Noel Ashley (1929–1939) arrived as the resident after nearly 20 years in Nigeria, where he served under Moorhouse, also as a resident. His successor, William Marchant (1939–1943), spent 21 years as an administrator in the East Africa Protectorate, Zanzibar, Tanganyika Territory, and Kenya (he called Solomons villages "kraals"). Owen Cyril Noel (1943–1948) also came from East Africa, and J D A Germond, who had been nearly 20 years in the Bechuanaland Protectorate, replaced him from late 1948 into early 1950 in an acting capacity. Germond stepped aside for Henry Graham Gregory-Smith (1950–1952), who spent two decades in Kenya. In 1952 the Western Pacific High Commission moved to Honiara, headed by Robert C S Stanley, another Nigeria veteran.

3. Lugard 1970, 296; Hailey 1944, 46. See Bertram 1930, 80–81; Hyam 2006, 13–15.

4. In 1929 Great Britain adjusted this policy and began funding some improvements in agriculture and industry in some colonies. Then, with the Colonial Development and Welfare Act of 1940, support significantly increased and some debts were waived (Hailey 1944, 52).

5. Bull 1963, 47; Lugard 1965, 225; Afigbo 1972, 46–47; Oliver and Fage 1973, 200.

6. Bertram 1930, 81; Cartey and Kilson 1970, 74; Lugard 1970, 298; Lackner 1973, 127; Schoettler 1984, 113; Mamdani 1996, 74.

7. Afigbo 1972, 3.

8. Cameron 1926, 8; Lugard 1965, 214–218; and quoted in Hailey 1950, 212; Gilmour quoted in Lugard 1965, 228; see Bertram 1930, 82–83; Hogbin 1933; Campbell 1978, 54.

9. For example, Lugard 1965, 217; 1970, 11, memo 9; see Afigbo 1972, chapters 1, 3; Falola and Heaton 2008, chap 5.

10. Bertram 1930, 70–71; Lugard 1965, 267, and chapters 10, 11; Iliffe 1979, 318; see Ranger 1984; Newbury 2003; Nugent 2008.

11. Bertram 1930, 72 (but cf 73); see Lugard 1970, 298, 317.

12. Wallerstein 1961, 64–65; Mair 1963, 107; Fulani quoted in Lugard 1965, 216; Lackner 1973, 128; Bodley 1982, 77; Foster 1987, 363; Mamdani 2001, 35; see Wieschhoff 1944, 70–72; Fields 1985, chap 1; cf Steinmetz 2003, 47; Newbury 2003; Pierce 2006.

13. Bertram 1930, 74; Hailey 1939, 202; Falola and Heaton 2008, 110–116.

14. Scott 1998; Pierce 2006.

15. Davies nd, 26. Re colonial officers trying to deal with such systems, see Vaskess 1937, 53; Hailey 1950, 351–356; Ranger 1984; Foster 1987, 362. For Malaitan examples, see Ashley 1929a, 3; 1934; 1938a; Hogbin 1944, 45; A Sandars 1950; G Sandars nd, 134. I thank Tony Hopkins for underscoring for me how relatively late indirect rule was attempted in the Solomons (2011 pers comm).

16. Lugard 1965, 133–136, 220, and see chapters 5, 6, 11; 1970, 14–15. Malaita's first officer, Edge-Partington, said he learned Roviana "perfectly" during three years

as Gizo district magistrate, and that he "was speaking nothing else all day long" and held court in it (1910j). But he learned no Malaitan language (see notes 59 and 60, below).

17. See Ashley 1929a, 1–2; Hilliard 1969, 61–62; Campbell 1978, 77n11; Russell 2003, 32.

18. For writings on the Vaukolu, see Wilson 1894–1896, April 1896, 4–6; Comins 1897, 1902; *SCL* 15 Jan 1901, 113; 1 Oct 1902, 59–62; 1 Jan 1904, 102–104; 7 March 1905, 10; and see *SCL* Nov 1910; Awdry 1902, 88–90; Penny 1903, 222–223; Coombe 1911, 315–316; Hilliard 1978, 95; and White 1978, 207.

19. AR 1897–1898, 14, 15; see *SCL* 15 Nov 1898, 3; Comins 1897; Woodford 1897b, 1913.

20. AR 1898, 14–15; *SCL* 7 March 1905, 10; Beattie 1906, 41 (quote); Moorhouse 1929, 21; Jackson 1975, 73–74; Campbell 1978, 266; see Hopkins 1927, 35.

21. Steward 1926, 14–15; see also Awdry 1902, 88; Workman 1918h; Fowler 1959, 41.

22. Bishop Selwyn had quickly determined that on Gela "women and pigs were the fruitful source of all troubles," and Vaukolu laws targeted them (Comins 1897). Bishop Wilson said women took no part in the 1894 Vaukolu he attended (indeed, only one Melanesian spoke) (1894–1896, April 1896, 5–6). At the 1901 Vaukolu, women reacted bitterly to moves to lower brideprice (which also served as a dowry), protesting: "Are we pigs that we should be sold for one string of money?" Afterward they refused to speak to the men (*SCL* 1 Jan 1904, 102–104; Wilson 1932, 176; see Bugotu 1969, 552). In 1902, Gela people simply added the church fine for paying higher brideprice to their brideprice demands, so payments were higher than ever. People said the marriage rule was "a 'teachers law' and not the people's" (*SCL* 1 Oct 1902, 61–62; see Awdry 1902, 94–95; Wilson 1932, 176; *SCL* 1 Oct 1938).

23. Comins 1897; 1902; Awdry 1902, 94–95; *SCL* 1 Oct 1902, 61–62; 1 Jan 1904, 102–104; 7 March 1905, 10; Penny 1903, 222–223; Beattie 1906, 41–41; Coombe 1911, 313–316; Wilson 1932, 176–177; Hilliard 1978, 95; Whiteman 1983, 143.

24. Over the years there were several schemes to divide Malaita into two zones, north and south, and even three, but none lasted (Moorhouse 1929, 22; see Bell 1920a, 1922a, 1926a; MAR 1930, 11–12; 1931, 15; 1941, 2; Hogbin 1944, 260; BSIP 1947d, 113; Germond 1948b). In mid-1949, the 32 sub-districts were reorganized into ten, based roughly on language groups, adopting divisions developed by Maasina Rule (see MAR 1949–1950, 5).

25. Ashley 1929a; see Guppy 1887, 20–25; Filose 1926; Roberts 1927, 63; Moorhouse 1929, 19; Corris 1973b, 37–38; Sayes 1976, 138–139; Bennett 1987, chap 4. Four years later, Ashley chided Malaita's Officer Sandars for writing in a report that Malaita had no "natural chiefs": "The most undeveloped form of society, even a herd of cattle, pack of hounds or wolves, must, in order to exist, have someone they look to as their head. Inherited race-characteristics cannot have made the Malaitaman different from anything else on earth." He then imparted an ersatz anthropology lecture that must have exasperated Sandars (1934; see Sandars nd, 134). Ideas of pre-European cultural decline may have been furthered by Malaita oral histories of older chiefly hierarchies. There is some evidence of more hierarchy there in the remote past, and Malaitans certainly had *conceptions* of powerful chiefs, later adapted to political activities (see Barley 1931a; Russell 1950a; Gegeo and Watson-Gegeo 1996; Keesing 1997; White 1992a, 233–237).

26. Southern Rhodesia 1910; BSIP 1918, 2; 1922b; Rodwell 1922a; Kakalu'ae testimony in BSIP 1947d, 12; Kaplan 1995, 70–78, passim.

27. Workman 1918h; Rodwell 1921b; 1922a; 1922b, 1; BSIP 1922b; WPHC 1922; see Hill 1924b; Pilling 1924a, 1924b; Moorhouse 1929, 19; Laracy and Laracy 1980, 133. Decades later, journalist Trevor Grundy wrote in an article on Robert Mugabe, "To this day, Mugabe lucidly recalls a conversation in 1933 between Father O'Hea [Jesuit supervisor at Kutama Roman Catholic Mission, where Mugabe was educated] and the British governor, Cecil Rodwell. When O'Hea pleaded for funds to build a hospital at Kutama, Rodwell retorted, 'Why do you worry about a hospital? After all, there are too many natives in the country already.' Mugabe never forgot or forgave Rodwell's remark" (2008, 2).

28. Kane 1922a.

29. Attempts to appoint headmen on Malaita in the 1910s had been unsuccessful. Decades later, in the midst of Maasina Rule and Malaitan rejection of loyalist headmen, a high official wrote, "It is doubtful whether anywhere in the Colonial Empire has the appointment of [headmen] been so haphazard as in this Protectorate." He said future headmen had to be picked "from the ranks of the accepted ruling castes" and instructed officers to find out what these were, and to make sure all headmen belonged to them, in order to form a "proper class of Headmen" (A Sandars 1950, 13–14). In 1949, officers renewed the search for Malaita's "ruling castes" and "lines" from which government could pick leaders (eg, Allan 1949c, 4–5; Russell 1950a; Forster 1949b; see Hogbin 1958). Bell often blurred distinctions between headmen and constables. Hereafter, I use "headman," when unmarked, to label all of these offices. Later, other classifications were introduced (eg, A Sandars 1950, 15). Before 1920 there was little court enforcement of laws: the BSIP Police Report of 1917 recorded 128 convictions against natives, or about one per thousand.

30. Kane also moved to criminalize betel nut and tobacco, but Bishop Steward opposed this, knowing it would alienate people from the government. Kane said the Protectorate's Dr Critchlow, all other mission leaders, and all district officers but Bell and J C Barley would support such a law, but Rodwell struck it out. Also dumped were Kane's rule that every man had to plant a specific number of plants (eg, 100 plants each of bananas, yams, sweet potato, and others) with a penalty of £2 or two months prison for failure to do so (WPHC 1922; Kane 1922a; Rodwell 1922a; Hilliard 1974, 102). Officer Sandars later said Kane "made such a nuisance of himself in Fiji that they decided to promote him and send him to the Solomons" (nd, 9). Hogbin probably referred to Kane when he wrote that during a 1927–1928 visit, "A certain resident magistrate...told me that his idea was that, to govern natives, the first thing to do was systematically to violate all their *tapu*" (1930, 62; see also Keesing and Corris 1980).

31. Kane 1923b; Hill 1924a, 1924b; MAR 1944, 4; see BSIP [1948?]; Allan 1950a, 33; Marquand 1950, 5; Hogbin 1964, 96; Thomas 1994, 123–124, and see chap 3, passim; and Thomas 1990.

32. On headmen during this period, see Barley 1920, 2; Ivens 1928a, 86–87; MARs 1929; 1930, 10; 1944, 4; MQR Sept 1933; Lambert 1934b, 4; Hogbin 1944; A Sandars 1950; Allan 1950a, 19; Marquand 1950, 5; and for Nigerian parallels, Afigbo 1972, chap 2. Officer George Sandars later recalled having nearly been killed (at least he thought so) after he delivered a bad court verdict based on false information fed him by a headman with "an axe to grind" (nd, 184). In places in

the Solomons unofficial headmen had worked with district officers before the 1922 regulation, and through the early 1940s some officers created informal bodies of native administration as needed without the high commissioner's approval. While usually portrayed as government creations, some derived from Islander initiatives (see Campbell 1918, 42; BSIP 1922a, 37; Bennett 1974, 84; 1987, 111; White 1978, 208, 215–216).

33. Heffernan 1924a, 1924b; Hill 1924a, 3; Middenway 1924; Bell 1924, 1926a.

34. Workman 1918g; Moorhouse 1929, 21, 22.

35. Moorhouse 1929, 21–22. Re the Depression, see Allan 1950a, 22; 1957a, 50; BSIP [1948?], 18.

36. Ashley 1929a, 2–3, 8; 1930c quoted in Bennett 1987, 259; 1931a, 3; Allan 1950a, 22; Premdas and Steeves 1985, 35; see Boutilier 1982, 66. Most Europeans at this time appear to have thought Solomon Islanders stupid, and as in other colonial settings some worked out intelligence rankings for "racial groups." Barley determined that peoples north of Kwara'ae were the smartest Malaitans, followed by Kwara'ae, with Kwaio and 'Are'are at the bottom; he said that 'Oloburi on the Kwaio-'Are'are border was home to "possibly the lowest standard of mentality throughout the whole district" (1930–1932, 161; see MAR 1929; 1934). Innes wrote: "It is possible roughly to grade the inhabitants of Malaita in order of intelligence....First, the whole of the salt-water people, and the lagoon island people in particular. Second, the bush people whose centers are Malu'u, Matokalau, Bitama, and Foodo. Third, the bush people from Fauabu to Bina [Kwara'ae]. Last, the real bush people." He blamed higher leprosy rates among inland people partly on their mental inferiority (1938, 23; see also Muspratt 1931, 80–81). These rankings correlated roughly with degrees of cooperation with government. Later, when resistance became the norm across the island, some whites portrayed all Malaitans as dim-witted.

37. Barley 1920; Ivens 1928a, 87; Hopkins 1928, 225; Ashley 1929a, 4; Belshaw 1949a, 425–426.

38. MAR 1930, 7, 10–11 (extract), 25; Barley 1931a; Malaita District 1936, 1940.

39. Ashley 1929a, 6; 1929b, 17–18; 1935a; BSIP 1931; Fletcher 1930; Joy 1937; Campbell 1978, 282–283; Laracy and Laracy 1980, 144–145; Bennett 1987, 281; see Knibbs 1929, 58; Afigbo 1972, 195–196, 250–252.

40. Turner 1975, 146; see Hogbin 1933; 1934, 264; Hailey 1938, 309; Marchant 1942a; Forster 1948a, Germond comments 23 April; Epstein 1953, 94–95; Lingat 1973, 263–265; Larcom 1982; Allan 1989–1990, 15; Linnekin 1990, 163.

41. Sharon Tiffany described how later land court decisions in the Western Solomons worked to freeze fluid ownership rights at one historical moment, and how several concepts, some anthropological, were transposed from Africa to the colonial land-law system there and later adopted by locals: "tribe," "clan," and the primacy of patrilineal descent (1983, 283, passim; see also Allan 1960, 158).

42. See Akin 1999b, 2004.

43. Ashley 1935a; Barley and Richards in Campbell 1978, 283–284, and 312, respectively. In 1948, Resident Commissioner Noel gave new Malaita arrival Germond a confused history lesson saying that Barley had failed to gain Ashley's support for his own desires for real native administration (1948a, 2). Lambert's 1933 diary recorded the reaction when Ashley returned to Tulagi, after it was thought he might not do so: "Great disappointment to the service here, who all have their tails down since this man came back. Great blow to administrative affairs and all hold

him in contempt—and this is not too strong a term. Not trusted, judgement poor. As one man says 'Because he is such a damn fool Fiji thinks we are all damn fools and everything we propose, no matter how good, is looked at askance.'" Lambert felt that Barley, whom he admired and who had been acting resident commissioner, should have had Ashley's position; Lambert wrote, "To most of the natives of the group Barley is the Government" (21 May).

44. *Sydney Herald* 1933; Hogbin 1933; 1934, 264–265; 1944; 1945; 1970, 235–239; *PIM* 1934a; Trench 1943; Allan 1958, 5; Campbell 1978, 282–284, 312; Bennett 1987, 281–282. Hogbin in the late 1980s wondered if he should have advocated an assimilationist policy with local courts applying British and Australian rather than "customary" law (quoted in Beckett 1989, 26; see Allan 1960, 161).

45. Campbell 1978, 284, 288; Bennett 1987, 281. See also White 1991, 199.

46. MAR 1935; Bengough 1941a; Clemens 1998, 35; Feldt 1946, 31–32. Into the early 1950s Malaitan officers still carried out all of these duties, each of which had grown manyfold, and more. Officer Alexander MacKeith detailed the problem in a comprehensive proposal for change (1951c). As Clemens's remarks indicate, "cadets" soon gained experience and carried out most of the court and administrative duties of a full district officer (I thank Tom Russell on this point).

47. On colonial officer training over time, see Kirk-Green 1999; and see Davies nd, 12.

48. Sandars nd, 18–19, 28; Horton 1965, 14; Scarr 1967, 255; Davies nd, 25; various officers' personal files, BSIP 1/III/58.

49. Belshaw 1950a, 126, see 5–6; Garvey quoted in Knox-Mawer 1986, 61; Russell 2003, 90; Tedder 2008, 38; see Feldt 1946, 31; Germond 1948b, 4–5; Davies nd, 28. Lugard defended concurrent legal duties as necessary and also desirable since it seemed natural to "the primitive African, since they are combined in his own rulers" and avoided delays, which Africans detested (1965, 539). Davies empathized with Malaitans who gave up trying to understand when "the magistrate dismissed charges he had helped to frame and prosecute" (nd, 28). When for periods in the 1910s and 1920s, a European police officer rather than the district officer headed 'Aoke's constabulary, an uncertain division of authority caused its own problems.

50. Bell 1919c, 3; see Bell 1916a, 8; 1925d; Belshaw 1950a, 53.

51. Ashley 1929a, 8; Bengough 1939a, 6; Clemens 1992b; see Fowler 1959, 18.

52. Steinmetz 2003, 42; see Belshaw 1950a, 23; Ranger 1976, 121, passim.

53. May 1911a; Mason 1927, 10; Moorhouse 1929, 25; Sandars nd, 119, 133; 1947f, 4; Brownlees 1938; Johnson 1939; Osa Johnson 1945, 266; MacQuarrie 1948, 109; Firth 1983, 90; cf Davies nd, 150. On Hogbin, see Sandars nd, 161–162. Those setting rules in London were unaware that most districts had no one "principal dialect" (see Law 1916). Such problems spawned periodic proposals into the 1950s to propagate a single language for the Solomons, or for Malaita alone. Anglicans, faced with what Bishop Selwyn called "this terrible diversity of language," cultivated particular ones for teaching their faith (Melanesian Mission Occasional Paper, Aug 1894, 7; see also Deck 1931b, 3; Brewster 1937; Bengough 1941a, 4; Germond 1948b, 6; Noel 1948c, 3; BSIP 1950e, 4–5; *SCL* Feb 1954, 160–161; Fox [1948c?]; 1967, 68–69). On government officers and language, see *SCL* 1 Jan 1927, 10; Hopkins 1928, 237; Moorhouse 1929, 25; Hogbin and Wedgwood 1943, 6; Fowler 1959, 18; Sandars nd, 18; Rhoades 1982, 58; Russell 2003, 37. On the import of colonial linguistic knowledge, see Cohn 1996, chap 2.

54. Bell 1916a; Keesing and Corris 1980, chap 5. Sandars later wrote that Bell "knew native custom as no other man ever did" (nd, 167).

55. Sandars 1932; Odi 1932; Barley 1933a; *PIM* 1974; Boutilier 1982, 47–48; Bennett 1987, 260.

56. Eyerdam 1929–1930, 53; Coultas 1929–1930, 95; Hamlin 1929–1930, 143, see 145. Kwaio people were often subsumed under "'Are'are." Two days after Wilson's meeting with the ornithologists, Ashley scolded him for not having collected taxes on foot when MV *Auki* was unavailable (1930a). Wilson stayed in the Solomons for many more years and High Commissioner Luke found him on Vanikolo in 1941, "a rather disillusioned man of long service" (Luke 1945b, 188; Clemens 1992a, 57).

57. Lambert nd, box 5, folder 15, undated, untitled pages. For the Guadalcanal episode, see Moorhouse 1929. On fears of Kwaio unrest, see Ashley 1930d; Barley 1930a, 1930c; MARs 1930, 10–12; and 1935, 17–20; Bengough 1936c, 1936d; Sandars 1937c; MQRs March 1931, Sept 1938, June 1941; Davies nd, 138; Keesing and Corris 1980, 198. Kwaio resented the government due to the punitive expedition and other issues but hatched no conspiracies of violence, and most officers over the years came to realize there was no threat. As a more levelheaded Barley noted in 1930: "Most, if not all, of the rumours…were originated and deliberately fostered by members of other racial sections in the District, anxious to see the Koio natives once again embroiled in a clash with authority and the levying of another punitive expedition, under cover of which in the guise of Government volunteers they would be free to wreak their will upon the unfortunate people whom they both hate and at the same time despise" (MAR 1930, 10; see also Sandars nd, 100). Colin Allan later absurdly suggested that previous officers had fostered hatred of Kwaio in order to divide Malaita at its middle and keep it from uniting politically (MAR 1949–1950, 4).

58. Hutson 1928a, 3; Wilson 1927, 1928a, 1928b; Moorhouse 1929, 6–9; Amery 1929; Garvey quoted in Knox-Mawer 1986, 59; Lambert Papers box 5, folder 15; see Sandars nd, 118; Palmer 1970, 8, 14; Hogbin 1970, plate 17.

59. Barley 1926, 1930b, 1930–1932, nd, and quoted in Campbell 1978, 282–284; Hutson 1927a; Ashley 1929a; MAR 1930; Sandars 1937d; Lambert 1941, 106, 323, and see 326–327; Laracy 1983, 39; Bennett 1987, 179; Hviding 1996, 119; Mike Butcher 2008 pers comm. Lambert quoted Barley as saying Malaitan warriors "were proper men, and took no nonsense from anybody" (1941, 327). Barley's reports at times exhibit basic ethnographic errors (see Barley 1930b; nd). Fowler told of meeting an unnamed man in Tulagi in 1929, who was obviously Barley, who said he had "amused himself learning some of the languages" and advised Fowler to try to learn one "just for a rag, don't you know, just for a rag" (1959, 3). Barley guided Hogbin to select Malu'u as a field site (1970, xv). Sandars recalled Barley's enthusiasm for "local maidens," over which he "waged constant war with the head of the Mission" (nd, 24; see Golden 1993, 183), and another former officer told me wryly he never met Barley since the latter "was busy populating the islands" (Barley was concerned about Islander depopulation). In the 1920s Barley impregnated an Ontong Java woman whom he loved and was determined to marry, but, Lambert claimed, the engagement was deviously destroyed by Kane, himself known for an amorous zeal for local women (Lambert nd, box 3, folder 25; see Sandars nd, 17; Boutilier 1982, 48). For more on Barley, see Butcher 2012. Barley authored a chapter about Malaita in an unpublished manuscript by Ashley, which is held in the Library of Rhodes

House in Oxford, but I have not seen it. It may reveal more about Barley's knowledge of the island.

60. My compilations of periods of service have been aided by Judy Bennett's list of BSIP officers to 1940 (1987, appendix 7). My revised and significantly expanded list of Malaitan officers is available on request. One officer, William Fowler, served on Malaita for over a year in 1933–1934, under first Barley and then Sandars, and again for about eight months in 1935–1936, for a time heading the district as Bengough's superior. Fowler did little to interest us here, though he said he had studied cultures of Africa, hoped to be posted there, and claimed that in the Solomons he "continued to read widely on ethnology and anthropology." He said he found "no great difficulty in learning new languages," but appears not to have learned any Solomon Islands ones (Fowler 1936). An Isabel officer whom Fowler replaced in 1930 advised him against wasting time trying to learn a language since it would be useless if he were transferred (Fowler 1959, 18).

61. Deck 1948c, 3; Horton 1965, 116; Sandars nd, 18, 20, 23, 28, 121–123; and personal communications from Diki, Saetana, To'oni, Larikeni 1982, Ma'aanamae 1987, Riufaa 1996. In 1992 Martin Clemens told me that Sandars had gone to Australia after his father disowned him.

62. Sandars nd, 126; Clemens 1992b, 2000; see also Waddell quoted in Knox-Mawer 1986, 16–17. By "what they had written," Clemens may have meant their reports, for apart from a few pages that Sandars wrote about Kwaio I have found no other writings by either man (but see note 59, above). Or perhaps Clemens assumed they had written up what they had not.

63. Sandars nd, 43–44 (quote); MAR 1936, 15; MQR June 1937, 2; cf Deck 1934–1935, 488–489.

64. Sandars nd, 129. Comb artists plait rows by memorized number sequences, not marking each relative to the last as Europeans would. Whites often presumed Melanesians were bad with numbers and thus ignorant of the value of money. Anglican priest Welchman wrote, "Combination of figures is a great difficulty for them, each figure having a separate identity in their minds; individualism is quite a Melanesian characteristic, so it quite naturally follows that they should apply it to their sums" (quoted in C Wilson 1932, 23; see Hopkins 1934, 19, 22; E Wilson 1935, 106; and esp Feldt 1946, 83).

65. MAR 1937; Sandars 1938, 24; nd, 33, 81–82, 86–87, 133–134; see also Innes 1938, 23; Belshaw 1950a, 3, 4, 34.

66. Innes 1938, 17–18, 23 (quote); Belshaw 1950a, 10, and see 7–8; Sandars nd, 22, 25, 107–108, 117, 123, 126, 158; Davies nd, 24, 25; Waddell quoted in Sandars nd, 123, and see also Waddell's comments in Knox-Mawer 1986, 17. See also Ashley 1929b, 5, 16; MQR Sept 1931; MAR 1936, 15; Germond 1948b, 4–5; Ivens 1972, 237; Rhoades 1982, 19. Even in 1948, Germond wrote, "Most of the people live without fear of any interference from a Government whose officers merely touch the coastal fringe of their Island fastness" (1948b, annexure 'A'). Sandars's unfamiliarity with inland Malaita is clear from his statement that "there was practically no vegetation" at elevations above 2,000 feet (nd, 30, and see 116–117).

67. Innes 1938, 13; Clemens 1998, 35–36; see Russell 2003, chap 6; Tedder 2008, 34–35. On touring by boat, see Innes 1938, 17–18; Tedder 2008, 56; cf Russell 2003, 55.

68. See Barley quoted in Bennett 1987, 179. Ma'aanamae used *koomani fiifuru*,

a Pijin term from Maasina Rule. Bishop Steward advised missionaries to demand separate houses for whites in Christian villages and to declare they would not sleep there again without them (1926, 7).

69. Horton 1965, 98; personal communications from Larikeni and Le'aa 1982, and Fifi'i and Ma'aanamae 1987; see Innes 1938, 17. For Tom Russell's later, more accessible style of touring interactions, see his autobiography (2003, 58–60, passim). Sandars later said that he had been closest to people of the artificial islands of 'Adagege and Sulufou in the Lau Lagoon (Sandars nd, 166), the homes of powerful loyalist leaders Timi Kakalu'ae and Tome Wate, respectively.

70. Fifi'i 1988a, 224; Ngwadili and Gafu 1988, 208; Langabaea 1988, 101; Molaina'o 1996 pers comm; see Sisili 1949, 3; Lord 1977; Esau Hiele quoted in Laracy and White 1988, 114. Clemens, an Australian, said his patrols shared food with locals, and years later Malaitan Andrew Langabaea recalled serving under him in the war: "Major Clemens treated us very well. He was friendly with us. He wasn't like some of the British, who said that only they knew something, or that they only were big men." During the war Clemens spent months behind Japanese lines scouting, eating, and often starving with Malaitan and other Islander police (see Clemens 2000).

71. Forster 1945a; Sandars nd, 125; Davies nd, 41.

72. Hopkins 1928, 235; Sandars nd, 37–48; Hogbin and Wedgwood 1943, 6–7; Vuza 1970 (Akin transcription, 7); Zoleveke 1980, 41–42; Fifi'i 1987 pers comm. Concerning the 1920s, Hopkins said that officers' village visits "must be nearly always disciplinary; the D.O. has not time to give complimentary and friendly visits, except on rare occasions" (1928, 237). Some Malaitan police disliked Vuza, and in 1950, by then headmen, they told Allan, "He is remembered as a man who as station sergeant on Auki, before the war, operated so many rackets and oppressed so many people that he had to be removed" (Allan 1950l, 2). Allan was given to making false statements, especially about political leaders (as then Vuza was), and I do not know to what degree, if any, this statement was true.

73. Ashley 1929a, 8.

74. Davies nd, 24–25.

75. Forster 1946c, 4; Cochrane 1970; Boutilier 1982, 62, 67n55; see Belshaw 1947b, 8; Sandars 1947a; Germond 1948b, 4; Allan 1950g, 29; Campbell 1978, 270–274; Laracy 1983, 16. The problem continued into the 1950s; in 1951 Officer MacKeith at 'Aoke proposed a new system of rest houses that would get officers off ships and into communities. Writing soon after mass arrests of Maasina Rule adherents were suspended, MacKeith said they would need an official name: "The prewar ones became known as 'tax-houses,' and new rest-houses would very likely be called 'arrest-houses'" (1951c, appendix 2, page 5). Starting in 1948, officers based at Malu'u toured widely on foot (eg, Russell 2003, chap 5, and page 94). Keesing (1978a, 55) bluntly dismissed the portrayal of officers as big men as well as other aspects of a 1970 book by former Malaitan officer Glynn Cochrane, who published an angry retort in *Oceania* (1979). Colin Allan quoted and tried to revive Forster's idea in mid-1950, just after officers jailed thousands of Malaitans, to justify putting still more pressure on people to tax (1950g, 29).

76. See Moorhouse 1929, 21; cf Rodwell 1921b, 2. Overseas reaction to Bell's death was to blame excessive taxation (eg, *Argus* 1927a; 1927b; *Sydney Herald* 1927), and High Commissioner Hutson and Kane were keen to counter this. Hutson telegrammed London, "No general or specific complaints from natives or from mis-

sionaries on their behalf against tax have at any time been received by High Commissioner" (1927b; see Hutson 1928b, 3–4; Ivens 1925; Keesing and Corris 1980, 191–192). Five months earlier, Bell had sent Hutson a confidential letter reporting widespread Malaitan anger at taxes and threats of violent resistance to them, including killing Bell himself (Bell 1927; Moorhouse 1929, 12). Lambert reported from a conversation with Hutson, "He [Hutson] had been dreading that something would happen in Malaita for two years; that it had been threatened," and, "The natives had been promised that the [tax] money would be spent directly on them in the form of medical aid or education as in Papua and he had been trying to push Dick Kane to do something for them without result. He thought the cause of these murders was resentment at the unfulfilled promises of the Government to the natives" (Lambert 1933, 27 May; 1934b, 8).

77. MARs 1925; 1930, 6, 14; Bell 1927, 2; Russell 1950j, 18; see Hogbin 1946, 65; Allan 1950k, 7; Davies nd, 29.

78. Wright 1938, 1940; Campbell 1978, 284; see Belshaw 1950a, 29; Horton 1965, 159.

79. Similar difficulties plagued colonial officers in Africa who, though strangers to local societies, were expected to decide court cases based on "custom" (see Schoettler 1984, 11). Julius Lewin, a barrister-at-law in South Africa, complained of the lack of information available about the "native customs" applied to decide cases; he noted, too, the important yet legally awkward distinction between "technical knowledge of native law and general knowledge of native habits acquired through long experience" (1938, 16, 20).

80. Sandars writing in MAR 1937, 18; Steward 1939, 129; see Steward 1921; Hopkins 1928, 235–237; Strathern 1972, 129.

81. Sandars writing in MAR 1936, 18; re officers employing chants, divinations, and ordeals in disputes, Sandars nd, 144–150 (and see 23); Marquand 1947e, 3; Horton 1965, 94–96, 118; Allan 1989–1990, 150; see Clemens 1942, 87; 1998, 184; Russell 2003, 92. On ordeals: Ivens 1928a, 341–345; 1972, 341–345; Fox 1925, 339–341; Wilson 1932, 161–162; Clemens 1940b. Officers in 1956 proposed adapting a 1945 Papua New Guinea law that would punish with a year at hard labor divinations such as Sandars utilized (BSIP 1956, 27).

82. Hopkins 1928, 238; Brownlees quoted in Knox-Mawer 1986, 60; see Belshaw 1950a, 126; Barrow nd, part 2, 4; Sandars nd, 126. Forster in 1948 could still write of Baegu, "They usually produce a series of complicated and obscure disputes for settlement. Unfortunately little seems to be known about them and the settling of these disputes in an arbitrary manner cannot be regarded as satisfactory" (1948e).

83. On other aspects of oaths, including by women, see Akin 1993, 40–41, 68; 2003. Deck 1928c summarizes another, *offensive* type of Malaitan oath: curses, and their removal. Curses can take the form "So-and-so did X and he also did Y"; or "Whoever did X also did Y"; or simply "So-and-so does Y." These can entail slander against multiple descendants of ancestors evoked as well as group liability on the part of the curser's people. On oaths and curses, see Ivens 1928a, 197, 241–242 for Lau; and 1972, chap 12 for Sa'a. See Hogbin 1944, appendix A, 270, for To'abaita's Malu'u Native Court's "Law of Swearing."

84. Personal communications from Sulafanamae 1981, Larikeni 1982, Folofo'u 1982, Saetana 1982, Ma'aanamae 1983.

85. Ma'aanamae 1982 pers comm. See Woodford 1890b, 15, 23; Goodrich 1894,

7, 17; Scheffler 1964a, 399–400; McKinnon 1975, 305; Zelenietz 1979. Marilyn Strathern reported a similar function of courts in Hagen in early-1970s New Guinea, and she suggested that a magistrate's ignorance of details or nuances might facilitate simple decisions that "cut" otherwise irresolvable cases. Her excellent study brings out various other Hagener attitudes toward and uses of government courts that were also found on Malaita and elsewhere in Melanesia (Strathern 1972, 148, passim).

86. See Ivens 1928a, 205–206; Hearth 1956a, 5; Jack-Hinton 1958b; Akin 1993, 56–62; 1999b.

87. Woodford 1897b; see Sandars nd, 166–168; Tiffany 1983.

88. MQR June 1930; Fowler writing in MAR 1935, 10–11; and see MAR 1936, 4.

89. Bell 1925a, 1925f; Ashley 1929b, 10; BSIP 1931; MAR 1935, 10–11; Hogbin 1970, 147, chap 6, frontispiece, and plate 8; Frazer 1981, 97. Gori'i belonged to a famous SSEM community founded at Malu'u by teacher Peter Abu'ofa.

90. Allan 1949c, 5. Allan here made special note that this portrayal did not fit Cephae Ba'etalua, headman of nearby Fo'odo, who appears later in this book (see chapter 8). See also Marquand 1950, 35–35.

91. Barley 1930–1932, 187–188; MAR 1936, 18; Marquand 1950, 5.

92. MAR 1935, 20; see Marchant 1940b; Isabel AR 1941, 4; Tedder 2008, 30.

93. Hopkins 1934, 72.

94. Hogbin 1970, 158, 159, 165–168, 221.

95. Hogbin 1970, 157–159; see Russell 1950j, 3–4; Boutilier 1984, 40–42; Akin 1999b.

96. On Ulawa, people killed all their pigs, "in fear and uncertainty" according to Ivens, probably after Officer Frederick Campbell enforced penning laws by shooting most or all pigs in parts of nearby Makira. Ulawans also killed their dogs, and feral dogs thrived, making it impossible to raise chickens. Ivens found elsewhere that many misconstrued the law as a complete ban on pigs, and pig numbers plummeted. One man told him, "Our altars have grown cold, there are no pigs to sacrifice." Barley later imposed less draconian rules on Makira. On Malaita, in To'abaita, people were allowed to just fence villages from pigs. People on artificial islands already built pigpens over the sea. In 1952, Malu'u's Officer John Wrightson had pigs shot by (illegal) rules even stricter than before the war, until his district commissioner reigned him in (Barley 1919; 1921; 1930–1932, 54–55; Hill 1924b; see Pilling 1924a; Andersen 1952d; Ivens [1928b?], 5; 1972, 54; Riufaa 1996 pers comm; Molaina'o 1996 pers comm; Scott 2007, 106).

97. Belshaw 1949a, 378; Riufaa 1996 pers comm; Russell 2003, 52; see Hill 1924b; Bell 1927, 9–10; Ivens [1928b?], 4, 5; Malaita District 1941a, 17 July; [1941b?]; MQR 30 Sept 1950, 3; Allan 1951k, 3; Clemens 1962, 80.

98. See Moorhouse 1929, 13; Marchant 1940b.

99. See, eg, MAR 1940, 6; MQR June 1940; Malaita District 1945a; Marquand 1950, 34.

100. Marquand 1950, 34; Sandars 1937f, 2; see Bell 1925c. Some Malaitans still bar or limit cash use in marriage and mortuary exchange, but such enclaving was always less common in compensations (see Akin 1999a).

101. Hogbin 1970, 153–154, 200; Oliver 1961, 227; see Hogbin and Wedgwood 1943, 21.

102. Hogbin 1944; 1945; 1970, 154 (quote).

103. Hogbin 1970, 156; Burt 2004 pers comm.

104. BSIP 1940a; Hogbin 1970, 143–144, 158.

105. Edge-Partington 1913c; Woodford 1913; Bell 1923a; see Bell 1916a, 8; 1918b; Workman 1918c. Sandars erred in saying that Moorhouse instituted the adultery regulation (nd, 37).

106. Hogbin 1934, 258, 265; 1935, 19–20; Deck 1934–1935, 244; 1935, 2; see Raucaz 1923; Wicks 1923; Mason 1933; Sandars 1935; nd, 162; Ashley 1935a; Hogbin 1934–1935; Laracy and Laracy 1980, 141–142.

107. WPHC 1924, 1929a, 1929b; Hogbin 1933; Sandars 1937e; see Colley 1940; Laracy and Laracy 1980; Keesing and Corris 1980, 105; Bennett 1987, 277–278.

108. Ashley 1929b, 9; Fletcher 1932; Deck 1935; Sandars 1935, 1937e; Bengough 1939b; Malaita District 1939a; Marchant 1940b; Hogbin 1970, 154–155.

109. Malaita District 1931–1935; see Fletcher 1932; Osifelo 1985, 5.

110. Ashley 1935a; see Marchant 1940b, 4, 5; Laracy 1983, 135, A7. The High Commission's chief judicial commissioner assailed any further increase in penalties: "No doubt in communities such as the Solomons wherein women are really chattels, bought and sold, adultery may be considered almost as a species of larceny, but for the punishment for simple larceny, the maximum in the case of a hardened offender is but five years penal servitude" (WPHC 1929c). The Court of Appeals later fueled anger by routinely reducing penalties that Malaitan courts imposed (Bengough 1939b). The issue persisted for years, and decriminalization in 1960 caused an uproar (see, eg, *Malaita Newsletter* Oct 1960, 2; Malaita District 1961; Cochrane 1969, 287).

111. Ashley 1932c. See *SCL* 11 April 1905, 2–26; BSIP 1931; Barley 1932; White 1932c; Hogbin 1933; 1935; 1970, 151–157; Deck 1934–1935, 244; Mander 1954, 221–223; Fortune 1963, appendix 3. One of the first Islanders ever turned over to the government, from Savo in 1898, was accused of sorcery, but Woodford released him (AR 1898–1899, 17). A sorcery law was considered in drafts of the 1922 Native Administration Regulation, punishable by a £50 fine or two years in prison (BSIP 1918, 7; Workman 1918g; see Hopkins 1905, 25–26; 1910b, 89). An officer could tailor a sorcery case to prosecute it under British laws; Barley charged a Kwai man accused of performing sorcery via a grave with "violation of a burial place" (1933b). Decades later, section 183 of the Solomon Islands Penal Code, adopted in the early 1960s, allowed punishment with two months in jail or SI$40 of those performing, or possessing paraphernalia to perform, "magic which is believed by some people to cause harm" (BSIP 1956, 27; Solomon Islands Government 1979, 43).

112. Ashley 1929b. Interpretations of what was "repugnant to humanity" in colonial settings could be legally problematic (see, eg, Lewin 1938; Epstein 1953, 48–50; Afigbo 1972, 84). See also colonial prohibitions in Fiji on "bad custom" (Lal 1992, 14–16), or what Kaplan called "negative tradition" (1995, 78, 85); and see Thomas 1990, 157.

113. Luke 1945a, 19; see Bertram 1930, 83, 92–93.

114. Said 1979, 321, passim.

115. Deck 1932; 1934–1935; 1948c, 2; MAR 1949–1950, 12; Thomas 1990, 157; 1994, 116–125; see Clammer 1973. Thanks to David Gegeo for the Kwara'ae expression. Sandars even conjured up a "true custom" of cannibalism, eating only "the palm of the hand and the sole of the foot," as opposed to the false one of eating "human flesh for the sake of a meal" (nd, 84).

Chapter 3: Colonial Experiments and Mounting Resentments

1. AR 1933, 7; Barrow nd, part 3, 2; Allan 1950a, 22.

2. MAR 1930, 30; 1931, 10; *PIM* 1932; Bengough 1938a; Lasaqa 1972, 40–44; Bennett 1987, 204, 222; Frazer 1990, 193. From 1919 through 1928, an average 2,380 men signed contracts each year. The 2,176 recruits of 1928 were 500-odd fewer than in 1926; 1,459, almost 68 percent, were Malaitans, followed by Guadalcanal at 18 percent. Half worked for the largest three of 94 employers: Levers Pacific Plantations Pty. Ltd., the Malayta Company Ltd., and Burns Philp. About 75 percent did copra-related work (Barley, Hetherington, and Hewitt 1929, 2). On staff shortages during the Depression, see Boutilier 1982, 59.

3. Barley, Hetherington, and Hewitt 1929, 65–66, quotes except for MacQuarrie 1948, 151; Frazer 1990, 191, passim; Bennett 1993, 154–158; see Hogbin 1970, 183. Older Kwaio told me approvingly how by the mid-1930s the government had gotten rid of the most bullying overseers (except, many noted, for Levers's manager Charles Widdy, whom we will meet later) and tried to protect them from others. For admirable studies of plantation life, see Bennett 1987, chap 8; 1993.

4. On the regulation, see *PIM* 1934b; Bengough 1936e; Bennett 1987, 164. Bell warned that the change would exacerbate depopulation: young men would give nothing to families and would cease to be an asset to parents, children would no longer be wanted, and abortion or infanticide would follow (Bell 1921b; see also Bell 1916a, 9; 1918c; 1918e; 1922a). Workers also received quarters, food, tobacco, soap, and clothing, and were repatriated. Accompanying dependents were also supported, but most employers refused to hire married couples, and women needed a husband's or male relative's permission to enlist (AR 1927, 12; Barley, Hetherington, and Hewitt 1929, 8–9, 14, 31–34).

5. On refusals, see AR 1934, 7; MARs 1935–1937. Re other events, see MQRs June and Oct 1934; June 1936, 3; *PIM* 1935, 1936; MAR 1935, 19; 1937; Hill 1936a, 1936b; Bengough 1936e, 1938a; Palmer 1970, 12; Bennett 1993, 159–160, 273–274. Recruiters in the 1920s and 1930s often let men return to their village with their wage advance on pledge to meet the boat at an arranged place, days, weeks, or even months later, and they at times gave them money to offer an advance to others (AR 1927, 12; Barley, Hetherington, and Hewitt 1929, 8–9, 14, 31–34; Vandercook 1937, 334). Guadalcanal and Santa Cruz men also refused the new wage (Bennett 1993, 159).

6. Bell 1922a; MQR June 1930, 21; White 1932a; *PIM* 1932; AR 1934, 6; Bengough 1936a, 1936e (quote); Sandars 1937b; nd, 114; Malaita District 1937; Frazer 1973, 59, and figure 3.1. Except for east Kwara'ae, which ranked with 'Are'are and Kwaio as Malaita's poorest places, Malaitans in the north, especially coastal groups, were not as pressed for cash as southerners. Fewer had refused the halved wage, and in any case they depended less on plantation work. Some around Fo'odo and Malu'u had coconut plantings and access to traders buying copra, and others sold trochus shell. Saltwater people of the Te Lagoon in Lau, and in Langalanga, had for years earned higher wages as non-indentured stevedore teams working overseas steamers. John Vandercook described the system: "The work is organized. Several clan groups have over a period of years contributed their wages and bought sailing-schooners. They follow the shipping schedules, and every month or so a different communally

owned ship takes a complement into Tulagi. There they go aboard the steamer and camp on its deck during the fortnight it spends going through the group picking up copra from the estates. They handle the shore boats, the launches, the winches, and the work below decks. When the trip is over they are dropped off again at Tulagi and return by schooner to the artificial islands" (Vandercook 1937, 355–356). Stevedores spent shorter periods away than indentured laborers, and so this was less disruptive of communities. The government used prisoners as its stevedores at Tulagi. See *Planters' Gazette* 1922, 8; Mason 1925, 139; Hopkins 1928, 222; BSIP 1940a; Ivens 1972, 46; Bennett 1987, 163, 187, 220–223, 274, 442; Lever [1990?], chap 2, 2.

7. Rodwell 1921b, 3; Steward 1921; Palmer 1970, 7; Hilliard 1974, 102; Campbell 1978, 270–274; see Collinson 1926, 195; MAR 1932, 33; Hogbin 1970, 170–171; Keesing and Corris 1980, 76–80. Frazer observed that imposition of the tax did not in fact appear statistically to have a clear, long-term impact on the number of men who became indentured (1973, 59, and figure 3.1). Of course the tax was just one of many factors affecting how many did so at a given time.

8. Mason 1925, 134; Ashley 1932a, 1936b; Lambert 1933, 29 May; Bengough 1936e; Sandars 1937b; nd, 115–116; Allan 1951k, 2; Hogbin 1970, 150; see Bell 1922a, 3; International Labour 1932; A Sandars 1950, 18; Keesing and Corris 1980, 74–76.

9. Bell 1922b; MAR 1935, 14; Bengough 1936e, 1938a; Sandars 1937b; nd, 114; Belshaw 1949a, 444; Hogbin 1970, 168.

10. See Hogbin 1970, 167–171, 213; MAR 1930, 30; 1934, 8; Akin 1999a. Barley in 1930 had noted a growing preference for cash in brideprice and compensations where once only local currencies were accepted. In many places shell and teeth currencies subsequently regained ground, perhaps owing in part to the dearth of cash during the Depression and then Maasina Rule. Also important were political meanings that came to be ascribed to shells as *kastom* money, and to brideprice, compensation, and other exchanges, as *kastom* transactions symbolically opposed to cash-based market exchange. Today cash payments are again the norm in most of Malaita, accompanied by a smaller but necessary payment in local currencies. Only in inland Kwaio does shell money still dominate (MAR 1930, 30; see Akin 1999a).

11. Hogbin and Wedgwood 1943, 10–12; see Hogbin 1930, 207–208; MAR 1940, 6. *Ara'i* (or *ala'i*) or *ara'ikwao* became common Pijin terms for white people.

12. MQR March 1934; MAR 1935, 1938; Ashley 1932a, 1936a; Bengough 1936e, 1938a; Sandars 1937b, 6; nd, 116–117; Hogbin 1970, 150. Sandars said Ashley remained unhappy until the high commissioner visited and confirmed Sandars had the right to cut the tax (nd, 117).

13. Ashley 1936b; Brownlees quoted in Knox-Mawer 1986, 61; Fox 1962, 139; Bennett 1993, 169. European residents in the 1930s were liable for any tax imposed by local enactments and paid a £1 residential tax.

14. Ashley 1936b; Bengough 1936b, 1936e; MQRs March and June 1936; see Sandars 1937b. The Kwaio and 'Are'are tax had also been lowered to 2 shillings in 1932–33.

15. Malaita District 1937; Sandars 1937b; Ashley 1938b.

16. Ashley 1931b; and quoted in Bennett 1987, 273; see also *Sydney Herald* 1934; Deck 1937; Kennedy 1946.

17. Forster 1950, 1. Marau area people maintained close political and other links with 'Are'are, and many were 'Are'are immigrants or their descendants.

18. MAR 1930; 1932, 33; Bengough 1936a, 1936e (quote); Sandars 1937b, 6. Vandercook described a trading boat and its wares (1937, 351–352).

19. On different pricing, see Ivens [1928b?], 2; Hopkins 1928, 245; BSIP 1939; and BSIP file 49/11; Malaita District 1939a; Sandars 1939b; Hilliard 1974, 102; see Bell 1922a, 1922c.

20. MQR Sept 1940; Isabel Annual Report 1941, 8, 13; on postwar plantations, see Bennett 1987, 302–303.

21. Lambert 1934b 8; and see Lambert 1933, 3 June; Mytinger 1942, 21.

22. See Belshaw 1950a, 24; Saunders 1979, 170, 183; Saetana 1980 pers comm.

23. MAR 1931, 18; 1935, 19–20; see Hogbin 1944, 264.

24. Sandars 1932; 1933a; 1933b, 3; BSIP 1933; Odi 1932; Barley 1933a; BSIP file 14/89; Hubbard 1933; Ashley 1938c; Fowler 1959, 39–41; Fallowes 1966; Hilliard 1974, 113; 1978, 282; Whiteman 1983, 206–208; Bennett 1987, 260; White 1991, 191–196, passim. On Filose, see also Boutilier 1982, 47–48.

25. Ashley 1938c; Fallowes 1971; Hilliard 1974, 115; Bennett 1987, 260–261; White 1991, 196–198.

26. Ashley 1939a, 1939b; see White 1978, 236–237.

27. Pidoke 1939 (and see version in Laracy 1983, A6, A7); see BSIP 1940c.

28. Pidoke 1939; Fallowes 1939a; White 1992 pers comm; see Bennett 1987, 261. Frazer noted that the average monthly pay of European plantation assistants in 1932–1933 was £12 (1990, 198).

29. Fallowes 1939a; BSIP 1940c. See Laracy 1976, 88; Hilliard 1978, 279–285; Whiteman 1983, 210–211. For Fallowes's influence on north Guadalcanal and Makira, see Bennett 1987, 262–263 and Scott 2007, 106–108.

30. Fallowes 1939b, 1939c, 1966, 1971; Sandars 1939a; Vaskess 1939; Hilliard 1974, 112–116; White 1978, 236–238; 1991, 198; Bennett 1977, 262–263; Fifi'i 1989, 40–41. Sandars first wrote "mental strain," but it was changed to "excitement." For more on Fallowes and related activities, see White 1978, 219–240; 1991, 190–199; Hilliard 1978, 281–285; Keesing 1980, 102–104; Whiteman 1983, 205–211; Bennett 1987, 259–263. Allan erred in saying the church withdrew Fallowes from the Solomons in 1939 (1950a, 77). Isabel's Officer Fowler published a belittling account of his 1930 dealings with Fallowes, giving him a pseudonym (1959, chap 2). Baddeley had sought Fallowes's deportation since April (Ashley 1939). Fallowes later said that of church colleagues only Charles Fox showed any sympathy (1966). The Colonial Office later repealed Fallowes's deportation. He returned in 1959 and was pleased to find many reforms he had advocated being instituted. He later worked in South Africa and died in 1992. I thank Geoff White and Hugh Laracy for documents about Fallowes, and White, Terry Brown, and especially David Hilliard for sharing his letters to them. Baddeley supported the racial status quo, for example, by forbidding the *Southern Cross*'s black crew to worship at a white Rabaul church (Fox 1962, 134; Hilliard 1978, 272–273; Fallowes 1981 pers comm to Terry Brown; Whiteman 1983, 212–214). Baddeley later received the US Medal of Freedom and an honorary doctorate from Columbia, and the US press lauded him as a war hero (see, eg, several *New York Times* stories of Nov 1944). Archbishop of Canterbury Cosmo Gordon Lang had picked Baddeley as bishop to exemplify "muscular Christianity" and to "discipline" Melanesia's clergy after his predecessor, Frederick Molyneux, was removed due to a homosexual scandal (Terry Brown 2004 pers comm).

31. Clemens 1940a; Horton 1940; Allan 1950a, 77; White 1991, 198–199; Hill-

iard 1978, 285. A rumor circulated in Makira, attributed to a Fallowes follower there, that he would return with an airplane filled with money to raise copra prices (Marchant 1940c, 1940d; Baddeley 1940).

32. Waddell writing in Eastern District Quarterly Reports, 31 July 1939, 5; 19 April 1940, 2; Waddell, Trench, and Bentley 1945.

33. Belshaw 1950b; Lanternari 1963, 175; Malefijt 1968, 338; see White 1991, 198.

34. *PIM* 1934b; Fallowes 1939b, 3; Laracy 1976, 102–107; Bennett 1987, 243–248, 263, 274.

35. Brownlees 1940; Allan 1950a, 29, 77; see Malaita District 1939a; Baddeley 1940.

36. Bengough 1939e; BSIP 1947d, 81; Anifelo quoted in Keesing 1980, 104; Anifelo 1980 pers comm; Ma'aanamae 1987 pers comm.

37. Horton 1940; Belshaw 1949a, 431; 1950a, 119; Hilliard 1974, 115; Hogbin 1976, 122–123.

38. As late as 1941 Bengough counted east and west Kwaio coastal populations as 100 of 3,750, and 20 of 1,820 people, respectively (1941a, 5). Few Christians lived inland.

39. MAR 1937; Deck 1940, 3; Sullivan 1944. Fifi'i, later Maasina Rule's head chief for east Kwaio, was working in Tulagi when the Gela meeting took place and its ideas were in circulation, but he was only 17 years old and did not attend (see Fifi'i 1982b; 1989, 40–41).

40. Bengough in this report (1939e; and in MAR 1939, 8–10) misspelled Uogwari as "Guagware" and "Gwaagware." 'Atobala is within 'Ole'olea, which is part of Uogwari.

41. Siufiomea quoted in Keesing 1980, 104; personal communications from Siufiomea 1982, Su'umete 1983, Safaasafi 1983, Peter Soea'adi 1996. Some say Noto'i's brother Bole was with him.

42. Tagii'au here metaphorically conveyed the idea that Noto'i became possessed. Betel nuts are chewed to open communications with ancestors, especially La'aka, who at times send fireflies into houses to announce to descendants their presence and their desire to connect through possession or divination (see Ivens 1930; 1972, 189–190; Codrington 1973, 221; Akin 1993, 711–712).

43. Keesing 1980, 107; Fifi'i 1989, 73–74; Tagii'au 1981 pers comm to author and Kathleen Gillogly (extract); personal communications from Ma'aanamae of 'Ai'eda 1987 and 1996, and from Siufiomea 1987. Speaking in tongues is now common in South Sea Evangelical Church communities, where it is called *'atorenisi* (probably from English "audience"), but this and related practices only became central to church practice on Malaita during a 1969 revival movement and so would not have inspired Noto'i (see Griffiths 1977). Several Kwaio recalled to me their disgust at the time of that revival, since they felt this behavior was proper only for those worshipping ancestors. Before this, Christians were sometimes possessed, but usually by their ancestors, requiring exorcisms.

44. Bengough 1939c, 1939e; MQR Sept 1939, 3; Siufiomea quoted in Keesing 1980, 105–107; Siufiomea 1982 pers comm; Su'umete 1983 pers comm. No one ever paid an entry fee. There is a common pattern of dual prophets in Malaitan political-religious movements. 'Airumu is within the territory of Age'eriufa, which is within Kwa'ilalamua.

45. Today La'aka is one of the two most widely propitiated ancestral spirits in

Kwaio, having spread to many groups since the 1930s through affinal connections. She is sometimes referred to as "'Afe" (wife). See Akin 2003, 393, re a mechanism for such ancestral proliferation. Her spread reflects, in part, her association with anticolonial activities that began with Noto'i, as well as the powers she grants in towns and on plantations—there, where some ancestors are apathetic or inactive, she protects her descendants (see also Fifi'i 1989, 74–75). La'aka when alive controlled powerful fighting magics that she learned through dreams and drew on to strengthen her kin group, and today she is renowned for bestowing martial strength on descendants who pray for it. For more on La'aka, see Keesing 1982c, 76, 96, 100–101.

46. Bengough 1939c, 1939e; MAR 1939, 10; MQR Sept 1939, 3–4; Siufiomea 1982 pers comm.

47. Siufiomea quoted in Keesing 1980, 106; Martin Clemens 1992 pers comm.

48. In October 1931, Norman Deck had spread word on Malaita that a recent severe earthquake was a sign the world would soon "turn upside down," and that people had to join his church to be saved. This frightened many and, at least in Kwaio, some killed and ate their pigs and felled Canarium almond trees. In one hamlet, incest occurred. In Langalanga and perhaps elsewhere, some did become Christians (Kuper 1933, 3; personal communications from Ma'aanamae 1983, Fifi'i 1988, and David Gegeo 1988). Fifi'i gave an account that omits Deck's role (1989, 23–26), which he included in an earlier version he told to me (and see Deck 1927b, 1; Vandercook 1937, 348–349; Fifi'i 1988b; for earthquake-inspired conversions in Kwara'ae, see Burt 1994, 155–156; on the earthquake, see M Deck 1931, 6; MAR 1931, 5–8; Richards 1932b; Grover 1949, 54–55; Palmer nd; Green 1976, 44–46; Griffiths 1977, 86–88; Lever [1990?], chap 2, 22; Sandars nd, 180; Davies nd, 327). Laracy said that just before the war some north Malaitans "feasted extravagantly, lest the Japanese deprive them of their pigs and gardens" (1976, 111; see MQR June 1940). Such destruction has been reported from elsewhere in Melanesia linked to activities lumped as "cargo cults," at times explained as due to not wanting others to enjoy one's property after one is gone. Some Malaitans after the war explained American destruction of surplus goods and equipment in similar terms: soldiers are said to have told them, "If we leave everything around the government will make business out of them" (Wa'ii'a 1987 pers comm). Property was destroyed or consumed on Malaita and Makira during stages of Maasina Rule due to rumors of another war (see this book, chapter 7). See Rohorua 1898, 7; Field 1943, 15; Trench 1945b; Crass 1947b; Davies 1947a; nd, 206, 208; and quoted in Laracy 1983, 151; Fifi'i 1951b; Campbell 1978, 300.

49. Bengough 1939c, 1939e; BSIP 1940b; Sandars nd, 142; Ma'aanamae quoted in Keesing 1978a, 261; 1982 pers comm; Fifi'i 1988 pers comm; 1989, 72–73; Clemens 1992 pers comm. Along with the others Noto'i spent six months in jail, but after their release the following March he and a few followers quietly continued their activities for several years. Later they refused to take part in some Maasina Rule activities, particularly one mass descent to the coast to await American ships said to be coming (Ma'aanamae 1982 pers comm; Gwanu'i 1996 pers comm; see Keesing 1978a, 260; Fifi'i 1989).

50. Bengough 1939c; 1939e, 3; MQR Sept 1939; Joseph Pali quoted in Sanga 1989, 24; see Siufiomea quoted in Keesing 1980, 107. Bengough wrote, "Rumours, notable mainly for their wildness, circulated through the District, having their ori-

gin for the most part in stories brought by natives returning from plantations or labour on the overseas steamer" (MQR 30 Sept 1939, 3).

51. Keesing 1978a, 46–47; Bennett 1987, 279–280; personal communications from Ma'aanamae 1982, Ri'ika 1982, Tagii'au 1987, and Laete'esafi and Waneagea 1987; see Guppy 1887, 15, 17; Wilson 1908, 5; Lindstrom 1981, 102–103. Bennett, and Keesing, tied Noto'i's movement to earlier Kwara'ae movements based around *bulu* spirits, because some Kwaio said Noto'i was speaking to a *buru* spirit. These activities shared some features but were minimally connected and had very different meanings. Kwaio *buru* are a type of spirit that impersonates true ancestors, and Kwaio who said Noto'i's spirit was a *buru* were by self-definition movement critics, dismissing it by charging that the spirit possessing Noto'i was not really La'aka and should be ignored (Keesing 1978a, 260; Siufiomea and Folofo'u quoted in Keesing 1980, 106–107; Bennett 1987, 278–279). Allan later claimed the Fallowes, Maasina Rule, and Federal Council movements all were extensions of the Kwara'ae *bulu* (MQR 30 June 1951, 5; 1957a, 250; 1974). He likely influenced Davies (1951b) to claim that 'Are'are *bulu* legends about "cargo" were key in "determining the form of the original Marching Rule." Neither Allan nor Davies knew what he was talking about and both claims are fatuous. For a study of Kwaio *buru*, see Akin 1996; for the early Kwara'ae *bulu*, see Burt 1994, 135–139, and 198. See also Russell 1954b, 2; Laracy 1983, 33.

52. See Mayr 1931, 1943; Eyerdam 1933a, 1933b. Their visit to Malaita had been delayed due to Bell's death, but the ornithologists knew no details of that prior to their arrival in the Solomons, and their ending up at 'Aulola under Babaamae's sponsorship was unplanned. In 1927 and 1928, refugees from government attacks had sheltered at 'Aulola under the protection of Babaamae and another leader, Kwaloamae, who were made constables (Coultas diary, 31 March 1930; Hamlin diary, 7 March 1930; 'Elota quoted in Keesing 1978b, 127; Keesing and Corris 1980, 174–175; Arugeni 1982 pers comm; Wadoka 1982 pers comm; Fifi'i 1989, 12). This refuge from foreign invasion likely inspired the La'aka movement leaders to specify that 'Atobala and 'Airumu would be similar "safe areas" during the predicted American invasion. (People near there, at Farisi, had erected a palisade to stop government soldiers 12 years before, and Kwaio had once built fortified refuges [*labu*] during feuds.) Babaamae was later made an assistant headman. Bobo'efuufuu was a six-hour walk from 'Aulola at the Americans' slow pace in this most difficult of Malaitan terrains, but Kwaio conceive of the two places as lying within a single general locale. A sketch map and general itinerary of the trip is in Mayr 1931, 2–3. Hamlin returned to the coast after the move to Bobo'efuufuu.

53. The other men arrested were Logari'i, Wadoka, Oritabu, Maarua'au, and Gi'okwala. The relationships to Babaamae are in large genealogies I collected in 1996 from Wadoka's son Safaasafi and nephew 'Inisafi in relation to another project. One friend of mine, Tome Toloasi Teoboo, later a Maasina Rule leader, from 1932 through 1933 was on the *France*'s crew under Coultas and traveled to Micronesia, Manila, Nauru, and Rabaul (Teoboo 1982, 1983).

54. Diaries: Eyerdam 1929–1930; Coultas 1929–1930; Hamlin 1928–1930; hereafter cited by 1930 dates. On locals' wonder and food, see Eyerdam 1933b, 434, 436 (and see 435); Basiberi 1996. Long quote: Eyerdam, 17 March.

55. Eyerdam 1933b, 435, 438; diary 4 April. This chant is still performed in Kwaio. I knew Ofomauri until his death in the early 1980s. Suuburigeni and another man named 'Adimae guided the birders throughout most of their visit to Kwaio.

56. Eyerdam, 17 March; see AR 1928, 11; Basiberi 1996 pers comm; on rifles and ammunition, see Teoboo 1982.

57. On shrines, see Coultas, 28 March; re the priest, see Coultas, 9 and 22 March. Quote: Eyerdam, 12 March; see Coultas, 15 March. See Eyerdam 1933b, 436.

58. Eyerdam, 25 Jan, 16 March; 1930, 77; 1933b, 436; Coultas, 26 Feb, 5 March, 15 April; see Mayr 1943, 33.

59. Coultas, 15 April; Eyerdam, 19 March. American soldiers sometimes addressed Islanders as "Joe," also.

60. Coultas, 1, 5, and 15 April.

61. Coultas, 15 and 17 April; Basiberi 1996; see Eyerdam, 15 April. It is conceivable that Noto'i and his brother Bole might have traveled on the *France* in 1930, an idea suggested to me by Ben Burt. Unfortunately, the expedition diaries from the Kwaio visit contain only a smattering of names. It is even possible that Noto'i claimed this is when he got La'aka's message, directly from Eyerdam and Coultas, but one can only speculate. One Kwaio version of the story says Noto'i met the Americans while "at Levers," but this phrase was sometimes a generic Malaitan label for "abroad" (Safaasafi 1982 pers comm).

62. Eyerdam 1933b, 434, 436; Bennett 1987, 280. On friction, see, eg, Coultas, 26 Feb, 7 March, 8 and 15 April; on standard weight, see Grover 1957, 300. Kwaio did not know why the team collected bird skins (1,060 specimens of 62 species in all on Malaita, and many other creatures). Eyerdam told Teoboo "the birds were going to be pictures in a book," and that a particular owl (*Ninox jacquinoti malaitæ* = Kwaio *kooko'afuto*, a new subspecies) would be valuable in the United States (Mayr 1931, 2, 14; Teoboo 1982). Tobacco was then a common currency for procuring labor—that year the Solomons imported 119,115 pounds of it, and it brought a good portion of BSIP import duties (Bell 1918e; *Blue Book* 1930, 58). Bell said a desire for tobacco was the main reason communities urged their young men to recruit in the 1910s (1918c, 3). Lambert recalled Hamlin's expertise in selecting trade goods (1941, 287).

63. J London 1911, 1913; C London [1910?]; Norden 1925; Johnson 1945; see Eyerdam 1933b.

64. Eyerdam, 15 Feb; 1934b, 434. Babaamae quote in Eyerdam 1933a, 6.

65. Vandercook 1937, 357. Vandercook and his wife crossed Malaita through the Kwaiba'ita river valley along the Kwaio-Kwara'ae border, north of where the ornithologists had been. They spent an evening at a village talking with their hosts in Pijin, during which three men asked eagerly to "sign on" in their employ so they could visit America (1937, 359–366).

66. Herbert 1979, 14. Herbert, later a well-known Australian novelist, was only at Tulagi Hospital from late February until dismissed at the end of May. The BSIP Annual Medical Report of 1928 says he "was compelled to resign owing to ill health" (BSIP 1928, 1; see Herbert's explanation in Keesing and Corris 1980, 206–209; see Boutilier 1982, 48). The sort of colonial social dynamics that could produce attitudes like those Herbert recalled were explained by the earl of Elgin in his mid-nineteenth-century diary description of European relations with Calcutta servants: "One moves among them with perfect indifference, treating them not as dogs, because in that case one would whistle to them and pat them, but as machines with which one can have no communion or sympathy.... When the passions of fear and hatred are grafted on this indifference, the result is frightful: an absolute callous-

ness as to the sufferings of the objects of those passions" (quoted in Mishra 2004, 33). See also Nelson 1982, chap 19.

67. Ivens 1907; *You and the Native* 1943; Grover 1958, 1; see Steward 1926; Knibbs 1929, 69, 191; Mytinger 1942, 32–34; Hogbin 1970, 164; Barley quoted in Bennett 1987, 179. Ivens's attitudes later grew more humane. Furse argued that familiarity meant "punishment, when it becomes necessary, may have to be harsher than it need otherwise be" (1962, 303; cf Bertram 1930, 62). See Stoler 1992 on the importance of racial boundaries to uniting colonial communities with diverse interests, and of keeping "subversives" from disrupting categories crucial to those communities.

68. Barley, Hetherington, and Hewitt 1929, 64; Rhoades 1982, 59; White 1928–1931, 15 Feb 1929; see Belshaw 1949a, 290; *PIM* 1935.

69. E Forster 1984, 7; see Stoler 1992.

70. Horton 1940; Belshaw 1949a, 431; 1950b, 118; Kennedy 1967, 3; Hilliard 1974, 115; Hogbin 1976, 122–123; White 1978, 240; see Marchant 1941. Resident Commissioner H G Gregory-Smith in 1951 wrote that Marchant "based his whole administrative policy on the Kenya lines," and cited the need for continuity in justifying doing the same thing himself (1951c, 3).

71. Woodford quoted in Scarr 1967, 293; Allan 1957a, 45; see Woodford 1890b, 188; Murray 1916, 15–16; Ivens 1929, vi; Scarr 1967, 293–294; Laracy 1976, 91; Keesing and Corris 1980, 33; Bennett 1987, chap 6; Thomas 1990; McGregor 1993. Wilson's successor Steward wrote, "God forbid that the Melanesian should die out; but this would be better than that he should be utterly degraded by contact with us and all his native virtues exchanged for imported vices, till he becomes the 'nigger' that some of his visitors from civilisation appear to think he is" (1939, 135). On ideas about depopulation and colonial policy in Fiji, see Thomas 1994, chap 4.

72. Somerville 1897, 361, 411; Deck quoted in Laracy and Laracy 1980, 137; Lambert 1934b, 20; see Hopkins 1927, 111–112; Scarr 1967, 292–297; Pratt 1986, 144–145; Thomas 1990, 153.

73. *NIV* Annual Report 1919–1920, 3; Bell 1924 (cf Bell 1918c); Ivens 1927; 1972, xvii, 25; Crichlow 1929, 181; Lambert 1934a, 16; Hogbin 1970, 127; Crosby 2003, 233–241; Sandars nd, 104; see McArthur 1967, 1970; Lal 1992, 57–59; Bennett 1993, 143; Jolly 1994, 29–34. For early estimates, see Edge-Partington 1911a; Murray 1916, 12. We have better, grim figures from Malaita's neighbors. In 1924, Ivens found Ulawa's population down a quarter since 1909, and on Makira an officer estimated nearly half died of dysentery in a 1914 epidemic. Michael Scott has summarized the great mortality from disease there and government attempts to counter it, particularly with spatial reorganization and sanitary regulation (Ivens 1927; 1972, xvii; Crichlow 1929, 181; Kuper 1933, 10–14; Fox 1962, 103, 142; Green 1976, 42–43; Scott 2007, 82–95). The government checked incoming ships to try to certify that they carried no diseases (see, eg, Sinker 1907, 29).

74. MAR 1930, 25; 1931, 4–5; see Ivens 1970, 42, 44; Fox 1967, 47. On periodic epidemics, see *NIV* and especially *SCL,* and Eastern District Annual Reports during the 1920s. The latter are comprehensive, especially for the 1910s and 1920s, when statistics for Malaita are unavailable. I thank Michael Scott for several of these.

75. Thomas 1990; 1994, chap 4, quote on page 119. See Clammer 1973 on the importance of order in Fiji and the imposition of a European concept of "communalism" in this context. Martha Kaplan analyzed "colonial constructions of disorder" in Fiji (1995, chap 5).

76. Goldie 1914, 564. Goldie was later harshly criticized for ignoring warnings that his gathering people to celebrate an anniversary of his own appointment would spread an ongoing typhoid epidemic (Carter 1990, 50–51; see Lambert 1934a, 12). For attributing depopulation to Islander shortcomings, see Romilly 1886, 68–70; Woodford 1890, 188; Colony of Fiji 1896, 5; Somerville 1897, 410–411; Carver 1911, 6; Campbell 1918, 42; Durrad 1922, 34; Rivers 1922; Roberts 1927, 63; AR 1932, 5; Hogbin 1930, 49; Harrisson 1937, 261–280; Wilson 1938, 25; Fox 1967, 47; see also Mander 1954, 227–228; Scarr 1967, 293; Thomas 1990; Jolly 1998, 183–187.

77. Wilson 1932, 184–185 (quotes). Jolly analyzed condemnation of mothers in Fiji and Vanuatu; officials intervened less in the maternal practices in the latter (1998). They took even less action on Malaita, though Christians radically transformed childbirth practices by barring observance of related ancestral taboos (see Akin nd). On Malaita, the government kept its distance, partly to avoid entanglement in intense religious conflicts over these practices, until the 1950s when it began constructing maternity centers in some places where they were wanted. See Romilly 1886, 68–70; Montgomery 1892, 2; Colony of Fiji 1896; Deck 1909, 3; E Wilson 1915, 47–50; 1936; Raucaz 1928, 177; Murray 1932, 212; *Mothercraft* [1949?]; Fox 1962, 142; Manderson 1987; cf Bell 1922a; Kuper 1933, 13–14. For blame on the labor trade, see Wilson 1905, 6; 1932, 184–185, 250; 1938, 25; Goldie 1914, 564; and see Hopkins 1927, 11, 113–120; Barley 1930–1932, 54; Hilliard 1978, 156.

78. *NIV* 1921 (nd), 3; Bell 1922b; Deck 1931a, 5. BSIP file I/III/49/3 details the *Southern Cross* taking disease to Ontong Java in the 1930s and Anglican denials and protests; Proclamation 11 of 1939 required all visitors there to first undergo a medical exam. On missions and health, see *SCL* 16 Jan 1899, 31; Durrad 1922, 5–6; Woodford 1922, 71; MAR 1925; 1931, 3; Ivens 1928a, 47; Eastern District Quarterly Report, July–Sept 1931, 3; Wilson 1932, 184–185; Luke 1945a, 20; Deck 1948d, 2; Green 1976, 45–46; Hilliard 1978, 156, 268. On early Christian health, see *NIV* Annual Report 1920–1921, 6–7; Baker 1928; Innes 1938; Hogbin 1970, 135, 139, 199; Hilliard 1978, 268.

79. Barley 1931b; MAR 1931, 10; Sandars quoted in Innes 1938, 16; Hogbin 1935, 28, passim; 1970, 156; see also Bengough 1934, 3; Ivens 1972, 25.

80. Colony of Fiji 1886, 6. See Darwin 1874, 206–218; Hopkins 1908b; Burnett 1911, 84; Murray 1916, 16; Rivers 1922; Macmillan Brown 1927, chap 25; Pitt-Rivers 1927; Roberts 1927; Harrisson 1937, 269–274; Malinowski 1961, 465–467; Fox 1967, 46–49.

81. Rivers 1922, 92; Roberts 1927, 154; see Hogbin 1930; Murray 1932; Williams 1932, 220–221, 226; Innes 1938, 6, 28. Hogbin had once put forth psychological theories as an explanation for disease susceptibility (1930), but in a 1939 book, in a chapter devoted to depopulation, he attacked such theories and argued that introduced diseases were the problem and better diets and medical services the only effective responses (1970, 132–136). Re late nineteenth-century investigations into depopulation's causes in Fiji, Thomas noted: "It is astonishing that such a limited amount of consideration was paid to what has since been demonstrated to have been the most important factor: the longer-term consequences of introduced disease" (1990, 155).

82. Im Thurn 1922, xvii; Roberts 1927, 154. See Hopkins 1922, 64–65; Malinowski 1961, 466–467; Rivers 1922; Williams 1977, 380; Roberts 1927, 70; Austen 1945, 22, 59–60; Horton 1965, 163; McArthur 1967, xvi. On mechanisms prompting mortality, see Pentony 1953; see also Wallace 1956, 270.

83. Im Thurn 1922: xvii; Roberts 1927, 389–390. On wholesome substitutes, see Rivers 1922, 107–109; Salisbury 1922, 708; Puxley 1925, 108–109; Hopkins 1928, 179; Wilson 1932, 235; Mander 1954, 278; Fox 1962, plate facing page 64. On more work as the solution, see Colony of Fiji 1896; Macmillan Brown 1927, 248; Hogbin and Wedgwood 1943, 7.

84. Ashley 1930b, 7; Murray 1932 on Ashley, citing British Colonial Office 1931, 189; see also Campbell 1978, 281–282.

85. Fortes 1940; see Lambert 1934a, 35; Ranger 1976, 119. Even in the 1950s, Malaita's District Commissioner Allan drew on such theories but used them to explain population *increases*. He wrote that due to ten years of excitement from World War II and Maasina Rule, "The Malaitaman of the forties whiffed the scent of his pristine past and decided that life was worth living after all and so through the jungles and hills, the lagoons and islets a spirit of excitement and reawakening has resulted in a primitive urge to racial preservation and rejuvenation" (MAR 1951, 2–3). But, inspired by Bengough's 1930s reports, Allan thought Kwaio and 'Are'are still suffered from "cultural fatigue" (MQR 30 June 1951, 8; 30 Sept 1951, 8). The next year, Officer John Wrightson at Malu'u quoted old Roberts and Goldie texts and argued for shooting people's pigs, violating colonial law, and forcefully destroying birth huts and introducing "some cultural substitute," all to reverse the severe depopulation he perceived (1952d; 1952f; 1952k, 3). However, by 1952 northern populations had been growing for decades. The indefatigable Charles Fox expounded cultural fatigue and substitution ideas well into the 1960s (1967, 47–49).

86. Some anthropologists supported indirect rule policies as a means to minimize disruption of colonized societies (see, eg, Roberts 1927, section 4; Mair 1936; Malinowski 1945, 138–150; 1961, 466; Horton 1965, 14; Porter 1975, 292–293; see also Bertram 1930, 92; Bodley 1982, 81).

87. Bengough 1936a, 3–4.

88. Sandars 1938b. Ashley cited in Bennett 1987, 237–238.

89. Barrow nd, part 3, 55; see BSIP 1940a.

90. That this project might have influenced Maasina Rule was first noted in passing by Keesing (1978a, 47), apparently as suggested by Ian Frazer. See also the master's thesis by Frazer's student, Naitoro (1993).

91. MAR 1931, 5; Hogbin 1934, 263; see Bell 1922b; Ivens 1927; *Sydney Herald* 1933; Lambert 1934b, 8. In 1925, Bell had noted that all Malaitans were "retaining their virility" except those "northwest of the Maramasike Passage" (MAR 1925). Fowler, who served under Barley, referred to the "apathetic, zestless and declining people of Ariari" (1936, 3). The BSIP Annual Report of 1936 gives statistics showing overall births significantly outpacing deaths for 1934, 1935, and 1936, despite high influenza tolls in 1936, but provides no Malaita-specific numbers (AR 1936, 6).

92. Barley writing in MAR 1931, 3; MQR June 1931; and Lambert 1933, 3 June; 1934a; 1934b, 8; and 1941, 330, based on talks with Barley; see Fox 1925, 7; MAR 1930, 25; 1950, 2; Innes 1938, 8.

93. Ashley 1929b, 9; MAR 1929, 1930, 1931; MQR June 1930, March 1931, June 1931; Barley 1931a, 1931b; Fletcher 1932.

94. MQR June 1931; Barley 1931b; Horton 1965, 97; Lasaqa 1972, 295; see MAR 1931, 4; Chinnery 1932.

95. MAR 1929; Lambert 1934a, 31–33; Innes 1938, 23; Ashley 1934; 1935b; see

Allan 1949c, 19. Barley on Makira had set penalties of 10 shillings or a month in jail for failure to report births, deaths, or marriages to salaried "district chiefs" (1920). Malaita's 1931 census counted only 603 boys and 285 girls between the ages of 6 and 16, of an estimated 40,067 total people (Lambert 1934a, 32). Though the census spawned repopulation efforts throughout south Malaita, only on Small Malaita did it indicate a significant sex imbalance (Barley 1931b). In 1937, tax lists led Sandars to greatly undercount mountain populations even in more accessible north Malaita (Innes 1938, 8, 23). Counting problems continued for decades. In mid-1947, when very few Malaitans were abroad, Sandars found at 'Oloburi and neighboring Maanawai in 'Are'are that women outnumbered men 371 to 331, and in every age category, while at nearby Takataka 336 men outnumbered 258 women, a contrast on which he made no comment (1947d). In 1948, citing the still-standing 40,000 number, Germond wrote, "I submit that this figure is a fiction and that the last census does not in any way reflect the true figures," and, "How many...hill villages there are and how numerous their inhabitants is not known but it is certain that there are far more than will be admitted by the headmen" (1948b, annexure A).

96. Bengough 1934, 3, 10, passim; Malaita District 1939b; BSIP 1940a; see *SCL* Nov 1910, 744; May 1937, 68; MQR June 1934; Deck 1937; Naitoro 1993, 38–44, 54–55; de Coppet 1981, 189–191; 'Are'are 2005b. The 'Are'are word *houra* or *houraa* (Sa'a *houlaa*, Kwaio *foulaa*) literally means fame, renown, and prestige—what participants seek for their groups and their leaders (Geerts 1970, 38; Ivens 1972, 100, 160). Charles Fox was a rare European who appreciated the value of feasts, writing, "European influence has been against these feasts, condemning them as a heathen custom, a waste of time, and so on. The people's time would be better given to making copra. But our Church helped to keep them, by and large, turning them in some islands into Christian festivals" (1962, 55; see Hogbin 1970, 214–216). Ivens 1972, chapter 7, summarizes types of feasts in the Sa'a area of neighboring Small Malaita. One of Deck's SSEM teachers, Hamuel Hoahania, compiled a list of 17 negative effects of *houraa* and said that current practice was not true custom. Deck submitted the list to Sandars (Deck 1937).

97. See Bennett 1987, 275; Akin 1999, 124–126; cf Naitoro 1993, 76.

98. MQR March 1941, 2; see MQR Oct 1934; Deck 1937; Bengough 1941b.

99. Marchant quoted from Malaita District 1939b.

100. BSIP 1947e, 54, 60. Even in 1957, District Commissioner W St G Anderson was telling Malaitans that until brideprice had been reduced to the "absolute minimum...your country will be unable to develop its natural resources" (1957b).

101. See, eg, Ashley 1932b; White 1932b; Deck 1932, 1948c; Sandars 1937a, 1938b; Bengough 1940a; MAR 1941, 3; Germond 1948f. Allan later wrote that on Malaita, "Failure of the District Officer to conform to the 'Mission Line' in matters of marriage dispute, illicit fornication disputes, divorce, feasting, bride price, the authority of teachers, and the such like would result often in threats from the worthy heads of the mission like the Decks, that pressure would be brought to bear and the wretched young man would lose his job. The mission authorities through the Young family who ran the Malaita Company...had direct and powerful access to the High Commissioner and to the Colonial Office. Often the wretched young man would have to comply" (1951b, 7). There is no truth in this. Allan loathed the SSEM.

102. Sandars 1938b; Hogbin 1970, 211–212. More than once young men, on hearing such explanations for bachelorhood, have whispered to me with a smile, "The real reason he didn't get married is that he was afraid of vaginas."

103. Bengough 1934, 10; 1935; 1940a; 1941b; MAR 1936, 9; 1941; Deck 1937; MQR June 1939; June 1941, 22; Malaita District 1941a, 22 May and 18 July; Sandars 1943b; Allan 1950a, 77; Bennett 1987, 275; cf Fox 1962, 55.

104. Bengough 1941b, 1. Naitoro summarized aspects of the Haumatana project and gives a table of government population figures 1934–1940 (1993, 76–83). He argued that the further decline was likely due more to a severe 1936–1937 flu epidemic than to the cultural practices Bengough blamed. This west 'Are'are area still has one of Malaita's lowest population densities. Cadets in charge at Haumatana were Martin Clemens (Feb–July 1940), Michael Forster (Oct 1940–March 1941), and David Trench (touring May and July 1941). Native Medical Practitioner Geoffrey Kuper was there July 1940–July 1941, except when Guso Rato Piko relieved him from December to March. Later, Jock Beveridge was the agricultural officer. Plans for a second "central camp" inland along the "road" to Takataka never materialized (Marchant 1940b; Bengough 1941b). Piko was from Choiseul and in 1936 had graduated from Suva training and taken over 'Aoke's hospital. He later carried 'Are'are project ideas to Santa Cruz, where, when war came, the district officer left him in charge of Nidu. Piko there imposed rules including slashing brideprice and abolishing sexual compensation. Apparently against his wishes, people took his ideas further as "Guso's New Law," a fuller rejection of marriage and sexual rules, which sparked copulatory abandon in places. When Bill Davenport and I compared notes, we realized that the Haumatana project was thus an antecedent of not only Maasina Rule but also the Santa Cruz movement (see Innes 1938; Davenport 1970, 1989).

105. Bengough 1941b, 2.

106. Marchant 1940a; MQR March 1941; Bengough 1941b, 3, 7; and see Bengough 1939a, 6.

107. Thomas 1990, 164–167; 1994, 120–122; Scott 1998, 1. On nucleated villages, see Ivens 1918, 191; Campbell 1918, 42; Kane 1923b; AR 1933, 7; Deck 1948c; Chapman and Pirie 1974, 236–240; Nelson 1982, 37–38; Bennett 1987, 112; Scott 2007, chap 2. On Melanesians' fleeting residence in them, see Barley 1921, 2; Thurnwald 1936, 351–352; Eastern District Annual Report 12 Jan 1945, 3; Oliver 1967, 15–17; Thomas 1994, 122; Tedder 2008, 79.

108. Marchant 1940b; Bengough 1941b; MQR March 1941; Clemens 1988; 1992 pers comm.

109. MAR 1925 (cf MQR June 1931); Garvey quoted in Knox-Mawer 1986, 61; various Kwaio personal communications; see Bengough 1938b; Sandars nd, 113–116; Keesing and Corris 1980, 103. For a broader discussion of the problems that fluid systems of personal naming have historically caused political regimes, and attempts to impose legibility through standardized naming practices, see Scott 1998, 64–71.

110. Bengough 1939a, 5, 6; 1941b; see Colley 1940; Deck 1948c.

111. Bengough 1934; Deck 1940; Luke 1945b, 90; Forster 1946c, 4; Laracy 1983, 18; Fifi'i 1989, 62; Clemens 1992 pers comm; Davies nd, 72. Fifty years later, Clemens asserted that he, not Bengough, deserved the major credit for the 'Are'are project, adding, "I believe I was really responsible for Marching Rule as I made them stand up and do something for themselves" (1988; see also Clemens 1998). Decades after, Davies wrote, weirdly, that in the mid-1940s Hoasihau was virtually alone in being concerned about Malaitans' future (nd, 72).

112. Malaita District 1941a, 17 July; Sandars 1943b; MAR 1944, 5; Forster 1946c, 6; Naitoro 1993, 75; 'Are'are 2005b, 3; Davies nd, 72. Davies asserted that Sandars

later banned *houraa* completely, due to a brawl at one (nd, 308). The partially finished roads were completed in 1964 as part of a cocoa-farming endeavor (Naitoro
1993, 123). On 24 July 1943, Bengough, while acting resident commissioner, was
killed at age 36 when Japanese Zeros downed a plane he was aboard as a Defense
Force observer over the Western Solomons (Cooper 1946, 56; Homewood 2005).

113. See Isabel Annual Report 1941; Trench 1941; Wright 1941; Barrow nd, part
3, 22.

114. Marchant 1940b; BSIP 1941; [1947f?]; Kennedy 1967, 5; Campbell 1978,
286; Bennett 1987, 281–282. Hogbin later (1946, 38) said these early bodies were
modeled on his proposals in *Experiments in Civilization* (1970), but I found no reference to that book in relevant government records, and councils were started in the
second quarter of 1939, the year it was first published. He did influence the process,
however (see Trench 1943; Hogbin 1944, 1945; Allan 1960, 161).

115. Malaita District [1941b?]; MQRs June 1939, March and June 1940, and
March, June, Sept 1941; MAR 1941, 2–3; BSIP [1947f?]; Marchant 1940b, 7; Hogbin
1946, 38, 65. In mid-1940, Marchant asked Officer Donald Kennedy to design an
experimental native administration scheme on Gela to respond to "passive resistance to Government," likely referring to Fallowes's meetings and discontents in
their wake. In 1941, Kennedy initiated a structure of courts (with power only to refer
cases to district officers) and village delegates who attended meetings presided over
by headmen. Kennedy later said "enthusiasm was remarkable," and he blamed wartime discontent on Gela on officers Sandars and Forster—posted there for a time—
having failed to revive his program. He linked his project to Maasina Rule since
Tulagi policemen from Malaita and Guadalcanal participated in it. Kennedy even
proposed that the name "Maasina Rule" derived from his having called his initiative
"Marchant's Rule" when meeting with disgruntled Gela people in early 1944 (1967,
3, 6–9). Brian Murdoch later published an article about Kennedy's claim and, like
Kennedy, exaggerated the Gela scheme's relevance to Maasina Rule's origins, if
indeed it had any (1980).

116. MQRs June 1939, June 1940, and March, June, Sept 1941; Bengough
1940a, 1941a, 1941b; MAR 1941, 2; see Clemens 1941; Campbell 1978, 287; White
1991, 199.

117. Marchant 1940a; MAR 1940, 6; MQRs June 1940, March 1941; BSIP 1941;
Bengough 1941a; Sandars 1941a.

118. Bengough 1941a, 2; see Forster 1946c, 12; A Sandars 1950, 14, 16–17.

119. Bengough 1941a, 2–3.

120. Marchant 1942a; BSIP 1942b, 1943a; Campbell 1978, 286.

121. Hogbin 1946, 65.

Chapter 4: The Wartime Opening

1. Malaita saw scattered fighting incidents. A week before the US invasion, a
boatload of Japanese soldiers raided 'Aoke, purloined a still-warm ham from Bengough's breakfast plate (a crime for which it was said he never forgave Japan), and
defecated on his table. While Bengough, clerk Alec Maena, sergeants Sau and
Irofiala, and Tome Toloasi Teoboo watched with binoculars from atop a hill, the
Japanese used sign language to direct 26 Langalanga men, under Sale "One-Arm"

Fotarafa (or 'Abakomu), to carry loot to their ship. To the bemusement of these sea-soned stevedores, the Japanese rewarded them with a sea biscuit for each box car-ried. Maena took down the men's names and Bengough later had them imprisoned. Japanese also looted Anglican Fauaabu hospital (Marchant 1942–1943, 31 July 1942; Baddeley 1943; Fox 1962, 122; Teoboo 1982 pers comm to author and Kathleen Gil-logly; Osifelo 1985, 21; Waleanisia 1987; Fifi'i 1989, 45; see White 1989, 56–57). On 7 August, US planes bombed Laulasi and Fo'odo islands in the Langalanga Lagoon, killing as many as 30 people (including 19 women and children) and destroying a shell money mint. The attack was due to navigational error, but many Langalanga today still believe it was punishment for their men having carried those boxes for the Japanese, and since the 1950s they have been calling for government compensa-tion for the attack. In the 1980s, the Laulasi Cultural Committee demanded SI$14.7 million from the British government, which they claimed had received US repara-tions but kept the money. The SSEM's Joan Deck detected the hand of God in ancestral Laulasi being bombed rather than a nearby Christian island, but that same day the SSEM launch *Arosi* was bombed at Onepusu. The SSEM's Robert Vance said US bomber pilots told him, "They were given to believe that there was no one on Malaita…apart from 'Nips' and cannibals" (Bentley 1944b; J Deck [1943?], 3; WPHC 1943; Vance 1945, 9; Laracy 1988 pers comm; 1988a, 24; Guo 2001, 98–100; see Marchant 1942–1943, 13 Aug 1942; Anderson 1958b; Solomon Islands Broad-casting 1987; Waleanisia 1987; Laracy 1988a, 24; Gegeo and Watson-Gegeo 1989, 370; Fifi'i 1991, 44). At Afufu on 5 November 1942, people of Malu'u and Fo'odo led police and US Marines to wipe out a Japanese observation post that had been there since July, and Headman Maekali hunted down and killed three Japanese who escaped (Bentley 1944a; Fox 1962, 123–124; Gegeo and Watson-Gegeo 1989, 358–359; Fifi'i 1989, 45–46; Clemens 1998, 232; see Akin 1993, 407). Later, a US bombing at Uru in Kwaio killed the man Diki in his canoe, after people had play-fully pointed sticks like rifles at the plane. Everyone there fled to the mountains (Noel 1944a; *NIV* Sept 1944, 4; Saelasi Lounga 1987 pers comm; Riufaa 1996 pers comm). Malaitans watched spectacular nighttime displays of firepower from Gua-dalcanal and sea battles, and people decades later recalled the war as "the time when planes filled the sky like whiskered tree swiftlets," a metaphor later used to describe an apocalyptic war that some feared would follow campaigns to suppress Maasina Rule (see this book, chapter 7). The 1st Fijian Commando unit trained 200 Solomon Islands Defence Force men at Baunani on the west coast of 'Are'are in early 1943 (Trench 1956, 260; Ravuvu 1974, 32).

2. BSIP 1943d; Forster 1946c, 3; see Laracy and White 1988, appendix A; Laracy 1988a, 19.

3. On the Solomons conflict and its larger context, see several works and col-lections edited by Geoffrey White and Lamont Lindstrom; Laracy 1988a; and Ben-nett 1987, chap 13. For the war's impacts on neighboring New Guinea, start with Read 1947; Wolfers 1972, 107–112; and Nelson 1980; 1982, 171–173, chap 22. In the 1980s, Hawai'i's East-West Center ran a project to study Pacific Islanders' war-time experiences, directed by White and Lindstrom, which published many oral accounts (eg, Laracy and White 1988; White and Lindstrom 1989; Lindstrom and White 1990). The British Colonial Office published an "Official Story" of the war in the Solomons and Gilberts, by Public Relations Officer Harold Cooper, con-taining much false propaganda but also useful information. A theme was that all

Solomon Islanders had displayed undying loyalty toward the colonials: "These backward people, clutching the humblest hem of the democratic heritage, could not be persuaded to loose their hold" (Cooper 1946, 30; see *PIM* 1943; *PIM* Oct 1950, 101). This idea was dear to many hearts, and in 1948 Resident Commissioner Noel pointed to it as a vindication of prewar "native policy" (1948a, 2; see Allan 1950a, 78). In 1988, White and others published *The Big Death,* a collection of Solomon Islander oral histories of the war often critical of behaviors of some officers. Former officers in letters berated its translator-editors (myself included) for publishing pernicious distortions. Many Islanders did display great loyalty to British officers, some with great valor, particularly former policemen who surrounded the "coastwatchers" working behind Japanese lines. Nevertheless, as this chapter makes clear, many saw in the war an opportunity to resist and reform the colonial system or even expel the government. Some war heroes later became resistance leaders, and the government canceled the war medal of at least one for that. Some Defense Force veterans later refused or returned war gratuities offered them (Marquand 1950, 40; George Maelalo 1987 pers comm).

4. See Deck 1942a; Baddeley 1943; Feldt 1946; Trench 1956; Lasaqa 1972, 45; Lord 1977; Rhoades 1982; Bennett 1987, 288–290; Ngwadili and Gafu 1988; Gegeo and Watson-Gegeo 1989, 358; Laracy 1988b; Clemens 1998; Barrow nd. Marchant later downplayed the hardships of his war experience, including scanty rations at Fulisango, but it left him with permanent health problems that forced his departure from the Protectorate in May 1943 and an early retirement (Marchant 1943f; Porter 1949; Teoboo 1982 pers comm to author and Kathleen Gillogly).

5. Tulagi evacuation officer "Spearline" Wilson in a 1942 report recorded his disgust as Levers Plantation manager Charles Widdy and companions prepared to flee to Australia and told Wilson "they did not care what arrangements the government had made, or might make" (Wilson 1942). Fellow plantation manager "Snowy" Rhoades later credited aspects of the evacuation to Widdy's "organizing prowess" (1982, 1). Widdy returned after the US invasion as a second lieutenant in the Royal Australian Air Force and took command of the Labour Corps. Most Chinese residents were not evacuated but were sent to southern Makira under Forster's supervision. On the evacuation, see Wilson 1942; 1946; Baddeley 1943, 24–25; 1945, 8; Hogbin 1943c, 5; Fox 1962, 119–120; Bennett 1987, 288; Boutilier 1989, 332–333; Laracy 1988a, 20–21; Clemens 1992a, 55–57; 1998, 61, 322, 57–70. After the fighting, the Adventists pushed to return to the Solomons, and missionary Norman Ferris in mid-1943 met with Sandars in Sydney, and in mid-1944 with Widdy. Sandars told Ferris that the Adventists could not return since they had "deserted" their flocks, while Widdy told him that the government "appreciated" those missionaries who had obeyed evacuation orders and would support their bids to return (Reye 2006, 50, 52).

6. Clemens 1942, 15 and 17 April; 1992a, 57; see also Clemens 1998, 70, 86, 97; Deck 1942a, 5; 1942b, 3; Kennedy reports summarized in Marchant 1942–1943, 6, 11, and 20 March 1942; Marchant 1942a; Belshaw 1947a, 190; 1949a, 447; Sisili 1949, 1; Fox 1962, 120; Laracy 1976, 111; 1983, 15; 1988a, 22; Rhoades 1982, 2, 56–57; Bennett 1987, 288; Boutilier 1989, 333–335; cf Cooper 1946, 14, 20. Marchant in a secret report told London that Australian servicemen started the looting (Laracy 1988a, 22, 26; see Nelson 1982, 196–197; Clemens 1992a, 57–59). Gela suffered some bungling or bullying officers and police before the war (Hogbin 1943c, 2–4;

Belshaw 1947a, 189; Kennedy 1944; 1967, 5; Campbell 1978, 292; Butcher 2012). Deck said that as the Japanese approached Tulagi, the Burns Philp and Carpenter stores were thrown open to locals to take what they wanted (1942a).

7. Klerk 1941–1944, 14 and 21 Jan 1943; BSIP 1942a; 1943d, 5; Bengough 1942; Marchant 1942–1943, 3 Nov, 21 and 26 Dec 1942; Hogbin 1943b; Widdy 1943a; Sandars 1943b; Crass 1947d; Belshaw 1949a, 448; Lord 1977, chap 4; Rhoades 1982, 27, 58; Bennett 1987, 291; White and others 1988, 177–178; Joseph Pali quoted in Sanga 1989, 24; Frazer 1990, 195; Clemens 1998, 184; cf Hogbin in Beckett 1989, 28. In an extreme case, Belshaw jailed three headmen for discouraging recruiting (Allan 1989–1990, 70; see Belshaw 1949a, 24; 1950a, 68). He later pushed for conscription on Gela after antigovernment sentiments made finding volunteers there "a farce" (Belshaw 1945b). Bengough ran SILC recruiting on Malaita; Clemens thought he did a terrible job and sent only men seeking material gain (1989; cf Bentley 1944a). By mid-1945, there had been over 8,000 recruitments, though many of those were reenlistments.

8. Wa'ii'a 1987. Some groups walked overland to 'Aoke, while ships collected others. Davies described recruiting and returning procedures at 'Aoke just before SILC recruiting ceased in May 1945 (nd, 48–49).

9. The name came from the US "First Marine Division," which was gradually replaced by the Second Division from the end of 1942 into 1943.

10. MQRs Sept 1939, June 1940; Orite'elamo 1982 pers comm; Riufaa 1996 pers comm; Wa'ii'a 1987; see Lansner 1987, 33; Lindstrom and White 1990, 169–170; Fifi'i 1991, 37, 39.

11. Widdy 1942; 1943a; Marchant 1942b; 1943d; Ngwadili and Gafu 1988, 208; White and others 1988; Fifi'i 1989, 49; 1991, 40–41; Akin 1993, 408; cf Cooper 1946, 34.

12. A bombing of Tulagi on 4 March wounded six. Soon after, Dikwa of Kwaio was killed and several others wounded when a Tulagi ammunition dump exploded, purportedly sparked by a discarded cigarette (Fifi'i 1991, 40; Riufaa 1996 pers comm; see Akin 1993, 408).

13. Barrow 1942–1947, part 1, 12; Marchant 1942–1943, 28 Jan–17 Feb 1943; 1943a; 1943b; 1943d; Widdy 1943a, 1943c, 1943d; Deck 1943, 6; *Time* 1944; Ngwadili and Gafu 1988, 208; Fifi'i 1989, 49; 1991, 41.

14. BSIP 1943d, 3; Hogbin 1943b; 1943c, 6; Bengough 1943; Klerk 1941–1944, 13–16 Jan 1943; Widdy 1943b, 1943d, 1943f, 1943g; Deck 1944, 6; Crass 1947b; Fifi'i 1982b; 1991, 41; Alaikona 1987, 3, Akin translation from his Pijin; see Trench 1956, 233; White and others 1988, 130–131, 199; Clemens 1998, 169, 290–291; Davies nd, 34, 48.

15. Bengough 1942; 1943; Widdy 1943b, 1943c, 1943d, 1943f, 1943g, 1943h; Marchant 1943a; 1943c; Fifi'i 1982b; 1987 pers comm; 1991, 41–42. Widdy told Marchant they had to grant a demand for Sundays off since a US officer in charge of labor had promised it (Widdy 1943b, 1943c; Marchant 1943c). Fifi'i said some Kwaio talked of killing British SILC officers, but that he dissuaded them (1988 pers comm; 1991, 43; see Rhoades 1982, 19). The government's official history lauded Solomon Islanders as "reluctant to accept wages" (Cooper 1946, 35; see Luke 1945a, 68), much as Resident Commissioner Noel later told the Advisory Council that during the Depression Islanders had "realized the situation and accepted lower wages" (BSIP 1945–1949, 22 Nov 1945).

16. BSIP 1942a; Widdy 1943b; Marchant 1943e; cf Trench 1956, 233. According to Ian Frazer, SILC officers prosecuted 783 disciplinary actions, three-quarters for "disobedience or insubordination," but he provided no breakdown by year (1990, 196).

17. Widdy 1943b; 1943d; Ngwadili and Gafu 1988, 209; see Noel 1946b, 1; Fifi'i 1989, 51–53; Russell 2003, 40–41.

18. Many Gela houses had been destroyed in the war. Hopkins 1934, 36; Belshaw 1949a, 340; 1950a, appendix 2, 69n; Keesing 1978a, 65; Ma'aanamae 1982 and 1987 pers comm; Ngwadili and Gafu 1988.

19. Bowman 1946, 427–431; Lasaqa 1972, 45–49; Ngwadili and Gafu 1988, 205, 211; see Burt and Kwa'ioloa 1991, 97. A 1945 aerial photo of Honiara is in *B.S.I.P. News Sheet* 6, 31 March 1969, 1. The main farm was at Ilu, about 20 kilometers from the center of present-day Honiara.

20. See Holton 1945; Lindstrom 1981, 104; Lindstrom and White 1990, 77; Frazer 1990, 196; cf Sandars nd, 79. In places, "native trading posts" were erected where soldiers bought curios. So lucrative was the business that Americans, especially "Seabees," began manufacturing "native artifacts" to market to greenhorn sailors off ships. One Australian veteran told Michael Quinnell of fights on Bougainville between Yank and Aussie entrepreneurs over art-marketing territory (Quinnell 2003 pers comm). On the art trade, see BSIP 1942a; Hogbin 1943a, 1943b; MAR 1945, 3; Stansfield 1946, 97–101, photos; Belshaw 1950a, 68; Oliver 1961, 383; Tippett 1967, 370; Lasaqa 1972, 48; Knox-Mawer 1986, 117; Akin 1988–1989. Bennett wrote that US soldiers told Islanders that the government had taken wages meant for them (1987, 292). The government rebuilt its ship fleet with £79,706 in Colonial Development and Welfare funds (Marquand 1950, 18).

21. Waddell, Trench, and Bentley 1945, 7; Laracy 1979, 99; Fifi'i 1988a, 224; see also Fifi'i 1988b; 1989, 51; Ngwadili and Gafu 1988, 208, and see 211–212. To communicate with Islanders, some US soldiers learned Pijin, while others employed a rough sign language.

22. Sisili 1949, 2, 4; Ngwadili and Gafu 1988, 209. Few Malaitans had contact with Japanese on Guadalcanal, but some saw prisoners and several told me they pitied their miserable condition. On Gela, Japanese quickly made enemies of locals by taking clothing and food (Fox 1943, 13; Bingiti quoted in Clemens 1998, 124). Re Sisili's bitterness over his lack of education in English, see Keesing 1978a, 63n29.

23. Norden 1925, 91; J Deck [1943?]; Read 1947, 107; Keesing nd, handwritten, undated 1962 note, in archival box 34, folder 5; Leckie 1965, 315; Lansner 1987, 32; Buckley 2001, xxiv, 260–261; Bielakowski 2007, 18–19, 44–45. Read described a similar scene in New Guinea's Eastern Highlands, but there Australian soldiers were the preferred whites, and people referred to unpopular Australians as "British" (1947, 106–110; see Trench 1947h, 1).

24. Keesing 1978a, 49; personal communications from Sulafanamae 1980, Siufiomea 1987, Biri 'Asu'ani 1996, and Riufaa 1996; Titiuru 1987; Fifi'i 1988a, 224; 1989, 52–53. See Nelson 1982, 173. Burt was told that some Malaitans identified blacks "biblically as 'Egyptians'" (1994, 173).

25. Trench 1947h, 1; Fifi'i 1982b; 1989, 53–54; Titiuru 1987; Vaea quoted in Lansner 1987, 32; Biri 'Asu'ani 1996 pers comm; see Ngwadili and Gafu 1988, 205; Davenport 1989, 271–272.

26. See, eg, White 1989, 58; Fifi'i 1991, 38.

27. Knibbs 1929, 69; see Lindstrom and White 1990, chap 2; see Widdy 1943e, 2; 1943d. Fifi'i thought these officers likewise despised Malaitans (1989, 49). Widdy, as leader of the infamous volunteer "Whisky Army" during the 1927 punitive expedition to Kwaio, complained of Colin Wilson's oversight, and claimed that Resident Commissioner Richard Kane had promised him that the volunteers would be given complete freedom "to shoot any native seen on sight." Kane sent the high commissioner a denial (Wilson 1927; Kane 1927b; see Keesing and Corris 1980, chap 11). The brutality of Donald Kennedy, who led Defence Force men, is well documented (Hogbin 1943c, 3, 8; Islander accounts in King 1985; W Bennett 1988; Boutilier 1989; Garrett 1997, 52–56; Laracy nd; Reye 2006, 54–55; see Kennedy 1946; Belshaw 1947a, 190). But such men were atypical of officers of the period.

28. Patch 1943; see Widdy 1943a, 1943g; BSIP 1945b; Aston 1948, 28; Wolfers 1972, 111–112. District-officer-turned-anthropologist Glynn Cochrane made this same assertion about gift perception in contending that Islanders did not admire Americans as they did colonial officers (1970, 95–96; 1971, 284; see also Fox 1962, 126, but cf 129). Belshaw defended restrictions on socializing and exchange by arguing that men would otherwise have refused to work for £1 per month (1950a, 69). But SILC men could earn as much or more than many freelancers, as Belshaw conceded; Allan said it was more, and claimed that this was why later "recruiting became extremely popular," though in fact it lost popularity (1950a, 84). Officers did try to restrict SILC men more, most notably by seizing or destroying American gifts and payments, which stoked Islanders' anger and undermined recruiting. This aside, officers clearly saw much more at stake than getting enough recruits.

29. *You and the Native* 1943, 1–3; Hogbin 1943c, 7, 9; see Wolfers 1972, 107–112. One author of *You and the Native* might have been Papua's government anthropologist Francis E Williams—he lectured Australian troops arriving there in words similar to some in the booklet, though Williams did not believe in innate white superiority (see Griffin, Nelson, and Firth 1979, 90).

30. Reynolds 1985; Pershing quoted in Buckley 2001, 163; Bielakowski 2007, 26.

31. Hogbin 1943c, 10; 1945, 69; 1951, 19; Fifi'i 1989, 49; Buckley 2001, 260; Bielakowski 2007, 26; Guglielmo 2010. On the failure of rules against fraternization, see also Trench 1943, repr in Hogbin 1944, 276; Zoleveke 1980, 26; Fifi'i 1989, 51. Re Islanders "passing," see Jim Bennett account in Laracy and White 1988, 109.

32. Titiuru 1987, 6; Fifi'i 1989, 50; 1991, 41; see Luke 1945a, 20; 1945b, 89; Lindstrom and White 1990, 29; cf Harrisson 1937, 153. The rule against pants was less enforced, and native constabulary wore shorts; over time the shirt rule was often violated. See Steinberg 1981, 44–45, for a (misdated) photo of sergeant stripes tied to arms and medals hung from necks, on Guadalcanal, 14 October 1943.

33. Belshaw 1945b, 1945d; cf Belshaw 2009, 27–28; BSIP 1945b; Keesing 1978a, 48; Bennett 1987, 292; Titiuru 1987, 6; Fifi'i 1988a, 225; 1989, 57–58; 1991, 42–43; Ngwadili and Gafu 1988, 210; Allan 1989, 90; Burt 1994, 174; personal communications from Molaina'o, Riufaa, and Ma'aanamae, all 1996; Clemens 1998, 51; see Wolfers 1972, 109. In an 11 May 1945 memo, Sandars gave the limits on SILC returnees' baggage: one box 30 x 18 x 18 inches and one blanket roll 3 feet x 3 inches. These were set in early 1944 but only strictly enforced later (BSIP 1945b). Clemens recalled, "The Labour Corps boys had so much loot there was only room for four [versus the usual six] to a tent, and the Americans could not spare any more tents" (1989). Wartime workers' property was similarly destroyed in New Guinea, for

"sanitary reasons" (Belshaw 1945b; Read 1947, 110; Mair 1948, 202; Kiki 1968, 60; see Wolfers 1972, 76–77). Fifi'i charged that Frank Moore, a police officer whom many Malaitans detested, later ran a store selling confiscated goods back to Islanders (1989, 58). Tom Russell told of Malaitans 25 years later seeking compensation for destroyed property, which he misconstrued as anger that ships returning them to Malaita had no room for it. In 1949 Russell proposed charging Federal Council men with sedition for having alleged in a document, "British officials took for themselves materials given by Americans to natives" (and that British had held back wages given to SILC men). The document, by Ariel Sisili, noted the burnings; Russell did not (1949c, 2; 2003, 41; Sisili 1949, 5). Almost a year later, at an 'Ataa meeting, Resident Commissioner Henry Gregory-Smith faced a man who "got up and at length referred to the burning of goods belonging to enlisted men in the Labour Corps in 1943. Some say that this is a festering sore and if removed could do some good. Chief Kakaluai thinks it is a 'blind' and even if an injustice and removed would do no good. But I promised to look into the whole thing and…let them know the result of my enquiry" (1950–1952, 8 Sept 1950, 5). I found no record that he did so, and if not he missed a golden political opportunity. Hodgess, owner of Guadalcanal's Paruru plantation, later urged a resident commissioner to combat Maasina Rule by publicly flogging leaders and minimizing prisoners' food (1950c).

34. Belshaw 1945b; Fox 1962; O'Connor 1973, 298; Fifi'i 1982b; 1989, 58; accounts of Bisili in King 1985; and Jim Bennett, Nathan Oluvai, Roy Kimisi, and John Lotikena accounts in Laracy and White 1988, 109–111; Bennett 1987, 292; Davenport 1989, 272; Russell 2003, 56.

35. Personal communications from Orite'elamo 1982, Bati 1983, Ma'aanamae 1987, and Molaina'o 1997; Homewood 2005; see Kennedy 1944.

36. Wa'ii'a 1987; see also Fifi'i 1982b; 1988a; 1989, 50–57; Hogbin 1943c.

37. Stansfield 1946, 76, 100; Belshaw 1950a, 70, 132; Fox 1962, 130, and quoted in Coates 1970; see Allan 1950a, 82–83; Caulton 1950, 1955; Worsley 1968, 178. Some white Americans in wartime England likewise "took consolation from the belief that only the British lower classes were friendly to African Americans" (Bielakowski 2007, 26). There was US pressure on Britain to grant joint rights over the Gela, Guadalcanal, and other bases, but at war's end Congress cut funding and the issue was dropped (Grattan 1961, chap 15; Johnson 1976, 233; Lindstrom 1989, 399–400). Policy experts bandied about various schemes for US control over Pacific islands (eg, Lasker 1944; Hobbs 1945). For examples of officers providing intelligence, see Holton 1945; BSIP 1945c; this book, chapter 8.

38. Deck [1943?]; Van Dusen 1945; Morehouse 1945; Baddeley 1945, 11–13; Forster 1946c, 5; Fox 1962, 125; Lindstrom and White 1990, 163–169; Garrett 1997, 48; see Kennedy 1944; Hogbin 1970, 164.

39. Barnett 1916a, 3; WPHC 1917; Workman 1918e; Bengough 1939d, 1940b; Marchant 1940b; White 1991, 253–254.

40. Hogbin 1943c, 1, 3, 9; *Red Cross Courier* 1943, 14; Trench 1944; Belshaw 1944, 1945a; Forster 1946c, 7–8; Sipolo testimony in BSIP 1947d, 112–113; Allan 1957a, 252; Murdoch 1980; Laracy 1983, 16–17, and see F5. See Allan 1982a for his interpretation of Gela Red Cross activities.

41. Belshaw 1945a; Sandars 1947a; Marquand 1950, 11; Lindstrom 1979, 41; Laracy 1983, F5; Wa'ii'a 1987; Fifi'i 1988 pers comm; 1989, 56–57; Riufaa 1997 pers comm.

42. Most Malaitan donations were from the north. At Sinalagu, the man Sikufi solicited Red Cross funds but few gave. Cadet Peter Cameron later mistakenly reported much money was being given for the Red Cross throughout east Kwaio and in 'Are'are's Takataka and Maanawai sub-districts, and that Kwaio Maasina Rule Chief Fifi'i was a "prime mover" in the collections, though he warned that his information was "very second hand." Fifi'i hotly denied this to me and his denial is backed by independent sources. The charge is an example of how officers confused various Malaitan groups collecting money and contributor lists with activities of Maasina Rule (Cameron 1947a, and 1947h–k; see Bentley 1945; Holton 1945; Trench 1945c; Davies nd, 38).

43. Cameron 1947a; Waleanisia 1987, 2–3. Another Gela Red Cross "chief" was Wiri Giripiru (Giripiru 1943), and a key Kwara'ae collector was Gafutu. On Guadalcanal in mid-1947 it was said Vuza possessed an American Red Cross book that he claimed assured protection from the British, and officers believed he was collecting funds (Crass 1947d, 4; Masterman 1947b, 1947c). In the 1980s, Kwaio who had served in SILC sections under sergeants 'Akwasigwaru and Suamae on Gela told me they all pooled money and gave it to Kabini and a north Malaitan associate named Diki Madikoe. Others gave to similar efforts on Guadalcanal, as did people from 'Are'are. Some believed the money would be returned after the war with interest. Apparently Madikoe had collected names and money for the north Malaita list Belshaw seized. In Lau, sometime headman Timi Kakalu'ae was involved with Kabini and Diki's activities, and he apparently tried to extort Kwaio contributions, but after Sipolo reported this, Trench "warned him off" (Trench 1944; Belshaw 1944; BSIP 1947d, 113; 1947e, 51). Fifi'i thought many Red Cross collections were confidence games (1988 pers comm).

44. On flight to the bush: Fox 1942–1949, 5 May 1942; Hogbin 1943c, 5; Field 1943, 14; MAR 1941, 1; Hokelema 1947; Waleanisia 1987, 1; Gegeo and Watson-Gegeo 1989, 356; Gegeo 1991, 30–31; Guo 2001, 98–100. On shortages: NIV March 1943, 2; Sandars 1943b; Zoleveke 1980, 26; Fifi'i 1988 pers comm; 1991, 42. Scarcities during wartime and then Maasina Rule invited entrepreneurship. One dearth was of the clay tobacco pipes people had bought from traders. People used bamboo pipes until 'Ai'eda people in Kwaio found an outcrop of stone suitable for making fine pipes. An industry burst forth and they earned a shell money fortune marketing pipes across central and southern Malaita (John Laete'esafi 1996 pers com; Ma'aanamae 1996 pers com; for the pipe-making process, see Akin 1995–1996, video 3). When a US warplane crashed near Fauaabu on 25 August 1942, people made metal pipes from it and sold them across the island. After a Japanese plane ditched in the Malu'u lagoon that same day, locals "turned the whole thing into rings, crosses, hearts and clothes lines" (Marchant 1942–1943, 25 Aug 1942; Vance 1945, 10).

45. On over-recruiting, see Bengough 1936e; Sandars 1937b, 5; 1943a; 1943b; Hogbin 1943a; 1943b; Widdy 1943i; Forster 1944b; Deck 1944, 1, 2; NIV Sept 1944, 3–4; Noel 1945; MAR 1945; Palmer 1970, 4; Beckett 1989, 28; Gegeo 1991, 30–31. Davies wrongly claimed officers easily got as many SILC men as were wanted (nd, 48–49). Wartime New Guinea also suffered problems from over-recruitment of labor (see, eg, Mair 1948, chap 10).

46. BSIP 1943d; Hogbin 1943b; Hogbin and Wedgwood 1943, 5–6; Hodgess 1943; Crass 1947d; Bennett 1987, 289.

47. Sandars 1943b; Hogbin 1943a, 1; Bentley 1944a; Akin 1988–1989.

48. Clemens 1942, 186; 1998; BSIP 1943c; Fox 1943, 14; Belshaw 1944; 1950a, 144; Cooper 1946, 18, 32; Allan 1950a, 78; Hogbin 1976, 113; White 1978, 243; Davenport 1989.

49. Sandars 1943b; see MAR 1944, 5; Naitoro 1993, 83. On Europeans who stayed on Malaita, see Cross nd; Baddeley 1943; Vance 1945, 9–10; Fox 1962, 120; 1985, 134; Laracy 1976, 114; Griffiths 1977, 129–135; Bennett 1987, 288.

50. Sandars 1943b; and see Sandars nd, 94; Hogbin 1944, 268; Malaita District 1944b; MAR 1944, 1–2, 4; 1945; Holton 1945. Unlike northern Malaita, in Kwaio *totonga* is compensation for sexual offenses.

51. 'Elota quoted in Keesing 1978b, 153. 'Ala'ota hid in the jungle, a fugitive with two bounties on his head—one sponsored by the dead man's relatives, the other by the government—until he hanged himself in 1945. He had come unhinged after the 1927 punitive expedition murdered his father (Malaita District 1944c; Keesing nd, 1964, 6332; Ma'aanamae 1982 pers comm; see 'Elota quoted in Keesing 1978b, chap 14). Few of the wartime native courts of "elders" led by headmen seem to have operated as planned. Officers—Bengough on Malaita—presided over higher-level "special courts" as "special commissioners."

52. BSIP 1943b; Sandars 1943b; nd, 94–95; MAR 1944, 5; *NIV* Sept 1944, 4; Fox 1962, 123. At the murder trials, Sandars used four elderly Malaitans as assessors (nd, 95). A later book by Fox seems to describe the same scene when recounting what Fox supposed were murderous intentions of inland people who descended to the coast after, he claimed, US planes had bombed mountain hamlets (1985, 134), but I know of no such mountain bombings on Malaita. In 1944 the murder rate returned to prewar levels (MAR 1944, 5; Sandars nd, 95).

53. Griffiths 1943, 4; see *NIV* March 1943, 2–3; Maefa'asia quoted in *NIV* Sept 1944, 4; David Irofanua and Seth Noofimae quoted in *NIV* Dec 1945, 7; Vance 1945, 10.

54. Trench writing in Malaita District 1944b; MAR 1945, 2; Forster 1946c, 8; see Davies 1947i.

55. Wieschhoff 1944; Hailey 1947, 90; Noel 1947a, 6; WPHC 31 July 1948, quoted in Mander 1954, 329; Marquand 1950, 20; Hyam 2006, 139–146; see Bennett 1987, 301–310.

56. See McDonald 1949; Easton 1960, 31; MacDonald 1976, 245–246; Bedford 1980, 35–36, 39; Foster 1987, 361, 366.

57. Huxley and Deane 1944, 26; Luke 1945a, 13; see also Luke 1962, 126; Baddeley 1947; Stanley 1975, xiv.

58. Masterman 1950f, 12; see Hemming 1946; Noel 1947a; 1946b, 2; 1947c, 2; Sisili 1949, 4; Forster 1950; Marquand 1950, appendix 6.

59. Moorhouse 1929, 25; Titiuru 1987, 3. Even at the time of the Protectorate's creation Woodford wrote about parts of Malaita, "I find there is a growing desire among the natives…to learn reading and writing. Many of them returning from Queensland and Fiji can do so already" (1896). In 1939–1940 the government spent A£12,000 on all health services, and less than A£1,000 on education (BSIP 1946, 2). Levers Plantation Ltd built the first hospital in the Solomons and employed its first doctor, who at times helped the government; Bennett described more effective medical policies on large 1920s plantations, which benefited Malaitan workers (Bennett 1993, 143–144; Stuart 2002, 101). On the Depression stifling change, see Lambert

1934b, 19–20; Mander 1954, 327–329, 347; Hilliard 1974, 108; Boutilier 1978, 156. Moorhouse advised very modest increases in medical service (1929, 24–25).

60. Bell writing in MAR 1925; BSIP 1934, 3; Bengough 1938b; Fox writing in *SCL* 1 Oct 1938, 11; Sisili 1949, 3; see Deck 1931b; Elkin 1936, 162–163; Hogbin and Wedgwood 1943, 7; Allan 1951b, 5 (cf Allan 1950a, 51); Hilliard 1969, 63; 1978, 265; Hogbin 1970, 178–179; Boutilier 1978; Watson-Gegeo and Gegeo 1992, 15–17; Wasuka 1989, 100–102; Davies nd, 32.

61. Noel 1944c; Sandars writing in MAR 1945, 3; Kirakira 1946; Belshaw 1948, 96; Allan 1950a, 50, 89. Boutilier pointed out that missionaries kept their best Islander students for mission work (1982, 59).

62. Ashley 1929a, 25; Marquand 1950, 51.

63. Sandars writing in MAR 1945, 2; Creech Jones 1946; Wasuka 1989, 103; see also Hall 1946.

64. Rodwell 1921b; Bell 1926b; 1; Ivens [1928b?] (see also Ivens 1925); Ivens 1927; Hutson statement attributed by Lambert 1933, 27 May; 1934b, 8; Sandars writing in MAR 1945, 3–5; Silifa'alu 1947; see Grantham 1946; Germond 1948a; Allan 1950a, 51; Mander 1954, 344; Hilliard 1974, 111–112; Laracy 1976, 107–109, chap 8; Davies nd, 84. Keesing and Corris quoted Bell as reporting that Malaitans told him that Kane (on a 1925 tour while Bell was away) had promised them medical care in return for taxes (1980, 104); Keesing mistakenly thought this misunderstanding was "probably because of Kane's defective Pidgin" (1992a, 126–127).

65. On government aid, see Hilliard 1978, 267–270; Bell 1927, 13. On Fauaabu, see *SCL* 1 July 1931; June 1933, 84–91; Maybury 1932; Lambert 1933, 21–27 May; 1934b 7, 19; 1941, 328–329; Hopkins 1934, 19; Wilson 1936; Innes 1938, 24; Hemming 1947, 1993; *Leprosy in Melanesia* 1949; Russell 1949a, 4–5; 2003, 60; Fox 1967, 71.

66. BSIP 1928, 4; Innes 1938, 15; *NIV* June 1941, 4–5; Hilliard 1969, 63; 1974, 111; 1978, 268; MacLaren 2007, 70 (quote on SDA), passim. Deck barred SSEM lepers from using the rival mission's colony (Lambert 1933, 21 May). On SSEM homeopathy, see file BSIP 12/I/13.

67. MQR March 1932; Innes 1938, 24; Forster 1950; Clemens 1992 pers comm; Sandars nd, 101–105. On officers giving care, see Bell 1921b; 1927, 7–8; Steward 1921; Mason 1925, 134; Davies nd, 29–31, 91–92; Bennett 1987, 210. On Islander medical men, see Lambert 1933c; Germond 1948b, 6; Zoleveke 1980, 51 (cf 46); Boggs and Gegeo 1996, 285.

68. Bell 1927; White 1928–1931; Crichlow 1929, 181–182; Moorhouse 1929, 24; Barley 1933c; Wilson 1936, 71; Hipkin 1936; Innes 1938, 2, 14, 50; Bengough 1940a; Lambert 1941, 282, 326, 328–331, 282; and see Lambert 1933; 1934b, 7–8; Laracy 1976, 78; Nelson 1982, 40, 205; Knox-Mawer 1986, 62–63; Bennett 1987, 210; Stuart 2002, chap 5. For the 1920s medical scene, see Kane 1923a; Moorhouse 1929, 23. Lambert first came with the Rockefeller Foundation, then with the 1933 Templeton Crocker Expedition.

69. Deck 1948c, 3. On accepting medicine during Maasina Rule, see Sandars 1947b; Cameron 1947b, 1947e; Allan 1950a, 51; and Zoleveke 1980, 44, 48. When Resident Commissioner Gregory-Smith visited the Fokanakafo loyalist enclave of Rakwane, "I promised them a dresser which they asked for in return for their loyalty" (1950–1952, 19 March 1950). In early 1947, Kwai people refused a medical officer, to Sandars's surprise, as, he said, "The doctor was usually well received

everywhere." Headman Siru had lied to people that Sandars planned to take their land, and they thought the officer was connected to that (Sandars 1947f, 2; cf MAR 1947, 6B; BSIP 1947d, 80; see also Zoleveke 1980, 57). Malu'u leaders in July 1947 told people to boycott a clinic brought by Cadet Wilfred Marquand since, Marquand guessed, they feared he would use it as a political lever, but many came anyway. While Russell was at Malu'u two years later, many boycotted the government's hospital there. Sadly, Ratu J A R "Tom" Dovi (a once-popular, Auckland-trained Fijian doctor) was made part of a squad that arrested Maasina Rule people, but Belshaw's claim that Dovi commanded "a force of the Fijian Army" to make such arrests holds no truth whatsoever (2009, 18; see *PIM* May 1951, 60). On refusals of medicine, see Marquand 1947b, 1; 1950, 18; Crass 1947a, 4; Davies 1947j, 2 (cf Davies nd, 150–151); Deck 1948a, 1 Feb; Whiteman 1983, 271; Russell 1986, 2; Sandars nd, 102–103). On linkage of medical care and oppression in colonial contexts, see Fanon 1965, chap 4.

70. Mander 1954, 344; see Lambert 1933, 21 May; Belshaw 1947b, 14; Forster 1948f; MacKeith 1950a; MAR 1952; Boutilier 1978; Bennett 1987, 210; Akin 1993, 470–474; MacLaren 2007.

71. Waddell, Trench, and Bentley 1945, 8–10; cf Barrow 1946, 4–5. The overseas training scheme was attempted but failed because the missionary societies forbade their teachers from participating (BSIP 1951c, training college proposal, 2–3; see *SCL* April 1951, 303–304).

72. Deck 1932, 2; SSEM 1942; Marquand 1947e, 4; Belshaw 1950a, 114; Caulton 1951, 301, 304 (and see Caulton 1950); Hilliard 1969, 63. On mission education trepidation, see Deck 1927a; 1948a, 22 July; Innes 1938, 17; Deck [1943?]; BSIP 1945–1959, 1 Oct 1949, 7; *SCL* April 1951, 303–304; Mander 1954, 344–347. In 1950, Russell was told, Catholic priests instructed flocks to avoid government schooling (1950k).

73. BSIP 1946, 11; Russell 1949a, 3; Marquand 1950, 32. The Ten Year Plan projected spending A£275,000 for education and A£229,000 for medical services over the period (BSIP 1946). In the first five years the respective amounts spent were A£25,000, and A£100,000 (Chamberlain 1952, 3). The lack of serious interest in improving education through the 1940s, which eventually drew embarrassing attention from the popular press, is summarized in Mander 1954, 344–348.

74. Belshaw 1949b, 12; see also Belshaw 1950a, 91; see Gregory-Smith 1950–1952, 4–19 Sept 1950, 2–3.

75. Hogbin 1944, 257; MAR 1944; BSIP 1945e; 1947a; 1945–1959, 26 Nov 1945. The Tenaru conference revised a guide for "native administrations" originally written by David Trench. Hogbin published both versions in *Oceania* (1944, 1945).

76. MAR 1944, 2. For examples of early codes, see Codes 1944a, 1944d, [1945b]; Hogbin 1944, appendix A; and codes in BSIP files 12/VI/6 and 12/VI/11. See also Belshaw 1948, 96.

77. Sandars 1943b (quote); Hogbin 1944, 268; BSIP 1945–1959, 26 Oct 1945, 107–108; Marquand 1950, 6.

78. MAR 1944, 2–3; Noel 1944c; Hogbin 1944; 1945; 1946, 38; BSIP 1945–1959, 26 Oct 1945, 107; Belshaw 1949a, 431–432; Marquand 1950, 6; Davies nd, 41. Bengough had suggested fines be "paid into a Native fund, for their benefit" (1941a).

79. MAR 1945, 2, 5.

80. Forster 1946c, 1–2, 4; MAR 1947, 3; Belshaw 1948, 96; Laracy 1976, 122. Ben-

nett wrote that Western Solomons people, too, saw councils as government instruments (1987, 293–294).

81. Trench writing in MAR 1944, 2; John Laete'esafi 1996 pers comm.

82. MQR March 1940; Trench 1941, 1943; Forster 1946c, 4; Tom Titiuru 1987 pers comm; cf Kennedy 1967, 7; Rhoades 1982, 58. Trench was later high commissioner (1961–1963), and governor of Hong Kong (1964–1971).

83. One target of anger was Frank Keeble, likely due to a failed government scheme he was placed in charge of to collect Malaitan artwork to sell to Americans. A notorious alcoholic, he had been the Protectorate's chief sanitary officer, an assessor for the trial of Basiana's codefendant Fuufu'e, and, he claimed, Myrna Loy's chauffeur. People told to make things to sell became irate when Keeble never showed up at some passages and at others ignored the standard labor recruitment practice of waiting for inland people to descend to the coast, now with their art. The Small Malaita threats somehow revived the eternal rumor that Kwaio were planning another massacre (BSIP 1928, 1; Clemens 1942, 7, 15, 16, 24; Noel 1944b; Malaita District 1944a; Akin 1988–1989; see PIM March 1953, 131; Davies nd, 138).

84. Marchant 1940b; Noel 1944b; MAR 1945; Forster 1946c, 5; Davies 1947i; Ma'aanamae 1996 pers comm. In mid-1949 it was announced BSIP plantations would get no war damage reparations and most of the smaller ones were never reopened (see Bennett 1987, 302–304; and most issues of PIM from 1949 into the early 1950s).

85. MAR 1945, 2; 1946, 29; see Akin 1993, 413.

86. Malaita District [1948?]; Noel 1946b, 1–2; Forster 1946c, 5, 7, 9; Cameron 1947i; Germond 1948d; Fifi'i 1988a (Akin translation from original Kwaio manuscript version).

87. AR 1944, 4; Forster 1945b; Malaita District 1945b, 1945c, [1948?].

88. Trench 1944; Hogbin 1944, 264–266; 1945, 62; Forster 1946c, 5, 8; BSIP 1947d, 113; [1947f?].

89. Hogbin 1944, 266; Marquand 1950, 48; see Davies nd, 317.

90. Bita Saetana 1981 pers comm to author and Kathleen Gillogly. See Eastern District AR 1944, 3; Forster 1946c, 5; Noel 1946a; Allan 1950a, 33. Boggs and Gegeo said that, before the war and later, some headmen in west central Kwara'ae, where Gegeo is from, were respected as mediators between their communities and the government. This area surrounds 'Aoke station, and in places there, Maasina Rule was relatively weak (see MAR 1946, 18; Deck 1948a; cf Davies nd, 98). Boggs and Gegeo explained that this partly reflected desire to forestall 'Are'are dominance that might weaken west Kwara'ae's long-privileged position near the government and its projects (1996, 287, 290). After the war some headmen there did have to distance themselves from the government or be ostracized, and a senior headman, Shadrach Dio, was the area's Maasina Rule head chief. After Maasina Rule, some recouped government positions and peer respect through the Malaita Council and other institutions. Some more radical movement leaders, such as Nelson Kifo and Sukulu, did come from west Kwara'ae.

91. BSIP 1940a; Forster 1946c, 4; Kennedy 1967, 4; Laracy 1976, 110.

92. Bengough writing in Malaita District 1936; MAR 1941, 4; Forster 1946c, 9; Hogbin 1944, 262–269; Marquand 1950, 6; Hilliard 1969, 61; see also Workman 1918b; Moorhouse 1929, 20–21; Allan 1958, 7; Campbell 1978, 290; Davies nd, 78; Beckett 1989, 25. Any knowledgeable reader will be baffled by Sandars's recalling in

his autobiography that SSEM people had always been loyal subjects and that he had puzzled "right up to today" over why they turned antigovernment during Maasina Rule (nd, 138). Davies said that SSEM head Norman Deck "contended fiercely with the Government and the representatives of other faiths alike," and that Sandars's last act on Malaita in mid-1947 was "telling Deck in words of one syllable exactly what he thought about him and the S.S.E.M., while I sat cringing and the RC gasped for air" (nd, 116, 292; see Steward 1926, 12; Raucaz 1928, 70; Hogbin 1970, 218–219). Doug Oliver wrote, "The native's dilemma was pathetically sharpened when, too frequently, he heard the white masters commit that worst of all caste crimes: criticizing one another within native hearing. The ideological differences between official and missionary were particularly unfortunate; occasionally the wretched Solomonese had to choose between a mild but immediate calaboose and a drastic but distant Hell" (1961, 220).

93. Deck 1970–1971, 26 July 1971; see also Deck 1943; 1948a, 1 Feb; Forster 1946c, 5; *NIV* March 1948, 4–5; Fox 1962, 131–132; Hilliard 1969, 61–64; Hogbin 1970, 179; Cochrane 1970, 80. Other missions paid stipends, which became crucial in 1931 when teachers lost their head tax exemption (Ivens 1918, 196; Sullivan 1933, 5–6). Ivens told of an ancestral priest who applied, unsuccessfully, for the same exemption as Christian teachers (1928a, 151). Higher-level mission teachers and their assistants remained excused from roadwork (Malaita [1941b?]).

94. Sandars writing in MAR 1945, 2; 1946, 4; see Hogbin 1944, 268; MQR March 1941; Forster 1946c, 5.

95. See Noel 1946b; Davies 1947f.

96. See Cameron 1947b, 1947d, 1947g; Sandars 1947f, 2; Noel 1946b. Davies recalled how on Makira in June 1947, just before he took control of Malaita, he in one area refused unanimous pleas that he dismiss a "violently anti-Marching Rule" headman who had "isolated himself," only because "he was my sole source of information in the area." In the same manuscript Davies brushed aside criticisms of councils and courts led by headmen, arguing that if people did not like their members, "they had only to ask if they wanted them replaced" (nd, 236, 219).

97. Barrow nd, part 3, 23, 54; see Barrow 1946, 1. Since the fighting ended, antigovernment sentiments similar to those on Malaita had spread to varying degrees through parts of Guadalcanal, Gela, Makira, and Isabel. See, for example, BSIP 1943c; Fox 1948a, 21; 1948b (cf 1962, 132); Mander 1954, 331; Allan 1982a, 225–227; Macdonald-Milne 2003, 139.

98. BSIP 1946, 10; Noel 1946a; see MAR 1945, 3.

99. Noel 1946b, 1, 4; see Belshaw 1944; see Barrow 1946, 1.

Chapter 5: The Rise of Maasina Rule

1. Keesing, note from 28 Sept 1963 interview, cassette 62, my translation from Pijin; Bati 1996 pers comm; see Fifiʻi 1989, 55. "Nonoʻoohimae couldn't talk with the Americans like Nori could," Kwalafanaiʻa said in the Keesing interview; "It was Nori who learned everything from the Americans."

2. Nonoʻoohimae and Nori testimony in BSIP 1947e, 86, 94; see Codes 1944b, 1945a, 1946b; Forster 1946c, 6; Sandars nd, 88, 157; Laracy 1983, 17–18, C1; Naitoro 1993, 84–85. Many older publications speak of Harisimae (often as "Arisimae"),

especially his strength as a *ramo,* and for his having taken the Rohinari Catholic mission under his protection in the 1910s. See Bell 1915c, 1916a; Raucaz 1928, 219–228; Forster 1945c; 1946c, 6; Naitoro 1993, 84–85; O'Brien 1995, 177–181; Davies nd, 38–39. Sandars wrote, "He was extremely helpful to me in matters of native custom." He became Christian just before dying, and Sandars carved a cross for his grave (nd, 82–83, 87–88).

3. Keesing 1978a, 49; Naitoro 1993, 83; Terry Brown 2006 pers comm; see Oloi'a quote later in this chapter.

4. For statements on the name (some useful, others laughable), see Forster 1946a, 1 July; Noel 1946b; *PIM* 1946a, 1946b, 1947b; BSIP 1947e, 85; *Canberra Times* 20 Sept 1947, 1; *Time* 1947; Fox 1948b; 1962, 127; Pope 1949; Allan 1950a, 27; Gibbins 1950, 4; Belshaw 1950a, 127; 2009, 21; Kennedy 1967; Tippet 1967, 205; Worsley 1968, 173; Cochrane 1970, 95; Geerts 1970, 57; Keesing 1978a, 49; 1981; Murdoch 1980; Laracy 1983, 18–20; Fulbright 1986, 1–2; Waleanisia 1987; Guidieri 1988, 187; Fifi'i 1989, 56; Naitoro 1993, 83; Burt 1994, 277; Russell 2003, 42–44; Scott 2007, 110.

5. BSIP 1947e, 94; Laracy 1983, 18, D5; 'Are'are 2005d. See Naitoro 1993, 87–88, which includes material from Namohani'ai's diary. Nono'oohimae was away for part of this period, again in the Labour Corps.

6. Forster 1946c, 6; Clemens 1992 pers comm; Naitoro 1993, 85.

7. Laracy 1983, 18; Fifi'i 1988 pers comm; 1989, 51, 69. During the war, Hoasihau and a clerk named Timeas Teioli tracked and killed a murderer, and in 1943 Hoasihau became Christian to try to escape the effects of curses the dead man's family made against him. He left 'Are'are for a time and was influenced by SSEM teacher Timothy Anilafa. Davies speculated, plausibly but without evidence, that Hoasihau's political plans were influenced by the SSEM's organizational structure, and implausibly, that this was his first encounter with it (Forster 1946c, 6; Davies nd, 72).

8. Codes 1944a; Takataka 1946; Crass 1946c, 2; BSIP 1947d, 65; Laracy 1983, C2; 'Are'are 2005d; see Codes ndb, ndc, [1946h?], 1947b.

9. BSIP 1947e, 64, 70, 94; Naitoro 1993, 77, 87; 'Are'are 2005d.

10. Government warnings to 'Are'are reached and were given directly to Kwaio people (Keesing nd, 8 Jan 1964). In Kwaio and northern 'Are'are, one phase of post–Maasina Rule *kastom* political activity was called Bobolesina (Population) (Sulafanamae 1980 pers comm). Kwaio today blame epidemics (*maemaenga*) on ancestors angry at shrine desecrations by the 1927 punitive expedition, Christian incursions, lax taboo observance, and foreign spirits. All are also powerful metaphors for catastrophic foreign infiltrations. Naitoro said 'Are'are blamed a devastating 1936–1937 flu epidemic on a foreign spirit. At their first contacts with them, 'Are'are, Kwaio, and probably others believed European ships were spirits bearing *maemaenga*. Kwaio elders recall that many people used to live until they were ancient, mere skin and bones propped by crutches (see Colony of Fiji 1896, 31; de Coppet 1981, 177–178; Akin 1993, 158; 1996; Naitoro 1993, 79; Burt 1994, 86).

11. MAR 1944; Forster 1946c, 8; Codes 1947c; 'Elota quoted in Keesing 1978b, 157. Salaimanu was an Anglican, trained at Norfolk Island, and appointed headman by Bell. In 1937 Sandars sacked him for obstructing the work of fellow Lau headman Timi Kakalu'ae. After Kakalu'ae was fired in 1941 for abusing his position, Salaimanu was reappointed. Many distrusted Salaimanu, and Forster called his council

"reactionary." Sandars wrote of him and others who had been to Norfolk, "I know of five such men over here and each one has the most exalted opinion of himself." Davies found him "gentle and sincere." He formally resigned in October 1945, and in mid-1946 Kakaluʻae regained the position (Sandars 1937f; Forster 1946c, 7–8; BSIP 1947e, 10; Fox 1958, 175; Davies nd, 77, 81; Keesing 1992b, 181–182.

12. Trench 1945c; Forster 1946c, 7–8; Cameron 1947a; Waleanisia 1987; Burt 1994, 176; see Gilbird [1947?]; Crass 1947c, 4; Mair 1948, 68; Sisili 1949, 2; Laracy 1979, 99. At a 1987 Honiara conference of World War II veterans I attended, speakers used this same "they got the meat, we the bones" metaphor to describe the burden of inequality in their relations with Europeans. Tome Waleanisia told me that before "Maasina Rule," the initial political activity in Langalanga was called "Union Council," as was some of the early ʻAreʻare work (1987).

13. Forster 1946c, 7; Crass 1946a; Fifiʻi 1946; 1989, 62–63; BSIP 1947d, 1, 69, 113; 1947e, 30A; Waʻiiʻa 1987 pers comm; Fifiʻi 1988 pers comm; Naitoro 1993, 87–88; ʻAreʻare 2005d. On the prior connection between Walade and ʻAtaa, see Ivens 1972, 40. The island of Ulawa was considered part of Malaita due to its deep cultural and historical links to Small Malaita (see Ivens 1929, 1972). In early 1947, Crass was told that Small Malaita canoes visited nearby Ugi island, whose people were outside of Maasina Rule, to try to bring back to Malaita some people related to Malaitans via kin links two and more generations old. Davies said that in 1947 several Malaitans still living in Fiji asked to return home, he believed to join Maasina Rule (Crass 1947a, 5; Davies nd, 171, 206, 210).

14. Davidson 1947; Noel 1947a, 1; Barrow and Davies 1947, 1–2; BSIP 1947c; 1947d, 1; 1947e, 86; Tomasi Leo testimony in BSIP 1947d, 74, 75; Crass 1947a, 5; Davenport 1998 pers comm; see Deck 1948b; Marquand 1950, 55; Scott 2007, 109–110. By the end of 1946, Maasina Rule was "almost universal" on Makira and along Guadalcanal's north coast (Crass 1946c; Eastern District AR 1947, Native Affairs, 3; Noel 1947a; Barrow and Davies 1947; Laracy 1983, 22–25). Later, Davies hoped Hoasihau and Nonoʻoohimae were advising visiting Makirans to cooperate more with the government since ʻAreʻare Maasina Rule had "the most reasonable brand to offer" (Davies 1947a, 4; MAR 1948, 7; see Allan 1989–1990, 124).

15. BSIP 1947e, 75; ʻAreʻare Community Website 2005c, 3 (re Nori being away in the Labour Corps). Many colonial divisions imposed on Malaita were artificial, but that between north and south along the Kwaraʻae-Kwaio border had long been salient for Malaitans. On plantations, ʻAreʻare and Kwaio congregated and distinguished themselves from northerners. In the early 1930s, the government planned to split Malaita into north and south districts (Barley argued for three districts) and opened a base at Maka in the south with this in mind. It was closed in 1933 due to costs, but in the late 1940s a dual administrative division was for a time imposed along similar lines (Bell 1922a; Moorhouse 1929, 22; Fletcher 1931; MAR 1931, 1; Naitoro 1993, 59–60).

16. Codes 1945b, 1946e; Akin 1993, 416.

17. Naitoro 1993, 88; Burt 1994, 177. ʻOloburi Maasina Rule Chief ʻUnuamae was made that area's government headman in 1952 and was a government-nominated Malaita Council member into the 1960s. In 1982 I attended a huge mortuary feast for his death.

18. See Leo testimony in BSIP 1947d, 66; ʻElota quoted in Keesing 1978b, 156; Burt 1994, 177–178; Molainaʻo 1996 pers comm.

19. Fox 1942–1949, 15 June 1946; Heber 1945–1947; Mariko 1946; Forster 1946a; 1946c, 10; BSIP 1947e, 76–77; Deck 1948b; Waleanisia 1987.

20. Forster 1946c, 6; BSIP 1947e, 76; Allan 1980b, 111; Fifi'i 1989, 66.

21. Noel 1947a, 3–4; BSIP 1947d, 66; Trench 1947h, 3; see Marquand 1950, 48, 49; Ivens 1972, 32; Scott 1990–1991; Burt 1994, 178. It was illegal to possess US money, and the government later prosecuted leaders for this and seized dollars as well as pounds. At 'Ataa, for example, an officer seized a "Maasina Rule bank" of nearly "£1000," some 80 percent of it from contributions (the rest thought to be from court fines). Years later the money was returned to contributors (Tedder 1954). Some communities carefully recorded expenses of their movement work, hoping eventually to be reimbursed by either Maasina Rule or maybe Americans (see, eg, Takataka 1946; Noel 1947a, 2; Laracy 1983, C22–24). Annual Reports later claimed, "All members of Marching Rule were forced to pay £1 into Marching Rule funds" (see, eg, AR 1948, 26).

22. Noel 1946b; Forster 1946c, 4, 8; McBride quoted in Deck 1948b; Kaakalade 1982 pers comm; Geni'iria 1982 pers comm; Waleanisia 1987.

23. Bell 1919a; Marquand 1950, 8; Sandars nd, 99; Guo Pei-yi 2004 pers comm.

24. See Bell 1924, 1926a; Hill 1924a, 4; MQR June 1930; Russell 1949a, 1; Keesing [1964?]; 1968, 277; 1978a, 251; 1992a, 103; Laracy 1983, xii.

25. AR 1947, 8; Fifi'i 1982 pers comm; see Laracy 1983, 20. Kwarekwareo (also called "Dorio") is home to a blend of 'Are'are and Kwaio languages and cultures, as well as much that is unique to the area.

26. As Keesing observed, "lines" were first formed as a basis of Bell's tax rolls and only partly reflected meaningful groups, but people adopted them as one basis of identity in political affairs, and Maasina Rule used the line concept in its structure (1968; 1978a, 251–252; 1992a, 103). Lines remained a basis of tax and voting rolls and political groupings for decades after, though often with different members than in the government designations.

27. BSIP 1947d, 24, 36, 78; 1947e, 54, 61; MAR 1947, 4b; Davies 1947f; nd, 91; Fox 1962, 129; Teoboo 1982; Burt 1994, 178. Armbands were inspired by those of US military police and others worn by church members; since before the war, Adventist "missions volunteers" had sported "MV" bands, and participants in SSEM "Young People's Bands" wore "YPB" ones (Lambert 1933, 31 May; see BSIP 1947e, 29, 65).

28. Davies 1947f; BSIP 1947e, 61.

29. Handwritten, no author or date, spelling slightly corrected, in BSIP 12/I/2/7.

30. Davies writing in Malaita 1945b, 11, and in MAR 1947, 4B; Davies nd, 38, 40, 41, 52, 75; and attributed by Allan 1980b, 110. Noel 1946b, 4; Sandars nd, 137; Forster 1946c, 7; see Forster 1945c; Trench 1947f, 2. At the time of Davies's visit, Maenaa'adi had already joined Maasina Rule, the activities of which, Davies later recalled, officers still understood "in terms of confidence tricks and protection rackets" (nd, 38).

31. Fifi'i 1982b (see Fifi'i 1989, chap 4); personal communications from Ma'aanamae 1987, Biri 'Asuani 1996, and Molaina'o 1996; see MAR 1947, 4B; Laracy 1971, 107–108. Keesing quoted Sandars's estimation of Nori as "ordinary" to support his own argument that creators of innovative political responses on Malaita did not need to be "charismatic," and that being at the right time and place with the right message was more important, especially since their messages were thought to come not from them but from spirits. Timing and message are important, and Keesing's portrayal of leaders does fit some cases, but not Nori, and not Ariel Sisili (see

this book, chapter 8), concerning whom Keesing said he has "no firm evidence" for the argument (1978a, 63). To my knowledge, neither of these leaders claimed spirits as sources for their messages, though Sisili had an SSEM background and at times cited tenets of Christian morality (see also Burt 1994, 198–199). It was *Europeans,* who resented leaders they did not control, that Nori failed to impress. If one believes most officers' appraisals of Malaitan leaders (and Sandars was much kinder than most in this regard), particularly after the government decided to suppress the movement, then only Nono'oohimae was exceptional; the rest were scoundrels of distinctly low character, and the Malaitans who elevated them were simply blind to this. Nono'oohimae was certainly an impressive man, but he alone possessed "traditional" social standing as a leader in the 'Are'are "chiefly" system, something crucial to the British that they often highlighted. Sometimes when a leader began to cooperate with the government his character as assessed by district officers miraculously improved. Kaplan described how the British similarly delegitimized Fijian resistance leaders in the 1860s and 1870s (1995, 81–92). In my view, Keesing's 1978 article, excellent in many respects, wrongly ascribes mediocrity and sameness to leaders across very different movements in the service of composing an overarching analysis that is flawed.

32. Holton 1945; BSIP 1945b, 1945c; Gregory-Smith 1950e, 1; Laracy 1983, 17; Saelasi Lounga 1982 pers comm (story); Ba'efaka 1996 pers comm; see Forster 1946c, 4. For a Kwara'ae story of Nori meeting MacArthur, see Burt 1994, 175–176. On the letters to Martin, see this book, chapter 8.

33. Nono'oohimae's views of Maasina Rule may be in the papers of the late Daniel de Coppet, an anthropologist who worked with him for years but published little on the movement. Palmer, whom we will encounter again, lived in the Solomons from 1919 until his death in 1976, as a Levers manager and plantation overseer but most famously as a labor recruiter. Older Kwaio and 'Are'are fondly recalled him to me for his kindness, fairness, and phenomenal Pijin fluency. It was said that on Guadalcanal he learned a language and took part in village affairs including initiation ceremonies. Not surprisingly, given his occupation, he later tried to help officers break Maasina Rule's labor strike (see Noel 1947f; Palmer 1970; Golden 1993, 103–106). His friend William Davenport recalled to me in 1988, "There was bad blood between him and the Levers administrative crowd, mainly, I think, over his attitude toward Solomon Islanders."

34. Forster 1946c, 7; Allan 1950g, 8; 1980b, 110. The same year Allan said Nono'oohimae was a former headman and mission teacher, confusing him with Timothy George (1950a, 77).

35. Noel 1947f; Trench 1947d, 2; MAR 1947, 4; Davies nd, 40, 75. For more on Waiparo, see this book, chapters 8 and 9.

36. Forster 1945c; BSIP 1947e, 76; Laracy 1983, D5; Scott 1990–1991; Naitoro 1993, 88.

37. Bell 1924, 1925e; Deck 1940, 4; Forster 1946c, 7; see Hilliard 1969, 62; Davies nd, 44; Tedder 2008, 40. Corris 1973a, drawn on here, summarizes George's life.

38. Forster 1944c; 1945c; 1946c, 7; see Noel 1946b, 4; Trench 1947f, 2; MAR 1947, 4B; Corris 1973a, 51; see Keesing 1978a, 50; Fifi'i 1989, 63. George's testimony at his 1947 trial was distinctly insincere, unlike that of most chiefs. He falsely distanced himself from other chiefs and movement decisions. His denials read not as clever but clumsy to anyone familiar with his actual role (BSIP 1947e, 91–93).

39. See Cameron 1947i. Fifi'i gave an interview to *Pacific Islands Monthly* (1982a) and published two accounts of World War II and its impacts that I translated and edited (1988a, 1991). Beginning in 1979, Fifi'i worked extensively with me on a range of topics including Maasina Rule. We also taught together at the Kwaio Cultural Center School until 1983. During a 1988 visit to Honolulu we worked through my archival materials, awakening for him many memories he soon recorded in his autobiography. His name would phonetically be written "Fiifii'i"; but in the 1940s he wrote it Fiifii, and later Fifi'i.

40. Sandars 1946, 7; BSIP 1947e, 70, 76–84; Fifi'i 1982a; 1982b; 1987 pers comm; 1989, 61–63; see Naitoro 1993, 88; cf Forster 1946c, 7. Officers apparently never realized Sirifa was a movement supporter (eg, Davies nd, 79), as was Kwarialaena.

41. MAR 1947, 4; Davies 1948a; see Allan 1950g, 7; Teoboo 1982 pers comm; Anifelo 1982 pers comm. A late-1930s photo of Teoboo, with Fifi'i and others, is in Fifi'i 1989, facing page 90, second from right.

42. BSIP 1947e, 72; Sandars 1947c; Cameron 1947d; 1947i; 1947k, 3; Davies 1947f, 1948a; see Forster 1948a; Teoboo 1982. Perhaps Davies felt a need to single out Fifi'i as dangerous because he knew that at Fifi'i's pending trial there would be no evidence against him. Davies claimed that in mid-1947 the chiefs came into conflict, giving as example that Fifi'i "began to extend his extremist brand of Marching Rule to Anoano, hitherto the territory of Nonohimae, and even into Eastern Kwara'ai" (MAR 1947, 8). The former claim was likely based on reports of a 1947 Fifi'i tour of towns reaching into west Kwaio; the latter derived from pure speculation by Cameron as to why Fifi'i attended a Kwai meeting. I have discussed this with people who were with Fifi'i on both occasions, and he had no expansionist intent (Laefiwane 1982 pers comm; Ma'aanamae 1996 pers comm). Nono'oohimae and Ganifiri remained Fifi'i's close friends. Marquand said, "There was a great deal of jealousy" between head chiefs, but I have seen no one else claim this or any evidence of it, and much against it (1950, 10). Officers' assertions of chiefly infighting seem to have been wishful thinking. A partial break between southern chiefs and some northern chiefs did occur in mid-1947, over policy, and this is examined in chapter 6.

43. Davies writing in MAR 1947, 4; and in nd, 150; Allan 1950g, 12; Notes on the Records [1953?]; Maranda 1973, 3–4; Fifi'i 1988 pers comm.

44. Hopkins 1934, 37; Forster 1946c, 4; Sandars 1946, 3–4; Marquand 1950, 6; Hilliard 1969, 58; Laracy 1971, 104; 1976, 126; Davies nd, 73; Burt 1994, 182, 199–200; 2006 pers comm.

45. Nearly 20 years before, Medical Officer Gordon White echoed common European complaints when he wrote, citing demands for payment for services, "It seems that the more missionized the place is the harder the people are to deal with" (nd, 12 Nov 1929). When SSEM missionary McBride toured the east coast after Nori's 1946 patrol, many expressed to him their distrust of missionaries and told him, "White man he rob'im boy" (quoted in Deck 1948b). We will see that both missionaries and officers tried to persuade Malaitans that Maasina Rule was un-Christian.

46. Pritt 1901, 183; Sisili 1949; Worsley 1957, 28; Laracy 1971, 105–106; 1976, 127; 1979, 100; Fulbright 1986; Burt 1994, 182–185; Russell 2003, 44.

47. *NIV* Sept 1944, 3; Mariko 1946; Cameron 1947d; Davies writing in MAR 1947, 4; BSIP 1947d, 1947e; Ganifiri 1956; Burt 1994, 97, 128–129, 157–158, 181–183. Norman Deck said Ganifiri was dismissed as teacher at Sandars's request, but I have

not confirmed this and it does not tally with Sandars's other writings and actions in early 1947 (Deck 1948b; Burt 1994, 191).

48. Marquand 1947c; Davies writing in MAR 1947, 4; and nd, 150; Gregory-Smith 1950–1952, Nov 1951; Notes on the Records [1953?]; Frazer 1973, v, 3. For 12 years after Maasina Rule, starting in 1951, 'Atoomea was headmaster at the government's Malu'u school (*Malaita Newsletter* Feb 1971).

49. Forster 1946c, 9; Marquand 1946c, 1947b; MAR 1947b, 4; BSIP 1947e, 78; Hilliard 1969, 61; Laracy 1979, 106; Davies nd, 89; cf Davies 1947g, 2. On Abu'ofa, see Moore 2009.

50. Sandars 1945b; Davies writing in MAR 1947, 4; Forster 1948e; Russell 1950j, 21; Wrightson 1952k, 2; Fifi'i 1987 pers comm; Tedder 2008, 53; see also this book, chapters 6 and 7. Keesing was told that Heber was born in Walade in southern Lau (1978a, 253). Some have written or said his name as "Hedley Heber" and others as "Heber Hedley." Such flexibility is common on Malaita where in the past there were no formal "first" and "last" names.

51. *NIV* Sept 1947, 3; March 1948, 4–5; Sept 1949, 11; Deck 1947a, 1947b; BSIP 1947d, 80; Tomlinson 1949; Clark 1950; Gibbins 1950, 1952a; Hilliard 1969, 61; Laracy 1971, 104, 107; 1976, 128; Burt 1994, 191. For a similar, Adventist missionary perspective, see Newman 1947.

52. Sandars 1947f, 3; see Hilliard 1969, 61. At Kwai the people collected funds to buy back land the SSEM had purchased at Naafinua (BSIP 1947d, 80). After the leaders' arrest later that year, Davies complained that SSEM missionaries were still avoiding troublesome Malu'u, with over 20 of them remaining ensconced at One-pusu; this continued into 1948, with only Deck touring regularly (Davies 1947i, 2–3; nd, 92, 327; Noel 1948g, 6).

53. Baddeley 1947, 30, 32; Marquand 1947b, 2; Reynolds quoted in Fox 1942–1949, 30 April 1948; Deck 1948a, 20 March; Caulton in *SCL* Oct 1950, 245; and 1955, 61; *SCL* April 1951, 296; Fox 1958, 176; 1962, 131–132; Laracy 1971, 108–109; 1983, 26; Whiteman 1983, 268–271, 314n68; cf Keesing 1978a, 250. By mid-1950, Allan thought the Anglican Church had become so weak that he suggested Methodists be invited in from the Western Solomons to run Malaita schools (1950i, 2).

54. Germond 1949a; Laracy 1971, 104, 107–114; 1976, 121–143 (Van de Walle quoted on 129); 1983, 26–27; see Crass 1946c, 3; Forster 1948e, Lau; Tomlinson 1949; Allan 1949c, 7; 1950i; Fox 1962, 132; Garrett 1997, 45–48, 204. For varying takes on relations between various churches and Maasina Rule, see Allan 1950a; Whiteman 1983, 266–273; White 1991, 198–202; Burt 1994; and Scott 2007, chap 3. For other tensions between Catholic priests and Maasina Rule, see Laracy 1971, 109–111.

55. Crass 1947a, 4; Noel 1948g, 5–6; Fox 1948b; Garrett 1997, 202; see Laracy 1976, 128–130.

56. Marquand 1948b, 1; 1950, 27; Allan 1950a, 40, 53, 89; 1950d; Keesing 1978a, 254.

57. Marquand 1948b, 1; 1950, 27; Allan 1951b, 1951d, 1950i; see this book, chapters 6–8. In 1949, District Commissioner Masterman declared an Adventist school at Kwai a fake and his police tore it down (1949a). One must also be cautious about inferring the degree of ideological influence of Christianity on Maasina Rule from writings of movement scribes. Though perhaps half of the moment's followers were non-Christians, very few of those were literate, and thus Christian scribes wrote most

documents; in them Christianity is sometimes to the fore and non-Christian perspectives are invisible or opaque. Furthermore, like missionaries, European academic writers have sometimes attributed all mentions of brotherhood, kindness, charity, peace, and the like fully to Christian influences, as if Malaitans did not value or perhaps did not even conceive of such ideas until churches taught people about them.

58. BSIP 1947d, 67; Deck 1948b; Laracy 1983, C5; Waleanisia 1987; Naitoro 1993, 89.

59. Later, District Commissioner Davies hoped the government could use seized Maasina Rule census records and vital statistics, which he suspected were complete, because loyalist headmen were able to collect data only for their own kin (1947g, 3; 1947i). On movement "road" making, see Davies 1947i, 1–2; 1947j, 1; Sandars 1947b; Marquand 1950, 40; Naitoro 1993, 93.

60. See MAR 1947, 5. 'Are'are had begun coastal building in early June 1945 (Davies nd, 39). Reading Naitoro (1993, 92–94), one might get the impression that 'Are'are built towns only in late 1948 and 1949, working with Eriel Sisili's Federal Council, but what he describes is a later phase of building (see this book, chapter 8).

61. Fifi'i 1982b; 1989, 65, 66; Ganifiri quoted in Burt 1994, 179.

62. See D.R.D.V. [1947?]; MAR 1951, 10; Fifi'i 1989, 64; Burt 1994, 180. Beginning in 1949, the label "colony" referred to a turning over of the BSIP to Australia, which some greatly feared (see this book, chapter 8).

63. See Edge-Partington 12–15 Aug 1911 letters in BSIP 14/40; Bell 1920b; Malu'u 1947; MAR 1947, 5; Sisili 1949, 3; Allan 1950a, 60; Marquand 1950, 12; Keesing 1978a, 54–55; Davies nd, 124; Laracy 1983, C29; Fifi'i 1989, 64; Bennett 1993, 129–130; Burt 1994, 179–180. By 1918, the Malayta Company had plantations at Baunani, nearby Hulo, Su'u, and Maanaoba. Christians saw their coastal land rights as particularly tenuous (Keesing 1978a, 57; Moore 2009, 28).

64. See Holton 1945; Barrow 1946; 4; Forster 1946c, 2; Marquand 1947d; Sandars 1947b; D.R.D.V. [1947?]; Davies writing in MAR 1947, 5; and nd, 88, cf 124; Allan 1950a, 46; Burt 1994, 179–180; see also this book, chapter 7. Colin Allan later told Resident Commissioner Gregory-Smith that land alienation fears were due to "loose American talk in the war," to which Gregory-Smith observed that such fears were "a hardy annual anywhere that native administration functions" (Gregory-Smith 1950–1952, 4 May 1951; and see Gregory-Smith 1951d).

65. Barrow 1946; see Scott 2007, 100–129, passim.

66. For good summaries of early BSIP land laws and alienation, see Allan 1957a, chap 3; and Bennett 1987, chap 8. In mid-1947, loyalist east Kwara'ae Headman Siru, whom Tedder later called "an original smooth 'con man,'" caused a stir by telling people there that Sandars planned to take land (Sandars 1947f, 2; Deck 1947b; Tedder 2008, 26). Davies soon after did lobby Noel to seize Kwai land for a government station (1947j, 3). Davies's 1947 Malaita Annual Report, one of the most distorting government documents ever written about Maasina Rule, stressed fear of land loss as a motivation for creating towns. Davies had recently transferred from Makira, formed many of his ideas about the movement there, and at times insisted it was exactly the same on both islands. In reports he was keen to place rumors and fear at the heart of Maasina Rule thought, often asserting without evidence that leaders calculatedly concocted and spread them to manipulate the "primitive" populace (see MAR 1947, 5; and see this book, chapters 6 and 7).

67. Marquand 1947c; Trench 1947a; Russell 1950j, 18. Allan claimed that Rame'ai town in Makwanu District in Baelelea had nearly 1,000 residents. Burt was told that at least some inland Kwara'ae hamlets were neglected and "fell down," and that when people ascended to tend bush gardens they stayed in small garden houses (John Gamu 1983 pers comm to Burt). Kwaio people have told me they minimally maintained their hamlets, but some may not have.

68. See Marquand 1950, 55; Russell 2003, chap 6. Malu'u officer Russell later got his intelligence from headmen: "Many had been suborned by the Movement and were virtually double agents reporting to the Government what the Marching Rule was up to, and vice versa" (2004, 5).

69. Clark 1947; Burt 1994, 181. A photograph of Clark is in *PIM* June 1952, 51.

70. Barley writing in MQR June 1930; Allan 1950a, 45; Zoleveke 1980, 43. Town-residence choices in east Kwara'ae are detailed in Burt 1994, 82–83, 180–181.

71. Clark 1947, 5, 6; see Marquand 1950, 40; Naitoro 1993, 93.

72. Clark 1947, 6; see Barrett 1947, 29 Jan; Allan 1950a, 45; Burt 1994, 181; Molaina'o 1996 pers comm. Officer Alexander MacKeith in 1951 still found A'arai "the largest MR town I have seen on Malaita" (1951b, 2).

73. Marquand 1947c; Allan 1950a, 44; Fox 1962, 130–131; Burt 1994, 180 (told by Gamu in 1983); Ma'aanamae 1996 pers comm; Molaina'o 1996 pers comm. There was much variation by area and over time; for example, in 1948 in inland Kwaio many towns behind Sinalagu had fences and towers, while fewer behind Uru and 'Oloburi did (Laefiwane 1982 pers comm; Ma'aanamae 1996 pers comm). But in about 1950 Tome Waleanisia passed through several towns in the mountains behind 'Oloburi that had towers he estimated at some 21 meters high, each with a two-square-fathom house at the top (1987, 7). See Scott 1998 for discussions of the importance in social engineering schemes of resettlement models and the imposition of grids and other structural plans on cities, towns, and villages.

74. On marketing plans, see Forster 1948c; Russell 1949a, 2; Zoleveke 1980, 43; Titiuru 1987; Fifi'i 1989, 66; Burt 1994, 179. On suspicions of fund misuse by avaricious chiefs, see Davies 1947f, 1947h, 1947i; Noel 1947a, 3; Zoleveke 1980, 43.

75. MAR 1947, 5; Forster 1948a; personal communications from Sulafanamae 1982, Ma'aanamae 1996, and Riufaa 1996.

76. See, eg, Hopkins 1904a; Sullivan 1933, 6–7; Deck 1943, 4–5; Marquand 1947e, 6; Russell 1949a, 2; Hogbin 1970, 216; White 1991, 191. Deck said Malaitans stopped supporting teachers this way during Maasina Rule (1947b), but many teachers had become chiefs.

77. Codes [1946f?], [1946g?], 1947a; Fox 1948, 22; 1962, 129; Zoleveke 1980, 44.

78. Clark 1947, 5; Noel 1947a, 2–3; 1947b; 1947c; Codes 1947a; Marquand 1947e, 1; 1948b; Russell 1949a, 2; Burt 1994, 183 (John Gamu 1983 pers comm); see Davies 1947f, 1948a.

79. Noel 1947a, 2; Russell 1949a, 2; Zoleveke 1980, 43; Buloli 1997 pers comm to Guo Pei-yi; Davies nd, 31; cf Marquand 1950, 44. Except for rice and cocoa, Malaitans had planted these sorts of crops within inland taro and potato gardens long before Maasina Rule.

80. Davies 1947i. Today people have coastal gardens where weary soils allow but suffer low yields and erosion. In some places coastal residents have for decades trekked miles inland to work better land. Mountain soils were once fallowed 10–20 years between crops. Soil degradation was a problem for coastal Christians by the

early 1920s (*NIV* 1921, nd, 3; Northcote Deck 1923, 3; Frazer 1987; Tedder 2008, 32). Frazer reported that the blight *Phytophthora colocasiae* crippled To'abaita taro production in 1957–1958. The disease was first reported in north Malaita in early 1950. In 1949 Russell found sweet potato surpassing taro as the staple in the north, probably reflecting needs of Maasina Rule gardening and residence patterns, the fact that only men grew taro, and that, more than potatoes, proper taro gardens required rituals for ancestors (Russell 1949a, 1–2; 1950b, appendix B; Frazer 1973, 26). In Kwaio the 1950s blight ruined taro that had not yet recovered from ruinous diseases of the 1920s and 1930s (see Allan 1989, 91; Akin 1993, 230–234).

81. Davies 1947f; 1947i, 1; see Noel 1947a, cover letter; Marquand 1947e, 1948a; Fox 1962, 129.

82. MAR 1946, 4; Davies 1947j (cf Davies 1947i); Cameron 1947d, 1947e, 1947j; see Cameron 1947i, 1; Marquand 1947e, 1; Sandars 1947b; Malu'u 1947; Worsley 1968, 181. In mid-1949 Russell thought farms, by then mostly abandoned in the north where he was, might be usefully revived later if they could be depoliticized (1949a, 2). Malaita suffered a plague of rats in 1947 that damaged some farms.

83. Sandars 1947b, 1947c; Ma'aanamae 1987 pers comm; see Zoleveke 1980, 43. Penned pigs could not forage, so people had to feed them more and thus had to plant more gardens.

84. Forster 1948c; Cameron 1947j, 1947k; Allan 1950a, 46; Zoleveke 1980, 43; cf MAR 1947, 6B; Tedder 2008, 58–59. Forster visited Furi'itolonga town in central Kwaio and spent a friendly night with chiefs at nearby Go'isi'ini. He also visited Looa town under chief Laefiboo, ordered it torn down, and took three men to jail for two months. Before they returned, Looa was abandoned (Ma'aanamae 1996 pers comm; Siufiomea 1996 pers comm). Marquand thought towns should be encouraged. He said in 1947 that some were poorly planned with unhygienic houses of bad design but that more permanent ones were planned. He was based along the northeast coast to Malu'u, where more towns lacked permanent residents. In early 1948 he toured 54 towns and found them improved, but he considered the bush-style dirt-floor houses unhealthy and some sites malarial (1947e, 1948b; see Russell 1949a, 4, and Masterman comments). In June 1948, Forster by arrests and fines forced people, mostly Adventists, to abandon Lau's Sulione town since, he said, it was at an unhealthy location (1948d). Later Russell reported during mass arrests, "Imprisonment is now given as the stock excuse for dirty villages, bad health and neglect of any kind" (1949a, appendix 3).

85. Cameron 1947e, 1947i, 1947j; Sandars 1947b, 1947c; Russell 1949a, 4. Remo Guidieri said that Maasina Rule wished to protect Malaitan languages and therefore rejected English and Pijin (1988, 189), but most Malaitans saw more English literacy as a long-term movement goal, and many codes were written in Pijin or English to target readers across languages and, sometimes, colonial officers.

86. BSIP 1947e, 94.

87. Noel 1946b; Zoleveke 1980, 44; see Codes [1946i?]; Clark 1947, 5; BSIP 1947e, 43; Naitoro 1993, 93. Hedley Heber testified at the chiefs' trial that Sandars when asked in 1947 agreed "That no man could be absent from his village for more than one day without permission of his headman or chief" and "that people should work as directed by the village chiefs." Extant law required one's headman's permission to travel outside one's district (BSIP 1947e, 80). Zoleveke was on Malaita from May 1951 into 1955, first at Hauhui in west 'Are'are, then at Malu'u, and for six

months of 1952 at Rerede Hospital in the north. In 1953 he toured the south and east, based for a time at Naafinua. His description of Abu town sounds to be from an earlier phase of Maasina Rule and may be at least partly secondhand.

88. Frazer 1973, iii, 99.

89. Forster 1945b, 1948c.

90. Willingness to hand murderers over to the government was Malaita-wide, but I do not know intricacies of ancestral death compensation in the north. Sandars thought people there wanted the government to prosecute both murder and rape; Allan said assault cases as well, though in 1947 Maasina Rule courts heard assault cases. All could spark intergroup violence (Sandars 1947f, 4; Allan 1950a, 43; see Codes 1944d). Hopkins related a 1904 case at Fiu, before the government had a presence on Malaita, in which relatives of a man accused of conspiring to murder mission teacher Arthur Ako paddled him the 40 kilometers to Tulagi to surrender himself to Woodford, apparently to escape vengeance by Ako's relatives (1934, 48; see BSIP 1947d, 23).

91. On codes, see "Codes" in References; Laracy 1983, E1, E3, E5; Akin 1993, appendixes 4–8. On meanings of codification, see Akin 1996, 170; 2004.

92. Deck 1940, 3; Bengough 1940b; Sullivan 1944; *NIV* Dec 1945, 6; Sandars 1947f, 5; see Ganifiri [1940s?]. For examples of these types of codes, see Codes ndd, 1944c, 1944d, 1946d; Akin 1993, appendixes 4–7.

93. Personal communications from Lounga 1982, Folofo'u 1982, and Fifi'i 1987; see Codes 1944c.

94. In 1942 some 18,000 Malaitans belonged to the three largest churches: 9,000 SSEM, 5,000 Anglicans (of 25,000 in the Solomons), and about 4,000 Catholics (in 1946, 5,410 Catholics). Overall, two-thirds of Solomon Islanders self-identified as Christian (Hilliard 1974, 93, 111; Laracy 1976, 126). There were fewer Adventists in the Solomons then. Dennis Steley (1990, 617) gave a Solomons SDA number in 1940 of 1,151, and Anderson and Anderson (1980–1981, 6 April 1981, 10) counted 4,128 in 1950, 1,628 of them in the Protectorate's eastern half (see also Ross 1978b, 185–187). Whiteman, citing mission sources, estimated that from 1942 to 1950 the proportion of Malaitans who were Christian rose from under one-half to three-quarters (1983, 315). Colin Allan in late 1951 thought two-thirds were Christian (1951m), and Tom Russell four years later thought about 60 percent were (1955c, 3). Roy Davies said that on Malaita "there had certainly been few conversions to Christianity in the war years" (nd, 32). Caution is in order; tallies almost always undercounted inland non-Christians, who were harder to count and often disliked being counted. For example, even in 1961, Malaita's District Commissioner Michael Townsend wrote to Roger Keesing that there were between one and two hundred people living in inland Kwaio, with a caution that his estimate might be "inaccurate in the extreme" (1961b). There were thousands there. Sandars in the mid-1930s estimated 10 percent of Malaitans were Christian, certainly an undercount, but wrote, "If you could believe the mission figures they claimed that everybody on the island was a Christian" (nd, 30). Another complication is that mission tallies of "Christians" often include only their own denomination.

95. For example, Codes nda, 1944b, [1944e?], [1946f?]; Russell 2003, 45.

96. Michael Scott 2001 pers comm; see Sandars 1947f, 4; Burt 1994, 184. In some contexts Malaitans distinguish between affairs and rules of ancestral spirits and those of "living people," and Christians between "God's law" and "church law."

These divisions can be crucial to how rule violations and disputes are managed, and people, particularly Christians, sometimes disagree as to where such lines should be drawn. Moreover, ancestors or God can be quickly drawn into "secular" disputes if disputants curse, kill each other, or evoke spiritual powers (see Akin 1999b, 46, 53). Nonetheless, it is a distortion to apply the Western concepts of "religious" and "secular" as distinct realms to Malaitan life overall.

97. Compare Babadzan 2004, 326, with Akin 2005, 81.

98. Re brideprice limits, SSEM founder Florence Young had warned Norman Deck of "a danger in encouraging the native church to lay down 'laws,' even when the object is desirable" (1932). But Deck and his colleagues continued to advance legalistic views of mission rules.

99. Clark 1947; Davies 1948a; Fifi'i 1987 pers comm; Ma'aanamae 1987 pers comm; Akin 2004. 'Elota in his autobiography (Keesing 1978b, 160–168) described disputes during Maasina Rule, though most of them occurred later, when people had returned inland; Kwaio in oral histories often extend the "Maasina Rule" period well into the 1950s or later. Though Kwaio produced many codes, they did not keep written case records. Before, specific compensation amounts had been negotiated or sometimes coerced. In 1987, Fifi'i told me they set amounts to be low so that even those with little wealth could pay them—codes served as a social-leveling tool. There was also concern to avoid divisive compensation disputes (Teoboo 1982).

100. On fear of spies: personal communications from Inaarobo (re Baegu) 1982, and Mariano Kelesi (Lau), Waleanisia (Langalanga), and Biri (Kwara'ae), all 1987. Re confusions over the status of courts, see, eg, Cameron 1947i, 1947j; see Codes 1946c; Russell 2003, 60.

101. Forster 1946c, 4; Fifi'i [1947?]; Burt 1994, 185; see BSIP 1947d, 1947e; and this book, chapters 6 and 7.

102. Cameron 1947f, 1947i; Marquand 1950, 14, 35; and see this book, chapters 3, 4, and 6; see Cameron 1947e.

103. Clemens 1941; BSIP 1942b, section 13–14; 1942c, number 13; 1947e, 81; 1945e; Hogbin 1944, 262; 1964, 96; Tomlinson 1949; Belshaw 1950a, 125; Osifelo 1985, 22; Tedder 2008, 157. Such a sentence to labor was sometimes called a *koda-lake* (from "contract"). Years before, Legal Adviser J G Bates, citing a Native Affairs Regulation draft, wrote, "The new definition of 'imprisonment' will permit of an offender being in a proper case sentenced to a limited term of compulsory labour in connection with 'public works.' This form of punishment, which can be effectively supervised by the local native authorities, will be more efficacious in certain cases (particularly cases of convictions for breaches of the 'Local Rules') than imprisonment in the usual sense of the term: the particular community to which the offender belongs will be directly benefited and the ends of justice will be equally served" (1918, 2). Sentences over a month had to be served in a government jail, and after the war native courts tried to keep to that or shorter sentences so that those they convicted could stay home (Davies 1947k, 2).

104. For examples from around Malaita, see Ivens 1928a, 62; Hogbin 1970, 17–18, 113–115; Ross 1973, chap 6; Keesing 1982c, chap 5; Burt 1994, 56–58; Guo 2001, 120–130; Akin 2003.

105. Clark 1947, 4; see Norman Deck 1923; Northcote Deck 1923, 5–6; Hogbin and Wedgwood 1943, 4. Some Lau, Langalanga, and related ancestral communities from small islands relocated to towns on the coast during Maasina Rule.

106. Clark 1947, 4; see Northcote Deck 1923, 5–6; Innes 1938, 16; *SCL* June–Sept 1957, 48.

107. Laracy 1971, 103.

108. Marilyn Strathern's concept of "partibility" is useful toward understanding the nature of big men and big ancestors and the exchanges they are party to and generate (1988, chap 8, passim). For Malaitans, the construction of personhood need not end at death; for those who become active ancestral spirits it continues through their evolving relations with expanding or contracting constellations of descendants who exchange with them (see Fox 1987, 174–175; Bloch 1993).

109. Fox 1962, 128–129; Akin, 1996, 170; 2004, 305, passim; see Ross 1973, 263–264; Keesing 1978b, 21. Dzenovska and Arenas analyzed events in Latvia and Mexico to show how material "practices of protest" themselves shape social movements and create collective identities that bridge formerly deep ethnic and political divisions (2012). During Maasina Rule, this became still more important after the government used mass arrests to suppress Malaitan abilities to pursue constructive social projects together (see this book, chapters 6–8).

110. For a few examples of conflicts, see MARs 1935, 11; 1936, 15; Horton 1965, 28.

111. Laracy 1983, 109; see Clark 1947; Marquand 1947c, 1948a; Allan 1950a, 44–45; Burt 1990, 214–215. On the use of oaths in disputes, see this book, chapter 2.

112. Marquand wrote, "The Marching Rule leaders 'came to an agreement' with the ancestor devils, that lies told, even on heathen oath, for the benefit of the Marching Rule, would be forgiven" (1950, 35). No Malaitans I asked had heard of this, but that something of the sort was done in places is plausible, for Malaitans have an entire genre of magics that allow one to utter ancestral oaths with impunity (see this book, chapter 2). Davies, unaware of this, read such false oaths as indicating a terrible psychological hold Maasina Rule had over adherents (nd, 90).

113. Oloi'a quoted in Keesing 1987, 41. Oloi'a's husband, a priest, died in 1982 (several years after this interview), and she and their children became coastal Christians to flee further punishment by ancestors still angry over past taboo violations, including that her husband had visited Christians too often and eaten their food (personal communications from Molaina'o 1982 and 1996, Maeana 1982, and Oloi'a 1982 and 1996).

114. Personal communications from Riufaa, 'Oitalana, and 'Otaalea, all 1996; see Clark 1947, 4; Akin 1996; 2004; nd.

115. Lewis 1986; see Fox 1962, 131; Akin 1996, 2003, 2004, nd.

116. Noel 1944c; MAR 1944; Clark 1947, 4; BSIP 1947e, 58–59; Burt 1994, 185; see Codes 1944c, 1944d; Allan 1950o, 5; Akin 1999b, 54.

117. Clark 1947, 6; personal communications from To'oni 1982, Kwailoboo 1982, and Ma'aanamae 1997.

118. Burt 1994, 41, 164; see Codes 1944c, 1–4.

119. Personal communications from Kwailoboo 1982, and Siufiomea, Ma'aanamae, Maenaalamo, Basiberi, and Gwanu'i, all 1996; see Akin 1999a, 127–130. For another marriage exchange innovation, see Davies 1948a, Uru notes.

120. Later, as religious divisions reemerged, all rejected this payment method as illegitimate, but since the 1980s some Christians, including Malaitans, have revived this and other strategies to mitigate church brideprice limits (see Akin 1999a, 127–130).

121. See Akin 2003, 396–398; nd.

122. For example, Codes 1946b; Allan 1980b, 112; see Codes 1944c, 1944d.

123. Personal communications from Sangosoea 1981; from Basiberi, Sulafana-mae, Geniilefana, and Le'aa, all 1982; from Ma'aanamae, Na'oni'au, and To'oni, all 1983; and from Wa'ii'a 1987; see Naitoro 1993, 93.

124. Thomas 1992c, 81, passim; see Thomas 1992b; Sahlins 1993.

125. For example, MAR 1947, 5B–6; Davies 1947c; nd, 241; AR 1948, 26, 38; Allan 1957a, 153, 251–253; 1989–1990, 154; BSIP 1945–1959, 20 Feb 1948, 27; Hearth 1956a; Laracy 1976, 124; Russell 2004.

126. See Akin 1996.

127. Kaakalade 1982 pers comm, in conversation with Geniilefana.

128. Wa'ii'a 1987 pers comm; John Naitoro 1995 pers comm. A similar argument on the need to approach development projects through *kastom* opens an early statement of Maasina Rule's purpose, likely written under Nono'oohimae's and Nori's direction (see Codes 1945b).

129. There are Malaitan concepts that partly overlap with "custom," such as Kwara'ae *falafala* or Kwaio *tagi*.

130. Barrow nd, part III, 55; see Belshaw 1947b, 10–11; MAR 1947, 5B–6; Allan 1957a, 253; 1960, 162; Davies nd, 70, 90, 132. It is also likely that officers and Malaitans often thought they were talking about the same thing—focusing on the partial overlap—when they were not, a type of miscommunication also common between missionaries and Malaitans.

Chapter 6: Maasina Rule and the Government

1. MAR 1945, 3; Forster 1946c, 9; Noel 1946b, 1; see BSIP 1947e, 51; AR 1947, 3; Allan 1950a, 25; Davies nd, 245.

2. Davies nd, 38–43; see Marquand 1950, 15. As late as October 1946 Forster had to write about Maasina Rule, "Details are difficult to obtain and much of the evidence is of a circumstantial nature." In 1946 Malaita's officers spent just 169 man-days on tours, most of them by Forster (Forster 1945c; 1946c, 6–7; Davies nd, 40–43, 74, 93–94). Ironically, District Commissioner Andersen a decade later bemoaned that Hoasihau, still headman, "just cannot adapt himself to indirect administration and he is being ejected from Wairokai" (1954a, 1; see Hoasihau 1951).

3. Forster 1945b, 1945c (quote). Davies later claimed Forster returned from 'Are'are telling them there was "a large scale conspiracy afoot...and thought that the movement should be smashed at all costs" (1948d, 44–45). This is contradicted by Forster's more positive and nuanced appraisals after the tour, just summarized. As we will see, Forster's views of Maasina Rule shifted back and forth over time. On this tour he learned Hoasihau had not given up the idea of a regional chief and that Assistant Headman Timothy George had been chosen as leader (Forster 1945b, 1945c).

4. Forster 1946c, 1; BSIP 1947e, 75 (and see 105); Davies nd, 41–45.

5. BSIP 1947e, 94; Davies nd, 83–84. Sandars later said he first met Nori on his return when Nori asked to see him, and that he told Nori he did not object to the movement's work (nd, 137).

6. In December Sandars met with Kwara'ae and then Malu'u council mem-

bers and, Davies said, lectured them against contacting Americans, embarking on "patrols," or levying fines, and forbade any relocations to the coast without his permission. According to Davies, at Malu'u Sandars railed at Nori's stupidity, warned that government would not tolerate his meddling, and ridiculed the idea that he offered what government could not; the government, he told attendees "had always been solicitous of the people's welfare" (Davies nd, 83–84; cf BSIP 1947e, 105).

7. MAR 1945, 3–4; Sandars 1945b; cf Davies nd, 46, cf 81. In 1950 Resident Commissioner Gregory-Smith was still blaming "Negro troops" for Maasina Rule (1950f, 4).

8. MAR 1947, 6.

9. Crass 1946a, appendix B, 29 May; BSIP 1947d, 132–133; 1947e, 54–55, 65, 75–79, 105, 110; Marquand 1950, 11; Davies nd, 95.

10. Forster 1946c; Crass 1946a, 1; Pulei quoted in Crass 1946a, appendix B; cf Belshaw 1946, 1; see Kane quoted in White 1991, 189; Russell 2003, 36; Scott 2007, 106. As late as 1951, Resident Commissioner Gregory-Smith thought the Malaitan village of Bina, on the western Kwara'ae coast, should all be "pulled down" as unsanitary and asked Colin Allan to look into his legal powers to do this (1950–1952, 10 May 1951).

11. Belshaw 1946, 2–3; Crass 1946a, 2; Loloito, Waneunga, Taheolo, Pule, and Matanigabu quoted in Crass 1946a, appendix C. Years later Davies claimed that Belshaw was "surrounded and threatened and jostled" (nd, 186), but all accounts refute this.

12. This paragraph's quotations and attributions are from telegrams appended to a confidential Crass report (1946a, appendix B): Belshaw, 23 May; Forster, 29 May; Barrow, 31 May; Acting RC Trench, 2 June. Laracy, citing a letter of priest T Parsonage, identifies catechist John Apui as leader of Ulawan resistance at this time, but though Parsonage and Belshaw suspected Apui of anti-government activity (and he had been jailed), he was that May on Malaita and not involved in this episode (Belshaw 1946, 1–2; Laracy 1971, 110; 1976, 130–131; see Laracy 1983, 27; Apui 1947). Belshaw later said George's "words had been distorted and exaggerated to a degree that can be imagined only by those who have had experience with native rumours" (1947a, 192), apparently referring to stories he and Parsonage heard after the event. A son of Kuper later assaulted a Maasina Rule man and threatened to shoot others who stayed in the movement, but the officer Val Andersen on Makira recommended he not be prosecuted since to do so would give Maasina Rule a victory (Andersen 1947; 1948; see Burrows 1950; Davenport 1970, 166–170).

13. Crass 1946a. Men had canoed to visit George on Malaita shortly before Belshaw's return to Ulawa. Ulawa District Headman Loloito, as a government witness in October 1947, testified they likely brought back instructions to not do any government work (but that he had not actually heard anyone say this) and that he thought this led to the row with Belshaw. Loloito himself later went to Malaita and spent two or three months with George who, he testified, told him that as headman he should work with officers but let people go ahead with Maasina Rule, and that if the government saw their work was going well they would leave the Solomons. He said George told him Americans would send material help (Loloito 1947; see Fifi'i 1989, 67).

14. Crass 1946a, 1, 3, and Loloito, Timothy, Maria, and others quoted in Crass's appendix C.

15. Noel 1946b, 2; Belshaw 1947a, 191–192; see Allan 1950a, 25–26; 1951a, 99; 1989–1990, 70; Davies nd, 186. Elsewhere, Belshaw foregrounded enforcement of sanitary rules as a necessary but lacking response to Maasina Rule needed to inculcate respect for law and order, and social responsibility (1947b, 11; see Belshaw 1950a, 79; 2009, 40, 50; Allan 1982a, 222). Headman Loloito told Crass that Belshaw was the only officer who went inside people's houses to inspect them and that people did not like it. Village Headman Lugu testified, "Mr Belshaw's conduct was not the same as other Governments [ie, officers]"; Government Councillor Asehu Pulei said that other officers had been kind (and Ulawans had compared Belshaw specifically and unfavorably with Alexander Waddell), but that Belshaw was a "Larrikin man" (Pijin for "troublemaker" or "lawbreaker"; see also Maria, all in Crass 1946a, appendix C). The point is that Ulawans reacted here against not government policy but rather Belshaw's actions, and they had discussed confronting him the previous December, before they joined Maasina Rule. Belshaw for his part told investigator Crass that his house burnings "did not effect in the slightest the warmth of the welcome, which was accompanied by dancing and singing" (1946, 1). Of those whose statements Crass collected, only Parsonage, who traveled to Ulawa with Belshaw, and Parsonage's Makiran "boss boy" Haga (the Wainoni headman but later a Maasina Rule leader there) supported Belshaw's reading. They said they had heard that George was stockpiling weapons for a violent revolt and that people were defying government rather than Belshaw personally. Parsonage declared Belshaw's conduct "admirable," and said, "I felt proud of this representative of the Government" (Crass 1946c, appendix C; on Haga, see Barrow nd, part 3, 30). In years to come, Belshaw, as an anthropologist, published influential statements on Maasina Rule, sometimes asserting its violent nature. His writings, with those of Allan and Cochrane, contributed to Maasina Rule being pigeonholed as a "cargo cult" (eg, Belshaw 1947a; 1950b; 1950a, 74, 126–129; 1972; 1976). Then again, some of his writings on the period, even on Maasina Rule, were insightful and valuable, particularly his prescriptions for economic reforms to improve the Protectorate's economic health and Islanders' lives, and I cite his work often in this book (see Belshaw 1948; 1950a; 2009, 63). He began his recent autobiography with a baffling account of this same Ulawa incident (Belshaw 2009, chap 1).

16. White 1928–1931, 8 Oct 1929; Lambert 1933, 31 May; Forster 1946c, 9–10; BSIP 1947e, 55; Waleanisia 1987. In Kwaio during Maasina Rule, a famous area artist, Sulafanamae, finely carved wooden rifles (Sulafanamae 1982 pers comm). In 1979 I watched elders there perform a smart drill with stick-rifles as a playful reenactment of Maasina Rule times. Today government police still perform creative drills that look like dances. On drilling, see Edge-Partington 1910d, 1914a; Hopkins 1911, 30; 1928, 177–178; 1934, 42; Young 1925, plates facing 160 and 180; Marchant 1940b, 18 July; Widdy 1943b, 1943e; Barrow and Davies 1947, 2; BSIP 1947e, 30A, 55, 77; 1947f, 14; Vance 1963, 23; Hogbin 1970, 180 plate 22; Keesing 1978a, 47; Saunders 1984, 230; Laracy and White 1988, 14. At the chiefs' trial, a good deal was made of duties wearing sashes. Sandars had told Kakalu'ae (while Kakalu'ae was still a Maasina Rule head chief) to allow duties to wear sashes with white calico, "but not with khaki" (BSIP 1947e, 81, 82). When he was still a police corporal, in 1920, Fotarafa lost his symmetry to a dynamite stick while reef fishing on Makira. In 1927 Bell sent Fotarafa back to 'Aoke when his patrol proceeded to Sinalagu. He toured with Lambert, White, and others working to eradicate yaws and hookworm,

and served two jail terms in the 1930s. Sandars wrote, "In the ordinary way he was a very pleasant fellow but a complete rogue and he had been in prison on numerous counts during the course of his career." When Fotarafa told him he was a chief, Sandars recorded, "I told him that if Marching Rule chose to accept a fellow of his caliber as chief I had no time for them." Sandars depicted him as one of "many bad hats" that exploited Maasina Rule for personal advancement (nd, 139). In 1946 officers were still angry with Fotarafa for organizing the Langalanga men whom Japanese employed to carry boxes when they looted 'Aoke in 1942 (see this book, chapter 4, note 1). He was later imprisoned for refusing to pay tax and be censused during Maasina Rule. On Fotarafa, see Eyerdam, 26 Jan 1930; Lambert 1941, 17, 283; Forster 1946a, 10; Trench 1946; Allan 1951j; BSIP 1951a; Waleanisia 1987; Fifi'i 1989, 45.

17. Forster 1946c, 10; Davies nd, 98; Waleanisia 1987, 3–5. Davies later claimed that Fotarafa had held an illegal court, but a woman who reportedly complained to a headman subsequently said it was mere arbitration. Sandars's and Forster's reports and letters say nothing of this. Later, Catholic Father Jim Wall heard and believed the complaint of the prisoners, by then in jail in Honiara, that they received no proper trial, and he protested to the government (Davies nd, 97, 112; Fotarafa was Catholic). In October, *Pacific Islands Monthly* fibbed, "One prominent native who lived near the Administration station on Malaita would not join [Marxian Law], and he was savagely beaten. He was rescued, after a sharp fight, by District Officer Foster [*sic*] and his native police, and 40 of the aggressors were arrested and gaoled. The strength and tact being displayed in an ugly situation, by DO Foster, a young Englishman, are warmly praised" (1946b). In 1949, Forster was reprimanded for illegal summary arrests and jailings in 'Are'are, which the legal adviser called "a travesty," and those prisoners were later released (see this book, chapter 7).

18. Forster 1946a, 15 June, 1 July; 1946c, 10; Noel 1946b; Trench 1946.

19. Forster 1946a, 15 June; Deck 1948b; Davies nd, 100–101. People who knew Kifo remembered him to me as brash and impetuous, but even his political enemies seem to have kept a fond spot for him amidst derisive humor about his outlandish political moves (personal communications from Toloasi Teoboo 1982, Ma'aanamae 1987, Fifi'i 1988).

20. Forster 1946a, 17 June; Davies nd, 110. Maena (see figure 2.4), illegitimate son of Harry Wickham of Gizo and a Roviana woman, married a Langalanga girl. He died in 1948 in a drunken brawl. Two sons of F M Campbell, Malaita's first police officer in 1912, were acquitted of his murder (Allan 1989–1990, 26). Fifi'i said that when he and other head chiefs were arrested in September 1947 Maena treated them cruelly and told them they would die on Guadalcanal and never see their families again (1989, 82–83).

21. Forster 1946a, 15 and 17 June; Waleanisia 1987; Davies nd, 110. Davies gave a rousing blow-by-blow account of both incidents, especially the Langalanga episode (and another less serious one in October at Lau). He urged that Fotarafa be banished to distant Vanikolo on completing his sentence but was told that it would be "gross interference" with Fotarafa's rights. Davies told the legal adviser and secretary to government that if they insisted the law be followed then the law should be changed: "If we had to rely solely on the law as it then stood, there seemed a good chance we should lose the struggle with Marching Rule entirely." This previewed Davies's attitude toward law when he battled Maasina Rule as district commissioner

in 1947–1948 (nd, 101–110, 112, 136; see this book, chapter 7). In an interesting twist of oral history, by the 1960s some Langalanga were claiming that Langalanga people never took part in Maasina Rule, which some still assert (Cooper 1966; Guo Pei-Yi 2005 pers comm).

22. Forster 1946a, 1946b; BSIP 1947d, 81–83, 120; 1947e, 77–78; Davies nd, 111, 113, 123; Fifi'i 1982 pers comm.

23. BSIP 1947d, 133; 1947e, 3, 14, 54, 63, 65, 75–78, 83–84, 105, 110–111; Germond 1948b, 1; Davies nd, 124–126, 134, 139, 143. Later Noel credited the "easing of tension" during this period to four British naval vessels casually passing through at various times in later 1946. Crews socialized with locals on shore, and rumors later spread that they were American. These visits were scarcely noted in reports at the time, and Noel's later claim for their pacifying effect was made as part of his efforts to convince the high commissioner to send warships to attend arrests of Maasina Rule leaders (Noel 1947h, 7). In January 1947, Sandars asked Nori to convince people of Uru in east Kwaio to allow land for an Adventist hospital, but they refused (BSIP 1947e, 78; Sandars nd, 140).

24. Forster 1946a; see BSIP 1947e, 55; Davies nd, 81, 96, 138, 139, 141–142.

25. Forster 1946c, 1, 10–11; see MAR 1946, 18; 1947, 3. Forster had just met with a conference of headmen at 'Aoke and with SSEM teachers at nearby Abu. Davies decades later dismissed this Forster report (which he had at hand while writing his own account that contradicted it) as "out-of-date and over-optimistic" (nd, 134), but in late 1950 he opined that it contained "the surest reflections on Marching Rule" yet written (1950c).

26. Asa Hoe 1946; Belshaw 1946, 3; Crass 1946c; 1947d, 3; Noel 1947a, 1947o; BSIP 1947d, 43; Sandars nd, 139–141; Davies nd, 139–140, 145–146, 180; Allan 1980b, 111; Laracy 1983, C10. Davies's and Allan's statements about Sandars must be read cautiously, but archival and oral evidence confirm that such ideas were rife. Marquand said that chiefs also tried to hire a government medical officer for £300 a year, but, oddly, in the same paragraph wrote that that they expected Europeans "to provide efficient medical services, free of course" (1950, 9; see Allan 1950a, 51).

27. Forster 1946c, 10; BSIP 1947d, 133, 139–140; 1947e, 78; Sandars 1947f; nd, 139–141; Davies nd, 110, 121–122; Laracy 1983, C10; Naitoro 1993, 91.

28. Sandars nd, 137; Trench writing in MAR 1944, 3; see Woodford 1890b, 23; Ivens 1928a, 28–29; Grantham 1947; Noel 1947a, 4; Belshaw 1950b, 116. With their "force of character," Bell wrote of Malaitans, "The lack of cohesion among them makes the Mala problem much more simple than it otherwise would be. It is to be hoped that no native will arise with criminal tendencies and sufficient personality to bring about any material cohesion" (1916g, 9). Even after Malaitans had organized a potent political system some officers still voiced the prewar regret that there were no chiefs or groupings on which to build indirect rule (eg, Germond 1948b, 3). The BSIP 1948 Annual Report (pages 34, 39) said that Maasina Rule expressed "the anarchistic tendencies natural to the Solomons Islanders," and that "Mission teachers and catechists acquired over the years a dominating position rivaling that of the traditional elders. This loosened the bonds, based mainly on magic and superstition, that had united the elders with their people."

29. Fox 1962, 128–129; see Noel 1946b, 1; MAR 1946, 5; BSIP 1945–1959, 10 Nov 1947, 28; Mair 1948, 67; Fox 1948a, 20; Hogbin 1964, 98.

30. Codes 1946e; MAR 1946, 5.

31. MAR 1946, 6, 7; Grantham 1947; BSIP 1947e, 80, 82, 109; Charles 1948a, 3–4. Later, against the charge of holding illegal courts, Heber testified, "I only did what Mr. Forster had taught us" (BSIP 1947e, 80, 81).

32. MAR 1946, 7; Sandars 1947f; Laracy 1983, 21; see Fifiʻi 1989, 67–69. Visiting ʻAoke was Sale Vuza, now retired from the police. He had engaged in nongovernment political activity, but after this visit came out openly for Maasina Rule, and the movement spread rapidly through Guadalcanal with Vuza as the key leader (see Crass 1947d, 2; Laracy 1983, 22–23). Later he was spared the arrest and imprisonment so many Malaitans suffered despite ample proof of his extensive anti-government actions. Instead, he was sent to visit Fiji to be shown how things worked there (contra Keesing 1981, 133, he was not "exiled" to Fiji). Vuza and Steven Sipolo, then head of Malaitan police and later dismissed for Maasina Rule involvement, were married to sisters—Salome (see figure 2.4) and ʻAeringi—from Kafusiisigi in east Kwaio.

33. Davies nd, 151–152, 153; Personal communications from Toloasi Teoboo 1982, Tagiiʻau 1982, Maʻaanamae 1987, Fifiʻi 1988, Molainaʻo 1996.

34. MAR 1946, 4, 5; Noel 1947a, 3, 4. Marquand guessed 80 percent of Malaitans were "active members or fellow travellers" (1950, 2). There are no accurate numbers, and they changed through time, but Marquand worked in the far north, home to the only large anti-Maasina Rule factions.

35. Davies nd, 157.

36. Grantham 1947. Alexander Grantham was later governor of Hong Kong.

37. Bengough 1941a, 1; Sandars 1947f, 5; [1966?], 21; Deck 1948b; see Masterman 1947a; BSIP 1945–1959, Feb 1947; Davies nd, 81.

38. Forster 1946c, 6; Marquand 1950, 37; see Noel 1946b, 2; BSIP 1947e, 92. Sandars said ʻAtoomea "half-concealed" his Toʻabaita activities (BSIP 1947e, 3). Allan exaggerated the secrecy, and then offered it as typifying Melanesian religions, cults, and "secret societies" (1950a, 56–57, 91).

39. Davies nd, 96. See Forster 1945c; Takataka 1946; Codes 1946d; MAR 1947, 3; Barrow and Davies 1947; Cameron 1947d, 1947i; Davies 1947f; Trench 1947d, 3–4; BSIP 1947d, 133; Marquand 1950, 35; Nori quoted in Allan 1980b; Laracy 1983, C2; Russell 2003, 44; cf ʻOtalifua 1947.

40. Marquand 1950, 20.

41. BSIP 1945e, 1947a; Marquand 1950, 36.

42. BSIP 1945e, 1947a; Marquand 1950, 57.

43. Rutter 1947.

44. Insightful in many ways, Marquand's paper (1950) also displays a striking lack of knowledge of Malaitan lives and aspirations, of what had occurred before his arrival on Malaita, and even of Sandars's Maasina Rule policies while he was there. This would seem to substantiate Clemens's complaint, quoted in chapter 2, that Sandars did not collaborate or share information with his cadets. Marquand went to England for the Devonshire training with Colin Allan, whose anthropology thesis written there (1950a) contrasted starkly with his. Allan's thesis became influential, while Marquand's essay was mostly ignored and forgotten.

45. Davies also said neither man knew Pijin but does not explain how, then, they conducted in-depth conversations they reported having with a wide variety of Malaitans (nd, 265–266). Davies lobbied against Cameron's ideas for democratizing the native administration system, for which Marquand also argued (eg, Cameron 1947o; Davies 1947k, 1947l; Marquand 1950, passim).

46. See Sandars 1947b, 1947c, 1947f; BSIP 1947b.

47. Sandars 1947f, 1–2; nd, 136–138, 164; AR 1947, 6; BSIP 1947d, 81, 112–113; 1947e, 3, 47–48, 51; Davies nd, 51–52, 147; Keesing and Corris 1980, 169; Laracy 1983, 26–27. Davies said Forster told him Sipolo's and Sau's actions came to light when all employees were asked to declare they would not strike, and both refused (MAR 1947, 7; Davies nd, 203). Sipolo later testified he had no enthusiasm for a strike and was trapped in the middle, pressured by other Malaitans and afraid of losing his land if he snubbed them. He said he was not dismissed but resigned, giving a month's notice and leaving 30 April. Other testimony supports Sipolo's, which varies from impressions taken by Sandars, who probably overestimated Sipolo's role as a strike organizer (BSIP 1947e, 47–50). On Sipolo, see Hogbin 1943c; MAR 1944, 4; Kennedy 1967, 3; Laracy 1983, 25; 2000, 9; Gegeo and Watson-Gegeo 1989, 358. Both men lost their pensions. The police now came under Sergeant Paul Iromea of Agia, east Baegu, later a headman, then government appointee to the Malaita Council (Notes on the Records [1953?]).

48. Noel 1947a; Sandars 1947c; 1947f, 1, 4; 1947e, 79, 109; BSIP 1947e, 55–56; Laracy 1983, 25.

49. Laracy detailed how Malaitans still worked for the Catholic Church in places but did so decidedly on their own terms, sometimes refusing wages (1971, 109).

50. BSIP 1947e, 76; MAR 1947, 5; Noel 1947a, 4; Trench 1947d, 3; Allan 1950a, 52; see Russell 2003, 46. Trench reported Malaitans were perfectly happy with the old wage, since they did not really need money (1947d, 4–5). Belshaw, citing the £12 call, wrote, "In the meantime it must be recognized that the demands of local labour are at least in part legitimate: Industry in the New Hebrides, for instance, is able to pay six times the wage offered in the Solomons [the latter £2/month in 1947] with the same technical background" (1950a, 85). Even so, Noel instructed district commissioners to proffer the New Hebrides to Malaitans as an example of a colonized people working rather than striking (1947b, 3). The New Hebrides economy emerged from the war in better shape than the Protectorate's, but the contrast in wages is notable nonetheless.

51. Forster 1946c, 11; Noel 1947b, 4; Marquand 1950, 17, 21, 23; cf Allan 1950a, 52–53.

52. BSIP 1947b; Sandars 1947a; 1947d, 1; Noel 1947a, 2; Marquand 1950, 25–26, 31, cf 33; Russell 1986, 4. Davies described people telling him they had no money to pay the tax, but then when he forced them under threat of arrest to find and tender money he triumphantly declared this proved they were lying (nd, 215).

53. Bell 1921b, 1922c (quote); Meillassoux 1981, 91–98, passim; Bennett 1993, 149–151; see also Bell 1916a, 9. Another part of the argument is that capitalist states therefore benefit by preserving "traditional" communities. Allan, likely drawing on Ivens, supposed Malaita was purposely left undeveloped so as to preserve a populace dependent on laboring. I know no evidence of such an overt conspiracy regarding Malaita, excepting the early-twentieth-century worries about "pacifying" Malaita since warfare aided labor recruiting because people left to get guns or flee trouble. As seen earlier, Resident Commissioner Ashley and others cited Malaitan self-sufficiency to justify low wages. Allan's suggestions that Kwaio was left especially underdeveloped, and that officers encouraged hatred of Kwaio so as to divide Malaita down the middle, are concocted slurs on his predecessors (Ivens 1928a, 21; MAR 1949–1950, 4; Allan 1950a, 76; 1982b, 369; see Keesing 1992a, 165–166).

54. Barley, Hetherington, and Hewitt 1929, 38–39. Judith Bennett detailed economic repercussions of such labor legislation (1993, 150–151).

55. Crass 1948; Noel 1948g, 5; Laracy 1983, C5.

56. Forster 1948a. See *SCL* Sept 1925, 134; Hogbin and Wedgwood 1943, 9–11; Sandars 1947c; BSIP 1947e, 55; Marquand 1950, 24–25, 33; cf Allan 1950a, 52–53. See this book's chapter 4 re hardship from SILC over-recruitment. Though cash was scarce, Malaitans maintained their own local currencies, and shell money production increased during Maasina Rule. Hill was told in Lau that dolphin hunts and related social activities, which had declined since the mid-1920s, were revived during the movement to address dwindling supplies of dolphin teeth, a key island-wide currency (1989, 2; see Trench 1945a; Sandars 1945a; Akin 1993, appendix 2; 1999a). Most Maasina Rule donations were collected in cash since they were to be used for development projects. Later, in the 1950s, the Waiparo movement collected both cash and shell money (see this book, chapter 9).

57. Forster 1948b; and see Forster 1948c (Small Malaita). See also Bell 1918c; BSIP 1947e, 54, 76, 77; BSIP 1947d, 91, 94 (I do not know who translated and transcribed the court proceedings); Germond 1948g; this book, chapter 3, note 4. Fairymead Sugar Company already ran a profit-sharing scheme at Su'u. Allan wrote, "The traditional system on Malaita had always provided for the welfare of the aged and infirm. For many years before the war young men had gone off in their thousands to the plantations and had left the old people to look after themselves as best they could. Marching Rule preached against the evils of this exodus, and whilst expressly forbidding young men to go to the plantations said they must not leave their communities unless they were paid wages at the rate of £12 per month." Allan then portrayed the men who stayed home as pathetic loafers (1950a, 52; see Marquand 1950, 2). In his 1950 Malaita Annual Report, Allan said there was no longer a population problem in 'Are'are due to Bengough's brief repopulation project (page 2; and see Allen 1960, 159). Noel's successor Gregory-Smith, too, dismissed concerns about the impact of recruiting on communities when pressed by Catholic Bishop Aubin and others (see Gregory-Smith and Bentley 1951; and Germond's comments on Forster 1948a).

58. Thomas 1990; see Lal 1992, introduction and chap 1; Kaplan 1995, 70–74.

59. Forster 1948b; Nicoll cover to Noel 1947a; Bennett 1987, 308–309; 1993, 162–163; Frazer 1990, 199–203; see Naitoro 1993, chap 5. Frazer 1990 gives an excellent summary of later changes in the labor system. He observed that recruiting numbers had from 1931–1940 already dropped by 43 percent, though it is hard to know how much that reflected the Depression and how much Malaitan refusals to enlist (1990, 193; see also Frazer 1973, figure 3.1; this book, chapter 3). He wrote that against implacable planter demands for resumption of the old system, pressures from outside and above were dictating change, but, he said, "certain officials … could not tolerate … the idea of Solomon Islanders exercising any influence on the debate" as to "how much and at what pace it would change" (1990, 193, 200). He named no officers, but it is important to point out, and we will see, that in early 1947 certain key officials, especially Sandars and Noel, did think Malaitans might have a role in the debate, for example by unionizing. I have found no officers who dealt with the 1947 strike threat referencing the external pressures, though later officers did. Toward the end of the war, the Anglican *Southern Cross Log* published a glowing defense of indenture as of great benefit to Islanders and the only alterna-

tive to imported labor (Jones 1944–1945). Belshaw advocated abandoning indenture and partly blamed government's reluctance to do so on "the alarm of planters at the prospect of having to deal with free labourers, able to leave employment at any time they chose" (1950a, 86).

60. Palmer 1947; and quoted in Noel 1947f; Noel 1947d; see Bennett 1987, 288. Davies said Noel told him Nori also tried to arrange labor with Levers in Honiara in mid-July, and presents this as a shocking betrayal of the movement. He makes no mention of the pending arrangement with Palmer, which he must have known about (Davies nd, 264; see Belshaw 1949b, 12). It is unknown if Nori negotiated sincerely or was merely placating Noel. Nori later testified that he consulted with the other chiefs and they agreed to work with Palmer and to meet again on 2 September to discuss the issue, but arrests began on 31 August (BSIP 1947e, 84, 89). Many Kwaio Maasina Rule veterans recalled to me a universal enthusiasm for maintaining the strike.

61. A more basic problem was how to feed workers. In the same memo, Trench told Noel that some of the plantation workforce had recently "been paid off for lack of rations" (1948b, 1, 2). Davies recalled that a lack of overseas shipping in 1947 "made it virtually impossible to feed labourers in the numbers required even if they had been available" (nd, 160).

62. Noel 1947a, 3–4; 1947b; see Davies nd, 213.

63. Noel 1947c, and cover letter to Sandars; Charles 1947a; Sandars 1947f, 1; Cameron 1947f.

64. Noel 1947c.

65. Noel 1947c; see Crass 1947a, 1947b.

66. Cameron 1947b, 1947c, 1947d, 1947g; and see Cameron 1947h; *Sydney Herald* 29 Aug 1947, 1; BSIP 1947d, 80; 1947e, 57. Ganifiri was away during the water confrontation (BSIP 1947d, 83). As detailed in chapter 5 of this book, Cameron later determined Kwai area "courts" had been legal and their standard of justice high (1947f; see 1947e). Russell was told that "Cameron was picked bodily up and thrown back into his dingy at Kwai [or possibly Fokanakafo]" (1986, 1), but Cameron did not report this, as surely he would have had it happened. Davies later wrote that he always met "red-eyed hostility" at Kwai, and that Siru was "a dogmatic, domineering old reactionary" but with "a high sense of duty" (nd, 77, 79). Siru had been five years in the constabulary before Bell appointed him headman. In mid-June 1947 Sandars replaced Siru in acting capacity with David Dausabea of Fokanakafo, a former constabulary member and since 1930 an assistant headman in northern Kwara'ae. He was a movement adherent but later a loyalist and crucial mediator between government and movement leaders (Cameron 1947g; and see this book, chapter 8). Siru formally remained senior headman, and Forster visited him in mid-1948 and reported: "He is unpopular and distrusted by the people. He is rather weak and shifty and harbours desires for revenge against those who have humiliated him in Marching Rule" (1948e, Kwara'ae). Dausabea formally replaced Siru on 1 August 1952. Before that, Colin Allan again suggested Ganifiri to replace Siru, though Ganifiri had by then spent three years in prison for sedition for his Maasina Rule leadership (1952b, 8).

67. Sandars 1947d, 1947f; MAR 1947, 7B.

68. Waleanisia 1987. Writing this after mass arrests were ongoing, Marquand added, "Surely the Government owes such people better consideration than they

are at present receiving" (1950, 39). Government clerk Teioli described a similar protocol at a late-1949 'Aoke meeting (1951), but Tom Russell told me that men carried weapons at some later meetings (2010 pers comm). Allan described the meetings held before the arrests (which he did not see) as "accompanied by mass-hysteria" (1950a, 59).

69. Sandars 1947d, 1947f; BSIP 1947d, 95–96; 1947e, 2, 56–57, 84; Marquand 1950, 13, 38–39; Waleanisia 1987; Fifi'i 1982a, 1988 pers comm. Noel, still believing Nori was getting Palmer recruits, regarded the strike cancellation "as face-saving" and "therefore satisfactory" (1947d). He later told the BSIP Advisory Council the strike threat was dropped because "the workers were not prepared to tolerate inter-ference with their desire to work for themselves" (BSIP 1945–1959, 10 Nov 1947). Sandars testified that the chiefs "had taken my advice" (BSIP 1947d, 2). Palmer said Nori told him that before this meeting east Kwaio men were angry and "became very critical of their leaders, whom they accused of mismanagement, neglect," and that serious trouble was averted only by Nono'oohimae and George calming them (Noel 1947f). Nori was not at this 'Aoke meeting, and reliable Kwaio witnesses told me people were angry at leaders for failing to arrange for enough food, a basic duty of anyone calling people together on Malaita. Yams were taken from a local garden, which Fifi'i compensated the owner for, and there was no real danger of violence (Molaina'o 1996 pers comm; Ma'aanamae 1997 pers comm). Shadrach Dio and Kifo had warned the head chiefs not to bring all of their followers to meetings due to insufficient food (Laracy 1983, C28, C30). Fifi'i's book confuses the two 'Aoke meetings and wrongly puts Nori at the second (1989, 70).

70. Ivens 1918, 77; 1972, 57, chap 5; Sandars 1947d, 1947e; BSIP 1947e, 56.

71. Native council members later had to be "heads of lines." In practice, unof-ficially, young men often stood in for these "heads." When Cameron advised council membership be officially opened to others, Davies sharply opposed this, wanting to exclude men with political views he scorned. He evoked Ashley's old perspective: "I consider that it is important to maintain... traditional authority however slight. The Marching Rule has created hordes of 'New Men' without traditional authority, or roots in the social structure, and I suggest that it is important that the Marching Rule, in its present mood of destructiveness, not be allowed to destroy what such traditional hereditary authority exists" (1947k; see Forster 1948i; Germond 1948a).

72. MQR June 1940; Bengough 1941a; Waiparo 1944; Sandars 1947f, 3; Davies nd, 41–42.

73. Noel 1947h, 6; Germond 1948d; Forster 1948a, and Germond comments.

74. Sandars 1947c; 1947f, 3; BSIP 1947e, 56. The record is confused here since 'Are'are people used the terms *alaha* and *alaha'ou'ou* interchangeably, and *alaha* had been helping arbitrate cases there for years (BSIP 1947e, 68). People retroac-tively also applied *alaha'ou'ou* to leaders before July 1947, even where the title was not used before that (eg, BSIP 1947e, 69).

75. Sandars 1947c, 1947d, 1947f; BSIP 1947d, 134; 1947e, 2, 42, 56–57, 66, 95, 109. Nori, Heber, and George were not at this meeting. Helpful to Sandars on *alaha* was Anifelo of Kwaio, then in his late thirties. He had under Sandars been a young police bugler, a corporal, and then assistant headman. Sandars called him "a good man, loyal and fairly well educated." Anifelo outlined to him a plan for the *alaha* system, but it is unclear how much it was a Maasina Rule plan and how much his personal vision. Having known him well, I suspect it was partly the latter. He alone

told Sandars a paramount *alaha* would stand for all Malaita (Anifelo 1947; Sandars 1947f, 5). After the June meeting, Noel and Nicoll had to deny rumors in the international press that Malaitan "native warriors" had attacked Honiara "with spears and blowpipes" (*Chicago Daily Tribune* 1947).

76. Sandars 1947f, 4, 5; and see Sandars 1947c; BSIP 1947e, 95.

77. See Anifelo 1947; Forster 1948c, July; Marquand 1950, 15; Keesing 1978a, 65; cf Trench 1947d, 4.

78. See Marquand 1950, 15; Akin 1993, preface; Boggs and Gegeo 1996, 288–289. Geoff White described how people of neighboring Isabel, unified as Anglicans, have by contrast with Malaitans preferred to combine these bases of leadership in one person (1991, 203). This encapsulates a fundamental difference in the outlook of the two islands' peoples. Forster told of quite different generational relations toward Maasina Rule in east Guadalcanal (1950, 2).

79. In court, Kifo testified, "The chiefs tried to stop Alaha-ohu from being used but the people said they were to function." By this he meant that most chiefs wanted to wait until Sandars gave them Noel's reply, but the "common people" refused to wait (BSIP 1947e, 89; see also BSIP 1947d, 134). Sandars was unusual among senior officers in having an inkling of the meaning of *alaha'ou'ou*. Allan bizarrely wrote, "Alaha'ohus were appointed as a kind of gestapo to maintain unity in the ranks of the movement and ensure that the directions of the nine chiefs were fully understood and obeyed" (1950a, 32; see Trench 1947d, 4). In his 1970s manuscript, Davies said Maasina Rule "established alaha'ohu and held illegal courts throughout the length and breadth of the island," though in his 1947 Annual Report he described the position (highly distorted) as planned but never realized (nd, 243–255, 262; MAR 1947, 5B–6A).

80. Sandars 1947e; see Sandars 1947f, 4–5; MAR 1947, 7B; 'Elota quoted in Keesing 1978b, 157.

81. BSIP 1947d, 9, 21, 23; 1947e, 43. Later, in 1948 and 1949, there were occasional reports or rumors that men here and there had been chosen to be *alaha'ou'ou*. Anifelo later claimed to be Kwaio's *alaha'ou'ou* but was little recognized as such.

82. See BSIP 1947d, 112–113; 1947e, 3, 38, 47–51, 52. A "*kastom* book" by Ganifiri ([1940s?]) lists three offices below *alaha'ou'ou: alahaba'ina* (big *alaha*), *alaharamo* (*alaha* of fighting), and *alahatotora* (meaning unknown). These were likely the three "assistant *alaha'ou'ou*" positions. Belo was from the Tae Lagoon in northern Lau.

83. 'Atoomea 1947a; Marquand 1947a, 2; 1947b, 2, 4; MAR 1947, 8; BSIP 1947d, 21–22; 1947e, 44, 53, 80, 81; Ma'aanamae 1996 pers comm; cf M. R. Meeting 1947.

84. Cameron 1947g; see also Cameron 1947e.

85. Davies nd, 97, 139.

86. Davies nd, 94, 127, 136, 158.

87. Davies composed the work (which is nicely written) with his diary and his own and other officers' reports at hand. Though he rarely cited the latter specifically except when quoting them verbatim, their presence is evident to anyone with access to the same reports. Davies said he had read most academic writings about Maasina Rule (nd, ii).

88. Davies nd, 186, 215, 225, see also 306–308.

89. Davies nd, 343.

90. MAR 1948, 3; Davies nd, ii, 244, see also 157, 206, 215–216, 228. Belshaw, like Davies, said Malaitans did not understand their own movement: "The purpose and

program of the movement are not comprehended by the ordinary native, if indeed they are by the leaders" (1947a, 192).

91. Davies nd, 164.

92. Davies nd, 240, see also 234. As I mentioned earlier, Noel in May did cite intelligence from Davies and his superior Ken Crass when warning High Commissioner Nicoll that suppression might soon be required on Makira (1947c).

93. Davies nd, 267.

94. Cameron 1947h. Malaitans treat gravely curses by children due to the danger they pose to others, and responsible language use is a basic part of a child's education. A serious curse by a boy of nine would typically lead to his relatives paying compensation. In this case, five-shilling fines were levied. Noel later told the high commissioner that the court's crime was not in hearing the case but in imposing fines rather than compensation. This followed the practice of government-sanctioned courts: when parties were Christians whose church forbade paying or accepting compensation, a fine might instead be paid into the treasury. Noel later cited this aspect of the case to explain to the Advisory Council how Maasina Rule courts did not follow true "native custom" as claimed (Noel 1947h, 3; BSIP 1947e, 32, 101; 1945–1959, 10 Nov 1947).

95. Cameron 1947h, 1947k; Marquand 1947b; Davies 1947c; nd, 264, 267; Masterman 1947e; Noel 1947i, 3. Charles later found four of the justices (Lenisi, Taloi, Iduina'o, and Taba'ania) innocent of the charges but guilty of "attempting to effect a public mischief" (1947e).

96. Davies nd, 268–269.

97. Davies 1947c; nd, 268, 269, 271; Noel 1947e.

98. Charles 1947b; Noel 1947i, 5, 7.

99. Noel 1947g; Cameron 1947f.

100. Cameron 1947k; Marquand 1947b, 2.

101. Cameron 1947j, 1947k; Davies 1947c, 1947d; Nicoll 1947c.

102. Masterman 1947e; Marquand 1947a; Noel 1947g; 1947i, 7; Charles 1947e, 2; Deck 1948b, 2; Nori quoted in BSIP 1947e, 83, on people's answer to Sandars. After the arrests, Noel renamed anti–Maasina Rule factions "moderates" intent on resisting Maasina Rule's "extremist leaders" (BSIP 1945–1959, 10 Nov 1947, 27).

103. Cameron 1947k, 2; Noel quoted in Masterman 1947d.

104. Cameron 1947k, 3; 'Atoomea 1947b; Marquand 1947a; Noel 1947i, 1–2; BSIP 1947e, 54, 78, and esp 105–106; Idukana 1948. Maekali in 1947 resigned under pressure, but the next February Davies convinced him to reassume the position (Davies nd, 337). Six months later Cameron wrote, "Maekali's...conception of Government is that of a former era, almost of 'time belong Mr. Bell'" (1948g; Maekali headed Bell's constabulary for over a decade). Kwai was different: Headman Siru was scorned and almost everyone there belonged to Maasina Rule. Siru's continued presence impeded cooperative relations, but officers feared his dismissal would be read as the government backing down. The mid-June appointment of Assistant Headman Dausabea as Siru's de facto replacement had alleviated but not transformed the situation (see Cameron 1947e, 1947g, 1947k; BSIP 1947d, 79–82; 1947e, 54, 111; Allan 1952b, 8).

105. BSIP 1947d, 9, 20–23; 1947e, 10, 87–90, 91; Burt 1994, 193. Kifo did tell some that Sandars had said he had to ask Noel, but that he had replied that they would not wait. But he told others that the government had given them permission

to go ahead and hold courts. Bobongi and others at the chiefs' trial blamed Kifo for fooling them into holding courts, and Kifo, against court advice, took blame "for all that is wrong in Lau district." Kifo later blamed the other chiefs for not telling him and others what Sandars said, but he participated in both the 30 June and 1 July 'Aoke meetings (BSIP 1947d, 22, 37–38, 39, 125–126; 1947e, 43–45, 87–89).

106. Noel 1947g; 1947i, 2–6; Nicoll 1947a; Tomlinson 1949; see also Noel 1947h.

107. Noel 1947h; 1947i, 5, 6, 7; 1947j; 1947k; 1947m; Nicoll 1947b, 1947e, 1947f; Davies 1947d, 2; see *PIM* 1947a. For a photo of Nicoll, see *PIM* Jan 1953, 19.

108. Cameron 1947l; BSIP 1947d, 23–24; 1947e, 10–11, 99–100; AR 1947, 7–8. Lau's first head chief, Loea (who had just returned from prison), was Molea's father and approved his becoming assistant headman. Increased tensions at this time may have been fed by leaks of the arrest plans. For example, on 5 August, 'Aoke Hospital's Senior Dresser Sam Lamani wrote a letter to Maukona in the north, warning, "Take back your £1 from the Marching Rule.... The things I told you last time, it soon be happen, not very longer, not very soon," and saying that when he heard it *was* happening he was to "run quickly to 'Fauabu'" and say "I am not in M.R." This letter was circulated and soon came into Nori's hands. Arrests had already been made by Crass on Gela and by Colin Allan on Isabel (Lamani 1947; Noel 1947k; cf Trench 1947a, 1; BSIP 1947d, 124; see BSIP 1947e, 10–11; Davies nd, 273, 282).

109. See BSIP 1947d, 23–24; 1947e, 10–11, 99–100; AR 1947, 7–8. In finding Maasina Rule seditious, the judge Charles cited remarks by unknown persons in the crowd about not wanting Kakalu'ae as "we don't want the headmen," though there was testimony that Kakalu'ae alone was the target of the people's animosity there (BSIP 1947e, 100). In Pijin, a distinction between singular "headman" and plural "headmen" is unmarked, unless *oloketa* (from "altogether") is added to make it inclusive.

110. Davies 1947e; nd, 274–277; Noel 1947k, 1947l, 1947m, 1947n; Nicoll 1947d.

111. Davies nd, 274, longer quote 276.

112. Davies 1947f; nd, 280, 282.

113. Davies nd, 283; MAR 1947, 8b; BSIP 1947d, 32, 37. On Belo going to 'Aoke, see also BSIP 1947e, 99. Deck alleged that the previous spring there had been "a secret move of the people of north Malaita to 'fight' the Government," but that Nono'oohimae had stopped it (1948a). I know no evidence for this.

114. Noel 1947o.

115. Davies nd, 281, 282; Noel 1947o. Sandars remained "disappeared" in the archives for years; references to past Malaita administrations name Barley or Bengough, but rarely Sandars. Russell wrote in error that Sandars left Malaita to retire, "and it is arguable that he avoided any confrontations with the Movement while he was still in charge" (2004, 4), which might imply that he intended to pass the problem on to his successor. Russell told the facts as he knew them, and what his misreporting suggests is the degree to which Davies's view of events became the accepted one that later officers learned (see also Russell 1986). Sandars's autobiography refers to Davies only briefly, as "a very nice fellow," and says merely that Sandars decided to retire after his operation (nd, 124, 142).

116. Article 24 in the Order's original 1877 version allowed the high commissioner to demand a security from a British subject he thought "has committed or is about to commit an offence against the Pacific Islander Protection Acts of 1872 and 1875 or is otherwise dangerous to the peace and good order of the Western Pacific

Islands" (quoted in Boutilier 1984, 4). Charles did not cite this article, which was clearly targeted at unsavory Europeans.

117. Charles 1947d; BSIP 1947c; see also Allan 1950a, 26, 59.

118. Noel 1947p.

Chapter 7: Suppression and Resistance

1. Davies nd, 280 (re Fijian soldiers). Many Malaitans for decades after resented people of the west, especially Choiseul, for their role in suppression, and some blamed Nori's early death from meningitis on 30 November 1952 on Choiseu-lese sorcery (see, eg, Russell 1950e; Andersen 1952o; *Parliamentary Debates* 1981, 225–227; see Zoleveke 1980, 44). Allan later took pains to play down the legacy of divisiveness caused by the use of Western Solomons police (1989, 96–98; cf Allan 1950m, 4; Germond 1949b). Assisting in early arrests were European "special con-stables" from Honiara: Harvey Gorrie, Charles Lamond, and John Bergelin.

2. Trench 1947a, 1947b, 1947e; Cameron 1947m; MAR 1947, 9; Noel 1947s; BSIP 1947d, 33–35. Noel falsely told Nicoll that the only exceptions to his "native complaint" reason were two men who obstructed arrests. By early October arrests totaled 100 on Malaita (most in the north), 10 on Guadalcanal, 20 each on Gela and Isabel, and 40 on Makira. By the end of October, 230 had been jailed, and by early December, 380 (Noel 1947x). After that, most of those arrested would be Malai-tans, followed by Makirans (Noel 1947s; MAR 1947, 9). Allan later perpetuated the "native complaint" justification and a falsehood, passed on to later officers, that the chiefs were all arrested in a one-day operation (1950a, 61; see Russell 2003, 47).

3. Trench 1947a, 1947b; Cameron 1947m; Noel 1947r, 1947s; Marquand 1947d, my translation of his Pijin; 1947e, 4; 1950, 15; *PIM* 1947a; BSIP 1947e, 97; Lamond testimony in BSIP 1947e, 39; Allan 1950a, 61 (cf Davies 1947l, 2). Nicoll, concerned to distance the warships from the punitive actions, told the press that the visit of *Warramunga,* and by implication the other warships, was coincidental and had been planned for months. Submarine HMS *Amphion* called at Santa Ana off the eastern tip of Makira (*PIM* 1947a; *Manchester Guardian* 19 Sept 1947, 8).

4. Cameron 1947m, 1947n; Davies nd, 304.

5. Cameron 1947n; BSIP 1947e, 59; personal communications from Sulafana-mae 1982, Laefiwane 1982, Ma'aanamae 1987, Gwanu'i 1996, anonymous 1996; see BSIP 1947e, 59, 72. Fifi'i's uncle Kwarialaena, who translated Cameron's speech, and the other headmen feigned surprise when Cameron told them he had come to take Fifi'i. In 1982 and 1987 Fifi'i gave me detailed accounts of his arrest, and his book has another (1982b; 1987; 1989, 78–81). I verified with several witnesses Fifi'i's claim to have averted a clash, perhaps saving the lives of Cameron, his party, and many Kwaio. Fifi'i's account matches Cameron's on most of the points that both cover. One man pressing Fifi'i to resist was Alefo, who had spent 14 years in prison for killing one of Bell's soldiers. A close friend of his told me that he was still bitter over his time in jail. Cameron guessed the crowd at 400, but a much larger group, including most of the women, was in a nearby clearing (Fifi'i 1982b; 1987; 1989, 78–81; personal communications from Tagii'au 1981, Ri'ika 1982, Ma'aanamae 1996). For more on Alefo, see Keesing and Corris 1980, 142, passim. Davies said Cameron told him that Kwaio "had been working themselves up into a frenzy" when

he arrested Fifiʻi, while Wairokai people met his "Maasina Rule must finish" speech as he arrested Nonoʻoohimae with "puzzlement" (nd, 301, 304).

6. Davies 1947f (see also Davies nd, 347); Nicoll writing in BSIP 1945–1959, 10 Nov 1947, 27. See also AR 1948 (page 27), from which the *Manchester Guardian* published quotations (24 Aug 1949, 4). In his later manuscript Davies said Basi "was supported.... by a band of very aggressive thugs and maintained his position by threat of force, which was not a remark one could conscientiously make about most of the other main Marching Rule leaders" (nd, 12). The yellow press, most notably the reactionary *Pacific Islands Monthly,* often outdid even Davies's portrayals, stressing communist inspiration and guidance (eg, *PIM* 1947c, 1948a, 1948b).

7. Noel 1946b; BSIP 1947e, 61 (Ganifiri), and 86 (Nori); Marquand 1947a; 1947b, 4; 1950, 29 (quote).

8. Noel 1947d; Trench 1947h, 3; Marquand 1950, 29; ʻAtoomea 1947b; BSIP 1947d, 47, 57; 1947e, 45, 54, 61, 82, 105, 109; Cameron 1947o; cf Allan 1950a, 28, 41–42, 90. Laracy noted the popular nature of the movement (1983, 31). For a broader statement of this colonial perspective re African leaders, see Furse 1962, 306; see also Guha 1989. The court verdict on the chiefs said they were guilty of conspiracy regardless, since, "If the real leaders were the rank and file of the movement, as the nominal leaders have alleged, [they were bound] to them not to disclose the criminal objects of Marching Rule" (BSIP 1947e, 131). Russell later wrote, "While Chiefs and a hierarchy of sub-chiefs were appointed island wide they were, I believe, representative rather than a cabinet of policy makers" (2004, 9). For Allan, chiefs embodied "the rise of the hero-leader" typical of messianic movements (1950a, 95–96). Belshaw portrayed followers' relationship with leaders as, "We'd cut off our hands if he told us to" (1947a, 192).

9. Marquand 1950, 27. Marquand argued that headmen were "paid tools of the Government" and so should no longer be heads of councils, and that in any case they would never be accepted as such (1950, 48). Allan advocated reviving the long and fruitless colonial search for a hereditary Malaitan leadership on which to base indirect rule and explained the chiefs' popularity and headmen's unpopularity by asserting that few headmen had hereditary status while more chiefs did (1950a, 40–42). The nonhereditary chiefs, he said, were mere "upstart politicians" (MAR 1949–1950, 12; cf Allan 1960, 163).

10. Davies 1947g; Marquand 1947c; Noel 1947s; Newman 1947; BSIP 1945–1959, 10 Nov 1947, 26–27; *Sydney Herald* 18 and 19 Sept 1947.

11. Nicoll in BSIP 1945–1959, 10 Nov, 26, and Noel on page 28; Noel 1947b; Davies 1947i (but cf Davies 1947k); Cameron 1947o; Trench 1947h, 5, 6; AR 1948, 26; see also Caulton 1950. Councils and courts were suspended on Malaita, Makira, and Guadalcanal in September, although a few continued with ambiguous status (BSIP [1947f?]). On how difficult it was for Islanders to complain about prewar labor conditions, see Frazer 1990, 194.

12. Trench 1947h, 4–5, 7; Allan 1950a.

13. Noel 1947j, 1947q, 1947t, 1947u; Davies writing in MAR 1947, 9; Marquand 1948b, 1; Waleanisia 1987, 6; see Nicoll 1947e and 1947h for measures he wanted taken to resume normal relations.

14. Trench 1947d, 1947f; Nicoll 1947i; Noel 1947v, 1947w; Charles 1947b. Charles in the new year advised that some prisoners be charged not with conspiracy but with "public mischief" or assault and false imprisonment, and he laid out evi-

dential guidelines, which were contradicted by much of the evidence he would soon
accept in the sedition trial (Trench 1948a; see Charles 1948a).

15. Noel 1947w; Moore 1947; Trench 1947g, 1947h, 2; BSIP 1947e, 1; see Fox
1942–1949, 20 May 1948; Sisili 1949, 1. Davies later wrote, "The accused were not
provided with legal aid, nor did they ask for it, although Marching Rule funds could
have well afforded the cost.... It was of course not a satisfactory situation to have as
examining magistrate a person like myself who had been responsible for the arrest
of the accused and unearthing all the evidence against them. While I did my best to
conduct the hearing as if I knew nothing about the case I was privately convinced of
the guilt of most of them.... My original understanding had been that Headquarters
would deal with this case and most of the other legal work involved in the arrests,
and my personal view was that not only had I been let down but that it was wrong
in principle to involve me in the case" (nd, 321–322). I can find no evidence that
Davies protested at the time. On Charles's guilty verdict, Davies said: "At least now
an independent judge had found that Marching Rule was a subversive conspiracy,
and that it did not exist solely in Davies' fevered imagination. Charles was no tool
of the Administration either, even if he was concurrently its Legal Adviser, and I
had no doubt that he had done his damnest to be even-handed" (nd, 338). Fifi'i in
1987 told me that funds were set aside for legal defense or to pay fines, and later
(1989, 85) said it was Davies himself who refused their requests for a lawyer. Six
months after the trial, Charles wrote in reference to other cases that a sedition case
"is a difficult one to try, and one in which the accused should have benefit of a trial
before a lawyer who can also assist him in his defence" (1948e, 3). One key prosecution witness, John Siho of Small Malaita, testified that Davies had coached his
exam testimony, and complained that in the transcript Davies had attributed to him
more incriminating statements than he had actually made about a defendant. Siho
was bitter about Maasina Rule people's criticism of the Anglican Church, for which
he was a lay teacher. He remained an informant, receiving pay, at least into 1952,
reporting on Malaitans and Catholic priests. Allan called him a "self appointed spy.
Not usually reliable." By early 1949 he had been barred from every village in southern Malaita and moved to Honiara (BSIP 1947e, 32, 33; Siho 1949, 1950; Allan
1952b, 15).

16. As historical evidence, these transcripts must be used cautiously. Several witnesses testified to wrong dates or chronologies. Some for the prosecution obviously
distorted events to vilify defendants. Some defendants overstated their unequivocal
cooperation with the government, and Kifo, at least, lied. A few testified that they
had never heard anyone speak angrily about the government or that they had heard
nothing of Maasina Rule being on other islands, both clearly false claims, at least as
translated. The translation of multiple spoken Malaitan languages and Pijin into an
English transcript was fraught with hazards in this legal context where precise wording could be crucial. For example, a Pijin statement, "*Mi nating save long* Maasina
Rule on other islands," might be translated as "I don't know about," perhaps a true
statement, or alternatively, "I don't know if there is," surely a false one. The government thought such knowledge a key point to the charge of widespread conspiracy.
Some translators translated from languages that were not their own. Page numbers
on the trial transcripts are multiple, with errors and duplications; for citations I
numbered pages after the index consecutively.

17. One seized code was presented as asserting "the claim to impose the death

penalty," coupled with a separate "black list" of movement enemies. I have seen several 1970s and later codes that list a death penalty for certain offenses, but their group authors, people I know (and I watched some of these codes composed), gave the old penalty simply to stress the severity of offenses that had become more common (eg, incest) and the consequent need for serious penalties. Across Malaita from 1944 through 1947 individuals and groups produced many hundreds of documents stating varied opinions, and many were sent to chiefs. This is still common in *kastom* politics, and any chief receives unsolicited papers. I have watched groups compose codes targeted at and even sent to rivals to enumerate disagreements with them. This occurred during Maasina Rule as well, for example the codes discussed in chapter 5 compiled by Christians to protest *kastom* codes with ancestral rules. Thus any chief might hold documents that did not express and might attack his own ideas. Further, multiple copies of forged letters circulated purporting to be from everyone from US officers to head chiefs. The latter continued to appear after the chiefs were jailed (see, eg, Letter 1948a; 1948b, likely forged as Nono'oohimae's [see Allan 1950e; 1950g, 8–9; Masterman 1950f, 6]). The government presented writings in different hands, authors unknown, to incriminate chiefs in whose village they were seized as well as "the Marching Rule" writ large. Any lawyer would quickly have exposed their worthlessness as evidence (eg, BSIP 1947d, 33–35, 99–101; 1947e, 39–41).

18. This charge was at the top of each defendant's "Statement of the Accused," filed at the end of the preliminary exam record (BSIP 1947d), and also opens page 1 of the trial transcript (BSIP 1947e). Charles selectively applied the date change, presumably made because the movement was not forbidden until 15 August, and then only verbally. His verdict stated, "Although as to some of [the defendants], the evidence does not establish any active participation in Marching Rule activities after 14th August 1947, I have no doubt from their admissions as to the duration of their membership that they continued to be members after that date." Six lesser defendants he judged not guilty due to lack of evidence of participation after that date (BSIP 1947e, 131). Most defendants would have been unaware before their arrest that the movement had been verbally declared illegal, except perhaps through rumor. Indeed, the declaration was apparently not itself legal. After the trial Divisional Officer Germond indicated that it had *not* yet been made illegal (1948c), and High Commissioner Nicoll on 2 September suggested looking into whether it should be (1947g). Norman Deck told Germond the next May, "At present many are quite puzzled when a sweeping condemnation of the movement is made" (1948c; see also Geerts 1948). Germond replied, "I am not keen for the moment on defining what Government says is illegal in Marching Rule—My line is that Marching Rule is wrong—the whole of it! I am sure that the Native will understand that better than if we start saying that this is wrong and this is not and that can pass and that cannot!" (1948b, 7; see also Germond 1948f; Nicoll 1947g). Three years later Russell suggested Maasina Rule be declared "an unlawful society" (1950j, 11). Ian Frazer observed that the Unlawful Societies Act and the Seditious Meetings Act were used to suppress worker actions in early industrial England (1990, 191–192).

19. BSIP 1947e, 120, 122; MAR 1947, 9; Fifi'i 1982b, 36. More potent evidence was presented at the trial implicating Diote'e than most other head chiefs, including that he helped conduct a court and kept a prisoner sentenced in it. But Davies and

Forster "considered he did more good than harm," and he was kept as a headman. In 1949 and 1950 he was suspected of further movement activity, or at least of turning a blind eye (BSIP 1947d, 84; Trench 1949; Allan 1950k, 4–5; cf Davies nd, 320). Deck said George had renounced Maasina Rule at a September SSEM conference, and though conceding he likely did this to "save his own skin" (arrests were ongoing), argued that he should serve a shorter sentence than other chiefs (1948b, 2).

20. See Charles 1947b; for a post-trial explanation of this to chiefs, see Germond 1948d.

21. In 1950, when officials in London asked why so many people were being arrested (and they only knew about the tip of the iceberg), they were told that these courts had "imposed fines on those who were unwilling to co-operate with Maasina Rule" as part of movement "attempts to coerce the local population into obedience with its dictates" (Secretary of State 1950; see Tomlinson 1949; *Manchester Guardian* 6 Nov 1951, 6). Trench and Gregory-Smith also gave the press false propaganda (see Sullivan 1948; *PIM* 1950c). Colin Allan wrote in his master's thesis, "Offences which came under the notice of these tribunals included refusal to accept the principles of the movement, disobedience of communal orders, non-payment of marching rule taxes, and breaches of native custom which had been recognized by the movement" (1950a, 32).

22. See Charles 1948a for his instructions to officers on these issues. The month before the trial, Marquand had written, "There has been much talk of violence but since arrests of members of the Marching Rule organization began, there has been no charge of violence. The only approach to violence being one case of rape and several cases of duties carrying truncheons" (1947e, 4). I know of no rape connected to Maasina Rule. As noted earlier (this book, chapter 5), Marquand thought these courts better than the government ones (1950, 14, 35). Six months after the trial, Cameron recommended that courts be soon restarted in the north with participation by "former Marching Rule justices" (1948g).

23. Bobongi and Heber received the same sentences as the other head chiefs. Tried with them was Brown Zalamana of Santa Isabel, charged with carrying Maasina Rule there and to Gela from Guadalcanal. He had not been to Malaita since before the movement started. The government tried but failed to connect him directly to the Malaitan activities, despite one witness falsely placing him in 'Are'are during their organization. Since Brown was not so connected, I do not deal with him here (see Charles 1947c; BSIP 1947e, 35–37, 113–117; White 1991, 200–203).

24. BSIP 1947d, 3. Kakalu'ae, son of Kwaisulia, the most powerful late-nineteenth century "passage master" in the north, had been reappointed Lau's headman the week before Nori's visit. Sandars, whose brief testimony mostly favored defendants, was moved up to appear first in the actual trial since he was about to leave the Protectorate (BSIP 1947e, 1–4, 11). The timing of his departure was lucky for the government (or perhaps something other than luck) since defendants would surely have called him as a witness. Laracy published excerpts of trial testimony and cross-examinations, mostly of Kakalu'ae, Steven Sipolo, and John Siho (1983, 114–134).

25. BSIP 1947d, 4–13, 15–20; 1947e, 77, 86; see Fifi'i 1989, 66–67. Saeni testified he was Kakalu'ae's "servant," and said, "I am as his son," but denied that Kakalu'ae had told him what to say (BSIP 1947e, 8–10). Kakalu'ae acted as court translator for Lau witnesses and defendants. England Kwaisulia remained a Lau resistance leader into 1952, and later helped found the Remnant Church (see Burt 1983; Maetoloa

1985). After meeting England Kwaisulia in 1961, District Commissioner Michael Townsend wrote, "He appeared to be mentally deficient" (1961a).

26. Writing in the 1970s, Davies appears confused here; he struck out "June" and replaced it with "1945," but June 1946 was correct for Nori's tour of the North. Trench, the trial's prosecutor, thought Nori had patrolled Lau and spoken with Kakalu'ae in 1944 (Trench 1947h, 2–3; see Davies nd, 250, 328).

27. Davies nd, 115.

28. See, eg, Trench 1947h, 2–3; MAR 1947, 5B; Germond 1948b, 2; Davies 1948a; nd, 328; Allan 1950a, 56–59; Russell 2003, 44; 2004, 10. SSEM missionaries also propagated this tale (eg, *NIV* Sept 1949, 11). After this Davies often reported "usual bogus villages" where he visited, even after months of open defiance, but did not say what their new deceitful purpose was. By then, other officers were reporting *too many* people living in some towns. Russell later recalled many towns in the north "were not occupied all the time" from mid-1949 into 1950, a period of government raids and mass arrests, but he also thought they were deserted when he visited "as a deliberate act of unfriendliness toward Government," and because people were away during certain gardening cycles (MAR 1947, 5B; Russell 1949a, appendix III; 1986, 2; see Moore 1950). Again, many bush people had alternated between inland and coastal towns, and many lived primarily in the former after arrests began.

29. BSIP 1947d, 2; see also BSIP 1947e, 5–7, 24, 62–63, 70, 99, 102. Kakalu'ae may have recognized that being head chief would wreck his relations with his long-time benefactor the government, but defendant "Kabouie" (Kaoboe, "Cowboy") put it to him in cross-examination that he really resigned because the Lau people were about to depose him and he quit to avoid that humiliation. Kakalu'ae did not refute this and said perhaps people disliked him because he was cautious (BSIP 1947d, 11). It was England Kwaisulia, with Loia, who had informed Kakalu'ae that he was to be head chief (BSIP 1947d, 10–11; 1947e, 4). An officer later described Kakalu'ae as "Self-educated, reserved, the complete snob, yet a die-hard Tory.... imposing his own brand of enlightened despotism" (Notes on the Records [1953?]).

30. BSIP 1947e, 123, 128, 130, 131; see *PIM* 1948a.

31. Noel 1948b. Defendant Ifiamae was convicted with the others but put under a £5 bond and ordered to report regularly to Davies since "The only thing against him is that he was a member of Marching Rule," and he "did not participate in any harmful activities" (Charles 1948c; see note 18, this chapter.) For the full list of defendants and their sentences, see Laracy 1983, D1.

32. Vaughan, 4 Sept minute, encl in Freeston 1948a; Charles 1948g. Charles retained his BSIP position until May 1953, when he departed to become a Hong Kong magistrate (1953–1956), high court judge in Nigeria (1958–1963), then a judge in Northern Rhodesia, and (dates unknown) a puisne judge on the Zambian Court of Appeal. In 1966 he became a special lecturer in law at Australia's Monash University.

33. Davies 1947j; MAR 1947, 9; see Burt 1994, 190. Given the deep resentment of Siru in the area, the dismantling was probably a protest, but Davies said he did not know for sure.

34. Marquand 1947e, 2. He counseled against arrests for refusing communal work (eg, tax house repairs), which would "undoubtedly result in the arrest of a considerable number of people which, in view of our intention to collect tax, might not at the moment be advisable." Instead, Marquand said, if Charles approved, they

should fine "heads of lines" if men in their communities failed to do such work, and if they refused to pay, imprison them (1947e, 3).

35. AR 1947, 9B. As Tom Russell told Ben Burt in 1986, "It was a holy writ here in London that the tax was symbolic of fealty to the crown," and for this reason, even when it was destined for deposit in local council funds, it was seen to be crucial that government officers collect it (Russell 1986, 4; see also Russell 1950f, 4). Forster had censused 'Are'are, so they were not required to be censused now, but Masterman in April 1950 nonetheless used the census as a weapon to send 'Are'are men to prison (Masterman 1950f, 1–2, 6).

36. Noel had split the Protectorate into two "divisions," each headed by such an officer: The Southern, containing Malaita, Makira, and Santa Cruz, was run by Germond based at 'Aoke. The Northern, containing Western District (New Georgia, Isabel, Choiseul, and the Shortlands) and Central District (Gela, Russells, and Guadalcanal), was run from Tulagi by Peter Hughes, also fresh from Africa (Basutoland). The system proved unwieldy and the respective duties of district commissioners were poorly defined. In early 1949 a new system was adopted, with four districts: Western, Central, Malaita, and Eastern (AR 1948, 33; A Sandars 1950, 1).

37. Davies nd, 339; Germond 1948a, 1948b; Noel 1948a, 1948b, 1948c; see A Sandars 1950, 1–6.

38. Davies nd, 339. Davies on this same page suggested Noel was pressured to take a mild approach by the Labour government in London, and perhaps also by officials in Fiji due to their "personalities" or career worries. I have found no evidence of either, or of Davies having called for sterner measures that Noel rejected. Davies never returned to Malaita, but Noel soon made him district commissioner of the far more benign Western District.

39. Germond 1948a; 1948b and cover letter; see Davies nd, 324–328, 333, 339.

40. Germond 1948b, cover letter.

41. Marquand 1948a, 1948b; Deck 1948a, 4 and 21 March; Forster 1948a; Davies nd, 339.

42. Marquand 1948a; Forster 1948c, 1948e, 1948i; Ma'anamae 1987 pers comm. Allan, who was not then on Malaita, said the first fence was built at Irofa'alu's village near Malu'u. Some artificial island dwellers at Ferasubua, 'Ataa, and elsewhere moved from coastal towns back to their islands, which Forster thought had no political meaning. Later some of them occupied coastal towns yet again (Forster 1948e, Lau; Russell 1949a, 4; Allan 1950a, 63–64).

43. Marquand 1948a; Germond 1948e; Forster 1948a, 4; see Kwara'ae Native Affairs Book, 8 May 1952. The fences' cleaning function would be to demarcate the area that needed to be kept in order—bush hamlets have exact borders for this and for purposes of taboo application. Town populations typically included people with primary land rights there and, under Malaitan land tenure principles, the right to permit others with no such rights to live there. Christian villages had been settled on this basis for decades, often over objections of other primary owners.

44. Noel 1948d; Masterman 1948; A Sandars 1950 (quote, while acting RC). By mid-1948 only seven Malaitan policemen were serving on Malaita; in mid-1950, there were 23.

45. Noel 1948e, 1948f; Germond 1948k; Charles 1948d, 1949b; Forster 1948d; Germond 1949f. See Charles 1948e and 1948f on his expansive definition of "sedition."

46. Cameron 1948a, 1948b, 1948d; Germond 1948i; Allan 1952a. Allan (1949c,

15–17) and Russell (2003, 51–52) described Malu'u station in 1949; for Malu'u later, see Frazer 1973, 44. It had been hoped to also open a station at Kwai, but resources were insufficient.

47. Noel 1948f; 1948g, 4; Forster 1948b; Allan 1949c, 19; see *PIM* 1949.

48. Cameron 1948d; Noel 1948g, 2.

49. Germond 1948i; 1948l; Cameron 1948d; 1948e. Germond suggested that when the To'abaita soon surrendered officers should set up trade classes, run soccer games, and show movies to win over the young men (Germond 1948j). Allan said India's independence in August 1947 passed unnoticed in the Solomons (1989, 90), and I found no evidence that Malaitans had heard of Gandhi, or for that matter of colonial India.

50. Noel 1948g, 2, 3; Freeston 1948a; Germond 1949a. Newspapers often presented as fact government accounts of Maasina Rule, but in late 1949, after Noel had left and Germond was acting in his stead, the *Chicago Daily Tribune* reported, citing no source, "The Solomons, although governed by a resident, are administratively under Fiji, three days away by small ship. The resident can easily block Fiji from learning what goes on. His sole opposition comes from an advisory council. When the discussion there gets awkward, he shifts it into camera (secret), which means that no minutes are sent to Fiji for his boss to see." Consistent with this, the reporter said Freeston had just told the press, "Marching Rule is broken up and...whole districts have decided to accept British authority" (Pope 1949).

51. Cameron 1948f, 1948g, 1948h; Forster 1948e, 1948g; Marquand 1948c; Deck 1948e. Later, SSEM head K E Griffiths gave sermons with a similar message (MQR 30 Sept 1951, 2).

52. For example, in November 1948 Freeston reported to Secretary of State for the Colonies Creech Jones that the situation was much improved, though it demanded "unremitting surveillance." Freeston anticipated the time—"I trust that this will not be long delayed"—when people would stop regarding officers "as oppressors and not as advisers and friends" (1948b).

53. Marquand 1950, 15, 17, 22–23, 26, 47.

54. See Allan 1949c, 4; 1950a, 40–41; MAR 1949–1950, 8.

55. Forster 1948f, 1948g; Germond 1948m; 'Elota quoted in Keesing 1978b, 160; personal communications from Tagii'au 1981, Sulafanamae 1981, Saelasi Lounga 1982, Fifi'i 1982, Gwanu'i 1996, Basiberi 1996, Ma'aanamae 1997. Former policeman Titiuru told me in 1987 that some structures were so massive as to require a full day to destroy with axes, and Kwaio have boasted to me of their sturdiness. Russell saw some built of sunken logs over three meters high (1949a, appendix III, 2; 2003, 47). After this same tour Forster stated, "Marching Rule will come to an end in the Lau Lagoon in the near future" (1948e). For months officers sought Anifelo and his US carbine, which his younger brother Laefiwane kept in the Kwaio bush until the 1980s (Anifelo 1981 pers comm; Laefiwane 1982 pers comm).

56. Forster 1948h, 1948i; Hughes 1948; personal communications from Sulafanamae 1980, Anifelo 1981, Ma'aanamae 1987. Hughes called Naafinua people "passive but surly" and 70 were jailed. 'Aoke had a women's prison in the 1930s, mostly for adulteresses (Sandars nd, 36).

57. Forster 1948h (and Trench response); 1949b, To'abaita; Father Stuyvenberg to Dubois, 29 Oct 1949, in Laracy 1971, 101; Fox 1962, 131 (and see 129); see Russell 1949a, 3; 2003, 48; Allan 1949c, 5, 12; 1950g, 18; and Forikeo 1951. I have also

not found what befell women Marquand arrested for "inciting others" after they rebuilt Abu's fences, as noted earlier (1948c). Forster reported that in March 1949 men were assigned to stay home in the Malu'u area, where all the area's other men were soon jailed (1949b). Four months later, though, Russell saw malnutrition among northern women and children, and an Anglican doctor, George Hemming, was "gravely concerned by this result of Government policy" (Russell 1949a, appendix III). The next year, then–District Commissioner Masterman wrote, "The arrests and comparatively severe sentences on whole sections of the native communities have naturally led to misery in the villages; indeed, I have used this misery of the women and children to point the moral of the law-abider as against the law-breaker, and the Missions have not sought to influence my actions in principle" (1950f, 10; see Gregory-Smith 1950e). On 10 October 1948, Noel went on leave, then retired.

58. Germond 1948o; 1948p, 2 (quote); ARs 1948, 26; 1949–1950, 38. For the idea that "degradation of women was a measure for the degradation of a society," see Thomas 1994, 102, passim; see also Thomas 1992a.

59. Hughes 1949a; Allan 1949c, 7, 12 (and see 5); 1949a, appendix III; Titiuru 1987, 5.

60. Titiuru 1987, 5. This is probably the incident Fox referred to: "There was [an] occasion when a District Officer, threatened by a large and hostile crowd of armed men, had to retreat with his police into the sea." Fox, often unreliable, also said he saw police beaten in one town (1962, 131). I have found no other reports of either episode—a puzzle, given the eagerness of some officers to portray the movement as violent. Titiuru held sympathies toward Maasina Rule. He was at one time a warder over the head chiefs, who liked him for his kindness, especially in secretly giving them extra food (Titiuru 1987 pers comm; Fifi'i 1987 pers comm).

61. Belshaw 1947a, 190 (and see 192; 1950b, 128); AR 1949–1950, 38; Allan 1950a, 26, 59–61; 1951c, 96; 1951e, 3; Davenport and Çoker 1967, 128; Campbell 1978, 298; Zoleveke 1980, 44; Laracy 1983, 177; Guidieri 1988, 189; Davenport 1989, 274; see also Grover 1955, 13; Hogbin 1964, 98; Worsley 1968, 179–180; Coates 1970, 295; cf Stanley 1975, 180. Oddly, several scholars wrote that the Maasina Rule man killed the policeman (Worsley 1968, 180; Laracy 1976, 125; Campbell 1978, 300—all citing AR 1949–1950, 39, though that source has it correctly, ie, the other way around). Russell received a concocted history of violence from his predecessors or their reports (1950f, 13), and perhaps others did as well. Belshaw seemed to refer to the ineffectual Langalanga protests at 'Aoke in June 1946, described in chapter 6 (though he spoke of them as "demonstrations"). He then warned of flare-ups: "Sudden shouting by distant men, an action trivial in itself yet mystifying to natives in the vicinity, is enough to work them into a frenzy of excitement, which, in the presence of mass hysteria, can make them irrational and savage" (1947a, 192–193). Later the same year he wrote, "Two or three incidents occurred, but nothing of real importance" (Belshaw 1947b, 11). Against violent portrayals, the *New York Times* years later reported the "Marxist-tinged" movement had promoted a policy of "free love" (Durdin 1966; see Belshaw 2009, 14). The true numbers of arrests for civil disobedience were concealed from the press (eg, *Fiji Times* 1950).

62. Hughes 1949b; Russell 2003, 4. Malaitans had portrayed jail time as "eating government rice" since the 1920s (eg, Hogbin 1933), and such stoic portrayals bolstered a fallacy among some whites that Islanders did not mind imprisonment and required still harsher punishments like flogging.

63. Allan 1949c, 8; MAR 1949–1950, 9; Marquand 1950, 38; Russell 2004, 5. From March 1949 until he left in June, Marquand as DO Auki was relieved of most arrest duties (Germond 1949b).

64. Germond 1949a; 1949d; Allan 1949c, 3; Marquand 1950, 16, 17; Russell 2003, 47–48 (cf Russell 1949a). Leaf shelters slept 200 prison laborers each, overseen by one warder (Russell 1986, 2–3; see Allan 1949c, 16). District Commissioner Stanley Masterman later stopped work on the road and sent more prisoners to Honiara (1950c, 7).

65. Germond 1948p; see also Germond 1948n; Masterman comments on Russell 1949a, 6. Russell recalled the census was "not in any way related to taxation" and that it was illegal to use census data for that (1986, 2), yet Germond is clear here and elsewhere that for him the census was intended for tax roll compilation (see Germond 1949a, 2, 3). Allan claimed in mid-1950, "It was found in 1949 when it became necessary to execute mass arrests on the fence and census issues in North Malaita, the headmen in the different areas were able to sit down and write out the names of every adult male between 16 and 60 in their respective areas. This would have been sufficient for assessing the population for taxation purposes" (1950g, 26). After its use as a political weapon, it was years before the government could conduct a true census; Allan wrote in 1952, "Vital statistics cannot yet be collected as census is still politically blacklisted. The mere suggestion of counting heads sends the population running for miles" (1952b, 24). Some refused to be censused even in the 1980s.

66. Forster quoted in Malaita District 1949; Hughes 1949b; Germond 1949b. Cameron went to Fiji and never returned.

67. Cameron 1949; Forster 1949a; Charles 1949a; Germond 1949c; Hughes 1949a, 1949b. Three weeks later Freeston remitted the sentences but did not refer the cases to the appeals court. A few months later a "manifesto" by Ariel Sisili was labeled possibly "seditious" because it said, among other things, that people had been "arrested and sentenced without fair trial" and Sisili was later imprisoned partly for writing it (Sisili 1949, 1; Russell 1949c, 2; see Laracy 1983, 162).

68. Andersen 1954c, 2; Russell 1986; 2004, 10. For arrest numbers, see Noel 1947x; AR 1948, 21. The coming year would be no better in Eastern District, from which Fred Bentley reported an "appalling" figure, as of 31 May 1950, of 2,000 arrested without incident (1950).

69. This highlights the cost of discontinuity of knowledge across generations of officers, with no organized system to transmit it. At other times confusions or misrepresentations were passed down for years, a prime example being Davies's 1947 Malaita Annual Report, which taught officers into the 1950s about the tyrannical nature of Maasina Rule before Operation Delouse. This could lead them to continue policies that had generated the very problems they inherited.

70. Germond 1949a, 1949b; Allan 1949b. Langalanga and west Kwara'ae were under the district officer at 'Aoke until mid-1950, when the district commissioner was relieved of touring and he became responsible also for all of Kwara'ae, Kwaio, 'Are'are, and Small Malaita (Masterman 1950c, 2). Of 2,147 Jericho arrests by early March, 847 were for census refusal (Allan 1949a; Marquand 1949b; Germond 1949a). Keesing erred in saying Allan was Malaita's district commissioner in charge of Operation Delouse in 1947 (1992a, 148–149, 165).

71. Allan 1949b. Also popular at this time were beards, which Russell was told

would be kept unshorn until Maasina Rule prevailed (2010 pers comm). This played on an old practice of a murdered person's survivors adopting mourning dishevelment until the killing was avenged or compensated. The SSEM's Gibbins, too, noticed Maanawai and 'Oloburi men "wearing the Moscow beard and hat which is a tenet of their creed" (1950).

72. Allan 1949c, 7, 9–14, 18, see 19, and for detailed arrest statistics, appendixes I and II. The 1,060 would not have been 76 percent of men north of Kwara'ae; perhaps Allan meant the percentage of men arrested in just the To'abaita area that surrounded Malu'u station.

73. Germond 1949b; Freeston 1949b; Masterman 1949; Devlin 1949; A Sandars 1950, 6–7.

74. BSIP 1935; Masterman 1935; Ashley paraphrased in BSIP 1938; Russell 1986, 2; 2003, 57. Prison Superintendent E Nelson Turner, a man with his own malevolent reputation among Malaitans dating at least to the 1927 punitive expedition, reported, "There was not the slightest justification for this assault" (1935). Ashley answered Masterman with sympathy: "I am sure you regret your action and I realise that you did it in a fit of temper which, in this climate, it is not always easy to have under control, but I trust you will be more careful in future" (Ashley 1935c; see Masterman personal file BSIP 1/P1/M58/22/1, esp Masterman 1949c). Russell was told that Masterman was the oldest platoon commander at the Normandy landing (2003, 56).

75. Collins 1950. Masterman for a time headed the punitive expedition base camp at Sinalagu, and patrolled inland, in 1927–1928. There were no riots in east Kwaio.

76. Germond 1949e. Later, Resident Commissioner Gregory-Smith was upset that men jailed for refusal to pay tax were, on their release, ordered to pay it; he considered this illegal, as in fact it was (1950–1952, 19 Nov 1951; see BSIP 1951a; Russell 2004, 5).

77. Masterman 1949a; see Masterman 1950f; Fox 1951; and documents in BSIP 4/SF108/V. On rumors of violence, see Masterman 1949b. Masterman denied and Germond rejected Ulawan allegations. Witnesses whom Masterman interrogated in 'Aoke withdrew their statements. It is hard to know what really happened, but many Malaitans undoubtedly heard of and believed the charges.

78. Russell 1949b. Russell later described foot tours of the sub-district, which took 10–14 days (2003, 54–55). Masterman toured almost exclusively by ship (Russell 2010 pers comm).

79. Russell 1949a, 6, appendix III, 1, and Masterman comments; see Russell 2004, 10. Some small children still run screaming from unknown white visitors, for their parents have warned, "If you don't behave, a white man will come and get you," a remedial tactic predating Maasina Rule.

80. Proverb from Ivens 1928a, 280.

81. Lindstrom 1993a, chap 2. See Cochrane 1970; Belshaw 1972. Anthropologist Ian Hogbin did not revisit the Solomons after 1945 but portrayed Maasina Rule's later stages as a "millenary cult" that claimed to be "divinely revealed," with rituals that would bring cargo (1964, 96–98; see Lindstrom 1993a, 36–37). The cargo cult model attained perhaps its most pathetic crudity in the hands of John Gutch, high commissioner from 1955 to 1961 (1961, 77; 1987, 113; see also Belshaw 2009, chap 1), although his predecessor Harry Luke wrote that Bell had been assassinated by cargo cultists (1962, 133).

82. Noel 1947a, 4; 1947b; Trench 1947h, 1, 5; Belshaw 1950b; see Belshaw 1947a; 2001, "Messianic Movements"; 2009, chap 1; Davies 1950c. Elsewhere Belshaw said the movement's concerns were largely economic, and that it was "an irrational expression of legitimate grievances" (Belshaw 1948, 97). At times he advised sensible solutions to problems behind the grievances (see Belshaw 1947b). In his 1950 article, for information on Maasina Rule he said he was "indebted to conversations with administrative officials in London during 1949"; he did not say if they included Allan, then in England writing his thesis on Maasina Rule (Belshaw 1950b, 15). FE Williams's *The Vailala Madness* (1977) greatly influenced Allan (1950a) and, later, Officer Glynn Cochrane (1970).

83. Allan 1950a, 54, passim; 1952b, 1 (see 1957a, 52, 249–254; 1960, 162); Davenport 1998 pers comm; see Barrow nd, part 3, 5; AR 1968, 100; Gutch 1987, 113. Allan summarized his thesis in *Corona* and *South Pacific* (1951a), after approval by the then–resident commissioner, Gregory-Smith, who encouraged him to place it in popular venues (BSIP 1950c; see Allan 1950h, 3). The *Manchester Guardian* (1951) quoted the latter to praise government's handling of Maasina Rule (and see *PIM* April 1951, 90). The first BSIP usage of "cargo" per se appears in Davies's 6 April 1947 notes for a report to Crass on a US survey ship visit to Makira and beliefs that "Americans were soon coming back to drive out the Government, and that all the people must belong to the Masina Rule by that time; that free cargo would be distributed to members of the Masina Rule and that the Americans would kill those who were not members" (undated note in front of BSIP 8/IX/6; Davies 1947a [the report]; see Crass 1947b; Davies quoted in Laracy 1983, 150–151).

84. AR 1948, 28; Allan 1950a, 1. See also BSIP 1945–1959, 1 Nov 1949, 6; Kaplan 1995, xiv, passim. On Malaitan avarice and laziness, see Forster 1946c, 2; Barrett 1947, 1 Jan; Noel 1948a, 4; 1948c; Russell 1949a, Masterman comment; Allan 1960, 162–163; Burt 1994, 200. When Malaitans refused material lures to abandon resistance, this, too, could be attributed to the movement's "mystical appeal" (eg, Russell 1950f, 11). David Gegeo wrote that Salana Ga'a, Federal Council leader and then president of the Malaita Council, believed the British used the cargo cult portrayal to undermine the movement's legitimate platforms (1991, 32). See Guha 1983 for examples from British India of colonial portrayals of resistance movements as psychological or religious phenomena, which denied insurgents true political consciousness. Later, former District Officer Glynn Cochrane took the opposite view and argued Maasina Rule had little to do with material concerns and was about status deprivation (1970; see Belshaw 1972; Anderson and Anderson 1980–1981, 6 April 1981, 11). Cochrane's dissertation adviser, Kenelm Burridge, presented a broadly similar but far more sophisticated analysis of New Guinea movements (eg, Burridge 1970).

85. *Sydney Herald* 1951 (1st quote); 1950 (2nd). See *Fiji Times* 1950 for devious distortions, including Maasina Rule reduced to a cargo cult, attributed to Resident Commissioner Gregory-Smith. On "stock cargo themes," such as natives awaiting refrigerators, see Lindstrom 1993a, 139–142; 1993b. Refrigerators were included in Europeans' lists of cargo items Maasina Rulers were said to wait for, particularly lists provided to the press by Makira planter Henry Kuper. Also quoted by the press was Major H S N Robinson, the Melanesian Mission's general secretary, who told *Pacific Islands Monthly* that he saw a neat row of 43 houses built on Malaita's coast awaiting expected cargo (later quoted in Worsley 1968, 178; see *PIM* 1946a; *Sydney Herald*

1947; Tomlinson 1949; Gregory-Smith 1950e, 1). Robinson traveled with Kuper, and figure 7.1 shows the two holding a Maasina Rule flag described in the same *PIM* story (*PIM* 1947b; see *Time* 1947; *South Pacific* Sept 1947, 17; Burrows 1950). In 1950, Russell reported cargo houses at Sinalagu, and he may have been told that is what some structures were (1950f, 6), but I was unable to find any Kwaio who had ever heard of such houses. See Buck 1989, 158, on invention and exaggeration in "creating 'cargo cults' as an object of analysis," and links between this and New Guinea labor issues.

86. Russell, for example, noted that people erected "cargo houses for the American food" and "cut large stacks of firewood to cook it," and that this led to Maasina Rule being called a "Cargo Cult," but he said that such ideas "were always a peripheral element in the movement" (2003, 46; see Russell 1949a, 1–2, and cf Masterman comments; 2004, 3; see Osifelo 1986, 22. See also note 85).

87. Worsley 1968, 182; Keesing 1978a, 68, 243 (quote); Laracy 1983, 150; see Ross 1978a, 184; Fifi'i 1982a, 17; Osifelo 1986, 22.

88. MAR 1946, 5; Sandars 1947f. Sandars was that July the first Malaitan officer to use "cargo" in this connection, though *kago* was also an everyday Pijin word for goods or baggage. An informant report from Makwanu said Head Chief Loia "gave to the people a great deceiving that's on January 1st 1946 the cargo will come." The letter, which contains other dates, was written later, by "Gilbird Chief of Funafou," probably in early 1947 (Gilbird [1947?]). I do not know if Loia really said this.

89. Translated from Kwaio except for the Pijin terms. Lounga here likely condensed several rumors into one statement. At Maka in the south in March 1945, Melanesian Sisters and a Brother said they saw submarine silhouettes and heard engines, and Davies believed Japanese subs had recharged batteries there. More important, in mid-1946 Royal Navy subs *Tally Ho* and *Talent* visited the Solomons and one of them called at most of Malaita's main harbors (Bentley 1945; Trench 1945b; Davies nd, 35, 119–120). Some Malaitans had also seen submarines during World War II.

90. Lounga 1982 pers comm. Mountain people who helped build the palisades and towers, but did not live there, also told me that Forster accused people of preparing for war, and that this surprised them since they had not envisioned the structures serving that purpose (personal communications from Ma'aanamae 1981, 1982, Laefiwane 1981, Sulafanamae 1982).

91. Forster 1948i; Ma'aanamae 1987 pers comm (quote). Fewer non-Christian Kwaio families lived on the coast then; Lounga's was one. Some 'Oloburi bush people stayed on the coast for as much as a week, but police did not raid there then (personal communications from Sulafanamae 1980, Lounga 1982, and Basiberi 1996).

92. Keesing 1978a, 70; Laracy 1983, 150–151; Burt 1994, 200. Burt, too, collected multiple and contradictory perspectives on cargo, in east Kwara'ae (Burt 1983 personal communications, and his 1983 interviews with Ben Banau, Adriel Rofate'e, and John Gamu).

93. Field 1949b, 4; Russell 1954b, 3; 2003, 58; Keesing 1978a, 68–70; Davies nd, 83–84, 123–126, 134; Fulbright 1986, chap 4; Burt 1994, 200; see Davenport and Çoker 1967, 134. See this book, chapter 8, note 44, for one influential *PIM* article copied and circulated around Malaita, in a related context. Fulbright suggested that Allan brought the cargo idea to Malaita from the Western Solomons, but the timing denies this. Allan on 1 March 1947 reported Western District rumors that

Americans would bring a "political millennium," and people were planning to make curios to sell to them, but he said nothing of "cargo" ideas. He did note that rumors were on the rise with increased contacts with north Malaita, implying that they were flowing east to west (Allan 1947, 4; see Allan 1989).

94. *SCL* Oct 1950, 243; Teoboo 1982; Waleanisia 1987; Fifi'i 1988 pers comm; 1989, 71; Gegeo 1991, 32; Burt 1994, 194, and his 1983 interview with John Gamu; McDonald 2003, 72. Many archived letters tell of meeting Americans or claim they will soon arrive (eg, "To Every Passage" 1948; Laracy 1983, F1–F3). Those who spread rumors could be jailed (eg, Russell 1949a, appendix 3, 2). There were precedents of loyalist headmen starting rumors to rile people: Siru spread word that Sandars was about to seize land at Kwai (see this book, chapter 5, note 66), and later Headman 'Itea (from Fokanakafo) told 'Ataa people that "if they did not pay their taxes the Government was coming to kill the men, cut off the breasts of the women, steal all the pigs, burn the houses, slaughter the children and generally cause havoc far and wide" (Allan 1950o, 8). 'Itea, whom Russell (2003, 66–67) said was his main informant for his *Oceania* article, about this time suffered a mental breakdown. Allan blamed the illness on the guilt he guessed 'Itea must have felt for teaching Russell about "custom," and on the fear Allan imagined 'Itea had that "If the people persisted in holding the Government to custom, there would be no progress, no enlightenment, no development. The people would continue to be down trodden by ancient and useless taboos, embittered and jealous old men, pig headed priests, frauds and the like." However, there is no indication that 'Itea told Allan this. Two years later, 'Itea became an ancestral priest, until he became an Adventist in 1957 (Allan 1950o, 10; Clive Moore 2012 pers comm; see Russell 1950a; 2003, 65–67).

95. See Laracy 1983, 150–151; cf Cochrane 1970, 96. On the rationality of "cargo" responses in Melanesia, more broadly, see Worsley 1968. Burt, too, stressed that cargo was "not associated with spiritual forces" and was grounded in recent experiences (1994, 200). On predicted American punishment of loyalists, see, eg, Kenipuria 1949. Keesing discussed cargo ideas in terms of "anticipations of religious escape" (1978a, 67). While rumor and ignorance led some Malaitans to consider ideas that were erroneous and fantastic, the same was true for some officers; officials as late as 1950 considered plausible the idea that a white or black person, perhaps an American deserter, was orchestrating Maasina Rule operations in secret or from a mountain hideaway. Officers worried over secret communist ties, or that there might be a war during which an unnamed "reactionary force" would arm recalcitrant Malaitans (eg, Noel 1946b, 4; 1947d; *PIM* 1946a; 1947b; Gregory-Smith 1950e, 2; 1950f, 4–5; Masterman 1950f, 12; Germond 1950b; Russell 1950j, 3; Allan 1951k; see *PIM* 1950b, 83; Caulton 1950; cf Cameron 1948c).

96. AR 1948, 26, 38. See also Davies 1950c; Allan 1950a, 92–94; 1951a, 99.

97. Holton 1945; MAR 1945, 1; Trench 1945b; Burt 1994, 186–187; and 1983 personal communication to him from Ariel Rofate'e. Oral accounts I have are mostly Kwaio and Kwara'ae. Little history has been published on this topic from elsewhere on Malaita (for Makira, see Davies 1947a and esp Scott 2007).

98. Fifi'i 1982 pers comm; 1988 pers comm (quote); 1989, 70–71; and quoted in Keesing 1978a, 66. Fifi'i at times confused the two 'Aoke meetings with Sandars. Here, in a 1964 statement to Keesing, and in his book, he said that Kifo said Americans would come in January, placing it after the Boxing Day meeting. But

in parts of his book and in an interview with me he seemed to say Kifo's talk came after the 30 June meeting (Keesing 1978a, 65; Fifi'i 1987 pers comm; 1989, 70–71). Other Kwaio can provide no date except "shortly before Fifi'i's arrest." Davies said hopes of American arrival intensified in late 1946 and early 1947 (MAR 1947, 5), consistent with the earlier date. But that people emphasize that it was just before the arrests suggests the latter, which also coincides with north Malaitans' worsening relations with the government and Kifo's rise to prominence.

99. In Kwaio, only Noto'i's group at Uogwari stayed in the mountains, and some very old and young people (personal communications from Toloasi Teeboo 1982, Fifi'i 1988, and Gwanu'i, Ma'aanamae, Bebea, 'Otomoori, 'Otaalea, Molaina'o, and Riufaa, all 1996). Davies's 1947 Malaita Annual Report (page 5B) told of old people abandoned to starve, and burnings of houses of those refusing to locate to the coast in response to rumor. But this did not happen in Kwaio, nor is it reported anywhere else, and like much in Davies's report, it is probably a concoction. Davies also related that some old people were carried to the coast, and some Kwaio who were living near the sea did do this (Gwanu'i 1996 pers comm). Fifi'i said loyalists misled Kifo; Kifo was his friend, though he came to see him as a rascal (1982b; 1988 pers comm; 1989, 711; see Kwaio Native Affairs 1951, 17 Aug). Keesing guessed Kifo intended his actions to divert the movement from moderate southern leaders (1978a, 67), though I know of no evidence for this.

100. Fifi'i 1989, 71; and quoted in Keesing 1978a, 66. Accounts I have of this event focus squarely on liberation, not cargo. Around this time, Nono'oohimae told recruiter Palmer that they had heard about fighting in Indonesia and feared it might spread to the Solomons (Noel 1947e, 2). Fifi'i in 1982 told an interviewer, "I get angry when I hear about this cargo. The only cargo we know is the cargo that's imported by ship from Australia.... People said we were coming down to the coast to wait for cargo?... This is something we can't make any sense of. We are not a crazy, lunatic people.... We didn't expect other people to feed us. That is not our way. We have our own gardens" (1982a, 17).

101. Forster 1949b (Fataleka), 2; Ma'aanamae 1987 pers comm; Titiuru 1987, 4 (translated from Pijin); see 'Elota quoted in Keesing 1978b, 156–57; Toloasi Teeboo 1982 pers comm. In 1949, Protectorate officials arranged to fly in American anthropologist Felix Keesing (Roger's father) to tell Malaitans that Americans would not return, but the trip had to be cancelled due to scheduling problems (Maude 1970).

102. See, eg, MAR 1947, 5–6; Allan 1950a, 91; Marquand 1950, 16; Davies nd, 88, 140. Some people said they had heard the head chiefs say cargo or Americans would come or had heard other people say they had said this, but we saw earlier that many statements credited to the head chiefs did not originate with them (eg, BSIP 1947d, 66–68, and see also 102; 1947e, 23).

103. Fifi'i in 1964 said he heard that 'Atoomea spread a rumor that soldiers were hiding in the To'abaita bush, landed by US submarines. Whether 'Atoomea believed this, as Fifi'i did Kifo's stories at first, is unknown. Others blamed such rumors on Sukulu, the West Kwara'ae chief who, with Nori, was said to have met a US general on Guadalcanal, and whom Forster had arrested with Kifo in June 1946 (Waleanisia 1987; Fifi'i 1987 pers comm; and quoted in Keesing 1978a, 66; see Laracy 1983, F1). Fifi'i in 1987 told me people sneaked up to the prison fence to ask the chiefs about rumors about Americans, and they told them they were false. After Kifo was jailed, letters forged in his name continued to spread rumors and advise resistance (Dausa-

bea 1952). See this book, chapter 6, for a claim that Timothy George said Americans would send material help.

104. See, eg, Marquand 1949a; Forster 1949b; Russell 1949a, appendix III, and Masterman comments; 1949c; Allan 1950g, 22; 1950h; Laracy 1976, 125. There had been some rumors of this sort in the south early on (eg, Bentley 1945; Trench 1947b; Davies nd, 36–37). Some tales of evil government plans originated with loyalists (see Sandars 1947f, 2; Moore 1950, 3).

105. Marquand 1949a; Russell 1949a, appendix III, 2; 1949c, 1; 1950b; 1950j, 3; Forster 1949b (Fataleka); Gregory-Smith 1950e. In Kwaio, many thought building shelters a waste of time (Basiberi 1997 pers comm). By later 1950, Allan was saying cargo stories were no longer believed, but for some people hopes for American help never fully vanished, and in places they were for decades an undercurrent of some *kastom* politics, with new rumors surfacing sporadically (MAR 1949–1950, 8; see Ross 1978b, 184). Even now some voice them, though often in desultory or semi-sarcastic ways. But in one 1985 case, a Kwaio leader was able to convince some that Americans would help them to derail a controversial government election (personal communications from Busumae 1987, Dangeabe'u 1987, Basiitau 1987, Fifi'i 1988). Today some in north Malaita hold unrealistic expectations for help from Israel, which has in fact become involved in Malaitan politics through "development."

Chapter 8: Attrition and Compromise

1. BSIP 1949; Russell 1949a, IR, 1; 1949c, 2–3; 1950e; 2004, 1; Germond 1950a; Masterman 1950f, 1–3. Marquand, back in England, denounced men who had agreed to labor (about 300 by late 1949) as "a few weak-willed traitors to the Marching Rule who lack the courage of their convictions and who have been driven by the fear of gaol and the wrath of the Government creeping and crawling to the white man as labour. Such people can only be despised" (1950, 33; the labor count is from Masterman's comment on Russell 1949a).

2. Russell 1949b; 1949c, 2–3; 1950f, 4; 1950j, 11; Germond 1949a, 1949e, 1949f, 1949g; Masterman 1949c. Allan later said the leaders targeted were "holding the people against their will" (MAR 1949–1950, 12). Russell also started to post stenciled flyers, like Maasina Rule ones but criticizing the movement (see file BSIP 12/VI/10; Laracy 1983, I2–I5; Russell 2003, 69). On 9 February 1950, flyers of biblical quotes urging tax payment and avoidance of violence were airdropped. Wrote Russell, "The pamphlets, which were about four-inches square, stuck together as the print was not dry. Packed in bundles the size of bricks, they came hurtling down in one piece, bursting through thatched roofs before disintegrating. They were collected as souvenirs and stimulated the thought: 'What on earth is the Government going to do next?'" Officers spread word that a new technology let them see from planes through clouds and roofs and into houses (2003, 70; see Masterman 1950f, 4).

3. Allan 1949c, 3; (and see 1950c; 1950o, 2); Malaita 1949, 4; Russell 1949c, appendix III; 1950f, 11; 1950h, 5; MacKeith 1950b, 1–3. Allan repeated his prediction of continued resistance in his anthropology thesis the next year. But while in the just-quoted document he based this on people's determination not to surrender politically, his thesis explains it as a result of deep-seated "beliefs in magic,

superstition, sorcery, kinship, the complicated system of leadership, and customary law" (1950a, 92, see 26). On pressures emanating from London at this time to end indenture, decriminalize breaches of contract, and improve work conditions, see Frazer 1990, 201. Frazer here also pointed to a shift that occurred from coercive to positive incentives for completing contracts (see Davies 1951a). Allan explained the labor system as of early 1952: "A man...promises to work for his employer for six or twelve months as the case may be. In law, such an agreement is on the month to month basis and may be terminated by either party with a month's notice. That is the only contract which exists" (1952b, 21). Bennett described how the penal enforcement of indenture was dropped in 1948 after negotiations between the International Labour Organization (ILO) and the British government, though this did not immediately register with all officers. She also noted that postwar pressures from Levers and other planters to reinstitute the two-year indenture period failed (1987, 308–309); the government refused them, by the early 1950s citing ILO conventions (*PIM* 1953b; BSIP 1955, 3–4).

4. Masterman 1949d; Sisili 1949; MAR 1949–1950, 11, 13; Teioli 1951; BSIP 1951d, exhibits G1 and L; Laracy 1983, 30–31; Burt 1994, 195. Various manifesto versions appeared over time.

5. Russell's account of this meeting has Masterman coolly walking away from an angry crowd to take tea with his officers. Teioli later testified in court that Sisili led men off the field as Masterman rejected each point, and by the time he reached the last no audience remained. Allan, who was not there, later cited the latter as an intolerable Malaitan insult to justify blocking further meetings, but in his next Annual Report gave the tea-taking version (Russell 2003, 62–64; 2004, 5; and quoted in Knox-Mawer 1985, 115–16; Burt 1994, 195; Masterman 1950f, 3, 8–9; cf Russell 1950f, 12; MAR 1949–1950, 14; Teioli 1951; Allan 1950g, 23; 1951e, 3). Masterman's reply, "To All People of Malaita," is appendix 6 to his handing-over report (1950f); and in Laracy 1983, 18. For his Advisory Council picks, see Masterman 1950f, 6, 8–9. He also insisted the government's choices for any future district council had to be senior headmen (Masterman 1950f, 9–10). Allan counseled that the idea of such a body "has considerable difficulty in penetrating the native mind," but did not say why (1950g, 23). Advisory Council representation was a key goal of Matthew Belamataga's "Development Society for Native Races" movement on Guadalcanal, which had some parallels with Maasina Rule (see Laracy 1983, 156–161; Bennett 1987, 299).

6. Masterman 1949e; Russell 1950b, 1, 3–4; 1950f, 5; 2004, 5.

7. Russell 1950b, 4; 1950f, 6, 7; 1950j, 12; 1986, 3; Allan 1950k, 5; 1952b, 26; Bartle 1951a, 10; see Burt 1994, 195.

8. 'Itea 1950; Ridley 1950; Masterman 1950f, 2; Russell 1950f, 6; 2003, 65–67; 2004, 10 (quote); see Tedder 2008, 31. See correspondence in BSIP 12/V/12 on rumors and fears of attacks on 'Aoke and Malu'u in February and March of 1952. Allan later sometimes reported rumors of planned violence as established fact, which justified his policies (eg, MAR 1949–1950, 14).

9. Russell 1950c; 1950f; 2003, 67–70; Taburi 1950; see Masterman 1950f, 10. The meaning of the older man's exclamation came out later; Taburi did not understand it at the time. Assuming Taburi's statement accurate, it seems certain the men would have killed the wounded soldier. Russell was displeased when Masterman would not order an official inquiry.

10. BSIP 1950a; Bartle 1950; Russell 1950e, 1; 2003, 70; Masterman 1950f, 5; Tedder 2008, 17. Russell credited the muted Malaitan reaction to government actions, including the aforesaid pamphlet-dropping plane flight one day after the shooting (1950f, 7; see note 2, above).

11. WPHC 1950; BSIP 1950a. Masterman later presented both the decision to evacuate 'Aoke after Ramositau's death and the idea of releasing Nono'oohimae as his own (1950f, 4–6). Research into Gregory-Smith's Kenya experiences might illuminate the approach he brought to the Solomons. His photo is in *PIM* Feb 1950, 13.

12. BSIP 1949; 1950a, 1; Davies 1950a, 1950b; Gregory-Smith 1950a; Fifi'i 1989, 86–87.

13. Gregory-Smith 1950a; 1950b; 1950e; 1950–1952, 19 March–5 April 1950; Russell 1950f, 8. A photo by George Milner of officers meeting loyalists at 'Ataa on this tour is in Burt 1994, 193.

14. Gregory-Smith 1950–1952, 19 March–5 April 1950; Masterman 1950a; 1950f, 4, and appendixes 14 and 15. Most people also avoided Gregory-Smith's next major tour, and with his backing Allan had Moore arrest vulnerable Langalanga and 'Aoke-area people in punishment (Gregory-Smith 1950–1952, 4–19 Sept 1950, 12; Allan 1950k, 5). Masterman had just issued another "Administrative Order" forbidding anyone joining together to meet with an officer without invitation. Ten months later, Charles called this "of doubtful validity" (see note dated 21 Dec 1950 in front of file BSIP SF108/VIII/5).

15. Gregory-Smith 1950d, 1950e; Russell 1950d, 1, 4; 1950h, 4; Colchester-Wemyss 1950; Allan writing in MAR 1949–1950, 12; 1950g, 5; see MacKeith 1950b, 2. North Malaitan 1949 tax payment percentages by language group as of 10 May 1950 were Lau 100, To'abaita 94.2, Baelelea 55.2, Baegu 32.7, and Fataleka 19.4, totaling 64.7 percent. Russell thought there were many more taxable men than estimated, however, and that if exempted men were included the true proportion who had paid was significantly less than half, with "considerable numbers to tax even in To'abaita and Lau." Only 27 percent of northern people had been censused. Tax payment numbers fell quickly as one moved south across the island, especially in Kwara'ae areas away from 'Aoke, and in Kwaio (Russell 1950f, 8–9; 1993, 71; see 1950j, 15). Two months later, after many hundreds more had paid taxes, Allan in a letter to Gregory-Smith guessed Malaita payments might be nearing half of the lower 1930s tax numbers (1950h, 2; cf 1950g, 27). 'Are'are and Small Malaita were exempt from the census since Forster had already conducted one there, and tax collection focused on the north. See Masterman 1950f, 7–9, appendix 9, for his June tax calculations.

16. Allan 1950g; Burt 1994, 196. Fifi'i in 1982 told me Masterman goaded them when Gregory-Smith was not there, telling them that they would not really be freed. Fifi'i's autobiography employs a Malaitan narrative style that has the effect of collapsing shifts in government policy over a longer period into mid-1950 conversations with Gregory-Smith (see 1989, 87–93). A plea to be released by Nelson Kifo, whose wife and children died while he was in prison, was refused. He was let go, along with Belo and Maesiedi, in November 1951, on the same terms as the head chiefs had been. Kifo did then spread a message of cooperation, telling people the government had agreed to all of Maasina Rule's demands. Gregory-Smith, acting as high commissioner in June 1952, fully remitted the head chiefs' sentences so they could serve on a Malaita-wide council (Kwaio 1951, 17 Aug; MAR 1951, 17; Dausabea 1952; and see this book, chapter 9).

17. Russell 1950f, 10; 1950h; 1993, 72. The northern headmen's verbatim comments on the head chiefs' release are provided in Masterman 1950f, 6–7.

18. Russell 1950f, 12; Masterman 1950b; 1950f, 5–6, 13–14; Burt 1994, 196. Basi was rearrested in early 1951, suspected of antigovernment activity, but Allan saw he was too weak from tuberculosis to have done anything. He died the next year (Allan 1950g; Bartle 1951a, 3–4).

19. Russell 1950f, 1 (quote); 1950h, passim; 1950j, 1, 15; 2003, 72; Allan 1950c; 1950d; 1950g, 4, 8, 11, 15, passim; 1950h, 2; 1950k, 7; Masterman 1950f, 6. Masterman said that other chiefs had, like Nono'oohimae, sent letters to their people from jail, but he did not say which chiefs or if officers delivered their letters (1950f, 5). To know this might help explain different homecomings given different chiefs. In mid-1949, Malaita's 32 sub-districts had been reorganized into just ten, roughly following, and inspired by, those laid out by Maasina Rule, each headed by a senior headman with several assistants (MAR 1949–1950, 5; 1955, 10).

20. Allan 1950e; 1950g, 1, 2, 8–10, 27; 1980b, 111; Russell 1950g; 1950h, 3. Russell said there were fewer "extremists" but more "waverers" in Lau (1950j, 15), but by January, Bartle reported most had paid the tax (1951a). Just after noting George's key role in helping the government, Allan cited his record of "letting down" officers since Edge-Partington, and added, "one can do little but hope that he will soon die, and thereby solve the problem of his own accord" (MAR 1949–1950, 18). Elsewhere Allan said he thought Small Malaita was cooperating due more to Nono'oohimae's influence than George's (quoted in MacKeith 1950a). But it was soon arranged for George to visit Ulawa to try and help there. On the Catholic Welfare Society, which later reformed, see Allan 1950i; 1950k, 8; Gregory-Smith 1950f, 3–4; MAR 1954, 15, 18; Laracy 1976, 131–134; Campbell 1978, 304–306. Leaders of other missions sometimes encouraged officers' hostility toward Catholics (see, eg, Gregory-Smith 1951d; Gibbins 1952b). In 1977 Allan said he had come to recognize positive aspects of the society and that it was not necessarily subversive (Campbell 1978, 305).

21. Allan 1950f; 1950g, 3, 11–12; Russell 1950g; BSIP 1950d; Kwaio Native Affairs Book 1951, 4 June.

22. Allan 1950g, 8; see Allan 1950l.

23. Allan 1951e, 12; Bartle 1951b, 9; Luluakalo testimony in BSIP 1951d; Ridley 1951a; Bokelema statement in BSIP 1951d; see MacKeith 1950b, 2. Allan often portrayed Maasina Rule and the Federal Council as very different, based largely on his misunderstandings of both, but at other times said they were the same (eg, MAR 1951, 19; MQR 30 June 1951, 8; see Allan 1960, 159, note 1). He called those who still used "Marching Rule" in late 1950 "ignorants and diehards on the periphery" (MAR 1951, 5). Anifelo in the early 1980s always used "Maasina Rule" in telling me about the work he had led.

24. Field 1949a; Forster 1949b (Fataleka); Allan 1950g, 15–17; Russell 1950h, 4, 6; Davies nd, 50. In the early 1950s, Irofiala asked for his medal back, but officers could find no record of it. I do not know if he ever got it.

25. Mariko 1946; Russell 1950f, 7; Allan 1950g, 18; Sandars nd, 46; Anifelo 1981 pers comm. Another leader, Ramo'oli of Baelelea, was convicted with the head chiefs and given two years for sedition. Kakalu'ae had appointed him a full chief of the Kwarade area, and both he and Ramoalafa were charged with hearing illegal courts (BSIP 1947d, 1947e). For an account of Ramoalafa's capture of the Japanese pilots, see Fifi'i 1991, 38. On Alaikona's patrols, see Sandars 1942–1943, 7, 15.

26. Lambert 1933, 23 and 31 May; 1941, 287; Allan 1950g, 20; 1952b, 13; Andersen 1952o, 6; Zoleveke 1980, 44; Ngwadili and Gafu 1988, 205.

27. Among secondary leaders, Raurau of Mota in Baelelea, a relative moderate, had been the Makwanu headman and vice president of its native court and an original Maasina Rule leader there. He was tried with the head chiefs but found not guilty. He was later made an assistant headman, but in 1949 he was dismissed and jailed for three months for accepting donations on behalf of Maasina Rule and afterward avoided all contact with officers (MQR 30 June 1951, 6). SSEM teacher Jason Frankie had been a clerk to the government's Anoano Native Council and then a Maasina Rule chief and clerk at Uru. Nelson Foʻogau, from near ʻAoke, spent his childhood around Sandars and the constabulary and was an early Maasina Rule leader (see Osifelo 1985, 12; Allan 1950k, 3–4). Mamarodo of Toʻabaita, who became more important in 1952, was ex-constabulary, as was the leader Fuliʻoa. Funuga of Lau had been Sandars's cook and an early Maasina Rule activist, and had served several jail terms (Allan 1950g, 18). Irofiala, Sau, Alaikona, Ramoalafa, and Mamarodo had all fought as members of the Solomon Islands Defence Force.

28. Chamberlain 1948; see Dausabea 1951.

29. MAR 1949–1950, 13, 19; Allan 1950g, 18 (2nd quote); 1950k; 1950n; 1950o, 8 (1st quote); 1951e, 2; Kafebai and Dioteʻe statements in BSIP 1951d; Teioli 1951.

30. Russell 1950h, 4. John Naitoro detailed links formed by ʻAreʻare who attended meetings at Bina organized by Sisili and his brother Maekiki in 1948, and the work that sprung from them, including a resurgence of town building (1993, 92–94). See Kwaio Native Affairs Book 1951, 17 Aug.

31. MAR 1949–1950, 12; BSIP 1951d, exhibit M3; Ridley 1951a; Laracy 1983, 164, 172. In 1943, a US war propaganda campaign employed the Four Freedoms, and artist Norman Rockwell designed posters for each "freedom," which were massproduced. Solomon Islanders may well have been exposed to this campaign.

32. Noel 1947a; BSIP 1947d, 42; 1947e, 11, 56, 71; Marquand 1950, 22, 29; Kwaraʻae Council 1950; Russell 1950h, 3. Laracy's book also has Sisili's "Declaration," and "manifesto" (1983, section H). For the import of the Four Freedoms in Belamataga's Guadalcanal "Freedom Movement" in 1948, see Laracy 1983, 156–160, and Bennett 1987, 299. Later, officers tried to use the Freedoms for propaganda, arguing that people already had them (*Malaita Newsletter* July 1952). Thirty years later, government compensation for Maasina Rule's chiefs was still being discussed in Parliament (*Parliamentary Debates* 1981, 225–227; see Akin 1999b).

33. West Council Malaita 1950; Martin 1950; BSIP 1950b; Allan 1950g, 19; 1950k, appendixes I and II; Gregory-Smith 1950d; Andersen 1950; Russell 1950h, 4; 1950j, 2; Shone statement in BSIP 1951d. The June bundle is often called "the Shone letters" after the man they were handed to. They were later used to prosecute Sisili and are in the file for his trial, BSIP 12/V/9. For an account of a failed 1949 Sisili attempt to send money to Americans, see Burt 1994, 194.

34. MAR 1949–1950, 8, 20; MAR 1951, 6; Allan 1950k, 2–3, appendix I, passim; 1950n; 1951e, 16–17; MQR 30 June 1951, 1; Maekiki and Luluakalo statements in BSIP 1951d, exhibits B and C. Sisili's previous ideas about getting American help are unclear—Allan blamed him for all cargo rumors, but Allan routinely did so with all Maasina Rule leaders, including many with no links to rumors. Shone gave to Nelson Foʻogau Bertrand Russell's *Road to Freedom,* a source of more ideas found in

documents (MQR 30 Sept 1951, 2). Also drawn on was Albert DeLa Vergne's 1941 book, *U.S. Army Service Memories.*

35. Russell 1950j, 1, 5–6.

36. MacKeith 1950a; Gregory-Smith 1950f, 3, 6, passim. At the Sinalagu conference were Allan, Russell, Alexander MacKeith ('Aoke's cadet officer since April, who took notes), and John Bartle, who was about to take over Malu'u from Russell.

37. Allan 1950g, 20–21; Gregory-Smith 1950f, 8; 1950–1952, Sept 1950; MacKeith 1950a. Sandars had once hunted down a north Malaitan murderer using local men supervised by police, and young men of the party damaged taro gardens and stole pigs. Sandars made them compensate the owners. Missionaries complained to the resident commissioner that "enormous damage had been done and innocent people assaulted," but Sandars did not believe them. A formal inquiry sided with Sandars, and Sandars produced an old document authorizing Bell to "call out the population" to hunt murderers, which had never been canceled (nd, 95–96).

38. Allan 1950m, 1. This singular Allan report reads throughout as if written by a different officer than the man who usually penned angry, vicious ones, and was clearly composed in a moment of introspection. A reader familiar with his usual style is surprised by his expressions of understanding for Malaitans, their plights, concerns, and strengths. This report even argues for raising the plantation wage (unchanged since 1946); for giving the Federal Council a position, with a loyalist, on the Wages Advisory Board (Nono'oohimae was chosen), and for the government to work with SSEM teachers toward mass education (1950m, 6, 9; see Frazer 1990, 202). One detects here a longing to pursue positive development work rather than suppression, and it provides a glimpse of the officer that might have been.

39. Gregory-Smith 1950–1952, 14 Sept 1950; Allan 1950j; MacKeith 1950a, 3.

40. Gregory-Smith nd, 13 Sept 1950; Allan 1950j; 1950l, 1, 3; MAR 1953, 3; see Andersen 1954d, 2, 12. Malaita had had headmen for just 27 years.

41. Allan 1950j; Bentley comments attached to Allan 1950l; and see Allan 1960, 158. Eighteen months later Allan wrote of Malaita's headmen, "At present a good deal more than half are in no way respected. Many of them are hated" (1952b, 10; and see Allan 1960, 160).

42. Allan 1950g, 21; 1950o, 8; Russell 1950h, 5; 1950i; Dausabea 1951.

43. Allan 1951e, 1, 3 (quote), 4–8; see also note 5, above.

44. Russell, 1950h, 5; MAR 1949–1950, 21; Dausabea statement in BSIP 1951d; Gregory-Smith 1950–1952, 3 May 1951. Another paper was a copy of a *Pacific Islands Monthly* article that Nelson Fo'ogau had brought to Sisili from Honiara, which argued for the Solomons to be put under Australian administration. This was a change that many European residents hoped for and discussed widely, and that Malaitans feared as the establishment of a "colony" that would steal their land. The article was hand-copied and circulated around Malaita. High Commissioner Freeston had presented an argument for Australian administration to the secretary of state for colonies in mid-1949, noting, "It is idle to inquire whether such a change would be acceptable to the indigenous population of the Protectorate, the bulk of whom are too primitive to appreciate its significance" (Freeston 1949a; *PIM* 1950a; Allan 1951e, 3, 7; Gregory-Smith 1950–1952, 4 May 1951). For the larger context of this issue, see Hyam 2010, chap 7.

45. Allan 1951e, 8 (this report contains details of the arrest). Burt was told that police beat up Sisili's wife and that Sisili forbade resistance (1994, 197). Allan later

warned the arrest was an anomalous, "lucky case" not likely to be repeated with other hunted leaders (1952b, 2).

46. For the prosecution, see file BSIP 12/V/9; Burt 1994, 197. Legal Adviser Charles told the prosecution that the letter seeking weapons had been left out of the explicit charge because the letter was ambiguous, and "it seems to me undesirable to drag in our American Allies in connection with a charge of Treason Felony" (Charles 1951). But this and other letters sent to Guadalcanal were introduced as supporting evidence. Sisili was also convicted of illegally possessing US currency for the confiscated "bank." In mid-1952 that money was credited to Malaita Council funds, with close to £1000 Allan had taken at 'Ataa in 1949 (Allan 1952b, 6; see Tedder 1954; Frazer 1973, 61).

47. Allan 1951c; MAR 1951, 6.

48. Allan's 1951 Annual Report says officers took the notices lightly, but they did not at the time. His June Quarterly Report says they had a bad effect in Lau; the Annual Report says none were posted there. Much of this Annual Report, Allan's last, presents a much brighter picture than do the reports and correspondence surrounding it. 'Are'are were able to keep Rickwood out since Allan did not want to force the issue and undercut Nono'oohimae, who claimed he had tried to convince people to allow him in (MacKeith 1951a; Allan 1951h, 1951i; Bartle 1951b; Notices 1951; MQR 30 June 1951, 1–4, appendix A; MQR 30 Sept 1951, 1, 9; MAR 1951, 7–9, passim).

49. MQRs 30 Sept 1951, 9; 31 March 1952, 2; Allan 1951e, 16; 1952b, 1. The letter to Dugdale, "Malaita Decision for One Head of the Island," is in Allan 1982a; see it and Dugdale's speech in Laracy 1983, H6, I10. In 1982, Allan claimed that by August 1951 "headmen and the loyalists" embodied "60% of the male population," who "were satisfied with the firm statements of the Minister," but he would have laughed at this claim at that time. Dugdale also visited a new government education project at Hauhui and told the people "he did not think much of mass education," leaving Allan to pick up the pieces (Gregory-Smith 1950–1952, 30 Aug 1951; Allan 1982a). The antiestablishment *Pacific Islands Monthly* called Dugdale "a babbling fool" and said his "general conduct and deliverances are still a subject of hilarity among those who met him in BSI" (1953a).

50. Waiparo 1944; Allan 1951i; 1951l; 1951n, 2; 1952b, 4, 15; MQR 30 June 1951, 3, 4; MQR 30 Sept 1951, 7–8; MAR 1951, 8, 15–18; "Notices from Bina Council" 1951; personal communications from Anifelo, Sulafanamae, Lounga, and Fifi'i, all 1982. Once the *alaha* turn against the government, Allan's reports call them "petty chiefs." One cannot discount that Nono'oohimae, still on license (ie, parole), may have overstated his rivalry with Waiparo and inability to control people. Before Waiparo challenged the government, Allan wrote he "has considerable drive and ability and is extremely ambitious to bring some enlightenment to his pagan followers, besides of course raising his own power and prestige," and Allan had tried to bolster his position as a chief essential to the government's position (1950k, 18; 1950l, 11). On Waiparo, and Kwaio links with his activities at various times, see Fifi'i 1989, 103–105; Keesing 1992a, 123, 127–129; Naitoro 1993, 130–132; and this book, chapter 9. By the end of 1951, in east Kwaio nobody had paid taxes at 'Oloburi, and very few had done so at Uru. At Sinalagu, which Allan said was "under firm government control," a few coastal and no bush people had paid. Only a handful paid taxes in west Kwaio (Allan 1951n, 2; MAR 1951, 10).

51. Allan 1951n, 4; MAR 1951, 16.

52. Allan 1952b, 2, 4.

53. Allan 1989–1990, 7–8; anonymous personal communication. For a few examples of this attitude, see Allan 1950o, 10; 1950i, 1, passim; 1951d, 5; 1951e, 2; MAR 1949–1950, 5, 13, 19, passim; MQR 30 Sept 1951. The guess of 8,000 taxable Malaitans is Andersen's (1954e, 3). Allan cited Freud and Malinowski to suggest the high levels of psychosis were "due to psychology of a patrilineal society" and sexual repression (MAR 1949–1950, 5). Someone who knew Allan 25 years later told me that his antipathy for Malaitans was still palpable. In 1978 he called Malaitans "a malign influence throughout the Solomons…comparable to the Jews in medieval Europe, the Indian merchants in East Africa and Indian Ocean and the Chinese in South East Asia" (Allan 1978). For years Allan continued to portray Malaitans as psychotic and blinded by primitive magical thinking, bewildered by change (eg, 1960, 161–162). He reserved special contempt for Kwaio (eg, MAR 1949–1950, 4; Allan 1951m; 1982b; 1989–1990, 157, 158).

54. MQR 30 Sept 1951, 12; see also MQR 30 June 1951, 9; Marquand 1950, 26. The Hauhui project was carried out from 1950 under Onepusu Headman Japen Warahimae and Hamuel Hoahania. It was to be at Wairokai, but when resisted there Allan shifted it to the area's one loyalist community. For a project summary, see Naitoro 1993, 119–121, 125–129. Soon after this, Peebles left loyalist Hauhui and took over Malu'u and less pleasant duties, and his approach became as malign as anyone's. For example, he wrote in a letter to Allan: "On the bright side, there is an unconfirmed report that Basi is dead," and apropos two wanted men, "If I can't pinch them then I will line up their friends and relatives as accessories or at least for suspicion of felony, and make a thorough go of it" (1951). Basi, feeble from tuberculosis, had been politically inactive since his release from prison. A photo of Peebles with Germond is in *PIM* Nov 1949, 8.

55. Tedder 2008, 27; see Andersen 1954d, 11; Fifi'i 1989, 92.

56. Wrightson 1952b, 1952c, 1952d, 1952e, 1952f; Andersen 1952c, 1952d, 1952f; MQR 30 June, 1, 2; see Sandars nd, 44–46. Just before Allan left, Wrightson reported Malaitans were massing to attack Malu'u and 'Aoke and to kill him and headmen, causing a panic. What Allan called "the planned Malu'u putsch" turned out to have been a rumor (Allan 1952c, 1952d; Wrightson 1952a; Andersen 1952a, 1; Tedder 2008, 31).

57. Andersen 1952i; 1954d, 1, 4, 10; Tedder 2008, 27, 33. On the cocoa scheme in the longer term in 'Are'are, see Naitoro 1993, and in To'abaita, Frazer 1973, chap 3. For the funding application for that scheme, see Gregory-Smith 1951b, and those for the other projects are in the same file (BSIP 1951c). The acting resident commissioner wrote on Andersen's March 1952 Quarterly Report, "It must be impressed upon D.O. Malu'u that under no circumstances must he give the impression of trying to take another Census." Gregory-Smith had said in mid-1951 that Islanders had to be quickly brought into the administration, with opportunity to rise to its highest posts. When he in 1952 nonetheless suggested importing Fijian staff, Andersen insisted Solomon Islanders should fill the posts, even if they were not yet as efficient (Gregory-Smith 1951c, 2). Because Malaitans lacked ways to get cash crops to market, Andersen and Tedder toured on government ships to buy them (see, eg, Tedder 2008, 33).

58. MQRs 30 March 1951, 2; 30 June 1951, 1, 5, 7; Bartle 1951b; Ridley 1951b; Andersen 1952b.

59. Wrightson 1952g; 1952h, 1; 1952j, 4–5; Andersen 1952q, 25 Aug; 1952m, 1; *Malaita Newsletter* Aug 1952; Malaita Council 1952; Stanley 1975, 175.

60. MQR 30 June 1951, 8.

61. Andersen 1952h; 1952j; 1952m, 1.

62. Andersen 1952k; 1952m, 1; Wrightson 1952i.

63. Richardson 1952; Andersen 1952h, 3; 1952m, 1. After a brief career as a journalist in England and the United States, Stanley entered the Colonial Service as a cadet in Nigeria, where he spent ten years. Between Nigeria and Rhodesia he had served in Cyprus, Barbados, and Gibraltar. His photo is in *PIM* Aug 1952, 29; see also Stanley 1975.

64. Gregory-Smith 1950–1952, 18 Nov 1951; Stanley 1953, 5; 1975, 175–176.

65. Andersen 1952l; 1952m, 2; *Malaita Newsletter* Sept 1952, 3–5. Ga'a told Andersen that Takanakwao himself had requested the meeting with Stanley (Andersen 1952l).

66. Allan 1952e; Andersen 1952l, 3–4; *Malaita Newsletter* Sept 1952, 3–4; Tedder 2008, 32. Stanley ignored advice from loyalist headmen he met with at Malu'u to fight Maasina Rule with further suppression (1975, 176–177). On past taxes, Stanley said, "I think that those who have not paid in the past have been punished enough and 'I want you all to be friends now.'" This comment was likely added since some were saying they would not pay the 1952 tax if those who had not paid before were let off. Malaitans wanted as their symbol an eagle, a sacred bird on Malaita. Officers worried that it was an American symbol, but it was later incorporated into the Malaita seal. It was decided to distribute delegates proportionally by sub-district populations: Kwara'ae 7; Kwaio 6; 'Are'are and Lau 5 each; South Malaita and To'abaita 4 each; Baelelea and Baegu 3 each; and Fataleka and Langalanga 2 each; totaling 41. In the end, only 8 were government nominated (Andersen 1952n, 1). Selections by populations were technically nominations, requiring approval and official appointment by Stanley, but in practice government was loath to overrule popular choices. In October, Fiji's Supreme Court cut Sisili's sentence to three years, and in May 1953 Stanley commuted his sentence.

67. Andersen 1952m, 2; *Malaita Newsletter* Sept 1953, 3–5; Stanley 1975, 176–178. Stanley felt his success was partly due to his ability, since he had just arrived and had no history there, to separate himself from the BSIP government and present himself as the Queen's representative (1975, 175, 177). For several years most Malaita Council members were chosen in Melanesian fashion via public discussion with no Western-style vote. Allan, exaggerating as ever the power of leaders, erred in saying they appointed members without consulting the people. A whispered ballot was introduced in 1958 (see Allan 1960, 160; Stanley 1975, 180). Council members became entirely elected under the Local Government Ordinance of July 1963.

68. Stanley 1952; Wrightson 1952k.

69. Andersen 1952m, 3; 1952o, 8.

70. Andersen 1952m, 3; 1952n; 1952q, 4–27 Oct; Wrightson 1952k.

71. Andersen 1952o; Malaita 1952, 3; BSIP 1963; Fifi'i 1988 pers comm; 1989, 92; Tedder 2008, 31. It was emphasized that the council belonged to the people since it was rumored on the island that delegates were to be a sort of government headmen. The council voted against Ga'a joining the Advisory Council (Andersen 1952o, 5) but in 1953 reversed that decision.

72. Andersen 1952p; Bartle 1952; Stanley 1953, 2; 1975, 178–179; Malaita Dis-

trict 1953; Tedder 2008, 32, 34–35, 52, 65. See also MAR 1953, 4. Like other colonial officers, Stanley arrived in the Solomons with little knowledge or understanding of events preceding him, or of Maasina Rule, which in his memoir he portrayed as a cargo cult, thanking Allan as his primary source of information (1975, 172–175, and see 205–207).

73. MAR 1953, 1, 2; Andersen 1954b. Future Malaita Council presidents would include Fifiʻi and Kifo, and Sipolo and Ganifiri were later vice presidents. Sau declined to be on the council but in early 1954 became Fataleka's native court president, by accounts one of the island's best. Takanakwao became vice president of east Kwaraʻae's court under its President Ganifiri. Timothy George's not joining the council contributed to a decline in his popularity (Russell 1955b).

Chapter 9: Gains and Losses

1. See, eg, Allan 1960, 163; Ross 1973, 59; Keesing 1978a, 53; 1992a, 122; Campbell 1978, 301; Laracy 1983, 29–31; Standish 1984, 101; Premdas and Steeves 1985, 38–39; Bennett 1987, 296; Burt 1994, 196; Coppet nd, 4; see Naitoro 1993, 95. Burt's book, with its bird's-eye view from Kwaraʻae, stands out in stressing Maasina Rule–Federal Council continuity and the fact that Malaitans gained government concessions (1994, 192–198). Keesing acknowledged the ʻAoke school, the council (which he portrayed as relatively powerless), and stronger native courts as partial fulfillments of some Maasina Rule aims (1978a, 53).

2. See, eg, AR 1974, 135. The 1975 Annual Report, in a startling turnabout, describes Maasina Rule as "the most successful experiment in local government so far," which "in many ways was more effective than the colonial administration," and credits it with spurring the government to accelerate development of administrative bodies run by Solomon Islanders (150–151). Colin Allan's often-cited writings have been a wellspring of misrepresentation.

3. Hughes 1952; Wrightson 1952k; MAR 1953, 4; see MacKeith 1950a.

4. In the Solomons one sometimes hears Maasina Rule credited with starting the country on the road to independence. The connection is indirect at best, and Britain left for its own reasons that had little to do with Maasina Rule. The movement did accelerate district council formation without the once-planned intermediary step of sub-district councils (see, eg, Anderson 1957a), and in this way probably hastened higher-level Islander involvement in government. According to Allan (1980a, 385), in 1949 a former high commissioner, Arthur Richards, suggested there would be little need to worry about independence of possessions like the Solomons until near the century's end, and for years after administrators gave it little thought.

5. Maluʻu officer John Bartle reported, just after the Malaita Council agreement was made and in the midst of rumors that government would soon leave, that many people wanted it to stay, at least for a while, perhaps "without any political power, solely as a police force" that would deal only with murder, rape, and larceny (1952).

6. See, eg, BSIP 1946, 10; Crass 1946c, 4; Hall 1946; Creech Jones 1946; Grantham 1946, 2; 1947; Nicoll 1947a; Noel 1947r, 2; WPHC 1947; Tippet 1967, 207; Davies nd, 303. For an ambitious plan for change in the Solomons envisioned at the high commission level in 1943 but not enacted, see Bennett 1987, 301–302. Officers in the Solomons at that time entertained no thoughts of such rapid change

on Malaita. Recall, too, Marquand's complaint that BSIP officials hampered the advance of councils and courts and thereby refused or undermined basic principles of the secretary of state's directives to administrators in the colonies to hasten self-government (1950, 57).

7. Cameron 1948d; Russell 1949b.

8. Gregory-Smith 1950f, 3.

9. Allan wrote this during his fifth month on Malaita while based at Malu'u (1949c, 4). See also Fox 1962, 138; 1967, 48; and Timothy George's letter quoted in Corris 1973a, 51. For later Malaitan refusals to work unpaid on government projects, see Russell 1955d.

10. Forster writing in Malaita District 1949 (1st quote); Davies 1947f (2nd); Germond 1948p (3rd); Marquand 1950, 22–23; see A Sandars 1950, 15–16, 18; and, in this book, Noel statements in chapter 7, and, in chapter 8, Masterman's that Malaitans would get nothing until every man was taxed and censused. Missionaries and other Europeans pressed the government not to negotiate. Derek Rawcliffe, at the time headmaster at All Hallows School on the island of Pawa, in 2005 told me that most whites opposed the Malaita Council since "It was just giving in to the Maasina Rule people." But, like some others, when resistance subsided, he decided officers had made the right decision and that Malaitan aspirations were legitimate (see Robson 1952; BSIP 1954; Allan 1958, 7).

11. Marquand 1950, 15; see Allan 1950g, 5; MQRs 30 June 1950, 4; 30 June 1951, 5; Laracy 1983, 177.

12. Harwood 1966. Harwood also mentioned that officers' "anti-clerical" dislike for Methodist missionaries may have been a factor in the government's good relations with the breakaway Christian Fellowship Church. Davenport was asked to investigate the Moro movement; his report was restricted, but later most of it was published (Davenport and Çoker 1967). Moro and a few followers were arrested in 1957 after they surrounded and reportedly threatened a police patrol. Officers soon regretted the arrest for its having raised Moro's stature and changed their approach to instituting development projects in the area (Davenport and Çoker 1967, 133–139; see 131–132). The Christian Fellowship Church's leader Silas Eto was arrested for sedition in the early 1950s but then released when Methodist missionary Goldie threatened legal action (Bennett 1987, 299–301; see Harwood 1978). Richard Fallowes told David Hilliard that on his last visit to the Solomons in 1959 his main criticism of the government "was that it had become too sensitive of Melanesian opinion, and almost grandmotherly in its dealings with them" (Fallowes 1966).

13. Andersen 1952p, 1; 1954c, 1; Bartle 1952; Basiberi 1996 pers comm. In 1979, some Malaitans expected Solomon Islands independence would mean "no more government."

14. Bartle 1952; East Kwara'ae District Officer Diary, 6 Dec 1953; Andersen 1954d, 1; MAR 1955, 22; Anderson 1957a; Allan 1960, 162; see Jack-Hinton 1958.

15. See, eg, Cochrane 1970, 93; Keesing 1978a, 53; 1992a, 171; Naitoro 1993, 95.

16. Russell 1950f, 12; 2003, 48; Andersen 1954d, 1; cf Premdas and Steeves 1985, 39. High Commissioner John Gutch wrote in his memoir that in 1955 he considered rejecting Sisili's selection as Malaita Council president (1987, 113; he mistakenly says it was Salana Ga'a).

17. MAR 1953, 6; see Andersen 1954d, 1; see Fifi'i 1989, 92.

18. Russell 2003, 90; 2004, 5; Stanley 1975, 180.

19. An equivalent of 74 percent of Malaitan tax money was projected for Malaita Council salaries and administration in 1956. This was similar to budgets of other district councils in the Solomons at that time. Things improved in later years and more money was spent on development (National Administration Course 1955, 10; see Townsend 1961a; Premdas and Steeves 1985, 39).

20. Anderson 1957a.

21. Naitoro 1993, 95–96.

22. For example, Anderson 1957a; Tedder 2007 pers comm; 2008, 52.

23. Space constraints prevent examining here the economic projects that officers and the council worked to establish. Some succeeded and brought needed money into communities. Others failed, partly due to poor long-range planning and insufficient infrastructure. This is no surprise given the emergency nature of their implementation at the tail end of political unrest, but some project failures increased resentment of government and the council. Suspicion of the government led some to oppose the schemes from the start. Waiparo, discussed later in this chapter, was thought partly responsible for refusals in the south, which clearly frustrated Russell (see Russell 1954c, 1955a, 1955d; MAR 1954, 7; East Kwara'ae District Officer Diary, 30 Aug 1953; MAR 1954, 7; Naitoro 1993, 130–135). Some refused to allow projects on their land or disputed the ownership of the land required. Bennett noted consequences that deeply rooted protectiveness of land in the Solomons has had for the economy overall (2002, 13). I have dealt little with land issues and land courts in this book, but some of the same problems that weakened local courts also hampered local land courts, especially government neglect and failure to help them financially. For a recent study of their problems, see Futaiasi 2010. For detailed case studies of post–Maasina Rule economic development from opposite ends of Malaita, see Frazer 1973; Naitoro 1993.

24. Andersen 1954d, 1, 12.

25. Malaita District 1953; BSIP 1945–1959, 23 Feb 1953, 14–15; Andersen quote in East Kwara'ae District Officer Diary 28 May 1953; Tedder 2008, 52.

26. Lindley 1958. Waiparo and Nono'oohimae had already "vigorously" denied the claim that they told Kwaio not to tax (Russell 1955d; Teoboo 1982 pers comm). Most Kwaio really were cash poor and had few ways to earn money; most of the reasons they gave for being poor were legitimate (cf Malaita District [1959?]). Saltwater people of Langalanga were refusing to pay the tax until they were compensated for the 1942 US bombing of Laulasi (Anderson 1958b; and see this book, chapter 4).

27. Anderson 1958a.

28. *Malaita Newsletter* Nov 1959, Dec 1959; Malaita District 1960; Townsend 1961a; see Holland 1961. Section 85(1) of the Local Government Ordinance of 1963 allowed punishment of any tax default with a fine of up to £50 and/or up to three months in prison.

29. Russell 1954d, 1, 2.

30. Malaita Council 1953, 6, 12.

31. BSIP 1957, 24–25; cf BSIP [1965?]. For post–Maasina Rule examples of the critique that things Malaitans put forth as *kastom* were not old and were thus specious, see Hearth 1956a; Allan 1957a, 153; 1960, 162–163, 251–253; 1989–1990, 154. Colin Allan recommended that an exception be made regarding customary land ownership: that a piece of land's current ownership status should be regarded as its customary status (1957b).

32. East Kwara'ae District Officer Diary May 1953; Russell 1954d, 1; 1955c; see also BSIP 1956; Hearth 1956b, 1956c.

33. Russell 1954d; BSIP 1954.

34. Anderson 1958b; Glover 1958; Malaita District 1961; Turpin 1967; Mariano Kelesi 1987 pers comm. This book does not trace the later history of the courts, but, years later, they were little used on Malaita. Instead, "chiefs' courts" applied "*kastom* law" to hear cases that disputants could not manage by themselves. In 1988 police in the southern half of Malaita recorded only 30 offenses. In 1986, courts on the island, then home to some 70,000 people, heard a mere 104 cases. By comparison, during the previous year courts in the Western Province, with a much smaller population, heard 901 cases (Naitoro 1990, 21; see Akin 1999b, 50–52).

35. BSIP 1947e, 28; Laracy 1983, 85–86, 100; see this book, chapter 8. Attempts to arrest Waiparo during the Federal Council period failed (MQR 25 Oct 1951). Allan said Waiparo and Nono'oohimae became "arch-rivals" (1989–1990, 154), but it is hard to know the extent to which this was posed for the benefit of officers (see Russell 1954c, 1955a). In 1988 (pers comm), Fifi'i dismissed the idea of animosity between them and said neither was more powerful since they were about different things: Waiparo worked on *kastom* and was not a politician. This placed them in a dual leadership of the sort discussed in this book, chapter 6, in relation to *alaha'ou'ou*.

36. MAR 1953; Russell 1955a; MQR 31 March 1956; Hearth 1956a, 1956b, 1956c; Malaita District [1956?], 8–9. On Waiparo's influence in east Kwaio, which in the early 1960s spawned a rival but similar movement of Kwaio "committees," see Fifi'i 1989, 104–105; Keesing 1992a, chap 13.

37. Russell 1955a. On views of local and foreign knowledge, see Akin 1994.

38. Andersen 1954e, 2; MAR 1954, 3; Tedder 2008, 42; *Malaita Newsletter* July 1962. Kwaio men who visited Waiparo were told the same thing (Ta'ika 1982 pers comm; Ma'aanamae 1997 pers comm).

39. MAR 1954, 3; 1955, 22; Russell 1955b.

40. Russell 1955a, 4. During a 1950 meeting with 300 people at Takataka, Gregory-Smith had been told virtually the same thing—they wanted to straighten out their customs before deciding about other endeavors. At Allan's request, Gregory-Smith responded by asking them to write their customs down so the government could see them (1950–1952, 4–19 Sept).

41. Andersen 1954a, 2; Jack-Hinton 1958. In 2008 Tedder remembered Waiparo to me as "very secretive and only occasionally would he deign to meet with you. He was wily and I think rather intelligent but very conservative and in due course gave some support to the Malaita Council."

42. Malaita District 1968; see Akin 1999b; Kwa'ioloa and Burt 1997, 2007.

43. Non-Christians have at times also seen Christianity as part of a foreign package to be held at bay, and Christians have sometimes seen white missionary agendas in the same light. Today the anti-Christian side of *kastom* remains mostly in mountain areas of Kwaio, and as a result *kastom* ideology there is in some ways singular (see Keesing 1992a; Akin 1996, 2003, 2004, nd). For examples of how different Christians deal with perceived contradictions between *kastom* and Christianity, see Burt 1982, 1983, 1994; Kwa'ioloa and Burt 1997. See also Geoff White's book about neighboring Isabel (1991), and Michael Scott's about Makira (2007).

44. Keesing 1982a, 299; 1989; Tonkinson 1982a, 1982b; Babadzan 1988; 2004,

326; cf Akin 2005. As described earlier, Christian relationships with aspects of *kastom* as practice did have to be negotiated during Maasina Rule, as they still do today. For studies of this from Kwara'ae, see Burt 1982, 1983, 1994; and from Kwaio, see Akin 1999b, nd.

45. Sahlins 1992, 22; 1994, 380; Akin 2003, 2004. On *kastom* as a form of state hegemony (a model more plausible for Vanuatu than for Malaita), see Tonkinson 1982b; Philibert 1986; Keesing 1989; Babadzan 1988. For most Malaitans, the notion of "government *kastom*" would seem oxymoronic (see Akin 1999b, 2005). For a study of *kastom* in Vanuatu that examines very different usages there today and their history, particularly re *kastom*'s relationship to the Vanuatu state, see Bolton 1993.

46. See Akin 1999b, 35, 55–56. For discussions of corruption among Solomon Islands politicians, see Bennett 2002; Fraenkel 2004; Moore 2005.

47. See White 1991, 1992a, 1992b; Burt 1994; Foster 1995; Akin 1999a.

48. See Akin 1999b; Fraenkel 2004; Moore 2005; and, on militant motivations, Allen forthcoming. The situation is complicated because many public servants are themselves Malaitans who are sympathetic toward *kastom* political ideas and ambivalent about the government in which they serve. Many Malaitan policemen joined the ranks of militias during the crisis (see, eg, Kwa'ioloa and Burt 2007). On attitudes and ambivalence toward *kastom* among Malaitans living in Honiara, see Jourdan 1995; Gooberman 1999; Akin 2005.

49. Allen forthcoming.

References

Original titles of archival documents are in quotations; otherwise, titles are my descriptive ones.

Afigbo, Adiele E
  1972   *The Warrant Chiefs: Indirect Rule in Southeastern Nigeria 1891–1929.* London: Longman.
Akin, David
  nd   Good Women and Bad Women: Changing Taboos in a Solomon Islands Society. Book MS in preparation.
  1988–1989   World War II and the Evolution of Pacific Art. *Pacific Arts* 27:5–11; 28:11–12.
  1993   Negotiating Culture in East Kwaio, Malaita. PhD dissertation, University of Hawai'i.
  1994   Cultural Education at the Kwaio Cultural Centre. In *Culture, Kastom, Tradition: Developing Cultural Policy in Melanesia,* edited by Lamont Lindstrom and Geoffrey White, 161–172. Suva: Institute of Pacific Studies.
  1995–1996   Videotapes of Kwaio. Tuzin Archive for Melanesian Anthropology, Mandeville Special Collections Library, University of California, San Diego.
  1996   Local and Foreign Spirits in Kwaio, Solomon Islands. In *Spirits in Culture, History, and Mind,* edited by Jeannette Mageo and Alan Howard, 147–171. New York: Routledge.
  1999a   Cash and Shell Money in Kwaio, Solomon Islands. In *Money and Modernity: State and Local Currencies in Melanesia,* edited by David Akin and Joel Robbins, 103–130. Pittsburgh: University of Pittsburgh Press.
  1999b   Compensation and the Melanesian State: Why the Kwaio Keep Claiming. *The Contemporary Pacific* 11:35–67.
  2000   Lessons from the Dead: Comparing Oral and Written Histories of a Kwaio Past. Lecture to seminar on field methods, University of Chicago.
  2003   Concealment, Confession, and Innovation in Kwaio Women's Taboos. *American Ethnologist* 39 (3): 381–400.
  2004   Ancestral Vigilance and the Corrective Conscience in Kwaio, Malaita. *Anthropological Theory* 4 (3): 299–324. Repr in *The Making of Global and Local Modernities in Melanesia,* edited by Joel Robbins and Holly Wardlow, 183–206. Burlington: Ashgate, 2005.
  2005   Kastom as Hegemony? A Response to Babadzan [2004]. *Anthropological Theory* 5 (1): 75–83.

Alaikona, Jason
    1987   Tulagi Police Line: 1935–1939. MS in Pijin given to Akin by Alaikona.
            Solomon Islands National Archive, Honiara.
Allan, Colin Hamilton (DC Western 1947; DO Malu'u 1949; DC Malaita 1950–
1952; Governor Solomons 1976–1978)
    1945   Autobiographical service summary. 20 July. BSIP 1/III/58/197/I.
    1947   DC Western to SG, "Political Troubles Western District." 1 March. BSIP 4/
            C91.
    1949a   DO Malu'u telegram to SG on arrest figures. 10 March. BSIP 4/SF108.
    1949b   DO Malu'u to DC Malaita Forster. 3 April. BSIP 4/SF108.
    1949c   DO Malu'u report to SG on anti–Marching Rule activities. 25 May. BSIP
            4/SF108.
    1950a   The Marching Rule Movement in the British Solomon Islands Protector-
            ate: An Analytical Survey. MA thesis, Cambridge University.
    1950b   DC Malaita political situation report to RC. ca June. BSIP 12/V/4.
    1950c   Telegram to SG. 12 June. BSIP 12/V/4.
    1950d   Memo to SG and DOs 'Aoke and Malu'u. 16 June. BSIP 12/V/4.
    1950e   Memo to RC, SG, and DOs 'Aoke and Malu'u. 28 June. BSIP 12/V/4.
    1950f   Letter to SDNA. 24 July. BSIP 4/SF108.VIII/5.
    1950g   Report to RC on Malaita tour of 12 June to 31 July. 1 Aug. BSIP 12/V/5.
    1950h   Personal letter to RC. 13 Aug. BSIP 4/SF108/VIII/V.
    1950i   "The Missions and the Marching Rule" (secret). ca Aug. BSIP 12/V/5.
    1950j   "Status of Nonohimae and Timothy George," to RC. 25 Sept. BSIP SF108/
            8/5.
    1950k   "Report to RC on Political Situation since July." 10 Oct. BSIP 12/V/5.
    1950l   "Headmen's Conference," report to SDNA Frederick Bentley, with Bent-
            ley's comments attached. 10 Oct. BSIP 12/I/12.
    1950m   Report to SDNA on development plans for Malaita. 16 Oct. BSIP 12/V/5.
    1950n   Letter to SDNA. 30 Oct. BSIP SF108/VIII/5.
    1950o   Report to SDNA on political affairs. 27 Nov. BSIP 12/V/6.
    1951a   Marching Rule: A Nativistic Cult of the British Solomon Islands. *Corona*
            3:93–100. Repr in *South Pacific* 5 (5): 79–85 (1951).
    1951b   "Notes on the Historical Background and Development of the South Seas
            [*sic*] Evangelical Mission." 14 Jan. BSIP 1/III/23/9.
    1951c   Comment on DO Malu'u political report, to SDNA Davies. 3 Feb. BSIP 4/
            SF108/I.
    1951d   "Homeopathic Medicine—S.S.E.M.," to SDNA Davies. 14 March. BSIP
            12/I/13.
    1951e   Secret report to SDNA Davies on Malaita political situation. 15 March.
            BSIP 12/I/13.
    1951f   Miscellaneous notes on Kwaio affairs. 6 April. BSIP 27/I/9.
    1951g   Memo to SDNA Davies, "Native Tax." 7 April. BSIP SF108/VIII/5.
    1951h   Telegram to SDNA Davies on Rickwood visit to 'Are'are. 18 April. BSIP
            12/I/13.
    1951i   Telegram to SDNA Davies on postings (with Davies's reply). 18 April.
            BSIP 12/I/13.
    1951j   Memo to SDNA Davies, "Charlie Fotarafa." 25 April. BSIP SF108/VIII/5.
    1951k   Report on the need for a road to Kwai. 13 June. BSIP 1/III/S.185.

1951l Notes on Ridley, Fifi'i, Houasihau, and Nono'oohimae reports. Aug. BSIP 12/V/7.

1951m "Police Recruits from Malaita," to Superintendent of Police. 26 Oct. BSIP 1/111/19/8.

1951n "Top secret" telegram to SG. 14 Dec. BSIP 4/SF108/I/2.

1952a Letter to RC Gregory-Smith. 4 Feb. BSIP 12/V/12.

1952b Handing-over report to Andersen. 16 Feb. BSIP 4/SF108/I.

1952c Letter to SG. 18 Feb. BSIP 12/V/12.

1952d Message to DO Malu'u Wrightson. 24 Feb. BSIP 12/I/10/II.

1952e Two letters conveying instructions from HC Stanley on Sisili. 7 Oct. BSIP 12/V/13.

1957a *Customary Land Tenure in the British Solomon Islands Protectorate: Report of the Special Lands Commission.* Honiara: WPHC.

1957b Acting Chief Secretary to DCs, "Amendments to Native Administration Regulation 1952." 11 Sept. BSIP 29/IV/ADM/A/10.

1958 Memo by Acting Secretary of Protectorate Affairs, "Political and Racial Consciousness in the British Solomon Islands Protectorate." Aug. WPHC 11/19/SF178/5/7.

1960 Local Government and Political Consciousness in the British Solomon Islands Protectorate. *Journal of African Administration* 12 (3): 158–163.

1974 Some Marching Rule Stories. *Journal of Pacific History* 9:182–186.

1978 Confidential letter to Head of Foreign and Commonwealth Office John Michael Owen Snodgrass. 2 Feb. National Archives, London, FCO 32/1504.

1980a Bureaucratic Organization for Development in Small Island States. In *The Island States of the Pacific and Indian Oceans: Anatomy of Development,* edited by R T Shand, 383–403. Monograph 23. Canberra: Development Studies Centre, Australian National University.

1980b An Early Marching Rule Letter by Nori of Waisisi, 'Are'are, Malaita Manuscript XV. *Journal of Pacific History* 15:110–112.

1982a Further Marching Rule Documents: Manuscript XVI—Anaefolo of Uru and the Federal Council Decision 1951; XVII: The Special Lands Commissioner's Note on the Nggela People and Marching Rule. *Journal of Pacific History* 17:222–227.

1982b Review of *Lightning Meets the West Wind: The Malaita Massacre,* by Roger Keesing and Peter Corris. *Journal of Imperial and Commonwealth History* 10 (3): 369–370.

1989 The Post-War Scene in the Western Solomons and Marching Rule: A Memoir. *Journal of the Polynesian Society* 24 (1): 89–99.

1989–1990 *Solomons Safari, 1953–1958.* 2 vols. Christchurch: Nag's Head Press.

Allen, Matthew Grant

forthcoming Greed and Grievance: Ex-Militants' Perspectives on the Conflict in Solomon Islands, 1998–2003. Honolulu: University of Hawai'i Press (2013).

Amery, Leopold C M Stennett (Secretary of State for Colonies, 1924–1929)

1929 Letter to Acting HC, Suva. 4 June. WPHC CO225/226/54931/1.

Andersen, Valdemar A Jens (DC Malaita 1952–1954)

1947 DO Kirakira to SDNA David Trench re threats and violence by Henry Kuper. 5 Nov. BSIP 4/SF108/v.1.

1948 DO San Cristoval confidential letter to David Trench, on Kuper. 11 Jan. BSIP 4/SF108/v.1/II.

1950 SG letter to RC Gregory-Smith on letters to Captain Martin. 16 March. BSIP 4SF/108.

1952a Malaita "Quarterly Political Report." 31 March. BSIP 12/V/12.

1952b "Political Report for Malaita District" for April, to SG. 27 April. BSIP 12/I/10/II.

1952c Notes on talk with Ba'etalua. 9 May. BSIP 12/V/12.

1952d Confidential letter to DO Malu'u Wrightson on pig laws. 11 May. BSIP 12/I/10/II.

1952e Personal letter to unknown officer. 14 May. BSIP 12/I/10/II.

1952f Letter to DO Malu'u Wrightson. 9 June. BSIP 4/CF187.

1952g "Bina Meeting of 18–6–52 & Events Leading Up to It." 22 June. BSIP 12/V/13.

1952h "Future Policy on Malaita," to SG. 11 Aug. BSIP 12/V/13.

1952i "Economic Development on Malaita," to SG. 12 Aug. BSIP 12/I/23.

1952j "Projected Police Actions," to Commander Malaita police. 15 Aug. BSIP 12/V/13.

1952k Political report for August, telegram to SG and others. ca 1 Sept. BSIP 12/V/13.

1952l "Latest Political Information." 18 Sept. BSIP 12/V/13.

1952m "Quarterly Political Report—Malaita," written by James Tedder "for and by direction of" DC Valdemar Andersen. 2 Oct. BSIP 12/V/13.

1952n "Political Events on Malaita from 27th Sept. to 27th Oct. 1952," to SG. 28 Oct. BSIP 12/V/13.

1952o "Report of First Meeting of Malaita Council at Auki." 14 Nov. BSIP 12/I/10/II.

1952p Political report for Malaita, 1–21 Dec. 21 Dec. BSIP 12/V/13.

1952q DC's tour notes. Cited by date. BSIP 27/I/9, 12/V/13, and 27/VII/2A.

1954a "District Commissioner's Tour—Native Courts." 8–26 March. BSIP 27/VII.2A.

1954b Letter to SG Hughes. 15 April. BSIP 28/VI/CON2.

1954c Memo to Chief Secretary, WPHC, Honiara, "Malu'u and Administrative Postings on Malaita." 4 May. BSIP 12/I/15.

1954d "Handing Over Notes" to Tom Russell. 13 Sept. BSIP 12/I/15.

1954e "Note on Meeting at Auki 12th September." 13 Sept. BSIP 29/1/7.

Anderson, John David, and Guinevere Mary Anderson

1980–1981 To Melanesia with Love. Serialized in the Adventist magazine *Australasian Record*. Cited by date and page.

Anderson, W St G

1957a "The Future of District Headmen." July. BSIP 29/IV/ADM/A/10.

1957b DC Malaita to Kwara'ae District Christians Council. 23 Sept. BSIP 29/IV/ADM/A/3.

1958a DC to Chief Secretary, Honiara, "Native Tax Penalties." 10 March. BSIP 29/I/10.

1958b Malaita Intelligence Report for January–March. 11 June. BSIP 12/I/41.

Anifelo, 'Abaeata

1947 "Notes on Ala'aha [*alaha'ou'ou*] (as Given by Anafelo)," taken by DC Malaita Sandars. 1 July. BSIP 4/C91.

Apui, John
    1947   "The Teaching of the Catholic Church on Marriage." 5 April. English translation by Father Paul Geerts and Father Rances Mauli published in section E of *Pacific Protest: The Maasina Rule Movement*, edited by Hugh Laracy, 144–149. Suva: Institute of Pacific Studies, 1983.

Argus (Melbourne newspaper)
    1919   Solomon Islands: Pearls of the Pacific. Interview with Charles Workman. 21 April: 5.
    1927a Solomon Islands Massacre. Taxes Cause Unrest. 11 Oct: 17.
    1927b Solomon Islands Massacre. Taxation Probable Cause. 12 Oct: 23.

Asa Hoe (former DH, Ravo, Makira)
    1946   Letter barring recruiting. ca Sept. BSIP 4/C91.

Ashley, Francis Noel (RC 1929–1939)
    1929a "Native Administration No. 1," sent to DOs. 1 Sept. BSIP 9/V/5, folder E.
    1929b "Report on Malaita" to HC. 16 Sept. BSIP 2/II/1659/29.
    1930a Letter to Malaita officer Colin Wilson. 28 Jan. BSIP 14/28.
    1930b Letter to HC Fletcher. 5 May. WPHC 1160/30.
    1930c Letter to HC Fletcher. 25 June. WPHC 1160/30.
    1930d Letter to DO Malaita Barley on rumors of Kwaio trouble. 11 Sept. BSIP 14/39.
    1931a Notes and comments on MAR for 1930. 5 Feb. Author's copy.
    1931b RC's Notes and comments on quarterly report of 30 Dec, to DO Eastern Solomons. 6 March. WPHC film 131.
    1932a Comments to Malaita DO A John White on AR of 1932. 23 Feb. BSIP 27/VI/1.
    1932b Letter to DO Malaita A John White on brideprice. 5 April. BSIP 14/30.
    1932c Memo to DOs on possible sorcery law. 3 May. BSIP 9/V/5, folder D.
    1934   Comments on MAR for 1933. 3 April. BSIP 27/VI/1.
    1935a Letter to HC Fletcher on adultery. 22 May. BSIP 1/III/36/9/1.
    1935b Remarks on MAR for 1934. 15 Aug. BSIP 27/VI/1.
    1935c Letter to Stanley Masterman. 21 Nov. BSIP 1/P1/M 58/22/1.
    1936a Comment on MAR for 1935. 13 Feb. BSIP 27/VI/1.
    1936b Report on meeting held at Sinalagu on 10 March. BSIP 14/35.
    1938a Letter to DO Malaita Sandars. 26 Jan. BSIP 14/36.
    1938b Letter to DO Malaita Sandars. 1 March. BSIP 14/36.
    1938c Letter to Baddeley re Fallowes's return to BSIP. 3 Aug. BSIP 1/III/43/14.
    1939a Secret letter to DO Isabel Brownlees. 9 March. BSIP 1/III/43/14.
    1939b Note about Fallowes inside folder cover. 24 April. BSIP 1/III/43/14.

Aston, C W Whonsbon
    1948   *Polynesia Patchwork: The Tale of a Pacific Diocese.* Westminster, UK: Society for the Propagation of the Gospel in Foreign Parts. Archived at http://anglicanhistory.org/oceania/patchwork1948/ [accessed 9 Nov 2011].

Austen, Leo
    1945   Cultural Changes in Kiriwina. *Oceania* 16 (1): 15–61.

Awdry, Frances
    1902   *In the Isles of the Sea: The Story of Fifty Years in Melanesia.* London: Bemrose & Sons. Archived at http://anglicanhistory.org/oceania/awdry1902/ [accessed 9 Nov 2011].

Babadzan, Alain
    1988   *Kastom* and Nation Building in the South Pacific. In *Ethnicities and Nations,* edited by Remo Guidieri, Francesco Pellizzi, and Stanley Tambiah, 199–228. Houston: Rothko Chapel and University of Texas Press.
    2004   Kastom as Culture? *Anthropological Theory* 4 (3): 325–328.

Baddeley, Walter Hubert (Anglican Bishop of Melanesia 1932–1947)
    1940   Response to Marchant 1940c of 25 July, on Fallowes. 26 July. BSIP 1/III/43/14/1.
    1943   The Bishop's Report—1942. *SCL* July: 23–29.
    1945   Speech to Melanesian Mission at Westminster, 3 Jan. *SCL* Jan–April: 6–15.
    1947   Barge Memorial Address, Toowoomba, 9 March. *SCL* June: 28–33. PC.

Baker, John R
    1928   Depopulation in Espiritu Santo, New Hebrides. *Journal of the Royal Anthropological Institute* 54:279–299.

Ballantyne, Tony
    2008   Colonial Knowledge. In *The British Empire: Themes and Perspectives,* edited by Sarah Stockwell, 177–197. Malden: Blackwell Publishing.

Ballantyne, Tony, and Antoinette Burton, editors
    2005   *Bodies in Contact: Rethinking Colonial Encounters in World History.* Durham, NC: Duke University Press.

Banivanua-Mar, Tracey
    2007   *Violence and Colonial Dialogue: The Australian-Pacific Indentured Labor Trade.* Honolulu: University of Hawai'i Press.

Barley, Jack C (DO Eastern 1919–1923; Malaita 1930–1932, 1933)
    nd   "Notes on Malaita Native Custom." Notebook of Barley's and likely also G E D Sandars's ethnographic notes, begun ca 1930; back of book has notes handwritten by Malaitans, mostly codes, the last dated 1952. BSIP 27/I/1.
    1919   Letter to RC Workman on prohibition of kava. 9 Dec. BSIP 9/VII/3a.
    1920   Letter to RC Workman. 29 June. BSIP 9/VII/3a.
    1921   Letter to RC Workman. 20 Sept. BSIP 9/VII/3a.
    1926   "Application for a Transfer," to General Secretary, Tulagi. 20 Dec. WPHC 149/27.
    1930a   Letter to SG replying to RC Ashley 1930c. 9 Oct. BSIP 14/39.
    1930b   Letter to SG, "Adultery on Malaita." 11 Oct. BSIP 14/61.
    1930c   Letter to SG. 10 Dec. BSIP 14/39.
    1930–1932   "Native Affairs." In Malaita Native Affairs Book, kept by hand over time in the Malaita District Office. BSIP 27/I/3.
    1931a   Report to SG on Malaita Headmen. 6 May. BSIP 14/62.
    1931b   Report to SG on Malaita Census. 6 June. BSIP 14/62.
    1932   Acting RC letter to HC Fletcher on sorcery law. 28 Aug. BSIP 2/II/1659/29.
    1933a   Acting RC letter to HC Fletcher, and enclosed petitions asking for reinstatement of DO Filose to Isabel. 11 March. WPHC 1064/33.
    1933b   *Police v Kwaite'e.* Kwara'ae Courts File. 21 July. BSIP 60/33.
    1933c   Memo on Charles Gordon White. Nov. Lambert Papers, Tuzin Archive for Melanesian Anthropology, Mandeville Special Collections Library, University of California, San Diego, MSS 682.

Barley, Jack, Harry Brown Hetherington, and Frank Hewitt
    1929   Labour Commission Report. BSIP 3/II/1.

Barnett, Frederick Joshua (Acting RC 1909–1911, 1915–1917)
    1914   Letter to Edge-Partington re gun smuggling. 6 Oct. Author's copy.
    1915a   Letter to Malaita DO Ralph Brodhurst Hill on court procedure. 23 May. BSIP14/10.
    1915b   Letter to Malaita DO Hill. 30 June. BSIP14/10.
    1915c   Letter to Malaita DO Hill on wounding of Baunani overseer. 6 July. BSIP14/10.
    1916a   "Copy of address by Acting Resident Commissioner to the Chief and People of Alu, Shortland Delivered at Malaiai, 13 July." WPHC CO224/148, 2518.
    1916b   Letter to DO Malaita Bell. 15 Aug. BSIP 14/11.
    1917   Letter to HC Sweet-Escott. 25 Jan, encl 11, Western Pacific dispatch 99. 22 March. Author's copy.
Barrett, Helen (Fauaabu Hospital nurse)
    1947   Journal. MS in possession of Terry Brown.
Barrow, G Lennox (DO various districts 1942–1947)
    nd   Outlying Interlude—An Account of Life in the British Solomon Islands Protectorate 1942–47. MS. Pacific Manuscript Bureau film 517.
    1946   Asst DC, Kirakira, "The Work of Native Councils." Circular to Makiran people, 25 June. BSIP 8/I/1/1.
Barrow, G Lennox, and Roy Davies
    1947   Asst DCs to DC Central Crass, "Political Activity on San Cristoval and Ulawa." 8 Feb. BSIP 4/C91.
Bartle, John F (DO 'Aoke 1949–1950; DO Malu'u 1950–1951, 1952–1953)
    1950   DO 'Aoke telegram to SG. 13 Feb. BSIP 4/SF108.
    1951a   "A Report on North Malaita," 18 Sept–7 Jan. 28 Jan. BSIP 12/1/10/I/1.
    1951b   "A Political Report on North Malaita." 28 June. BSIP 12/I/10.
    1952   "Report on North Malaita," 29 Oct–31 Dec. ca 31 Dec. BSIP 12/V/13.
Basiberi
    1996   Interviews (Kwaio language) on Malaitan history tape recorded by David Akin in Kwaio. March. Tuzin Archive for Melanesian Anthropology, Mandeville Special Collections Library, University of California, San Diego.
Bates, J G
    1918   Legal Adviser's report on "The Draft Solomon Native Affairs Regulation 1918," prepared for HC Sweet-Escott. WPHC 228/19.
Beattie, John Watt
    1906   *Journal of a Voyage to the Western Pacific in the Melanesian Mission Yacht the Southern Cross, 25 August–10 November 1906.* A library MS version typed from handwritten original. Royal Society of Tasmania Library, Hobart (reference RS.29/3). PC.
Beckett, Jeremy
    1989   *Conversations with Ian Hogbin.* Oceania Monograph 35. Sydney: University of Sydney.
Bedford, Richard
    1980   *Perceptions, Past and Present, of a Future Melanesia.* Christchurch: Department of Geography, University of Canterbury.
Bell, William Robert (Government Labor Agent 1908–1915; DO Malaita 1915–1927)
    1908–1909   Log of Government Agent for ship *Clansman.* WPHC, no file number. Author's copy.

1915a   Letter to RC Barnett. 15 Oct. (misdated as 1916). WPHC CO225/153.

1915b   Letter to RC Barnett. 27 Nov. BSIP 14/11.

1915c   Report to RC Barnett on tour of southwest Malaita. 23 Dec. BSIP 14/43.

1916a   Report to RC Barnett. 17 Jan; copied to HC Sweet-Escott on 19 June. BSIP 14/44.

1916b   Letter to RC Barnett. 18 Jan. BSIP 14/44.

1916c   Letter to RC Barnett. 29 July. BSIP 14/44.

1916d   Report on raid by police at Bita'ama. 5 Aug. BSIP 14/44.

1916e   Report to RC Barnett on recent murders. 11 Sept. BSIP 14/44.

1916f   Letter to RC Barnett. 5 Oct. BSIP 14/44.

1916g   Letter to HC Sweet-Escott critiquing Malaita policy. 16 Dec. BSIP 14/44.

1917   Letter to RC Workman on adultery. 29 Sept. Author's copy.

1918a   Letter to RC Workman on police affairs. 30 Jan. BSIP 14/46.

1918b   Letter to RC Workman on adultery problems. 18 Feb. BSIP 14/46.

1918c   Letter to RC Workman on taxation. 19 Feb. BSIP 14/46.

1918d   Letter to RC Workman on bond by Irokwato. 13 April. BSIP 14/46.

1918e   Comments to RC Workman on Thomas J McMahon's article in *The Queenslander* (Brisbane weekly). 28 May. BSIP 14/46.

1918f   Reports to RC Workman on police action at Anoano. 18 Aug. BSIP 14/46.

1919a   Report to RC Workman. 19 May. BSIP 14/12.

1919b   Court sentence of "Akwai" (likely Akwaa'i). 25 and 27 Oct. BSIP 15/11/29.

1919c   Report of patrol around Malaita, 21 Oct–3 Nov. 1 Dec. BSIP RC W.48/1919.

1920a   Report to Acting RC. 14 Oct. WPHC IC 2408/1919; 2667/1920.

1920b   Letter to Acting RC. 24 Oct. BSIP 14/48.

1921a   Report to RC Workman, "Itinerary of Patrol on Mala by DO with Vessel 'Afa' from the 2nd to 18th of January." BSIP 14/49.

1921b   Letter to RC Workman re article in *Planters' Gazette.* 21 July. BSIP 14/49.

1922a   Letter to RC Kane re introduction of taxation. 8 Aug. WPHC 2667/1922.

1922b   Letter to RC Kane re census of north Malaita. 9 Aug. BSIP 14/55.

1922c   Letter to RC Kane re "King's Regulation 15." 16 Nov. WPHC 2667/1922.

1923a   Letter to RC Kane. 18 Feb. BSIP 14/56.

1923b   Letter to RC Kane. 2 Dec. BSIP 14/56.

1924   Report to Acting RC Hill re "Native Administration Regulation of 1922." 30 March. WPHC IC 849/24.

1925a   "Matters of Native Tax and General Administration," to RC Kane. 3 June. BSIP 14/58.

1925b   "Matters of Native Tax and Administration," to RC Kane. 14 Sept. BSIP 14/58.

1925c   "Report on the Capacity of the Natives to Pay the Tax Assessed," to RC Kane. 15 Dec. BSIP 14/58.

1925d   "Copy of Log of District Vessel 'Auki.'" Oct. BSIP 14/59.

1925e   Letter to RC Kane re DH Timothy George. 16 Dec. BSIP 14/58.

1925f   Letter to RC Kane re Stephen Gori'i discharge. 17 Dec. BSIP 14/58.

1926a   "Division of Sub-Districts," to RC Kane. 12 April. BSIP 14/57/26.

1926b   Letter to RC Kane. 16 June. BSIP 14/58.

1927   Letter to HC Eyre Hutson re Malaitan complaints. 11 June. WPHC 287/27.

Belshaw, Cyril S

1944   Letter to DC Malaita David Trench. 30 Dec. BSIP 8/I/3/1.

1945a Letter to DC Malaita Trench. 9 Jan. BSIP 8/I/3/1.

1945b Letter to RC Noel re SILC recruiting problems. 9 Jan. BSIP 4/69c.

1945c Acting DC Tulagi to DC Malaita Trench, "Native Trade." 23 June. BSIP 8/I/3/1.

1945d Letter from Assistant DC Tulagi to DC Central Alexander Waddell, "Disturbance SILC A'ama, 6 August 45." 6 Aug. BSIP 1/III/9/86.

1946   Assistant DC to DC Central Crass, "Disturbance Ulawa." 6 June. BSIP 9/I/8.

1947a Native Politics in the Solomon Islands. *Pacific Affairs* 20 (2): 187–193. Revised version published in *South Pacific* 1 (12): 19–21 (1947).

1947b Post-War Developments in Central Melanesia. MS produced at the International Institute of Pacific Relations, New York. Author's copy.

1948   The Postwar Solomon Islands. *Far Eastern Survey* 17 (8): 95–98.

1949a Economic Aspects of Culture Contact in Eastern Melanesia. PhD dissertation, University of London.

1949b Trends in Motives and Organisation in Solomon Island Agriculture. Manuscript archived at http://www.anthropologising.ca/writing/agriculture.htm [accessed 9 Nov 2011].

1950a *Island Administration in the South West Pacific.* London: Royal Institute of International Affairs.

1950b The Significance of Modern Cults in Melanesian Development. *Australian Outlook* 4:116–125. (Excerpted from *Australian Intelligence Digest*, 1 Sept.)

1972   Review of Glynn Cochrane's *Big Men and Cargo Cults. American Anthropologist* 74:49–51.

2001   Personal website. http://www.anthropologising.ca/ [last accessed 9 Nov 2011].

2009   *Bumps on a Long Road.* Vancouver: Webzine.

Bengough, Charles Norman Frederick (DO Malaita intermittent 1934–1943)

1934   Report to Acting DO Sandars on 'Are'are depopulation. 3 July. BSIP 1/III/19/6.

1935   Letter to Acting DO Sandars. 10 Jan. BSIP 1/III/19/6.

1936a Letter to SG on registration of native marriages. 7 May. BSIP 29/I/1.

1936b Letter to SG, "Recruits' Taxes." ca late May. BSIP 29/I/1.

1936c Letter to SG on rumors of Kwaio unrest. 10 July. BSIP 29/I/1.

1936d Letter to SG on alleged unrest in Kwaio. 30 Sept. BSIP 29/I/1.

1936e Report to SG on Malaita District financial resources. 1 Oct. BSIP 29/I/1.

1938a Letter to RC Ashley. 11 Nov. BSIP 29/I/3.

1938b Letter to SG on literacy testing on Malaita. 15 Nov. BSIP I/III/43/19.

1939a Report on 'Are'are depopulation. 3 March. BSIP 1/111/19/6.

1939b Letter to Secretary to WPHC Vaskess. 11 July. BSIP 29/I/4 and 1/III/36/9/1.

1939c Letter to SG, "Unrest in Central Koio." 12 Sept. BSIP 14/39.

1939d Letter inviting donations to newly formed Red Cross branch. 29 Sept. BSIP 14/51.

1939e Letter to SG on unrest in Kwaio. 1 Nov. BSIP 14/39.

1940a Letter to Norman Deck on setting compensations. 16 Feb. BSIP 14/68.

1940b Cover letter, donation list, to Red Cross Treasurer, Tulagi. 25 May. BSIP 14/68.

1941a Letter to SG on native court plans. 4 Feb. BSIP 1/111/49/19.

1941b   Report to SG on 'Are'are population project progress. 29 Aug. BSIP 1/
        111/19/6.

1942   Letter to Charles Widdy re first Malaitan SILC recruits. 3 Dec. BSIP 5/I/
        1/3.

1943   Statements made by Jared Ramo'ifaka and Ata. 6 April. BSIP 5/I/1/3.

Bennett, Judith

1974   Cross-Cultural Influences on Village Relocation on the Weather Coast
        of Guadalcanal, Solomon Islands, c. 1870–1953. MA thesis, University of
        Hawai'i.

1987   *Wealth of the Solomons: A History of a Pacific Archipelago, 1800–1978.* Hono-
        lulu: Center for Pacific Islands Studies and University of Hawai'i Press.

1993   "We Do Not Come Here to Be Beaten": Resistance and the Plantation
        System in the Solomon Islands to World War II. In *Plantation Workers: Resis-
        tance and Accommodation,* edited by Brij V Lal, Doug Munro, and Edward D
        Beechert, 129–185. Honolulu: University of Hawai'i Press.

2002   *Roots of Conflict in Solomon Islands; Though Much Is Taken, Much Abides: Lega-
        cies of Tradition and Colonialism.* Discussion Paper 2002/5. Canberra: State,
        Society and Governance in Melanesia Project, Australian National Uni-
        versity. Archived at http://ips.cap.anu.edu.au/ssgm/papers/discussion_
        papers/bennett02-5.pdf [accessed 9 Nov 2011].

Bennett, William

1988   Behind Japanese Lines in the Western Solomons. Edited by David Gegeo
        and Geoffrey White. In *The Big Death: Solomon Islanders Remember World War
        II,* edited by Geoffrey White, David Gegeo, David Akin, and Karen Ann
        Watson-Gegeo, 137–148. Suva: University of the South Pacific.

Bentley, Frederick John (DO and DC Malaita 1944, 1945)

1944a   Letter to SG summarizing Malaitan contributions to war effort. 4 Aug.
        BSIP 1/43/60.

1944b   Memo to SG detailing Malaitan bombing casualties. 1 Dec. BSIP 1/111/
        9/59/2.

1945   Letter to DC Trench on rumors of impending invasion. 14 April. BSIP 1/
        III/19/9.

1950   DC Eastern "Handing Over Report." 30 June. BSIP 4/SF108/Vol. 4/part
        VII.

Bertram, Anton

1930   *The Colonial Service.* Cambridge, UK: Cambridge University Press.

Bielakowski, Alexander

2007   *African American Troops in World War II.* Oxford: Osprey.

Bloch, Maurice

1993   Zafimaniry Birth and Kinship Theory. *Social Anthropology* 1:119–132.

Bloch, Maurice, and Jonathan Parry

1989   Introduction. In *Money and the Morality of Exchange,* edited by Jonathan
        Parry and Maurice Bloch, 1–32. New York: Cambridge University Press.

Blue Book of the British Solomon Islands Protectorate

1930   Suva: WPHC.

Bodley, John

1982   *Victims of Progress.* Palo Alto, CA: Mayfield Publishing.

Bogesi, George

1948   Santa Isabel, Solomon Islands. *Oceania* 18 (3): 208–232; (4): 329–357.

Boggs, Stephen, and David Welchman Gegeo
 1996   Leadership and Solomon Islanders' Resistance to Plantation-Based
        Political Economy. In *Leadership and Change in the Western Pacific,* edited
        by Richard Feinberg and Karen Ann Watson-Gegeo, 272–297. London:
        Athlone.
Bolton, Geoffrey
 1963   *A Thousand Miles Away: A History of North Queensland to 1920.* Canberra:
        Australian National University.
Bolton, Lissant
 1993   *Unfolding the Moon: Enacting Women's Kastom in Vanuatu.* Honolulu: Uni-
        versity of Hawai'i Press.
Boutilier, James
 1978   Missions, Administration, and Education in the Solomon Islands, 1893–
        1942. In *Mission, Church, and Sect in Oceania,* edited by James Boutilier,
        Daniel Hughes, and Sharon Tiffany, 139–161. Ann Arbor: University of
        Michigan Press.
 1982   The Government Is the District Officer. In *Middlemen and Brokers in Ocea-
        nia,* edited by William Rodman and Dorothy Counts, 35–67. New York:
        University Press of America.
 1984   The Law of England Has Come: The Application of British and Custom
        Law in the British Solomon Islands Protectorate, 1893–1942. Paper pre-
        sented at Association for Social Anthropology in Oceania annual meet-
        ing, Molokai, Hawai'i.
 1989   Kennedy's "Army": Solomon Islanders at War, 1942–1943. In *The Pacific
        Theater: Island Representations of World War II,* edited by Geoffrey White and
        Lamont Lindstrom, 329–352. Honolulu: Center for Pacific Islands Studies
        and University of Hawai'i Press.
Bowman, Robert G
 1946   Army Farms and Agricultural Development in the Southwest Pacific. *Geo-
        graphical Review* 36 (3): 420–446.
Breckenridge, Carol, and Peter van der Veer
 1993   *Orientalism and the Postcolonial Predicament: Perspectives on South Asia.* Phila-
        delphia: University of Pennsylvania Press.
Brewster, A B
 1937   *King of the Cannibal Isles.* London: Robert Hale.
British Colonial Office
 1931   *Papers Relating to the Health and Progress of Native Populations in Certain Parts
        of the Empire.* London: Her Majesty's Stationery Office.
Brittain, Arthur (Melanesian Mission)
 1894   On the Melanesians in Queensland, with Suggestions for Future Work.
        Melanesian Mission Occasional Paper, Christmas: 5–8. PC.
Brownlees, John Kilpatrick (DO Malaita 1935–1937, 1940)
 1938   Acting DO Isabel letter to SG on literacy testing. 23 Dec. BSIP I/III/43/19.
 1940   Letter to SG. 8 Oct. BSIP 14/89.
Bruce, James (Commander)
 1883   Reports of 1 and 30 July 1881 to John C Wilson, commanding Australian
        Station, on proceedings of HMS *Cormorant.* Repr in *Correspondence Respect-
        ing the Natives of the Western Pacific and the Labour Traffic,* 45–55, 57–58.
        London: Great Britain Colonial Office.

BSIP, British Solomon Islands Protectorate

1897–1975 BSIP Annual Reports. Cited by "AR" and year. London: Her Majesty's Stationery Office."

1911 *Handbook of the British Solomon Islands Protectorate*. Tulagi: BSIP.

1917 Police Report for 1917. Author's copy.

1918 Draft of "The Solomons Native Affairs Regulation 1918." WPHC 228/19.

1922a Advisory Council Minutes. 8 Dec. WPHC 185/23.

1922b Draft of "Native Administration (Solomons) Regulation." nd. WPHC 2290/22.

1928 "Annual Medical and Sanitary Report" (ending 31 Dec). Under Senior Medical Officer Harry Brown Hetherington. Author's copy.

1931 Notes on HC Fletcher discussion with RC Ashley and DO Barley on establishing native courts on Malaita, and on sorcery legislation. 21 July. BSIP 2/II/1659/29.

1933 Testimonies relating to assaults by Richard Fallowes, collected by G E D Sandars. 28 Feb–4 March. Attached to Sandars 1933a. BSIP 1/3/43/14.

1934 "Education in the British Solomon Islands Protectorate." Report to Advisory Committee on Education in the Colonies. 12 Nov. Author's copy.

1935 Inquiry, Stanley Masterman assault on prisoner Ulani. 7 Nov. BSIP 1/P1/M58/22/1.

1938 Acting SG to Stanley Masterman re request for promotion. 18 Feb. BSIP 1/P1/M/58/22/1.

1939 File on different prices charged to Europeans than to Islanders. nd. BSIP 49/11.

1940a Document describing Malaita development to 1940. nd. BSIP 12/I/8.

1940b Letter from Acting Director of Prisons to DO Malaita. 21 March. BSIP 14/90.

1940c Translation of letter credited to John Pidoke. 23 Dec. WPHC 43/14/1.

1941 Circular from SG to all DOs, "Native Courts." 13 Jan. BSIP 1/111/49/19.

1942a "Military Units Regulation." 30 Nov. BSIP 5/I/1/3.

1942b "Native Courts Regulation. Special Regulation No. 2." 8 Dec. BSIP 29/11/7.

1942c "Special Courts (Establishment) Regulations. No. 1 of 1942." nd. BSIP 12/I/4.

1943a Warrants establishing native courts. 18 March. BSIP 25/VII/1.

1943b Document with list of executions in 1943. ca pre-Sept. BSIP 5/I/1/5.

1943c Acting RC to HC, cover letter for Sandars 1943b. 15 Sept. BSIP 1/III/19/8.

1943d Secret RC memo on SILC recruitment and labor. ca Oct. BSIP 1/III/9/44.

1945a SG's memo. 31 March. BSIP 1/III/19/16.

1945b Commanding Officer SILC letter to DO Malaita. 21 July. BSIP 10/I/34/10.

1945c Report on letter from American US troop commander. 17 Dec. BSIP 10/1/34/10.

1945d Acting SG memo to DC Malaita Sandars. 29 Dec. BSIP 1/III/19/9.

1945e "Native Courts Regulation No. 1." Summarized in *Journal of Comparative Legislation and International Law,* 3d series, 27 (1/2): 95–99.

1945–1959 Minutes of Advisory Council Meetings. Supplements to *Western Pacific High Commission Gazette*. Cited by date. Hamilton Library, University of Hawai'i.

1946   "British Solomon Islands Protectorate Ten Year Plan of Reconstruction and Development and Welfare, 1946." 30 Nov. Hamilton Library, University of Hawai'i.

1947a   "Native Administration Regulation." King's Regulation 2. 31 Jan. BSIP 12/I/5. (Pijin and English 1945 drafts are in BSIP 2/II/1659/29.)

1947b   "Native Tax Regulation, 1947." King's Regulation 3. 1 Feb. BSIP 12/I/5; repr with schedule of rates, in *Western Pacific High Commission Gazette* 5 (11 Feb): 29–30 (1947).

1947c   "Public Order (Recognizance) Regulation." Aug draft. BSIP 4/S.103.

1947d   Proceedings of Preliminary Examination of *Rex v Bobongi* and thirty-two other Maasina Rule leaders. 17 Nov–5 Dec. BSIP 4/SF108/I/1B.

1947e   Marching Rule—Proceedings of *Rex v Bobongi* and thirty-two other Maasina Rule leaders. 15 Dec–14 Feb 1948. BSIP 4/SF108/I/1A. (Excerpts are in Laracy 1983, D.)

[1947f?] "Native Councils on Malaita." Handwritten MS. BSIP 12/I/8.

[1948?]   "Historical" (section of report draft, likely by Colin Allan). BSIP 12/I/8.

1949   "Notes of Discussion" held in Acting RC's office. 16 Nov. BSIP 4/SF108.

1950a   "Minutes of Discussion" in RC's office. 10 Feb. BSIP 12/V/3.

1950b   "Minutes of Discussion" of letters to Captain Martin. 13 March. BSIP 4/SF108/VI/3.

1950c   SG personal and confidential to DC Malaita Allan. 19 June. BSIP 4/SF108/pt. IV/4.

1950d   Political section, monthly newsletter. 11 Sept. BSIP 12/V/4.

1950e   Confidential précis of DC conference discussions, for RC. 5 Dec. BSIP 4/FS154.

1951a   Superintendent of Police and Prisons to SG, DC Central, and Malaita Police. ca Jan. BSIP 12/I/9.

1951b   "Native Tax (Amendment) Regulation." 30 March draft. BSIP 12/I/13.

1951c   Applications for Colonial Development and Welfare Funds for elementary schools, teachers' training college, and cocoa scheme. April. BSIP 12/I/13.

1951d   *Rex v Ariel Sisili.* Sept. BSIP 12/V/9. (Statement files are in BSIP 12/I/13.)

1954   Native court warrants. 17 March. BSIP 3/VI/2.

1955   "Minutes of Discussion Held at Government House." 7 Nov. BSIP 12/I/16.

1956   Minutes of DCs' meeting in Honiara. 6–8 June. BSIP 29/IV/ADM/A/10.

1957   "Courts and Laws in the Solomon Islands, Issued to District Headmen and Presidents of Native Courts." March. Author's copy.

1963   "A Brief History of the Malaita Council." 26 Jan. BSIP 27/II/24.

[1965?]   "A Handbook for Native Courts" in the BSIP. BSIP 25/VII/6.

Buck, Pem Davidson

1989   Cargo-Cult Discourse: Myth and the Rationalization of Labor Relations in Papua New Guinea. *Dialectical Anthropology* 13:157–171.

Buckley, Gail

2001   *American Patriots: The Story of Blacks in the Military from the Revolution to Desert Storm.* New York: Random House.

Bugotu, Francis

1969   The Impact of Western Culture on Solomon Islands Society: A Melanesian Reaction. In *The History of Melanesia,* 549–556. Canberra: Australian National University and University of Papua New Guinea.

Bull, Mary

    1963   Indirect Rule in Northern Nigeria, 1906–1911. In *Essays in Imperial Government,* edited by Kenneth Robinson and Frederick Madden, 47–88. Oxford: Basil Blackwell.

Burnett, Frank

    1911   *Through Polynesia and Papua.* London: G Bell & Sons.

Burns Philp & Company

    1899   *Handbook of Information.* Sydney: John Andrew.

Burridge, Kenelm

    1970   *Mambu: A Study of Melanesian Cargo Movements and Their Social and Ideological Background.* New York: Harper & Row. First published 1960.

Burrows, William

    1950   The Background of Marching Rule: Late Henry Kuper Gives Some Curious Solomons History. *PIM* 20 (11): 37–38.

Burt, Ben

    1982   Kastom, Christianity and the First Ancestor of the Kwara'ae of Malaita. In *Reinventing Traditional Culture: The Politics of Kastom in Island Melanesia,* edited by Roger Keesing and Robert Tonkinson. Special issue, *Mankind* 13 (4): 374–399.

    1983   The Remnant Church: A Christian Sect of the Solomon Islands. *Oceania* 53:334–345.

    1990   Tradition and Christianity in East Kwara'ae, Malaita: The Colonial Transformation of a Solomon Islands Society. PhD dissertation, University of London.

    1994   *Tradition and Christianity: The Colonial Transformation of a Solomon Islands Society.* Langhorne, PA: Harwood Academic Publishers.

    2002   The Story of Alfred Amasia: Whose History and Whose Epistemology? *Journal of Pacific History* 37 (2): 187–204.

Burt, Ben, and Michael Kwa'ioloa, editors, with contributions from the Kwara'ae chiefs

    2001   *A Solomon Islands Chronicle, as Told by Samuel Alasa'a.* London: British Museum Press.

Butcher, Mike

    2012   *"When the Long Trick's Over": Donald Kennedy in the Pacific.* Bendigo, VIC: Holland House.

Cameron, Alastair Robin Peter Patrick Keith (Cadet and DO Malaita intermittent 1947–1949)

    1947a   Appendix to travel report to DC Malaita Sandars, "Collection of Monies for American Red Cross." 25 April. BSIP 27/VII/1.

    1947b   "Reports of A.R.P.P.K. Cameron from Nafinua." 3 June. BSIP 10/I/34/10.

    1947c   Letter to Sanders re Naafinua incident. 4 June. BSIP 10/I/34/10.

    1947d   Kwai political report to DC Sandars. 10 June (misdated 1946). BSIP 27/VII/1.

    1947e   "Travel Report Kwai Sub-District." 1 July. BSIP 10/I/34/10.

    1947f   "Some Notes on the Holding of Allegedly Illegal Courts in the Kwai Area." 1 July. BSIP 1/III/14/33 and 10/I/34/10.

    1947g   "Report on Political Situation in Kwai Sub-District." 2 July. BSIP 10/I/34/10.

1947h "Notes on Possible Prosecutions in Malu'u Area." 24 July. BSIP 4/C91.

1947i Travel report from Sinalagu. 6 Aug. BSIP 10/I/34/12.

1947j Travel report from 'Oloburi. 6 Aug. BSIP 10/I/34/12.

1947k "A Report on Political Conditions on the East Coast of Malaita, area from Oloburi to Kwai." ca post-4 Aug. BSIP 10/I/34/10.

1947l Report to DC Davies on Sulianu visit (Tai Lagoon). 19 Aug. BSIP 4/SF108.

1947m Report to DC Davies on actions of Delouse II. 31 Aug. BSIP SF108/I.

1947n "Report on Government Action at Sinarago, Kwai and Ata." 20 Sept. BSIP 27/VII/1.

1947o "Memorandum on Post-Marching Rule Reconstruction in Malaita," to DC Malaita Davies. 12 Oct. BSIP 12/I/1.

1948a Letter to "Bill" in Honiara. 19 June. BSIP 12/I/4.

1948b Report from Malu'u to Forster. 24 June. BSIP 12/I/4.

1948c Report from Malu'u to Germond. 26 June. BSIP 12/I/5.

1948d "A Memorandum on the Implications and Consequences of the 'Fences' Order in Tobaita," to Germond. 22 July. BSIP 4/SF108.

1948e Bali area report to Germond. 25 July. BSIP 12/I/4.

1948f Summary of plan for Phase II, Operation Jericho, to Germond. 17 Aug. BSIP 12/I/5.

1948g "Interim Political Report, Malu'u," with Germond comments. 4 Sept. BSIP 12/I/4.

1948h "Civil Disobedience Campaign," at Malu'u. 22 and 24 Sept. BSIP 12/I/4.

1949 Memo to Divisional Officer Tulagi Peter Hughes and DC Michael Forster. 11 Jan. BSIP 12/I/4.

Cameron, Donald

1926 Report on Tanganyika for 1926. Author's copy.

Campbell, Frederick M

1913 Letter to Edge-Partington on 'Aoke police. 17 Oct. BSIP 14/8.

1918 District Officer's Annual Report for Eastern District. Repr in The History of Post-Spanish European Contact in the Eastern District before 1939, by Kaye Green. In *Southeast Solomon Islands Culture History: A Preliminary Survey*, edited by Roger Green and Mary Meyerhoff Cresswell, 42–43. Bulletin 11. Wellington: Royal Society of New Zealand (1976).

Campbell, Michael John

1978 The Development of Local Responsibility under Colonial Rule: A Comparative Study of Papua New Guinea and the Solomon Islands. PhD dissertation, University of Papua New Guinea.

Carter, George G

1990 *Yours in Service: A Reflection on the Life and Times of Reverend Belshazzar Gina of Solomon Islands.* Honiara: University of the South Pacific.

Cartey, Wilfred, and Martin Kilson, editors

1970 *The African Reader: Colonial Africa.* New York: Random House.

Carver, E C

1911 Commander HMS *Torch* report to Vice-Admiral G King-Hall on Farisi punitive actions after the murder of Daniels. 11 Nov. WPHC IC 1398/1911.

Caulton, Sidney Gething (Anglican Bishop of Melanesia 1948–1954)

1950 The Marching Rule Delusion. *PIM* 21 (1 [Aug]): 77, 79.

1951 Report on Solomon Islands. *SCL* April: np.

1955   The Marching Rule: A Political Development in Melanesia. *Pan-Anglican* (Worldwide Episcopal Church semiannual magazine, Hartford, CT) 6 (1): 61–62.

Chamberlain, G D

1948   Assistant HC Memo to Secretary of State for Colonies Arthur Creech Jones on stripping Jasper Irofiala of British Empire Medal. 28 June. BSIP 4/S28.

1952   Acting HC letter to Secretary of State for Colonies on progress of 1946 ten-year plans of BSIP and Gilbert and Ellice Islands Colony. 3 June. BSIP 4/C82.

Chapman, Murray, and Peter Pirie

1974   *Tasi Mauri: A Report on Population and Resources of the Guadalcanal Weather Coast.* Honolulu: East-West Center Population Institute.

Charles, William T (BSIP Chief Magistrate and Legal Adviser 1946–1953)

1947a   "Legality of a Threatened Strike—Advice Sought" by DC Malaita, to RC Noel. 23 April. BSIP 12/1/2/7.

1947b   Memo to RC Noel, "Illegal Courts on Malaita." 31 July. BSIP 4/C91.

1947c   Memo to DC West Solomons Allan, "Consent to Prosecute one Brown for Spreading Alarm in Ysabel." 13 Aug. Author's copy.

1947d   Legal Report on "Public Order (Recognizance) Regulation." 29 Aug. BSIP 4/S.103.

1947e   Judgment in *Rex v Idunao* [Iduina'o] *and Others.* 2 Oct. BSIP 4/SF108/v.1.

1948a   Memo to divisional officers, "Trials for Holding Unauthorized Courts." 3 Feb. BSIP 12/I/5.

1948b   Follow-up to 1948a. 15 Feb. BSIP 12/I/5.

1948c   Letter to Germond re Ifiamae, with judgment against him and terms of his bond. 16 Feb. BSIP 4/SF108.

1948d   "Enclosure of Villages on Malaita." Legal guidance to RC Noel to facilitate destruction of fences. ca 11 Aug. BSIP 12/I/5.

1948e   "Marching Rule Activities," to Germond. 26 Aug. BSIP 4/SF108.

1948f   Draft order re fence removal, to Noel. 30 Aug. BSIP 4/SF108/I.

1948g   "Marching Rule Activities," and "The Conduct of Political Trials," opinions to Acting RC Germond, with cover letter. 15 Oct. BSIP 4/SF108.

1949a   Memo to Germond, "Criminal Trials in Respect of Certain Incidents at Maroa, Malaita on 16th February." 18 March. BSIP 4/SF108/IV.

1949b   Memo to Germond, "Marching Rule Watch-towers and Fences." 30 Aug. BSIP 4/SF108.

1951   "Prosecution of Ariel Sisili," to Superintendent of Police Colchester-Wemyss. 4 May. BSIP 12/V/9.

Chicago Daily Tribune

1947   British Can't Find a "War" on Guadalcanal. 11 July: 6.

Chilver, Elizabeth

1963   Native Administration in the West Central Cameroons 1902–1954. In *Essays in Imperial Government Presented to Margery Perham,* edited by Kenneth Robinson and Frederick Madden, 89–139. Oxford: Basil Blackwell.

Chinnery, Ernest William Pearson

1932   Census and Population. *Oceania* 3 (2): 4–17.

Clammer, John
    1973   Colonialism and the Perception of Tradition in Fiji. In *Anthropology and the Colonial Encounter,* edited by Talal Asad, 199–220. London: Ithaca Press.
Clark, Wilbur T
    1947   Island News. *NIV* June: 4–7.
    1950   News from Malaita. *NIV* March: 7.
Clemens, Warren Frederick Martin (DO Malaita 1938–1940; Eastern 1941–1942)
    1940a   "The 'Fallowes Movement.'" Response to SG's 20 June circular. 14 Oct. BSIP I/III/43/14/1.
    1940b   The Custom of Mau: An Account of Trial by Ordeal of Hot Stones Witnessed in South Malaita. *Folklore* 51:72–74.
    1941   Acting DO Eastern letter to SG on native courts. 15 May. BSIP 1/III/49/19.
    1942   "District Officer's Diary, Guadalcanal." Hamilton Library, University of Hawai'i.
    1962   Two Decades Have Brought Big Changes to Malaita, BSIP. *PIM* Oct: 79–81.
    1988   Letter to Geoffrey White. 8 Nov. Author's copy, courtesy G White.
    1989   Letter to Geoffrey White. 3 Feb. Author's copy, courtesy G White.
    1992a   Watching the Coast. In *Guadalcanal, 1942–1992,* edited by Des Dugan, 55–64. Chatswood, NSW: Mace Marketing.
    1992b   Letter to David Akin. 13 Dec.
    1998   *Alone on Guadalcanal: A Coastwatcher's Story.* Annapolis: Naval Institute Press.
    2000   Letter to David Akin. 4 Jan.
Coates, Austin
    1970   *Western Pacific Islands.* London: Her Majesty's Stationery Office.
Cochrane, D Glynn (DO Malaita 1962–1964)
    1969   Conflict between Law and Sexual Mores on San Cristobal. *Oceania* 39 (4): 281–289.
    1970   *Big Men and Cargo Cults.* Oxford: Clarendon Press.
    1979   Mr. Keesing's Gulag Archipelago. *Oceania* 49 (3): 235.
Codes and Maasina Rule Documents
(NB: Malaitan scribes during Maasina Rule and later hand-wrote dozens of copies of codes and documents for messenger distribution around the island. Copies are often not identical. Only one of each is listed here.)
    nda   Several undated codes from Baunani and probably 'Are'are. BSIP 12/VI/11.
    ndb   "Notice." List of crimes and penalties, probably from 'Are'are. BSIP 12/VI/9.
    ndc   "Native Custom." List of crimes and penalties. BSIP 12/VI/11.
    ndd   "Pray put out, Before Govern. Restitutions." Christian code. BSIP 12/VI/11.
    1944a   "Native Custom, Alailau" (Arairau, Nono'oohimae's village). 5 Jan. BSIP 12/VI/7.
    1944b   "The Law of Our Custom." ca Jan. BSIP 12/VI/9.
    1944c   "Mission Rules" Code from Anoano, west Kwaio. ca May. BSIP 10/1/34/25.
    1944d   "Native Rules, Kwaa Council." 22 May. BSIP 10/I/34/25.
    [1944e?] "Law, Alailau." Code, west 'Are'are. BSIP 12/VI/9.
    1945a   "Tabu Customs." Code from 'Are'are. ca early in year. BSIP 12/VI/9.

1945b   Maasina Rule Statement. 10 April. BSIP 12/VI/7/43. (Similar to 1945c, and to Laracy 1983, C3, where labeled "probably written at Arairau, Nono-'oohimae's village.")

[1945c?]   "Council Paper of Bina." Anoano, west Kwaio. BSIP 10/I/34/26.

1946a   "Customary Paper." From Malu'u, by "Sukubaea, Agwailalo, and Luiao-fia." June. BSIP 12/VI/8/56.

1946b   Code from Takataka, 'Are'are. 22 June. BSIP 12/VI/10.

1946c   "Gov. Counsel Money." 20 Sept. BSIP 12/VI/4. (Partly similar to "Answers from Alick (Nono'oohimae) in the Arairau Counsel [sic]," of same date, in Laracy 1983, C14.)

1946d   "The Customs Work." Probably from 'Are'are. 22 Nov. BSIP 12/VI/9.

1946e   "The Heads of M.R. Council Decision," from Makwanu, north Malaita. Handed to Sandars at 26 December 'Aoke meeting. BSIP 12/VI/7/42. (Sandars's translation is in MAR 1946, 5–6; a close version is in Laracy 1983, E2.)

[1946f?]   Lists of "Chiefs," "Araha," "Leaders," "Gardeners," and "People" of "Heathen Panuniuna Taoni," and "R. C. Mission Pauniuna," 'Are'are. BSIP 12/VI/11.

[1946g?]   Lists of Maasina Rule "Chiefs," "Gardeners," "Letter Men," members, etc. Maanawai, 'Are'are. BSIP 12/VI/11.

[1946h?]   "The Work of Custom." BSIP 12/VI/7/54. (Similar to Laracy 1983, E3, 138–140, which he says is likely from Fusea or Suu'aba, north Malaita. Several close versions exist. A typed version in same file was "Exhibit M" at the trial of Maasina Rule's Head Chiefs, and was seized near Malu'u.)

[1946i?]   "The Work of the Native Customs." BSIP 12/VI. (Similar to Laracy 1983, E3. Several like documents are in BSIP files.)

1947a   "Farmer Book." April. BSIP 12/VI/6/38.

1947b   "The Native Custom." From Maanaoba, several codes in different writing in local language, some with author's names—"M. Dioko, Clerk Dominiko Selofae, Government Chief Alabeti, Chief Farmer Anibasa"—one dated Dec. BSIP 12/VI/6/37.

1947c   Letter on Salaimanu critique of Maasina Rule and Nori. 12 Aug. BSIP 12/VI/4.

Codrington, Robert Henry (Head, Melanesian Mission 1871–1877)

1969   *The Melanesians: Studies in Their Anthropology and Folk-Lore.* Oxford: Clarendon Press. First published 1891.

Cohn, Bernard S

1996   *Colonialism and Its Forms of Knowledge: The British in India.* Princeton: Princeton University Press.

Colchester-Wemyss, E J H

1950   Secret telegram to Superintendent of Police, Honiara. 10 March. BSIP 12/I/9.

Colley, P

1940   Acting DO Gela to SG on Gela legal resolutions. 18 June. BSIP 1/III/36/9/1.

Collins, P V (Assistant Superintendent Police, 'Aoke 1950)

1950   Report to Colchester-Wemyss, "Shot Fired in Auki Station." May. BSIP 12/I/9.

Collinson, Clifford W
1926   *Life and Laughter among the Cannibals.* New York: E P Dutton.
Colony of Fiji
1896   *Report of the Commission Appointed to Inquire into Decrease of the Native Population.* Suva, Fiji: Government Printer.
Comins, Richard Blundell (Melanesian Mission)
1893   Letter from Wano to Robert Henry Codrington. 7 Sept. *Melanesian Mission Occasional Papers,* March 1894: 21–22. PC.
1897   "Minutes of Inquiry Held at Gavutu, 28 June 1897." Copy with Woodford letter to Bakeley at WPHC. 12 July. WPHC Series 4, inward correspondence 376/1897.
1902   The Vaukolu of 1902. *SCL* 1 Oct: 59–62.
Commonwealth Parliament of Australia
1901   The Pacific Island Labourers Act (Commonwealth) No. 16. 17 Dec. In *Selected Documents in Australian History 1851–1900,* edited by C Manning H Clark, 232–233. Sydney: Angus & Robertson.
Coombe, Florence Edith (Melanesian Mission)
1911   *Islands of Enchantment: Many-Sided Melanesia.* London: MacMillan. PC.
[Cooper, Harold]
1946   *Among Those Present: The Official Story of the Pacific Islands at War.* London: Prepared for the Colonial Office by the Central Office of Information.
Cooper, Matthew
1966   Letter to Harold Scheffler. 31 Dec. Scheffler Papers, Tuzin Archive for Melanesian Anthropology, Mandeville Special Collections Library, University of California, San Diego, MSS 481.
Coppet, Daniel de
nd   For a Portrait of the 'Are'are Society. MS. Translator from French unknown. Held in Solomon Islands National Museum, Honiara.
1977   First Exchange, Double Illusion. *Journal of the Cultural Association of the Solomon Islands* 5:23–39.
1981   The Life-giving Death. In *Mortality and Immortality: The Anthropology and Archaeology of Death,* edited by Sarah C Humphries and Helen King, 175–204. London: Academic Press.
Corris, Peter
1970   Kwaisulia of Ada Gege: A Strong Man in the Solomon Islands. In *Pacific Island Portraits,* edited by James W Davidson and Deryck Scarr, 225–265. Canberra: Australian National University.
1973a   The Man Who Lived before His Time. *PIM* 44 (10): 49, 51.
1973b   *Passage, Port and Plantation: A History of Solomon Islands Labour Migration 1870–1914.* Melbourne: University of Melbourne Press.
Coultas, William F
1929–1930 Journal and Notes from Whitney South Sea Expedition, May 1929–Nov. 1930. Vol P. MS held by Department of Ornithology, American Museum of Natural History, New York.
Crass, A G Kenneth
1946a   "A Disturbance on Ulawa." DC Central report to RC Noel, with appendix of Belshaw 1946, "Relevant Telegraphic Correspondence," and testimonies. 18 June. BSIP 12/I/2.

1946b DC Central letter to SG re Asa Hoe November letter on Makira. 4 Nov. BSIP 4/C91.

1946c DC Central to SG, "The Marching Law Movement—San Cristoval." 26 Nov. BSIP 4/C91.

1947a "D.C.'s Tour report San Cristoval—MARCHING LAW." 30 April. BSIP 4/C91.

1947b DC Central to SG, "U.S. Activities—San Cristoval," and "Marching Rule, San Cristoval." 3 May. BSIP 4/C91.

1947c DC Central to SG, cover letter to Alec FS Davidson's "Tour Report—Longgu District, Guadalcanal; April." 30 May. BSIP 8/I/43/4.

1947d DC Central memo, "Activities of Vouza G. M., District Headman, Tasiboko." 13 July. BSIP 4/C173.

1948   Letter to RC Noel from London. 22 Jan. BSIP C4/82.

Creech Jones, Arthur (Secretary of State for Colonies 1946–1950)

1946   Telegram to HC Grantham. 30 Nov. BSIP 4/C91.

Crichlow, Nathaniel (BSIP Medical Officer)

1929   The Prevalent Diseases of the British Solomon Islands. *Transactions of The Royal Society of Tropical Medicine and Hygiene* 23 (2): 179–184.

Cromar, John

1935   *Jock of the Islands: Early Days in the South Seas.* London: Faber & Faber.

Crosby, Alfred

2003   *America's Forgotten Pandemic: The Influenza of 1918.* 2nd ed. New York: Cambridge University Press.

D'Arcy, Paul

1987   Firearms on Malaita—1870–1900. In *Wansalawara: Soundings in Melanesian History,* edited by Brij Lal, 50–87. Working Paper Series. Honolulu: Pacific Islands Studies Program, University of Hawai'i.

Darwin, Charles

1874   *The Descent of Man.* Revised 2nd ed. New York: A L Burt.

Dausabea, David (HM Kwara'ae)

1951   Report to DC Allan. 4 April. BSIP 12/I/3.

1952   Report on "Meeting at Fiu" (noted by unknown officer). 25 March. BSIP 12/V/12.

Davenport, William

1970   Two Social Movements in the British Solomons that Failed and Their Political Consequences. In *The Politics of Melanesia,* edited by Marion W Ward, 162–172. Canberra: Research School of Pacific Studies; Port Moresby: University of Papua New Guinea.

1989   *Taemfaet:* Experiences and Reactions of Santa Cruz Islanders during the Battle for Guadalcanal. In *The Pacific Theater: Island Representations of World War II,* edited by Geoffrey White and Lamont Lindstrom, 257–278. Honolulu: Center for Pacific Islands Studies and University of Hawai'i Press.

Davenport, William, and Gülbün Çoker

1967   The Moro Movement of Guadalcanal. *Journal of the Polynesian Society* 76 (2): 123–175.

Davidson, Alec F S

1947   Report on April visit to Longgu. 30 May. BSIP 8/I/43/4.

Davies, Roy J (DO Malaita 1945–1946; DC Malaita 1947–1948)

nd   Marching Rule: A Personal Memoir. MS, possibly completed 1979. Pacific Manuscript Bureau film 1076.

1947a   Asst DC Kirakira to DC Central A G Kenneth Crass, "Visit of U.S. L.S.T. 340 to Star Harbour and Political Situation There." 12 April. BSIP 4/C91.

1947b   Telegram to DC Central forwarded to SG (with commentary by A G Kenneth Crass). 3 May. BSIP 4/C91.

1947c   DC Malaita report to RC Noel, "Illegal Courts on Malaita." 31 July. BSIP 4/C91.

1947d   Top secret letter to RC Noel on arrest plan. 13 Aug. BSIP 4/SF108.

1947e   Telegram to SG on Malaitan courts and defiance. 19 Aug. BSIP 4/SF108.

1947f   "Political Situation in North Malaita." 22 Aug. BSIP 4/SF108.

1947g   Report to SG on Operation Delouse. 10 Sept. BSIP 4/SF108/1.

1947h   Letter to SDNA David Trench, with Marquand report on Malu'u, Matakwalo, and Fo'odo. 6 Oct. BSIP 27/VII/1.

1947i   Comments on Marquand's tour report of Malu'u, Matakwalao, and Fo'odo, to SDNA. 10 Oct. BSIP 27/VII/1.

1947j   "Tour Report—Kwai Sub-District, 6–8 Nov." 1 Dec. BSIP 1/III/14/33/1.

1947k   Memo to Germond, comments on "Memorandum on Post MR Reconstruction in Malaita" by Cameron (Cameron 1947o). 10 Dec. BSIP 12/I/1.

1947l   Memo to Germond, "Comments on attached report by Mr. Marquand entitled 'Political Notes on Marching Rule'" (Marquand 1947e). 28 Dec. BSIP 12/I/1.

1948a   Notes on east coast tour, Maanawai to Uru. 31 Jan–2 Feb. BSIP 10/I/34/11–14.

1948b   Letter to RC Noel. 7 Feb. BSIP 12/I/2.

1950a   DC Western telegram and memo to SG. 4 Jan. BSIP 4/SF108.

1950b   DC Western to SG re conversation with Head Chiefs. 24 Jan. BSIP 4/SF108.

1950c   DC Western comments to SDNA on Belshaw's "Native Movements in Melanesia." 6 Dec. BSIP 4/SF151.

1951a   SDNA for RC Office to DC Malaita Allan, confidential. 10 Feb. BSIP 12/I/13.

1951b   Comments on DC Malaita Allan MQR. 30 June. Note at front of file BSIP 4/CF187.

Dawbin, W H

1966   Porpoises and Porpoise Hunting in Malaita. *Australian Natural History* 15 (7): 207–211.

Deck, Joan B

[1943?]   What Amazed the Americans. MS. SSEM Archive.

Deck, Mary Alice

1931   Letter to mother and Norman Deck. 13 Oct. SSEM Archive.

Deck, Norman C

1923   Letter to Florence Young. 22 June. SSEM Archive.

1927a   Letter to Florence Young. 13 Sept. SSEM Archive.

1927b   Letter to Florence Young. 10 Dec. SSEM Archive.

1928a   Letter to Florence Young. Feb. SSEM Archive.

1928b   Letter to Florence Young. 10 April. SSEM Archive.

1928c   Memo to RC Kane on Malaitan oaths, "Lulu Fa'abua." May. Encl III in WPHC dispatch 273 from HC Hutson to Secretary of State for Colonies Leopold Amery, 4 July. CO225/225/56/22A.

1931a   Letter to Wallis, from Ngongosila. 26 Nov. SSEM Archive.

1931b   Letter to Florence Young. nd. SSEM Archive.

1932   Letter to "Dear Friend." 26 April. SSEM Archive.

1934–1935   Exchanges with H Ian Hogbin. *Oceania* 5 (2–4): 242–245, 368–370, 488–489.

1935   Letter to RC Ashley on adultery regulation. 3 May. BSIP 1/III/36/9/1.

1937   Letter to G E D Sandars attaching letter from Hamuel Hoahania on destructive impacts of 'Are'are *houraa* feasts. 18 July. BSIP 14/18.

1940   Letter to Kathleen Deck, from Onepusu. 26 Feb. SSEM Archive.

1942a   Letter to Mary Deck. 6 Feb. SSEM Archive.

1942b   Letter to Kathleen Deck, from Naafinua. 28 April. SSEM Archive.

1943   Letter to Kathleen Deck, from Tulagi. 27 Feb. SSEM Archive.

1944   Letter to Mary Deck, from Naafinua. 10 May. SSEM Archive.

1947a   Letter to Mary Deck, from Naafinua. 28 Dec. SSEM Archive.

1947b   Letter to Roy Davies. 30 Dec. BSIP 12/I/2/7.

1948a   Letters to Mary Deck. Feb–Aug. Cited by date. SSEM Archive.

1948b   "A Few Chronological Details on the Rise of the Marching Rule." nd. BSIP 12/I/5.

1948c   Letter to Acting RC Germond. 7 May. BSIP 12/I/5.

1948d   Letter to Michael Forster. 23 May. BSIP 10/I/34/23.

1948e   Letter to DO Malu'u Cameron. 4 Oct. BSIP 1/III/19/9/1.

1970–1971   E Knox notes on interviews with Norman Deck. Cited by date. SSEM Archive.

Deck, Northcote

1909   SSEM Letter for December. *NIV* Dec: np.

1910a   Across Malaita. SSEM Letter for May. *NIV* March: np.

1910b   "The Tragedy of Borasu [Borasu'u]." Letter for December. Woodford Papers, bundle 15, series 7/36/4 (encl in 9/28), Australian National University Library.

[1921?]   Letter to *NIV* nd: 5.

1923   Report on mission work. *NIV* April: 3–7.

Deringil, Selim

2003   "They Live in a State of Nomadism and Savagery": The Late Ottoman Empire and the Post-Colonial Debate. *Comparative Studies in Society and History* 45 (2): 311–342.

Devlin, Arthur T (Catholic priest)

1949   Letter to DC Malaita Masterman. 29 Oct. BSIP 12/V/2.

Dickinson, Joseph

1927   *A Trader in the Savage Solomons*. London: H F & G Witherby.

Dirks, Nicholas B

1996   Foreword. In *Colonialism and Its Forms of Knowledge: The British in India,* by Bernard S Cohn, ix–xvii. Princeton: Princeton University Press.

2001   *Castes of Mind: Colonialism and the Making of Modern India*. Princeton: Princeton University Press.

D.R.D.V.
[1947?] "The Kwara'ae District Advising by D.R.D.V." BSIP 10/2/34/16.

Durdin, Tillman
1966 Solomon Islands Emerging from Primitivism after Long Post-War Distress. *New York Times*, 25 Jan: 14.

Durrad, Walter John (Melanesian Mission)
1922 The Depopulation of Melanesia. In *Essays on the Depopulation of Melanesia*, edited by William H R Rivers, 3–24. Cambridge: Cambridge University Press.

Dzenovska, Dace, and Iván Arenas
2012 Don't Fence Me In: Barricade Sociality and Political Struggles in Mexico and Latvia. *Comparative Studies in Society and History* 54 (3): 644–678.

East Kwara'ae District Officer Diary
1953–1954 Cited by date. Author's copy.

Eastern District Quarterly and Annual Reports
1931–1947 Individual reports cited by date. BSIP 9/III/1.

Easton, Stewart C
1960 *The Twilight of European Colonialism: A Political Analysis*. New York: Holt, Rinehart and Winston.

Edge-Partington, Thomas W (District Magistrate, Malaita 1909–1912, 1913–1914)
1909a Letter to Acting RC Barnett. 12 Oct. BSIP 14/140.
1909b Letter to RC Woodford on pacification challenge. 18 Dec. BSIP 14/60.
1910a Letter to RC Woodford on gun smuggling. 28 March. BSIP 14/40.
1910b Letter to RC Woodford on tour behind Bina. 3 May. BSIP 14/40.
1910c Letter to RC Woodford on prisoner Joe Maekali. 19 May. BSIP 14/40.
1910d Letter to RC Woodford. 14 July. BSIP 14/40.
1910e Letter to RC Woodford on Sili murder and punishment. 14 Sept. BSIP 14/40.
1910f Letter to RC Woodford on Sili murder aftermath. 19 Sept. BSIP 14/40.
1910g Letter to RC Woodford on expedition behind Fo'odo. 1 Nov. BSIP 14/40.
1910h Letter to RC Woodford on captured deserters from Levers. 1 Nov. BSIP 14/40.
1910i Letter to RC Woodford on station personnel. 1 Nov. BSIP 14/40.
1910j Letter to RC Woodford on Kapahana murder case. 10 Nov. BSIP 14/40.
1910–1911 Court Minute Book, Government Station, Mala. BSIP 15/II/30.
1911a Letter to RC Woodford on census. 30 March. BSIP 14/40.
1911b Letter to Acting RC Frederick Barnett. 25 June. BSIP 14/40.
1911c Personal letter to Acting RC Barnett. 26 June. BSIP 14/40.
1911d General Report on Mala. 7 July. WPHC IC 1398/1911.
1913a Letter to RC Woodford. 4 May. BSIP 14/41.
1913b Letter to RC Woodford on fining Suu'aba natives. 9 July. BSIP 14/41.
1913c Letter to RC Woodford on adultery. 19 Sept. BSIP 14/42.
1914a Letter to RC Woodford on drilling at 'Aoke. 23 March. BSIP 14/42.
1914b Letter to RC Woodford on Roviana fluency. 22 May. BSIP 14/42.
1914c Letter to Acting RC Barnett. 15 Sept. BSIP 14/42.
1914d Letter to Acting RC Barnett. 12 Oct. BSIP 14/42.

Elkin, A P
1936 Education of Native Races in Pacific Countries. *Oceania* 7 (2): 145–168.

Epstein, A L
    1953   *The Administration of Justice and the Urban African: A Study of Urban Native Courts in Northern Rhodesia.* London: Her Majesty's Stationery Office.

Eyerdam, Walter J
    1929–1930   Journal, from Whitney South Sea Expedition, 17 August 1929–10 July 1930. Vol P. MS held by Department of Ornithology, American Museum of Natural History, New York City.
    1930   Correspondence to Mr F S Hall. *Murrelet* 11 (3): 76–78.
    1933a   Among the Mountain Bushmen of Malaita. Handwritten version of 1933b, which was in places politically sanitized before publication. Author's copy.
    1933b   Among the Mountain Bushmen of Malaita: Invading a Primitive Wilderness in the Cause of Science. *Natural History* 33 (4): 430–438.

Fabian, Johannes
    1983   *Time and the Other: How Anthropology Makes Its Object.* New York: Columbia University Press.

Fallowes, Richard Prince
    1939a   Letter to HC Luke, with enclosures. 15 June. BSIP 1/3/43/14/1. (Enclosures also repr in Laracy 1983, A5.)
    1939b   Letter to Secretary to H A Vaskess (Secretary WPHC). 19 June. BSIP 1/3/43/14/1.
    1939c   Letter to HC Harry Luke. 17 July. WPHC 43/14/1.
    1966   Letter to David Hilliard. 25 Jan. Author's copy, courtesy D Hilliard.
    1971   Letter to David Hilliard. 8 Jan. Author's copy, courtesy D Hilliard.

Falola, Toyin, and Matthew M Heaton
    2008   *A History of Nigeria.* Cambridge, UK: Cambridge University Press.

Fanon, Frantz
    1965   *A Dying Colonialism.* New York: Grove Weidenfeld.

Feldt, Eric A
    1946   *The Coast Watchers.* New York: Ballantine Books.

Field, John D
    1949a   Acting DO Malu'u to Masterman, "Cancellation of award of B.E.M. J. Irofiala." 8 July. BSIP 12/I/4.
    1949b   Acting DO Malu'u handover notes to Tom Russell. 19 July. BSIP 12/V/1.

Field, Sister (Melanesian Mission)
    1943   Excerpts of 15 Sept 1942 letter. *SCL* May: 14–15.

Fields, Karen
    1985   *Revival and Rebellion in Colonial Central Africa.* Princeton: Princeton University Press.

Fifi'i, Jonathan (East Kwaio Head Chief)
    1946   Letter to Nono'oohimae. 15 Nov. BSIP 12/VI/3/13.
    [1947?]   Undated letter to Nono'oohimae, confiscated at Kiu Custom house on 23 Sept 1947 by Peter Cameron. BSIP 12/I/6.
    1951a   Kwaio affairs report. 17 Aug. BSIP 27/I/9.
    1951b   Statement. 25 Oct. BSIP 12/V/8.
    1982a   Setting the Record Straight on "Marching Rule" and a 1927 Murder. *PIM* July: 15–18.
    1982b   Interviews (Kwaio language). Transcription by David Akin of interviews on Maasina Rule and related topics. Ngarinaasuru, Kwaio. Oct. Melane-

sian Archive, Mandeville Special Collections Library, University of California, San Diego.

1988a World War II and the Origins of Maasina Rule. Translated and edited by David Akin. In *The Big Death: Solomon Islanders Remember World War II*, edited by Geoffrey White, David Gegeo, David Akin, and Karen Ann Watson-Gegeo, 220–226. Suva: University of the South Pacific.

1988b Norman Deck and the Earthquake. Transcription of interview translated and edited by David Akin. Tuzin Archive for Melanesian Anthropology, Mandeville Special Collections Library, University of California, San Diego.

1989 *From Pig-Theft to Parliament: My Life Between Two Worlds.* Translated and edited by Roger Keesing. Suva: Institute of Pacific Studies.

1991 Remembering the War in the Solomons. From a 1988 interview and Fifi'i's own notes. Translated and edited by David Akin. In *Remembering the Pacific War,* edited by Geoffrey White, 37–46. Occasional Paper 36. Honolulu: University of Hawai'i Center for Pacific Islands Studies.

Fiji Times & Herald

1950 "Marching Rule Is Wound Up" and "British Tact and Sympathy are Back Again in Solomons." 8 Aug. Copy in BSIP 12/V/5.

Filose, Francis B (DO Malaita 1928–1929)

1926 Letter to SG. 29 July. BSIP 1/III/MP2203/1922.

Firth, Raymond

1983 A Comment on "Killing the Government...." In *The Pacification of Melanesia,* edited by Margaret Rodman and Matthew Cooper, 89–90. New York: University Press of America.

Fletcher, Arthur George Murchison (HC 1929–1936)

1930 Letter to RC Ashley. 7 March. BSIP 2/II/1659/29.

1931 Letter to Secretary of State for Colonies P Cunliffe-Lister. 14 Dec. BSIP 2/II/1659/29.

1932 Letter to Secretary of State for Colonies on adultery law. 5 Jan. BSIP 2/II/1659/29.

Foana'ota, Lawrence A

2012 The Culture or *Kastom* of Compensation: Payment Practices and Abusing the Applications in Solomon Islands Contemporary Society. MS.

Forikeo (Senior HM, west Kwaio)

1951 Handwritten report. 18 March. BSIP 12/I/13.

Forster, Edward Morgan

1984 *A Passage to India.* New York: Harcourt Brace.

Forster, Michael James (DO Malaita 1940–1941, 1943–1944, 1945–1947; DC Malaita 1948–1949)

1944a Letter to Defence Force Major Ragnar Hyne. 2 Feb. BSIP 1/III/19/9/1.

1944b Letter to Defence Force Major Ragnar Hyne. 16 Feb. BSIP 1/III/19/9/1.

1944c DO Malaita letter to SG, "Timothy George." 31 March. BSIP 1/III/19/9/1.

1945a Personal letter to Sandars, sent from Hobu Hobu. 14 Feb. BSIP 1/III/F58/68/II.

1945b "Bush tour behind Oloburi and Sinarago, 9–14 Sept." 18 Sept. BSIP 10/I/34/12.

1945c Notes from late August tour of western 'Are'are. 21 Sept. BSIP 8/I/34/22.

1946a   Three handwritten letters to David Trench. 15 and 17 June, 1 July. BSIP 1/III/19/9.

1946b   DC Malaita memo to SG on Ulawa incident. 11 July. BSIP 12/I/2/7.

1946c   "Political Activity on Malaita." Report to RC Noel on Maasina Rule attached to 1946 MAR. Dec. BSIP 27/VI/11 and 27/6/1.

1948a   April tour report, nd, with Germond's 23 April and 3 May comments. BSIP 12/I/1.

1948b   "Notes by District Commissioner Malaita." June. BSIP 12/I/5 and 4/SF168.

1948c   Malaita tour reports, with Germond comments. May–July. BSIP 1/III/14/33/1.

1948d   Memo to Germond. ca June. BSIP 12/I/5.

1948e   Malaita tour reports from August. Cited by area toured. BSIP 10/I/34/9–11.

1948f   "Urgent" letter to Germond on Uru situation. 27 Aug. BSIP 12/I/5.

1948g   Handwritten letter from Malu'u to Germond. 19 Sept. BSIP 4/SF108.

1948h   Telegram of 22 Oct to Acting RC Germond, with Trench response. BSIP 12/I/2.

1948i   Reports for east Kwaio and Small Malaita tours in Oct. 7 Nov. BSIP 12/I/1.

1949a   Report to Germond on arrests at Takataka on 26 Feb. 7 March. BSIP 4/SF108.

1949b   March tour reports. Cited by specific areas. 16 March. BSIP 29/III/5/file 2.

1950   DC Central "Tour Report of Marau Saltwater." 14 Feb. BSIP 4/SF108/pt 5.

Fortes, Meyer

1940   Review of H I Hogbin's *Experiments in Civilization. Man* 40:170–171.

Fortune, Reo F

1963   *Sorcerers of Dobu: The Social Anthropology of Dobu Islanders of the Western Pacific.* New York: E P Dutton. First published 1932.

Foster, George

1987   Colonial Administration in Northern Rhodesia in 1962. *Human Organization* 46 (4): 359–368.

Foster, Robert

1995   *Social Reproduction and History in Melanesia: Mortuary Ritual, Gift Exchange, and Custom in the Tanga Islands.* New York: Cambridge University Press.

Fowler, Wilfrid (DO Isabel 1930–1932; DO Malaita 1935–1936)

1936   Letter to SG asking for transfer from BSIP. 4 Feb. BSIP 1/III/58/27.

1959   *This Island's Mine.* London: The Adventurers Club.

Fox, Charles Elliot (Melanesian Mission)

1925   *The Threshold of the Pacific.* New York: Alfred Knopf.

1942–1949 Diary. MS. Pacific Manuscript Bureau film 550.

1943   From Malaita. Extracts from letter of 15 Aug 1942. *SCL* May: 13–14.

1948a   A Journey on Gela. *SCL* April: 20–22.

1948b   Letter from Fiu, to Reverend W J Durrad. 17 Aug. Turnbull Library, Wellington.

[1948c?] Extracts from letter on establishing Solomons "lingua franca." nd. Annexure C to Germond 1948b. BSIP 4 SF108/1.

1951   Letter to W J Durrad. 6 April. Author's copy.

1958   *Lord of the Southern Isles.* London: A R Mowbray.

1962   *Kakamora.* London: Hodder and Stoughton.
1967   *The Story of the Solomons.* Taroaniara: Diocese of Melanesia Press.
1985   *My Solomon Islands.* Honiara: Provincial Press.
Fox, James
    1987   The House as a Type of Social Organisation on the Island of Roti. In *De la hutte au palais: Sociétés "à maison" en Asie du Sud-Est insulaire,* edited by Charles Macdonald, 171–191. Paris: Centre de la Recherche Scientifique.
Fraenkel, Jon
    2004   *The Manipulation of Custom: From Uprising to Interventions in the Solomon Islands.* Wellington: Victoria University Press.
Frazer, Ian L
    1973   *To'ambaita Report: A Study of Socio-Economic Change in North-West Malaita.* Wellington, NZ: Department of Geography, Victoria University.
    1981   Man Long Taon: Migration and Differentiation amongst the To'abaita. Solomon Islands. PhD dissertation, Australian National University.
    1990   Maasina Rule and Solomons Islands Labour History. In *Labour in the South Pacific,* edited by Clive Moore, Jacqueline Leckie, and Doug Munro, 191–203. Townsville: James Cook University.
Freeston, Leslie Brian (HC 1948–1952)
    1948a   Confidential dispatch to RC Noel, with attachments by WPHC Legal Advisers "B.D.," and J H Vaughan. 14 Sept. BSIP 4/SF108.
    1948b   Letter to Secretary of State for Colonies Arthur Creech Jones. 30 Nov. BSIP 4/SF108.
    1949a   Dispatch to Secretary of State for Colonies. 30 June. WPHC 11/19/SF10/9.
    1949b   Telegram to Secretary or State for Colonies, re Masterman. 24 Dec. BSIP 1/P1/M/58/22/1.
Fulbright, Tim
    1986   The Marching Rule: A Christian Revolution in the Solomon Islands. MA thesis, University of British Columbia.
Furse, Ralph
    1962   *Aucuparius: Recollections of a Recruiting Officer.* New York: Oxford.
Futaiasi, Derek Gwali
    2010   An Assessment of Adjudicative Elements Dealing with Customary Land Disputes and Its Challenges in Malaita, Solomon Islands. Research Project toward Master of Law degree, University of the South Pacific, Vanuatu.
Ganifiri, Justus Jimmy (East Kwara'ae Head Chief)
    [1940s?]   Falafala ana Taki (The tradition of law). Code given by Ganifiri to Adriel Rofate'e, copied and translated by Ben Burt. Author's copy.
    1956   Out of the Miry Clay. *NIV* June: 4–5.
Garrett, John
    1997   *Where Nets Were Cast: Christianity in Oceania since World War II.* Suva: Institute of Pacific Studies; Geneva: World Council of Churches.
Geerts, Paul (Catholic priest)
    1948   Letter to DO Malaita. 15 June. BSIP 12/I/2.
    1970   *'Āre'āre Dictionary.* Canberra: Linguistic Circle of Canberra, Australian National University.

Gegeo, David Welchman
   1991   World War II in the Solomons: Its Impact on Society, Politics, and World
          View. In *Remembering the Pacific War,* edited by Geoffrey White, 27–36.
          Occasional Paper 36. Honolulu: University of Hawai'i Center for Pacific
          Islands Studies.
Gegeo, David Welchman, and Karen Watson-Gegeo
   1989   World War II Experience and Life History: Two Cases from Malaita. In
          The Pacific Theater: Island Representations of World War II, edited by Geof-
          frey White and Lamont Lindstrom, 353–371. Honolulu: Center for Pacific
          Islands Studies and University of Hawai'i Press.
   1996   Priest and Prince: Integrating Kastom, Christianity, and Modernization
          in Kwara'ae Leadership. In *Leadership and Change in the Western Pacific,*
          edited by Richard Feinberg and Karen Watson-Gegeo, 298–342. London:
          Athlone.
Germond, J D A (Divisional Officer Southern District 1947–1948; Acting RC
1948–1950)
   1948a Confidential letter to RC Noel. 7 Feb. BSIP 12/I/2.
   1948b "Political Situation on the Island of Malaita and Suggested Changes in the
          Present Administrative Policy," and three annexures. 15 Feb. With "strictly
          confidential" cover letter to RC Noel, "Subject—Native Affairs." 21 Feb.
          BSIP 12/I/5.
   1948c "Administrative Districts: Southern Division," to SG. 3 March. BSIP 12/I/5.
   1948d "Summary of a statement by the Divisional Officer at a meeting of Line
          Chiefs and Alahas of the Auki and Fiu Districts." 17 April, but summary
          undated. BSIP 12/I/5.
   1948e "Administration of Justice—Malaita." 22 April. BSIP 29/IV/4.
   1948f Letter to Norman Deck. 21 May. BSIP 12/I/5.
   1948g Memo to Trench on Malu'u situation. 21 June. BSIP 12/I/5.
   1948h Letter to DC Forster. 25 June. BSIP 12/I/5.
   1948i "Administrative Affairs—Malu'u District," to Trench. 15 July. BSIP 12/I/5.
   1948j Letter to Trench. 21 July.
   1948k "Legal Machinery for Dealing with M.R. Offences in Malaita," sent to
          BSIP Legal Adviser W T Charles. 11 Aug. BSIP 12/I/4.
   1948l Report to RC Noel, "Malu'u Sub-District—Anti M.R. Campaign." 27 Aug.
          BSIP 12/I/5
   1948m Message to DC Malaita Forster on Uru situation. 13 Sept. BSIP 12/I/2.
   1948n Memo to Forster prior to Germond's departure to be Acting RC. 5 Oct.
          BSIP 12/I/5.
   1948o Acting RC report to HC Freeston. 28 Oct. BSIP 4/SF108.
   1948p "Administrative Policy on Malaita with Special Reference to Marching
          Rule." 26 Nov. BSIP 12/I/1.
   1949a Acting RC secret dispatch to HC Freeston. 11 March. BSIP 4/SF108.
   1949b Memo to Divisional Officer Peter Hughes, Tulagi, "Marching Rule—
          Counter Activities in Malaita." 16 March. BSIP 12/V/1.
   1949c Telegram to HC Freeston on Forster arrests at Takataka. 31 March. BSIP
          4/SF108.
   1949d Telegram to HC Freeston on cost for arrests. 2 April. BSIP 4/SF108.
   1949e Secret memo to DC Malaita Masterman. 17 June. BSIP 12/V/1.

1949f   Telegram to DC Malaita Masterman. 12 Sept. BSIP 4/SF108.

1949g   Hand-written entry number 194 at beginning of file. 13 Sept. BSIP 4/ SF108.

1950a   Memo to Superintendent of Police, Honiara, re prisoner work and rations. ca 4 Jan. BSIP 4/SF108.

1950b   "Memorandum on Marching Rule." 11 April. BSIP 12/V/3.

Gibbins, William

1950   After Thirty Years. *NIV* Dec: 3–4.

1952a   A Portend of Victory. *NIV* March: 3.

1952b   SSEM Director's letter to DC Malaita Andersen. 25 Aug. BSIP 12/V/13.

Gilbird, "Chief of Funafou"

[1947?]   Informant report, "The Report Point from Makwanu District." ca spring. BSIP 12/I/2.

Gilchrist, Alexander

1927   *From the Middle Temple to the South Seas.* London: John Murray.

Giles, W E

1968   *A Cruize in a Queensland Labour Vessel in the South Seas.* Edited by Deryck Scarr. Honolulu: University of Hawai'i Press.

Giripiru, Willie

1943   Letter to chief of Kia, Western Isabel, re gathering of Red Cross contributions. English translation. Oct. Author's copy.

Glover, J N

1958   BSIP Attorney General commentary on "Native Courts." Nov. BSIP 10/II/ DA/I/16.

Goh, Daniel P S

2007   States of Ethnography: Colonialism, Resistance, and Cultural Transcription in Malaya and the Philippines, 1890s–1930s. *Comparative Studies in Society and History* 49 (1): 109–142.

Golden, Graeme A

1993   *The Early European Settlers of the Solomon Islands.* Mentone, VIC: privately published.

Goldie, John Francis (Methodist missionary, Western Solomons 1902–1951)

1914   The Solomon Islands. In *A Century in the Pacific,* edited by James Colwell, 559–585. London: Charles H Kelly.

Gooberman, Rachael

1999   The Constraints of "Feeling Free": Becoming Middle Class in Honiara (Solomon Islands). PhD dissertation, University of Edinburgh.

Goodrich, James E

1894   Commander's report to Commander-in-Chief on activities of HMS *Royalist.* Public Record Office, London. Document ADM1/7252.

Grant, Jonathan

2007   *Rulers, Guns, and Money: The Global Arms Trade in the Age of Materialism.* Cambridge, MA: Harvard University Press.

Grantham, Alexander William George Herder (HC 1945–1946)

1946   Letter to Secretary of State for Colonies Arthur Creech Jones re Maasina Rule. 10 Sept. BSIP 4/C91.

1947   Letter to Acting Secretary of State for Colonies Ivor Bulmer-Thomas. 15 Jan. BSIP 4/C91.

Grattan, C Hartley
    1961   *The United States and the Southwest Pacific.* Cambridge, MA: Harvard University Press.
Great Britain Colonial Office
    1883   *Correspondence Respecting the Natives of the Western Pacific and the Labour Traffic.* London: Great Britain Colonial Office.
Green, Kaye
    1976   The History of Post-Spanish European Contact in the Eastern District before 1939. In *Southeast Solomon Islands Culture History: A Preliminary Survey,* edited by Roger Green and Mary Meyerhoff Cresswell, 31–46. Wellington: Royal Society of New Zealand, Bulletin 11.
Gregory-Smith, Henry Graham (RC 1950–1952)
    1950–1952   Tour reports. Cited by date. BSIP 3/II/8.
    1950a   Handwritten "Note to file." 17 Feb. BSIP 4/SF108.
    1950b   Memo to SG, "Interview with Nono'oohimae." 23 Feb. BSIP 4/SF108.
    1950c   Note to SG re meeting "Viv" Hodgess. 25 Feb. BSIP 4/SF108/3/V, front of file.
    1950d   "Extract from Memorandum." 16 March. BSIP 12/I/7.
    1950e   Memo on Marching Rule ("strictly confidential"). 11 April. BSIP 12/V/3.
    1950f   Secret report to HC Freeston on "the Malaita situation." 25 Nov. BSIP 12/V/6.
    1951a   Explanatory notes on new District Councils. nd. BSIP 27/II/31.
    1951b   Application under Colonial Development and Welfare Act for cocoa project. 2 April. BSIP 12/I/13.
    1951c   Confidential letter to HC Freeston, "Native Administration." 2 Aug. BSIP 12/V/7.
    1951d   "Notes of Discussion with Rev. W. Gibbins, S.S.E.M." 11 Oct. BSIP FS166.
Gregory-Smith, H G, and Frederick Bentley
    1951   Exchange over recruiting of married men. 28 Nov and 2 Dec. BSIP 4/SF108/8/5/notes at front of file.
Griffin, James, Hank Nelson, and Stewart Firth
    1979   *Papua New Guinea: A Political History.* Richmond, VIC: Heinemann Educational Australia.
Griffiths, Alison
    1977   *Fire in the Islands! The Acts of the Holy Spirit in the Solomons.* Wheaton, IL: Harold Shaw.
Griffiths, K E
    1943   Present and Probable Changes in the Solomons. *NIV* Dec: 4–5.
Grover, John C (BSIP geologist)
    1949   *Some Aspects of Mining Development in the British Solomon Islands Protectorate.* Honiara: Geological Survey of the BSIP.
    1955   *Geology, Mineral Deposits and Prospects of Mining Development in the BSIP.* London: WPHC.
    1957   Some Geographical Aspects of the British Solomon Islands in the Western Pacific. *Geographical Journal* 123 (3): 298–314.
    1958   Geological Survey of the B.S.I.P. Plans for Visit of HMS "Cook." 30 March. MS. Author's copy.

Grundy, Trevor
  2008   Mugabe Birthday: No Cause for Celebration. "Report News: Zimbabwe Crisis Reports." Institute for War & Peace Reporting website, 10 April. http://
          iwpr.net/report-news/mugabe-birthday-no-cause-celebration [accessed 9
          Nov 2011].
Guglielmo, Thomas A
  2010   "Red Cross, Double Cross": Race and America's World War II-Era Blood
          Donor Service. *Journal of American History* 97 (1): 63–90.
Guha, Ranajit
  1983   The Prose of Counter-Insurgency. *Subaltern Studies: Writings on South Asian
          History and Society* 2:1–42. New Delhi: Oxford University Press.
  1989   Dominance without Hegemony and Its Historiography. *Subaltern Studies:
          Writings on South Asian History and Society* 6:210–309. New Delhi: Oxford
          University Press.
Guidieri, Remo
  1988   Two Millenaristic Responses in Oceania. In *Ethnicities and Nations,* edited
          by Remo Guidieri, Francesco Pellizzi, and Stanley Tambiah, 172–198. Austin: University of Texas Press.
Guo, Pei-yi
  2001   Landscape, History and Migration among the Langalanga, Solomon
          Islands. PhD dissertation, University of Pittsburgh.
Guppy, Henry B
  1887   *The Solomon Islands and Their Natives.* London: Swan Sonnenschein, Lowrey.
Gutch, John (HC 1955–1961)
  1961   Excerpt from address to Melanesian Mission 112th anniversary meeting
          in London, 14 June. *SCL* 69 (3): 65–81.
  1987   *Colonial Servant.* Padstone, Cornwall: T J Press.
Hailey, William Malcolm
  1938   *An African Survey.* London: Oxford University Press.
  1939   Some Problems Dealt with in the "African Survey." *International Affairs*
          18:194–210.
  1944   *The Future of Colonial Peoples.* Princeton: Princeton University Press.
  1947   British Colonial Policy. In *Colonial Administration by European Powers,* edited
          by Jose de Almada and others, 83–97. London: Royal Institute of International Affairs.
  1950   *Native Administration in the British African Territories. Part I: East Africa:
          Uganda. Kenya, Tanganyika.* London: Great Britain Colonial Office.
Hall, George Henry (Secretary of State for Colonies 1945–1946)
  1946   Telegram to HC Grantham on BSIP education needs. 15 Sept. BSIP 4/
          FC91.
Hamlin, Hannibal
  1928–1930 Journal and Notes, from Whitney South Sea Expedition, 8 Nov
          1928–8 Aug 1930. Vol P. MS held by Department of Ornithology, American Museum of Natural History, New York City.
Harrisson, Tom Harnett
  1937   *Savage Civilization.* New York: Alfred A Knopf.
Harwood, Frances
  1966   Letter to Harold Scheffler. 30 Nov. Scheffler Papers, Tuzin Archive for

Melanesian Anthropology, Mandeville Special Collections Library, University of California, San Diego, MSS 481.

1978   Intercultural Communication in the Western Solomons. In *Mission, Church, and Sect in Oceania,* edited by James Boutilier, Daniel Hughes, and Sharon Tiffany, 231–250. Ann Arbor: University of Michigan Press.

Healy, Allan
1966   Administration in the British Solomon Islands. *Journal of Administration Overseas* 5 (3): 194–204.

Hearth, John D M (DO 'Aoke, 1956)
1956a   "Survey of Small Malaita and other Sub-Districts of Malaita." 23 Feb. BSIP ADM29/IV; ADM/A/14.
1956b   Report to DC Malaita Russell, "Small Malaita Native Courts." 9 April. BSIP 10/II/ADM/A/9.
1956c   Report to DC Malaita Anderson, "Native Courts." 27 Dec. BSIP 10/II/ADM/A/9.

Heath, Ian
1978   Charles Morris Woodford: Adventurer, Naturalist, Administrator. In *More Pacific Islands Portraits,* edited by Deryck Scarr, 193–209. Canberra: Australian National University.
1981   Solomon Islands: Land Policy and Independence. *Kebar Sebran Sulating Maphilindo* 8/9:62–77.

Heber, Hedley (Fataleka Head Chief)
1945–1947   Diary, 1 Jan 1945–10 March 1947. BSIP 12/V/3/12.

Heffernan, N S (DO Isabel 1917–1918, 1924–1925)
1924a   Report to Acting RC on native affairs for 1923. 3 March. WPHC IC 849/24.
1924b   Report to Acting RC on the working of "Native Administration Regulation of 1922." 21 March. WPHC IC 849/24.

Hemming, George Radcliffe
1946   Extracts from his circular letter from Fauaabu, north Malaita. 15 Dec. Sent by WPHC to RC Noel with cover letter. BSIP 4/C101.
1947   The Mission Hospital, Fauabu. *SCL* June: 24–27.
1993   A Pacific Life. Archived at http://anglicanhistory.org/oceania/hemming_memoir.pdf. [accessed 9 Nov 2011].

Herbert, A Xavier
1979   Interview by Peter Corris, Townsville, 22 May. Keesing Papers, Tuzin Archive for Melanesian Anthropology, Mandeville Special Collections Library, University of California, San Diego, MSS 427.

Higginson, Robert Cyril (Judicial Commissioner)
1928   "A Short Statement of the Matters Leading up to the Murders of Messrs Bell and Lillies...." nd. BSIP 27/I/14B.

Hill, H
1936a   Letter to Malaita DO Fowler on trouble while recruiting. 14 Jan. BSIP 29/I/1.
1936b   Letter to Malaita DO Fowler on Sinalagu recruit desertions. 17 Jan. BSIP 29/I/1.

Hill, Lance
1989   Traditional Porpoise Harvest in the Solomon Islands, Preliminary Report—March 1989. MS held by Solomon Islands National Museum.

Hill, Ralph Brodhurst (DO Malaita 1915; later Acting RC)

1915   Letter to Acting RC Barnett on problems at Baunani. 29 June. WPHC CO225/153.

1924a   Letter to HC Cecil Rodwell on working of "Native Administration Regulation of 1922." 22 Feb. WPHC IC 849/24.

1924b   Letter to HC Cecil Rodwell on section 19 of "Native Administration Regulation of 1922." 28 April. WPHC 849/24.

Hilliard, David

1969   The South Sea Evangelical Mission in the Solomon Islands. *Journal of Pacific History* 4:41–64.

1974   Colonialism and Christianity: The Melanesian Mission in the Solomon Islands. *Journal of Pacific History* 9:93–116.

1978   *God's Gentlemen: A History of the Melanesian Mission, 1849–1942.* St. Lucia: University of Queensland.

Hipkin, Howard Stockdale (Melanesian Mission)

1936   Evangelising in Central Mala. *SCL* June: 89–92.

Hoasihau

1951   Report to DC Allan on political situation. ca Aug. BSIP 12/V/7.

Hobbs, William H

1945   *Fortress Islands of the Pacific.* Ann Arbor: J W Edwards.

Hodgess, C H V "Viv" (Captain in charge of SILC camp, A'ama, Gela)

1943   Report re recruiting native labor on Guadalcanal. nd (with 12 Dec handwritten note by Noel). BSIP 1/III/9/44.

Hogbin, Herbert Ian Priestley

1930   The Problem of Depopulation in Melanesia as Applied to Ongtong Java. *Journal of the Polynesian Society* 39 (153): 43–66.

1933   Indirect Rule for Native Peoples. *Sydney Morning Herald,* 8 Dec:16.

1934   Culture Change in the Solomon Islands: Report of Field Work in Guadalcanal and Malaita. *Oceania* 4 (3): 233–269.

1934–1935   Exchange with Norman Deck. *Oceania* 5 (2–4): 242–245, 368–370, 488–489.

1935   Sorcery and Administration. *Oceania* 6 (1): 1–36.

1943a   Preliminary Report to Acting RC Trench. 1 Oct. BSIP 1/11/F9/44.

1943b   "Report to Acting RC Trench" (and commentary on BSIP 1943d). 10 Oct. BSIP 1/14/F9/44.

1943c   Report to RC Noel, "Big Gela and Olevuga-Vatilau Subdistricts, Florida, in October, 1943." 30 Oct. Author's copy.

1944   Native Councils and Native Courts in the Solomon Islands. *Oceania* 14 (4): 257–283.

1945   Notes and Instructions to Native Administrations in the British Solomon Islands. *Oceania* 16 (1): 61–69.

1946   Local Government for New Guinea. *Oceania* 17 (1): 38–65.

1951   *Transformation Scene: The Changing Culture of a New Guinea Village.* London: Routledge & Kegan Paul.

1958   Review of Colin Allan's *Customary Land Tenure in the British Solomon Islands Protectorate. Oceania* 28:336.

1964   *A Guadalcanal Society: The Kaoka Speakers.* New York: Holt, Rinehart and Winston.

1970   *Experiments in Civilization: The Effects of European Culture on a Native Community in the Solomon Islands.* New York: Schocken Books. First published 1939.

1976   *Changing Melanesia.* Westport, CT: Greenwood Press. First published 1954.

Hogbin, H Ian, and Camilla Wedgwood

1943   *Development and Welfare in the Western Pacific.* Canberra: Federal Capital Press. Repr in *Pacific Affairs* 17 (2): 133–155 (1944).

Hokelema, Timothy

1947   Contribution to, The Stories of the Crew. *NIV* June: 9.

Holland, John (Sub-inspector, 'Aoke Police)

1961   Comments on 13 April patrol report by Captain 'Adifaka. BSIP 12/IV/M130/4/2C.

Holton, Russell G (Major, IGD, Inspector General)

1945   Memo to Colonel R G Howie, Commander, US Island Command. 23 Nov. BSIP 1/III/19/8.

Homewood, David

2005   Trevor Edward Ganley DFM. Wings over Cambridge website. http://www.cambridgeairforce.org.nz/Trevor%20Ganley.htm [accessed 9 Nov 2011].

Hopkins, Arthur Innes (Melanesian Mission)

1903   Some Experiences on a New Station in the Solomons. *SCL* nd (early in year): 7.

1904a   District of N. Mala. *SCL* April: 25–28.

1904b   A Bush Village. *SCL* May: 20–21.

1905   District of North Mala. *SCL* April: 23–29.

1906   North Mala Report, 1905. *SCL* May: 7–10.

1907   The Kanakas' Return. *SCL* Dec: 97–99.

1908a   North Mala. *SCL* Supplement, Annual Report, April: 32–39.

1908b   Mala and Its People. *SCL* May–Aug: np.

1909   Letter from Rev A H Hopkins, Ngore Fou. Trinity Sunday. *SCL* Oct: 536–537.

1910   Diary of Rev A H Hopkins. 2 June. *SCL* 12 Nov: 89–91.

1911   Mala Diary. *SCL* Feb: 27–30.

1922   Depopulation in the Solomon Islands. In *Essays on the Depopulation of Melanesia,* edited by William H R Rivers, 62–66. Cambridge, UK: Cambridge University Press.

1927   *Melanesia To-day.* London: Society for Promoting Christian Knowledge. PC.

1928   *In the Isles of King Solomon: An Account of Twenty-Five Years Spent amongst the Primitive Solomon Islanders.* Philadelphia: J B Lippincott.

1930   *From Heathen Boy to Christian Priest.* St Christopher Books, no 33. London: Talbot Press (SPCK). PC.

1934   Autobiography. Typescript in Church of Melanesia Archive. Solomon Islands National Archive, Honiara. Page numbers refer to Akin's retyped copy. PC.

Horton, Dick Crofton (Cadet, Malaita, 1938; DO Guadalcanal 1939–1941)

1940   Letter to SG on influence of Fallowes on Guadalcanal. 2 Sept. BSIP I/III/f43/14/1.

1965   *The Happy Isles: A Diary of the Solomons.* London: The Travel Book Club.

Hubbard, P C
 1933   BSIP Chief Magistrate and Legal Adviser letter to RC on Richard Fallowes
        trial. 26 June. BSIP 1/III MP380/33, encl 10A.

Hughes, Peter (Divisional Officer Northern District 1947–1949; then SG; then
Acting RC)
 1948   Note to Acting RC Germond on Naafinua raid. 10 Dec. BSIP 4/SF108.
 1949a Secret telegram to Germond. 1 Feb. BSIP 4/SF108.
 1949b Memo to SG re DO Conference in ʻAoke. 5 Feb. BSIP 4/SF108.
 1952   Acting RC note to SG Philip Richardson, front of file. 20 Oct. BSIP 4/
        CF187.

Hutson, Eyre (HC 1925–1929)
 1927a Letter to Secretary of State for Colonies Leopold Amery on Barley request
        for transfer. 14 Feb. WPHC 149/27.
 1927b Telegram re Bell killing. 12 Nov. WPHC CO225/223/34/05.
 1928a Letter to Secretary of State for Colonies Amery. 5 July. C0225/54/22A.
 1928b Recommendations re Moorhouse report. 10 Oct. WPHC CO225/226/
        54139/1.

Huxley, Julian, and Phyllis Deane
 1944   *The Future of the Colonies.* London: Pilot Press.

Hviding, Edvard
 1996   *Guardians of the Marovo Lagoon: Practice, Place, and Politics in Maritime
        Melanesia.* Honolulu: Center for Pacific Islands Studies and University of
        Hawaiʻi Press.

Hyam, Ronald
 2006   *Britain's Declining Empire: The Road to Decolonization 1918–1968.* Cam-
        bridge, UK: Cambridge University Press.
 2010   *Understanding the British Empire.* Cambridge, UK: Cambridge University
        Press.

Idukana
 1948   Informant statement to the government. 21 Aug. BSIP 12/I/5.

Iliffe, John
 1979   *A Modern History of Tanganyika.* Cambridge, UK: Cambridge University
        Press.

Im Thurn, Everard F (HC 1904–1911)
 1913   Review of Douglas Rannie's *My Adventures among South Sea Cannibals. The
        Geographical Journal* 41 (2): 159–160.
 1922   Preface. In *Essays on the Depopulation of Melanesia,* edited by William H R
        Rivers, v–xviii. Cambridge, UK: Cambridge University Press.

Innes, James Ross
 1938   *Report of the Leprosy Survey of the British Solomon Islands Protectorate.* Suva:
        WPHC.

International Labour Office
 1932   Convention Concerning Forced or Compulsory Labour, 1930. I.L.O. No.
        29, 39 U.N.T.S. 55, Entered into Force 1 May. Human Rights Library web-
        site. http://www1.umn.edu/humanrts/instree/n0ilo29.htm [accessed 9
        Nov 2011].

Irschick, Eugene
 1994   *Dialogue and History: Constructing South India, 1795–1895.* Berkeley: Uni-
        versity of California Press.

Ivens, Walter George (Melanesian Mission)

1899   Ulawa and Mala. *SCL* 16 Jan: 28–32.

1902   A Visit to Mwala Paine. *SCL* 1 Dec: 78–80.

1903   Mala and Ulawa. *SCL* March: 21–25.

1905–1906   The Bishop's Visitation, 1905. *SCL*, serialized, cited by entry date.

1907   *Hints to Missionaries to Melanesia.* London: Melanesian Mission. PC.

1918   *Dictionary and Grammar of the Languages of Sa'a and Ulawa, Solomon Islands, with Appendices.* Washington, DC: Carnegie Institution of Washington. PC.

1921   *Grammar and Vocabulary of the Lau Language, Solomon Islands.* Washington, DC: Carnegie Institution of Washington. PC.

1924   The Melanesians: Effect of White Impact. *Argus* (Melbourne), 29 Nov: 9.

1925   The Solomon Islands. Declining Population. *Argus* (Melbourne), 10 Oct: 6.

1927   Letter to Dr Stanton at Colonial Office. 13 Jan. Lambert Papers, Tuzin Archive for Melanesian Anthropology, Mandeville Special Collections Library, University of California, San Diego, MSS 682.

1928a   *The Island Builders of the Pacific.* Philadelphia: J B Lippincott Company.

[1928b?]   "Memorandum on the British Solomon Islands," to Secretary of State for Colonies Leopold Amery. WPHC CO225/226/54139/6545.

1929   *A Dictionary of the Language of Sa'a (Mala) and Ulawa, South-east Solomon Islands.* Melbourne: Melbourne University Press.

1930   Snake Worship on North Mala. *SCL* Oct: 150–151.

1932/1934   *A Vocabulary of the Lau Language, Big Mala, Solomon Islands.* Polynesian Society Memoir, Journal of the Polynesian Society Supplements 41–43. New Plymouth: Thomas Avery.

1972   *Melanesians of the South-east Solomon Islands.* New York: Benjamin Blom. First published 1927.

Jack-Hinton, Colin (DO Malaita 1958)

1958   Tour Report, Kwara'ae and Kwaio, 26 Feb–7 March. BSIP 29/V/M11/1/2/I.

Jackson, K B

1975   Headhunting in the Christianization of Bugotu 1861–1900. *Journal of Pacific History* 10:65–78.

Johnson, Donald D

1976   American Impact on the Pacific Islands since World War II. In *Oceania and Beyond: Essays on the Pacific since 1945,* edited by Frank P King, 232–243. Westport, CT: Greenwood Press.

Johnson, F E (Acting RC)

1939   Letter to HC Harry Luke on literacy testing. 18 July. BSIP I/III/43/19.

Johnson, Osa

1945   *Bride in the Solomons.* London: George G Harrap.

Jolly, Margaret

1994   *Women of the Place: Kastom, Colonialism and Gender in Vanuatu.* Langhorne, PA: Harwood Academic Publishers.

1998   Other Mothers: Maternal "Insouciance" and the Depopulation Debate in Fiji and Vanuatu, 1890–1930. In *Maternities and Modernities: Colonial and Postcolonial Experiences in Asia and the Pacific,* edited by Kalpana Ram and Margaret Jolly, 177–212. Cambridge, UK: Cambridge University Press.

Jones, F L
  1944–1945   The Indentured System of Native Labour. *SCL* 1 Oct: 7–8, 34–35; 1
              Jan: 8–11.
Jourdan, Christine
  1995   Stepping Stones to National Consciousness: The Solomon Islands Case.
              In *Nation Making: Emergent Identities in Postcolonial Melanesia,* edited by
              Robert Foster, 127–149. Ann Arbor: University of Michigan Press.
Joy, G A
  1937   Letter to HC for the New Hebrides on establishment of native courts in
              northern areas. 23 Feb. New Hebrides dispatch 42. BSIP 1/III/49/10.
Kane, Richard Rutledge (RC 1921–1928)
  1922a   Letter to HC Cecil Rodwell. 6 May. WPHC 1448/22.
  1922b   Cover letter attached to 8 Aug letter from Bell. 24 Aug. WPHC IC 2667/
              1922.
  1923a   Comment on petition from "Settlers of the British Solomon Islands." 13
              July. WPHC 4/IV.
  1923b   "Instructions to Native District Headmen" sent to DOs. 13 Aug. BSIP 9/V/5.
  1928   Letter to HC Hutson on punitive expedition. 22 Aug. WPHC 1849/28.
Kaplan, Martha
  1989   *Luve Ni Wai* as the British Saw It: Constructions of Custom and Disorder
              in Colonial Fiji. *Ethnohistory* 36 (4): 349–371.
  1995   *Neither Cargo nor Cult: Ritual Politics and the Colonial Imagination in Fiji.* Dur-
              ham, NC: Duke University Press.
Keesing, Roger
  nd   Unpublished field notes. Keesing Papers, Tuzin Archive for Melanesian
              Anthropology, Mandeville Special Collections Library, University of Cali-
              fornia, San Diego, MSS 427. Cited by date and, where appropriate, page
              number.
  [1964?]   Letter to DO 'Aoke Robert Spivey on Kwaio political divisions. Keesing
              Papers, Tuzin Archive for Melanesian Anthropology, Mandeville Special
              Collections Library, University of California, San Diego, MSS 427.
  1968   Chiefs in a Chiefless Society: The Ideology of Modern Kwaio Politics. *Oce-
              ania* 38:276–280.
  1978a   Politico-Religious Movements and Anti-Colonialism on Malaita: Maasina
              Rule in Historical Perspective. *Oceania* 48:241–261 (pt 1); 49:46–73 (pt 2).
  1978b   *'Elota's Story: The Life and Times of a Solomon Islands Big Man.* New York: St
              Martin's Press.
  1980   Antecedents of Maasina Rule: Some Further Notes. *Journal of Pacific His-
              tory* 15 (2), pt 2: 102–107.
  1981   Still Further Notes on "Maasina Rule." *Journal of the Anthropological Society
              of Oxford* 12 (2): 131–134.
  1982a   Kastom in Melanesia: An Overview. In *Reinventing Traditional Culture: The
              Politics of Kastom in Island Melanesia,* edited by Roger Keesing and Robert
              Tonkinson. Special issue, *Mankind* 13 (4): 297–301.
  1982b   Kastom and Anticolonialism on Malaita: "Culture" as Political Symbol.
              In *Reinventing Traditional Culture: The Politics of Kastom in Island Melanesia,*
              edited by Roger Keesing and Robert Tonkinson. Special issue, *Mankind* 13
              (4): 357–373.

1982c   *Kwaio Religion: The Living and the Dead in a Solomon Islands Society*. New York: Columbia University Press.

1985   Killers, Big Men, and Priests on Malaita: Reflections on a Melanesian Troika System. *Ethnology* 24 (4): 237–252.

1986a   Plantation Networks, Plantation Cultures: The Hidden Side of Colonial Melanesia. *Journal de la Société des Océanistes* 82–83:163–170.

1986b   The Young Dick Attack: Oral and Documentary History on the Colonial Frontier. *Ethnohistory* 33:268–292.

1987   Ta'a Geni: Women's Perspectives on Kwaio Society. In *Dealing with Inequality: Analyzing Gender Relations in Melanesia and Beyond*, edited by Marilyn Strathern, 33–62. Cambridge, UK: Cambridge University Press.

1989   Creating the Past: Custom and Identity in the Contemporary Pacific. *The Contemporary Pacific* 1:12–42.

1992a   *Custom and Confrontation: The Kwaio Struggle for Cultural Autonomy*. Chicago: University of Chicago Press.

1992b   Kwaisulia as Culture Hero. In *History and Tradition in Melanesian Anthropology*, edited by James G Carrier, 174–192. Berkeley: University of California Press.

1997   Tuesday's Chiefs Revisited. In *Chiefs Today: Traditional Leadership and the Postcolonial State*, edited by Geoffrey White and Lamont Lindstrom, 253–263. Stanford: Stanford University Press.

Keesing, Roger, and Peter Corris
1980   *Lightning Meets the West Wind: The Malaita Massacre*. Oxford: Oxford University Press.

Kenipuria
1949   Speech at 'Aitomu, Takataka meeting. 15 Dec. BSIP 1/V/3.

Kennedy, Donald
1944   The Solomon Islander Wants to Be Sophisticated! *PIM* 15 (1): 17–18.

1946   This Is the Solomon Islander. In W*here the Trade Winds Blow*, edited by R W Robson and Judy Tudor, 168–170. Sydney: Pacific Publications.

1967   Marching Rule in the British Solomon Islands Protectorate: A Memorandum on the Origin of the Term. MS prepared for Institute of Colonial Studies at Oxford.

Kiki, Albert Maori
1968   *Ten Thousand Years in a Lifetime*. New York: Praeger.

King, Robert, editor
1985   Untitled collection of World War II accounts by people of Western Province, Solomon Islands. MS. Western Provincial Government, Gizo.

Kirakira (Makira)
1946   Notes on tour of Arosi, no author. March. BSIP 9/I/1.

Kirke, B (Commandant Armed Constabulary, Tulagi; Sub-Inspector on special duty, Malaita)
1917   Report to RC Barnett on Baunani plantation troubles. 30 Jan. WPHC CO225/153.

Kirk-Green, Anthony
1999   *On Crown Service: A History of HM Colonial and Overseas Services 1837–1997*. London: I B Tauris.

Klerk, Fr Emery de
1941–1944   Diary. US Naval Historical Center, Washington, DC. File 34(19)(A).

Knibbs, Stanley G C
  1929   *The Savage Solomons as They Were and Are*. Philadelphia: J B Lippincott Company.
Knox-Mawer, June
  1986   *Tales from Paradise: Memories of the British in the South Pacific*. London: Ariel Books and BBC Publications.
Kuper, Henry
  1933   Report on Eastern District. ca after May. BSIP 8/IX/6.
Kuva, Aduru
  [1974?]   *The Solomons Community in Fiji*. Suva: South Pacific Social Sciences Association and United Nations Development Program.
Kwaio Native Affairs Book
  1951   Cited by date. BSIP 27/I/9.
Kwara'ae Council
  1950   Unsigned letter given to 'Ataa Headman 'Itea. ca July. BSIP 12/V/4.
Kwara'ae Native Affairs Book
  1951–1952   Cited by date. BSIP 27/I/8.
Kwa'ioloa, Michael, and Ben Burt
  1997   *Living Tradition: A Changing Life in Solomon Islands*. London: British Museum Press.
  2007   "The Chiefs' Country": A Malaitan View of the Conflict in Solomon Islands. *Oceania* 77:111–127.
Labour Party
  1933   *The Colonial Empire*. London: Victoria House.
Lackner, Helen
  1973   Social Anthropology and Indirect Rule, the Colonial Administration and Anthropology in Eastern Nigeria: 1920–1940. In *Anthropology and the Colonial Encounter*, edited by Talal Asad, 123–151. London: Ithaca Press.
Lake, Marilyn, and Henry Reynolds
  2008   *Drawing the Global Color Line: White Men's Countries and the International Challenge of Racial Equality*. Cambridge, UK: Cambridge University Press.
Lal, Brij V
  1992   *Broken Waves: A History of the Fiji Islands in the Twentieth Century*. Honolulu: Center for Pacific Islands Studies and University of Hawai'i Press.
Lamani, Sam
  1947   Letter from 'Aoke to P Maukona. 5 Aug. BSIP 12/I/2/7.
Lambert, Sylvester M
  nd   Papers held at Tuzin Archive for Melanesian Anthropology, Mandeville Special Collections Library, University of California, San Diego. MSS 682. Items cited by box and folder number.
  1933   Diary of Solomons visit. May–June. Lambert Papers, Tuzin Archive for Melanesian Anthropology, Mandeville Special Collections Library, University of California, San Diego, MSS 682.
  1934a   *The Depopulation of the Native Races*. Special Publication 23. Honolulu: Bernice P Bishop Museum.
  1934b   *Health Survey, 1933* [of the BSIP]. Suva: J J McHugh.
  1941   *A Yankee Doctor in Paradise*. Boston: Little, Brown and Company.
Langabaea, Andrew
  1988   Untitled account of World War II. In *Taem Blong Faet: World War II in*

Melanesia, edited by Hugh Laracy and Geoffrey White. Special issue, *'O'o* 4:99–105.

Lansner, Tom
  1987   Black and White Memories of the Pacific War. *Far Eastern Economic Review* 6 Aug: 32–33.

Lanternari, Vittorio
  1963   *The Religions of the Oppressed: A Study of Modern Messianic Cults.* New York: Alfred A Knopf.

Laracy, Hugh
  1971   Marching Rule and the Missions. *Journal of Pacific History* 6:96–114.

  1976   *Marists and Melanesians: A History of Catholic Missions in the Solomon Islands.* Canberra: Australian National University.

  1979   Maasina Rule: Struggle in the Solomons. In *Race, Class and Rebellion in the South Pacific,* edited by Alexander Mamak and Ahmed Ali, 98–107. Sydney: George Allen & Unwin.

  1988a   War Comes to the Solomons. In *Taem Blong Faet: World War II in Melanesia,* edited by Hugh Laracy and Geoffrey White. Special issue, *'O'o* 4:17–26.

  1988b   Missionaries and the European Evacuation of the Solomon Islands, 1942–1943. In *Taem Blong Faet: World War II in Melanesia,* edited by Hugh Laracy and Geoffrey White. Special issue, *'O'o* 4:27–35.

  nd   Donald Gilbert Kennedy: A Refractory Outsider in the Colonial Service. In Watriama and Co.: Further Pacific Islands Portraits. Book ms in preparation.

Laracy, Hugh, editor
  1983   *Pacific Protest: The Maasina Rule Movement; Solomon Islands, 1944–1952.* Suva: Institute of Pacific Studies, University of the South Pacific.

Laracy, Hugh, and Eugenie Laracy
  1980   Custom, Conjugality and Colonial Rule in the Solomon Islands. *Oceania* 51 (2): 133–147.

Laracy, Hugh, and Geoffrey White, editors
  1988   *Taem Blong Faet: World War II in Melanesia.* Special issue, *'O'o* 4.

Larcom, Joan
  1982   The Invention of Convention. In *Reinventing Traditional Culture: The Politics of Kastom in Island Melanesia,* edited by Roger Keesing and Robert Tonkinson. Special issue, *Mankind* 13 (4): 330–337.

Lasaqa, Isireli Q
  1972   *Melanesians' Choice: Tadhimboko Participation in the Solomon Islands Cash Economy.* Canberra: New Guinea Research Unit, Australian National University.

Lasker, Bruno
  1944   Planning for Oceania. *Far Eastern Survey* 13 (2): 13–14.

Law, A Bonar
  1916   Letter to RC on requirements for DO promotions. 14 July. BSIP 14/12 1918.

Leckie, A
  1965   *Challenge for the Pacific.* New York: Doubleday.

Leprosy in Melanesia
  1949   Southern Cross Booklet 6. London: Melanesian Mission. PC.

Letter to 'Are'are *araha*
  1948a Signed "Erehau" (a name of Head Chief Aliki Nono'oohimae), but likely
         forged. 14 Nov. BSIP 10/I/34/16. (An English translation is in Laracy
         1983, C35.)
  1948b Letter said to be from Nono'oohimae, but likely forged. 22 Dec. BSIP 8/
         I/29/1.
Lever, R A
  [1990?] Crusoe among the Coconuts. MS held by Dep. of Africa, Oceania and
           the Americas, British Museum, London.
Lewes, Vaughan (Captain HMS *Cambrian*)
  1908 Two reports to Commander-in-Chief, Australian Station on punitive
        actions. 11 Aug. Australian National Library, film G1839, Royal Navy, Aus-
        tralian Station, vol 44, Northern Division Box.
Lewin, Julius
  1938 The Recognition of Native Law and Custom in British Africa. *Journal of
        Comparative Legislation and International Law,* 3d Ser, 20 (1): 16–23.
Lewis, I M
  1986 Possession Cults in Context. In *Religion in Context: Cults and Charisma,*
        23–50. Cambridge, UK: Cambridge University Press.
Lindley, Allan R (Sub-inspector in charge of Malaita Police)
  1958 Report on Kwaio tour of 15–28 May. 5 June. BSIP 12/I/40.
Lindstrom, Lamont
  1979 Americans on Tanna. *Canberra Anthropology* 2 (2): 36–45.
  1981 Cult and Culture: American Dreams in Vanuatu. *Pacific Studies* 4 (2):
        101–123.
  1989 Working Encounters: Oral Histories of World War II Labor Corps from
        Tanna, Vanuatu. In *The Pacific Theater: Island Representations of World War
        II,* edited by Geoffrey White and Lamont Lindstrom, 123–151. Honolulu:
        Center for Pacific Islands Studies and University of Hawai'i Press.
  1993a *Cargo Cult: Strange Stories of Desire from Melanesia and Beyond.* Honolulu:
         Center for Pacific Islands Studies and University of Hawai'i Press.
  1993b Cargo Inventories, Shopping Lists, and Desire. In *Talking about People,*
         edited by William Haviland and Robert Gordon, 25–39. Palo Alto: Mayfield.
Lindstrom, Lamont, and Geoffrey White
  1990 *Island Encounters: Black and White Memories of the Pacific War.* Washington,
        DC: Smithsonian Institution Press.
Lingat, Robert
  1973 *The Classical Law of India.* Translated by Duncan Derrett. Berkeley: Univer-
        sity of California Press.
Linnekin, Jocelyn
  1990 The Politics of Culture in the Pacific. In *Cultural Identity and Ethnicity in
        the Pacific,* edited by Jocelyn Linnekin and Lin Poyer, 149–173. Honolulu:
        University of Hawai'i Press.
Loloito (HM Ulawa)
  1947 Testimony on Maasina Rule events taken by Makiran Officer Valdemar
        Andersen. 31 Oct. BSIP 9/I/8.
London, Charmian
  [1910?] *A Woman among the Headhunters: A Narrative of the Voyage of the 'Snark' in
           the Years 1908–1909.* London: Mills and Boon.

London, Jack
  1911   *South Sea Tales*. New York: International Fiction Library.
  1913   *The Cruise of the Snark*. New York: Macmillan.

Lord, Walter
  1977   *Lonely Vigil: Coastwatchers of the Solomons*. New York: Viking Press.

Lugard, Frederick John Dealtry
  1965   *The Dual Mandate in British Tropical Africa*. London: Frank Cass. First published 1922.
  1970   *Political Memoranda: Revision of Instructions to Political Officers on Subjects Chiefly Political and Administrative, 1913–1918*. London: Frank Cass. First published 1919.

Luke, Harry Charles (HC 1938–1942)
  1945a *Britain and the South Seas*. London: Longman's, Green & Company.
  1945b *From a South Seas Diary 1938–1942*. London: Nicholson & Watson.
  1962   *Islands of the South Pacific*. London: George G Harrap.

MacDonald, Barrie K
  1976   Imperial Remnants: Decolonization and Political Change in the British Pacific Islands. In *Oceania and Beyond: Essays on the Pacific since 1945,* edited by F P King, 244–255. Westport, CT: Greenwood Press.

Macdonald-Milne, Brian
  2003   *The True Way of Service: The Pacific Story of the Melanesian Brotherhood 1925–2000*. Leicester: Christians Aware and The Melanesian Brotherhood.

Machiavelli, Niccolò
  1963   *The Prince*. New York: Washington Square Press.

MacKeith, Alexander A (DO 'Aoke 1950–1951)
  1950a "Minutes of a Conference Held at Sinarango" on 11 Sept. 19 Sept. BSIP 12/V/4.
  1950b "Report on the Political Situation in Kwara'ae." 17 Oct. BSIP 4/SF108/I.
  1951a Report to DC Allan on Rickwood prospecting tour. 20 April. BSIP 12/I/13.
  1951b Tour Diary, 22–28 May. BSIP 12/I/13.
  1951c "(Re)organization of District Services." 10 Sept. BSIP 12/I/12.

MacLaren, David
  2007   Culturally Appropriate Health Care in Kwaio: An Action Research Approach. PhD dissertation, Griffith University.

Macmillan Brown, J
  1927   *Peoples and Problems of the Pacific*. London: T Fisher Unwin.

MacQuarrie, Hector
  1948   *Vouza and the Solomon Islands*. New York: Macmillan.

Maetoloa, Meshach
  1985   The Remnant Church: Two Studies. In *New Religious Movements in Melanesia,* edited by Carl Loiliger and Garry W Trompf, 120–148. Suva: University of the South Pacific.

Mahaffy, Arthur W (Deputy Commissioner to RC Woodford)
  nd   Introductory text to his artifact collection. MS, copy typed by Aoife O'Brien. Author's copy.
  1902   Report to RC on HMS *Sparrow* actions, Savo and Malaita. 2 Oct. WPHC IC 7/1903.

Mair, Lucy P
  1936   *Native Policies in Africa*. London: G Routledge & Sons.

1948   *Australia in New Guinea*. London: Christophers.

1963   *New Nations*. Chicago: University of Chicago Press.

Malaita Council

1952   Minutes of first meeting. 6–7 Nov. BSIP 28/VII/B/1.

Malaita District

1909   DO Malaita Diary. 16 July. BSIP 15/VIII.

1930–1954   Malaita District Annual Reports. Cited by "MAR" and year. In files BSIP 1/III/14/7–21; 14; 27/I/20; 27/VI/1–17; 29/I/9.

1931–1935   Criminal Cases, Quarterly Returns, 31 March 1931–31 Dec 1935. BSIP 14/68.

1936   "District Headmen, Malaita" (with Bengough cover note). 17 Aug. BSIP 29/I/1.

1936–1954   Malaita District Quarterly Reports. Cited as "MQR" and closing date; tendered every third month's end. In files BSIP 1/III/19/3; 4/CF187; 12/V/7–8; 14; 28/VII/1; 29/I/1–5.

1937   "Matters to be brought up by the Natives for discussion with His Excellency," prepared for HC Arthur Richard's visit of 14 July. nd. BSIP 29/I/2.

1939a   "Matters to be brought up by Headmen for discussion with High Commissioner" (HC Harry Luke, visiting Malaita in July). nd. BSIP 29/I/4.

1939b   Notes on RC Marchant's Malaita tour. Dec. BSIP I/III/19/11.

1940   "District Headmen, Malaita." nd. BSIP 29/I/5.

1941a   District Officer's Diary. 21 May–18 July. BSIP 15/VIII/158.

[1941b?]   Malaita District Journal. nd. Chief Magistrate's Office (Ben Burt notes).

1944a   ZGJ (wartime coded call-sign for 'Aoke) to RC Noel. 23 June. BSIP 1/III/19/9.

1944b   Uru tour notes (likely by DC David Trench). 24 June. BSIP 10/I/34/11.

1944c   ZGJ to RC Noel. 23 Dec. BSIP 1/III/19/9/1.

1945a   "Native Administration Estimates, Malaita District." nd. BSIP 12/I/8.

1945b   Uru, Sinalagu, and 'Oloburi files. Cited by entry dates. BSIP 10/I/34/11, 12, and 13.

1945c   "Case of Fulaiasi Ground." 10 Sept. BSIP 10/I/34/13.

[1948?]   "List of headmen showing relationship to MR." ca May. BSIP 12/I/6.

1949   Notes on DO conference, 'Aoke, 31 Jan–1 Feb, with attached "List of Marching Rule Towns Still Fenced," and "Proposed Programme" to destroy towns. BSIP 8/2/4/3.

1953   "Meetings with Takanakwau, Irofiala, and Sau at 'Aoke." 27 Jan. BSIP 12/I/29.

[1956?]   Langalanga District Survey. nd. BSIP 10/II/ADM/A/31.

1958   Letter from DC Malaita to member for local government, Tanganyika. 13 Oct. Malaita M10/13/5.

[1959?]   Note on taxation problems in east Kwaio. nd. Malaita M50/9/9.

1960   Malaita Intelligence Report, 6 Oct–23 Dec. BSIP 12/I/42.

1961   Malaita Half-Yearly Report, 1 Jan–30 June. Malaita M10/14/1/1.

1968   Report on discussion, "Custom Movements on Malaita." 12 Sept. Malaita CF100/9/2.

Malaita Newsletter

1952–1971   Printed irregularly at 'Aoke by the Malaita District Administration starting in June 1952. Cited by date.

Malefijt, A de Waal

1968   *Religion and Culture: An Introduction to Anthropology of Religion.* London: Collier-Macmillan.

Malinowski, Bronislaw

1945   *The Dynamics of Culture Change.* New Haven: Yale University Press.

1961   *Argonauts of the Western Pacific.* New York: E P Dutton. First published 1922.

Malu'u (To'abaita)

1947   Diary of January events (likely by 'Atoomea). BSIP 12/I/1.

Mamdani, Mahmood

1996   *Citizen and Subject: Contemporary Africa and the Legacy of Late Colonialism.* Princeton: Princeton University Press.

2001   A Brief History of Genocide. *Transition* 10 (3): 26–47.

Manchester Guardian

1951   The Cargo Myth. 7 March: 4.

Mander, Linden A

1954   *Some Dependent Peoples of the South Pacific.* New York: Macmillan.

Manderson, Lenore

1987   Blame, Responsibility and Remedial Action: Death, Disease and the Infant in Early Twentieth Century Malaya. In *Death and Disease in Southeast Asia,* edited by Norman Owen, 257–282. New York: Oxford University Press.

Mann, William M

1948   *Ant Hill Odyssey.* Boston: Little, Brown and Company.

Maranda, Elli Kaija Köngäs

1973   Five Interpretations of a Melanesian Myth. *Journal of American Folklore* 86 (339): 3–13.

1974   Lau, Malaita: "A Woman Is an Alien Spirit." In *Many Sisters: Women in Cross-Cultural Perspective,* edited by Carolyn J Matthiasson, 177–202. New York: Free Press.

Marchant, William Sydney (RC 1940–1943)

1940a   Letter to DO Guadalcanal. 11 July. BSIP 1/III/36/9/1.

1940b   Notes on Malaita tour. 6–21 July. BSIP 1/III/19/11.

1940c   Letter to Bishop Baddeley on rumors about Fallowes. 25 July. BSIP 1/III/43/14/1.

1940d   Handwritten note in file re Fallowes. 13 Sept. BSIP 1/III/43/file 14.

1941   Letter to SG on Rendova Society. 2 June. BSIP 1/III/49/21.

1942a   Cover letter to all DOs for special regulations 1–4. 12 Dec. BSIP 29/11/7; 1/1.

1942b   Letter to Charles Widdy on SILC. 18 Dec. BSIP 5/I/1/3.

1942–1943   RC's Diary, 2 Jan 1942–6 May 1943. BSIP 5/4/1.

1943a   Letter to HC. 9 Feb. BSIP 5/I/1/3.

1943b   Letter to Charles Widdy on SILC strike. 10 Feb. BSIP 5/I/1/3.

1943c   Letter to Charles Widdy on SILC. 25 Feb. BSIP 5/I/1/3.

1943d   Letter to HC. 11 March. BSIP 5/I/1/3.

1943e   Letter to Charles Widdy on SILC strike. 23 March. BSIP 5/I/1/3.

1943f   Letter to Charles Widdy re his departure. 28 April. BSIP 5/I/1/3.

Mariko, Ni

1946   Notes on various Maasina Rule events at Malu'u and Kwai. BSIP 12/VI/7.

Marquand, Wilfred James (Cadet at Malu'u 1947–1948; DO 'Aoke 1948–1949)

1947a   "Report Number One from Malu'u." 18 July. BSIP 4/SF108.

1947b   "Report No. 2 from Malu'u." 24 July and 5 Aug. BSIP 4/SF108.

1947c   Report from Malu'u. 12 Sept. BSIP 12/VII/1.

1947d   Letter to Headmen re HMS *Theseus* and *Cockade* visits. 20 Sept. BSIP 12/ I/2/7.

1947e   "Political Notes on Marching Rule." 10 Dec. BSIP 12/I/1.

1948a   Tour Reports from Kwai, 'Ataa, Fokanakafo. 12–21 Feb. BSIP 10/I/34/ 9–11.

1948b   Preliminary report on tour of north Malaita. ca Feb. BSIP 12/I/4.

1948c   Telegram to Germond on Abu trouble. 7 Sept. BSIP 12/I/2/7.

1949a   DO 'Aoke to Peter Hughes, "Marching Rule Activities." 24 Jan. BSIP 1/ 24/49.

1949b   Telegram to SG on arrest figures. 10 March. BSIP 4/SF108.

1950   Community Development in the British Solomon Islands Protectorate with Particular Reference to the Marching Rule Movement on the Island of Malaita. Paper for 2d Devonshire Course, London 1949–1950. BSIP 4/ S108/VII/4.

Martin, John E (Captain, Commander 30th Engineer Base Topographic Battalion)

1950   Letter to West Council of Malaita Property Owners. ca 14 March. BSIP 12/V/4.

Marwick, J G

1935   *The Adventures of John Renton.* London: Kirkwall Press.

Mason, Albert (Melanesian Mission)

1925   North Mala Report, 1924. *SCL* Sept: 134–139.

1927   Riilana Longania, North Mala. *SCL* 1 Jan: 10–11.

1933   Report from North Mala. *SCL* July: 102–104.

Masterman, Stanley George (DC Malaita 1949–1950)

1935   Letter to SG explaining his assault on a prisoner. 8 Nov. BSIP 1/P1/M 58/ 22/1.

1947a   Acting SG to DCs Central, Malaita, and Western, "Marching Rule." 18 Feb. Circular 17/C91.

1947b   Minute on Jacob Vouza. 16 July; with Noel comment of 17 July. BSIP 4/ C173.

1947c   Report on meeting with Jacob Vouza. 21 July. BSIP 4/C173.

1947d   SG sending RC Noel minute to DC Malaita Davies. 21 July. BSIP 4/ unnumbered CF.

1947e   Telegram to SG on plans for arrests in north. 5 Aug. BSIP 4/C91.

1948   Acting SG to officer in charge of Constabulary on recruiting. 19 May. BSIP 12/I/5.

1949a   Letter to SG. 23 June. BSIP 4/S108/III & IV.

1949b   DC Malaita telegram to Germond. 7 July. BSIP 4/SF108.

1949c   "Interim Political Report" to SG. 6 Sept. BSIP 4/SF108/5/V.

1949d   "All People Read these Words and Know that this Is the Truth." Circular after 22 Nov 'Aoke meeting. 23 Nov. BSIP 4/SF108.

1949e   Telegram to Germond on 'Aoke meeting. 22 Dec. BSIP 4/SF108.

1950a   "Read and Remember My Words Again You People of Malaita." 22 April. BSIP 4/SF108/Pts IV/vol 3; and appendix 10 to 1950f.

1950b   Letter to Father Bernard Van de Walle, Rohinari, 'Are'are. 20 May. BSIP 12/V/3.

1950c   DC Malaita handing-over report. 9 June. BSIP 12/I/10/2/I.

1950d Report to SG and DOs Malu'u and 'Aoke. 12 June. BSIP 12/V/4.

1950e Report to SG and DOs Malu'u and 'Aoke. 16 June. BSIP 121/V/4.

1950f Political appendix to DC Malaita handing-over report. 20 June. BSIP 4/
       S108/VII/4.

Maude, Harold

1970   Letter to Roger Keesing. 14 Feb. Keesing Papers, Tuzin Archive for Mela-
       nesian Anthropology, Mandeville Special Collections Library, University
       of California, San Diego, MSS 427.

May, Francis Henry (HC 1911–1912)

1911a "Instructions…for the Guidance of District Magistrates," and HC minute
       "Defining Duties of Police Officer." 3 and 4 Nov. BSIP 14/41.

1911b Letter to Secretary of State for Colonies Lewis Vernon Harcourt on impos-
       ing Pax Britannica in BSIP. 8 Dec. WPHC MP 2162/11.

1911c "Memorandum for Guidance of Officers in Dealing with Outrages." 15
       Dec. WPHC MP 2162/11.

Maybury, L M (Doctor, Fauaabu Hospital)

1932   Where and What Is Qaibaita? *SCL* 1 Oct: 34–36.

Mayr, Ernst

1931   Birds Collected during the Whitney South Sea Expedition, XVII: The
       Birds of Malaita Island (British Solomon Islands). *American Museum Novi-
       tiates* 504:1–26.

1943   A Journey to the Solomons. *Natural History* 52:30–37, 48.

McArthur, Norma

1967   *Island Populations of the Pacific.* Canberra: Australian National University.

1970   The Demography of Primitive Populations. *Science* 167:1097–1101.

McClaren, Jack

1928   *My Odyssey.* London: Ernest Benn.

McDonald, A H, editor

1949   *Trusteeship in the Pacific.* London: Angus & Robertson.

McDonald, Ross

2003   *Money Makes You Crazy: Custom and Change in the Solomon Islands.* Otago:
       University of Otago Press.

McGown, W J (Secretary, Malayta Company)

1920   Letter to RC Workman. 6 Sept. BSIP 18/I/I.

McGregor, Russell

1993   The Doomed Race: A Scientific Axiom of the Late Nineteenth Century.
       Australian Journal of Politics & History 39 (1): 14–22.

McKinnon, J M

1975   Tomahawks, Turtles and Traders. *Oceania* 45:290–307.

Meek, A S

1913   *A Naturalist in Cannibal Land.* London: Adelphi Terrace.

Megarrity, Lyndon

2006   "White Queensland": The Queensland Government's Ideological Posi-
       tion on the Use of Pacific Island Labourers in the Sugar Sector 1880–
       1901. *Australian Journal of Politics & History* 51 (1): 1–12.

Meillassoux, Claude

1981   *Maidens, Meal and Money: Capitalism and the Domestic Community.* New York:
       Cambridge University Press.

Meleisea, Malama
  1980   *O Tama Uli: Melanesians in Western Samoa.* Suva: Institute of Pacific Studies.
Melvin, J D
  1977   *The Cruise of the Helena: A Labour-Recruiting Voyage to the Solomon Islands.* Edited by Peter Corris. Melbourne: Hawthorn Press. First published 1892.
Mercer, Patricia, and Clive Moore
  1976   Melanesians in North Queensland: The Retention of Indigenous Religious and Magical Practices. *Journal of Pacific History* 11:66–88.
Metcalf, Thomas R
  2007   *Imperial Connections: India in the Indian Ocean Arena, 1860–1920.* Berkeley: University of California Press.
Middenway, Arthur (DO Gizo 1923–1925)
  1924   Report to Acting RC on workings of "Native Administration Regulation of 1922." 8 April. WPHC IC 869/24.
Miklouho-Maclay, Nikolai Nikolaevich
  1883   Notes *in re* Kidnapping and Slavery in the Western Pacific. Encl A in *Correspondence Respecting the Natives of the Western Pacific and the Labour Traffic.* London: Great Britain Colonial Office.
Mir, Farina
  2010   *The Social Space of Language: Vernacular Culture in British Colonial Punjab.* Berkeley: University of California Press.
Mishra, Pankaj
  2004   The Empire under Siege. *New York Review of Books,* 15 July: 33–35.
Montgomery, Henry Hutchinson
  1892   Bishop of Tasmania's letter on the conditions of recruiting native labor in the New Hebrides and Solomon Islands. 14 Nov. WPHC 4/IV, 249.
  1904   *The Light of Melanesia: A Record of Fifty Years' Mission Work in the South Seas.* 2nd revised ed. London: Society for Promoting Christian Knowledge. PC.
Moore, Clive
  1985   *Kanaka: A History of Melanesian Mackay.* Boroko: Institute of Papua New Guinea Studies.
  2005   *Happy Isles in Crisis.* Canberra: Asia Pacific Press.
  2007   The Misappropriation of Malaitan Labour: Historical Origins of the Recent Solomon Islands Crisis. *Journal of Pacific History* 42 (2): 211–232.
  2009   *Florence Young and the Queensland Kanaka Mission, 1886–1906.* Brisbane: School of History, Philosophy, Religion and Classics, University of Queensland.
Moore, Frank C
  1947   Superintendent Police and Prisons memo to SG, and BSIP Legal Adviser Charles, "Legal Counsel—Application for, by Persons in Custody." 3 Oct. BSIP4/SF108/1.
  1950   Police Officer in charge of Malaita's report for October. 4 Nov. BSIP 12/V/4.
Moorhouse, Harry C
  1929   *Report of Commissioner Appointed by the Secretary of State for the Colonies to Inquire into the Circumstances in which Murderous Attacks Took Place in 1927 on Government Officials on Guadalcanal and Malaita.* London: His Majesty's Stationery Office.

Morehouse, Clifford P
    1945   From the Editor. *The Living Church,* 21 Jan: 15. PC.
Mothercraft: The Solomon Islands and the New Hebrides
    [1949?]   Southern Cross Booklet 8. Oxford: Church Army Press. PC.
"M. R. Meeting"
    1947   Unsigned note about the 30 June 'Aoke meeting. Early July. BSIP 12/VI/1.

Murdoch, Brian
    1980   On Calling other People Names: A Historical Note on "Marching Rule" in the Solomon Islands. *Journal of the Oxford Anthropological Society* 11 (3): 189–196.

Murray, Hubert
    1916   Report on visit to Solomon Islands. 29 April. WPHC CO225/248/2518.
    1932   Depopulation in Papua. *Oceania* 3 (2): 207–213.

Muspratt, Eric
    1931   *My South Sea Island.* New York: William Morrow.

Mytinger, Caroline
    1942   *Headhunting in the Solomon Islands.* New York: MacMillan.

Naitoro, John Houainamo
    1990   Customary Dispute Settlement and Local Courts. In *A Feasibility Study on the Penal System,* conducted for the Solomon Islands Government by Eidawn Consultancy Services, np. Swansea: Center for Development Studies, University of Swansea.
    1993   The Politics of Development in 'Are'are, Malaita. MA thesis, University of Otago.

National Administration Course, Honiara
    1955   Minutes. 26 Sept–1 Oct. BSIP 29/IV/ADM.

Nelson, Hank
    1980   Taim Bilong Pait: The Impact of the Second World War on Papua New Guinea. In *Southeast Asia under Japanese Occupation,* edited by Alfred McCoy, 246–266. New Haven: Yale University Press.
    1982   *Taim Bilong Masta: The Australian Involvement with Papua New Guinea.* Sydney: Australian Broadcasting Corporation.

Newbury, Colin
    2003   *Patrons, Clients, & Empire: Chieftaincy and Over-rule in Asia, Africa, and the Pacific.* New York: Oxford University Press.

Newman, J H (Adventist pastor)
    1947   Happenings on Malaita, Solomon Islands. *Australasian Record,* 17 Nov: 3.

Ngwadili, Arnon, and Isaac Gafu
    1988   Malaita Refuge, Guadalcanal Labour Corps. Translated and edited by David Gegeo and Karen Watson-Gegeo. In *The Big Death: Solomon Islanders Remember World War II,* edited by Geoffrey White, David Gegeo, David Akin, and Karen Ann Watson-Gegeo, 202–215. Suva: University of the South Pacific.

Nicoll, John F (Acting HC 1947)
    1947a   Note to RC Noel. ca 12 Aug. BSIP 4/SF108.
    1947b   Telegram to RC Noel. 13 Aug. BSIP 4/SF108.
    1947c   Telegram to RC Noel. 18 Aug. BSIP 4/SF108.
    1947d   Telegram to RC Noel. 20 Aug. BSIP 4/SF108.

1947e Telegram to RC Noel. 25 Aug. BSIP 4/SF108/I&II/I.

1947f Telegram to Secretary of State for Colonies. 28 Aug. BSIP 4/SF108.

1947g Telegram to RC Noel on actions to be taken. 2 Sept. BSIP 4/SF108.

1947h Telegram to RC Noel on actions to be taken. 12 Sept. BSIP 4/SF108.

1947i Telegram to RC Noel of delays of Maasina Rule trial. 11 Nov. BSIP 4/SF108.

NIV, Not in Vain

1918–1971 South Sea Evangelical Mission journal. Authored articles are listed under authors' names and others are cited by issue and pages. Early issues are unpaginated.

Noel, Owen Cyril (RC 1943–1950)

1944a Letter to G3, forward area, "Bombings at Uru and Sinalagu." 23 May. BSIP 1/111/19/9.

1944b Letter to DC Malaita David Trench. 20 June. BSIP 1/III/19/9.

1944c Letter to Acting HC Mitchell. 15 Oct. BSIP 1/III/19/9/1.

1945 Memo to DC David Trench. 4 Jan. BSIP 1/III/19/9/1.

1946a "Speech Made by Resident Commissioner to the Native Councils in Malaita, on August 30 1946 at Auki." BSIP 4/C91.

1946b "Memorandum on Local Political Affairs," to HC Grantham. Aug. BSIP 4/C91.

1947a Political report to HC and cover letter. 27 March. BSIP 4/C91.

1947b "Memorandum on Current Native Affairs." 9 April. BSIP 4/C91.

1947c "Marching Rule." RC memo to HC Nicoll, with cover letter to DC Malaita Sandars. 14 May. BSIP 12/I/4 and 4/C91.

1947d Telegram to HC Nicoll re false rumors of Malaita trouble. 9 July. BSIP 4/C91.

1947e Letter to DC Malaita Roy Davies on *alaha'ou'ou.* 21 July. BSIP 4/C91.

1947f Memo on Nori, Nono'oohimae, and labor. 26 July. BSIP 4/107.

1947g Letter to DC Malaita Davies on BSIP Legal Adviser Charles's opinion re decision to charge Malu'u Maasina Rule court officials. 1 Aug. BSIP 4/C91.

1947h "Top Secret" telegram to Acting HC Nicoll. 10 Aug. BSIP 4/SF108/I/1.

1947i "Top Secret" report to HC Nicoll, Maasina Rule situation. 11 Aug. BSIP 4/SF108.

1947j Telegram to HC Nicoll. 13 Aug (handwritten version). BSIP 4/SF108.

1947k Telegram to HC Nicoll on plans to combat Maasina Rule. 19 Aug. BSIP 4/SF108.

1947l Telegram to DC Malaita Davies. 19 Aug. BSIP 4/SF108.

1947m Telegram to HC Nicoll. 20 Aug. BSIP 4/SF108.

1947n Telegram to DC Malaita Davies. 20 Aug. 4/SF108.

1947o "Personal and Confidential" letter to G E D Sandars. 30 Aug. BSIP 4/SF108.

1947p Radio announcement of arrests. 31 Aug. BSIP 12/I/5. (Also in Laracy 1983, I1.)

1947q Telegram to HC Nicoll on meeting at Malu'u. 9 Sept. BSIP 4/SF108/1.

1947r Telegram to HC Nicoll on progress battling Maasina Rule. 16 Sept. BSIP 4/SF108.

1947s "Interim Report on the Disorders in the BSIP" to HC Nicoll. 4 Oct. BSIP 4/FF108.1.

1947t   Telegram to HC Nicoll. 10 Oct. BSIP 4/SF108/1.

1947u   Telegram to HC Nicoll. 17 Oct. BSIP 4/SF108/1.

1947v   Telegram to HC Nicoll. 7 Nov. BSIP 4/SF108/1.

1947w   Telegram to HC Nicoll. 13 Nov. BSIP 4/SF108/1.

1947x   Summary of court proceedings, for HC Nicoll. 2 Dec. BSIP 4/SF108/1.

1948a   "Personal and Confidential" letter to J D A Germond. 11 Feb. BSIP 12/I/5.

1948b   Confidential letter to Germond. 15 Feb. BSIP 12/I/5.

1948c   Minute of RC on Germond memo of 15 Feb (Germond 1948b). nd. BSIP 12/I/5.

1948d   "Secret" letter to Germond. 28 April. BSIP 12/I/5.

1948e   "Order" for the removal of fences at Malu'u. Approved 9 June. BSIP 4/SF108.

1948f   Confidential "Political Situation Report" to HC Freeston, with announcement of order to tear down fences around Malu'u. 29 June. BSIP 4/SF108.

1948g   Letter to HC Freeston on Maasina Rule policy. 13 Aug. BSIP 4/SF108.

Nolan, Janette

1978   *Bundaberg: History and People.* St Lucia: University of Queensland.

Norden, Hermann

1925   *Byways of the Tropic Seas.* London: H F & G Witherby.

Northam, J

1913   Savage Malaita. *Argus* (Melbourne), 27 Dec: 6.

"Notes on the Records and Backgrounds of North Malaitan Delegates to the Malaita District Council"

[1953?]   Likely by DC Malaita Andersen. BSIP 28/VII/B/1.

"Notices from Bina Council"

1951   Summary of impact, likely by Allan. 18 April. BSIP 12/I/3.

Nugent, Paul

2008   Putting the History Back into Ethnicity: Enslavement, Religion, and Cultural Brokerage in the Construction of Mandinka/Jola and Ewe/Agotime Identities in West Africa, c. 1650–1930. *Comparative Studies in Society and History* 50 (4): 920–948.

O'Brien, Claire

1995   *A Greater than Solomon Here: A Story of Catholic Church in Solomon Islands.* Honiara: Catholic Church Solomon Islands, Inc.

O'Connor, Gülbün Çoker

1973   The Moro Movement of Guadalcanal. PhD dissertation, University of Pennsylvania.

Odi (of Sugarege, Bugotu)

1932   Testimony at Tulagi on charges against DO Filose. 13 Dec. WPHC handwritten document, no reference data. Author's copy.

Oliver, Douglas

1961   *The Pacific Islands.* New York: Natural History Library.

1967   *A Solomon Island Society: Kinship and Leadership among the Siuai of Bougainville.* Boston: Beacon Press.

Oliver, Roland, and J D Fage

1973   *A Short History of Africa.* Baltimore: Penguin Books.

Osifelo, Frederick
1985 *Kanaka Boy*. Suva: Institute of Pacific Studies.

Palmer, Ernie
nd Tidal Wave on San Cristoval 4th Oct. 1931. Eyewitness description...copied by Mate. Encl in *Some Aspects of Mining Development in the British Solomon Islands Protectorate*, by John Grover. Honiara: Geological Survey of the BSIP (1949).
1947 Report to RC Noel on 14 April meeting with chiefs. 28 April. BSIP 4/C91.
1970 The Bell Affair. Transcript of 20 July interview (from tape 109) by Roger Keesing. Keesing Papers, Tuzin Archive for Melanesian Anthropology, Mandeville Special Collections Library, University of California, San Diego, MSS 427.

Palmer, George
1973 *Kidnapping in the South Seas*. Edinburgh: Edmonston and Douglas. First published 1871.

Parliamentary Debates, National Parliament of the Solomons
1981 Second Session–Second Meeting, vol II, 6–13 April. Honiara: Government Printer.

Parnaby, Owen
1964 *Britain and the Labor Trade in the Southwest Pacific*. Durham, NC: Duke University Press.

Patch, Alexander M (US Major General)
1943 Memo on "Native Labor." 29 March. BSIP 5/I/1/3.

Patteson, John Coleridge (Anglican Bishop of Melanesia 1861–1871)
1871 South Sea Island Labour Traffic. Appendix to *Journal of the New Zealand House of Representatives*. PC.

Peabody, Norbert
2001 Cents, Sense, Census: Human Inventories in Late Precolonial and Early Colonial India. *Comparative Studies in Society and History* 43 (4): 819–850.

Peebles, A P "Sandy" (DO 'Aoke; then DO Malu'u)
1951 Letter to DC Allan. 16 Sept. BSIP 12/I/6/1/1.

Penny, Alfred
1903 *The Headhunters of Cristabel*. London: Society for Promoting Christian Knowledge.

Pentony, B
1953 Psychological Causes of Depopulation of Primitive Groups. *Oceania* 24:142–145.

Philibert, Jean-Marc
1986 The Politics of Tradition: Toward a Generic Culture in Vanuatu. *Mankind* 16:1–12.

Philp, John Ernest
1978 *A Solomons Sojourn: J. E. Philp's Log of the Makira 1912–1913*. Edited by R Herr and E A Rood. Hobart: Tasmanian Historical Research Association.

Pidoke, John Plant (or Palmer)
1939 Statement presented to visiting HC Luke, translated by Richard Fallowes. June. WPHC 43/14/1. (Also in Laracy 1983, A6.)

Pierce, Steven
2006 Looking Like a State: Colonialism and the Discourse of Corruption

in Northern Nigeria. *Comparative Studies in Society and History* 48 (4): 887–914.

Pilling, H (Acting Secretary to WPHC)

1924a "Report on the Working of the Native Administration Regulation." 11 April. WPHC 849/24.

1924b On HC Rodwell response to RC Ashley's 22 July request re "Native Administration Regulation." 28 Aug. WPHC 849/24.

PIM, Pacific Islands Monthly

1932 Solomon Islands: Recruiters Have Lean Days. Jan: 41.

1934a Tropicalities. Feb: 35.

1934b Solomon Islands Grievances. Feb: 7.

1935 Unrest on Malaita. 6 (4): 56.

1936 Repudiationists in Malaita, S. I. Jan: 47.

1943 Solomons Aid Allies. July: 8.

1946a Communist Busy in the Solomons. March: 22.

1946b "Masinga Lo" Anti-British Native Movement Is Sweeping over Solomons. Oct: 7.

1947a Navy Showed the Flag in British Solomons. Oct: 71.

1947b "Marching Rule." Nov: 9.

1947c Marching Rule Leaders on Trial in BSI. Nov: 64.

1948a 23 "Marching Rule" Leaders Sent to Gaol. March: 29–30.

1948b Marching Rule: Police Raids on Fortified Villages in Solomons. Dec: 44.

1949 Marching Rule Activities in Solomons. March: 2.

1950a Future of Solomon and Gilbert Islands. March: 27–28.

1950b Gift to Chinese Traders in the Solomons. Aug: 81, 83.

1950c Marching Rule is Petering Out in Solomons. Sept: 75.

1953a Depressing Picture in Solomons and New Hebrides. April: 13–14.

1953b BSIP Finds It Difficult to Spend Its Money. Dec: 31.

1954 "Marching Rule" Nationalism is Not Dead in BSIP. March: 59–60.

1974 BSI Outlaws' Manifesto Comes to Light. June: 105.

Pitt-Rivers, G H

1927 *The Clash of Culture and the Contact of Races*. London: Routledge.

Planters' Gazette (1920s periodical of the BSIP planter community)

1922 Untitled article. May: 8.

Pope, Quentin

1949 British Reveal Solomons Rule Creates Crisis: But Charge of Native Revolt Denied. *Chicago Daily Tribune*, 5 Dec: B8.

Porter, Bernard

1975 *The Lion's Share: A Short History of British Imperialism 1850–1970*. New York: Longman.

Porter, K R D

1949 Memo about the health of Sydney Marchant. 30 Aug. BSIP 1/III/58/78I.

Pratt, Mary Louise

1986 Scratches on the Face of the Country; or What Mr. Barrow Saw in the Land of the Bushmen. In *"Race," Writing, and Difference*, edited by Henry Gates, 138–162. Chicago: University of Chicago Press.

Premdas, Ralph, and Jeffrey Steeves

1985 *The Solomon Islands: An Experiment in Decentralization*. Working Paper Series. Honolulu: Pacific Islands Studies Program, University of Hawai'i.

Price, Charles, and Elizabeth Baker
  1976   Origins of Pacific Island Labourers in Queensland, 1863–1904: A Research
          Note. *Journal of Pacific History* 11:106–121.
Pritt, Lonsdale (Melanesian Mission)
  1901   The Melanesians in Queensland. *SCL* 15 April: 182–185.
Puxley, W Lavallin
  1925   *Green Islands in Glittering Seas*. New York: Dodd, Mead & Company.
Ramoi, Stephen
  1928   By Order of the Governor. *SCL* April: 62–63.
Ranger, Terence
  1976   From Humanism to the Science of Man: Colonialism in Africa and the
          Understanding of Alien Societies. *Transactions of the Royal Historical Society*
          26:115–141.
  1984   The Invention of Tradition in Colonial Africa. In T*he Invention of Tradi-
          tion*, edited by Eric Hobsbawm and Terence Ranger, 211–262. Cambridge,
          UK: Cambridge University Press.
Rannie, Douglas
  1912   *My Adventures among South Sea Cannibals*. Philadelphia: J B Lippincott.
Raucaz, Louise-Marie
  1923   Letter from Catholic Vicar Apostolic of the Solomons to RC Kane on adul-
          tery legislation. 18 Sept. BSIP 1/III/MP2203/1922.
  1928   *In the Savage South Solomons: The Story of a Mission*. New York: The Society
          for the Propagation of the Faith.
Ravuvu, Asesela D
  1974   *Fijians at War 1939–1945*. Suva: University of the South Pacific.
Read, Kenneth E
  1947   Effects of the Pacific War in the Markham Valley, New Guinea. *Oceania* 18
          (2): 95–116.
Red Cross Courier
  1943   October issue. Washington, DC: American National Red Cross.
Reye, Arnold
  2006   They Did Return! The Resumption of the Adventist Mission in the Solo-
          mon Islands after World War II, Part I. *Journal of Pacific Adventist History* 6
          (1): 49–56.
Reynolds, David
  1985   The Churchill Government and the Black American Troops in Britain
          during World War II. *Transactions of the Royal Historical Society* 35:113–133.
Rhoades, F Ashton ("Snowy")
  1982   *Diary of a Coast Watcher in the Solomons*. Fredericksburg, TX: Admiral Nim-
          itz Foundation.
Richards, Ceredig
  1932a   Sanctuary. *SCL* April: 8–10.
  1932b   Details of the October Earthquake. *SCL* May: 69–71.
Richardson, Philip A ("Pip")
  1952   Acting RC memo to DC Malaita Andersen on arrest plan (communicated
          by SG). 12 Aug. BSIP 12/V/13.
Ridley, David Kapitana (HM east Kwaio)
  1950   Letter to DC Malaita Masterman. 5 Feb. BSIP 4/SF108.
  1951a   Statement to DC Malaita Allan. 11 Feb. BSIP 12/V/6.

1951b Notes from his report on Federal Council activities. ca Aug. BSIP 12/V/ 7.

Rivers, William H R
1922   The Psychological Factor. In *Essays on the Depopulation of Melanesia,* edited by William H R Rivers, 84–113. Cambridge, UK: Cambridge University Press.

Rivers, William H R, editor
1922   *Essays on the Depopulation of Melanesia.* Cambridge, UK: Cambridge University Press. PC.

Roberts, Stephen H
1927   *Population Problems of the Pacific.* London: George Routledge.

Robson, R W
1952   New Administration Faces Muddled Conditions in Solomons. *PIM* March: 97–99.

Rodman, Margaret
1983   Introduction. In *The Pacification of Melanesia,* edited by Margaret Rodman and Matthew Cooper, 1–23. New York: University Press of America.

Rodwell, Cecil Hunter (HC 1918–1925)
1921a Cover letter for proceedings of recent murder trials, with commutations of death sentences. nd. WPHC 1261/1921.
1921b Memo to Acting RC Workman. 10 Oct. WPHC 2049/1921.
1922a Cover letter to Acting Chief Judicial Commissioner attached to "Native Administration Regulation" draft. nd. Author's copy.
1922b Cover letter to RC Kane, attached to "Native Administration Regulation" draft. 24 Aug. WPHC 2290/22.

Rohorua, Luke
1898   Tales of Ulawa in Heathen Days. *SCL* 15 Sept: 6–10.

Romilly, Hugh H
1886   *The Western Pacific and New Guinea: Notes on the Natives, Christian and Cannibal, with Some Account of the Old Labour Trade.* London: John Murray.

Ross, Harold
1973   *Baegu: Social and Ecological Organization in Malaita, Solomon Islands.* Urbana: University of Illinois Press.
1978a Baegu Markets, Areal Integration, and Economic Efficiency in Malaita, Solomon Islands. *Ethnology* 17 (2): 119–138.
1978b Competition for Baegu Souls: Mission Rivalry on Malaita, Solomon Islands. In *Mission, Church, and Sect in Oceania,* edited by James Boutilier, Daniel Hughes, and Sharon Tiffany, 163–200. Ann Arbor: University of Michigan Press.

Royal Commission on Sugar Industry Labour
1906   Report. In *Selected Documents in Australian History 1851–1900,* edited by C Manning H Clark, 233–235. Sydney: Angus & Robertson.

Russell, Tom (DO Malu'u 1949–1950; DC Malaita 1954–1956)
1949a "Report on Tour of Fataleka and Baegu Areas," and appended intelligence report. 27 Aug (with Masterman comments of 24 Sept). BSIP 4/ S108/III.
1949b "Political Policy, Malaita," to Masterman. 1 Sept. BSIP 4/SF108/5/V.
1949c "Intelligence Report, Marching Rule ... North Malaita." 24 Nov. BSIP 12/ V/2.

1950a The Fataleka of Malaita. *Oceania* 21 (1): 1–13.

1950b "Intelligence Report on Marching Rule Activities in North Malaita." 24 Jan. BSIP 12/V/3 and 4/SF108.

1950c "Preliminary Report on Incident near Faurere, Suava Peninsula, North Malaita." 9 Feb. BSIP 12/V/3.

1950d "Monthly Political Report—North Malaita—May 1950." 5 May. BSIP 12/V/3.

1950e Malu'u Monthly Political Report. 10 May. BSIP 12/V/3.

1950f "Monthly Political Report—North Malaita—June." 11 June. BSIP 12/VI/4.

1950g Report to DC Malaita Allan and DO 'Aoke MacKeith. 23 June. BSIP 12/V/4.

1950h "Political Report for Malu'u Sub-District." 13 July. BSIP 12/V/4.

1950i Administrative Order to Jasper Irofiala. 13 July. BSIP 12/I/10/2/1.

1950j Malu'u Monthly Political Report. 14 Sept. BSIP 4/SF108/VIII/5.

1950k Letter to DC Malaita Allan re complaint by Father Devlin against HM Iromea. 19 Sept. BSIP 12/I/10.

1954a Letter to east Kwaio Headman David Riddley. 15 Sept. BSIP 29/I/9.

1954b Political Situation for September letter to Chief Secretary. 4 Oct. BSIP 12/I/29.

1954c Letter to Malaita Council Member Aliki Nono'oohimae. 9 Nov. BSIP 29/I/7.

1954d Letter to Chief Secretary, "Native Courts on Malaita." 19 Nov. BSIP 29/I/7.

1955a Malaita Political Report for March. nd. BSIP 12/I/30.

1955b "Malaita District—Political Report for April-May." 15 June. BSIP 12/I/34.

1955c "Police Stations and Their Relation to Patrolling on Malaita." 1 Sept. BSIP 12/I/16.

1955d "Malaita District Political Report for October." 9 Nov. BSIP 12/I/3.

1986 Interview by Ben Burt. April. MS. Author's copy.

2003 *I Have the Honour to Be.* Spennymoor, UK: The Memoir Club.

2004 The Post-War Marching Rule Movement in Solomon Islands: Reminiscences of a District Officer. Address to Pacific Islands Society of the United Kingdom and Ireland. 27 Oct. Author's copy.

Rutter, Allen G (Senior Medical Officer)

1947 Medical Certificate for Michael Forster. 1 March. BSIP 1/III/F58/69 II.

Sahlins, Marshall

1992 The Economics of Develop-man in the Pacific. *RES* 1:12–25.

1993 Cery Cery Fuckabede. *American Ethnologist* 20 (4): 848–876.

1994 Goodbye to Tristes Tropes: Ethnography in the Context of Modern World History. In *Assessing Cultural Anthropology*, edited by Robert Borofsky, 377–395. New York: McGraw-Hill.

Said, Edward

1979 *Orientalism.* New York: Vintage Books.

Salisbury, Edward

1922 Napoleon of the Solomons. *Asia* 22 (9): 707–720, 746.

Sandars, A (Acting RC 1950)

1950 "Native Affairs in the BSIP during the Year 1949." 12 Jan. BSIP 1/111/49/29.

Sandars, George Eustace Drysdale (Constabulary; DO Malaita; DC Malaita, intermittent 1928–1943, 1945–1947)

nd   Untitled MS on his Solomons years. In "Papers on the Solomon Islands,
          1928–1943." MS. Pacific Manuscript Bureau film 553.

1932   Statements collected on DO Isabel Filose beating Islanders. 7 Dec. BSIP
          1/3/43/14.

1933a   Letter to Acting RC Ashley on visit to Isabel. 5 March. BSIP 1/3/43/14.

1933b   Letter to Acting RC Ashley on whippings by Richard Filose. March. BSIP
          1/3/43/14.

1935   Letter to SG on adultery regulation. 14 March. BSIP 1/III/36/9/1.

1937a   Letter to SG on brideprice trouble at Sinalagu. 1 Feb. BSIP 29/I/2.

1937b   Annual Report on Taxation, Malaita. 3 Feb. BSIP 29/I/2.

1937c   Letter to SG on "Unrest on Malaita." 17 Feb. BSIP 29/I/2.

1937d   Letter to SG on kidnapping. 6 May. BSIP 29/I/2.

1937e   Letter to RC Ashley on criminal fee collection. 20 June. BSIP 29/I/2.

1937f   Letter to RC Ashley on Salaimanu and Kakalu'ae. 24 Dec. BSIP 14/39.

1938a   Letter to SG on resignation of Asst DH Fa'ani of Uru. 14 Feb. BSIP 29/I/3.

1938b   Letter to RC Ashley. 12 Sept. BSIP 29/I/3.

1939a   "Minutes of interview between Reverend R. Fallowes and the Resident
          Commissioner." 3 March. Author's copy.

1939b   Circular from SG to all DOs, "Prices Charged to Europeans and Natives."
          1 Dec. BSIP 29/II/4.

1941a   Acting RC to HC Luke, cover letter for replies from DOs on native courts.
          30 April. BSIP 1/III/49/19.

1941b   Letter to RC Trench. 17 May. BSIP 1/III/49/20.

1942–1943 Handwritten diary, 23 Nov 1942—7 April 1943. Pacific Manuscript
          Bureau film 553.

1943a   Letter, probably to Acting RC Marchant. 18 Aug. BSIP 5/I/1/3.

1943b   Report on Malaita situation. 1 Sept. BSIP 1/III/19/8.

1945a   Memo to DC Central. 19 March. BSIP 1/III/19/16.

1945b   DC Malaita letter to SG. 12 Dec. BSIP 1/III/19/9.

1946   DC Malaita to RC Noel re Forster. 15 Dec. BSIP 1/III/F58/68 II.

1947a   Letter to SG, and DCs Central and Western, "Collection and Disposal of
          Native Taxes." 2 Feb. BSIP 29/III/4.

1947b   Reports on 'Ataa and Fataleka visits of 10–11 Feb; 'Ataa Council questions
          and Sandars's replies. 20 Feb. BSIP 10/I/34/9.

1947c   DC's tour reports from eastern 'Are'are. ca early June. BSIP 10/I/34/14.

1947d   "Meeting of Marching Rule Leaders and Members at Auki, Malaita on 30
          June, 1947." nd. BSIP 4/C91; BSIP 12/I/2/7.

1947e   Handwritten letter to RC Noel. 3 July. BSIP 4/C91.

1947f   Report to RC Noel, Malaita political situation since 26 Dec. 6 July. BSIP 4/
          C91.

[1966?]   Short autobiographical account, 1896–1923. In "Papers on the Solo-
          mon Islands, 1928–1943." MS. Pacific Manuscript Bureau film 553.

Sanga, Jan

1989   Remembering. In *Ples Blong Iumi: Solomon Islands, the Past Four Thousand
          Years*, edited by Hugh Laracy, 16–30. Suva and Honiara: University of the
          South Pacific.

Sankoff, Gillian
  1985   Touching Pen, Marking Paper: Queensland Labour Contracts in the 1880s. In *History and Ethnohistory in Papua New Guinea,* edited by Deborah Gewertz and Edward Schieffelin, 100–126. Sydney: University of Sydney Press.

Saunders, Kay
  1979   "Troublesome Servants": The Strategies of Resistance Employed by Melanesian Indentured Labourers on Plantations in Colonial Queensland. *Journal of Pacific History* 14 (3): 168–183.
  1980   Melanesian Women in Queensland, 1863–1907: Some Methodological Problems Involving the Relationship between Racism and Sexism. *Pacific Studies* 4 (1): 26–44.
  1982   *Workers in Bondage: The Origins and Bases of Unfree Labour in Queensland 1824–1916.* New York: University of Queensland.
  1984   The Workers' Paradox: Indentured Labour in the Queensland Sugar Industry to 1920. In *Indentured Labour in the British Empire 1834–1920,* edited by Kay Saunders, 213–259. London: Croom Helm.

Sayes, Shelley
  1976   The Ethnohistory of San Cristobal. MA thesis, University of Auckland.

Scarr, Deryck
  1967   *Fragments of Empire: A History of the Western Pacific High Commission 1877–1914.* Canberra: Australian National University.
  1968   Editor's Introduction. In *A Cruise in a Queensland Labour Vessel to the South Seas,* by W E Giles, 1–32. Canberra: Australian National University.
  1970   Recruits and Recruiters: A Portrait of the Labour Trade. In *Pacific Island Portraits,* edited by James W Davidson and Deryck Scarr, 225–251. Canberra: Australian National University.

Scheffler, Harold
  1964a   The Social Consequences of Peace on Choiseul Island. *Ethnology* 3:398–403.
  1964b   The Solomon Islands: Seeking a New Land Custom. In *Land Tenure in the Pacific,* edited by Ron Crocombe, 273–291. New York: Oxford University Press.

Schoettler, Gail
  1984   The Genial Barons. In *The British in the Sudan, 1898–1956: The Sweetness and the Sorrow,* edited by Robert O Collins and Francis M Deng, 105–133. Stanford: Hoover Institution.

Schwartz, Theodore
  1962   *The Paliau Movement in the Admiralty Islands, 1946–1954.* Anthropological Papers of the American Museum of Natural History, vol 49, pt 2. New York: AMNH.

SCL, Southern Cross Log
  1895–1957   Newsletter of the Anglican Melanesian Mission. Authored articles are listed under authors' names and others are cited by issue and pages. After 1900, Auckland and London published separate editions, with most articles in both; most of my copies do not indicate which they are from.

Scott, James
  1985   *Weapons of the Weak: Everyday Forms of Peasant Resistance.* New Haven: Yale University Press.

1998   *Seeing Like a State: How Certain Schemes to Improve the Human Condition Have Failed.* New Haven: Yale University Press.

Scott, Michael W

1990–1991   Constitutions of Maasina Rule: Timothy George and the Iora. *Chicago Anthropology Exchange* 19:41–65.

2007   *The Severed Snake: Matrilineages, Making Place, and a Melanesian Christianity in Southeast Solomon Islands.* Durham, NC: Carolina Academic Press.

Secretary of State to the Colonies

1950   Telegram to HC Freeston. 4 July. BSIP 4/SF108.

Seymour, A W (Acting HC)

1928   Review of Bell affair and taxation. 8 Feb. WPHC 3251/27.

Shineberg, Dorothy

1999   *The People Trade: Pacific Island Laborers and New Caledonia, 1865–1930.* Honolulu: Center for Pacific Islands Studies and University of Hawai'i Press.

Shlomowitz, Ralph

1989   Epidemiology and the Pacific Labor Trade. *Journal of Interdisciplinary History* 19 (4): 585–610.

Siegel, Jeff

1987   *Language Contact in a Plantation Environment: A Sociolinguistic History of Fiji.* New York: Cambridge University Press.

Siho, John

1949   Informant report to David Trench. 12 March. BSIP 4/SF108.

1950   Informant report. 10 Oct. BSIP 12/I/9.

Silifa'alu, Jaspar (Clerk to Head Chief 'Atoomea)

1947   Letter to Malu'u Headman Ariel 'Otalifua. 10 Dec. BSIP 12/I/6. (Both original and English are in file; see Laracy 1983, C33.)

Simmons, Robert J A (Melanesian Mission)

1917   North Malaita. *SCL* July: 7–10.

Sinker, William

1907   *By Reef and Shoal.* London: Society for Promoting Christian Knowledge. PC.

Sisili, Ariel

1949   Manifesto. Appendix A to DO Malu'u Russell "Intelligence Report" of 24 Nov. BSIP 4/SF108. (Also in Laracy 1983, H1.)

Solomon Islands Broadcasting Corporation

1987   *World Belong Yumi* radio show interview with Adrian Bataeofesi on Langalanga compensation claims. 4 June. Author's copy of audio recording.

Solomon Islands Government (see British Solomon Islands Protectorate for pre-1978 references)

1979   *Local Court Handbook.* Honiara: The Judiciary.

Somerville, Lt Boyle T

1897   Ethnographical Notes in New Georgia, Solomon Islands. *Journal of the Anthropological Institute of Great Britain and Ireland* 26:357–412.

SSEM, South Sea Evangelical Mission

1942   Circular to Prayer Partners. March. SSEM Archive.

Southern Rhodesia

1910   "Proclamation 55 of 1910" by HC Southern Rhodesia (Native Regulations), with HC Rodwell letter. nd. WPHC 2290/22.

Standish, Bill
1984   *Melanesian Neighbours: The Politics of Papua New Guinea, the Solomon Islands and the Republic of Vanuatu.* Canberra: Parliamentary Library.

Stanley, Robert Christopher Stafford (HC 1952–1955)
1952   Instruction to DC Malaita Andersen. 7 Oct. BSIP 12/I/11.
1953   Letter to J B Sidebotham, Colonial Office, on Malaita political situation. 10 Jan. BSIP 6/II/16.
1975   *King George's Keys: A Record of Experiences in the Overseas Service of the Crown.* London: Johnson.

Stansfield, Robert E
1946   *Bitter Bellies.* Portland: Beattie & Hofmann.

Steinberg, Rafael
1981   *Island Fighting.* Chicago: Time-Life Books.

Steinmetz, George
2003   "The Devil's Handwriting": Precolonial Discourse, Ethnographic Acuity, and Cross-Identification in German Colonialism. *Comparative Studies in Society and History* 45 (1): 41–95.

Steley, Dennis
1990   *Unfinished: The Seventh-Day Adventist Mission in the South Pacific, Excluding Papua New Guinea, 1886–1986.* Ann Arbor: University Microfilms.

Steward, John Manwaring (Anglican Bishop of Melanesia 1919–1924)
1921   Letter to Acting RC. 18 Feb. WPHC 2049/21.
1926   *Hints on District Work.* Melanesian Mission Occasional Paper 4. Guadalcanal: Melanesian Mission Press. PC.
1939   *John Steward's Memories: Papers Written by the Late Bishop Steward of Melanesia.* With an introduction by M R Newbolt, editor. Chester: Phillipson & Golder. PC.

Stoler, Ann Laura
1992   Rethinking Colonial Categories: European Communities and the Boundaries of Rule. In *Colonialism and Culture,* edited by Nicholas Dirks, 319–352. Ann Arbor: University of Michigan Press.

Stoler, Ann Laura, and Frederick Cooper
1997   Between Metropole and Colony: Rethinking a Research Agenda. In *Tensions of Empire: Colonial Cultures in a Bourgeois World,* edited by Frederick Cooper and Ann Laura Stoler, 1–56. Berkeley: University of California Press.

Strathern, Marilyn
1972   *Official and Unofficial Courts: Legal Assumptions and Expectations in a Highlands Community.* New Guinea Research Bulletin 47. Canberra: Australian National University.
1988   *The Gender of the Gift: Problems with Women and Problems with Society in Melanesia.* Berkeley: University of California Press.

Stuart, Annie
2002   Parasites Lost? The Rockefeller Foundation and the Expansion of Health Services in the Colonial South Pacific, 1916–1939. PhD dissertation, University of Canterbury.

Sullivan, Violet May
1933   The Indigenous Church in the Solomon Islands. *NIV* April: 5–8.
1944   *Wild Warriors of Koio.* Melbourne: S John Bacon for SSEM.

Sullivan, Walter
    1948   Natives Restless in South Pacific. *New York Times*, 20 Nov: 5.
Sydney Herald
    1927   Malaita, Recent Massacre. Taxation Resented. 12 Oct: 17.
    1933   Solomon Islands. Anthropology and Missions. Scientist's Studies. 6 Dec: 12.
    1934   Life in the Solomons. Human Flesh and Indigestion. Paying Poll Tax. 14 Feb: 15.
    1947   British Win Strange Battle of Flags in Solomons Rising. 19 Sept: 3.
    1951   Candid Comment, by Onlooker. 26 Aug: 2.
Taburi, Frank (Sergeant, Armed Constabulary)
    1950   Statutory Declaration. 9 Feb. BSIP 12/VI/3.
Takataka (west 'Are'are)
    1946   Record of Maasina Rule's start there. 12 Nov. BSIP 12/VI/1.
Tedder, James Lionel O'Neil
    1954   DO Malu'u to DC Malaita Andersen, "Ata'a Marching Rule Bank." 6 Jan. BSIP 12/I/15.
    2008   *Solomon Island Years: A District Administrator in the Islands, 1952–1974.* Stuarts Point, NSW: Tuatu Studies.
Teioli, Timeas
    1951   Statement for *Rex v Ariel Sisili.* 7 March. BSIP SF108/I/1.
Teoboo, Tome Toloasi
    1982   Interview tape recorded (Kwaio language and archaic Pijin) by David Akin and Kathleen Gillogly, on archaic Pijin and historical topics. 12 Aug. Tuzin Archive for Melanesian Anthropology, Mandeville Special Collections Library, University of California, San Diego.
    1983   Letter to American Museum of Natural History, New York, re Whitney South Sea Expedition. Jan. English translation sent on his behalf by David Akin.
Thomas, Julian
    1886   *Cannibals and Convicts: Notes of Personal Experiences in the Western Pacific.* New York: Cassell & Company.
Thomas, Nicholas
    1990   Sanitation and Seeing: The Creation of State Power in Early Colonial Fiji. *Comparative Studies in Society and History* 32 (1): 149–170.
    1992a   Colonial Conversions: Difference, Hierarchy, and History in Early Twentieth-Century Evangelical Propaganda. *Comparative Studies in Society and History* 34 (2): 366–389.
    1992b   The Inversion of Tradition. *American Ethnologist* 19 (2): 213–232.
    1992c   Substantivization and Anthropological Discourse: The Transformation of Practices into Institutions in Neotraditional Pacific Societies. In *History and Tradition in Melanesian Anthropology,* edited by James Carrier, 64–85. Berkeley: University of California Press.
    1994   *Colonialism's Culture: Anthropology, Travel and Government.* Princeton: Princeton University Press.
Thomson, Andrew (Melanesian Mission)
    1927   Letter to RC Kane, with letter from John Doraweewee. 17 Oct. Keesing Papers, Tuzin Archive for Melanesian Anthropology, Mandeville Special Collections Library, University of California, San Diego, MSS 427.

Thurnwald, Richard
  1936   The Price of the White Man's Peace. *Pacific Affairs* 9 (3): 347–357.

Tiffany, Sharon
  1983   Customary Land Disputes, Courts, and African Models in the Solomon Islands. *Oceania* 53 (3): 277–290.

Time Magazine
  1944   South Sea Bishop. 4 Dec: 62.
  1947   Martin Lo. 29 Sept: 40.

Tippett, A R
  1967   *Solomon Islands Christianity.* London: Lutterworth.

Titiuru, Tom (Armed Constabulary 1947–1950)
  1987   Experiences of Maasina Rule, recorded in English and Pijin mix, and transcribed and translated by David Akin. Solomon Islands National Archive, Honiara.

"To Every Passage"
  1948   Unsigned letter about American submarine arrival. 20 March. BSIP 12/I/6.

Tomlinson, J E
  1949   Marching Rule. *NIV* Sept: 11.

Tonkinson, Robert
  1982a Kastom in Melanesia: Introduction. In *Reinventing Traditional Culture: The Politics of Kastom in Island Melanesia,* edited by Roger Keesing and Robert Tonkinson. Special issue, *Mankind* 13 (4): 302–305.
  1982b National Identity and the Problem of Kastom in Vanuatu. In *Reinventing Traditional Culture: The Politics of Kastom in Island Melanesia,* edited by Roger Keesing and Robert Tonkinson. Special issue, *Mankind* 13 (4): 306–315.

Townsend, Michael M (DC Malaita 1959–1962)
  1961a "Conversation with 'Remnant Church' Leaders." 21 April. BSIP 12/I/42.
  1961b Letter to Roger Keesing. 24 April. Malaita (MII Series) M10/13/5.

Trautmann, Thomas
  1997   *Aryans and British India.* Berkeley: University of California Press.
  1999   Inventing the History of South India. In *Invoking the Past: The Uses of History in South Asia,* edited by Daud Ali, 36–54. Oxford: Oxford University Press.

Trautmann, Thomas, editor
  2009   *The Madras School of Orientalism: Producing Knowledge in Colonial South India.* New Delhi: Oxford University Press.

Trench, David Clive Crosby (DO Malaita 1941; DC Malaita 1944–1945; SDNA 1947–1948)
  1941   Acting DO Shortlands's letter to SG, "Native Courts." 10 March. BSIP 1/III/49/19.
  1943   Document by DO Guadalcanal for native officials. nd. Repr in Hogbin 1944.
  1944   DC Malaita memo to DO Gela Cyril Belshaw. 19 Dec. BSIP 8/I/3/1.
  1945a Letter to SG on shell money management. 15 March. BSIP 1/III/19/16.
  1945b Letter to SG on rumors of Japanese invasion. 27 March. BSIP 1/III/19/9.
  1945c Letter to SG on unauthorized money collections. 20 May. BSIP 1/III/19/9.

1946   Acting RC Trench to DC Malaita Forster on lecture to Langalanga prisoners. 19 July. BSIP 12/I/2/7.

1947a   Operation Delouse Phase II Operation Order. 26 Aug. BSIP 4/SF108.

1947b   Signals to RC Noel on arrests for "Operation Delouse." 31 Aug. BSIP 4/SF108.

1947c   Letter to DCs on plans for Maasina Rule trials. 27 Sept. BSIP 4/unnumbered CF.

1947d   Trench to all DCs. 27 Sept. BSIP 4/unnumbered CF.

1947e   Report to DC Davies on "Force C Actions on 31 Aug." 3 Oct. BSIP 4/SF 108/I.

1947f   Telegram to DC Davies. 8 Nov. BSIP 4/SF 108.

1947g   Telegram to DC Davies. 10 Nov. BSIP 4/SF 108.

1947h   Memo to RC Owen Noel on Maasina Rule. 31 Dec. BSIP 12/I/2/7.

1948a   Telegram to "SOSOLS" (code word). 9 Jan. BSIP 4/SF108.

1948b   Memo to RC Noel, "Economic Recovery of the Protectorate." 16 Feb. BSIP 4/C82.

1949   Remarks on Shadrach Dio, entry 21 of 31 Jan, at front of file BSIP 4/SF108/IV.

1956   Marchant on Malaita. *Corona* 8 (5–7): 186–189, 230–233, 258–261.

Turner, E Nelson

1935   Superintendent of Prisons letter to SG. 13 Nov. BSIP 1/P1/M 58/22/1.

Turner, Victor

1975   Symbolic Studies. *Annual Review of Anthropology* 4:145–161.

Turpin, Richard (DC Malaita 1964–1967, 1969–1970)

1967   Memo to Chief Secretary, "Native Courts Ordinance." 5 Oct. Malaita 100/8/1.

Vance, Robert C (SSEM)

1945   The Invasion of the Solomons. *NIV* Dec: 9–10.

1963   *The Hunter Hunted: The Story of God and One Man.* Sydney: J Bell.

Vandercook, John

1937   *Dark Islands.* New York: Harper Brothers.

Van Dusen, Henry

1945   *They Found the Church There: The Armed Forces Discover Christian Missions.* New York: Charles Scribner's Sons.

Vaskess, H A (Secretary to WPHC)

1937   *Public Services Reorganization Report, 1937.* Sydney: Government Printer.

1939   Letter to Richard Fallowes. 18 June. WPHC 43/14/1.

Vuza, Sale (also known as Jacob Vouza)

1970   Interview by Roger Keesing (Solomon Islands Pijin). 4 June. Recording and Akin transcription. Keesing Papers, Tuzin Archive for Melanesian Anthropology, Mandeville Special Collections Library, University of California, San Diego, MSS 427.

Waddell, Alexander N, David Trench, and Frederick J Bentley

1945   Report to RC Noel on five-year planning for BSIP. 8 Oct. Author's copy.

Wagoner, Phillip

2003   Precolonial Intellectuals and the Production of Colonial Knowledge. *Comparative Studies in Society and History* 45 (4): 783–814.

Waiparo (also known as Haiware)
  1944   "Takataka Council to Report to Alic Nonoohimae." 23 Nov. BSIP 12/5/6/
         n. 36. (Also in Laracy 1983, C2.)
Waleanisia, Tome
  1987   Interview by David Akin on various topics. 2 July, Honiara. Record-
         ing (Kwaio language and archaic Pijin). Tuzin Archive for Melanesian
         Anthropology, Mandeville Special Collections Library, University of Cali-
         fornia, San Diego.
Wallace, Anthony
  1956   Revitalization Movements. *American Anthropologist* 58 (2): 264–281.
Wallerstein, Immanuel
  1961   *Africa: The Politics of Independence.* New York: Vintage Books.
Wasuka, Moffat
  1989   Education. In *Ples Blong Iumi: Solomon Islands, the Past Four Thousand Years,*
         edited by Hugh Laracy, 94–111. Suva: University of the South Pacific.
Wawn, William Twizell
  1973   *The South Sea Islanders and the Queensland Labour Trade.* Edited by Peter
         Corris. Honolulu: University of Hawai'i Press. First published 1893.
Wa'ii'a, Ansene
  1987   The Second World War Two. Handwritten account given to David Akin.
         Solomon Islands National Archive, Honiara, and author's copy.
Welchman, Henry Palmer (Melanesian Mission)
  1894   Letter to John R Selwyn. *Melanesian Mission Occasional Paper,* March:
         23–24. PC.
West Council Malaita Property Owners
  1950   Letter to US Army Captain John E Martin. 13 March. BSIP 12/V/3.
White, A John F (DO Malaita 1930–1933)
  1932a Letter to RC Ashley. 5 Feb. BSIP 14/63.
  1932b Letter to RC Ashley on SSEM brideprice limits. 3 May. BSIP 14/63.
  1932c Letter to RC Ashley on potential regulation on sorcery. 28 July. BSIP 14/
         63.
White, Charles H Gordon
  1928–1931 Medical tour diaries. Cited by date. Lambert Papers, Tuzin Archive
         for Melanesian Anthropology, Mandeville Special Collections Library,
         University of California, San Diego, MSS 682.
White, Geoffrey M
  1978   Big Men and Church Men: Social Images in Santa Isabel, Solomon
         Islands. PhD dissertation, University of California, San Diego.
  1983   War, Piece, and Piety in Santa Isabel, Solomon Islands. In *The Pacification
         of Melanesia,* edited by Margaret Rodman and Matthew Cooper, 109–139.
         New York: University Press of America.
  1989   Histories of Contact, Narratives of Self: Wartime Encounters in Santa
         Isabel. In *The Pacific Theater: Island Representations of World War II,* edited
         by Geoffrey White and Lamont Lindstrom, 43–71. Honolulu: Center for
         Pacific Islands Studies and University of Hawai'i Press.
  1991   *Identity through History: Living Stories in a Solomon Islands Society.* Cambridge,
         UK: Cambridge University Press.
  1992a The Discourse of Chiefs: Notes on a Melanesian Society. In *Chiefs Today:*

Traditional Leadership and the Postcolonial State, edited by Geoffrey White and Lamont Lindstrom, 229–252. Stanford: Stanford University Press.

1992b   Three Discourses of Custom. In *Custom Today*, edited by Lamont Lindstrom and Geoffrey White. Special issue, *Anthropological Forum* 5 (4): 474–495.

White, Geoffrey M, David Gegeo, David Akin, and Karen Ann Watson-Gegeo, editors

1988   *The Big Death: Solomon Islanders Remember World War II*. Suva: University of the South Pacific.

White, Geoffrey M, and Lamont Lindstrom, editors

1989   *The Pacific Theater: Island Representations of World War II*. Honolulu: Center for Pacific Islands Studies and University of Hawai'i Press.

Whiteman, Darrell

1983   *Melanesians and Missionaries*. Pasadena: William Caren Library.

Wicks, H B P

1923   Letter to RC Kane on adultery legislation. 26 Sept. WPHC 190/23.

Widdy, Charles V (Commander SILC)

1942   Letter to RC Marchant. 17 Dec. BSIP 5/I/1/3.

1943a   Report to RC Marchant on activities of SILC. 1 Jan. BSIP 5/I/1/3.

1943b   Letter to RC Marchant. 22 Feb. BSIP 5/I/1/3.

1943c   Letter to RC Marchant. 27 Feb. BSIP 5/I/1/3.

1943d   Letter to RC Marchant. 11 March. BSIP 5/I/1/3.

1943e   Memo to SILC Commanders, "Enforcement of Discipline." 19 March. BSIP 5/I/1/3.

1943f   Letter to RC Marchant. 19 March. BSIP 5/I/1/3.

1943g   Letter to RC Marchant. 3 April. BSIP 5/I/1/3.

1943h   Letter to Bengough on Jared Ramo'ifaka. 5 April. BSIP 5/I/1/3.

1943i   Letter to RC Marchant, "Native Members of the Corps. Expiration of Term of Service." 23 July. BSIP 5/I/1/3.

Wieschhoff, H A

1944   *Colonial Policies in Africa*. Philadelphia: University of Pennsylvania Press.

Williams, Francis Edgar

1932   Depopulation and Administration. *Oceania* 3 (2): 218–226.

1977   The Vailala Madness and the Destruction of Native Ceremonies in the Gulf Division. In *"The Vailala Madness" and other Essays*, edited by Erik Schwimmer, 331–384. Honolulu: University of Hawai'i Press. First published 1923.

Wilson, Alexander Herbert ("Spearline") (BSIP Commissioner of Lands and Works)

1942   Report on Tulagi evacuation. 6 Feb. MS held by British Museum, London.

Wilson, Cecil (Anglican Bishop of Melanesia 1894–1911)

1894–1896   Old Scenes Viewed through New Glasses: Bishop Wilson's Journal of His First Voyage in the Melanesian Islands, 1894. *SCL*, serialized, cited by date. PC.

1899   Report on a visit to Malaita. *SCL* 15 Nov: 2–7.

1905   Article about mission's work in Melanesia (no title available). *SCL* 11 April: np.

1908   General Report of the Melanesian Mission for 1907. Supplement to *SCL* 11 April.

1932 *The Wake of the Southern Cross: Work and Adventures in the South Seas.* London: John Murray. PC.

1938 Bad Old Days in the Pacific, Bishop's Narrative. *SCL* 1 July: 25–27.

Wilson, Colin E J (DO Malaita 1927–1928, 1929–1930)

1927 Report to RC Kane on punitive expedition to Kwaio. 3 Nov. WPHC 3029.

1928a "Malaita Affairs." Punitive expedition report. 15 May WPHC C0225/56/22A.

1928b Encl with report to SG, Tulagi. 8 June. CO225/54/22A.

Wilson, Ellen

1915 *The Isles that Wait.* London: Society for Promoting Christian Knowledge. PC.

1935 *Dr. Welchman of Bugotu.* London: Society for Promoting Christian Knowledge. PC.

1936 White Women Workers and Their Work; and Healing the Sick. In *The Church in Melanesia*, edited by Stuart Artless, 41–50, 65–73. Sydney: Melanesian Mission. PC.

Wolfers, Edward

1972 Trusteeship without Trust: A Short History of Interracial Relations and the Law in Papua New Guinea. In *Racism: The Australian Experience; A Study of Race Prejudice in Australia.* Vol 3: *Colonialism*, edited by F S Stevens, 61–147. New York: Taplinger.

Woodford, Charles Morris (RC 1896–1914)

1888 Exploration of the Solomon Islands. *Proceedings of the Royal Geographical Society*, New Series 10:351–376.

1890a Further Explorations in the Solomon Islands. *Proceedings of the Royal Geographical Society*, New Series 12:393–418.

1890b *A Naturalist among the Headhunters: Being an Account of Three Voyages to the Solomon Islands in the Years 1886, 1887, and 1888.* New York: Longman's, Green & Company.

1896 Reports to HC John Thurston. 26 June. WPHC inward correspondence 292/96.

1897a *Report on the British Solomon Islands.* London: Her Majesty's Stationery Office.

1897b Letter to H S Bakeley at WPHC. 12 July. WPHC IC, Series 4, 376/97.

1901 "Story of Amisia." Told at Tulagi. 3 Nov. WPHC IC 7/03.

1903 Letter to HC Henry Jackson. 26 March. WPHC IC 7/03.

1913 Letter to District Magistrate Malaita Edge-Partington. 18 Sept. BSIP 14/8.

1922 The Solomon Islands. In *Essays on the Depopulation of Melanesia*, edited by William H R Rivers, 69–77. Cambridge, UK: Cambridge University Press.

Workman, Charles Rufus Marshall (Acting RC 1917–1921)

1918a Letter to Acting DO Bell re return of shell recognizance deposit. 28 Jan. BSIP 14/12.

1918b Letter to Acting DO Bell. 4 Feb. BSIP 14/12.

1918c Letter to Acting DO Bell re punishment of adultery. 16 March. BSIP 14/12.

1918d Letter to Acting DO Bell re recognizance by Irokwato. 18 April. BSIP 14/12.

1918e Letter to DO Malaita Bell, with Red Cross attachment, from Secretary of

State for the Colonies Walter H Long, sent by HC Sweet-Escott. 9 June. BSIP 14/12.

1918f Letter on a claim for compensation made by Araiasi of Tarapaina, with a list of goods Native Constabulary took from his house. 16 Aug. BSIP 14/12.

1918g Cover letter to HC Cecil Rodwell for Solomons "Native Affairs Regulation" draft. 18 Nov. WPHC 228/1919.

1918h Memo to HC Rodwell (sent with Workman 1918g). 18 Nov. WPHC 228/1919.

Worsley, Peter

1968   *The Trumpet Shall Sound: A Study of "Cargo" Cults in Melanesia.* New York: Schocken Books.

WPHC, Western Pacific High Commission

1917   "British Red Cross Gift from Ysabel Natives." WPHC 4/II/10/1674.

1922   "Memorandum on Native Code—Criticisms by His Lordship of Melanesia" (Anglican Bishop John Steward). 14 June. WPHC 1448/22.

1924   "Native Adultery Punishment Regulation. King's Regulation No 7." WPHC 190/23.

1929a Acting HC letter to Acting RC on new adultery regulation. 13 April. BSIP 1/III/MP2203/1922.

1929b "Native Adultery Punishment (Amendment) Regulation 1929." King's Regulation 3. 23 April. BSIP 1/II1/MP2203/1922.

1929c "Memorandum by His Honour the Chief Judicial Commission for the Western Pacific" on proposal for adultery penalty increase. 17 Dec. BSIP 2/II/1659/29.

1943   Telegram from Acting HC Mitchell to Acting RC Bengough on Laulasi and Fo'odo bombing casualties. 30 May. BSIP 1/III/9/59/2.

1947   Acting HC letter to RC Noel. 15 Nov. BSIP 4/SF108/I.

1950   Acting HC confidential telegram to Acting RC Germond. 3 Feb. BSIP 4/SF108.

Wright, Leonard William Sydney (DO various islands, especially Guadalcanal)

1938   Notes on the Hill People of North-eastern Guadalcanal. *Oceania* 9 (1): 97–100.

1940   The "Vele" Magic of the South Solomons. *Journal of the Royal Anthropological Institute* 70:203–209.

1941   Letter from DO Isabel to SG, "Native Courts." 7 Feb. BSIP 1/III/49/19.

Wrightson, John W (DO Malu'u 1951–1952)

1952a Telegram to Allan. 24 Feb. BSIP 12/I/10/II.

1952b Secret telegram to DC Malaita Andersen. 4 May. BSIP 12/I/10/II.

1952c Letter to DC Malaita Andersen 8 May. BSIP 12/I/10/II.

1952d Letter to DC Andersen. 14 May. BSIP 12/I/10/II.

1952e Letter to DC Andersen. 18 June. BSIP 12/11/13.

1952f "Notes on Population in North Malaita." Appendix 5 to MQR. 30 June. BSIP 4/CF187.

1952g "Political Situation—Toabaita," to DC Malaita Andersen. 12 Aug. BSIP 1/V/13.

1952h Secret telegram on situation in north, to DC Andersen. 18 Aug. BSIP 12/V/13.

1952i "Projected Police Actions—North Malaita," to DC Andersen. 6 Sept. BSIP 12/V/13.

1952j "A Review of the Political Situation in North Malaita during the Period from 1st March to 30th September 1952." 30 Sept. BSIP 12/V/13.

1952k Handing-over notes for Malu'u, to John F Bartle. 20 Oct. BSIP 12/I/12.

You and the Native

1943 *You and the Native: Notes for the Guidance of Members of the Forces in Their Relations with New Guinea Natives.* World War II pamphlet. np: Allied Geographical Section, Southwest Pacific Area.

Young, Florence Selina Harriet

1925 *Pearls from the Pacific.* London: Marshall Brothers.

1932 Letter to Norman Deck. 20 May. SSEM Archive.

Zelenietz, Martin

1979 The End of Headhunting in New Georgia. In *The Pacification of Melanesia,* edited by Margaret Rodman and Matthew Cooper, 91–108. New York: University Press of America.

Zoleveke, Gideon

1980 *Zoleveke: A Man from Choiseul.* Suva: Institute of Pacific Studies.

'Are'are Community Website

2005 (a) Solomon Islands Indentured Migration: 1904–1942; (b) First Development; (c) Solomon Islands Labour Corps: 1942–1945; (d) Maasina Rule History. (Most of this website was adapted from Naitoro 1993.) Author's printed copy.

'Atoomea, Arnon Rinalu (To'abaita Head Chief)

1947a Letter to Shem Irofa'alu. 5 July. Author's copy.

1947b Letters to DO Malaita Marquand. 16, 18, and 21 July. BSIP 4/SF108. (21 July letter also in Laracy 1983, C32).

'Itea (HM Fataleka)

1950 Letter to DO Malu'u Russell. 5 Jan. Appendix A to Russell 1950b.

'Otalifua, Ariel (HM Malu'u)

1947 Letter to DC Malaita Sandars. 30 March. BSIP 12/I/2/7.

Index

Page numbers in **boldface** type refer to illustrations.
The glottal stop (') is ordered as the last letter in the alphabet.

About the Author

David W Akin is an anthropologist and independent scholar living in Ann Arbor, Michigan. He is the managing editor of the journal *Comparative Studies in Society and History* and teaches at the University of Michigan. He has spent over five years living inland in the Kwaio area of Malaita. His publications about Kwaio include studies of spirits, taboos, politics, currencies and exchange, dispute management, suicide, art, educational development, and anthropological data repatriation. He is currently writing a book about changing women's taboos in Kwaio.

Malaitan Language Groups